PORT TOWN

How the People of Long Beach Built, Defended, and Profited From Their Harbor

By George and Carmela Cunningham

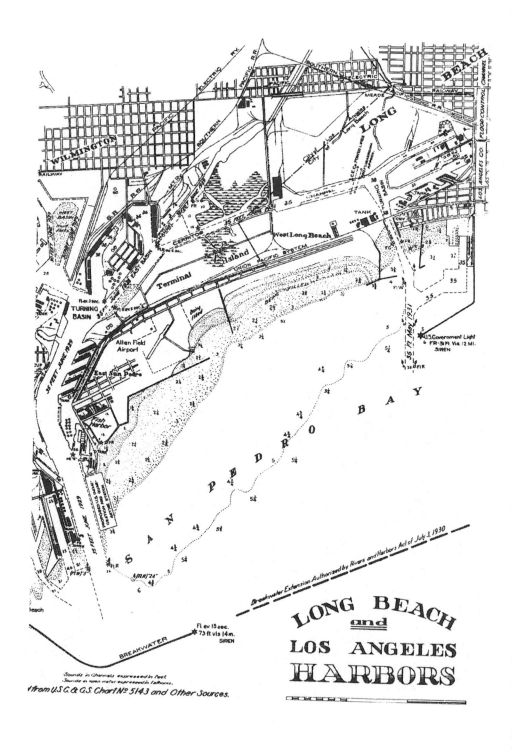

Dedicated to the people of
Long Beach – past, present, and future.

Copyright © 2015 by City of Long Beach
All rights reserved.

For ordering information contact:
Port of Long Beach
PO Box 570
Long Beach, CA 90802
www.polb.com

Printed in the United States of America
Queen Beach Printers Inc.
937 Pine Ave.
Long Beach, CA 90813

Written by George and Carmela Cunningham
Project management by Jen Choi
Production coordination by Donna Shipman
Editing by Chris Berry, Art Wong, Yvonne Rehg Smith, and Harold Glicken
Index by Julianne Alfe and Chris Berry
Map illustration by Jared Blando
Cover, book design, and production by Eden Parrish

Photography credits:
Friends of the Ballona Wetlands page 25
LA Public Library page 79
Library of Congress pages 35, 51, 95, 119, 261
Historical Society of Long Beach pages 109, 145, 245, 273, 325, 347
Port of Long Beach pages 2, 15, 123, 131, 139, 159, 160, 179, 195, 221, 235, 245, 255, 273, 283, 317, 321, 325, 329, 337, 347, 363, 377, 381, 391, 417, 423, 427, 429, 457, 473, 479, 489, 497
University of Southern California page 55

ISBN 978-0-692-46848-7

Table of Contents

Foreword 6

Preface 8

Acknowledgments 12

June 24, 1911 14

PART ONE: Historical Heritage 19

Chapter One: The Land and the People 20
Chapter Two: The Spanish Colonizers 26
Chapter Three: Revolution and Politics 44
Chapter Four: California Statehood 56
Chapter Five: Old Issues, New Opportunities 66
Chapter Six: Railroads and Salesmanship 88
Chapter Seven: Birth of a City 106
Chapter Eight: Free Harbor Fight 120
Chapter Nine: Birth of a Port 136

PART TWO: The Early Years 181

Chapter Ten: The Port and the City 182
Chapter Eleven: Oil, Prosperity, and the Navy 212
Chapter Twelve: Big Crash, Big Quake, and Big Labor 250
Chapter Thirteen: The War Years 276

PART THREE: The Postwar Years 301

Chapter Fourteen: Swords into Plowshares 302
Chapter Fifteen: A New Beginning for Old-Style Ports 342
Chapter Sixteen: No Longer the Little Sister 372
Chapter Seventeen: Cargo, the Navy, and Mickey Mouse 402
Chapter Eighteen: Cutting Through the Urban Maze 436

PART FOUR: Challenges of the 21st Century 481

Chapter Nineteen: A New Age with Some Old Problems 482

Bibliography 502

About the Authors 508

Index 510

FOREWORD

This is how the story ends. Here in Long Beach, we have what I will describe as the finest seaport in all of the United States of America. It's easy to summarize the story in a few words. Our City of Long Beach Harbor Department started with a voter-approved bond issue in 1911 that provided the seed money for a huge omni-port that would eventually handle containers, wet and dry bulk cargo, automobiles, and virtually every type of cargo that moves by sea. But what's the back story, the secret to Long Beach's implausible success? Today, we have the deep water to accommodate huge vessels, and we have access to two of America's largest railway systems – the Union Pacific and the Burlington Northern Santa Fe. But why build such a port in Long Beach? It's easy to understand building a port in the sprawling metropolis that is Los Angeles. But little Long Beach? San Pedro Bay is home to the ports of both Los Angeles and Long Beach, and it's the dominant U.S. gateway of choice for trade from Asia. How did that happen?

The Port of Long Beach was built out of the mighty mud, which threatened again and again to swallow the Port before it really began. Skip ahead one hundred years and industry leaders repeatedly vote for Long Beach as North America's finest seaport. Why? Part of the answer is that Long Beach is a landlord port. We develop and rent cargo facilities. That's our unique expertise. We do not operate terminals – our customers are the premier operators, the ones in front of the curtain. Our magic is in finding the right performers to put on that front stage.

After a century we rival the greatest ports in the world. It isn't only our business acumen. Los Angeles, for example, is still bigger and moves more cargo. At least for now. In Long Beach we operate with about half the number of employees and earn about three times as much as our bigger neighbor. Our aim is to be the world's best port, the world's most innovative port, the world's most socially and environmentally responsible port. Of course, that's one of our secrets, too. We always aim high.

In 2011 the Port of Long Beach celebrated 100 years of phenomenal success. We completed that celebration and our Board of Harbor Commissioners came away with a greater understanding of our history – and yet we wanted to know even more. We acted just like any governmental agency would. We sent out a "Request for Proposals," and the search was on. Who would write our history?

We found George and Carmela Cunningham. George had covered the waterfront for decades as a reporter for the Long Beach Press-Telegram, and his own Cunningham Report – which he published with his wife, Carmela – covered ports and the trade and transportation community for fifteen years. George and Carmela know the waterfront. Their access to information is unsurpassed. Here they chronicle our history. They unearth the secrets of our success. And, they have a fine flair for prose – their style is colorful, and they have made our past and the people in it come to life.

This is also a story about the City of Long Beach. George and Carmela describe our love affair with the Navy, shipyards, oilfields, manufacturing plants, downtown Long Beach, and the Pike waterfront amusement center. They show that we were an industrial city and how we are now evolving into a diverse, cosmopolitan community – as well as a key hub for the world's major trade routes. The Port of Long Beach has become a vital center of international trade, and this is the story of how that happened.

Doug Drummond
President, Long Beach Board of Harbor Commissioners

PREFACE

To write a history is to tell a story. A story about places, about people, about events. But a good history has to be more than just a compilation of facts and a recounting of occurrences, no matter how accurate they may be. A good history has to put those facts into perspective, to point out the patterns that manifest themselves, and the motivations that led the people involved to take the actions they took.

Our goal was to write a good history – a history that the reader will not only enjoy, but that will be worth his or her time to read. This is an adventure story, a story with both comedic and tragic elements, a story of people with unlimited vision, and of those whose vision went no further than their own self-interest. Most of all, it is a story about how a river delta mudflat was transformed – for better or for worse – into a world-class port.

We called it *Port Town*. The name did not come easily. We won't mention our working title, except to say it was badly flawed. Our friends and associates were not reticent in sharing that opinion with us, and we thank them for it.

Port Town is the name we finally chose, because perhaps above all else, Long Beach is a port town. The port and the city complement one another, even if the relationship is sometimes contentious. The Port of Long Beach is not supported by tax dollars. It gets its money by leasing out terminals to shipping lines, stevedoring companies, oil importing companies, and other businesses. The port generates jobs for city residents and economic well-being for others who don't work directly in the freight-moving business. It eases the burden on taxpayers by yearly transfers of cash to maintain beaches and waterfront that would otherwise come from taxpayers' pockets. When the city is in economic trouble – as it was during the 1990s – the port is there to help.

Los Angeles is not a port town. Los Angeles is a city that happens to have a port. In Los Angeles, the port is an appendage, dangling like a pendulum far below the city, connected only by a shoestring strip. San Pedro and Wilmington could have been port towns, but in 1909 the citizens of those two communities voted to become part of the City of Los Angeles, connected to a city government more than 20 miles up the shoestring strip. Long Beach was offered the same deal. Long Beach said no.

The Port of Los Angeles is run by the massive City of Los Angeles. The members of the harbor board – a post often awarded as a political favor – can come from anywhere in the city – from the San Fernando Valley to Pacific Palisades. Sometimes the Los Angeles commissioners even come from the local communities, but not always. The people of San Pedro and Wilmington may live next to a port, but they do not control it. Their interest in the port, and their control over it, are diluted by the sheer size of the mega entity to which they belong.

It has been the people of Long Beach who built our port, who developed it, who defended it from attempts by both the state and the city of Los Angeles to take it over, and who have an ownership interest in it.

When river floods clogged the harbor with mud during the early years, it was the people of Long Beach who pushed for a channel to divert the river and save local jobs. When subsidence threatened to sink the entire downtown, it was the people of Long Beach who helped find a solution. The people of Long Beach live with the port. Residents can see the ships and the cranes from City Hall or from the Belmont Pier. Residents of high rises along the beach can hear a nightly symphony of fog horns, train whistles, and tugboat engines. Everybody is aware of the trucks on the freeway – each one of them representing a job – and the ongoing construction project that is the port. And when people in Long Beach have a problem with the port, they can take it to the people they elect or go straight to the port itself without a long and costly 45-minute ride up the freeway.

The story of the Port of Long Beach is a story of success and of failure, and how each success led to new problems for subsequent trustees of the land. We did not make moral judgments about the people in our story or point out the heroes or the villains. We leave that to the readers. Our challenge to ourselves and our promise to our readers was to be fair, to present the conflict of ideas that mark all human endeavors in an open and balanced way, and to be relevant. There were heroes and villains, of course, as there are in every story. In history, however, the heroes and the villains often turn out to be the same people – the people who got things done, the people who moved the world forward, and the people who, along the way, enriched themselves as well.

To tell the port's story, we had to go beyond just what happened in and around what is now the Port of Long Beach. We had to tell what was happening in the world because that dictated, in ways both large and small, what was happening in the port at any given time. So we periodically included an overview of what the world was like along with the attitudes and circumstances that were reflected in what happened in Southern California and at the port.

If we have a bias to confess, it is that we are advocates of both the port and international trade. The Port of Long Beach is one of the largest and most successful ports in the United States. It is a dominant factor in the United States' trade with other nations. It provides thousands of jobs locally, and beyond the local area, it provides access to consumer goods for millions of Americans. It helps provide strong economic and trade ties with other countries, and it is a force for peace. Nations that trade together, that depend on one another for goods and services, are much less likely to go to war than those that do not. Trade consists of mutually beneficial agreements between buyers and sellers. Taking up arms is rarely in the interest of either side of that equation.

We would be remiss, however, not to point out the downside of all that trade, all those jobs, and all the economic benefits that accrue to the local and regional community. The goods that flow through the port carry with them congestion on the highways, pollution in the air and water, and sometimes the outsourcing of jobs to other lands.

Most economists agree that the benefits for Long Beach, Southern California, and the nation outweigh the costs. Some people, however, do not.

The arguments and conflicts over how to best utilize and exploit the land that is now the port are part of the history that continues to this day. Some of the issues have changed as time has gone on, and the old stewards of the land have been replaced by new generations. Other issues – such as how to protect and conserve water and how best to invest in necessary infrastructure – have remained the same throughout subsequent generations.

This book is an effort to tell the history of a place – the Port of Long Beach – and how the visions of yesterday left us with all the benefits and liabilities that we grapple with today. It is dedicated to the people of Long Beach with the hope that after they read this account they may appreciate all that it means to live in a port town.

George and Carmela Cunningham

ACKNOWLEDGMENTS

Writing a book is a lonely and often difficult task. When the sun is shining outside the window and the songs of birds fill the air, it is most difficult to sit at the computer, reading old books and composing and editing what one hopes will be a story to delight, and perhaps even inform, the reader. They say it takes a village to raise a child. We're not sure about that. But it does take an entourage of friends, associates, colleagues, and family to write a book. Of that there is no doubt in our minds. We had those people and we thank them for their patience and their encouragement.

First and foremost, we have to recognize the Long Beach Harbor Commission, all of whom supported this project – Doug Drummond, Rich Dines, Lori Ann Farrell, Lou Anne Bynum, and Tracy Egoscue.

Commission President Doug Drummond and former Commissioner Susan Anderson Wise pushed the idea of a history book on the port – not a coffee table, large-format extravaganza, full of grainy photos and skimpy copy blocks, but a real narrative on how the port came to be. They wanted the real story, not a whitewashed version of the same. They promised not to interfere, and they were true to their word.

Commissioner Drummond, a lover of history, has championed the project. He offered much encouragement, but no demands on what to put in and what to leave out. We thank him for that and have responded with a commitment to fairness to all sides.

We had secret readers, people who followed our progress and told us what they liked about the book and what they did not, where they were confused and where they were intrigued. Along the way they caught some of the typos that snuck into our copy and hid among the type, mistakes that are easier than one might think to overlook.

Ken Cable read every word of the copy as it came off our computers. Sometimes he read at midnight or at 6 a.m. – doing his part to make sure we told our story well – and that we met our deadlines. Al Shore also read along as we wrote – asking questions and making suggestions all along the way. Chris Berry, of the Port of Long Beach, read over our shoulders, caught the most obscure mistakes, and also took on the huge responsibility of selecting photos and writing captions. A very special thank you to these three gentlemen.

We had other readers, each of whom brought an eye for detail, a special knowledge of the port, or an understanding of history, to our task. Thank you to Natalie Shore Peterson, Paul and Shelly Castorina, and Michael Castorina. Much appreciation goes to former Long Beach Port Communications Director Yvonne Rehg Smith and former Press-Telegram editor Harold Glicken for their excellent proofreading work on the book. Our gratitude also goes to the Port of Long Beach design team of Jennifer Choi, Eden Parrish-Adams, and Donna Shipman, who created a book design that well represents *Port Town*.

Support, love, and understanding throughout the process were liberally provided by our families and friends – Bill Cunningham, Joe Castorina, Nicki Shearn, Lisa Roth, Cathy Ayres, Dorothy Cable, Susan Tucker, Larry LaRue, Grant Young, and Art Wong, an old pal from our newspaper days who is now with the Port of Long Beach. Their encouragement and excitement about the book spurred us forward on many long nights.

And special thanks must be given to Bailey Roth for her contribution to keeping the book on track and making us laugh when the task seemed overwhelming. We thank you all. *Port Town* would not have been possible without you.

George and Carmela Cunningham

June 24, 1911

At 1 p.m. that day, more than 200 automobiles lined up at Pine Avenue and Ocean Boulevard for a parade down Second Street to the new city docks. The parade was led by the Long Beach Municipal Band – formed in 1909 by bandleader Harry Wiley. Wiley's music had proved so popular that two years after he formed the band, the residents of the young city had voted a special tax on themselves to fund the band and its music, making it the first municipal band to be funded year-round by any city in the nation.

That's how people were in Long Beach in 1911. In 1900, Long Beach had a little more than 2,000 people. Ten years later it had 17,809 souls, and it was growing. In fact, Long Beach was the fastest growing city in the U.S., and the people who lived there had a sense of being part of something big.

June 24 was to be a grand day in Long Beach. Thousands of residents were turning out to witness the dedication of the new city docks. The weather was mild – a typical June day in the city by the sea, some twenty miles south of Los Angeles – and the crowd was excited.

The steamer *Santa Barbara* had arrived the evening before with 350,000 feet of Pacific Northwest pine earmarked for delivery to the Long Beach Improvement Co., which had been formed three months earlier and had already established a lumber yard and mill near the city docks. Master of the *Santa Barbara*, Captain F.B. Zaddart, from Grays Harbor, Washington, told the local folks that the recently dredged channel was easy to maneuver. He had inspected the harbor in May and said at that time that he could come in with his eyes shut.

"Well, I almost did that last evening," he told people. "There is plenty of water here, and I never thought of having any trouble from the time I started in through the jetties until our lines were thrown out on the municipal docks."

The *Santa Barbara* was a good-sized ship, 250 feet long and loaded to a depth of eighteen feet. Captain Zaddart was treated to an automobile ride around the city, and then taken to a luncheon in his honor at the beachfront Virginia Hotel.

By the time the parade from downtown arrived with the band playing tunes as it marched, a crowd had already gathered at the waterfront near the new city docks. The band continued to play as the crowd grew to an estimated 3,000 people – an impressive number for a city the size of Long Beach in 1911.

Then it was time for the speeches.

William H. Wallace, vice president of the Chamber of Commerce, was the master of ceremonies and the first to speak. It was an important day for Long

FIRST SHIP: *Workers unload the* SS Iaqua *after its arrival at Long Beach Harbor on June 2, 1911. Redwood lumber from Northern California was the cargo, destined for the Southern California building boom. Twenty-two days later, the steamer* Santa Barbara *brought in more lumber amid the fanfare of an official opening day parade.*

Beach, he told the crowd. It was the formal opening of the city's docks, built by the city on land owned by the city, and bought and constructed with money from the voters of the city, who had approved a $240,000 issue of bonds.

Construction of the docks made practical use of the Long Beach Harbor possible, he said, pointing out the size of the ship at dock and noting the arrival some twenty-two days earlier of the steam schooner *Iaqua* with 280,000 feet of redwood, also consigned to the Long Beach Improvement Co.

The *Iaqua* would later be noted as the first cargo-bearing ship to arrive at the new harbor, but the official date for the port opening would always be considered the June 24 day of dedication.

Next to speak was Charles Henderson Windham, the popular 45-year-old mayor of Long Beach, who received cheers and applause from the crowd as he strode to the dais. Windham told how the city docks came to be, why he favored building them and how the city would benefit.

Windham had lived in the city for only nine years. He, his wife, Angelica, and their three children had come to Long Beach in 1902 from Costa Rica, where he had owned and operated a coffee and sugar plantation. He had been one of the leaders in pushing for development of the port, and for those efforts he would be acknowledged by the generations to follow as the "Father of the Port of Long Beach."

In a very short time Windham had gone from a newcomer to one of the most important people in the city. That's the way it was in Long Beach then. The young city was in the middle of an adolescent growth spurt, and men of purpose and vision quickly rose to positions of leadership.

There were more speakers to come. Clinton J. Curtis, the president of the Los Angeles Dock and Terminal Co., which had built the harbor, talked about the vast sums his company had spent on the project to bring international commerce to the city. Dr. L.A. Perce, who had been president of the Chamber of Commerce for almost ten years, had been suffering from a severe cold and confined to bed, but his interest was so great, he told the crowd, that he could not resist the desire to attend. Realty Board President J.A. Rominger said the port would do much to boost the real estate business, but that the Realty Board was also interested in the city's welfare and progress. Job Barnett of the Long Beach Improvement Co. noted that the Panama Canal would be opening in the next few years and the port would benefit from easier access to East Coast and European cargo. Captain Zaddart explained once more how easy access to the harbor had been and predicted that great things lay ahead for the new port.

After the speeches, the band gave an impromptu concert, and many remained at the docks to listen to the music and watch the unloading of the ship. It was a great day for Long Beach, although perhaps greater for some than for others.

In 1911 Long Beach, what was good for business was good for everybody. The lumber that had arrived onboard both the *Iaqua* and the *Santa Barbara* was for the Long Beach Improvement Co., a venture founded by prominent businessmen in town. The company planned to use the lumber to build houses and apartment buildings for new residents. But before it bought the land, built the mill, and ordered the lumber, the company had the harbor sounded to make sure it could handle the lumber ships to come.

The directors for the new company read like a who's who of Long Beach movers and shakers. They included Mayor Windham, National Bank of Long Beach President P.E. Hatch, Farmers and Merchants Bank President C.J. Walker, First

National Bank Director J.D. Cate, State Bank Director J.P. Cortis, Exchange Bank Director R.H. Young, L.A. Dock and Terminal Co. President Curtis, Long Beach Improvement Co. Manager Louis Purcell, real estate agents Stephen Townsend, John H. Betts, and T.J. Harriman, attorney Herbert M. Haskell, and others.

It was a time for civic pride, for building a new city and a new port, but it was also a time for making money and building fortunes, and one didn't necessarily get in the way of the other. And through it all, many grand things were accomplished.

By the end of the day on June 24, 1911, Long Beach was a port city.

That gala beginning – full of music and speeches and optimism – celebrated the transformation of a useless mudflat into a port and center of industry in a city that seemed destined for greatness. But it certainly wasn't the end of the story. The port they celebrated that day would in the years to come surpass the wildest expectations of even the most optimistic of those gathered on the city docks.

But it was also not the beginning. That useless mudflat had a long history and many stewards stretching back more than a thousand years. This is the story of the people, the land, and the changes that the people wrought upon the land. It is a tale at times tragic, at times inspiring, and at times both at once. It has heroes and villains, winners and losers, and often they were the very same people.

It's the story of the Port of Long Beach, and we hope you enjoy it.

PART ONE:
HISTORICAL HERITAGE

Chapter One:
The Land and the People

Native people had lived in the area of what is now the Los Angeles basin for at least 12,000 years before the first Europeans arrived. In the late 15th century, when Christopher Columbus landed in the Antilles with the mistaken belief that he had reached the Indian Ocean and subcontinent, he dubbed the descendants of those early peoples of the Americas "Indians." Although his error was discovered fairly soon thereafter, the name stuck, and for centuries the native people of the Americas were collectively called Indians, and so they are called here.

These early people of the American continents were descendants of people who, during an era in which sea levels were lower than usual because so much water was trapped as ice, had migrated from Northern Asia to America across a land bridge that existed over what is now the Bering Strait. When they arrived in the basin, wooly mammoths and sabre-tooth tigers still roamed the area. It was a time when the prehistoric people of Europe were still living in small bands that sustained themselves, as did the Indians, by hunting animals and gathering wild plants. It was thousands of years before the rise of the Egyptian civilization, before the Greek and Roman empires rose and fell, before Stonehenge was raised in England, and before Jesus Christ walked the dusty streets of Jerusalem.

But those early migrants were not of the same line of Indians that were residing in the Los Angeles basin when the European explorers first arrived. The later Indians had come to the L.A. basin a mere 1,000 years prior to that first encounter. Although they had no written history, historians and archeologists have pieced together much about their origins, who they were, and how they lived. By studying their language, scholars have deduced that the people who greeted the Spanish when they arrived were part of the Shoshone people, also known as Uto-Aztecan.

It is thought that these people migrated to California from the Great Basin, an arid and alkaline land stretching from Reno and the Eastern Sierras into Utah. The migration probably didn't happen all at once. It likely occurred about 2,000 years ago with successive waves of newcomers trying to find a more hospitable environment than the one they were leaving behind.

The Shoshone arrival in Southern California, according to Bruce W. Miller in his book *The Gabrielino*, "drove a wedge through California from the desert to the sea, driving out and separating peoples of the Hokan [Amerindian language] family..." It is unclear whether the newcomers conquered the former residents or just slowly replaced them and claimed the territory for their own, but claim it they did.

Around 1,000 to 1,300 years ago, the Indian coastal population began evolving into communities with distinct social classes and hereditary chiefs. They had established cultural standards of behavior, methods of resolving disputes, and alliances between various groups.

It remains unclear how the early Indians referred to themselves as a group. They were given the name "Gabrileños" by the Spanish after the Mission San Gabriel, but the spelling "Gabrielino" didn't become common until the 1870s. The early Indians were thought to have used the name of their village with a "vit," "bit," or "pet" attached to the end. The name Tongva, meaning "the people," was adopted by some Indian descendants in the early 1900s.

Portrayals of the Early Indians

Life for the Gabrielinos before the arrival of the Europeans has been portrayed in different lights by different people – usually according to what was the politically correct philosophy of the day. Some have referred to the early Indians' life as idyllic, but that is almost certainly not true. Although the Gabrielinos were among the most affluent of the California Indian tribes, life was far from easy. They had no metal. Their tools and weapons were made of stone, wood, and carved bone. They had neither beasts of burden, such as horses or oxen, nor wheeled carts. If they wanted to go overland from one place to another, they walked. And if they lived close to nature, they were also at the mercy of it.

Grizzly bears and rattlesnakes were common. Having a ready supply of water was an issue during periods of drought. Floods threatened during periods of rain. The Gabrielinos adapted to the harshness of life as humans have always done, but it was hardly a carefree existence.

Some mid-20th century archeologists suggested that the reason the Indians were not more advanced in their social development was that they lived in such a bountiful area that all the necessities of life – game, water, fish, acorns, and other edible plants – were plentiful. However, others think that claiming that the Indians' primitive lifestyle was the result of them being too placid or unmotivated to advance their lot in life is both patronizing and racist.

By the late 20th century, many experts had come to view the Indians not as happy, satisfied primitives, but as masters of their environment. In this perspective of pre-European history, the Indians did much to make life easier with what was available to them at the time. They understood the world around them. They burned off fields in order to more easily catch and kill small game. They pruned oak trees and other plants to ensure a steady supply of acorns and berries. And if they had not yet reached the stage of development where they planted crops, they did broadcast seeds onto the ground to promote the growth of new, life-sustaining plants. They were active participants in maintaining a biologically diverse and sustainable environment that provided for their needs.

Archaeologist L. Mark Rabb calls such interpretations of Indian life "political ecologies" that tend to reflect the times in which the theories gained credence more than the reality of Indian life itself. Scholars who were optimistic about where the world was headed tended to see the early Indians as primitives. Scholars who were anxious about the future and the environment tended to see the Indians as wiser about nature and the world in which they lived than modern man.

Rabb argues that both of these perspectives are flawed. Recent evidence suggests that over the long term, Indians struggled with environmental issues and scarce resources. Examinations of food bones unearthed at archaeological sites have indicated that as time went on, California Indians were eating smaller game, fewer fish, and more staples such as acorns. This evidence may indicate the overhunting of larger species, changes in the natural environment, or growth in the human population. There are some who argue that after the Europeans arrived with their cattle and other livestock and the size of the Indian population was reduced due to European diseases and the loss of the Indians' hunting culture, there was actually a rebound in wild animal populations in the area.

The recovery of thousands of Indian skeletons from 8,000 years prior to the first contact with Europeans in the 16th century indicates that the long-term health of the Indian population declined over the period, Rabb says. This decline is evidenced in the rise in bone lesions from disease and fractured bones as the result of violence on one another. This evidence also indicates that the Indians who lived in California at the time of first contact with Europeans may have been almost four inches shorter than their ancestors from more than 7,000 years before.

Wherever the truth lies in these different perspectives about the Indians who inhabited California when the Spanish arrived, it seems clear that their lives were – as were the lives of most people throughout time – less than idyllic.

Life Before the Spanish

Although the Indians were not as technically or socially advanced as the Europeans, they were certainly not savages living outside of any civilized standards. They had mastered many practical skills and adopted a complex legal, political, and religious philosophy. William McCawley, in his book *The First Angelinos*, estimates there were more than 5,000 Gabrielino Indians living in fifty to 100 settlements at the time of first European contact. These communities typically ranged from 100 to 150 residents each.

It seems clear that Indians had a relatively complex culture. There were well-defined social classes with an elite class of chiefs, elders, and shamans; a middle-class of craftsmen; a lower class of commoners; and below them poor people and slaves who existed on the fringes of the group, but who were accorded certain entitlements.

The commander-in-chief – known as the Tomyaar – administered the affairs of his community, dispensed justice, and managed the food supply. Hunters and gatherers of the community would deposit a portion of their bounty with the chief, who was responsible for making sure the poor were fed. Being chief was hereditary, passing from the father to the eldest son. If there was not a son to take the position, it went to the nearest male relative, or in rare instances, to a daughter with a male relative appointed regent.

The elders were men older than 40 who had wealth and status and who advised the chief – especially in issues of war – and punished him if he mismanaged the food supply. The punishment for such an offense could be death. The elders often had specific duties such as overseeing the community finances, delivering moral lectures, or supervising preparation of maanet – the hallucinogenic datura drink used in puberty rituals. Membership as an elder was also mostly passed down from father to son.

The shamans attended to the community's medical and spiritual needs and wielded great political and religious power. They were thought to be able to take on the form of animals, such as wolves or bears, live to be up to 200 years old, and leave their bodies on magical flights. The magical flights usually involved taking the drug maanet. The shaman was the person the community consulted during periods of illness or when individuals or communities needed supernatural help with various individual or community problems. They were predominantly men, although some women also attained the status. The shamans leveraged their power by membership in a regional association of shamans, trained and tested others seeking to join the association, and expelled those who abused their power.

The middle class was composed of craftsmen and people who had gathered some material wealth. The commoners had little wealth or power, and the poor were seen as unreliable and dishonest. Slaves were usually women and children captured in war, who might sometimes be returned to their families as part of a negotiated settlement.

There were rules of conduct that resulted in bonds between members of the community and sometimes with members of other communities. Lineage groups consisted of related people who shared a common ancestor and typically owned hunting and gathering territories that would be shared by members of the group, but not by outsiders. Trespass onto that territory was a serious offense. A community would consist of one or more lineages. Every lineage belonged to one of two moieties – kinship groups – that were called either the wildcat or the coyote. Since no single moiety possessed all of the songs, stories, and paraphernalia required for ritual performance, the two moieties of a lineage would have to come together to perform such events. The ritual events also provided an opportunity to redistribute the food supply of each lineage and help strengthen the regional economic base.

If a lineage territory became inadequate to sustain the members of the lineage – either because of flood, drought, or other natural problems or because the population had grown too large – it would split in two. The portion that was split off would have to leave and find a new living area. The offshoot would also adopt deliberate changes in language and tradition to establish its individual identity. This dividing of lineages may have been one of the prime factors that led to the migration of Shoshone Indians from the Great Basin to Southern California.

The moral code forbade hunters from eating their own kill and fishermen from eating their catch. This rule prevented the hunters and fishermen from hoarding food and mandated that they share their food with others.

Most punishments for misbehavior were in the form of fines or execution. Whipping was not used as a punishment, although murder, incest, and mismanagement of the food supply could result in execution. In the case of adultery, the wronged husband could kill or wound his wife if he caught her in the act, and anybody who attempted to avenge her would have to deal with the chief. A more common solution, however, was for the husband to reject his wife, turn her over to her lover, and take the lover's wife as his own.

Wars were declared for a variety of reasons, including to capture new women, for robbery, in trespass, and as a response to insult. Once the chief – in consultation with the Council of Elders – made the decision to go to war, men were ordered to prepare their weapons, women were told to prepare food, and allied communities were invited to join in. The chief led the warriors. The women, children, and old men followed. The warriors fought with clubs, stones, and arrows dipped in rattlesnake poison. The shamans would care for the wounded. Captured enemy warriors were decapitated on the battlefield or taken back to be tortured and killed. Enemy scalps were taken as trophies and put on display, while captured women and children were taken as slaves. Relatives of the dead warriors could sometimes pay a ransom to get the scalps returned.

A less violent dispute between communities took the form of a "song duel" in which the opposing sides took part in a multi-day ceremony in which participants would stamp their feet and sing obscene songs to ridicule their enemies.

The coastal Gabrielinos, such as the ones around San Pedro Bay, were at the center of an Indian trade network that extended across the water to the Channel Islands and to inland Indian communities.

They carved fish hooks and harpoon tips out of bones. They chiseled driftwood into planks, sanded down those planks with shark skin, sewed them together with coarse fiber, caulked the cracks between planks with tar and other waterproofing materials, and took to the ocean to gather fish and sea mammals. The canoes were sturdy enough to take goods from the mainland to the Channel Islands and bring traded goods back. Small boats would hold perhaps three people – a man at both ends paddling and a boy in the middle bailing out the water that seeped in during the journey. Some larger canoes were big enough to carry more than twenty people, but there was always a need for someone to bail water.

The coastal Indians traded items from the mainland with their fellow Gabrielinos who lived on the Channel Islands. The island Gabrielinos supplied manufactured goods, such as soapstone bowls and pipes, roots, paints, and beads. In exchange they received various plant foods, stone tools and other manufactured goods.

There were also well-defined trade routes between the coast and inland communities. The coastal Indians supplied the inland Indians with fish, shellfish, and marine mammals in exchange for minerals, gemstones such as opals and crystals, and mined ores. Shell beads were used as money and sometimes in ritual exchanges. Known trade routes reached as far as the Colorado River – more than 200 miles to the east as the crow flies, fifteen or sixteen days on foot one way. From the Colorado Indians, the Gabrielinos received soft blankets and deer and antelope skin clothing in exchange for soapstone and shells.

The Gabrielinos had strong beliefs about almost every aspect of life, including religion, family, hunting, warfare, and trade. They cremated their dead before burying the remains. They were religious, they believed in magic, and they passed on the legends and myths of their people through storytellers who memorized such tales word-for-word. They made art, music, jewelry, and weapons. Both men and women had tattoos. They danced, sang, smoked, took ritualistic drugs, gambled, and painted their bodies.

The Gabrielinos had a long-standing and complex culture, but by the early 16th century, the Indians' reign upon the land was about to end. After thousands of years as the residents and stewards of this land by the sea, they were about to receive an eviction notice.

FIRST ANGELENOS: *Indians living in the Los Angeles basin before the arrival of Europeans had a complex culture and traded with other native groups both along the coast and inland. Dubbed the Gabrielinos by the Spanish, their way of life was largely destroyed by the mission system.*

Chapter Two:
The Spanish Colonizers

Before the coming of the Europeans, Los Angeles was a much different place than it is today. The land itself was a plain, marked by marshlands and creeks and seeping tar pits. When the winter rains came, marshy areas became full wetlands; when rains ceased, the water would evaporate or seep into the ground and become part of the aquifer.

It was a place of floods and droughts. Ground squirrels and rabbits riddled the landscape with burrows. Antelope, deer, and elk roamed the grasslands. Grizzly bears dug up and aerated the soil looking for underground prey. What we now call the Los Angeles River was a tramp, often changing direction and routes during periods of flood, sometimes emptying into the sea near what is now Marina del Rey, sometimes where it empties now in Long Beach, and sometimes into Alamitos Bay.

The plant life varied from year to year, according to the amount of rainfall. Flowers would blanket the ground with color along the creeks and streams during spring, then die out in the summer. Their seeds would fall to the ground, where they would remain until the next year to take root. If there was a drought, only a few seeds would sprout up from the ground. When the waters returned the following years, or sometimes several years later, more seeds – some of which had been dormant for years – would suddenly flower.

Wide-ranging estimates say that between 5,000 and 10,000 Indians lived in what is now Los Angeles and the San Fernando and San Gabriel valleys, down along the coast past Laguna Beach and north along the coast to Topanga Canyon. The environment as it existed then was well-suited to the culture and lifestyle of that relatively small hunter-gatherer population. But could it have supported the tens of thousands of new settlers that would eventually begin pouring into the area? Certainly not.

The Life and Death of Juan Cabrillo

By the time Spaniards landed on San Pedro Bay in October of 1542, it had been fifty years since Christopher Columbus had set sail from Spain, traveling west in search of a new route to Asia. Eight months earlier, the Tudor King Henry VIII had executed his fifth wife, Catherine Howard, on charges of adultery, and it would be another seventy-eight years before the pilgrims landed at Plymouth Rock. Germany was embroiled in a fierce religious battle that had grown out of the Reformation; the massacre of St. Bartholomew had not yet taken place in France, and Hernando De Soto was making his way up into the Mississippi. William Shakespeare's father had just begun courting Mary Arden.

Of course Juan Rodríguez Cabrillo wasn't thinking about any of that on June 27, 1542, as he sailed out of the port of Navidad with his three small ships. His fleet included his own ship, the *San Salvador*, which was about 100 feet long and had two or three pieces of artillery, plus crossbows and small weapons; the *La Victoria*, which was smaller, round-bellied and square-rigged; and the *San Miguel*, a frigate with lateen sails and twelve pairs of oars. Two hundred and fifty men sailed with Cabrillo on this trip that was expected to last two years. He had provisioned the ships himself with food, arms, and horses. He further planned to stop often along the coast to get fresh game and fish.

Cabrillo's voyage to Alta California took him far from the land and circumstance into which he was born. A street urchin who came into the world around 1498 or 1500, Juan Rodríguez – as he was called until he reached middle age – was pulled off the street by a merchant named Alfonso de Ortega. By the time he was 11 years old, Ortega had sent the boy to Cuba, where he acted on the merchant's behalf. He learned to read and write and keep accounts in Cuba, but more importantly, he learned the craft and met the powerful people who would eventually ensure his place in history.

In 1516, Cuban Governor Diego Velazquez and his agent Panfilo de Narvaez received permission from the King of Spain to begin a shipbuilding industry at Puerto de Carenas – present day Havana. Still in his teens, Juan Rodríguez became part of that new industry and learned shipbuilding, which eventually helped him to become both rich and famous.

When Rodríguez was about 18 years old, Hernán Cortés was in Cuba recruiting men and preparing for his invasion into what is now Mexico. Cortés and Cuban Governor Velazquez had been entangled in a power struggle which had become so contentious that by the time Cortés had left Cuba and claimed Mexico for the Spanish crown in March of 1519, Diego Velazquez had sent Panfilo Narvaez in pursuit with orders to bring back Cortés at any cost. Although Juan Rodríguez didn't sail with Cortés, he did sail with Narvaez. When Narvaez finally encountered Cortés, Cortés and his soldiers defeated Narvaez, even though Narvaez had many more men and weapons. The triumphant Cortés invited Narvaez's men to join him in the quest for Aztec gold, and Juan Rodríguez agreed. He was put in charge of a regiment of crossbowmen as Cortés turned back to his main objective – the Aztecs.

Cortés' conquest of the Aztecs was brutal, but it was not without a heavy toll on the Spanish invaders. After defeating Narvaez, Cortés had to rush back to the Aztec capital to reinforce the part of his army that had been left there under the command of Pedro de Alvarado. Alvarado's men were under siege, and Cortés could do little to rescue them. About 900 Spanish soldiers were killed, captured or sacrificed along with about a thousand Tlascalan Indians who had allied with the Spanish. Alvarado's unit lost almost all of its artillery. The small lake-going boats built with the help of Indian carpenters were destroyed, and most of its crossbows and muskets were lost.

Cortés jumped into action. He commandeered a ship that happened to be in the area as he waited for reinforcements from Spain that brought gunpowder, muskets, crossbows, horses, arms, and more soldiers. The supply ships also brought iron, threaded bolts, anchors, sails, and rigging – everything necessary to build the new fleet that Cortés so sorely needed. Juan Rodríguez – about 21 years old at the time but with the shipbuilding skills he had learned in Cuba – was put in charge of the operation.

Re-supplied and refreshed, Cortés renewed his attack on the Aztecs. Vicious battles, the death of reigning emperor Montezuma, and an epidemic of smallpox that devastated the population combined to leave the empire in ruin. By August 13, 1521, the Aztec Empire was for all practical purposes ended, and Cortés was made the first governor of Mexico. Cortés' conquest of the Aztecs is one of the most infamous in Mexican history; it also marked the beginning of an upward spiral for the street child from Seville. As Cortés conquered the Aztecs, Rodríguez became "more than moderately rich" at the same time that he built his reputation with the powerful conqueror and made his reputation as one of the best shipbuilders in the New World. His inadvertent enlistment into Cortés' army would eventually make Rodríguez the first European to set foot in California.

With the Aztecs conquered, Cortés planned excursions into Honduras and Guatemala. He sent his lieutenant Pedro de Alvarado. Rodríguez went with Alvarado – and for better and sometimes for worse – he linked his fortunes to this man of big ideas, although not necessarily the best judgment or character.

After the first Alvarado campaign, Rodríguez settled in Guatemala. By then he had become a Hidalguia – a title of gentry earned by service to the crown. The title brought with it honor, land, servants, and power. Hidalgos were passed from father to son, but there's no record at all of Rodríguez's parents, and it's clear from court records that he earned the honor himself. A stout-hearted man who could read and write did well in Guatemala. Over the next years, Rodríguez was awarded several ecomiendas – whole villages that were granted by the governor in return for favors to men who could tax the villagers in exchange for providing protection and religious training to them. The reality was that the people living in the ecomiendas became slaves to the gentry, spending their days mining gold and working fields and then turning all the wealth over to the ecomiendas owner. Rodríguez grew very rich from gold and cacao – the most profitable crop in Guatemala.

On a trip back to Spain, Rodríguez secured himself a good Spanish wife – Beatriz Sanchez de Ortega, the daughter of his old benefactor – who bore him two good Spanish sons. He also had a number of common Guatemalan "wives" – likely Tzutuhil Indian women – who produced several daughters and other sons. By the time he was 40, Juan Rodríguez was one of the richest men in Guatemala, with an established "casa poblada" – a complex household that included his legal wife and children, his Indian wives and their children, relatives, servants, and poorer friends.

Well-established in Guatemala, Rodríguez poured his riches into building ships and buying goods from Spain to ship to Peru where the conquistadores with their newly acquired Incan gold would pay outrageous prices for Spanish goods. He built the *Santiago* – one of the finest ships of its time – and filled it with goods to sell in Peru, but before Rodríguez could sail, Pedro de Alvarado took control of the ship and everything on it for an expedition he was outfitting. Although Rodríguez filed papers in court suing for the ship's return, he also agreed with Alvarado's proposition, which was to let Alvarado take the ship on his voyage and when he returned, Rodríguez could have back the ship and share in the profits of all new discoveries. Things didn't go well, however, and two years later Alvarado was back with the ship, which was so damaged that Rodríguez sold it outright to Alvarado for pennies on the dollar. Alvarado did grant Rodríguez two more ecomiendas, although the entire deal got tangled up in court because it wasn't certain that Alvarado owned the things he was promising to Rodríguez.

By 1536, Juan Rodríguez sailed as captain with Alvarado on an exploration into Honduras. This is when he added the name "Cabrillo" to Juan Rodríguez, which had been his name of record up to this point. Being named "Juan Rodríguez" in 16th century Spain was similar to being named "John Smith" in modern-day America. Now that he had become a man of wealth and position, he was entitled to set himself off from others. It was also around this time that Alvarado talked Cabrillo into helping him outfit a major excursion that Alvarado and Viceroy Antonio de Mendoza were planning for the king of Spain.

The voyage was to be part of a pincer incursion in which Alvarado would sail up the northern coast of the continent while another fleet would sail directly west. The plan was that the two fleets would meet in the islands of the western Pacific. Unfortunately, the geography of the time was poor. Navigators had figured out latitude but could not measure longitude. They also believed the northern continent to be much narrower than it is and the world altogether to be much smaller. They figured that China and the Spice Islands were not a far distance from the northern part of the continent on which they stood. They also planned to look for the legendary Strait of Anian, which was believed to be a convenient waterway across the northern part of the continent that would take them to what would eventually be known as Hudson Bay.

While Alvarado went to Spain to secure approvals from the king, Cabrillo worked to build the fleet for the voyage.

"It has been perhaps six years since the Señor Adelantado (Alvarado) went to Spain, and at the time he left, he ordered that I should build him an armada while he was in Spain, and so I built it," Cabrillo wrote.

During the time, Cabrillo also built himself a new ship, called the *San Salvador*, which he and Alvarado sailed on a "practice" voyage to Peru around 1539 or 40, and on which he made an immense profit selling Spanish goods. Eventually Cabrillo built about seven or eight of the thirteen vessels for the planned Alvarado-Mendoza coastal voyage. A report to the king of Spain said that Cabrillo's ships were "built the best of any that sail the seas."

As time for the voyage came close, Alvarado and Mendoza convinced Cabrillo to go with them to Mexico to get the fleet ready for the voyage. While they were preparing, Alvarado was killed in an Indian uprising, leaving Mendoza to figure out how to keep to the agreement he and Alvarado had made with the king of Spain, and Cabrillo to figure out how to recoup all the money Alvarado owed him.

To fulfill part of the agreement with the crown, Mendoza eventually sent Hernando de Alarcon up the Gulf of California on what would turn out to be a fruitless quest to contact Francisco Vásquez de Coronado, who was moving up the Colorado River in search of the Seven Cities of Gold. Mendoza approached Juan Rodríguez Cabrillo to sail north up the coast of California in order to fulfill the rest of the promise to the king. Around that same time, a massive earthquake struck Santiago, wiping out much of Cabrillo's fortune. Cabrillo likely saw the proposed voyage as a way to rebuild his wealth.

"The things the Lord Adelantado (Alvarado) owes me. This is an obligation that he neglected to declare in his will because of his grave injuries … I hope to be able to collect from his estate and his heirs," Cabrillo wrote as he tried to collect from Alvarado's estate, but when he saw the futility of his claim, he was willing to say "yes" to Mendoza and began preparing to sail north himself.

Cabrillo's orders were simple. Discover the route up the northern coast of the continent and over to China and the Spice Islands. Along the way, avoid other vessels, be guarded but friendly with the Indians, and don't endanger ships or your men. If you meet natives and they're friendly, go on land and do a full reconnaissance. If you find a good place for a settlement, build it and remain settled there.

A merchant called Lázaro de Cárdenas accompanied Cabrillo on his historic voyage to the bay that would eventually become home to two of the busiest, most important trade ports in the modern world. Cárdenas eventually provided much of the information we have about Cabrillo's trip. Today the Port of Lazaro Cárdenas is the largest seaport in Mexico.

The voyage reached its historic apex in October 1542, when Juan Rodríguez Cabrillo landed at what is now San Pedro Bay. It had been a slow, hard journey with many other discoveries and milestones along the way. On July 2, 1542, the name "California" was used for the first time for the land on the west coast of the continent. The word comes from "Califia," the name in a popular novel of the day of a beautiful queen of an all-female island who let men visit once a year for a sex ceremony necessary to continue the race.

Although he was sailing through charted territory for the first part of the voyage, Cabrillo named many points along the way – always for the saint's day that came nearest to the date of the landing. He noted thousands of sea lions near Asuncion Point and logged the vegetation, talking about the Isla de Cedros being covered with tall cedars and pines on the crests of the western slopes of the mountains, along with grass, shrubs, and dwarf oak on the rest of the island. The mainland was noted as being plains, nice valleys, some groves of trees and open country. After passing Rosario Bay and Baja Point, the land was new, and Cabrillo stopped frequently to take possession of the land in the name of New Spain.

There had been different Indian lineages living in the area for about 12,000 years, and descendants of those peoples were still making their home in and around the coast. Some of those Indians greeted Cabrillo when he landed at different points along the coast. Although they didn't speak the same language and had no interpreters, the Indians used sign language to tell stories of other men with beards and clothes that they had heard about. Most likely these other men were from Alarcon's trip up the Gulf of California – or perhaps even hearsay from inland Indians who had passed along stories of Francisco Vásquez de Coronado and his men who were moving up the Colorado River.

Of course, the Indians Cabrillo met were not aware that the land they had considered their own for so many thousands of years was at that very moment being discovered by these men from a place called Spain. The encounters were predominantly friendly, but the reputation for Spanish swords and cruelty had been well-established by that time, and not all the encounters were genial. Sometimes the Indians fled in fear; sometimes they attacked.

As the explorers continued north, the countryside became richer. "It is red earth and better looking," according to oral descriptions of the sailors years after the voyage. "There are good savannahs and vegetation is like that of Spain." Summaries of the voyage went on to describe ash, sycamores, flocks of animals that looked like cattle, and "very beautiful valleys, groves of trees and low, rolling countryside." They were describing the Coronado Islands. By September 28, 1542, Cabrillo made his first landfall in Upper California at "a sheltered port and a very good one," to which he gave the name San Miguel. Today we call it San Diego.

During his stop in San Diego, three of Cabrillo's men were wounded by Indian arrows. But Cabrillo was perhaps wiser and less confrontational than some of the other Spanish commanders – he most certainly followed his orders to be friendly to the Indians, whom he met, presented with gifts, and tried to reassure that his purpose was peaceful.

After San Diego, the expedition headed north, past modern-day San Clemente, anchoring at an island Cabrillo called San Salvador after his flagship. Today it is called Santa Catalina Island. As they approached, a large number of Indians – who would eventually be named the Gabrielinos by the Spanish – emerged from the bushes, dancing and shouting and making signs for the Europeans to come ashore. Although some of the Indian women fled, Cabrillo and his men made signs that they had come in peace, and the Indians put their weapons on the ground and dispatched a canoe with eight or ten men out to the ship. The Spanish gave them beads and other presents.

Cabrillo and his men went ashore and once again were told stories of men with beards and European clothes being seen inland from the coast.

The next day, Sunday, October 8, the expedition sailed across the channel to what is now San Pedro, which Cabrillo named "Bahia de Los Humos y Fuegos" — the Bay of Smokes and Fires. Cabrillo described it as "a good port and a good land with many valleys and plains and wooded areas," even though the area was covered with thick clouds of smoke from the chaparral fires that the Indians set to chase small animals out into the open so they could be easily hunted.

In San Pedro, the voyagers encountered more Gabrielino Indians who came in a canoe. These also talked of other Europeans who had been encountered inland from the coast. Such reports are evidence that although the Indians had no written language or mass communication, news of unusual events spread rapidly from one tribe to another over great distances. Those stories of such encounters probably happened during both casual contact and trade between the tribes.

Cabrillo left the San Pedro area the next day, never to return. He headed north, stopping several times along the way, visiting both islands and mainland. He found the country "more than excellent – good country where you can make a settlement." He sailed past Point Conception and on to Point Reyes, north of San Francisco Bay, which he missed altogether as did other explorers for the next 200 years. He went north as far as the Russian River and then, with ships damaged from foul weather, he headed back south to San Miguel Island, part of the group that Cabrillo had called the Islands of San Lucas. The fleet planned to winter there before heading home.

But Cabrillo, the poor son of Spain who left his home as a child only to become rich in the New World, never made it back from his voyage of discovery. Although relations with the Indians on what is now called the Channel Islands had been friendly for the most part, on December 24 some Indians attacked a group of sailors on Catalina Island. In the hours just before dawn on Christmas morning, Cabrillo fell and broke his arm while going ashore to help his men. The wound became gangrenous. By January 3, 1543, Juan Rodríguez Cabrillo was dead – eighty-seven days after his visit to San Pedro and more than 5,000 miles from home.

At the age of 43, Cabrillo had become the first European to set foot in California when he led what some historians have called the "most productive" voyage in world exploration. But Cabrillo's contemporaries did not see his voyage in the same light. They saw it as a failure. Andres de Urdaneta, a scribe who in 1566 summarized the voyage for the king of Spain, labeled Cabrillo's exploration "no ymporta" and filed the records away. It was considered a failure for the simple reason that it did not accomplish its mission, which was to find the route to China. And although Cabrillo kept a log for the first five months of the journey, and others kept the log after he died, Cabrillo's log never reached Spain, and the log of the last part of the trip didn't make it there until 1559. In 1560, a crown chronicler named Juan Leon took accounts from sailors to form a summary of the voyage, which Andres de Urdaneta used to create the official voyage record in 1566. In the 17th century, historian Antonio de Herrera y Tordesillas used Leon's records to write two chapters on the Cabrillo voyage in his "Historia General." Because the logs were lost and the voyage was considered a failure, the names that Cabrillo created along the way were mostly forgotten, leaving it to Sebastián Vizcaíno to rename most places when he made his voyage sixty years later. Much of what is known about Cabrillo was put together from thousands of pages of court records that came from litigation his family brought to try to repair his estate after his death.

The heritage and the name of Juan Rodríguez Cabrillo – memorialized on street signs, schools, museums, monuments, and beaches throughout California – is shrouded in some confusion. Portugal, the United States and California all call Cabrillo a Portuguese explorer, but that may not be the case. He was much more a shipbuilder and merchant than an explorer, and his primary biographer, Harry Kelsey, provides compelling evidence that he was more probably Spanish than Portuguese. The first record of Cabrillo traces him to the streets of Seville, Spain. He may have been born in Seville or possibly in the nearby area called Cuellar. Then his name was Juan Rodríguez. Even so, some histories still call him by the Portuguese translation – João Rodrigues Cabrilho.

Cabrillo was born poor, but he didn't stay that way. He was a man of big ideas who could lead other men. He was a man who made the most of his short time. His California discovery eventually became home to the Port of Long Beach and the Port of Los Angeles – two of the busiest and most profitable ports in the world. It's somehow fitting that the street urchin from Spain was the man to discover San Pedro Bay. Juan Rodríguez Cabrillo was a warrior and an adventurer, a traveler, and a trader. He was a master shipbuilder, and he was a merchant. He was a man who could make a deal.

There's no way Cabrillo could have imagined what would someday lie in Bahia de Los Humos y Fuegos, but it's not hard to imagine that if he'd been born 475 years later, he would be sitting in an office overlooking that same bay – making deals and moving cargo.

The Voyage of Sebastián Vizcaíno

Juan Rodríguez Cabrillo earned a place in history for his twenty-four-hour visit to San Pedro Bay, but the visits of the two explorers who followed him are arguably more noteworthy. Sixty years after Cabrillo's voyage and brief stop in the harbor that would one day become home to the Port of Long Beach and the Port of Los Angeles, Sebastián Vizcaíno – a Spaniard who during his life traveled from his birthplace to New Spain, the Philippines, Baja California, and Japan – followed Cabrillo's path.

In 1601, the merchant and diplomat was ordered by the Spanish Viceroy in Mexico City – the Conde de Monterrey – to explore Alta California and identify safe harbors where Spanish galleons making the return voyage to Acapulco from Manila could put in for wood, water, and repairs. His mandate was also to create a detailed map of the California coastline. Vizcaíno left Acapulco in May of 1602 with three ships – the *San Diego*, the *San Tomas* and the *Tres Reyes*. Six months later, he entered the port Cabrillo had called San Miguel and named it for his own flagship – *San Diego*. All along the California coast, Vizcaíno used the same naming convention that Cabrillo had used when he sailed the California coast. Islands, harbors, capes, and mainland were named for the ships each man had sailed or after saints' days that fell closest to the voyagers making landfall. Vizcaíno sailed into the Bay of Smokes and Fires on November 26, 1602 – the Catholic Feast Day of St. Andrew, and he called the harbor Ensenada of San Andres – the inlet of Saint Andrew. Later the cosmographer Cabrera Bueno discovered that Vizcaíno had gotten his saints' days mixed up. November 26 was actually sacred to St. Peter, the third-century martyred bishop of Alexandria. And so the bay was given its third – and so far permanent – name, San Pedro.

If the Indians along the coast of Alta California were fearful of the Spanish visitors' intentions after Cabrillo's visit in 1542, those concerns faded over the next few decades. The Indians who had greeted Cabrillo were surely dead by the time of Vizcaíno's visit, but there were some who likely had heard about the first Spaniard's visit from their fathers and grandfathers. The new generation of natives – like their forebears – did not understand or care what the visitors wanted to call the land, as long as the intruders didn't cause any trouble, didn't stay too long, and left them in peace.

Vizcaíno's first encounter with the Indians occurred on the island he renamed Catalina, and the people there welcomed him. Reports from Vizcaíno's log and a detailed journal by Father Antonio del la Ascensión both described the Indians in the same way. The men were "well-built and robust" and the women were "well-featured and well-built, of good countenance and modest in their looks." The children were noted as being "white and blond," "affable and smiling." Later explorers also documented that these Indians in and around what became the L.A. basin seemed to have been lighter-skinned than Indians who lived farther south.

The Indians that Vizcaíno met were said to be fascinated by Spanish clothes and tools and were "very light-fingered and clever in stealing anything." Father del la Ascensión's journal also documents the Indians using "well-made canoes of boards fastened together," and writes of "canoes so large that they would hold more than twenty people."

The account also talked about the natives' fishing equipment, including harpoons made of fishbone, reed-constructed vessels and pitchers, and domesticated dogs that were the size of "spotted retrievers," that "do not bark, but howl like coyotes." The island Indians maintained a strong trade with the mainlanders. Father Ascension's observations about religious practices went into some detail describing a "place of worship or temple where the natives perform their sacrifices and adorations."

Vizcaíno's voyage provided the first good map of the coast of California, along with excellent notes of the ecological features of the California coast such as the

Monterey cypress forest at Point Lobos. His discovery of Monterey Bay ignited a great deal of interest in establishing a Spanish settlement there, but that wasn't to happen for another 167 years.

Spanish Soldiers and Spanish Priests

When the Spanish decided in the late 1700s that they needed to secure the land far up the coast of Alta California in order to create a buffer zone between other European intruders and their own holdings in New Spain, the world had changed a great deal from the day Cabrillo first sailed that same coast. From the 1500s through most of the 1600s, Spain was clearly the most powerful state in all of Europe. But that power structure began to change dramatically in the 18th century. In 1700, when Spain's last Hapsburg ruler – Charles II – died without an heir, the country was thrown into a war over Spanish succession. By the time it ended, the Bourbon pretender Philip V was on the throne, and Spain had become a second-rate power.

In 1725, Peter the Great had begun creating a belated Renaissance in the massive Russian Empire, which by then sprawled across three continents. It's likely that the young Russian tsar's direction to naval officer Vitus Jonassen Bering to explore the northeastern coast of the Asian continent and from there on to the western coast of the North American continent, pushed the weak Spanish king to see how vulnerable the Spanish Californias were to intrusion by other powers. Philip V ordered Spanish expeditions north and began establishing Jesuit missions throughout Baja California with the goal of converting, educating, and "civilizing" the indigenous population so they could eventually become Spanish colonial citizens.

But by 1768, the Russians were pushing even more aggressively onto the Northern California coast, and the British were also threatening. Britain had already colonized the eastern coast of the continent and had also just conquered Canada. It was obvious that Spain would need to act if it wanted to both protect its New World holdings and continue its own exploration and colonization into Alta California. With a string of twenty-three missions already stretching through Baja California, Philip's son Carlos III ordered the Franciscan, Father Junípero Serra, to establish a mission system in Alta California. In July of that year, Father Serra sailed north with explorer Gaspar de Portolà, who was also the Governor of Baja California and Founding Governor of Alta California.

The plan remained the same as it had always been – to convert, civilize, and eventually make Spanish citizens of the Indians, all with the overarching goal to stave off foreign incursion and settle Alta California for Spain. The type of mission established in Alta California was known as a reducción, which was supposed to "reduce" or consolidate the Indians roaming the countryside into one central community.

Father Serra established his first mission in San Diego in 1769 and planned to establish the second mission at Monterey. Sixty-three of Portolà's troops, along with 100 provision-laden mules, were sent north to scout the bay that Vizcaíno had discovered more than a century and a half earlier. After six months and a march of 400 miles from San Diego, the soldiers came to the bay, but it was shrouded in fog, so they didn't actually see it. They marched north all the way up to San Francisco Bay before turning back and missing Monterey Bay again. Father Serra and Portolà decided they'd make a joint expedition by land and sea to locate

CULTURAL OUTPOST: *Missions such as San Juan Capistrano, seen here in the early 1920s, some 150 years after its construction, and San Gabriel were used to secure the Spanish foothold on Alta California. In addition to teaching Christianity, the missions concentrated the local Indian populations in one place to exploit their labor.*

Monterey themselves, which they did. Father Serra established the Mission San Carlos Borromeo de Carmelo, and Portolà founded the Presidio of Monterey. At that point, Portolà put Lieutenant Colonel Pedro Fages in charge at the presidio and sailed away – never to return to Upper California. On that foundation, Father Serra ultimately established twenty-one missions in Alta California.

Portolà's journey was the first recorded land expedition to explore Alta California, and it led directly and relatively quickly to the decline of the Indian culture, which had evolved in the area over more than a millennium.

The original plan for the missions was full of good intentions. It was summarized in Spain's Laws of the Indies, which governed colonization and colonial ownership and use of land. W.W. Robinson in his book *Land in California* explains:

> *These laws were full of pious recognition of the rights of Indians to their possessions, the right to as much land as they need for their habitations, for tillage, and for the pasturage of their flocks. So far as the California Indians were concerned, this meant, practically, that when they were 'reduced,' that is converted to Christianity and established with or around a mission area, they would have these theoretical property rights. There was, of course, no recognition of Indian rights to land not actually occupied or necessary for their use, nor was there any policy of purchasing Indian titles. Obviously only Christianized California Indians could share in any of the provisions of Spanish law.*

The good intentions were a far cry from reality. Long-existing Indian communities in the mission-controlled areas were abandoned almost overnight, as most Indians chose to continue their traditional lifestyle. For these Indians, there were no property rights recognized under Spanish law, and so they left the land their people had lived on for 12,000 years. For those who stayed, mission life turned out to be more like slavery than a path to Spanish citizenship.

Mission San Gabriel is a good illustration.

When Portolà's land expedition went searching for Monterey, it passed twice through the territory of the Indians the Spanish would dub "Gabrielinos." At first, the Gabrielinos were friendly and shared food and beads with the soldiers. But as time wore on, they grew tired of the soldiers, and by the time Mission San Gabriel was founded, the Gabrielinos had become openly hostile to the Spanish intruders on their land.

One missionary, Father Pedro Benito Cambón, describes the resistance the missionaries encountered but attaches an almost mystical resolution, saying:

> *The Gabrielino, who in full war paint and brandishing their bows and arrows, with hostile gestures and blood-curdling yells, tried to prevent them from crossing the river. Our people finally fought their way to the chosen spot, dangerously pressed ... the Padres took out from one of the cases a canvas picture of Our Lady of Sorrows...*
>
> *At the sight of it, they became as if transfixed in wonderment, and all of them threw their bows and arrows on the ground. Two chiefs took from around their necks the necklaces they value so highly and are accustomed to wear in those distant lands, and placed them at the feet of the Sovereign Queen of the Angels.*

On September 8, 1771, the first Mass was celebrated at Mission San Gabriel, and "increasing numbers of men, women and children" came to offer gifts to the "Sovereign Lady." Unfortunately, things didn't go well after that. The Spanish missionaries piled insult upon misunderstanding, and seemed to alienate the Gabrielinos at every turn. Violence and bloodshed governed the first weeks of the mission establishment, and although things eventually settled down, the Gabrielinos, who had always been friendly and welcomed their Spanish visitors, now shunned them, making conversion and the path to citizenship a difficult endeavor. Many Gabrielinos left the area altogether, and it was several months before they returned. But, by 1773, seventy-three adults and children had been baptized and were living in the mission.

Life on the mission was like nothing the Gabrielinos had known before. The neophytes were required to adopt European dress and eat a poor diet that consisted mostly of mush, pozole (barley and beans boiled together) and some meat, which was much less appealing than the bounty they had been used to. The Gabrielinos, who had previously worked as hunters and gatherers of seasonal crops were put to work long hours each day doing mission work – generally herding animals, farming, cooking, cleaning, and other mission upkeep – much of which was foreign to their previous lifestyle. Baptism was required, and the neophytes (beginners in Christianity) were expected to turn their backs on their spiritual and cultural heritage and lifestyle to embrace Christianity and become Spanish subjects. The Indians were regarded as "adult children," who were expected to change their sexual mores, work ethics, and religious beliefs and were subject to corporal punishment if they didn't toe the mission line. The most brutal and demeaning aspect of the mission system was that once an Indian was baptized, he could never renounce conversion or leave the mission to return to his home. If an Indian fled his mission, he would be hunted down, flogged, and returned in irons.

A clear indicator of how destructive the mission system was for the Indians was the toll it took on their health. Overcrowding, poor sanitation, and a nutritionally deficit diet – that in the early years of the mission was sometimes reduced to half-rations because of crop failures – weakened the population's resistance to disease. Venereal disease was rampant, and measles, influenza, tuberculosis, and dysentery all plagued the Gabrielino population.

University of California physiology professor Sherburne Friend Cook found in his research that there were 29,100 births among Indians in missions between 1779 and 1833, and 62,600 deaths. Perhaps the truest legacy of the mission system is the fact that after thousands of years living in the region, the Indian culture collapsed within thirty-five years of Father Junípero Serra's arrival.

Much of what we know about the early Indians and the natural environment when Europeans first arrived has been found in journals of Portolá's expedition, kept by his captain Pedro Fages – who would become governor of California after Portolá – and a priest called Padre Pedro Font.

The arrival of the Spanish settlers also took its toll on the land and rapidly – and permanently – altered the existing ecology of the Los Angeles basin. The Indians had been hunters and gatherers. The new stewards of the land were farmers and ranchers who brought plants, seeds, livestock, insects and pests with them from Europe.

Over thousands of years a balanced ecosystem had evolved in the area, and that was sent askew with the arrival of new animals – such as cattle, sheep, and horses – that grazed indiscriminately on every growing thing. When the droughts came, the new animals overgrazed, causing large-scale damage to the prairie ecosystem. Native animals did not graze in large herds and each kind of animal had specific plants it preferred, but the horses, cattle, and other livestock imported into the basin grazed the land, eating a variety of plants and spreading the seeds from those plants in their stool. Particularly destructive pests that thrived in the new ecosystem were the grasshoppers, with their voracious appetite for the native plants. They become so prolific that early Los Angeles residents called what is now South Figueroa Street "Calle de las Chapules" – street of the grasshoppers.

Many of the new species of flora and fauna took root and then destroyed and replaced the native grasses and plants, changing forever the animals, the water, and the land that the Indians had long called home.

The First Settlers
The colonization plan for Alta California was to install a Spanish-style civilization that rested on three interconnected components – missions, presidios, and pueblos. The military was responsible for securing new territory and keeping order; the pueblos were established as housing, farming, and ranching communities; and the missions were built to spread the Christian faith to the local population, who would also be co-opted as cheap labor. It was important that the missions, presidios, and pueblos be in a location suitable for farming and raising animals so the soldiers, settlers, and mission population would not have to import their food and other supplies.

This tri-fold foundation gave the Spanish a valuable toehold on the California frontier and represented the first major effort by Europeans to colonize the Pacific Coast region. The missions and presidios were established first, and then the farming pueblos grew around them. Spanish settlers, enticed into the new territory with promises of land and subsidies, introduced European livestock, fruits, vegetables, cattle, horses, and ranching to the region. Each pueblo was entitled to four square leagues of land. A Spanish league was about 2.6 miles long; four square leagues comprised 17,700 acres.

Convincing settlers to move to new pueblos in Northern California was a fairly easy task, as most of those settlers already lived in the area. However, recruiting new settlers for the pueblos in the south – including the one that would eventually become the City of Los Angeles – was more difficult. The people who first settled Los Angeles were from the Sonora and Sinaloa areas in New Spain, hundreds of miles from where they were being encouraged to begin a new life in a land of which they knew practically nothing. The goal was to entice twenty-four settlers and fifty-nine soldiers to what is now the Los Angeles basin. The government offered potential settlers ten pesos a month and daily rations for three years from the date of enlistment. In addition, each settler would get "two cows, two oxen, two mares, two horses, one mule, two ewes, two goats and the tools and utensils necessary for the labors of the field." The settlers would not have to pay any taxes for the first five years, but they had to build homes, plant fruit trees, till the soil and be willing to fight to defend the pueblos.

On September 4, 1781, after an arduous cross-country journey, a group of settlers headed for what is now the Los Angeles basin established El Pueblo de Nuestra Señora La Reina de Los Angeles de Porciúncula – The Town of Our Lady the Queen of the Angels of Porziuncola. Porziuncola is a small but famous chapel built in the fourth century outside the town of Assisi in central Italy.

Five years later, the settlers received clear title to the lands they had been assigned, and five years after that, the population had grown to 139 residents, living in twenty-nine adobe homes, and producing more grain than any of the missions in California with the exception of the Mission San Gabriel.

Land for Service

The actual rancho movement in California began in 1784 when Governor Pedro Fages gave land grants to three veteran soldiers who had served with him on the Portolà expedition through California in 1769.

Juan Jose Dominguez was given more than 74,000 acres. His grant spread over what now comprises the communities of San Pedro, Wilmington, Lomita, Gardena, Torrance, Carson, Compton, Redondo Beach, and the Palos Verdes Peninsula. In the fall of 1784, the 65-year-old Dominguez drove a herd of horses and 200 head of cattle up from San Diego to his new holdings. He built dwellings for the people to live in and corrals for the animals, and called his property Rancho San Pedro.

Corporal Jose Maria Verdugo, who was on detached duty at the San Gabriel Mission, heard about what Fages had given Dominguez and requested a similar grant for himself, a few miles north of the Los Angeles Pueblo. On October 20, 1784, Fages granted Verdugo 36,000 acres in a roughly triangular shape with the southern tip at the confluence of the Los Angeles River and the Arroyo Seco. Known as Rancho San Rafael, the grant covered what is now Glendale and parts of Burbank and Los Angeles. Verdugo remained in the military for another ten years while his brother cared for his cattle.

Manuel Perez Nieto, a Royal Presidio of San Diego solider of mixed race, also applied to Fages for one of the grants. He explained that he had a herd of horses and some bovine stock at the Presidio of San Diego and because his animals were multiplying in number, he was running out of land to graze them. He asked to be assigned a property to graze his animals at a place called La Sanja, three miles distance from the San Gabriel Mission.

These men, who requested and received grants, were not sophisticated or educated people. They were soldiers. Nieto concludes his request to the governor for land with an admission that he does not know how to sign his name:

> *To Your Worship I humbly beg and request that you be pleased to decide along the tenor of my petition or as it may be to your superior pleasure, and I swear to all the necessary and that this my petition is not done in malice, nor least of all to injure any one, and not knowing how to sign I made the sign of the Cross.*

On October 21, 1784, Fages granted his request:

> *San Gabriel, October 21, 1784*
> *I grant the petitioner the permission of having the bovine stock and horses at the place of La Sanja, or its environs; provided no harm is done to the Mission San Gabriel nor to the Pagan Indians of its environs in any manner whatsoever; and that he must have someone to watch it, and*

> *to go and sleep at the aforementioned Pueblo.*
> Pedro Fages

Nieto received the largest grant of all – 300,000 acres that butted up against Dominguez's Rancho San Pedro on the west, curved around San Pedro Bay to the east and south, and extended north many miles inland. He retired to his Rancho Los Nietos, built an adobe home southwest of what is now the City of Whittier, and grew wealthy raising horses and cattle and growing wheat and corn.

There seems to have been little in Spanish colonial law that gave Governor Fages the right to give to his military comrades lands that had been claimed in the name of the king of Spain. In fact, Fages apparently had some doubts about it himself. About a month after he presented his first grant, the one to Dominguez, he put the question before the Commandante General as to whether he had the authority to do what he had just done. What he got back the following year was an opinion from legal authorities in Chihuahua.

The opinion said that the governor did have the right to make such grants as long as the land wasn't within the four-square leagues set aside for a pueblo; there was no injury to pueblos, missions, or Indian villages; and that the land remained "for the common advantage." The settler was obligated to actually use the property for the intended purpose, build a house, keep cattle, and establish possession.

These were not grants of ownership – the king still owned the property. They were basically provisional cattle-grazing permits. But the king was a long distance away, and so were the authorities to the south. They may have merely been permits, but people began to treat the land grants as their own property. The rancho era owes its beginnings to veterans such as Dominguez, Nieto, and Verdugo and others that followed. These men had endured years of hardships and disease representing Spanish interests in the New World. They had fought Indians and seen many of their comrades fall. Land was their reward for that service.

The granting of other ranchos to military veterans up and down the state followed. It was not as clean and easy as it may seem. Nieto's grant was challenged by the Mission at San Gabriel, which claimed a portion of his grant intruded on the property the mission held in trust for the Indians. He lost almost half his property to the mission, reducing his share from 300,000 acres to 167,000 acres. It was still a huge property that extended to all or part of what is today Long Beach, Lakewood, Los Alamitos, Cerritos, Seal Beach, Huntington Beach, Artesia, Cypress, Downey, Norwalk, Whittier, Buena Park, Garden Grove, Santa Fe Springs, Fullerton, and Anaheim. Other grants were lost by grantees who failed to comply with the provisions for improvements or residency.

When Nieto died in 1804, he was by many accounts the richest man in Alta California. In 1806, his oldest son, Juan José Nieto, built a home on the site of the former Indian village of Puvunga – a sacred site for the Indians with a fresh water spring that provided water for many generations. Between the spring and the nearby San Gabriel River was a stand of cottonwood trees. Juan Jose Nieto called the site Los Alamitos, which translates to the "little cottonwoods."

In 1809, the first land grantee, Juan Jose Dominguez, died at 90 years old. Although he had no legal ownership of the property itself, he left it to his nephew Cristobal, the commander of the military detachment at San Juan Capistrano. Manuel Gutierrez, Juan Dominguez's old friend and the executor of his estate, stayed on to manage the property.

The American Traders

Trade around the Pacific Rim had taken place for centuries before Europeans arrived on the North American continent. It was mostly local trade between neighboring islands or communities, such as the trade between the mainland Gabrielino Indians and their fellow Indians on the Channel Islands, or trade among the various islands that are now the state of Hawaii. But there was also some medium- and long-distance maritime trade between various cultures, such as China's trade with Burma, Siam, Borneo, and Sumatra.

Most long-distance trade in the pre-European days was driven by necessity – people traded for things they didn't have or could not easily produce in their own territory. Seal and sea otter pelts from the north, handicrafts or special foods from various islanders, and wooden tools from places where the proper kinds of woods were available, all changed hands. Asia had traded goods with Europe for centuries, mostly through the overland silk route that extended over the mountains to the eastern Mediterranean. The arrival of the Spanish galleons in the Pacific connected Asia to the Americas, and on to Europe by sea. To protect its economic interests, Spain tightly restricted trade by foreign nations with its Pacific colonies in New Spain, Peru, and the Philippine islands. This was an effort to protect industries in Spain and also to seek a profit by selling Spanish goods to colonists abroad. Because of the great distances involved, the king appointed viceroys to represent him in the distant lands.

The viceroy in New Spain had authority over Spanish colonies on the West Coast of North America plus the Philippines; a different viceroy administered the king's holdings in Peru.

The colonists in Alta California had much to trade, including the valuable skins of seals and sea otters, as well as bovine hides and tallow – rendered fat used in the production of candles, soap, and as a lubricant. At the same time, the Spanish settlers were dissatisfied with the exorbitant prices and poor quality of household goods and other necessities being imported from Spain, and would have welcomed trading opportunities with other European nations. But foreign ships, which did have the goods the colonists desired, were prohibited from calling at Alta California ports unless they were in need of water or repairs. The result was the establishment of a robust smuggling industry, widely acknowledged and participated in by the settlers, including the mission padres.

The first recorded foreign trader to call at San Pedro was 32-year-old Captain William Shaler aboard his ship the *Lelia Byrd* in 1805. Shaler was born in Bridgeport, Connecticut. His mother died when he was 8 years old; his father died when he was 12, and the trustee of his father's estate lost the entire family fortune either through mismanagement or embezzlement, leaving William, his two brothers, and his sister on their own. Shaler secured a job as an apprentice to a mercantile firm, embarked upon a course of self-education to make up for his lack of formal schooling, was sent abroad by the company to supervise the purchase and shipment of goods, and learned to speak French. He subsequently became a ship captain, a smuggler, an author, a spy, and a diplomat. He is remembered in history as a visionary, a scoundrel, a troublemaker, a jingoist, and a shady character.

Shaler was not popular with the Spanish authorities. Two years before he landed in San Pedro, he had clashed with them in what may have been the first battle between an American ship and the colonial government of New Spain.

The episode began on March 22, 1803, when Commander Manuel Rodríguez discovered three members of Shaler's crew on a beach near the presidio, trying to buy a pile of sea otter pelts from some of his soldiers. Rodríguez was outraged – some skeptics claim it was probably because he had been cut out of the deal – and ordered the three sailors to be placed under armed guard. He then left.

As dawn approached, an armed party from the *Lelia Byrd* rowed ashore, freed their fellow crewmen, and returned to the ship. They then disarmed the six soldiers that Rodríguez had stationed as guards on the ship, and Shaler gave orders to weigh anchor and get out of San Diego. The *Lelia Byrd* sailed slowly past the presidio as the presidio fired its cannons at the ship, and the ship fired back. It wasn't until the Spanish realized that Shaler had lashed his six hostages on the near side of the *Lelia Byrd*, so that they couldn't fire on the ship without risking the death of their own soldiers, that they ceased fire. Shaler later put the hostages safely ashore and sailed away.

The story illustrates the growing tension between the imperial regulations imposed by the government of New Spain and the early American ideal of free trade. It also demonstrates the attitude by the Alta California colonists toward such restrictions. A year later, Shaler was back trading furs with the people of Alta California. He merely stayed away from the major ports, such as San Diego and Monterey, and did business at lesser ports with both European and indigenous people outside the direct control of the government – places such as San Luis Obispo, Refugio, the Channel Islands, and what was to become a hotbed of contraband, the San Pedro Bay harbor, south of the Los Angeles pueblo.

Shaler was not the only American creeping into Alta California. In his *Journal of a Voyage between China and the North-Western Coast of America Made in 1804*, he noted that other American ships were engaged in the same trade and that the people who resided in Alta California were reaping the benefits. In fact the Spanish authorities in Monterey in 1804 ordered the *Lelia Byrd* and three other American ships – the *Alexander*, the *Hazard*, and the *O'Cain* – to leave California and not return. The order was largely ignored.

Shaler was doing more than just trading, however. He was gathering intelligence on the area as he visited various ports – although not at that time as a paid agent of the United States. His observations, while racist by the standards of modern America, were not at all shocking in a period when white supremacy was a common assumption. The military, with the exception of the officers, contained very few white people, Shaler noted in the journal of his voyage, which was published in the American Register.

> *It principally consists of a mixed breed. They are of an indolent, harmless disposition, and fond of spirituous liquors. That they should not be industrious is not surprising; their government does not encourage industry.*

Shaler went on to observe that under good government, "California would soon rise to ease and affluence…" and that "The conquest of this country would be absolutely nothing; it would fall without an effort to the most inconsiderable force."

Although the term "Manifest Destiny" would not be adopted for another forty years, for many of the forward-thinking people of time, the philosophy associated with the term – the idea that the expansion of America was part of its destiny

– had already taken root. For Shaler and people like him, that philosophy and sense of destiny was more than just an academic theory. It was a concept that he would believe in, pursue, and work toward for the rest of his life.

Chapter Three:
Revolution and Politics

From the destruction of the Aztec Empire by Cortés in 1521 to the early 19th century, the people of New Spain were under the authority of the Spanish crown, and although there was a great distance between the two lands, the Spanish overlords managed to keep a tight rein on its colony and territories in the Americas. The power on the ground in New Spain was a viceroy who directly represented the king and made day-to-day decisions based on the overarching desire of the crown. Sometimes, though, the viceroy ruled according to his own personal interpretation of what the authority in Spain wanted, and it wasn't totally unheard of for some of the viceroy's dictates to serve his own and his cronies' best interests more than the people in New Spain or the king sitting in old Spain. Business enterprises and activities in the colony almost always had to take a back seat to the best economic and political interests of Spain. For example, the cultivation of grapes for wine was banned in New Spain because it competed with Spain's lucrative business of exporting grapes and wine.

New Spain society was based on the old Spanish model and divided into classes based on racial background and where a person was born. To be a member of the ruling class in the colony, one not only had to be of Spanish blood, but had also to have been born in Spain; those born in New Spain were barred from top leadership positions. Below that Spain-born nobility was a hierarchy of clearly defined social classes, ranging from people of Spanish blood who were not born in Spain to the Indians, imported Africans, and the mixed race people called Mestizos, Mulattos and Zambos. Although the various classes all had issues with one another, they did all tend to agree on one thing – they felt disenfranchised and exploited by their overlords in Spain.

By the early 1800s, that resentment bubbled over into violence. The willingness of the people in New Spain to revolt after almost 300 years of subjugation was driven by several factors. A Frenchman was sitting on the Spanish throne, and the Spanish Empire had become weak and vulnerable to the rest of Europe. Subjugated people around the globe were seeking more individual rights within their own homelands and people in colonies – many inspired by the American Revolution in 1776 – were seeking and winning full independence from their own "mother countries."

Mexican Independence
The Mexican War of Independence began as an uprising of Indians and mixed

race people in 1810 that through a complicated series of maneuvers and intrigues ended in 1821 with the establishment of the Mexican Empire. The new empire was independent of Spain, but much of the social structure and privilege that had been established in New Spain over the previous three hundred years was still intact, and having a home-grown version of that oppressive old-world system wasn't acceptable to the people who had just fought off their overlords. The Mexican Empire was dissolved in less than a year, and by 1824 it was replaced by a constitutional republic – the United Mexican States.

As a northern territory of New Spain, the people of California had been largely untouched by the War for Independence, and they weren't particularly excited about the liberation of Mexico from Spanish rule. Nor were they all that interested in the turbulent politics and intrigues that rocked the new Mexican nation.

During those years of being part of the Mexican Republic, California mostly ran itself. The Mexican federal government's role in the affairs of its northern province amounted to little more than sending a string of governors and a small number of soldiers to keep peace among feuding interests within California and head off growing dissatisfaction with the federal government in Mexico City.

There was some benefit for the Californios. With Mexico's independence came the lifting of the stringent Spanish trade restrictions, which almost immediately led to international trade at California harbors rising sharply. Even so, steep import and export taxes by the new Mexican government continued to make smuggling a common basis for the exchange of California goods. Cattle hides and tallow continued to be the big export from Alta California, although sea otter skins, which had long been a profitable export, were no longer widely traded since the otters had been hunted almost to extinction. Ships continued to call at the harbor at San Pedro Bay, but because of the shallow water, they were forced to anchor offshore and row their goods ashore on small boats.

By the time Mexico won its independence, there had been at least thirty grants of ranchos in California – lands bestowed by governors and military commanders to loyal soldiers, much as the original grants had been made by Fages to Dominguez, Nieto, and Verdugo. Although the land still officially belonged to the king during the Spanish years, and the grants were merely cattle-grazing concessions, they were treated by the Californios as personal property and passed down from father to son. These grants covered most of the best open grazing and valley lands from Northern California south.

As soon as Mexico became an independent nation, the holders of the grants were able to seek clear title to the property that they had held as concessions during the Spanish years. Others also came seeking new land grants from the Mexican government. There were some conditions attached – a residence would have to be built on the granted property within a year. The land could not be subdivided or rented out, and public roads across the property could not be closed to traffic.

Things did not always go smoothly in the quest for personal ownership of Alta California. Cristobal Dominguez, who had inherited Rancho San Pedro after the death of his uncle in 1809, had a problem asserting his authority over the entire property following the War of Independence. The property was being managed by his uncle's executor, Manuel Gutierrez. When the new commander of the Los Angeles garrison, Jose Delores Sepulveda, arrived, he procured some horses and cattle and asked Gutierrez for permission to graze them on the rancho. Gutierrez granted the request, but when Cristobal Dominguez found out, he demanded that Sepulveda remove the animals from the property. Sepulveda not only refused, he claimed a large portion of Rancho San Pedro as his own, which he named Rancho Los Palos Verdes.

The legal dispute between the two continued from about 1817 until 1824, when Sepulveda rode to Monterey to argue his case with Governor Pio Pico. On his way back home, Sepulveda was killed by Indians. Cristobal Dominguez himself died the following year, and two years after that the governor granted Rancho Los Palos Verdes to Sepulveda's five children. Rancho San Pedro, by then reduced to only 43,119 of its original 74,000 acres, went to Cristobal's 22-year-old son, Manuel Dominguez. Manuel married Maria Engracia de Cota and had a successful career raising cattle and serving in a variety of elected and appointed positions.

In the area around San Pedro Bay, the four grown children of Manuel Perez Nieto had been working to confirm their title to Rancho Nieto since 1817. In 1833 they petitioned Governor Jose Figueroa for the right to divide their property into five smaller ranchos, and the governor agreed to their request.

Jose Antonio Nieto's widow, Catarina Ruiz, was awarded Rancho Las Bolsas, at 33,460 acres; Antonio Maria Nieto's widow, Josefa Cota, received Rancho Santa Gertrudes, at 21,298 acres; Manuela Nieto de Cota and her husband, Guillermo Cota, received Rancho Los Cerritos, at 27,054 acres; and the eldest son, Juan Jose Nieto, was given two grants – Rancho Los Coyotes at 48,806 acres and Rancho Los Alamitos at 28,612 acres. As soon as the property was divided up among the heirs, Juan Jose Nieto sold Rancho Los Alamitos to the governor for only $500 – less than two cents per acre – a great price even back then. Figueroa died a year and three months later and Rancho Los Alamitos was sold to settle his estate.

Rancho Los Alamitos was located on what became the eastern side of Long Beach, Los Alamitos, Seal Beach, and part of Garden Grove. Rancho Los Cerritos covered what was later the western and northern side of Long Beach, and part of Cerritos.

The Americans

The breaking away of Mexico from Spain and the takeover of the tracts of mission lands coincided with a growing international demand for California cattle products. Latin America had always been the main supplier of hides and tallow, but political instability in those countries prompted traders to seek new markets. The traders brought fabrics, food items, and manufactured goods to California, enriching both the economy and the owners of the vast ranchos with their thousands of head of cattle grazing on the open range. The traders signed multi-year contracts to buy the hide and tallow, providing the ranchers with a stable future market for their goods and driving the economy forward.

Abel Stearns was one of the early Americans to establish himself as a prominent figure in the affairs of Alta California. A man with a long face and sad eyes, Stearns started as a trader and smuggler, who progressed over the years into being a major landowner, political figure and civic leader of California while it was still part of Mexico, and later as California became part of the United States.

Stearns was born in Lunenburg, Massachusetts, about forty miles west of Boston, one of eight children born to Levi and Elizabeth Stearns. Both his parents died in 1810, when Abel was 12. He ended up going to sea and serving aboard merchant ships on voyages to China and the East Indies. He honed his skills at trading and negotiations by serving as "supercargo" on voyages to South America and the Caribbean islands. As supercargo he represented the owner of the cargo. He negotiated the sale of the cargo when the ship arrived at its destination and the purchase of goods or materials for the return voyage.

By the time Stearns was 23, he was in command of a schooner named the *American Ranger*, although it is not clear whether he owned the ship or merely sailed aboard on behalf of someone else. In 1826 he received permission to reside in the newly independent Mexico and remained there for four years, although he apparently didn't find the opportunities he sought.

By 1828, he had converted to Catholicism, been naturalized as a Mexican citizen, and applied with fellow smuggler George Washington Eayrs for a grant of land in what was then the territory of Alta California. In the summer of 1829, he moved to Monterey, then the principal port of California. The Mexican government, in order to encourage settlement of the Alta California territory, had passed a law shortly after independence allowing the governor to grant unused public land to anybody who would live on it and cultivate it. But the process for actually getting a grant could be painfully slow. It took two years for the governor, Jose Maria de Echeandia, to even notify the Mexican government that Stearns had arrived in California and was awaiting a grant. Stearns grew frustrated.

While he waited, he worked for John Cooper, trading with the missions up and down the coast for hides, otter skins, salt, and tallow. Stearns and partner Eayrs had been asking for a grant along the Sacramento River with the plan to establish a town. When it was tentatively approved in October 1830, it was for property along the San Joaquin River, which flows through California's Central Valley. But the deal wasn't final. A report on the grant by the Diputación – a governing group that checked out such grants – still needed to be sent to the Mexican Supreme Court and approved before the grant could be made official. Stearns and Eayrs continued to wait.

During this time, the liberal faction in Mexico City fell to the conservatives, and Manuel Victoria became the political chief. He did not approve of land grants to encourage settlement of the territory, and what's more, he did not like Stearns. He thought Stearns was a radical and subversive, and he feared that Stearns would attempt to turn his grant into an American colony that would threaten Mexican rule. In truth, Stearns was neither radical nor subversive. He was a businessman who wanted stability in government and the opportunity to earn a profit.

The Diputación was supposed to meet in April of 1831, but Victoria made no attempt to convene it. When Stearns pushed to get the grant approved, Victoria told him he was unable to resolve the matter, and when Stearns pushed some more, Victoria told him to get out of Alta California. Stearns was stubborn, but after some more wrangling and contentious communications between him and the governor, he boarded a ship and set sail for the Mexican port of San Blas. Three days later, however, the ship put ashore at San Diego, and Stearns got off to wait while the ship made a trip back up the coast to Santa Barbara. During the two-month delay, Stearns made an important decision. He would not leave Alta California. While Stearns fumed in San Diego, Victoria's arrogant manner and performance as governor was becoming increasingly unpopular among the Californios, who considered him a despot and unfit for office. Revolt against Victoria broke out in Southern California with the leaders of the action being Pio Pico, Juan Bandini, Jose Antonio Carrillo, and the American-born Abel Stearns.

The revolt reached its climax on December 5, 1831, at a battle northwest of the Los Angeles pueblo in the Cahuenga Pass – near what is now Studio City – with rich landowners on one side and the governor's forces on the other. There are several versions of the event as related by the various participants, but the following seems to be a reasonable account.

As battles go, it was more of an armed standoff between combatants – many of them friends and families on opposite sides of the battlefield. Victoria ordered his men to fire a volley at the revolutionaries – which they did, almost to the man firing over the heads of the enemy in fear of hurting a cousin, brother, uncle, or friend. The revolutionaries fired back in the same spirit. Then there was a lull in the battle. That's when things went wrong.

When Victoria ordered his men to fire, Captain Jose Antonio Romualdo Pacheco thought he had ordered them to charge, so he spurred his horse forward, armed with a lance and ready for battle. When he realized his mistake, he halted between the two forces. By this time, Jose Maria Avila on the rebel side of the battlefield, also armed with a lance, spurred his horse forward and went to meet Pacheco in solitary man-to-man combat. People on both sides stopped to watch. Some climbed trees to get a better view. Pacheco and Avila charged each other on horseback three times, and three times they failed to engage with their lances. On the fourth charge, Pacheco knocked Avila's lance out of his hand. Avila became so angry, he pulled out his pistol and shot Pacheco dead. Victoria, upset at Avila's behavior, shot Avila dead. A Captain Portillo, in an effort to avenge Avila, charged Victoria with a lance, struck him in the face, tearing away flesh and cartilage. Victoria fell to the ground screaming in agony and was thought to be near death. But Victoria survived his wounds and was taken as a prisoner to the San Gabriel Mission, where he resigned as governor and left Alta California. The previous governor, Echeandia, took his place.

Meanwhile, Stearns was accepted by the leaders in Southern California. He later attempted to revive his claim for a land grant, but all the documentation for which he had waited so long had disappeared. With the promise of the land grant gone, Stearns decided on a new strategy. He would become a middleman in the commerce between ranchos, missions, and traders on ships. The rancho owners and mission padres would bring the hides and tallow to him, he would exchange them with the traders for goods they had aboard ship and offer those goods for sale in his store in the Los Angeles pueblo.

The traders would no longer have to transact business rancho by rancho up and down the coast, negotiating each deal one at a time. With Abel Stearns as the middleman, they could arrive at one place, load up the hides and tallow stored there, and offload the goods from the holds of their ships. Consumers would no longer have to wait for the next ship carrying the specific goods they desired. They could merely go to the store and buy them. Warehousing and retailing the fabrics, household goods, and other necessities at a store made the trading system both more efficient for traders and convenient for consumers.

John Temple was another New Englander who converted to Catholicism and became a Mexican citizen when he arrived in San Diego in 1824. He was born in Reading, Massachusetts, in 1796, and before arriving in California, he spent several years as a merchant in Hawaii, then better known as the Sandwich Islands – so named by British Captain James Cook in honor of John Montagu, the fourth Earl of Sandwich and First Lord of the Admiralty.

Temple, a stocky man of medium height, moved the following year to the Los Angeles pueblo, where he opened a store. In 1830, he married Rafaela Cota, who gave birth to a daughter in 1831. Temple partnered with George Rice in the trading business in 1833, and as part of the growing business community in the pueblo, he became good friends with Abel Stearns. It was an alliance that would last for years.

Two Years Before the Mast

Among the merchant seamen who called at California ports gathering goods for both the American East Coast and foreign lands, there was an educated young man whose account of his travels up and down the California coast during those years would make him famous. Richard Henry Dana turned his 1834-1836 voyage from Boston to California and back into a book – *Two Years Before the Mast* – and a campaign to expose the cruel exploitation of merchant seamen. It is through his eyes and the prejudices and biases of his day that we learn much about California in the days of Mexican rule and in particular, the San Pedro Bay harbor, which Dana called the "Hell of California."

In one section, he recalls calling aboard the brig *Pilgrim* at San Pedro. Dana and his companions had to anchor offshore, load the cargo into a small boat, which they rowed ashore, then carry the goods across slippery stones on a rocky beach. Two Indians waiting with an ox cart full of hides refused to come down to help. Such was the "California fashion," they were told by the captain. So the seamen rolled heavy casks up the steep and slippery slope and toted large crates of sugar – balanced on makeshift litters using oars placed atop their shoulders – "slowly up the hill with the gait of a funeral procession." Throughout the ordeal, which took "an hour or two," the Indians squatted on their haunches, watching the process. On arriving at the top of the hill, the seamen had to unload the hides from the cart and load their goods onboard, Dana wrote. They asked the Indians to help, but the only answer was "no quiero" – I don't want to.

The hides were thrown down the hill – although some got snagged part way down and the seamen had to slide down the hill to dislodge them, tearing their clothes and covering themselves in dirt.

> *After we had got them all down, we were obliged to take them on our heads, and walk over the stones and through the water to the boat. The water and stones would wear out a pair of shoes a day, and as shoes were very dear, we were compelled to go barefooted. At night we went on board, having had the hardest and most disagreeable day's work that we had yet experienced. For several days we were employed in this manner, until we had landed forty or fifty tons of goods, and brought on board about two thousand hides, when the trade began to slacken, and we were kept at work on board during the latter part of the week, either in the hold, or upon the rigging.*

Dana, a New Englander who grew up in a culture with a strong work ethic, was not impressed with San Pedro or with the people of California. There was no village of San Pedro at the time of Dana's visits, just a hide house that had been built in 1823 by the trading firm of McCulloch and Hartnell – where the hides were stored in preparation for shipping. The nearest residence was the

Dominguez family's Rancho San Pedro, about three miles distant.

Scotsman Hugh McCulloch and Englishman William Edward Petty Hartnell were two of the early traders who were successful in establishing a network of hide-and-tallow suppliers. Their company was commonly called Macala y Arnel – easier for the Spanish-speaking residents to pronounce – causing Hartnell to eventually adopt Arnel as his last name. Construction of the hide house marked the first development of port infrastructure on San Pedro Bay. By the time Dana arrived in San Pedro, however, the McCulloch and Hartnell trading firm was no longer in business. Hartnell had deeded the hide house to the San Gabriel Mission, and it had fallen into disrepair.

The End of the Mission System

One of the steps taken during the years that Mexico governed California was the secularization of the mission system. The mission system established under the Spanish was supposed to be holding the land in trust for the Indians while the Indians were learning the Christian religion and becoming Spanish colonial citizens. It was originally going to be a ten-year process, but sixty years later, the missions were still going strong, and the land was still being administered by the padres. The liberal faction in Mexico argued that the mission system was a paternalistic holdover from the days of Spanish rule that had degraded the Indians and prevented them from joining the mainstream of society. It was time to shut down the missions and divide the property and equipment up among the Indians, they argued.

The result was passage of the Secularization Law of 1833.

Many of the politicians in Alta California also supported secularization of the missions, but with a somewhat different motive. They saw it as a way to gain access to the mission lands and goods. Despite the failure of the padres to baptize and educate the Indians to the satisfaction of the Spanish, the missions themselves had become quite prosperous operations. As an example, the Mission San Gabriel at its peak operated seventeen ranchos, which included 3,000 Indians, 105,000 head of cattle, 20,000 horses, and 40,000 sheep.

As author Carey McWilliams observed in his 1946 book, *Southern California, An Island on the Land*, "the pressure to plunder these estates soon became much stronger than the capacity or willingness of the weak Mexican Government to enforce the secularization decrees."

In the end, the majority of the mission lands went to the rich and privileged people in California – generally non-Indians. Within thirteen years, there had been a total of 700 rancho grants made to private landowners. The Indians, many of whom had grown up on a mission, had neither a culture to which they could return nor any place to go. Following the breakup of the mission system, most of the Indians ended up moving on to find new homes in town, in the wilderness, or working on the ranchos as cheap labor – the same role they had played during the mission years. Although they were officially free people, in reality they were little more than slaves. There were some exceptions where Indians were granted a measure of property, but most of those lands were lost or sold off within a few years. The decline of that ancient Indian culture in California was complete.

Respected but Not Respectable

Abel Stearns had bought the hide house from the Mission San Gabriel – which

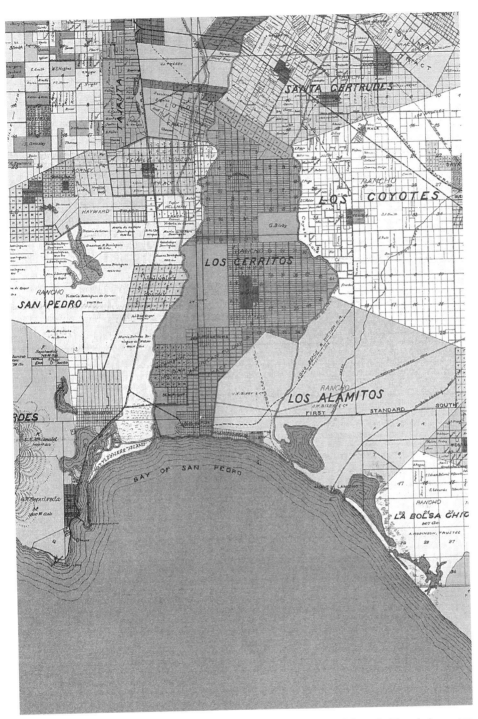

LAND GRANTS: *Politicians and landowners in Alta California welcomed the end of the mission system in the 1830s as an opportunity to gain prosperous church properties for themselves. When this map was completed some 50 years later, long after statehood, Southern California and the San Pedro Bay region were dominated by these large ranchos and their owners, some of whom would be critical to the development of the Port.*

was about to lose its property because of pending secularization – for 150 pesos. He was putting the hide house into good operating order when Dana called in San Pedro. Although Stearns had become a respected member of the Los Angeles community, he continued to have enemies in high places. Smuggling goods was still a widespread and accepted practice in Alta California since the fees and tariffs imposed on goods by the government in Mexico were so high they made it economically unfeasible to trade legally. By avoiding those charges, smuggling benefited importers, merchants, and consumers. Of all the traders, Stearns with his Casa de San Pedro hide house was one of the most successful, which also made him a target.

In early 1835, a local representative of the customhouse in Monterey wrote to the customhouse administrator that he was suspicious of Stearns' operation in San Pedro. The hide house was in a remote area near the shore, and Stearns was known to be ready to deal with any ship that called there, the report said. Smugglers could anchor during the day at Santa Catalina Island and then bring their goods over at night to be unloaded under cover of darkness. The report was passed along to Governor José Figueroa, who passed it on to the Los Angeles town council. The governor also received a report from a group of about twenty citizens who said their cattle were being rustled and that they thought Stearns was buying stolen hides from the thieves. After a lengthy investigation, it was concluded that if the customhouse officials were worried about smuggling going on at the hide house, they should post a sentry there and find out if it were true. And if the cattle owners thought that Stearns was buying stolen hides, they should prove it rather than just make accusations. The report neither convicted Stearns nor exonerated him.

Both Stearns and Temple were tough, hard-headed men, and they took advantage of whatever opportunity presented itself to make a profit. In his early years in Los Angeles, Stearns became a surveyor, although he had no instruments or knowledge of the subject. In fact, he requested that his brother in Boston send him a book on land surveying to help him figure out if he was doing it right.

Then there was the incident with saloonkeeper William Day in 1835 – about the same time that Stearns was fighting the smuggling charges. Day had bought some wine from Stearns' store, but wasn't satisfied with the way it tasted, although he had been warned that it had turned sour. After several confrontations over the wine, the two men ended up in a fight, during which Day pulled a knife and cut Stearns on the hand, shoulder, and face, disfiguring him and almost severing his tongue. Day later bragged about his action, telling people that if they wanted to see the blood of old Stearns, they should go to the store and have a look because he had left him bleeding like a pig. Stearns was seriously wounded and might have died if he had not gotten prompt medical attention. Day was arrested, tried, and sentenced to five years in jail, but Stearns was left with an ugly scar and a permanent speech impediment.

John Temple was making his own dubious mark on history. In 1836, he hosted a meeting in his Los Angeles home of about fifty members of the Vigilance Committee, who were outraged over the murder of farmer Domingo Félix by his wife, María del Rosario Villa, and her lover, Gervasio Alipás. The farmer's partially covered body was discovered in a ravine several days after his murder. Although California courts did not have the authority to sentence civilians to death, the Vigilance Committee members were adamant that the lovers should die, and a resolution was drawn up to that effect. The resolution was sent to the *Alcalde* (mayor), who called a special meeting of the *Ayuntamiento* (town council). By this time, Stearns had been elected to the council as its legal representative. Stearns was not a lawyer by training, but that was not a requirement in the small Mexican frontier town of Los Angeles at the time.

The town council issued a resolution opposing what the Vigilance Committee was planning and beseeching committee members not to do it. After the council meeting, Stearns and two others met with the Vigilance Committee and got the promise that the Committee would make every effort not to let things get out of hand. With that said, the two lovers were taken from the jail by members of the Vigilance Committee and shot. By the standards of the time, justice may have been done, but the affair would have troublesome consequences down the line for Stearns.

After the death of Governor Figueroa on September 29, 1835, and a short three-month rule by his replacement, José Castro, Mexican Congressman Colonel Mariano Chico became governor. Chico was similar in temperament and philosophy to former Governor Manuel Victoria. "Captious, tactless, and void of balance, and his administration, like that of his predecessor, was incisive and short," wrote historian Irving Berdine Richman.

Chico hated Stearns because of the part Stearns had played in the battle of Cahuenga Pass in which the former Governor Victoria had been wounded. One of Chico's first acts was to order Stearns to report to him in Monterey. Stearns hurried north, arriving in Monterey after sunset and going straight to the governor's office. When Chico met with Stearns, he flew into a rage, berating him for his actions against Victoria and vowing to hang him from the flagpole in the plaza in the morning. Despite his threat, Chico did not hang Stearns the following day, but he did order him back to Los Angeles and gave him a month to clean up his affairs before being sent back to Mexico.

Chico later learned of the lynching of the Los Angeles couple accused of murder and accused Stearns of being the ringleader who had convinced others to take the law into their own hands. He had several people arrested in the case and chartered a ship, the *Clementina*, to transport Stearns as a prisoner back to Mexico. Fortunately for Stearns, it was Chico who had to flee back to Mexico when the *Clementina* sailed – to escape the wrath of an outraged citizenry. He was governor for only ten months, but he had managed during that time to alienate almost every person of importance in the territory with his brash manner and foolish actions.

Despite his problems, Stearns was a respected and prominent member of the Los Angeles community. In 1841, at age 43, he decided it was time to take a wife. The wife he had in mind was Juan Bandini's daughter, Arcadia Bandini, age 14, who had the reputation of being one of the most beautiful young women in the California territory – a claim supported by her picture. Bandini gave his permission, and Arcadia said she was entering the marriage freely, signing a declaration to that effect with a cross – since she could not write her name. But Stearns – who was older than Arcadia's father – remained sensitive about the difference in their ages.

The church required that banns of matrimony be published on three successive Sundays to proclaim the coming nuptials to the community. In a letter to the presiding padre, Stearns asked that he and Arcadia be exempted from the banns. An excerpt from the letter demonstrates his concern – he subtracts three years off his actual age – and promises to give an appropriate amount of alms to the poor.

> ... *wishing to avoid the ridicule that the disparity in years might excite in the idle young, she being fourteen years of age and I forty, and in addition finding myself engaged in commercial affairs in Los Angeles and San Pedro as well as having other business that may suddenly require my attention, I beg of Your Reverence please to exempt me from the three banns, or at least two, pledging myself to satisfy the alms that may be imposed upon me.*

Abel Stearns and Arcadia Bandini Stearns – the scarred, sad-faced middle-aged man and the bright, sparkling young beauty – were wed on June 22, 1841, at the Mission of San Gabriel. Friends and families gathered for almost a week of parties and social events. The couple moved into Stearns' home in Los Angeles, a house so big and so fortified that it was known as *El Palacio de Don Abel*, The Palace of Don Abel. He was the shrewd and calculating businessman. She was the lovely hostess and party-giver who would welcome the important people of the day to dances in the home's 100-foot-long ballroom. They were an unlikely couple, but their marriage lasted for thirty years, and to all appearances it was a most happy and successful union.

Both Temple and Stearns had been quite successful as merchants, but both men were ready to become ranchers. When Governor Figueroa died, Rancho Los Alamitos – the section of the Nieto grant that he had acquired for $500 and a favor to the Nieto heirs – had to be sold by his estate to settle outstanding debts.

Stearns bought Rancho Los Alamitos in the summer of 1842 for just under $6,000. The purchase included 28,612 acres of land, 900 head of cattle, 1,000 sheep, and 240 horses. One of the other ranchos that had been part of the original Nieto land grant was Rancho Los Cerritos, which had gone to Manuel Nieto's eldest daughter, Manuela Nieto de Cota and her husband, Guillermo Cota – a second cousin to John Temple's wife, Rafaela. When Manuela died in 1840, the 27,000-acre property went to her husband, and in 1843 John Temple bought it from her heirs for $3,025 – $275 to each of Manuela's children, including $25 for the ranch branding iron and the right to use it.

There is one more thing of historic note in 1842 – not for its importance, but for its portent. In 1842, Abel Stearns became the first man to send California gold, about twenty ounces worth, to the U.S. Mint in Philadelphia. Contrary to what many think, the first gold to be discovered in California was not in the foothills of the Sierras in 1848, but in the San Francisquito Canyon about thirty-five miles north of Los Angeles in 1841. Placer mining for gold at the site continued until the 1848 gold discovery at Sutter's Mill sparked the California Gold Rush. When Stearns sent his twenty ounces to Philadelphia, the Gold Rush was still six years away – six years during which life in what was then Alta California would forever change.

LAND BARONS: *Abel Stearns, left, and John Temple, at far right with wife Rafaela and son-in-law Gregorio de Ajuria, owned Rancho Los Alamitos and Rancho Los Cerritos, respectively, the former Spanish land grants that would make up most of Long Beach. Both men were involved in violent incidents typical of the rough-and-tumble business climate of the era.*

Chapter Four:
California Statehood

The three decades between 1820 and 1850, in which Mexico was winning its independence from Spain and California was becoming an economic force, also ushered in a series of cultural, technological, and political changes in Europe. In 1824, Ludwig Van Beethoven wrote his Ninth Symphony, and in 1826 French physicist Joseph Nicéphore Niépce shot the first photograph, an image showing the view from the upstairs window of his estate in Burgundy. In 1830 two "romantic" revolutions occurred – the Belgian Revolution which led to the southern provinces seceding from the United Kingdom of the Netherlands and establishing the Belgian Kingdom, and the July Revolution in France. They were called "romantic" because in both cases, the upheaval left behind a political landscape in which a king's absolute authority over his kingdom changed to a king's rule of his subjects. But that was just the start. By 1848, France was again in revolt, as were many of its neighbors. Also called the "Spring of Nations," the Revolutions of 1848 saw a rise of the middle class across Europe, along with demands for democracy, liberalism, socialism, and nationalism.

During those three decades, things were changing all over the Americas. Like Mexico, most of the Spanish and Portuguese colonies in South and Central America took the opportunity of turmoil in the mother lands to become independent nations. The fledgling United States, which had just beat the British for a second time in the War of 1812, worried about keeping the Americas free from further intrigues by European colonizers. In 1823, the U.S. adopted a policy that came to be known as the Monroe Doctrine after President James Monroe, who first articulated it. The policy warned the European powers not to intervene in the Western Hemisphere and put them on notice that any attempts to do so would be regarded by the United States as acts of aggression.

Andrew Jackson became president of the United States in 1829. The Indian Removal Act, aimed at evicting all remaining Indians from the eastern states, was passed in 1830. A 30-year-old slave named Nat Turner led a two-day revolt in 1831 which resulted in the execution of Turner and fifty-six of his followers, the deaths of fifty-five whites, and almost 200 more blacks being murdered by white militias and mobs.

Wagon trains of pioneer settlers seeking a new life on the frontier began their long treks west along the Oregon Trail. They weren't the only ones moving west. Between 1831 and 1837 more than 45,000 Indians also moved west on a forced relocation to reservations west of the Mississippi. The mass migration of Indians

– during which thousands died from hunger, disease, and exposure – became known as the Trail of Tears. The removal of the Indians opened up 25 million acres of land for settlement by white families.

Many Americans in the mid-19th century believed in a concept that became known as Manifest Destiny – the idea that it was America's destiny to expand westward across the continent to the Pacific Ocean. It was never a written policy or even a political movement. It didn't even have a name until journalist John L. O'Sullivan used the term in an article he wrote in 1845. But a general feeling that it was America's mandate to spread civilization, democracy, and American values to the frontier and beyond was apparent well before that year in both words and deeds.

One tool in the Manifest Destiny battle was known as the filibuster, which involved private interests going to another country to stir up or abet revolution. An example was the 1812 Gutiérrez-Magee Expedition which went to the Spanish territory of Texas during the Mexican War of Independence with a plan to overthrow the Spanish government and establish an independent Texas republic. Although it was illegal for a private American citizen to wage war against another country, especially one that was at peace with the United States, President James Monroe secretly had Captain William Shaler support the efforts by the filibusters to overthrow the Spanish. The Expedition was successful – but not for long. The first Texas Republic was established, but it collapsed the following year. In the end, that didn't matter much. Before the middle of the century, Texas would become part of the United States, and the ramifications of Texas' road to statehood would be long-reaching. The road led both to the Mexican-American War and ultimately to California also breaking free of Mexico and joining the United States.

The Move Toward California Statehood

Because of the great distances involved, poor communication lines, and its sparse population, California developed somewhat independently from New Spain during the years of the Spanish rule. After Mexico won its independence, that gap between the new country and its Alta California territory continued to widen. Mexican society was divided into a strictly defined ethnic and racial caste system with pure-bred Spaniards in the upper class and mixed-race people, Indians, blacks, and others in the lower classes. Those distinctions were also observed in California, but to a lesser degree. Many of the Mexican people who settled in California had mixed blood, and a number of them rose to positions of wealth and power as landowners and political leaders.

The Mexican War of Independence was won in 1821 by an unlikely alliance of revolutionaries who demanded change and a ruling class who wanted to maintain the status quo that had been established in New Spain – even as it wanted to separate from its overlords in Spain. And although the strange coalition achieved victory that left Mexico independent of colonial control, it resulted in an unstable and polarized government that lurched from one crisis to another. Control of the government switched back and forth between factions, each anxious to implement its own ideology. The result was a weak and vulnerable country that was not well respected by other countries or by its own citizens.

The owners of the huge California ranchos who had benefited from the secularization of the missions became the economic and political elite in California, and they chafed under the autocratic attempts by their Mexican governors to exert authority over the territory. Rebellions were frequent, and the Mexican government, torn by internal political dissension, did not have the resources to enforce its decrees. The secularization of the mission lands also brought on a new host of problems in Alta California. Turned out from the missions and with their native culture and lands lost to them, many of the Indians started attacking the ranchos and pueblos. But the Californios had to deal with the Indian attacks themselves, as the government in Mexico had little resources to offer in protection of its northern territories.

At the same time that Mexico had less power to either protect or regulate its territory, trade between California and the rest of the world increased. That was due somewhat to the lifting of restrictions, but even more so to smuggling, which as it increased encouraged the overt disregard of Mexico's rules and regulations. Many Americans and some Europeans who visited California as traders ended up settling there. California's dependence on American traders as a market for its products and as a supplier for its own required household goods and supplies created an economy separate from the rest of Mexico.

Of all the Mexican provinces and territories, California was the least populated. The Spanish-speaking population was less than 10,000, consisting of about 800 major family lines. There were also about 1,300 Americans and 500 Europeans, who together dominated the trade sector. The rancho owners, with their Indian and peon labor, controlled the ranching and farming. In the north, the Anglo settlers were predominantly English-speaking whites who tended to cluster with others of their own kind. In the south, where Abel Stearns and John Temple made their homes, Spanish-speaking, Hispanic people were more dominant. Americans moving into the southern areas were likely to marry into Spanish families, creating an ethnic division between Northern and Southern California.

Meanwhile, the U.S. desire for an expanded presence across the North American continent was strong, and the tension between the Mexican government and its territories – California, New Mexico, and Texas – soon offered an opportunity to fulfill that desire.

Given the mindsets of the time, the Mexican-American War was inevitable. The territories had little loyalty to the central government in Mexico, and there were big prizes to be had by the United States – specifically Texas and California. Texas had a huge agricultural potential, especially for the production of cotton, and California's location with its natural ports on the Pacific Ocean made it a jewel worth fighting for. With the acquisition of California, the United States could become a continental power. The value of the in-between states, such as New Mexico, Arizona, Nevada, and Colorado, was mostly in the contiguous connection they formed between east and west.

The opportunity to acquire new territory arose first in Texas, which was largely occupied by American settlers who had come there in the 1820s seeking land. Although they were officially Mexican citizens, those settlers tended to think of themselves as Americans first, and by the mid-1830s they were in open revolt against Mexican rule.

Mexican General Antonio López de Santa Anna in 1836 went to Texas with a large force of men to quell the upstart Texans. During a thirteen-day siege of the Alamo Mission in San Antonio, he killed 189 Texan insurgents and their supporters in a bloody battle that would become a matter of both history and legend. But the Texans rallied, and on April 21, 1836, Santa Anna's Army was defeated in the Battle of San Jacinto. Taken prisoner the following day, Santa Anna signed a treaty calling for withdrawal of Mexican troops, an end to hostilities between Texas and Mexico, and noting the Rio Grande River as the border between the two. He was later returned to Mexico.

Both the Mexican government and Santa Anna himself disavowed the treaty he had signed. The government claimed Santa Anna did not have the authority to commit to such a treaty, and Santa Anna said that as a prisoner, he had no choice except to sign it. Texas' status as an independent nation was recognized by the U.S., Britain, France, Belgium, and the Netherlands – but not by Mexico. Particularly at issue was the border between the self-proclaimed republic and Mexico. Texas claimed the territory all the way south to the Rio Grande. Mexico set the border 150 miles to the north at Rio Nueces. The stalemate lasted for almost a decade.

Finally on November 10, 1845, President James K. Polk stepped in to offer a solution. The U.S. would pay the Mexican government $25 million for the "Nueces Strip," in Texas, plus the Mexican provinces of Alta California and Santa Fe de Nuevo Mexico. He further offered to forgive $3 million in debts that the Mexican government owed to American citizens for damages caused during the Mexican War of Independence. The Mexican government was insulted by the offer and responded that not only would they not give up the provinces or the Nueces Strip – but they were restating their claim that all of Texas was Mexican territory. The two countries held their positions until finally, on December 29, 1845, after much congressional debate, the Republic of Texas was admitted to the United States as the twenty-eighth state – further infuriating the Mexican government.

Meanwhile, President Polk ordered General Zachary Taylor south into the disputed Strip, and the Mexicans prepared for war. On April 25, 1846, a 2,000-man Mexican cavalry attacked a seventy-man American patrol in the disputed territory and killed sixteen U.S. soldiers. Eighteen days later, the United States declared war.

War!

It would take another three months for news of the Mexican-American War to make its way to the San Pedro Bay, but a lot went on as the Californios blissfully went about their daily lives. Around the same time that Polk had sent the offer to Mexico for the disputed Texas strip and the New Mexico and California territories, he also sent a secret message to U.S. Consul Thomas Larkin, who was based in Monterey. The specifics of the message are not exactly known – the messenger, U.S. Marine Lieutenant Archibald H. Gillespie, memorized it in case he was captured during the trip across Mexico on his way to California – but the gist of it was that war with Mexico was likely and that Larkin and the other Americans in the area should promote the idea among the settlers that California should secede from Mexico and join the United States. If the settlers took such action, the U.S. Navy was to support the settlers' efforts to escape Mexican control. Larkin had the message passed along to U.S. Navy Commodore John D. Sloat.

After delivering the message to Larkin, Gillespie also tracked down U.S. Army explorer Lieutenant Colonel John C. Fremont, and delivered the same message. Never a man to hesitate, and always a man to interpret things in his own unique way, Fremont took it upon himself to foment an uprising of settlers who took over the Mexican garrison in Sonoma and declared themselves the Bear Flag Republic on June 15, 1846. When the Navy received news of this newly declared California republic, it took action. On July 7, Commodore Sloat raised the American flag and took possession of government buildings in Monterey with no opposition from the Californios. Capt. John B. Montgomery did the same thing two days later in San Francisco (then known as Yerba Buena). With the United States in command in Monterey and San Francisco, the Bear Flag Republic was quietly disbanded, and the American flag was planted in Sonoma.

Meanwhile, the U.S. aggressively pursued the war against Mexico. A U.S. cavalry force under Brigadier General Stephen W. Kearney invaded Western Mexico, at the same time that General Zachary Taylor followed his orders to march as far south as the city of Monterrey, and the U.S. Pacific fleet under the command of Sloat patrolled the coast of California. On July 29, San Diego was taken without incident. On August 4, Santa Barbara also went over to the Americans. Two days later, the Marines sailed into San Pedro Bay. Word of the war had not yet reached the Californios in San Pedro and wouldn't for another week, but that didn't matter. The Americans had been unopposed all along the coast, and San Pedro was no different. The prominent people of Southern California had little love for the central government of Mexico and were more concerned with pursuing their business and personal affairs than getting involved in a war between their U.S. trading partners and their nominal governors. The coming of the Americans was viewed with curiosity more than resistance.

Everything was on track to go smoothly for an American takeover of Alta California, until the Americans became over-eager in asserting themselves. When Commodore Robert F. Stockton arrived in San Pedro with Consul Larkin onboard, he landed his troops, began to make preparations to march on Los Angeles, and established a military base – the first such American military base in Southern California. Stockton had taken command of American forces days earlier after Commodore Sloat had fallen ill. Stockton was more aggressive than Sloat had been, and the differences between the two men were soon apparent.

When Sloat had earlier seized Monterey, he issued a proclamation saying that he had come not as an enemy of California, but as a friend, promising the people of California an open and democratic society with religious and personal freedom.

> *I declare to the inhabitants of California, that although I come in arms with a powerful force, I do not come among them as an enemy to California; on the contrary, I come as their best friend – as henceforward California will be a portion of the United States, and its peaceable inhabitants will enjoy the same rights and privileges they now enjoy; together with the privileges of choosing their own magistrates and other officers for the administration of justice among themselves, and the same protection will be extended to them as to any other State in the Union. They will also enjoy a permanent government under which life, property and the constitutional right and lawful security to worship the Creator in the way most congenial to each one's sense of duty will be secured, which unfortunately the central government of Mexico cannot afford them, destroyed as her resources are by internal factions and corrupt officers, who create constant revolutions to promote their own interests and to oppress the people. Under the flag of the United States California will be free from all such troubles and expense, consequently the country will rapidly advance and improve both in agriculture and commerce; as of course the revenue laws will be the same in California as in all other parts*

of the United States, affording them all manufactures and produce of the United States, free of any duty, and all foreign goods at one quarter of the duty they now pay, a great increase in the value of real estate and the products of California may also be anticipated.

Larkin's plan had also been to settle things peacefully with the Californios. He was a businessman and trader in Monterey, who had been chosen consul because of his reputation for diplomacy and his personal connections with prominent people in California. One such person was Abel Stearns, whom Larkin had enlisted to be his confidential agent in Southern California. Stearns' job was to inform and advise Larkin on the true feeling and intrigues within the community. The two men had known each other when Stearns first arrived in California and lived in Monterey while he sought a land grant from the governor, and they agreed that California interests would be best served with a peaceful annexation by the United States. However well-intended, being a secret informant for the Americans was a dangerous role for Stearns to play since he was also a Mexican citizen who served as sub-prefect for Los Angeles under the Mexican government. Exposure of his American ties could have had dire consequences.

Larkin had hoped to convince local authorities of the benefits of seceding from Mexico and joining the United States. He had written to California territorial Governor Pio Pico and General Jose Maria Flores asking them to try to find a peaceful path for California. When the Americans landed at San Pedro, both Governor Pico and Military Commandante General D. Jose Castro were in Los Angeles, and the two were in a fierce political struggle over who would control California. When they heard of the Americans' arrival in San Pedro, however, the Mexican governors jointly sent a delegation south with a message in which Castro said he was willing to negotiate for peace if all hostilities were suspended by both sides. The fact was that up to that point there had really been no opposition to the Americans by Mexican forces. Larkin thought it was a reasonable request; Stockton did not. He wanted nothing short of unconditional surrender. Stockton sent Larkin back under a flag of truce on August 7, 1846, to deliver his answer.

> *I do not wish to war against California or her people; but as she is a department of Mexico, I must war against her until she ceases to be a part of the Mexican territory. This is my plain duty ... if, therefore, you will agree to hoist the American flag in California, I will stop my forces and negotiate the treaty.*

The Mexicans considered the demand humiliating and rejected it. Both Pico and Castro left Los Angeles on the night of August 10, 1846. Castro told his officers he was returning to Mexico to report what was going on to the supreme government and would return at some future date to deal with the Americans.

The following day, American sailors and Marines marched north to take Los Angeles. They met no resistance, and with Pico and Castro gone, found the government house abandoned. On August 15, the Americans entered the pueblo on foot with the band playing and set up headquarters on Main Street. On August 17, the same day the warship *Warren* anchored in San Pedro with the definite news that war had been declared three months prior, Stockton issued a proclamation to the people of California, declaring martial law and warning them to obey his rules. Unlike Commodore Sloat's earlier proclamation, which had been designed to reassure residents, Stockton's message was much harsher.

> The flag of the United States is now flying from every commanding position in the Territory, and California is entirely free from Mexican domination.
>
> The Territory of California now belongs to the United States, and will be governed, as soon as circumstances permit, by officers and laws similar to those by which other Territories of the United States are regulated and protected.
>
> But, until the governor, the secretary, and council are appointed, and the various departments of the government are arranged, military law will prevail, and the commander-in-chief will be the governor and protector of the Territory.
>
> In the meantime the people will be permitted, and are now requested, to meet in their several towns and departments, at such time and place as they may see fit, to elect civil officers to fill the places of those who decline to continue in office, and to administer the laws according to the former usages of the Territory. In all cases where the people fail to elect, the commander-in-chief will make the appointments himself.
>
> All persons, of whatever religion or nation, who faithfully adhere to the new government, will be considered as citizens of the Territory, and will be zealously and thoroughly protected in their liberty of conscience, their persons, and property.
>
> No persons will be permitted to remain in the Territory who do not agree to support the existing government, and all military men who desire to remain are required to take an oath that they will not take up arms against it, or do or say anything to disturb the peace.
>
> Nor will any person, come from where they may, be permitted to settle in the Territory who do not pledge themselves to be, in all respects, obedient to the laws which may be from time to time enacted by the proper authorities of the Territory.
>
> All persons who, without special permission, are found with arms outside of their own houses, will be considered as enemies and will be shipped out of the country.
>
> All thieves will be put to hard labor on the public works, and there kept until compensation is made for the property stolen.
>
> The California battalion of mounted riflemen will be kept in the service of the Territory, and constantly on duty, to prevent and punish any aggressions by the Indians, or any other persons, upon the property of individuals, or the peace of the Territory; and California shall hereafter be so governed and defended as to give security to the inhabitants, and to defy the power of Mexico.
>
> All persons are required, as long as the Territory is under martial law, to be within their houses from 10 o'clock at night until sunrise in the morning.
>
> R.F. Stockton
> Commander in Chief and Governor of the Territory of California

Stockton also declared victory – if somewhat prematurely – in a letter sent to George Bancroft, U.S. Secretary of the Navy, reporting how he had in less than three months routed and dispersed the Mexican Army, secured California for the United States, ended the war, and restored peace and harmony among the people. He then left Los Angeles after placing Lieutenant Gillespie in charge of the garrison with a small contingent of troops.

Stockton sadly overplayed the situation – and his own success.

Although the people of California were not especially loyal to the dysfunctional government in Mexico City, many resented the arrogant attitudes of the American intruders. The imposition of martial law and the appointment of 36-year-old Lieutenant Gillespie to run things in Los Angeles didn't make matters any better. Gillespie was brash, arrogant, and determined to make sure everybody understood who was in charge. It was an attitude sure to raise hackles in the proud and independent people – both Hispanic and Anglo – of early Los Angeles.

On September 23, a group of about twenty Californios attacked the government house, exchanging shots with the Americans. The act turned widespread resentment into action. By the end of the evening, others had joined the revolt, and Gillespie was in serious trouble. He withdrew from the government house and took up a position on Fort Hill, about a block north of what became the intersection of Temple and Hill streets. The problem was that Fort Hill did not have any water or supplies and Gillespie soon found himself surrounded by 600 armed and angry Angelenos. The young lieutenant did manage to send a courier through enemy lines with a message to apprise Stockton of the situation, but that message and Stockton's response would come too late to help Gillespie. He had no choice but to surrender. He and his men were taken to San Pedro and put aboard the U.S. ship *Vidalia*.

When Stockton got news of Gillespie's predicament just a few weeks after he, himself, had declared victory, he immediately sent reinforcements. On the evening of October 7, Captain William Mervine landed at San Pedro and joined Gillespie and his men, who were still aboard the *Vidalia*. The following day the combined forces began the march north to retake Los Angeles.

But the Californios were ready, and things did not go well for the Americans. When Mervine marched his men through a canyon with Gillespie's men securing the flanks, the enemy shot down on the Americans from the canyon rim. Gillespie's riflemen fired back, clearing the rim of enemy fire, but drawing Mervine's displeasure for wasting ammunition. The two men clearly did not like or respect one another. That night, they camped at Rancho San Pedro, drawing sniper fire throughout the night.

The following day Mervine proceeded toward Los Angeles. But the Californios, led by Captain José Antonio Carrillo, had a clever plan. With only about fifty men and a small cannon called the "Old Woman," Carrillo fooled the Americans into thinking he had closer to 200 men, a goodly amount of ammunition, and an anticipated 600 re-enforcements coming to fight in Los Angeles. The opposite was actually true – Carrillo's forces were pretty much out of ammunition, and there were no additional soldiers. The Americans lost the Battle of Dominguez Ranch. Fourteen U.S. Marines and sailors lost their lives and were buried on Deadman's Island at the entrance to San Pedro harbor.

The news of the American defeat was greeted with celebration and cheering in Los Angeles, but Mexico's military leaders understood that the victory was temporary. The Americans had better weaponry, better training, and vastly more resources. Even so, the Mexican military and the Californios fought on. The final taking of Los Angeles and California by the American forces would not come for three more months. U.S. forces coming up from San Diego joined with a battalion led by Fremont, who was moving southward, and the combined 607-man force marched into Los Angeles to face off against about 300 Californios in the Battle of Rio San Gabriel. On January 8, 1847, the Americans routed the Californios, and did the same again the next day at the Battle of La Mesa. On January 12, the Californios surrendered to U.S. forces, and on January 13, 1847, General Andres Pico – the younger brother of former Governor Pio Pico – met with the Americans at the Cahuenga Pass ranch house to sign the Articles of Capitulation and officially end the California resistance.

But the war with Mexico was not over. That didn't come until more than a year later, when Mexico and the United States signed the Treaty of Guadalupe Hidalgo on February 2, 1848, officially ceding about 900,000 square miles of territory – including California – to the United States. Mexico lost more than half of its territory. In exchange, the U.S. paid Mexico $15 million. The property rights of Mexican citizens within the transferred territory were guaranteed, and each Mexican citizen would be given the choice to become an American citizen, according to the treaty. The U.S. also promised to assume $3.25 million in debts owed by Mexico to American citizens.

The signers of the treaty were not aware of it at the time, but about a week before the treaty was formally signed, an event happened that would change California forever. Gold was discovered at Sutter's Mill on the American River, about thirty-five miles northeast of Sacramento.

The California Gold Rush

The discovery of gold had a huge impact both in California and around the world. Word of the gold strike started to leak out slowly then, as more and more people heard about it, explosively. Adventurous fortune seekers from all corners of the world raced to California in a quest for riches. San Francisco, a small community of around a thousand people in 1848, reached a population twenty-five times higher only two years later. About half of the newcomers came by sea; the other half came over land, but come they did, in a mighty gush of humanity – mostly young and mostly male. Author James Miller Guinn in his 1915 book, *A History of California and an Extended History of its Southern Coast Counties*, describes the scene in a colorful fashion typical of his day:

> *The tales of the fabulous richness of the gold fields of California spread rapidly throughout the civilized world and drew to the territory all classes and conditions of men, the bad as well as the good, the indolent as well as the industrious, the vicious as well as the virtuous. They came from Europe, from South America and from Mexico. From Australia and Tasmania came the ex-convict and the ticket-of-leave man; from the isles of the sea came the Polynesian, and from Asia the Hindoo and the "Heathen Chinee."*

The gold rush did not draw the meek or the mild. It promised adventure for the strong and the hardy, and on that score it delivered. It was a young and masculine society, not softened by the presence of sweethearts, wives, or children. Disputes were settled with fists, knives, and guns. Most of the women there were shared by all – if one could afford such pleasures. There were hostile Indians, thieves, flim-flammers, grizzly bears, and always somebody ready to cash in on somebody else's hard work or hard luck. San Francisco harbor was jammed with abandoned ships whose crews had gone ashore to join the mad dash. And the once-sleepy town of Yerba Buena – renamed San Francisco by U.S. Navy Lieutenant Washington Bartlett in 1847 – was suddenly a bustling, international city.

California's gold rush was as brief an event as it was monumental. It resulted in overnight riches for a few lucky prospectors, but the vast majority of fortune seekers discovered only hardship and disappointment for their hard work and sacrifice. And although gold was mined in California for many years, the easily accessible gold – the gold that could be gathered without substantial financial investment – was gone by 1850. Almost from the beginning, some of the newcomers drifted away from the gold fields to pursue other opportunities – not infrequently illegal ones. Others preferred never to join the rush, but to profit from selling goods and services to a growing population of consumers.

Most people arriving in California during the gold rush were traveling to Northern California, but many of those passed through San Pedro on the way, and some of those who planned only to pass through stayed on. Others did go north, but soon drifted back south when their dreams of riches proved false. By the time of the gold rush, San Pedro had grown into a small settlement of squatters and others who supported themselves through fishing, trading, and servicing the ships that arrived with supplies.

Among the businesspeople in San Pedro were John Temple, the merchant who bought Rancho Los Cerritos, and David W. Alexander, an Irish-born trader who had come to California from New Mexico in 1841. The two partners had bought the Casa de San Pedro hide house from Abel Stearns in 1845 for 2,000 pesos, paid in hides and tallow. The 1.75-acre property included a large storeroom, a house with seven rooms including a kitchen, and a walled-off corral. By the early 1850s, Temple and Alexander were operating a general store in San Pedro, a trading company, and a freight-moving service that used oxen-pulled wagons to transport goods between San Pedro and Los Angeles.

As the gold rush played out and commerce grew, there was still the matter of establishing a government to make California an official part of the United States. From 1847 until 1849 California was run by the military. In September 1849 a constitutional convention met in Monterey – the old territorial capital under Spain and Mexico – to set up civilian rule. The members of the convention voted to outlaw slavery and establish a temporary regional government. Following the September 9, 1850, congressional passage of the Compromise of 1850, which outlined the admittance of slave and free states, California was admitted to the union as a free state. The first state capital was created in San Jose, but it was soon moved to Vallejo, then Benicia, and finally, in 1854, to Sacramento.

From being a territory of Mexico to becoming the thirty-first U.S. state took less than three years for California. It was a time in which the California economy offered extreme opportunities to build wealth – at least for those willing and able to exploit the circumstances.

Chapter Five:
Old Issues, New Opportunities

California had officially become part of the United States. Gone was the ever-changing medley of politically appointed governors who, although largely ignored, remained a constant irritant for the Californios and their American associates. The political and cultural values of Mexico had been replaced by a system of laws based on English common law and a dominant culture rooted in Anglo values.

The Treaty of Guadalupe Hidalgo had committed to respect the property rights of the conquered land, but that was a promise easier to make than keep. Claims that had begun as little more than cattle-grazing permits, fraudulent claims of ownership, challenged claims of ownerships, and claims that required specific terms of ownership were suddenly open to question.

The new state had been flooded with people from around the world. The influx of foreigners – Europeans, Asians, Latinos, and Anglo-Americans – rushed to the state in search of new opportunities and new lives. There existed a passion to build, to take the raw material of a new land and transform it into something great, to bring order to the chaos of the frontier, and to build personal fortunes and influence.

And as the cities of California grew and order was achieved and personal wealth was accumulated, the nation stumbled toward a final confrontation over an old issue – the institution of slavery.

The American Civil War and the turbulent times leading up to it do not usually conjure up images of California. No abolitionists were hanged in Los Angeles; no underground railroad existed here. No decision over who was a slave, and who was not, was made in a California court. And later, no major battles were fought in the Golden State. There were no fields of dead bodies lying in the streets of Los Angeles or San Francisco or Monterey as there were in the aftermath of Gettysburg and Shiloh and Antietam. There were no mass movements of cavalry or infantry as Union and Confederate soldiers struggled to achieve geographic advantage. There were no stories of bigger-than-life California heroes showing courage and honor on the battlefield. There was no Stonewall Jackson or George Armstrong Custer to be revered. No great generals such as Ulysses S. Grant or Robert E. Lee rode the dusty trails of the Golden State. There was no march to the sea.

But the Civil War did come to California, and what happened in the state before, during, and after the war, had a significant impact on the development of the state. The Civil War was as pivotal an event for California as it was for the rest of the nation. The culture and civilization that existed before the war was forever changed, and what came afterward evolved in ways that few could have imagined a decade earlier. And even though no Civil War battles – great or small – took place in California, the war's impact on the state was profound, because the nation's pre-Civil War struggles over states' rights and slavery, along with the war itself, formed the backdrop for the development of a uniquely Californian economy and infrastructure that sets the state apart to this day. Much of California was developed in those pre-Civil War and War years by people whose names even now pepper our streets and towns and schools and parks.

A New Land of Opportunity

One of those people, one who would play a huge role in making San Pedro Bay a center of commercial shipping, was a strapping young man named Phineas Banning, who arrived by ship in 1851. Banning became such a bigger-than-life figure in the harbor community that it is sometimes hard to separate legend from fact. The popular perception is that he showed up at 21 years old with high hopes and little more. The truth is a bit more complicated.

The Banning family in Delaware was both prominent and successful. Although Phineas Banning's father found little success as a farmer, his grandfathers on both sides – John Banning and William Lowber – had been both successful and prominent as landowners, businessmen, and public officials. His own father was the exception, and life on the farm was both difficult and boring. At 13 years old, Phineas left home with fifty cents in his pocket and walked thirty miles to live with his brother William Lowber Banning, an attorney in Philadelphia. In the 1840s, Philadelphia was an extreme and dangerous place to be. But the tension between the rich and the poor, as well as between the various ethnic and racial groups that jammed into the city, combined with political incompetence and corruption to make Philadelphia a wonderful training ground for life on the frontier of California.

Phineas worked for several years at his brother's law firm near the docks, but by 1851, he had a job as a clerk at Siter, Price and Co., a firm that sold household goods imported from Europe. One of his assignments at the company was to pack some fragile china for George East, a client who planned to ship the items to California and sell them there. East agreed to pay Banning's passage to California if Banning would go with him and look after the goods. Banning agreed.

The two men sailed south to Panama, crossed the isthmus in canoe and wagon, and caught another ship up the coast to San Pedro – a journey that took many weeks – the difficulty magnified because of the fragile freight they were transporting. Once they reached San Diego they separated, with East going up the coast to find a buyer for his goods, and Banning temporarily remaining in San Diego. After several unsuccessful sales calls, East finally sold his shipment to the firm of Douglass & Sanford in San Pedro. Then he fell ill and died. Apparently aware that his end was near, East had signed a will a week before his death directing that his property be divided among his relatives. East's will, however, left several loose ends. The firm of Douglass & Sanford had not fully paid East for the shipment of crockery, and East had not fully paid Siter, Price and Co. for the goods. In addition, many of the fragile items had been damaged in transit and the time for filing a claim for insurance was long past. It fell to Phineas Banning to work out things between East's estate, Douglass & Sanford, and his former Philadelphia employer, Siter, Price and Co.

Los Angeles County Clerk Benjamin D. Wilson and David Douglass were named as executors of East's estate – Wilson to handle East's bequest to his relatives and Douglass to handle the question of the freight since his firm had agreed to buy the goods. It took many months to settle the estate. At the same time that Banning was settling the outstanding payments for the cargo, he also was hired as a clerk by Douglass & Sanford.

During this time, Los Angeles was a small frontier city with a permanent population of fewer than 2,000 people. The streets were unpaved, the buildings were made of adobe bricks – none more than two stories tall – and almost everybody knew everybody else. San Pedro, twenty miles south, was a tiny settlement with no schools or churches or other amenities. The harbor was shallow, and the cargo – as in Richard Henry Dana's time – had to be offloaded at anchor and taken ashore in smaller boats. Most of the cargo was landed on the beach, sometimes ending up drenched after being dropped in the water.

Banning's stint at Douglass & Sanford paid off more than just his salary; the young man learned the business and came to know the important people in the community. These people would play key roles in his future and in the future of the San Pedro Bay – either as adversaries or as business partners, and at various times both.

David Douglass of New York and his partner William Sanford of Missouri had been in California since before it became a state. They were in the business of buying and selling goods from seafarers to both wholesale and retail customers. They also supplied passenger service by coach between San Pedro and Los Angeles.

Augustus W. Timms, a Prussian officer on a ship calling in San Pedro, had disembarked in San Pedro, served in the war against Mexico, started a goat farm on Catalina Island, and then returned to the mainland. Shortly after Banning arrived, Timms bought the Sepulveda Landing property and a small dock from Juan and Jose Sepulveda, renamed it Timms' Landing, and arranged to represent several shipping firms that called at San Pedro Bay. He salvaged the lumber and deckhouse from the remains of the brig *Mary Jane*, which had blown ashore during a storm, and built a home. He quickly added a warehouse and other improvements. Timms would become a tenacious competitor who often provoked Banning.

John Temple, the owner of Rancho Los Cerritos and partner to David Alexander in the Casa de San Pedro hide house, was probably the second-richest man in Southern California at the time. The richest was the old trader and smuggler, Abel Stearns, who owned the adjacent Rancho Los Alamitos. Congress had recently certified San Pedro as a port of entry and named Stearns as Collector of Customs.

Benjamin D. Wilson, the Los Angeles County Clerk and executor of East's will, had been in California since 1841. His story reads like a pulp western. He was a former fur trapper, Indian fighter, explorer, soldier, rancher, and farmer. In 1844, Wilson married Doña Ramona Yorba. Her father, Don Bernardo Yorba, was one of the owners of the Santa Ana Ranch. Later that year, Wilson was almost killed while tracking a grizzly bear that had killed one of his cows. After recovering from his wounds, he hunted the bear down and killed it. Also known as Don Benito, Wilson was a frontiersman who had a head for business and politics. In 1851, he was elected as the third American mayor of Los Angeles. Wilson would play a big role in Banning's career as a business partner, mentor, and friend.

Although Banning arrived in Southern California with little money, he managed to save what he had and to earn more – a lot more. He landed in the middle of this frontier society in a situation that provided him with political and business connections, a job, and an opportunity to impress the leading members of the community with his acumen. He was young, but he was also ambitious and smart. He was the kind of person of whom other people took notice. He was the kind of person who managed always to dominate and control any circumstance. Horace Bell in his book *Reminiscences of a Ranger* tells of arriving in San Pedro from San Francisco in October 1852 aboard the steamer *Sea Bird* – at the time when Banning was still working as a clerk for Douglass & Sanford. Bell and other passengers, one of whom was Benjamin "Don Benito" Wilson, had just boarded two old stages pulled by teams of mules. Speed was important in those early days. The rutted road to Los Angeles was long and desolate, and bandits were known to rob both stages and passengers along the way. The stages were driven at high speed with riders on horseback whipping the mules forward from both sides.

> *Finally, when all hands were seated, a portly looking young man that Don Benito called Banning, came around with a basket on his arm and offered to each of the passenger an ominous looking black bottle, remarking, "Gentlemen, there is no water between here and Los Angeles," and then inquired, "all ready?" One surly looking sailor driver grumbled out in reply, "Is there going to be no betting?" When Banning laughingly remarked that the drivers expected the passengers to bet something on the trip, "just enough to make it interesting," whereupon a passenger who sat beside me, whose neat appearance showed him to be of recent importation, offered to bet $5 on our stage.*

As one of his sidelines to supplement his earnings during that period, Banning would bottle and sell fresh water to sailors onboard ship. It would seem that he may have done the same to passengers on the stage.

After little more than a year working as a clerk for Douglass & Sanford, Banning formed a partnership with George Alexander – the younger brother of David Alexander – and bought out the assets of his former employer. Although Banning had long saved his money, neither he nor George Alexander were wealthy men. But Banning's year-long employment had provided him with more than just a salary; it had also given him an entree to the movers and shakers of his day. To buy out Douglass & Sanford along with their horses, mules and rolling stock, Alexander and Banning had to borrow money. Probably some of the cash came from older brother David Alexander. William Sanford sold out his share of Douglass & Sanford, but joined the new firm, Alexander & Banning, as both an investor and associate. Things were moving forward quickly, as they always would with ventures involving the young Mr. Banning.

Merchant Harris Newmark, who would become both a friend and a financial angel for Banning, recalled his first meeting with Banning when he arrived in San Pedro in October 1853 – one year after Bell had arrived. Banning by this time was 23 years old and a partner in his own business. Newmark, who had arrived to join the family business, was only 19.

> *There stood before me a very large, powerful man, coatless and vestless, without necktie or collar, and wearing pantaloons at least six inches too short, a pair of brogans and socks with large holes; while bright-colored suspenders added to the picturesque effect of his costume. It is not my desire to ridicule a gentleman who, during his lifetime, was to be a good, constant friend of mine, but rather to give my readers some idea of life in the West, as well as to present my first impressions of Southern California. The fact of the matter is that Banning, in his own way, was even then such a man of affairs that he had bought, but a few months before, some fifteen wagons and nearly five times as many mules, and had paid almost thirty thousand dollars for them. I at once delivered the letter in which (business associate Jacob) Rich had stated that I had but a smattering of English and that it would be a favor to him if Banning would help me safely on my way to Los Angeles; and Banning, having digested the contents of the communication, looked me over from head to foot, shook hands and, in a stentorian voice loud enough, I thought, to be heard beyond the hills good-naturedly called out. "Wie geht's?" (How are you?) After which, leading the way, and shaking hands again, he provided me with a good place on the stage.*

The thing that had not changed from Bell's arrival to Newmark's was the betting on which stage would get to Los Angeles first. Newmark, in his excellent history, *Sixty Years in Southern California 1853-1913*, wrote that the stagecoach races had become the talk of the pueblo. The trips were made at "breakneck speeds" over roads that were "abominably bad." Total time: two-and-one-half hours. Fare: $5.

Banning was by this time a respected member of the community. On November 16, 1854, he married 19-year-old Rebecca Sanford, the sister of his associate and former employer William Sanford. They moved into an adobe house close to the San Pedro waterfront. Rebecca would give birth to nine children during their marriage, but only three would live beyond five years – a not uncommon experience at the time, even for well-to-do families.

Meanwhile, Alexander & Banning bought a piece of property from the Sepulvedas near Timms' Landing, where they erected a small wharf. The partners continued to expand their business, buying more flat-bottomed barge-like vessels to help load and unload cargo from ships anchored offshore – the harbor still being too shallow to allow access for ships. With each addition of capacity, the business grew. On September 1, 1854, David Alexander, George's older brother, joined the firm as a full partner, and the name was changed to Alexanders & Banning.

Earlier that year the Army had announced plans to build a fort at the Tejon Pass, between Los Angeles and the Central Valley, which offered lucrative opportunities to Alexanders & Banning. The company wanted the contract to deliver supplies to the fort. The project immediately ran into problems because of the primitive San Fernando Road, which connected Los Angeles to the fort site. The partners and other businessmen joined a campaign to convince the County Board of Supervisors to put up $1,000 toward a project to improve the road with the promise that private parties would contribute a like amount. It was an early example of a public-private partnership to build infrastructure and a strategy that Banning would employ in the future. Wealthy businesspeople agreed to contribute $2,900 toward the improvements. The fact that David Alexander was himself a county supervisor helped the project win county approval.

Once the road was open, Alexanders & Banning began using it to deliver supplies to Fort Tejon, seventy miles north of Los Angeles. With the Army contract in hand, the company extended its route north to include gold mines along the Kern River – connecting the Central Valley to the Los Angeles basin.

There were other developments around this same time that would have far-reaching impacts on the future development of harbors on both sides of San Pedro Bay. On December 22, 1854, Manuel Dominguez of Rancho San Pedro sold 2,400 acres of low-lying property north of San Pedro to a group of businessmen for $5 an acre. The group included Benjamin Wilson, William Sanford, and John G. Downey. Although Banning knew all the folks involved in the purchase, he did not participate. His money at the time was tied up in building his own business. An early mention of the businessmen's plan for the property appeared in the February 11, 1855, issue of the Los Angeles Star. The article optimistically predicted that the investors would build a town at the site and that ships would soon be tying up at the waterfront there. Unlike San Pedro, the new site had easy access to fresh water, fewer hills and bluffs with which to contend, and was seven miles closer to Los Angeles. In reality, it would be more than a little while before that prediction came true. The investors had envisioned their new city being served by a transcontinental railroad.

The idea of a transcontinental railroad that would link the Atlantic Coast to the Pacific had been talked about for decades, starting in the 1830s – when California was still a Mexican territory. But all the talk resulted in very little action. Even after California became a state, there was the question of exactly what the route for such a railroad would be. The Southern states favored a southern route; the industrialized Northern states favored a northern course. As always during those years, there was the question of slave versus free states and what the impact of each route would mean for that balance. With congressional funding for the railroad stalled, the new city sputtered with little work on the project actually taking place.

The road to Fort Tejon wasn't the only highway improvement going on during this period. The County also had agreed to fund road improvements between San Pedro, Los Angeles, and San Bernardino – the site of a Mormon colony. The Mormons had requested state and federal funding to improve the road through the Cajon Pass and on to Salt Lake City. The highway was seen by the Mormons as a supply route connecting their desert community to Southern California. Alexanders & Banning were quick to capitalize on the improvements, purchasing $20,000 worth of goods – much of it on credit – to sell in Salt Lake City. The company assumed a third of the debt for building the supply route. John Temple, William Sanford, and Benjamin Wilson took on the remainder.

In 1855, Sanford led a train of fifteen wagons each with a team of ten mules that pulled a combined thirty tons of merchandise to sell in Salt Lake City. The merchandise was all sold, and the trip was a monumental success, despite opposition from religious leaders who wanted to keep the business within the Mormon community. For a time it must have seemed that everything Banning touched turned to gold, but when the company attempted a repeat of its successful Salt Lake City venture the following year, it was a financial disaster. This time the freight being hauled included a large supply of liquor – something not welcome in a community that had a religious opposition to alcohol. In addition, the resistance by Mormon leaders to outsiders trading within the community had grown stronger. Alexanders & Banning suffered a significant loss on the trip, just at the same time that the fast-growing company had borrowed its way into trouble. Its creditors wanted their money, and when payment was not forthcoming, they turned to the courts.

In the end, people lost fortunes. David Alexander, who by then was also the Los Angeles County sheriff, had to resign his post and take a job working for his friend John Temple. Settlements were reached, many with a combination of cash, equipment, real estate, and promises for future service. Alexanders & Banning disbanded, but Banning himself seemed to suffer little more than a slightly damaged reputation. Later that same year, he formed a new partnership with Canadian trader Spencer H. Wilson doing precisely the same thing the old partnership did – importing and selling goods to people in Los Angeles and beyond. By the summer of 1857, they dissolved the partnership and Banning continued on his own. Although he was only 27 years old and had been in California for only six years, people were already recognizing him as the "stage and freight baron of Southern California."

By 1858, Banning had recovered enough from his earlier financial setback to buy several hundred acres of land at the head of what was known as the San Pedro Slough – a portion of the property purchased more than three years earlier from the Dominguez family as the site for a new city. Banning planned to move his operation from San Pedro north to the new site. Not only would that put it closer to Los Angeles and on flatter ground, but the presence of Rattlesnake Island – an east-west barrier island that separated the open ocean to the south from the marshy lagoon on the north – would shelter his operation from the southeaster storms that would periodically wreak havoc along the San Pedro waterfront. It would also give Banning a competitive advantage over his rivals in San Pedro.

On September 25, 1858, Banning held a ceremony in which he declared the founding of a new town – which he initially called New San Pedro – with the landing of freight and passengers at his recently completed dock. Any thoughts he may have had of continuing to do business in the first San Pedro were completely dashed less than a week later when a southeaster storm swept into San Pedro Bay causing widespread damage to the remains of his old San Pedro operation. The October 2, 1858, issue of the Los Angeles Star reported the devastation:

> *We are sorry to say that Mr. Banning's famous yacht Medora suffered from the envious winds and waves, whose swiftest course she has frequently out run. Laying quietly at anchor, they rose in their might against her, drove her from her moorings on to the beach, where they prevailed against her and broke her up, scattering her fragments on the shore. A large barge was also broken up; another, having dragged its anchor a considerable distance, was brought to by the anchor fastening against a rock.* "The wharf at San Pedro was very much injured, a large part of the flooring having been carried away by the violence of the sea. A large quantity of lumber stored on the beach was floated off by the high tide and the violence of the storm."

Banning was done doing business in San Pedro, even though some questioned whether his new location was a good idea. Floods would wash silt down from the mountains, clogging the channels to his new port landing, and extreme high tides often threatened to inundate the low-lying area. His operation was derisively called "Banning's Hog Waller" and "Goose Town," because of the large number of wild geese in the area. But such taunts did little to deter Banning and his partners, who continued to move forward, laying out town plots and cutting deeper channels where necessary. Banning asked the county supervisors to fund the building of a road from his new landing that would connect with the existing road to Los Angeles. In exchange, he would deed the road to the county and pay for construction of a small bridge along the way. They had a deal.

The Bixbys and the Flints

On the Fourth of July, 1851 – a little before the arrival of Phineas Banning in San Pedro – a sea captain who had had far too much whiskey almost ran his ship aground off the coast of what was to become Long Beach. The close encounter gave passengers Lewellyn Bixby (who had dropped the second "l" from the traditional spelling of his name in order to "Americanize" it), his brother, Amasa Jr., and their cousin Thomas Flint their first look at the area. What they saw was a bluff, rolling hills, pastures, and cattle. It must have been a pastoral and pleasant scene, but the Bixbys and Flint weren't stopping in Southern California – at least not then. They were on their way to San Francisco and then on to the town of Volcano, about fifty miles southeast of Sacramento, to join Thomas' brother Benjamin Flint.

Benjamin Flint had left Maine in 1849 to join the gold rush in California. Much as Banning would do two years later, Flint went by ship to Panama, crossed the isthmus, and took another ship up the coast to California. His fellow passengers included two men who would later play prominent roles in the history of Southern California – Collis Huntington, who would become a railroad tycoon, and James Irvine, who would become a landowner and rancher in what is now Orange County.

Gold had lured Flint to California, but what he found after spending long hours in freezing streams looking for it, was that the real money to be made was not in seeking gold, but in selling goods and services to other people who were seeking gold. So when his brothers and cousins arrived in 1851, they spent little time mining. Instead, the Flints and the Bixbys got jobs. Two years later, two more Bixby brothers arrived – Jotham and Marcellus. Life on the frontier could be difficult, but the Flints and the Bixbys were New Englanders. They believed in hard work and saving money. Within a year, Lewellyn Bixby and the Flints became partners in a butcher shop; Jotham and Marcellus were growing crops on a small farm and selling produce to miners, and Thomas Flint built a hotel.

In December 1852, Lewellyn Bixby and the Flint brothers left Volcano to return to New England with $5,000 in gold and a new plan. Once back East, they visited with family, and then boarded a train west to the end of the line – Terre Haute, Indiana, where they formed Flint, Bixby & Co. They spent the next two months buying sheep that they planned to drive overland to California. Southern California supplied all the beef needed to feed the thousands of people who poured into California in search of gold, but there was a waiting market for mutton and for wool. Sheep could bring $20 a head in California, but the trick was getting them there. Before they departed on their 2,000-mile journey west, the partners sheared their flock and sold the wool, earning $1,570. Then, along with their crew of hired help, they started the long trek, moving at the speed of sheep across dangerous and rough terrain, through hostile Indian country and a pack of hardships that included everything from bad weather to a swarm of locusts.

Along the way they met another party of sheep herders in Utah – headed by Colonel William Welles Hollister, his brother Joseph, and their sister Lucy A. Brown – that was driving a flock of 6,000 sheep from Ohio to California. The two parties worked closely during the rest of the trip, defending their flocks from Indians and negotiating their way through lands held by Mormons, who were suspicious of outsiders. The little band with their several thousand head of sheep moved over the Cajon Pass to the Los Angeles basin that fall and wintered at Rancho San Pasqual near what is now Pasadena. They spent a year in Southern California, pasturing and replenishing their flock before heading north for what was then Monterey County. In October 1855, Flint, Bixby & Company bought the 34,620-acre Rancho San Justo, south of San Jose, for $25,000, with the agreement that Hollister would buy half interest in the property two years later.

And there the Bixbys and the Flints became successful sheep ranchers.

There was no city of Long Beach at the time. But years later, when the hillsides and livestock that Lewellyn Bixby had first seen from the deck of that ship under the command of the drunken sea captain turned into a village by the sea, and later a city, Lewellyn and the Bixby family would play a leading role.

The Land Commission and the Ranchos

The Treaty of Guadalupe Hidalgo that ended the Mexican-American War in 1848 provided that the property rights of the people living in the conquered territory would be respected. In order to fulfill that obligation, the U.S. Land Commission was set up to resolve land claims. Settling those claims soon proved to be a more difficult and confusing task than it first seemed. Before the war, the Mexican governor of California, Pio Pico, had seen the writing on the wall and began selling off grants in order to put as much property in private hands as possible. These grants were so poorly documented that it was not clear exactly where the grant was, and sometimes the grants had conflicting boundaries. Some people presented claims for land that were clearly fraudulent. Many of the legitimate grants had stipulations about what improvements were to be made on the property, and the Land Commission had to study these agreements to see if the stipulations had been satisfied. In other cases, the land had been sold by the estates of owners who had died. Those sales were sometimes challenged by other possible heirs of the original owner, who felt they had not been given adequate notice to stake their own claims to the property. Then there was political pressure from people such as Senator Thomas Benton, whose son-in-law John C. Fremont held claim to a gold mine in the Sierra Nevada Mountains and was pushing for a quick resolution to land ownership disputes. There were also problems with squatters, who would arrive in California after a long overland trip, find a nice spot of undeveloped land, build a house and start living in it. There was a feeling that this was how land ownership worked in the West. When the squatters were told that the land belonged to someone else, they became angry – some so angry that the government feared the situation could turn violent.

Although the Land Commission was diligent in attempting to resolve property ownership, the legal and political morass that followed stretched out the process for more than two decades in some cases. The typical time from filing a claim of ownership to getting a clear title was about seventeen years in California. A lot of things could happen over that span of time, especially when the title to one's property was under a cloud.

It cost money to file a claim with the Land Commission, and it cost money to hire attorneys to represent the claim. While claims made their way painstakingly slowly through the courts, owners of the large tracts would continue to fight for their property in court as they attempted to operate their ranches. To finance their struggle, they would often promise their attorneys tracts of land in exchange for services.

Both Stearns and Temple were struggling to maintain their empires and not just because of exorbitant legal fees. The gold rush had sparked a boom in the cattle market to feed the folks looking for gold. It also inspired many of the California cowboys to head north to seek their own gold. Those who stayed behind demanded higher wages. The ranch owners tried to hire Indians as cheap labor, but many Indians preferred to become rustlers instead – letting the white men raise the cattle so they could steal and eat them.

By 1857, things were not going well for the leading families of Southern California. Legal and economic problems coupled with natural disasters threatened to overwhelm the rich landowners whose wealth depended on raising cattle on their huge tracts of land. The beef boom spurred by the gold rush was over. There was an 8.3 earthquake on the San Andreas Fault. There was a financial recession in 1860 and a plague of grasshoppers in 1861.

These were dark days for rancho owners, but what they didn't know, was that the worst was still yet to come.

The Wild West

In the 1840s and '50s, when the people who would become the "first families" of California were arriving on the scene to stake their claims, establish their businesses, and make their fortunes, California was at perhaps its most wild time ever. The territory was filled with men who had worked their way north from Mexico or west across the wilderness to mix with the Indians, soldiers, and Hispanics who came to establish pueblos during the time of Spanish rule. Many young men in the late 1840s came looking for gold and the other opportunities that could only be found on a new frontier. They were young men who had a certain fire in their bellies, young men who decided not to stick around and do what was expected of them. They were headed for the gold fields of California, although most of them failed in their quest and many of them died. Some of those would-be fortune seekers drifted south to Los Angeles. In the 1850s, California was a male-dominant world. Differences were solved with fists, knives, and guns.

It was a dangerous time to be in California. Between September 1850 and September 1851, there were thirty-one homicides committed in L.A. and the vicinity – in other words, two or three per month. That may not sound like a lot at this writing, but the population of the area at that time was only 2,500. To put it in today's terms, in a city such as Long Beach with a population of 466,000 people, it would be like having 5,779 murders a year or about sixteen per day. It is said that more than two-thirds of the state Legislature went armed to deliberations, and sometimes, when their disagreements turned personal, they challenged one another to duels. The winner would walk away, and the loser would be planted in the ground.

But, by the early 1860s, the worst of the murder and violence that plagued Southern California during the '50s had been brought under control, due largely to vigilante groups who would use a rope and a tree to dispense frontier justice to outlaws and murderers who threatened the civic order. In 1860, the last bullfight was held in Los Angeles, the first baseball team organized, and brick was replacing adobe as the building material of choice. The building boom of the 1850s had ended, but Los Angeles had emerged as a hub of business and finance with three hotels serving the public. Abel Stearns and John Temple were the two richest men in Southern California, but the days in which the raising of cattle dominated the economy were over. Grapes, wine, and oranges were rising to the top of the list as important local products.

As always in Southern California, water was a problem. The network of Zanja Madre irrigation canals still existed, but it was no longer sufficient to supply the city with clean water. Built in 1781, the Zanja Madre – which translates to "Mother Ditch" – is the original aqueduct that brought water to the Pueblo de Los Angeles from the Río Porciuncula. The city's water came from the Los Angeles River and from nearby springs. A waterwheel lifted it into a large waterway, where it was transported to a brick reservoir at the Plaza and from there by iron pipe to the downtown district.

In 1860, the Pony Express was created to speed mail delivery from the East to the West in an effort to connect California to that part of the nation east of the Mississippi River where most of the population lived. The price to send something by Pony Express was steep – $5 per half-ounce – but the mail would get from St. Joseph, Missouri, to Sacramento, and then on to San Francisco by steamboat in only ten days – barring Indian ambushes and other unforeseen dangers along the way.

As the California economy grew and civilization settled, there was still trouble brewing for the state. The country's dispute over slavery and the battle lines being drawn between the North and the South caused California to have its own North-South tension. Northern California – where the influx of gold seekers had resulted in a population boom including a number of Northern Anglos – tended to be anti-slavery and pro-North. Southern California, which included a large number of Southern immigrants, tended to favor the stand made by the Southern States. Adding to the geographical schism in the state, the Hispanic population, which had long held the greatest political and economic clout in Southern California, saw its power being eroded by the influx of settlers to the northern part of the state.

A year earlier, Los Angeles Assemblyman Andres Pico – who had fought against the Americans during the Mexican-American War – introduced a bill to split California in two. San Luis Obispo, Santa Barbara, Los Angeles, San Diego, and San Bernardino would become the Territory of Colorado and everything north would remain the state of California. (Ventura, Orange, Riverside, and Imperial counties did not exist at the time.) The Legislature passed the bill, but it died in Congress. The nation was teetering on the verge of civil war, and it was not the time to introduce such complications into the mix. So California remained one state, and the rift between North and South continued to simmer.

California had a majority of Democrats, but the strength of the party had been splintered by the Great Democratic Schism of 1860 – the split between slavery hardliners and moderates at the Democratic presidential convention in Charleston, South Carolina. Fifty hardliners walked out of the convention in protest after the majority of the party failed to provide explicit protection for the institution of slavery in its platform. With the departure of the Southern delegates, Senator Stephen A. Douglas – a moderate who felt each territory should be allowed to decide for itself whether or not to allow slavery – was nominated as the Democratic candidate. In a second Democratic Convention called in Baltimore two months later, an attempt to reconcile the party was unsuccessful. Douglas was again nominated as the party candidate, but the Southerners elected their own candidate, John C. Breckinridge, vice president to then-President James Buchanan.

In California, pro-Southern Democrats had already formed a Chivalry wing of the party that opposed attempts to limit slavery. The Chivalry wing backed Breckinridge for president, the remaining part of the body backed Douglas. Although Lincoln carried California by a plurality in 1860, the vote in Los Angeles was much different. The final Los Angeles tally showed Breckenridge getting 686 votes, Douglas receiving 494 votes, Lincoln receiving 350 votes, and third-party candidate John Bell receiving 201 votes.

Being a pro-Union Republican in Southern California in 1860 was a risky stance, both from a business and a political standpoint. But Phineas Banning, whose landing on the upper reaches of San Pedro Bay was dominating trade, was strongly pro-Union, and it ended up paying off for him both in business and in politics.

Phineas Banning in Business
Phineas Banning was never deterred by slurs or taunts. He was also not above enhancing his position, even by giving himself military titles, from Captain, a title he got in 1857 when he was elected commander of the Los Angeles Union Guard, to being named a General in the National Guard later in life. He had an innate ability to see beyond the naysayers of his time and to use appropriate terminology to sell people on his plans. An anecdote related by California historian W.W. Robinson tells of a visitor to the harbor calling out to the successful entrepreneur:

> *"Hey Banning! When is your tug coming up the slough?"*
> *To which Banning replied, "You mean, General, when do you expect your steamer up the estuary?"*

With a harbor facility and budding community at New San Pedro, Banning and partner Benjamin Wilson began to request that the federal government survey the inner harbor with an eye toward deepening the channels. In 1859, the U.S. Coast Guard was ordered by authorities to conduct the survey, which in years to follow, would attest to the potential for development of the inner harbor.

Banning had been shipping and selling supplies to Fort Tejon since he received the first Army contract back in 1854. In 1858, when the Army issued a request for bids to ship freight 114 miles from San Pedro to the fort, Banning submitted his bid to General Benjamin Beall, commander of the fort and a close friend. He won the contract with a bid price of $4.74 per hundred pounds – just one cent per hundred pounds less than the bid by chief competitor Augustus W.

Timms. Whether that was coincidence or the result of insider information can't be known for sure. That same year, Banning won a contract to transport supplies to Fort Yuma in Arizona, where the Army was engaged in protecting settlers from the Yuma Indians. He also accompanied Army explorers to the Colorado River to look for an appropriate site for a new fort, Fort Mohave.

By this time, Banning had 200 mules, one hundred horses, twenty-one freight wagons and six stagecoaches. He was elected to the L.A. Common Council, the forerunner of the City Council, and his fourth child, William Stanford Banning, was born. William would be the first of Phineas Banning's offspring to live to adulthood.

The following year, Banning won the contract to supply the newly established Fort Mohave. It was a sweetheart deal in which the Army paid Banning $210 a day for the trip, but with no schedule of how long the trip should take. Not surprisingly, the pay scheme created an incentive to move the freight across the desert in a leisurely fashion. It didn't take long for the Army to figure that out and start moving supplies by steamboat on the Colorado River.

Although San Pedro Bay was the major port for moving freight to and from Los Angeles, it was not the only choice. Beginning in 1857, a harbor opened up at a landing in what was to later become the Seal Beach Naval Weapons Station. It was known as the Anaheim Landing, since it quickly became the major harbor for the growers and merchants in the Anaheim Colony several miles inland. Building materials, consumer goods, and equipment were top inbound cargo; produce, grapes, and other goods were shipped out.

Meanwhile, Banning's business on the north end of the harbor continued to prosper. When his main rival in the harbor transport industry, Augustus W. Timms, sold his business, the buyers set up a new company – Goller and Tomlinson. The new company made a deal with Banning in which he would rent their warehouse, livestock, and equipment for six months. The deal ended up in court with Goller & Tomlinson suing over unpaid rent and misuse of their property.

When the telegraph line linking San Francisco to Los Angeles was being built, Banning got the contract to supply the poles for the southern portion of the route. In 1860, he took on a new partner, John Temple's brother-in-law August F. Hinchman, who brought what many of Banning's partners brought to the table – a reservoir of cash to help cover the ups and downs that were sure to come. It was Banning & Hinchman who enhanced the Banning legend when they agreed to transport a four-ton boiler from the harbor across the Cajon Pass to a site in the mountains for a mining company. Many local experts said it couldn't be done. Banning & Hinchman did it.

A Distant War with a Local Impact

On April 12, 1861, the Confederate Army began firing on Union soldiers at Fort Sumter in Charleston, South Carolina. The Civil War had begun. News of war reached San Francisco by Pony Express twelve days later, and it was relayed south to Los Angeles by telegraph. The telegraph line connecting the two cities had been completed the previous October. The cost of receiving news by telegraph from San Francisco was $100 per month. Since neither the Los Angeles Star nor the Southern News could afford such service, Phineas Banning, the Newmarks, and several other businessmen in the community agreed to pick up the tab.

California was important to the Union because it had gold that would help finance the war, and Lincoln needed the Republican electoral votes that California

CAPTAIN, GENERAL, BUSINESSMAN: *Through years of personal and financial triumphs and tragedies, Phineas Banning worked to develop Wilmington and San Pedro, paving the way for the modern San Pedro Bay port complex.*

represented in order to win re-election. California had been a Democratic Party state up until Lincoln's narrow victory. Because the same passions that drove the war between the North and the South were also present in California, it was important not to let those passions boil over into a shooting war on the West Coast.

The California Constitution required the formation of state militias that could be called to duty in case of war. Some of those militias were dominated by sympathizers to the Southern cause – enough to concern Captain Winfield Scott Hancock, quartermaster for the Army's Southern District for the Department of the Pacific. When Hancock heard rumors of a plan by secessionists to raid the government storehouse, he hid the Army's guns, ammunition, and other supplies under bags of grain, built an impromptu barricade of wagons and boxes, armed himself and his wife, and gathered a small group of pro-Union citizens to defend his post until help could arrive from Fort Tejon. Although some threats were made, no raid took place.

Another rumor concerned General Albert Sidney Johnston, commander of the Army Department of the Pacific and a native of Kentucky. There was some fear that Johnston planned to hand California over to the Confederacy. Although there was no evidence of such a plan, Lincoln ordered Johnston replaced by General Edwin Sumner. Johnston, who was almost 60, tendered his resignation, but remained at his post until he was relieved by Sumner two weeks later. Johnston moved with his wife to Los Angeles, where he originally planned to seek civilian employment, but after a month he decided it was his duty to defend his native state. Less than one year later he was dead, felled by a bullet at the Battle of Shiloh.

On May 14, 1861, troops from Fort Tejon arrived in Los Angeles, setting up camp along Fort Street (now Broadway) between First and Second streets. They were joined a few days later by troops from Fort Mohave. Southern California was key to the Army effort. If the Army could maintain the peace there, it would be able to avoid open warfare on the Pacific coast. With soldiers controlling Los Angeles, pro-Union people were able to safely express their opinions with little fear of violence. Union supporters organized a club and planned a Grand Union Demonstration to be held on May 25. There were threats that the pro-Union demonstrators would be shot and that pro-Southern groups would physically disrupt the rally, but these did not play out.

There was a parade to the courthouse. The Army band played music, and Phineas Banning was the first to mount the dais to deliver an impassioned address in support of the Union cause. Banning had been a life-long Democrat, but he had also been an ardent opponent of slavery dating back to his days as a boy working for his brother in Philadelphia. And he was against secession. By the time of the Civil War, he was openly identifying himself as a Republican. His speech that day left no doubt as to where his sympathies lay. Only one incident marred the day. When a pro-Union advocate attempted to read a patriotic poem from the second story of the Bella Union Hotel, some of the people who disagreed with his sentiments threw him out the window.

War, much like almost everything Phineas Banning touched, proved profitable for him. When news of the war arrived, Banning had decided to enlist in the Union Army and traveled to San Francisco to catch a ship for Washington, D.C. While he was there, however, he heard reports that the Confederate Army had advanced into the New Mexico territory and was planning to carry the war to California. He changed his plans, decided it made better sense to serve the Union by remaining in California, and returned west. It was a decision that would not only support the Union cause, but turn a profit for Banning as well.

The California Volunteers, new troops that had been gathered to replace Army regulars, were transported south from San Francisco to Banning's dock in New San Pedro, then marched north to a new camp near Ballona Creek, southwest of Los Angeles in what is now Culver City. The new camp was called Camp Latham after Senator Milton Latham.

Banning had worked with the Army on numerous occasions and knew how to secure military contracts. In 1861, he convinced General James Carleton, who commanded the Southern California district, to locate the Army supply depot in New San Pedro. Banning was then in a good position to get Army contracts to transport supplies to Union troops at various Western posts, including up the Colorado River by steamer to Fort Yuma. Early the following year, Banning and his partner, Benjamin Wilson, sold the Army thirty acres of land in New San Pedro for $1. Their generous sale won Banning a contract to construct an Army base on the land. An additional thirty acres was turned over to the Army in a separate transaction. The base was named Camp Drum after Richard C. Drum, who would serve for several years as adjutant general of the Army of the Pacific. Banning also built a depot and warehouse for the Army near his dock.

Doing business with the Army was lucrative, but it also highlighted some political conundrums. Benjamin Wilson was a long-time Democrat, who was openly sympathetic to the Southern cause, as was his wife, Margaret. He had aligned with the Chivalry wing of his party before the war and was a close associate of other pro-secessionist leaders. Perhaps he saw his association with the Union Army as business and his support for the South as politics. Banning's own wife, Rebecca, was an avid supporter of the Southern cause, so much so that when Union soldiers who were friends and associates of her husband came to their home for social visits, she refused to meet with them and retreated upstairs. California was far from the battlefield, but it was not immune from the conflicts that fueled the greatest bloodletting in the nation's history. The passions that tore apart the country also injured close relationships among friends and family thousands of miles away.

Despite the Army presence in Southern California and the harassment and sometimes arrests of people who spoke out against the Union, Southern California remained a hotbed of rebel sympathizers. There is strong evidence that the pro-Union forces and the federal officials were not above election tampering to try to ensure their political ends in the divided state.

The Democratic State Convention in Sacramento adopted a resolution calling for an end to the war, the reuniting of the Union if possible, and the recognition of the South as a sovereign nation if reunion were not possible. Democrats in Los Angeles echoed that sentiment and nominated two outspoken pro-South candidates for the state Assembly – Colonel E.J.C. Kewen and J.A. Watson. The Democrats carried the election, despite what appeared to be Republican election tampering at Camp Latham near Ballona Creek and Camp Drum north of the harbor.

The Los Angeles Star – a rabidly pro-South newspaper – accused the soldiers at Camp Latham of taking over the election process, stuffing the ballot box with votes by non-resident soldiers, and refusing to give Democratic voters access to the polls. In the San Pedro precincts around the harbor, Democratic voters were reported to have been intimidated by the military and others and barred from casting their ballots.

> We understand that the mob took full control of everything, requiring all who came forward to vote, not known and recognized by the powers that were, to vote an open ticket. By this means they kept down all expression of opinion opposed to the sentiments of that highly intelligent and refined community, who reside in New San Pedro. One gentleman, determined to assert the rights of an American citizen, he presented his ballot with one hand, holding his pistol on the other...

The Star was known for its hyperbole in attacking the Union cause, but the election results tended to support the charges. Results for the entire county showed Democratic Assembly candidates Watson and Kewen getting 718 votes and 701 votes respectively, while their pro-Union opponents Hayes and Johnson received 680 and 676. In the Ballona precinct where Camp Latham was located, Hayes and Johnson got 208 and 204 votes, while Watson and Kewen got 2 and 6 respectively. It was a similar story in San Pedro – Hayes and Johnson received 92 and 91 votes, respectively, while Watson and Kewen each got 4 votes. The county panel that canvassed the election subsequently voided the Ballona results because of the seizure of the ballot boxes by the Army and the illegality of more than 200 votes by soldiers, who were not legal residents of the area.

The *Ada Hancock*

Life for the Banning family would forever change on April 27, 1863, when they boarded the steamer *Ada Hancock* with family, friends, and other passengers for a short trip out to the coastal steamer *Senator*, which was ready to embark on a voyage to San Francisco. There was not a hint of trouble as the boat left the dock. The *Ada Hancock* – named after the daughter of Winfield Scott Hancock, the former quartermaster who had guarded the Army stores after the news of war reached California – was only three years old and in good working order. The Bannings were seeing off their friends Dr. Henry R. Myles and his fiancée, Medora Hereford, who were traveling to San Francisco to be married. Medora Hereford's sister, Margaret, was the wife of Banning's partner, Benjamin Wilson.

The sixty-foot-long boat had traveled only about half a mile when its boiler exploded, sending debris and body parts high into the air and sinking the small craft. Shredded remains of the boiler were found three-quarters of a mile from the wreck. Thirty people died in the accident. Among the dead was Rebecca Banning's brother, William Sanford, who had been an employer, mentor, and business partner of Banning through the years. Others included *Senator* Captain T.W. Seeley; *Ada Hancock* Captain Joseph Bryant; Banning & Company bookkeeper Tom Workman; Confederate General Albert Sidney Johnston's son, Albert Sidney Johnston Jr., and other businesspeople and workers. The happy couple that the Bannings were sending on their way to be married were also killed. Dr. Myles died immediately. Medora Hereford died nine weeks later, with the last few weeks of her life spent in agony.

Among the injured were Rebecca Banning; her sons William and Joseph; her mother, Hannah Sanford; Benjamin Wilson's daughter Ruth; and Rebecca's

18-year-old black servant, Harriet. Rebecca, who was three months pregnant, suffered a bruised scalp and internal injuries. Her mother broke an arm and a leg. Ruth Wilson suffered contusions; the boys' injuries were minor. Harriet, who was called "Darkness," is thought to have been a daughter of a slave back in Missouri, where the Sanford family had lived. She turned out to be one of the heroes of the day, holding the two young Banning boys above water until they could be saved and then helping other injured passengers, keeping their heads above water until rescuers arrived. Banning himself was the only survivor from the front part of the vessel. He was thrown several hundred feet by the blast, dazed and incoherent when he was found, but not seriously injured.

The cause of the explosion was ruled to be seawater hitting the hot boiler when a sudden gust caused the vessel to keel over sharply. When it righted, cold seawater rushed in and hit the heated engine and boiler, setting off an explosion. At least that was the official explanation. Conspiracy theories abounded, and there were, in fact, several curious circumstances.

Wells Fargo courier William Ritchie was reported to have been carrying $11,000 in gold dust bound for the mint in San Francisco. His body washed up several days later, but the gold was never found. Wells Fargo launched an investigation. Another passenger, Fred E. Kerlin of Fort Tejon, was reportedly carrying $30,000 in greenbacks, which was never recovered. Neither was the jewelry worn by several of the other victims.

"It was concluded that, even in the presence of death, these bodies had been speedily robbed," wrote Banning friend and sometime associate Harris Newmark in his book, *Sixty Years in Southern California.*

There was one other victim, one not counted in the official death toll of the accident. That was the child Rebecca was carrying when the explosion occurred. The injury sustained by the mother may have cost the life of her child. The baby was born in October, but did not survive long enough to be given a name.

Frontier Crime and Frontier Justice

Although the wild and wooly days of the frontier had quieted somewhat from when Phineas Banning arrived in San Pedro in 1851, there were still plenty of bad hombres loose in Los Angeles and plenty of citizens ready to take the law into their own hands if it seemed necessary. Lynchings were not uncommon, and there were several incidents in 1863 that were especially noteworthy. In November, four men were hunted down and arrested for the murder of a miner. A few days later, 200 armed vigilantes pulled them out of the jail in Los Angeles and hanged them from the portico of the old City Hall on Spring Street. A fifth prisoner – in jail for a minor offense and not an associate of the other four – was also hanged, seemingly just for good measure. There was some talk of tracking down the leaders of the mob, but public opinion was so in favor of the mob action that nothing ever came of it.

In the 1850s, Phineas Banning had helped found and finance the Los Angeles Rangers – a hard-riding group of men who would track down evil-doers and bring them to justice. Sometimes that justice was dispensed with a short rope and a tall tree. Banning himself was not the kind of man afraid of getting his hands dirty. A couple of weeks after the execution of the prisoners in Los Angeles, another lynching took place, this time on one of Banning's boats, the *Cricket.* Manuel Cerradel had been arrested in the killing of Rancho Cucamonga owner John

Rains. Cerradel was sentenced to ten years in San Quentin Prison, north of San Francisco. He was being escorted by Sheriff Tom Sanchez to the steamship *Senator* for transport to San Francisco, when a group of men overpowered the sheriff, put a noose around Cerradel's neck, and hanged him from the boat's flagstaff. After he was dead, they tied stones they had carried aboard to his feet and tossed his body overboard. Was Banning involved or did he have foreknowledge of the plan? There is no evidence that he did, but it is not beyond question.

One lynching in which Banning was definitely involved was that of Charles Wilkins, a hardened criminal with a long record of murder and mayhem. On December 6, 1863, Fort Tejon sheep rancher John Sanford, Rebecca Banning's brother, was driving his buggy near Elizabeth Lake, when he picked up the hitchhiking Wilkins and gave him a ride. Wilkins returned the favor by taking Sanford's gun, killing him, and stealing one of his horses. He was arrested six days later and held for trial. Rebecca had lost her brother William in the explosion of the *Ada Hancock* earlier that year; this second loss infuriated Banning. Harris Newmark, an eyewitness, recalled that when Banning first caught sight of Wilkins, he had to be restrained from shooting Wilkins to death on the spot. Wilkins later confessed to the crime and several others as well. On December 17, Wilkins was back in court for sentencing. Banning stormed into the courtroom with a band of followers, dragged Wilkins away, and hanged him. H.D. Barrows was a witness to the lynching.

"I remember as the people took him across Spring Street to Temple, he begged that they would shoot him and not hang him — but the people paid very little attention to his appeals, for he was a hardened villain of the worst class," Barrows wrote.

Many witnesses saw Banning at the head of the mob, and he never denied the act. But instead of being arrested, he was awarded $200 by the County Board of Supervisors for his public service in bringing a killer to justice.

Thirty years later, Barrows summed up the general feeling of that time in an article he wrote for the Historical Society of Southern California.

> *I have deemed it proper to say this much in vindication of the actors in the scenes of that day. Probably the only way in which people in our day, who condemn all vigilance committees and all revolutions can appreciate the overwhelming motives which impel men to take part in such movements, would be for them to take the places of those whose acts they so freely criticize.*
>
> *When in a new country, murder and robbery run riot, and regular and legal remedies utterly fail to protect society and stark anarchy threatens its very existence, society, if it possesses a spark of virtue or stamina, will protect itself, and if need be, by summary means. Most people who have been through these experiences, can say that it is better to take up arms against an anarchic sea of troubles and end them, even by summary methods, than to let them continue indefinitely — become chronic and unbearable.*

The Decline of the Ranchos

Despite the turbulent times, Banning continued to do well in business. By 1863, Banning and the New San Pedro community he helped found were both busy and ready for a new identity. It was too easy to confuse New San Pedro with the old San

Pedro a few miles to the south. A new name was needed, and Banning suggested the name of the Delaware town he had walked away from twenty years earlier – Wilmington. His partners agreed, and later that year, the State Legislature approved the change.

One of the keys to Banning's success was his ability to tap into government funding through contracts for services and through joint projects that benefited both the government and himself. One such project was the twelve-mile-long waterway from the San Gabriel (now Los Angeles) River to Wilmington. When the military first took over Fort Drum, it discovered that there was not enough fresh drinking water to supply the needs of the troops. Banning made a deal to build an aqueduct to bring water from the river to the camp. He then got legislation passed to allow him to dam up a section of the river, secure the right-of-way, and build a system of four-foot-wide ditches and flumes to bring the water to Wilmington. The water would be transported the last three miles on a raised wooden flume. Banning would supply 100,000 feet of lumber – a fraction of what was needed – and the Army would supply the manpower and the rest of the materials. In return, Banning got a franchise to sell surplus water in Wilmington. He also got access to a government-funded source of water to irrigate his fields where he grew feed for his drayage stock. As with many of Banning's government contracts, it was a sweetheart deal and sure to draw criticism. The Los Angeles News labeled the project "The Great Government Ditch," and other publications reported on lavish expenditures for supplies and structures at the camp. A government investigation was threatened, but headed off by Banning's Army friends.

An official investigation, conducted by Brigadier General James F. Rusling after the war, condemned the project and noted that although it was paid for by the government, it was controlled by Banning. The investigation disparaged the project as "a gigantic monument to the folly and extravagance of somebody." Although Rusling was candid in his criticism, he also provided a testament to Banning's persuasiveness and charm. In later writings, Rusling credits Banning as "a man of large and liberal ideas, with a great native force of character and power of endurance..."

While Banning prospered during the Civil War, many in Southern California did not. It was an especially tough time for cattle ranchers such as Abel Stearns and John Temple, who were still working their way through court to validate their claims for property, trying to keep squatters from settling on their land, and all the while, fighting to operate their ranches at a profit. Neither nature nor the economy was on their side.

In 1861, there had been a swarm of grasshoppers that had devastated the vegetation needed for grazing. The two previous years had been dry ones, and growers were hoping for a wet year. Then on November 11, the rain started and continued for fifteen days straight, cleared up for almost a month, than started coming down again on Christmas Eve and continued for more than a month. In all, sixty-six inches of rain fell during the season – the highest rainfall ever recorded for Southern California. The rain brought on floods, turned much of what is now Orange County into a lake with four-feet deep water up to ten miles from the Santa Ana River. Farms and vineyards were swept away, and up to 200,000 head of cattle perished. Great swathes of the Los Angeles basin were inundated from the mountains to the Palos Verdes Peninsula with high ground sticking up out of flooded lowlands. Harris Newmark recalled Los Angeles merchants, up to their waists in water, trying to save their merchandise before their stores were swept away in the deluge.

Despite the damage from the floods, the foliage returned to the hills during the spring and summer of 1862, but then things began once again to dry out. The deluge that had so devastated the countryside was followed by three years of drought. In the winter of 1862-63 no more than four inches of rain fell. The following winter it wasn't until March that the first rain fell. Cattle once again began to die, this time not from flooding, but from lack of water and food. Dead cattle littered the landscape. More than 70 percent of the cattle in Southern California were thought to have died during the drought with as many as 50,000 head dead on Rancho Los Alamitos alone.

The devastation of the cattle business resulted in a widespread recession. Credit, once given freely, was no longer available. Transactions were made in cash or not at all. The "greenback paper dollars" issued by the federal government were not universally accepted in California, where people preferred to do their business with gold. When the greenbacks were accepted, they were accorded only 65 to 70 percent of their face value. By 1864 property values in Los Angeles had plummeted with some land going for as little as ten cents per acre.

The drought and the economy were not the only problems. A smallpox epidemic hit Los Angeles in late 1862 and continued into the following year. The victims were overwhelmingly poor Hispanics and Indians, and as many as twenty died in a single day. There was no quarantine and no restrictions from bathing in the Zanja irrigation canals, so the disease spread quickly. The city carried victims to the hospital in Chavez Ravine – currently the site of Dodger Stadium – on a wagon dubbed the "Black Maria." The deaths were so many and the fear of infection so large that it was difficult to arrange for the burial of the victims. The epidemic ended in March 1863, but the death toll was high. It was estimated that the disease killed half of the Indians living in Los Angeles and many others in outlying areas.

Southern California remained politically polarized. During the election of 1864, Phineas Banning campaigned publicly at rallies for Lincoln. His partner, Benjamin Wilson, campaigned at rallies for Lincoln's opponent, former General George G. McClellan – the first commander of Union forces, relieved of command by Lincoln for his apparent unwillingness to take aggressive action. McClellan won the election in Los Angeles city but Lincoln took the county, at least initially until the County Board of Supervisors discarded four precincts – Wilmington, San Jose (now Pomona), Azusa, and Fort Tejon – with suspiciously lopsided returns.

News of General Robert E. Lee's surrender to General Ulysses S. Grant at Appomattox Court House reached Los Angeles by telegraph on the morning of April 10, 1865, touching off a round of celebrations. Five days later another message arrived, this one telling of the assassination of the president. The city was stunned, but not everybody was saddened. Some saw it as the just desserts for a tyrant. But expressions of joy at the death of the president were not to be tolerated.

Harris Newmark was with his family physician, Dr. John S. Griffin, when the news arrived. An outspoken Southerner, Griffin was ecstatic, Newmark recalled.

> *He gave evidence indeed of great mental excitement, and soon seized his hat and rushed for the door, hurrahing for the Confederacy. In a flash I realized that Griffin would be in awful jeopardy if he reached the*

street in that unbalanced condition, and by main force I held him back, convincing him at last of his folly. In later years the genial doctor frankly admitted that I had undoubtedly saved him from certain death.

Army commanders were ordered to arrest anyone "so utterly infamous as to exult over the assassination of the President." Six such citizens were so arrested; all but one shortly released. The strong passions that divided California before and during the war remained after the conclusion of the conflict. As time went on those lingering animosities faded, but things had changed.

By the end of the drought and the war, the fortunes of both Stearns and Temple had been reversed. Stearns in 1861 had mortgaged Rancho Los Alamitos for $20,000 to Michael Reese of San Francisco in order to cover his taxes and other expenses. In 1866, a year after the war ended, Stearns defaulted and lost the property. Temple had also found his business devastated by drought and circumstance. Although they both retained wealth, their glory days as landowners were over.

Like the antebellum plantation lifestyle in the South, the hospitable rancho lifestyle of the West had also come to an end. One civilization was built on the labor of black slaves, the other on the cheap labor of Indians and poor Hispanics. That was not the only parallel. The war was followed by Reconstruction in the South and the final subjugation of the Indians in the West. Both left scars that are still evident today.

The Union emerged as the dominant force in a federalized system. People who had long thought of themselves as citizens of Massachusetts or Virginia first and Americans second, no longer did. And if there were a few hangers-on who still looked first to their home state, their children and grandchildren did not. The cost was high – about 750,000 Americans were dead – but the issue was settled.

America was one nation.

Chapter Six:
Railroads and Salesmanship

The Civil War was over. President Lincoln was dead, felled by an assassin's bullet as he enjoyed a night at the theater with his wife, Mary. Vice President Andrew Johnson had taken his place. The point had been made and the principle upheld. The United States was one nation, not just a collection of states. Now it was time to reconcile the principle to the reality. The South as a political entity had to be re-established and brought back into the fold with the rest of the nation. The West had to be connected to the rest of the nation by commerce and infrastructure. It was a time to rebuild and reunite.

But the bloodletting was not over. The Indians, who had been driven from their home territories by the economic needs and desires of white settlers, were making their last stands against the encroachment of civilization as it moved westward.

The 13th Amendment – passed in 1865, the year the war ended – abolished slavery and involuntary servitude except as punishment for a crime. A year later, the Civil Rights Act of 1866 was passed by Congress. It provided that all people born in the United States were citizens, regardless of race or previous condition of servitude. It gave all citizens, white and black, the right to make and enforce contracts, sue and be sued, give evidence in court, inherit, purchase, own, and sell real and personal property, and to be protected by the law. However, the Act did little for Indians, specifically "excluding Indians not taxed." It also did not give black citizens the right to vote, sit on juries, or send their children to white schools. Those issues were left to the states to determine. A Civil Rights Act had been passed the previous year as well, but was vetoed by President Johnson. Johnson vetoed the Act again in 1866, but Congress was able to gather enough votes to override the veto.

That was the same year that the Ku Klux Klan was founded in Pulaski, Tennessee, as a vigilante group determined to enforce its white supremacy philosophy through threats, violence, and murder against black people and their white associates.

In 1868, the 14th Amendment to the Constitution was passed, including all citizens, white and black, in deciding the number of congressional representatives, and guaranteeing those citizens – at least the adult males – the right to vote in all federal elections.

Meanwhile, a new source of energy was rapidly being developed. Using petroleum for fuel had been going on for years, but refining crude oil into kerosene for lanterns was proving to be a cheap replacement for whale oil. By the end of the Civil War, entrepreneurs were drilling wells to extract crude oil from the ground.

Times were changing. The Old West was slowly giving way to the New West, and the old ways of doing business were being replaced.

Banning in the Oil Business

As the Civil War wound down, Phineas Banning and other prominent capitalists were already looking for new business opportunities. In January 1865, Banning and his partners and friends founded the Pioneer Oil Co., which quickly secured rights to drill at several sites in the area, including Wilmington, on the Palos Verdes and San Pasqual ranchos, and other locations. Joining him in the venture were former Governor John G. Downey, Benjamin D. Wilson, John S. Griffith, Mathew Keller, Charles Ducommun, General Winfield S. Hancock, and two officers from Camp Drum, J.S. Curtis and W.E. Swasey.

People had long known about the tar along the California beaches and the inland tar springs. The Indians had used it to seal the planks on their canoes, and the Hispanic and then the white settlers later used it to caulk the planks on their ships, waterproof their sails and rigging, and to seal the roofs of adobe homes during the rainy season. One major source was in the Hancock Park area – a tar spring that would later be known as the La Brea tar pits – where the asphalt or tar that bubbled to the surface was mined. It wasn't until much later that people realized that the troublesome bones in the tar pits were the remains of prehistoric beasts that had become trapped in the tar and perished. The tar from the pits in Los Angeles and on the beaches in the area was actually bitumen, a viscous form of petroleum sometimes called "oil tar."

For the most part, the tar was seen more as a nuisance than an asset, but that began to change in the mid-19th century, when people began experimenting with distilling coal oil and petroleum into a substance that came to be known as kerosene. Until kerosene became available, people had used whale oil to light their lamps. Kerosene turned out to be much cheaper. In 1858, former railroad worker Edwin Drake proved petroleum could be extracted from the ground by drilling for it. Drake's steam-powered rig struck oil at 69.5 feet deep in Titusville, Pennsylvania. Soon others across the nation were also drilling for oil, including folks in California.

Banning and his partners began drilling for oil in May 1865 and soon were producing kerosene for lanterns. The retail price for kerosene at the time was ten cents a gallon. Pioneer Oil, however, was not successful. The returns failed to match the investment, and the Los Angeles demand for lantern fuel was too low to support the production by Banning and several other oil companies with the same plan. The company quietly went out of business, but it was the forerunner of an industry that would play a critical role in the economy of the state and of the harbor area.

A Steam Engine on the Road of Iron

Phineas Banning had long advocated for construction of a railroad between Los Angeles and the San Pedro Bay harbor. When the winter rains came, the dirt roads between the harbor and the city would sometimes become so muddy that it was impossible to drive a wagon with passengers or freight on them. Banning had experimented in the summer of 1860 with a steam-powered tractor invented in England that could supposedly pull a thirty-eight-ton load at five miles per hour. It may have worked fine on the flat and manicured lanes of England, but in Southern California, it was a complete bust.

In February 1861, Abel Stearns, who was then representing the area as a state assemblyman, had heard that some eastern capitalists might be willing to back construction of a rail link between Los Angeles and San Pedro Bay if the city would subscribe $50,000 and the county would subscribe $100,000 toward the project. Stearns introduced two bills in the Assembly to provide such funding, one for the city and one for the county.

Both bills passed, but by that time the United States was deep into the Civil War and any plans for such a railroad died. In 1863, Assemblyman Edward J.C. Kewen introduced almost identical legislation and again it passed, but again no railroad project was built. In December 1864, Banning and his associates Benjamin Wilson, Dr. John Griffin, and former Governor John G. Downey supported construction of a rail line that would go from Los Angeles, through Wilmington, and on to Deadman's Island, where a wharf and breakwater would be built. But in the end, that plan too was a lot of talk and no action.

After the war ended, Banning decided it was time to get personally involved in politics. He had held elected office twice before, once as the justice of the peace for San Pedro in 1856, and once as a member of the L.A. Common Council in 1858. His term on the Los Angeles Common Council – the forerunner to the City Council – was undistinguished. Banning lived down by the harbor; it was a long and difficult journey downtown, and he was a busy man. Now Banning wanted to run for the State Senate, but this time he had a specific agenda. He wanted to build a railroad from Los Angeles to the harbor, get the federal government to improve the harbor, and bring a transcontinental railroad to Los Angeles. Having a rail line from the city to the harbor would help convince the large railroads to bring their lines to Los Angeles, he argued.

A lot of people argued back. Opponents to the rail line were worried about higher taxes to pay for the city funding of such a project. Farmers were worried that the railroad would replace dray animals and ruin the market for barley and other feed. Banning was accused of wanting to move the county seat from Los Angeles to Wilmington, and Banning's main competitor for freight from the port, businessman John J. Tomlinson, was adamantly opposed. Tomlinson had taken over August W. Timms' stage and freight business in San Pedro. The two companies were fierce competitors, often racing one another from the harbor to the city. A railroad to Wilmington would give Banning a competitive advantage and mean an end to Tomlinson's stage and freight business.

On September 5, 1865, Banning won his State Senate seat, and in January he introduced a bill that would authorize the County Board of Supervisors to subscribe $200,000 to the stock of the new railroad. A second bill would authorize the City of Los Angeles to subscribe $50,000. Foes of the idea were again vigorous in their opposition, and the bill died in the Senate Committee for Corporations. The defeat did little to dim Banning's enthusiasm for the project, but he was facing other problems as well. Although Banning had prospered during the Civil War, largely in part to his government contracts, he also made many enemies because of his pro-Union politics and the aggressive way he did business. His freight business between the harbor and Los Angeles had suffered, with much of that business being picked up by Tomlinson's stage and freight operation.

In 1865 Banning's former partner, David Alexander, again joined the business, which this time was named Banning & Company. The company began to upgrade its waterfront location in Wilmington to focus on its stage and freight business. Legend has it that among the company employees driving teams between Wilmington and San Bernardino were two brothers, Virgil and Wyatt Earp. That legend has been challenged. Tom Sitton, author of *Grand Ventures: The Banning Family and the Shaping of California*, says there are no records indicating that Wyatt Earp ever drove for the company. Allan Barra in his book, *Inventing Wyatt Earp: His Life and Many Legends*, agrees. Wyatt Earp would have only been 17 at the time. Barra says Virgil, who was 22, did drive for Banning and speculates that he let his kid brother ride along for the experience.

In 1866, the Army began mustering out troops at Camp Drum, and the lucrative contracts to supply military posts began to dry up. Fort Tejon had been closed, and Banning also lost the Fort Yuma contract in Arizona to another vendor. He also faced new competition in moving freight to and from the mines of Inyo County. But Banning remained committed to building the railroad. In 1867, he won re-election to the State Senate on the same platform he had run on before. This time around, Banning laid the groundwork for his second attempt to get his railroad bill passed. He got the County Board of Supervisors to endorse the railroad plan and put together a coalition of pro-railroad businessmen led by former Governor Downey. Former Los Angeles Mayor and Banning associate Benjamin Wilson joined the effort, as did Dr. John Griffin. Like Banning, these three were all landowners who stood to profit from establishment of the rail line.

In January 1868, Banning introduced two new railroad bills in the State Senate – one authorizing a $150,000 subscription by the county, and the other a $75,000 subscription by the city. Both city and county would share in the dividends from the railroad stock and appoint representatives to vote their shares at stockholders' meetings. Both bills required that the city and county public subscriptions be approved in votes by the residents of the two jurisdictions. This time the railroad bill passed the Legislature with little debate and was signed into law by Governor Henry H. Haight on February 1.

Before the bill was approved, however, Banning and his associates had agreed to incorporate a railroad company that would build and maintain the line. Two weeks after the governor signed the bill the first stockholders' meeting was held, and Downey was elected president. Others on the board of directors were Dr. Griffin, John King, Banning partner David Alexander, and Matthew Keller. The articles of incorporation for the Los Angeles & San Pedro Railroad Company were filed seventeen days after the governor signed the bill. Although Banning was a stockholder in the company, he chose not to participate publicly in the venture – at least not at the very beginning.

Public elections for approval of the city and county subscriptions were set for March 24, 1868, and the debate over the measure was spirited. In order to gather support, more directors, representing a cross-section of the community, were named to the railroad board – Deputy County Clerk Steven Mott, Benjamin Wilson, Ozro W. Childs, Prudent Beaudry, and Phineas Banning. Both Childs and Beaudry were downtown merchants and landowners.

Tomlinson, who stood to lose his stage and freight business if the railroad was built, led the opposition. Tomlinson alleged that Banning would put the terminus to the line at Wilmington, giving him a monopoly on lightering cargo and passengers between ship and shore. The company denied such charges and pledged that the railroad would extend all the way to a deep-water wharf. The opposition lost some momentum two weeks before the vote when Tomlinson suddenly died. The railroad was approved, but the county vote was close, 700-672; the city measure passed, 397-245.

Several bids to build the railroad were received, some of them from experienced railroad constructors. But Banning was determined to win the contract. Unfortunately, he had suffered some serious financial losses in an investment he had made in the La Abundancia Mining Company in Sonora, Mexico, so he was strapped for cash. But as always, he made a deal – this time with San Francisco lumber merchant Henry Baldwin Tichenor, who owned a fleet of coastal steamers and who had built a small railroad, saw mill and bridge in Northern California. Tichenor would supply funding and experience; Banning paid Tichenor in railroad stock.

The Banning and Tichenor partnership won the contract to build the Los Angeles & San Pedro Railroad. The contract called for the railroad to be completed by January 1, 1870; payment for construction of the twenty-one-mile railroad would be $19,000 a mile.

In the meantime, the partnership of Banning & Alexander immediately received $70,000 from Tichenor to cover the Wilmington property and equipment purchased by the railroad company. Included was $31,000 for four lighters, five boats and skiffs, three steamers, and miscellaneous beacons and buoys. Although the company had pledged to extend the track to a deep-water wharf on Deadman's Island, Wilmington would be the temporary terminus for the railroad until a breakwater could be built connecting Deadman's Island to Rattlesnake Island. The fact that Banning held 2,900 of the 5,000 shares of stock in the company likely had much to do with that decision.

There were problems and controversy right from the start. The San Diego Union noted that there was no natural harbor at San Pedro Bay, called Banning's facility in Wilmington a "goose pond," and declared it would make more sense for Los Angeles to connect to the harbor at San Diego. Meanwhile, Anaheim civic leaders pledged $25,000 to build a line from Anaheim Landing – where the Seal Beach Naval Weapons Station is located today – to Anaheim and on to San Bernardino. Businessmen in San Bernardino liked that idea and promised to contribute $5,000 per mile for such a project. Despite such pledges, the Anaheim Landing railroad idea soon fizzled and died.

Despite the problems, work began in the summer of 1868 on the Los Angeles to San Pedro line. The chief engineer, Colonel Edward A. Flint, began plotting the route. For a railroad, where grade changes matter, there were two potential ways to go – east of the Dominguez Hills or west. The eastern route was drier, and the maximum grade was twenty-six feet per mile. The western route was twice as steep and included a mile and a half of marshland, which would require a trestle. But the western route went through Rancho San Pedro, which was owned by Downey, and that was the route he favored. The other directors voted for the more economical eastern route, ignoring Downey's recommendation and eventually costing his support for the project. The beginning of construction was marked with a Grand Railroad Inauguration Ball at the Exchange Hotel in Wilmington on the evening of September 18, 1868, with Banning turning over the first shovel full of dirt at a groundbreaking the next morning.

Work had begun, but it didn't mean there weren't problems along the way. By the end of 1868 only three miles of track had been laid. There was a fatal accident on the job when a workman on a pile driver got his feet entangled in a rope and was pulled into the machinery. There were legal problems when some residents along Alameda Street went to court to stop construction of a rail line down their once peaceful street. By June 1869, only six miles had been completed, sparking fear among grain growers that the new line would not be ready to haul their crops to market in the fall.

On June 11, 1869, the first locomotive arrived – the *San Gabriel* – a small, open-cab "pony" engine painted black with its name on the side in gold leaf. The *San Gabriel* had been built several years prior for the Napa Valley Railroad, which had found it too small to be of value. Tichenor had picked it up at a bargain price, shipped it down to Los Angeles, and put it to work, hauling rails and ties to the work site. Banning put it to work too, hauling passengers and cargo from the dock to the construction site, and then loading the people and freight onto stages and wagons for the rest of the trip. Many people in Southern California at that time had never seen a locomotive, and the little *San Gabriel* was a novel sight. Banning also used Sunday harbor rail excursions to help promote the new line. By the end of summer, the little engine began to break down under the load and began requiring frequent repair and maintenance.

But Banning and Tichenor plugged on, despite delays in rail and lumber from San Francisco and a mishap when one of the supply ships ran aground. Banning, in a letter published by the Los Angeles Star, vowed that the line would be finished ahead of the January 1, 1870, schedule.

The Los Angeles & San Pedro Railroad bought a vineyard owned by Downey and businessman James Burnes on the southwest corner of Alameda and Commercial streets in Los Angeles, the same location now occupied by the federal Metropolitan Detention Center, not far from the present Union Station. Not long after the depot was built, property values in the neighborhood shot up as real estate speculators began buying up land for development.

On September 8, 1869 – three months ahead of schedule – the first train departed the Los Angeles depot for Wilmington, pulled by the little engine that had performed so gallantly during construction. The going was slow. The *San Gabriel* had been stressed beyond its limits during the building of the line, and nobody dared push it too hard. The stronger, more robust locomotive that would actually provide the power for the new railroad arrived in Wilmington in October – a beautiful engine named the *Los Angeles*. It was the first of two engines ordered from the Schenectady Works in New York State to be transported around Cape Horn to Wilmington. The arrival had been anticipated with some concern. In those early days, once a ship left port, there was little information on where it was until it arrived at its destination. Sometimes when a ship was lost at sea, nobody would know until it failed to arrive at all. The *Los Angeles* was a fine-looking sturdy workhorse of a locomotive. The only problem was that the artist in Schenectady who painted the name of the locomotive on its side must have known more about art than spelling or geography. The name was spelled *Los Angelos*. The artwork was corrected before the locomotive went into service.

The formal grand opening of the railroad was scheduled for October 26, 1869. A crowd of about 2,000 showed up for the event. The last spike was driven with Banning, Tichenor, and Downey taking turns with the hammer. People jammed onboard for a free trip to Wilmington. The complete trip took less than an hour, and then it returned to Los Angeles for another load. That night, when the riders returned to Los Angeles, a dance was held at the depot, with a military band providing the music. As much as anything else, the new railroad symbolized the end of one era and the beginning of another. A sign along the tracks of the new line read: Cuidado por la Maquina de Vaho del Camino de Fierro. In English it translated to: Look out for the steam engine on the road of iron.

The vaqueros who worked the cattle ranches along the tracks would enjoy racing their horses alongside the engine as it came past, and for a short distance they would speed past the locomotive, but only for a short distance. Then their horses would grow winded, and the engine would pull ahead and leave them behind. It was one more sign that their world was ending and a new one had begun.

Triumph and Tragedy

While Banning was busy fighting to build a railroad from Los Angeles to his docks in Wilmington, the rest of his life was eventful and often sad. After the Civil War and the tensions between husband and wife that the war caused, the Bannings settled down to a more stable relationship. Rebecca, her mother, and her servant Harriet handled the household and entertaining duties while Phineas took care of business. The dinner parties at the Banning Mansion for the business and civic leaders of the day became legendary.

In the fall of 1866, Rebecca gave birth to a daughter, named Elizabeth after Phineas' mother and sister. The child died a few months later and was buried on the mansion's grounds. Sadly, it was not a unique experience. The Bannings had been through the death of a child four times before. Within a few months, Rebecca was pregnant once more. In January 1868, she gave birth to a boy, Vincent Edgar Griffin Banning. A few days later, Rebecca died. She was 33 years old, and in the fourteen years she had been married to Banning, had been severely injured in the explosion of the *Ada Hancock* and given birth to nine children – only three of whom would live to adulthood. Those three children were William Sanford, born in 1858 and named after Rebecca's brother; Joseph Brent, born in 1861 and named after a friend, Joseph Lancaster Brent, who went on to become a Confederate general during the Civil War; and Hancock, born in 1865 and named after Union General Winfield Scott Hancock.

Banning was not a person to waste time mourning the dead. He was suddenly a widower with four young sons, the oldest only 9. The funeral for Rebecca was quickly arranged, so he could get to Sacramento for the opening of the legislative session. Within a month of Rebecca's death, he was looking for a new wife. The woman he settled on was Mary Elizabeth Hollister, daughter of Joseph Hubbard Hollister. Joseph Hollister, his brother William, and sister Lucy Brown were the family who in 1854 had driven a herd of 6,000 sheep across the desert from Ohio to California, joining up along the way with the Flint Brothers and their cousin Lewellyn Bixby, who were also driving a herd of sheep west. The families prospered in the sheep business, and Joseph Hollister bought large tracts of land north of Santa Barbara, eventually becoming one of the largest landowners in the state.

In the spring of 1868, Mary Hollister sailed away on a trip to New York. Banning wrote a letter to his old friend Harris Newmark, who happened to be in New York at the time. It read:

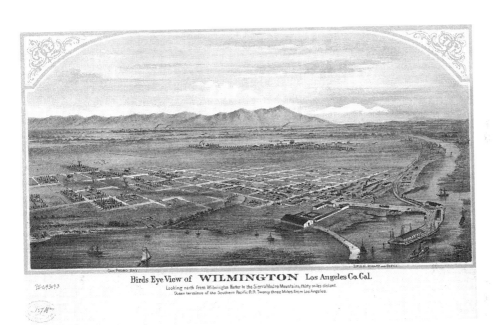

BAY BEGINNINGS: *An 1877 view of Wilmington looking north shows some of the harbor improvements spearheaded by Phineas Banning. At right is the Southern Pacific line stretching north toward Los Angeles. Rail connections were and still are crucial to the success of trade in San Pedro Bay.*

> *Dear Harris*
>
> *Herewith I enclose to you a letter of the greatest importance, addressed to Miss Mary Hollister (daughter as you know of Colonel Joseph H. Hollister), who will soon be on her way to New York, and who may be expected to arrive there by the next steamer.*
>
> *This letter I beg you to deliver to Miss Hollister personally, immediately upon her arrival in New York, thereby obliging*
>
> *Yours obediently*
>
> *Phineas Banning*

The sealed envelope that Newmark personally presented to Miss Hollister contained a written proposal of marriage. She declined. This did little to discourage Banning. He had much experience in getting rejected before getting what he wanted. He courted her in letters and in person. Her father, who was familiar with Banning through business and commercial dealings, was not in favor of the proposed marriage, but slowly Banning won over the object of his desire. On August 1, 1869, Mary accepted his proposal after a courtship that took more than a year. During the courtship of Mary Hollister, in June 1868, Banning's youngest son, Vincent Edgar Griffin Banning, died and was buried near the graves of his mother and deceased brothers and sisters.

Before the wedding, Banning evicted Rebecca's mother, Hannah, from his mansion in Wilmington and sent her to live with her sister, Marilda Prather, in Linden, California. Also removed to Linden was Rebecca's servant, Harriet, who had performed so heroically following the explosion of the *Ada Hancock* six years earlier. Banning didn't want his new wife and new marriage to be hindered by the ghosts of his former marriage.

Phineas Banning and Mary Hollister were joined in holy matrimony on Valentine's Day 1870 at the Goleta ranch home of her uncle, William Hollister. Banning was 40 years old; his bride was 24. There is no reason to believe that the bride and groom did not love one another, but as with so much in Banning's life, there also may have been a business angle involved. Mary's uncle William Welles Hollister wanted the County of Santa Barbara to finance an east-west railroad spur from Newhall to Santa Barbara. Banning was a politically connected transportation capitalist who knew how to get things done. Banning later testified to a reluctant Board of Supervisors about the benefits of such a project, but despite his recommendation, no spur line was built.

Although the Drum Barracks in Wilmington remained active as a supply center during the effort to bring the last of the warring Indian tribes under control, by the time of Banning's marriage to Mary Hollister, it had been deactivated and was not well maintained. Banning attempted to get the federal authorities to simply give the sixty-acre property and all the buildings to him and his partner Benjamin Wilson. Banning and Wilson had donated the properties to the military for a token sum in 1862, and then they had gotten the Army contract to construct the buildings. The Army favored dismantling the buildings and putting the materials up for auction. Banning took his case straight to Washington, D.C., in an effort to get Congress to sign the property and buildings over to Wilson and himself. Despite reports from the Army that Banning and Wilson had profited handsomely from building the Drum Barracks project, the Legislature agreed to return the original property to the two men, although not the buildings, which were to be put up for auction. When the auction was held, Banning and Wilson were in a good position to purchase the buildings that stood upon the land that they owned.

In 1871, Banning convinced Congress to contribute $200,000 toward harbor improvements, and with that funding, a breakwater was built connecting Rattlesnake Island to Deadman's Island. By the following year Congress had appropriated a total of $425,000 toward improving the harbor.

The Flint-Bixbys Go South

Phineas Banning wasn't the only one to exploit new opportunities following the end of the Civil War. The Flint-Bixbys were also seeking to build the family fortune. As had been the case for Banning, the Civil War had been a financial boon for the Flint-Bixby clan, and they profited mightily as the supply of Southern cotton declined and the demand and price for wool soared. The great drought of 1862-64 and the slow-moving machinations of the federal Land Commission as it sorted out land grants and claims had done much to drive down the price of land in Southern California.

Flint, Bixby & Co. – the partnership of brothers Benjamin and Thomas Flint and their cousin Lewellyn Bixby – began acquiring property even before the war, when they determined that their original Rancho San Justo property northwest of Monterey was too small to support their growing population of sheep. One of the first large properties they acquired was the 15,600-acre Huero-Huero Ranch, purchased in 1858 near Paso Robles, to which the company added 31,000 acres of government land.

Starting in 1864, Flint, Bixby & Co. partnered with wealthy San Francisco merchant and real estate investor James Irvine to buy land in what is now Orange County. By 1868, the partnership – half Flint and Bixby and half Irvine – had purchased ranchos San Joaquin, Rancho Lomas de Santiago, and part of Rancho Santiago de Santa Ana.

In 1866, Flint, Bixby & Co. on its own bought the 27,000-acre Rancho Los Cerritos for $20,000 from the aging John Temple – one of the pioneering American dons who had bought it from the Nieto family in 1843. Temple, who had moved to San Francisco with his wife by the time of the sale, died two months later at 70 years old. He had left a legacy as a merchant, a trader, a rancher, and a leader of the community. He had been the first alcalde (mayor) of Los Angeles following the American takeover of California. As a developer, he erected a downtown building that became known as the Temple Block. It was at his home in Los Angeles that the Vigilance Committee plotted the first lynching in the area, and his home at Rancho Los Cerritos was commandeered as a headquarters for the Mexican Army during the Mexican-American war. He was a true pioneer, and at one point, the second-richest man in Southern California. But the days of the pioneer were done in California, and his passing in San Francisco received minimal notice in the press.

After the Flint-Bixbys took over Rancho Los Cerritos, they had to find somebody to raise sheep on the property. The partners went to Lewellyn's younger brother, Jotham, with the proposal that Jotham would take charge of the operation in exchange for half of the profit each year, plus an option to purchase half the ranch for $10,000. The great drought of 1862-64 had been the final straw that decimated the cattle industry, and now that the rains had returned, the market for wool was strong. Jotham Bixby was able by 1869 to shear enough sheep and sell enough mutton to exercise his option and buy a half interest in Rancho Los Cerritos. The new partnership between Flint, Bixby & Co. and Jotham Bixby required organization of a separate business entity named J. Bixby & Co.

Connecting the Nation by Iron and Steam

In 1868, while Phineas Banning was getting started building his railroad and the Flint and Bixby brothers were expanding their empire of sheep in Southern California, Leland Stanford, the president of the Central Pacific Railroad and former governor of California, was pushing a plan to lure residents from the eastern states, from Canada, and from Europe to move to California. He convinced the San Francisco Chamber of Commerce to form an International Immigrant Union with an office in Baltimore that would promote the opportunities awaiting those bold enough to make the move. The selling pitch was good land at reasonable prices.

Early the next year, the Chamber formed the California Immigrant Union – a local version of the International Immigrant Union with a slightly different focus. The California Immigrant Union was to support the subdivision of large estates into smaller family farms that would be sold to new settlers at good prices and with easy terms. The one caveat was that new settlers must have at least a $1,000 stake in order to ensure their success. The California Immigrant Union was financed by business subscribers, including Jotham Bixby and banker John Temple, the nephew and namesake of the former owner of Rancho Los Cerritos.

Stanford may have been promoting the California economy when he proposed the International Immigrant Union, but he was promoting his own financial prospects as well. The Central Pacific Railroad, which was building the western portion of the transcontinental railroad, was about to link up with the Union Pacific, which was constructing the eastern portion of the line. When that happened, the East Coast and the West Coast would be connected by rail, and a new age would be born.

Stanford and three other California businessmen, known as the "Big Four," had been pushing the project forward since well before Stanford became governor in 1862. The Big Four, who also called themselves "the Associates," were a diverse group of merchants and dealmakers united only in their drive for wealth and power. Stanford was the politician, skilled at negotiating deals and obtaining the required government subsidies. Collis Huntington provided the ruthless and persistent energy and drive to make projects happen. His partner, Mark Hopkins, was a numbers man, who watched the bottom line and reined in Huntington when he stepped over the line. Charles Crocker, another Sacramento merchant who had been a farmhand, blacksmith, prospector, and local politician, rounded out the group.

But if anybody was responsible for giving life to the idea of a transcontinental railroad that would connect the country east and west, it was Theodore Judah, an engineer with an obsessive vision of the power of rail to unite the nation. Judah had campaigned in Washington to get political support for the rail line and met with the money men of San Francisco to get financial support. Everywhere he turned, he was rejected. His boundless energy and relentless enthusiasm for the project won him only a reputation as a lunatic. His luck changed in late 1860 when he met with a group of businessmen and farmers in Sacramento, a group not as wealthy or as influential as the San Francisco crowd that had rejected him, but folks who had money to invest just the same. Collis Huntington was at the meeting, and though he started out with a large dose of skepticism, he soon joined the effort to put together the financing to build the railroad. It may have been Judah who laid out the rail route and provided the engineering expertise, but it was Huntington who convinced the others to invest in the project. Huntington admitted that the risk was high, but the potential rewards were huge.

As huge as those rewards would turn out for Huntington and the other investors, it was not so much the case for Theodore Judah.

A new company, the Central Pacific Railroad, was organized in 1861, shortly after the start of the Civil War. Leland Stanford was elected president of the board, a move that irked Huntington, who had been the one to bring Stanford and the others into the venture. And Judah, whose vision Huntington had listened to and supported when no one else would, had voted in favor of Stanford. Huntington was not a person to forget a slight, and the day would come when he would extract his revenge. But not just yet.

The Central Pacific Board sent Judah back east in the fall of 1861 to begin lobbying for land grants and government bonds to help build the rail line. Abraham Lincoln, the new president suddenly enmeshed in the bloodiest war in the nation's history, had been a proponent of a transcontinental railroad that would unite the country economically and physically as well as politically. The rules and regulations of government were less rigid in the 1860s than they have evolved to in later times. Although a lobbyist for the Central Pacific, Judah was able to get himself appointed as clerk to the Senate and House committees on railroads. With Lincoln's backing, a bill to approve government support for a transcontinental line seemed assured.

Huntington, seeing Judah's lobbying effort beginning to show dividends, headed back to Washington. The art of political persuasion – especially when it was backed by financial incentive – came easily to Huntington, and he was soon at ease convincing the various political representatives what passage of the railroad bill could mean to them. The final bill was passed on June 24, 1862, and signed into law by President Lincoln a week later.

The Railroad Act called for the Union Pacific to begin laying tracks from the Missouri River west toward California and for the Central Pacific to start building eastward from Sacramento. The plan was for the two companies to meet at the California border, but if one company got there first, they were to keep going until they linked up with the other. In other words, the race was on. The Central Pacific had the toughest job. It had to build a railroad across the rocky and rugged Sierra Mountains. And the steel rails and locomotives for the job had to be shipped to California from the East. For each mile of track to the base of the Sierra, the Central Pacific would be advanced $16,000 in government loans; in the foothills, it was $32,000 a track-mile; and for the mountains, it was $48,000 a track-mile.

To stay on schedule and to maintain control of the project and the profits, the partners cut some corners. The Big Four were not the only directors in the Central Pacific, but they formed a clique on the board that ensured they'd keep tight control of the venture. One of the early decisions facing the board was hiring a contractor to construct the route. The Big Four decided to award that contract to themselves with Charles Crocker in charge. Judah objected over the fact that Crocker was on the board of directors. It would be an illegal conflict of interest for him to be the contractor as well as a board member. But the four associates found a way to get around that legal technicality. They held a secret meeting after which Crocker resigned as director to be replaced by his brother, Judge Edwin Bryant Crocker. Crocker was then free to form Charles Crocker and Co. and was immediately given a $400,000 contract to build the first eighteen miles of rail. Stanford, Hopkins, and Huntington were silent partners in the company, but not on paper. The whole deal was done with a handshake between partners.

Years later, when congressional investigators examined the possibility that fraud had been committed during the building of the railroad, they demanded that the Central Pacific turn over its books only to discover that the books no longer existed. Mark Hopkins had carried the company's financial records down to the basement of the Central Pacific's office and burned them in the furnace – bringing a whole new meaning to the term "cooking the books." Huntington, called to testify before the congressional committee, said Hopkins was a "peculiar man," who considered the books no longer worth saving.

When the Central Pacific ran low on cash, Stanford as governor was able to get the state Legislature to pass $15 million in state bonds toward the project. And when the contract called for a different payment for mountains and flat land, Stanford used his legal background to define exactly where the mountains began. The ploy won the company about $500,000 for laying rails on flat land that under Stanford's parsing was regarded as "mountainous."

In 1865, when workers were needed to lay tracks and there were not enough available men to do the job, Crocker brought in Chinese laborers – a very unpopular move in a nation where Asians were treated with suspicion and disdain – especially in California, where they could not attend public school, testify in court, or vote.

Stanford in his inaugural speech as governor in 1862 had warned:

> To my mind it is clear, that the settlement among us of an inferior race is to be discouraged, by every legitimate means. Asia, with her numberless millions, sends to our shores the dregs of her population ... There can be no doubt but that the presence of numbers among us of a degraded and distinct people must exercise a deleterious influence upon the superior race, and, to a certain extent, repel desirable immigration..

But three years later, faced with the urgent need for workers to lay tracks for the railroad, Stanford revised his early harsh assessment. He started referring to his thousands of Chinese employees as "the Asiatic contingent of the great army of civilization."

Meanwhile, Judah was slowly being cut out of any leadership role in the company. His continued complaints about cutting corners and shoddy workmanship, along with his idea that he was in charge of the project, served only to irritate the others who were risking their fortunes in the venture. He soon found himself the odd man out with decisions being made behind his back by men who would not seek his counsel. In the summer of 1863, Huntington returned from a trip to Washington to discover that Judah had rerouted the first mile of the rail line in Sacramento. Huntington had ordered the line to go along

I Street; Judah had routed it down B Street so it would be closer to the river. The board had approved the change, but Huntington was furious. He ordered work shut down and told Judah and his ally on the board James Bailey that they had two weeks to buy out the Big Four partners at a price of $100,000 apiece.

When an early prospect to fund the buyout balked at the last minute, Judah contacted Cornelius Vanderbilt to arrange for funds. Judah and his wife headed for New York to close the deal, but on the trip across the isthmus in Panama, he got caught in the rain and fell ill with yellow fever. By the time he got to New York, he was delirious. He died in November 1863 at age 37, his dream of a transcontinental rail line unrealized. The four associates sent their sympathy to the widow, expressing their sorrow at Judah's passing. But there is little doubt that his untimely death was a welcome relief from his interference in what they saw as their business. Now they could get back to work on the railroad unhindered by Judah's perceived prissiness about how things got done.

There were problems and setbacks, but work on the project progressed through summer heat and winter snows. On May 10, 1869 – four months before the Los Angeles & San Pedro line opened in Southern California – the Central Pacific and Union Pacific met at Promontory Point, Utah. The famous "golden spike" was driven to unite the tracks, and the United States was connected coast-to-coast by rail.

The human toll of the project was tremendous, although no one knows exactly how many people died constructing the transcontinental line. Some put Chinese casualties alone at more than 1,500, based on one newspaper report at the time that put the toll at perhaps 1,200 and then exaggerated it in subsequent accounts. But others say that such a high number is nonsense. A more reasonable number would be around 130 workers, with many of those dying from avalanches and other weather-related causes, the skeptics say. But even they admit that there may have been more than that who succumbed to disease, including those infected during a documented smallpox epidemic in Nevada.

In the end, what seemed an impossible task – constructing a rail line across the Sierra Mountains – was accomplished, and the nation was tied together by iron and steam.

Prior to the railroad, people wanting to journey to California from the East Coast had to go by ship on a dangerous voyage around the Horn or across the Isthmus of Panama to connect to another vessel, or across the country on horseback, on foot, or in wagons behind a team of horses or mules. Now they could buy a ticket, sit in a seat, and ride across the continent in relative comfort.

California was open for settlement.

William Willmore's Vision

Twenty-six-year-old William Willmore was on the road from Wilmington to Anaheim with a group of travelers in 1870 when they took a break not far from the ocean before moving on. Willmore, an English immigrant who had arrived in America as a boy fifteen years earlier, had no wife. His mother and father were dead, and he seemed to have no close friends. After the other travelers departed for Anaheim, Willmore and a young lad lagged behind. "Someday," he told the young man, "this place will be a great city and a great port." Or so the story goes.

That city supposedly envisioned by Willmore today is called Long Beach. But is that what really happened that day on the road to Anaheim? William Willmore said it was, and it is the kind of story that people want to believe. It is also the kind of story that people selling real estate like to tell. Whether that particular story is true or not, the dream of building a town where cattle used to graze among the mustard plants eventually would become Willmore's passion. But on that day in 1870, it seemed unlikely that the shy man with the big dream would ever accomplish his goal. It would be a decade before he came back to that spot, but when he did he was finally ready to turn his dream into a reality.

A Deal with the Railroad

Even before the Central Pacific and Union Pacific linked up in Utah, Collis Huntington was looking at the benefits of creating a web of rail lines with tentacles spreading throughout the state and the Southwest. If one company could dominate the transportation of goods and people for an entire state or region, the potential for power and profit would be immense. The Central Pacific had already bought some existing lines – the Western Pacific, connecting Sacramento and San Francisco, and a combination of financially ailing lines that linked the Sacramento area to Chico.

In 1868, Huntington, Stanford, Hopkins, and Crocker quietly bought the Southern Pacific Railroad, which had been founded by San Francisco businessman Timothy Phelps three years earlier. It had tracks and no equipment, but it did have the rights to property on the Oakland waterfront, as well as rights for land in the San Joaquin Valley, south of Sacramento. The Big Four kept their ownership of the company a secret, installing a group of front men to represent their interests.

After the Central Pacific hookup was complete, the partners decided to expand their enterprise by building new lines as part of their Southern Pacific holdings. The railroad's original charter was to build a line south along a coastal route, but the four new owners decided an inland route made more sense because it was shorter, flatter, and ran through rich valley lands well-suited for farming.

As the Southern Pacific continued pushing south through California, hoping to dominate both Northern and Southern California rail business, the Texas and Pacific Railroad was laying tracks from the other direction in an attempt to build a southern transcontinental line, one with fewer grades and milder year-round weather that would connect up to San Diego.

Huntington needed to get through California and over to Yuma, Arizona, before the Texas and Pacific got there in order for the Southern Pacific railroad to be the dominant line in California. The decisions he made on getting there were both ruthless and profitable. As the railroad proceeded southward, it would demand from each town along the route a large sum of money, a wide right-of-way, and a place to build a depot. If the city refused, the railroad would alter the route and bypass the city. Without the economic clout that the railroad would provide, the city's future was dimmed.

Los Angeles was no exception. It had a nearby harbor and a rail line from the harbor to the city, but it needed a rail connection to the rest of the country. Phineas Banning's partner, Benjamin D. Wilson, who had been elected to the State Senate, got a bill passed in 1870 that would allow certain counties to offer up to 5 percent of their assessed value as an incentive to attract railroads. Officials with the Southern Pacific, however, noted that routing the railroad to Los Angeles would require crossing the San Gabriel Mountains north of the city, making such a decision unlikely. In 1871, both Wilson and Banning went to Washington to plead their case. Congress was considering a bill to permit the Southern Pacific to build on public land, and the partners were able to get the phrase "by way of Los Angeles" inserted into the legislation. Although the Southern Pacific was now required by law to run through Los Angeles, it was clear that Huntington had the political connections to get the law changed if he so wished. If the city wanted the Southern Pacific connection – and it did – the city leaders would have to sweeten the pot.

A "Committee of Thirty," composed of business and civic leaders, was appointed to negotiate with the railroad. The Southern Pacific knew how much the city needed the railroad, and the railroad's demands were harsh. The best deal that the Committee could get from the railroad was to provide a subsidy equal to 5 percent of Los Angeles County's assessed valuation, all the city and county owned stock in the Los Angeles & San Pedro Railroad, the usual right-of-way, sixty acres of downtown property for a depot, and funding to build a spur line to Anaheim – a total of $602,000.

To add to the confusion, Texas and Pacific Railroad President Tom Scott showed up with a counteroffer. He already had a charter to build his line to San Diego. For only 5 percent of the assessed value and no transfer of ownership of the Los Angeles & San Pedro Railroad, he would extend the Texas and Pacific rail line up from San Diego to Los Angeles. The Committee of Thirty had problems with Scott's proposal. First there was no guarantee that the extension to Los Angeles would ever actually get built, and even if it was, it would put Los Angeles as a secondary destination behind San Diego.

There was much outcry over the proposed Southern Pacific deal, but for many it seemed a better opportunity than was being offered by the Texas and Pacific Railroad. The Southern Pacific may have had a reputation for its arrogance and ruthless tactics, but having a railroad that would connect the growing city with the rest of the state and nation was essential. On November 5, 1872, the public voted overwhelmingly to approve the Southern Pacific deal.

The following April, the city and county formally transferred its stock in the Los Angeles & San Pedro Railroad to the Southern Pacific. A month later, the Southern Pacific bought out Henry Tichenor's and Phineas Banning's interests in the line. By 1874, the Southern Pacific had laid a portion of the main line north from Los Angeles to San Fernando. By 1875, the Southern Pacific completed the spur line to Anaheim, and construction of the Southern Pacific line to Los Angeles was completed in 1876. That was the same year that a steep increase in freight rates from the harbor was announced. Freight transported between the harbor and the city went from about $8 per ton to as high as $30 per ton.

Huntington believed in charging all that the traffic could bear and so the Southern Pacific charged different rates for different shippers. The railroad required some shippers to open their books in order to be able to charge the maximum amount short of destroying the customer's business. Grain farmers complained that the price for transporting grain went up and down with the market price of the product. In effect, they were all working for the railroad.

Banning himself had been an ardent supporter of getting the Southern Pacific to come to Los Angeles, and he developed a good relationship with the railroad executives. He was a featured speaker at the ceremony marking the completion of the railroad's line to Los Angeles. Although the Southern Pacific's purchase of the Los Angeles & San Pedro Railroad had included the harbor operation in

Wilmington, in 1876 the railroad sold it back to Banning for $60,000. Banning incorporated the operation as the Wilmington Transportation Co.

A Final Indignity

Although Abel Stearns defaulted on his mortgage in 1866 and Michael Reese of San Francisco took over ownership of Rancho Los Alamitos, Stearns remained a wealthy man. On August 23, 1871, Stearns unexpectedly died at the Grand Hotel in San Francisco. He was 72 years old. He had been a smuggler, a merchant, a plotter against the Mexican governor, a confidential agent for the Americans, a rancher, mayor of Los Angeles, and a husband. His 14-year-old bride Doña Arcadia was now 46. His body was brought back to Los Angeles for interment at Calvary Catholic Cemetery. Harris Newmark recalled the bizarre scene at the grave.

> *Awesome indeed was the scene that I witnessed when the ropes sustaining the 800-pound metallic casket snapped, pitching the coffin and its grim contents into the grave. I shall never forget the unearthly shriek of Doña Arcadia, as well as the accident itself.*

Another California pioneer was gone.

Rancho Los Alamitos Under New Ownership

As always happens in Southern California, there were years of rain and years of drought. The rains came in 1867, but in 1872 the drought was back. Although sheep were more drought-tolerant than cattle, many of the sheep being raised by the Bixbys and Flints died as the range dried up. By this time, the market for wool was also in decline, and it was clear that open-range ranching was not the ideal way to make money in Southern California.

Meanwhile, real estate promoters were hard at work trying to entice folks from back East to move to California. The open land of the old ranchos started to be sprinkled with farms and towns, such as Pasadena, Santa Ana, Orange, Riverside, and Pomona. Jotham Bixby realized that the pastoral age of cattle and sheep was drawing to a close. A new agricultural age of small towns and farms was taking its place. Bixby became a board member of the California Immigrant Union and contributed generously to its objectives.

Jotham's cousin, a schoolteacher named John William Bixby, moved to Rancho Los Cerritos from Maine in 1871 to work on the ranch. He was tall, lean, a hard worker, and a violin player. One of the house guests at the ranch at the time was Susan Hathaway, the sister of Jotham Bixby's wife, Margaret. He was 22 when they met, she was three years older. When they married on October 4, 1873, she became the fourth of the five Hathaway sisters – the daughters of Reverend George Hathaway – to marry one of the Bixby men. Lewellyn Bixby had married Sarah Hathaway in 1859. He was 33; she was 18. Jotham Bixby met his wife, Margaret Hathaway, during an 1862 visit with his future in-laws during a trip back East. He was 31; she was 19, two years younger than Sarah. They were wed in San Juan Bautista on December 4, 1863. Sarah Hathaway Bixby died childless after six years of marriage. Six years later, Lewellyn married her 24-year-old younger sister, Mary. She died seven years later, leaving two daughters and a son. The oldest of the three, Sarah Hathaway Bixby, named after Lewellyn's beloved first wife and Mary's older sister, would later recall the details of her childhood in her book, *Adobe Days*.

After Mary's death, Lewellyn proposed to a third sister, Martha Hathaway. She declined, but agreed to come to California to help him raise his children.

John Bixby quickly learned the business of being a sheep rancher during his employment at Los Cerritos. After his marriage to Susan, the two moved to Wilmington, not far from Phineas Banning's mansion, where they lived for several years. The economic depression that lasted from 1873 to 1879 had sent wool prices plummeting, and everybody was feeling the pinch. In 1876, the Bixbys sold their share of the property they had bought with James Irvine to Irvine for $150,000. Despite the tough times, the Bixbys continued to look for new opportunities to build their financial holdings.

John Bixby in 1875 – the same year that his son Frederick Hathaway Bixby was born – purchased 2,155 acres of the property south and east of the Santa Ana River, in what today is Yorba Linda, expanding it gradually by 4,000 additional acres. Rancho Los Alamitos at the time was owned by Michael Reese of San Francisco, who got the property when Stearns defaulted on his mortgage.

In 1878, John Bixby subleased 1,000 acres of Rancho Los Alamitos from two brothers who in 1871 had signed a ten-year lease with Reese for the property. The brothers, who had been raising sheep on the land, had also been caught in the squeeze of drought and falling wool prices and were happy to sublease a portion of the land to Bixby. Bixby moved his wife, young son, and daughter into the old ranch house and began fixing it up. Reese died later that year during a trip to his German homeland. His will required that all his property be sold within five years. Rancho Los Alamitos was suddenly on the market. To purchase the property, John Bixby put together a three-way partnership among himself, J. Bixby & Co., and Los Angeles banker Isaias W. Hellman. Hellman was the founder and president of the Farmers and Merchants Bank in Los Angeles and a long-time investor in Southern California real estate.

Although times were tough, John Bixby was looking to the future. The arrival of a major railroad in Southern California promised to open up new markets and to facilitate the arrival of new residents to the state. Instead of depending on mutton and wool, maybe it was time to branch out into dairy cows and growing new crops to feed the coming settlers.

In 1871, the sale closed with the partners buying the 26,393-acre Rancho Los Alamitos for $125,000 in gold coin. The purchase of the property made the Bixbys the largest waterfront landowners on San Pedro Bay and would place the clan squarely in the middle of a future that was far beyond anything they could have imagined at the time.

Chapter Seven:
Birth of a City

The world was rapidly changing. The Wild West was just about gone, thanks to the growth of railroads, the rush of settlers looking for new land, the telegraph, the invention of the Bessemer converter to produce high quality steel from pig iron, and the pacification of the Indians. Along the way, General George Custer and 267 men of the 7th Cavalry lost their lives in a battle with Lakota, Northern Cheyenne, and Arapaho Indians at Little Big Horn. Iron rails for trains were replaced by steel. Wild Bill Hickok was shot in the back of the head while playing poker in Deadwood, South Dakota. And the international great depression, which began with the Panic of 1873, was pretty much over by 1879 – at least in the United States.

The giant Krakatoa volcano exploded in Indonesia in 1883, resulting in 36,000 deaths, mostly from the resulting tsunamis. The explosion – the largest ever in recorded history – was heard 3,000 miles away, and ash quickly circled the globe, causing average global temperatures to fall more than 2 degrees Fahrenheit during the following year.

It was called the Gilded Age. It was an age of dynamic economic growth, of technical advance, of widespread industrialization, of new immigrants – and of old prejudices. It was an age that witnessed – and contributed to – the rise of labor unions, political machines, and new ways to do old things.

The University of Southern California was founded in 1880, the same year that the recorded population of the United States passed the 50 million mark. Billy the Kid was shot and killed by Sheriff Pat Garrett in 1881. And in 1882, the Chinese Exclusion Act was passed by Congress, forbidding any further immigration of Chinese people into the United States for ten years. The exclusion of the Chinese was favored by labor unionists, who saw the Chinese as low-wage competitors for jobs, and opposed by capitalists for the same reason.

Giant tracts of land in California were being subdivided and turned into towns and small farms as the holders of such lands realized that the days of the big cattle and sheep ranches were coming to an end. The California Immigrant Union was sending out pamphlets and advertisements lauding the climate, the rich soil, and the available land at reasonable prices. For those willing to work hard and bold enough to make the move, California was a place with unlimited potential.

The Rise and Fall of William Willmore

William Erwin Willmore, upon his return from six years working in Washington and Oregon, was hired as a manager of the California Immigrant Union, an organization aimed at promoting California to new settlers. His first outreach was to a group of female teachers, who were interested in growing grapes in the Central California Colony, about three miles south of what is now downtown Fresno. Willmore had not forgotten that day on the road near the Pacific Ocean in 1870 on his way to Anaheim, when he had envisioned a future city by the sea.

Around 1880, Willmore proposed development of some waterfront property, which was part of the Rancho Los Cerritos oceanfront. Both the CIU and Jotham Bixby, whose J. Bixby & Co. owned Rancho Los Cerritos, were interested in the idea. Bixby was active in the California Immigrant Union, and he had already subdivided part of the rancho and other lands he owned for development into small farms and towns. He agreed to attempt the same thing on 4,000 acres along the coast – a development dubbed The American Colony. It would turn out to be Willmore's dream, his obsession, and ultimately his downfall.

The California Immigrant Union appointed Willmore as Southern California manager for the American Colony project. William H. Martin, the Union's general agent, would handle promotion of the development in Northern California. Surveyor Captain C.T. Healey, who had been hired by the Bixbys to draw up plans for the development, had included a townsite that was eight blocks wide, extending ten blocks back from the ocean – about 350 acres. There was a place for parks, schools, churches, and a college. Plans for the American Colony were announced on Christmas Eve 1880 in the Los Angeles Daily Herald.

> *The soil of the Cerritos is noted for its fertility and one of the most gratifying things about the programme is that lands are to be sold at reasonable rates, ranging from $12.50 to $25 an acre, according to location, quality of soil, etc. We don't see why, with such figures for the land, those who buy in the American Colony for purposes of actual settlement – and this is the desirable class of buyers – should not profit by the decided advance in the value of the real estate upon which they settle. Both corn and wheat will grow abundantly on this ranch and artesian water can be secured at trifling depths.*

Despite such optimism in this and subsequent press accounts, interest by buyers in the project failed to live up to expectations. Excursions planned to bring parties of prospective buyers west by rail ended up being delayed for months. And when an excursion of potential buyers finally took place in February 1882, it proved to be disappointing, both in size and in sales. By July 1882, the California Immigrant Union had pulled out of the deal. Undeterred, Willmore formed the American Colony Land, Water, and Town Association. But the members of the Association had little capital to back the deal. Willmore decided to enlist the help of Judge Robert M. Widney, the attorney for the American Colony Association. Widney was the founder of the University of Southern California, which had opened two years earlier, and he did have capital. Judge Widney with his brother, Dr. Joseph Widney, also had been involved in other development projects.

Widney decided to see the planned development for himself. He took the train down to Wilmington, got a horse and buggy there, and rode out to the site. Despite all the grand plans, there wasn't much to see – an eight-by-ten-foot wooden shack on the edge of a gully near what is now First Street and Pine

Avenue in downtown Long Beach. Both Widney and Willmore spent the night on makeshift beds pulled from a nearby pile of hay.

Widney agreed to become part of the undertaking, but only if he could reorganize the Association, bring in his own people, and have the ultimate say on all matters of policy. The reorganized Association had J.H. Lester as president, Willmore as secretary, and Widney and T.J. Morrison as the managing committee. In August, Willmore negotiated a deal with J. Bixby & Co. for an option on 4,000 acres at $25 an acre – $100,000. The property would be paid off as sales of property progressed.

The contract is revealing. Willmore promised to pay the J. Bixby & Co. $25,000 by December 1, 1882; a second payment of $30,000 would be made by June 30, 1883, and the remainder would be paid on June 1, 1884. It seemed an impossible goal to meet, but as is the case of many dreamers, Willmore may have been blinded by his own optimism for a real estate scheme that had not gone as well as expected up to that point.

An auction of property in what was now known as Willmore City was scheduled for October. One of the problems in selling property was providing easy access for potential buyers to see the property. The Southern Pacific provided train service to Wilmington, but the nearest station was still more than three miles from the properties for sale. Widney, acting quickly, formed the American Colony Railway Co., most of which he personally funded. He was to be compensated by five and a half blocks of land on each side of Chestnut Avenue for which he would only have to pay the $40 an acre demanded by the Bixbys. It was a daunting task. He had to lay three miles of track and build three bridges in two months. He obtained right-of-way, gathered whatever materials were available – three-by-four-inch redwoods formed the ties, connected by pine strips for rails – and began laying tracks.

Surveyor Healey, who had been working in Wilmington after initially laying the boundaries for the development, returned to help Willmore polish his plan, which included a 124-foot-wide main boulevard called American Avenue (now Long Beach Boulevard), parks, resort hotels, a downtown district, and a university campus. The university campus was excluded in the plan that Healey drew up. Despite best efforts, as the day of the auction drew near, the town was little more than dirt roads plowed through the brush and a few buildings.

On auction day, a special train with six carloads of passengers arrived. The American Colony Railway's horse-drawn train quickly filled with passengers and began its first three-mile trip from Wilmington to Willmore City. Along the way, one of the pine strips gave way under the strain, tipping over a railway car full of passengers. Everybody got out, tipped the car back on the track and gave it a push. Widney's railroad from that day on was nicknamed the GOP – the Get Out and Push – railroad.

Despite the problems with the train, Willmore sold thirty-six lots that day at prices ranging from $125 on Ocean Park to $25 inland. Included in the deeds – supposedly at the suggestion of Jotham Bixby's wife, Margaret – was a provision that if liquor was ever sold on the property it would revert back to the former owner. The only exemption to the rule was for property that was to be developed for hotels.

Although the auction was considered a success, big problems remained. Rains washed out Widney's rail line three times. He doubled the number of ties, covered the wooden tracks with iron strapping, and added two new cars. A water

CITY FATHER: *Beginning in the early 1880s, William Willmore developed what became downtown Long Beach. Unfortunately, his financial resources were not up to the long-term task of building city infrastructure. He returned to Long Beach impoverished in 1899 and died in 1901.*

system was installed, providing fresh water for the townsite. By the spring of 1883, visitors were beginning to arrive to spend the day at the ocean, and some of them ended up buying property. In June 1883, Mrs. George Reed gave birth to a little girl, the first baby born in Willmore City. Willmore offered the mother her choice of any piece of property in the townsite to be held in trust for the baby if she would name her daughter Wilmoretta. She declined, perhaps understandably, but instead named her daughter Yuba in honor of the small community of Yuba Dam, where the family had previously resided.

Development of Willmore City continued. Property owners began building homes on the lots that they bought and opening businesses. There were still amenities missing, but construction had begun on an ocean-front bathhouse and pavilion a little west of Pine Avenue. Willmore's problem was that the money that came in so slowly went out far too fast. What did come in was spent on such things as waterlines, pavilions, and advertising. In the end Willmore could not sell enough property quickly enough to meet his obligation to the Bixbys. The first two payments due were missed. The potential for success was apparent, but realizing such success often depends on having enough resources to get to the point where earnings exceed expenses. In May 1884, Willmore's resources ran out. He was forced to surrender what he worked so hard to build, buying his way out of his contract with the Bixby Company for $1.

Willmore left town a broken man. Within months an option on the land plus some additional acreage was purchased by the real estate firm of Pomeroy and Mills for $240,000. The new owners also paid Willmore $8,000 for the water system he had installed. One of the first orders of business was to find a new name for the town. Since Willmore was by this time gone, Willmore City no longer seemed appropriate. Several names were suggested and discussed. Belle Lowe, who with her husband had moved to the community earlier that year, suggested Long Beach, and when a vote was taken, that was the name that won. Within several months, Pomeroy and Mills had incorporated under the name of the Long Beach Land and Water Co.

The nine directors of the new company were many of the same men that Willmore had been dealing with during the prior three and a half years, according to historian Walter Case. They were A.E. Pomeroy, H.W. Mills, Judge Widney, George H. Bonebrake, George R. Crow, C.W. Woodherd, A.M. Hough, S.W. Mott, and P.M. Green. It was this collection of directors – all men of means – that helped push what Willmore had started in vain to success. Judge Widney continued to run his American Colony Railway between Wilmington and Long Beach and provided valuable continuity between the old management and the new. Construction was begun on the Long Beach Hotel – the first major building in the new town. Also that year, the new company was able to convince the Methodist Resort Association to make Long Beach the location for their annual camp meeting and to construct a church in which to hold revivals.

The Southern California Real Estate Boom

If Willmore had just been able to hold out a little longer, things might have been different for him. In 1886, a price war between the Santa Fe and Southern Pacific railroads dropped the price of a ticket from the Missouri Valley to Southern California from $125 to $100. As the competition between the two railroads continued, the price of a ticket at one point dropped to as low as $1, and people flocked to Los Angeles. In 1887, the Southern Pacific alone brought 120,000 people west.

The Great Southern California Real Estate Boom of 1887 was under way. It was driven by four factors, according to historian James M. Guinn – cheap train fares, a multitude of job opportunities at good wages, climate, and the boom itself. As news of the booming real estate market came out, land speculators and shady developers flocked to the area to cash in. Real estate was the business to be in.

"Land that sold at $100 an acre in 1886, changed hands in 1887 at $1,500 per acre; and city lots bought in 1886 at $500 each, a year later were rated at $5,000," Guinn recalled.

Under new management and with the rising demand for property from new settlers, the community that William Willmore envisioned became a reality. He just wasn't there to see it.

The Death of Phineas Banning

Phineas Banning had been a larger-than-life figure on the Southern California stage. He had driven stagecoaches, had taken tumbles from wagons, been injured on the docks, and had almost been killed when a boat he owned suddenly blew up. He had moved boldly in business, courted the right people, plotted and conspired, took a stand against slavery, led at least one lynch mob, lost one young wife and married another, and saw seven of his twelve children die before they reached the age of 5. He had been both criticized and praised, loved and hated, attacked and defended. He had built a railroad, launched a port, lobbied for port improvements, and entertained lavishly. He had lived a hardy life and ate and drank the same way. As a young man he was husky. In his middle years he became fat, his waistline expanding along with his appetite for fine food and drink.

By the late 1870s, his health began to fail, the beginnings of kidney and liver problems. His friend Benjamin Wilson died in 1878, a sad final note to a successful partnership of two men separated by politics, but united by business and personal respect. In June 1882, Banning resigned as commander of the First Brigade of the California National Guard – a military unit that was never activated, but which provided him with his highly prized title of "General." He said that the reason he had to step down was continued severe attacks of neuralgia in the head.

The Los Angeles Times responded with tongue-in-cheek sarcasm.

> *Every friend of his country – every lover of the dear flag of numerous stars and stripes – "old glory," as some infatuated people call it – will record the item with moistened eye! The General was a brave soldier; true he never killed anyone that we know of, and that's the kind of soldier we like...*
>
> *In the far future, when the slate of the braves is made up, there will be Geo. Washington, "the first in war, the first in peace, and the first in the hearts of his countrymen;" and one hundred years further down the column – General Banning, the last in war, the first with the Quartermaster and with the commissary's fluid stores...*

It was a harsh – although not entirely inaccurate – critique of one of the pioneers who helped carve a community out of raw and wild country and grew rich in the doing. The man most responsible for the development of San Pedro

Bay and who had worked throughout his adult life toward the development of Southern California as a trade hub was in his twilight years. But as often happens, those who inherit the benefits of the previous generation are often quick to judge how those benefits were secured.

Banning was in San Francisco in 1884 to discuss plans for buying Santa Catalina Island, when he stepped off a cable car and was knocked off his feet and run over by an express wagon. He was too bruised and battered in the accident to immediately return home, so he stayed in San Francisco long enough to heal before he headed back to Wilmington. Later that year, he took a trip to Catalina and then went back East to visit family and seek further medical attention. Before he left, he gave his son William power of attorney to manage his businesses. After he returned to California, still ill, he traveled to San Francisco in November to consult with a new doctor, improved somewhat, then came home to Wilmington for what would be his last Christmas. He returned to San Francisco for further treatment in January with his wife, Mary, son Joseph, and daughter Lucy. He caught a cold when he arrived and never recovered.

Phineas Banning, the brash 21-year-old who got his start on the San Pedro waterfront in 1851, died March 8, 1885, in his room at the Occidental Hotel. He was 54. His body was returned to Los Angeles by train, then down to Wilmington on the same line he had built fifteen years earlier. A funeral service was held on March 12 at the Banning home, and he was taken for burial at the Wilmington Cemetery. The funeral procession of people walking four abreast was said to have been a mile long.

He had accomplished much in his thirty-three years in Southern California. By sheer will, persistence, and sometimes shady dealings, he had secured a working port on San Pedro Bay. But the best was yet to come.

A Seaside Village with Big Plans

With the development of Long Beach under new management that had capital behind it and new residents moving in, improvements began to take place. By the summer of 1884, just weeks after William Willmore's departure, construction of a new two-level, wood-frame hotel was begun with three stories atop the bluff overlooking the sea and five stories on the sand below. The Long Beach Hotel, near what is now Pacific Avenue and Ocean Boulevard, had 130 rooms for guests, an eighty-by-twenty-foot piazza facing the beach, and all the modern conveniences, such as an electric bell in each room, a speaking tube on each floor, and a telephone connection to Los Angeles. Steam heat was added two years later.

A new wooden pier for boating and fishing was completed in 1885 with a walkway thirty-two feet wide, extending 700 feet into the ocean. The Long Beach Land and Water Co., which had taken over when Willmore had failed, invested about a quarter-million dollars into improvements – much of it in upgrading the water system – and spurred additional sales of properties.

Jotham Bixby and his family moved from his adobe house at Rancho Los Cerritos into a large home at the corner of Ocean Boulevard and Magnolia Avenue. Other homes were being built all over town. William Wallace Lowe, whose wife Belle had suggested the name Long Beach, had bought property on the northeast corner of Ocean Boulevard and Pine Avenue where the family made their home. Immediately north, he opened a grocery and general merchandise store where, according to his ad, "everything usually found in a first-class store may be had at low down figures for cash." He was appointed by President Grover Cleveland as the first postmaster for Long Beach.

Businesses and residences began to take the place of weed-overgrown lots. Most of the streets were still dirt lanes, but a community was clearly taking shape, and the Long Beach Land and Water Co. was making a profit.

Despite the success, the only rail connection between the Wilmington Southern Pacific Railroad station and Long Beach was still Judge Robert M. Widney's little horse-drawn American Colony Railway. Widney had extended the line all the way to the new Long Beach Hotel, but it was still a makeshift connection that needed to be upgraded or replaced. The Land and Water Co. replaced the narrow-gauge tracks with a wide gauge line and bought a small steam engine to replace the horse. Even with the improvements, the railway remained a popular source of good-natured jibes from passengers who sometimes still had to get out and push to get the little train going again.

The Long Beach Land and Water Co. sent a representative to San Francisco to meet with Charles Crocker – one of the four associates who had built the western section of the transcontinental railroad – and make the case for Southern Pacific service to Long Beach. The growing success of the new community and its obvious potential began to attract attention.

In July 1887, a new entity – The Long Beach Development Co. – was incorporated with the intent to buy out the Long Beach Land and Water Co. and take over development of the city. The directors of the new company were W.H. Goucher, C.F. Bragg, Edward Records, E.B. Cushing, H G. Wilshire, Fred Cowley and Charles D. Baker. Most of them were affiliated directly or indirectly with the Southern Pacific Railroad.

The Long Beach Development Co. paid the Long Beach Land and Water Co. $250,000 for the remaining unsold property, and the water system. As part of the deal, they were also required to buy 800 acres of saltwater marsh to the west of the community – a property in which they had no interest – but which would one day be the inner harbor of the Port of Long Beach.

In December 1887, Widney sold his "Get Out and Push" railway to the Land and Water Co., which immediately transferred the right-of-way to Southern Pacific. The three-mile rail line was reconstructed by Southern Pacific with heavier rails and sturdier bridges in order to accommodate full-size trains.

By January 30, 1888 – less than four years after Willmore City became Long Beach – the residents of the new community were ready to make it official. They voted, 103 to 3, to make Long Beach an incorporated city. Thomas Stovell, John Roberts, I.D. Fetterman, George H. Bixby, and M.H. La Fetra were elected as trustees – the equivalent of today's City Council. W.W. Lowe was voted city treasurer; W.H. Nash was the city clerk, and H.A. Davies became the city marshal and tax collector. Their first term in office was short. State law required all cities the size of Long Beach to hold their regular election in April. Bixby declined to run for re-election, and Kenyon Cox took his place; W.F. Hopkins was elected to replace Nash.

The first order of business was to pass an ordinance banning saloons, gambling houses, and other businesses dangerous to the public health or safety. It was a hot-button issue in 1888 Long Beach and one that would come back to haunt the city just a few years later.

The Woman in Black

In 1886 the Bixby family was making major plans to expand on the Long Beach idea. John W. Bixby, a one-third owner of the Rancho Los Alamitos property, and his cousin Jotham Bixby, had plans drawn up for a new 5,000-acre town site – twenty blocks long and two blocks deep – abutting the newly established community of Long Beach. The boundary line between the new community, which he called Alamitos Beach, and Long Beach would be Alamitos Avenue – which was also the boundary line between Rancho Cerritos and Rancho Alamitos. The plan was later expanded northward to Tenth Street. The avenues running north from Ocean Boulevard were given Spanish names in alphabetical order, such as Bonita, Cerritos, Esperanza, Gaviota, and Junipero. An area was set aside, on the north side of Ocean, for a park, later known as Bixby Park. Water for the new community would come from wells to the north and east on what is now Recreation Park.

John W. Bixby died on May 6, 1887, at age 39. He was survived by his wife, Susan, his 12-year-old son, Fred, and his 7-year-old daughter, Susanna. Cause of death is thought to have been acute appendicitis. His rich widow, with two small children, had no choice but to carry on. But from that day until her own death, nineteen years later, Susan Bixby – wherever she went, on business or pleasure – dressed only in black. She never remarried.

After his death, the owners of Rancho Los Alamitos – J. Bixby & Co., I.W. Hellman, and John Bixby's estate, formed the Alamitos Land Co. The town site was extended east to tidal lands that then existed. The 5,000 acres were set aside to be developed by the Alamitos Land Co., and the remainder of the Rancho Los Alamitos property was divided three ways – 7,200 acres each – with Hellman getting property along the coast, J. Bixby & Co. getting inland property, and Susan Bixby and her children getting the ranch site and surrounding property.

By that time, the real estate boom of 1887 was beginning to cool off, and plans for the new community were temporarily put aside. But only temporarily. California was still the land of boundless opportunity, and it would be only a short time before new possibilities spurred things forward once again.

The Charles Crocker Prospect

In March of 1888, Charles Crocker – one of the "Big Four" and former president of the Southern Pacific Railroad – bought controlling interest in the Long Beach Development Co., and the possibilities for Long Beach seemed assured. One of those possibilities was development of a port – not where the present-day port is, but on the east side of town, in the area of the present Alamitos Bay Marina and Naples Island. Such a port, it was thought, could easily compete with the port in Wilmington and San Pedro, especially if it had rail connections.

The area had already been used as a harbor to land both passengers and cargo in the past. Hide and tallow had been shipped through the area in the early years before California became a state, and later cargo would be offloaded from ships at anchor and taken ashore in small boats to be transported by wagons along the North Walk – an old Spanish trail that terminated in what is now Norwalk.

In an age of horse-drawn wagons, having a harbor as close as possible was an important advantage for the farmers in Anaheim – then still part of Los Angeles County. People wanted to provide an alternative to Wilmington and San Pedro, which was dominated by Phineas Banning and later by the Southern Pacific Railroad. When the Alamitos Bay location filled with silt following a rainy season, people explored the possibilities of building a "new port" in what is now Newport Beach, but that site lacked the rail connection and was too far from the Los Angeles urban center to compete with San Pedro Bay. Anaheim Landing was later developed with a wharf and warehouses at the current location of the Seal Beach Naval Weapons Station wharf. Wine, wool, and produce were among the early cargos exported from the landing. The major import was lumber.

But the 1880s was the time of the railroads. Rail connections between Anaheim and San Pedro made getting cargo to and from the larger port both easier and cheaper, slowly forcing the decline of Anaheim Landing. For an Alamitos Bay port in Long Beach to compete with Wilmington and San Pedro, it would need to have rail connections to link distant customers to the waterfront. The Southern Pacific had held a rail monopoly at San Pedro-Wilmington since 1873, but there were plenty of other railroads also anxious to get a port connection.

The Los Angeles and Ocean Railway was incorporated in September 1887 with nine directors, including General Edward Bouton, Jonathan Bixby, G.W. Elwood, Edward Records, M.L. Wicks, C.E. French, John W. Green, A.W. Barrett, and A.W. Francisco. General Bouton took an active role in representing the railroad's interest in the city. The company obtained the last of the right of way from Los Angeles to Alamitos Bay in 1888. It was granted permission to run its line along Second Street, despite protests from Southern Pacific, which already had established that right of way. The Los Angeles and Ocean Railway planned to service the new Alamitos Bay Port.

Another railroad – the Long Beach and San Pedro Railway – was incorporated in April of the following year with some of the same directors. Directors of the new company were General Bouton, James Campbell, J.M. Leach, Harvey L. Bissell, and John W. Green. The Long Beach and San Pedro Railway Co. planned to run a line from Los Angeles through Long Beach and across the island to the east side of the Wilmington-San Pedro Harbor. From there it could compete directly with the Southern Pacific Railroad terminal on the other side of the channel and break the Southern Pacific monopoly.

The two railroads – the Los Angeles and Ocean and the Long Beach and San Pedro – were affiliated. Both were represented by General Bouton and managed by James Campbell, a former engineer who had worked on the construction of the first transcontinental railroad. The plan was that the railroads would eventually be bought by one of the transcontinental lines. Some rumors said the Union Pacific was already in control; others claimed it was the Santa Fe.

As the boom years ground to a halt in 1888, so did the grand plans for a port at Alamitos Bay that would compete with San Pedro. Property values plummeted and early optimism about the city's future began to turn to gloom. Charles Crocker, whose investment in the city had been the cause of much rejoicing, died on August 14, and his heirs had little interest in continuing whatever he had planned for the city. The general depression was clinched in the wee hours of November 8, when the Long Beach Hotel, a symbol of the success of the fledgling community, went up in flames. The fire had started in the kitchen shortly after midnight, and an alarm was sounded, but the hose to fight the fire could not be made to work. Some furniture was carried out the door, including a billiard table, but the people who rushed to the scene were unable to contain the flames.

Onlookers stood by helplessly as the grand building burned to the ground. The Long Beach Development Co. announced plans the following day to immediately erect another hotel in its place within the year – one that would surpass the one that had burned. But those plans came to naught.

What the city did have, however, were rail connections. And those connections would prove to be invaluable in the future, when the opportunity arose for the city to at last have its own port.

The Terminal Island Connection

The dream of a major port at Alamitos Bay was gone, but there was still a great deal of interest in a competing rail line in gaining a foothold in San Pedro Bay, where the Southern Pacific controlled the waterfront in both Wilmington and San Pedro. The key would be to get control of Rattlesnake Island – the narrow east-west spit of land that separated the ocean on the south from the salt water marsh to the north. If somebody could control that island, they could build a bridge from Long Beach to the island, and then across the island to the east side of San Pedro harbor.

The rights to the island had been purchased by the Long Beach and San Pedro Railway, controlled at the time by James Campbell. In September of 1890, Campbell agreed to transfer ownership to the newly formed Los Angeles Terminal Railroad, including rights to land on the west end of the island for a terminal. Less than three months later, the Los Angeles Terminal Railway merged with two other lines – the Los Angeles & Glendale Railway and the Los Angeles, Pasadena & Glendale Railway – but kept the same name. The new company later changed the name of the island from Rattlesnake Island to Terminal Island.

Among the people with interest in the new company was a group of investors from St. Louis and two brothers from Montana, William Andrews Clark and his younger brother, Ross.

William Clark had made a fortune in mining and was one of the three so-called "Montana Copper Kings." Clark had been elected by the Montana Legislature to the U.S. Senate in 1899, but later had to resign after charges that he had spent more than $300,000 bribing state legislators in order to get elected.

"I never bought a man who wasn't for sale," Clark would later explain in his defense. The resulting scandal helped lead to the passage of the 17th Amendment in 1915, which called for the popular election of U.S. Senators. After his resignation, Clark went back to Montana, ran successfully to regain his seat, and served in the Senate from 1901 through 1907. Despite his tenacity and political skills, he was never popular with his fellow senators, who made little effort to hide their contempt.

"If you took away the whiskers and the scandal there would be nothing left," was an oft-repeated comment made about him within the Senate, not a body known to be squeamish when it came to corruption.

Senator Clark needed a way to ship his copper ore to the West Coast. At the time, Salt Lake City needed a rail connection to the growing metropolitan hub of Los Angeles. In 1900, Clark bought into the Los Angeles Terminal Railway in order to nail down that end of the line. Later that year he announced plans to incorporate the San Pedro, Los Angeles, and Salt Lake Railroad, which would finally give Utah its long-desired link to the West. But he wasn't the only one with the idea for a Salt Lake City-Los Angeles rail line. Edward Henry Harriman, the president of the Union Pacific and chairman of the Southern Pacific, also planned to build such a line. The race to Los Angeles was on, and the fight between Clark and Harriman raged in both courtroom and board room as the two lines jostled for right of way and advantage. In July 1902, the battle ended in compromise, with Clark selling half-interest in the San Pedro, Los Angeles, and Salt Lake Railroad to Union Pacific, and Union Pacific selling all the trackage and right of ways it owned on the route south of Salt Lake City to the San Pedro, Los Angeles, and Salt Lake company.

The Southern Pacific monopoly in San Pedro Bay was about to be broken, and Collis Huntington, who had taken over as president after ousting Leland Stanford in 1890, was not pleased. In fact, he would go to great lengths to keep out the competition, even if it meant moving his harbor operation to another location.

Long Beach and Liquor

Times had changed. The people who settled Long Beach where not the adventurers, the scoundrels, and the hard-drinking, hard-living frontier types who had first come to California. The new arrivals were a different sort. They came mostly by train from the Midwest and were hard-working, sober people – the kind of folks every settled country needs to work the farms and factories, the kind of folks who had made America great. They went to church, settled their differences in court, and believed in the American dream.

The scoundrels were still there – the get-rich-quick hustlers, the small- and big-time thieves, and people of low morals – but they were outcasts, looked down upon by the regular folks and punished severely when caught.

The burning issue in town was over the sale and use of liquor. The Long Beach Development Co. in 1887 had banned the sale of liquor south of Anaheim Road. A city ordinance passed the following year banned the sale of alcohol anywhere within city limits – even to painters or for use in home lamps. One exception was a saloon at Pine and Broadway run by Old Joe McPherson, which had been issued a county permit prior to the city's incorporation. A large sign along its south wall said "Wanted 1,000 Men to Unload Schooners at the Bar."

Alcohol was an issue that divided the city. Even William Willmore, who put in a reversion clause in the deeds of the property he sold – calling for the property to revert to the original owner if liquor was ever sold on the site – is said to have issued quitclaim deeds removing the stipulation after he left town in 1884 and started drinking himself.

In 1889, the city relented and allowed hotels of fifteen or more rooms to sell wine to their regular guests at dinner, and by 1890, the City Council agreed to license retail sales of liquor, providing there were no sales to children or to anyone whose wife, mother, father, child, or guardians had requested in writing that no liquor be sold to that person. That same year, a dry faction gained control of the council and passed a new ordinance banning all retail sales.

The other side retaliated by calling for an election to disincorporate the city. On July 27, 1896, the citizens voted 132 to 126 to disincorporate, but the council refused to canvass the vote. The council finally did so under pressure, but it did not report the results of the vote to the County Board of Supervisors. Delays mounted, and the case ended up in court. In May 1897 the State Supreme Court ruled, and the city was officially disincorporated.

During the more than nine months between the vote and the Supreme Court ruling, Long Beach was in limbo. It wasn't officially under county rule, but it also wasn't a city. There were no city services. The parks were not maintained, nor were the streets or the waterfront. Civic-minded folks tried to interest people in contributing money to keep the parks going, but people were clearly ready to reincorporate, even before the disincorporation was official.

Once the court ruled, the county took over governance of Long Beach. In order to pay the city's debts and build a new high school, the county levied the highest property taxes in the state. When people complained, the county simply eliminated everything it couldn't afford, including lights on the wharf.

In December 1897, residents voted to reincorporate the city, leaving out the farm land between Anaheim and Hill Street, but adding in the land east into the Alamitos Beach Colony all the way to Descanso Street (which is now Orange Avenue). The new city put a $600-a-year fee on liquor sales. In 1900 the Anti-Saloon League won every council seat in the city, and the city was once again alcohol-free.

It wouldn't be until 1920 that the entire nation followed Long Beach, when the 18th Amendment to the U.S. Constitution took effect, prohibiting the "transportation or importation into any state, territory, or possession of the United States for delivery of use therein of intoxicating liquors."

But in the fight against demon rum, Long Beach was clearly a leader.

BUSTLING TOWN: *The intersection of Ocean Boulevard and Pine Avenue in downtown Long Beach, 1909. After some growing pains (including incorporation, disincorporation, and reincorporation), the city was poised to grow. The First National building (at First and Pine, with clock tower) still stands.*

Chapter Eight:
Free Harbor Fight

The end of the 19th century and the first decade of the 20th century were times of great change for the United States. Technology, politics, and social institutions were all moving forward at a rapid clip to create an economic landscape that would underpin the creation of a whole new class of millionaires even as it helped build a larger middle class that had more conveniences, more power, and a higher standard of living than the country had known before. The introduction of the transcontinental telegraph during the Civil War and the building of the transcontinental railroad following that war were only the beginning of far-reaching developments that would forever change both the country and the world.

In 1878 Thomas Alva Edison formed the Edison Electric Light Co. Edison not only invented the first commercially practical light bulb, he also led the way in wiring the country to bring electric power for lights and other uses right to people's homes. The advent of electrically wired cities during the coming decades dramatically changed the way people lived and worked. Alexander Graham Bell invented the first telephone in 1876, and by the turn of the century telephones were common in cities across the country. Automobile manufacturing plants began opening in the mid-1890s, and within a decade people in cars and on motorcycles were zipping along American roads, getting speeding tickets and sometimes crashing into one another. Photography had emerged from crude and grainy black and white images to being commonplace in journalism, landscapes, and portraiture. And in 1903, Orville and Wilbur Wright made history when Orville flew the first airplane on the sands of Kitty Hawk in North Carolina.

But technology wasn't the only thing changing. So were people's attitudes. Great fortunes had been made by some, but the populace was beginning to question – and often to resent – the centralization of power and wealth within a small group of people. There was a growing perception that the wealthy industrialists were being pandered to by officials whose job it was to represent all the people.

The Gilded Age was giving way to the Progressive Era, which was defined by reform of what was seen as a corrupt political system and an effort to curb the influence of large corporations. It was not necessarily an anti-business movement – many businesspeople also identified themselves as progressives – but rather a movement that saw the need for government to break up monopolies, regulate business practices that limited competition, and bring balance back to society. Prohibition was a progressive reaction to the big-city political machines dominated by political bosses who often operated out of local saloons. Progressives included both Democrats and Republicans, and there was plenty of room for widespread differences of opinion within the progressive ranks.

It was also a time of labor unrest as working people organized in order to negotiate better pay and working conditions with the threat that they would withhold their labor if their employers refused to meet their demands. Employers, in the face of what they saw as insubordinate arrogance, fought back with every tool they could command.

Numerous events occurred between 1890 and 1911 that place the time in historic perspective. In 1893, U.S. Marines intervened in the independent Kingdom of Hawaii, culminating in the overthrow of the government of Hawaiian Queen Liliuokalani. In 1896, the U.S. Supreme Court decided that racial segregation was appropriate under the "separate but equal" doctrine. In 1898, the U.S. declared war on Spain after the U.S. battleship *Maine* exploded in Havana harbor. And, in 1901, President William McKinley was assassinated and Vice President Theodore Roosevelt stepped up as chief executive.

The world was changing and so was Long Beach. With the change came opportunity, and opportunity brought money and investment. If you were looking for a place to make your fortune at the turn of the century, California was the place to be.

The Search for a Port Site

Southern California needed a port. The population was growing, and it was essential to ship lumber from the Pacific Northwest and Latin America so a burgeoning Southern California population could build houses and other structures. It was also essential to import household goods for those continually arriving consumers. Local growers were interested in selling their products – oranges, lemons, and tangerines; wine and brandy; vegetables and grains – to foreign markets. And all those new residents moving West would need jobs to support their families. Access to a major port was essential to ensure and sustain the growth and economy of a booming area.

It seemed clear that San Pedro Bay, with its long history as the port of call for everybody from the Spanish to the traders and early smugglers, to the U.S. Navy during the Mexican-American and Civil wars, was the obvious place to develop a major port. But there were challenges that made people consider a variety of options.

From the beginning, the biggest problem that plagued development of a harbor at San Pedro was the depth of the water and a shallow bar that stretched across the channel blocking passage to all but small vessels. Even small boats sometimes had to be dragged across the bar in order to gain access to the inner harbor, and there are reports of the bar being completely above water during some periods of low tides.

By the time people were seriously considering where to build a Southern California port, some of those problems had been solved, or at least alleviated. In 1870, the state Legislature had petitioned Congress, asking that $350,000 be set aside to make needed improvements to the harbor, including removal of the sandbar that separated the outer and inner harbors. The solution proposed by Colonel George H. Mendell of the Army Corps of Engineers was to build a 6,700-foot breakwater from the western tip of Rattlesnake Island south and east to Deadman's Island. This would block off the main channel on the east side and isolate it from ebb tides that caused the bar to form. A $200,000 appropriation was approved, and construction of the timber and stone breakwater began the following year. That breakwater, which became known as the east jetty, changed the tidal patterns and increased the channel to a depth of ten feet.

The other problem that plagued the San Pedro harbor was the dominance of one railroad – the Southern Pacific – which had a monopoly on the harbor and charged excessive prices for serving harbor businesses. The Southern Pacific charged almost as much to transport freight from San Pedro to Los Angeles as it cost importers to ship that same cargo from Asia to San Pedro.

By the 1880s, however, the ten-foot depth that was created by the east jetty could no longer accommodate either the growth in trade or the need to bring larger ships into the port. Another appropriation by Congress – this one for $425,000 – funded a deepening of the channel to sixteen feet at mean low tide. This opened up the port to more traffic, but there was competition.

In 1888, a new pier was built in Redondo Beach, and that new facility succeeded in siphoning off much of the ship traffic that had once gone to San Pedro. Redondo Beach offered several benefits. It was located at the head of an underwater canyon, providing deep water for large ships coming straight to the pier. Like Santa Monica, it was connected by the Santa Fe Railroad's line to Los Angeles and was closer than San Pedro for passengers traveling between Los Angeles and San Francisco.

Despite such advantages, San Pedro had features to offer that Redondo Beach did not. San Pedro had rail connections that offered year-round access all the way east with few high mountain passes that would be blocked during winter storms. Although Redondo Beach was a good fair-weather port of call, it was unprotected from the open ocean during stormy weather and offered little opportunity to scale up to a full-sized harbor.

Almost everybody agreed that Southern California needed a major port. But where? There were few natural, sheltered, deep-water ports available, and the ones that were available – such as San Diego or Newport Beach – had no rail connections or were remote from major population centers. Any port development would require jetties, breakwaters, dredging, and other enhancements.

Best Location for a Port

In 1890, Congress got involved in the growing debate by providing for the appointment of a board of three Army engineers – Colonel George H. Mendell, Colonel G.L. Gillespie, and Colonel W.H.H. Benyaurd – to survey the Southern California Coast from Point Dume to Capistrano to determine the best place for a deep-water harbor.

That action sparked the interest of investors who saw the possibility of building a railroad line from Rattlesnake Island on the other side of the channel from San Pedro to Los Angeles. That rail line, the Los Angeles Terminal Railroad, would break the Southern Pacific's monopoly in San Pedro. The plan was to extend the new line from Los Angeles east to the rest of the country by way of Salt Lake City.

That possibility did not sit well, however, with Collis Huntington, the politically powerful president of the Southern Pacific Railroad, which had dominated the harbor since the Southern Pacific arrived in Los Angeles almost twenty years earlier. Huntington had always backed San Pedro harbor improvements in the past, but he was not in a mood to share the harbor with another railroad.

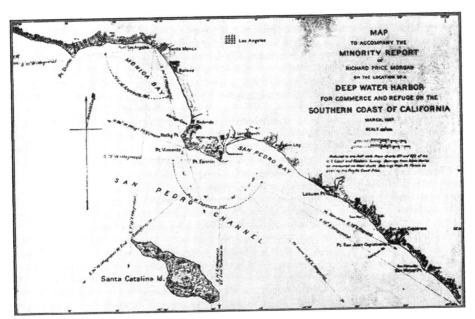

TRY, TRY AGAIN: *San Pedro Bay or Santa Monica Bay, where to build a port? Magnate Collis Huntington campaigned for Santa Monica in order to preserve his railroad monopoly, and his political influence proved a major obstacle for backers of a San Pedro Bay port. This "minority report," filed in 1897 during the third engineering study of the issue, favored Santa Monica, but San Pedro was the final choice, on March 1, 1897.*

Moving to ensure his own dominance in the harbor, Huntington bought a tract of land at Santa Monica Canyon, about three miles north of Santa Monica, where the present-day Chautauqua Boulevard ends at Pacific Coast Highway, and applied for a wharf franchise.

The general assumption at the time was that San Pedro was the logical place for a port, but when the engineering panel began taking testimony, much of discussion centered on the benefits of building an 8,250-foot breakwater off the coast of Santa Monica. It was the beginning of the Free Harbor Fight, which would play out over the next eight years and determine the course of harbor development in Southern California. The Free Harbor Fight was about more than just location. It was about having an open harbor that wouldn't be controlled by any one railroad or private interest. Government would provide the basic infrastructure, but private businesses would build the docks, warehouses, and rail facilities needed to conduct business.

After careful consideration, the three-member board of Army Engineers concluded that San Pedro was the best location to develop into a deep-water port. The engineering panel's report filed in 1891 recommended construction of a breakwater in two parts to protect the harbor.

> *In view of the fact that San Pedro Bay in its natural condition affords better protection both from prevailing winds and from dangerous storms than Santa Monica Bay; that protection can be secured at less cost for equal development of breakwater at the former than at the latter; that larger area of protected anchorage from the prevailing westerly swells can be secured, the severe storms from the southwest being, infrequent; and that there is already an interior harbor that will be a valuable addition to an outer harbor; the Board considers San Pedro Bay as the better location for the deep water harbor provided for by the Act.*

Huntington was not deterred. Despite the unanimous decision by the engineers, Southern Pacific began building a huge rail wharf just north of the Santa Monica Canyon site that would extend 4,720 feet out to deep water. Southern Pacific purchased right-of-way along a narrow strip at the bottom of the bluffs and started laying tracks for a new rail line to Santa Monica, running along what is now Pacific Coast Highway. At Santa Monica the new line would connect with Southern Pacific's existing rail line to Los Angeles and beyond.

Huntington then brought the full weight of his political influence to opposing any federal appropriations for a breakwater at San Pedro, and began lobbying instead for a breakwater off the coast of his new wharf.

In February 1892, the members of the U.S. Senate Commerce Committee were deliberating a $250,000 appropriation for the harbor at San Pedro. Huntington sent a telegram to Committee Chairman Senator William B. Frye of Maine – an ally and friend – saying he was no longer interested in developing a harbor in San Pedro. The ground there was not suitable for developing a harbor, he told the senator, and he (Huntington) was developing a port in Santa Monica instead.

The committee not only rejected the San Pedro appropriation, but they began to question whether a harbor was really necessary at either location. But, in typical political fashion, they decided to put together a second board of Army engineers – this time a five-member panel led by Colonel William P. Craighill – to do a new study of whether the new harbor should be at Santa Monica, San Pedro, or Redondo Beach.

Although each site had its advocates, the Redondo Beach site was rejected early on because it was unprotected from the open ocean and the underwater canyon leading up to the shore made construction of a breakwater across it virtually impossible.

As his Santa Monica Canyon site was being built, Huntington began conducting special train tours to the wharf in order to win public support for his plan. The train would transport visitors out on to the wharf where they would be treated to a view that stretched from Point Dume to the Palos Verdes Peninsula and Santa Catalina Island. A spokesman would talk about the size of the project and the important role the port was to play in the future of Southern California. It was difficult not to be impressed by the project, and it did win some public support.

On October 27, 1892, the five engineers on the Craighill board filed their report, taking into account the need for a major harbor in the region, the topography of each site, each harbor's potential for commercial and military use, the meteorological conditions unique to the two locations still being considered – Santa Monica and San Pedro – and the character of the harbor floor as demonstrated by test drillings at each place. Although there was not enough demand at that time for a major port in Southern California, the potential for such a port was readily apparent, they said. Point-by-point the engineering report compared the two sites, and in the end all five engineers came to the same conclusion that the three-man board led by Colonel Mendell had reached a year earlier. San Pedro was clearly the best site.

> *Having made a careful and critical examination for a proposed deep-water harbor at San Pedro or Santa Monica bays, as required by law, the Board is unanimously of the opinion that the location selected by the Board of Engineers in 1890, at the present anchorage at the westerly side of San Pedro Bay under Point Fermin, is the "more eligible location for such harbor in depth, width, and capacity to accommodate the largest ocean-going vessels and the commercial and naval necessities of the country."*

The study focused on the engineering and technical aspects of where to build a harbor. No comment was made of the fact that Huntington's Santa Monica Bay location would allow the Southern Pacific exclusive access and control of the site.

Despite having eight senior Army engineers on two different panels agree that San Pedro was the logical site for a port, construction on the Southern Pacific wharf north of Santa Monica continued. Some people who opposed the San Pedro site claimed that the engineers had erred in their recommendation, but after months of discussion and two separate studies, debate on the matter began to fade away.

The Los Angeles Chamber of Commerce sent a representative to Washington to lobby for a harbor appropriation for San Pedro. Although he took along petitions from businesses in California, Arizona, and New Mexico, and resolutions from cities and from the State Board of Trade, the bill never got out of the Senate Commerce Committee. Chairman of the committee was Huntington ally Senator Frye. Also on the same committee was Senator John P. Jones of Nevada

– who mostly resided in Santa Monica. Jones was a millionaire miner and former California state official, who had built the original wharf in Santa Monica and later sold the rail line he built between Santa Monica and Los Angeles to the Southern Pacific. Jones had requested that if the subject of money for development of a harbor in Southern California came up, that it be tabled until he returned. That request was granted as a matter of senatorial courtesy.

Port Los Angeles

Meanwhile, Huntington continued work on the mammoth wharf complex Southern Pacific was building north of Santa Monica. The last 1,300 feet of the wharf – where the ships would dock – expanded out from twenty-eight feet, two tracks wide to 130 feet, seven tracks wide. It also contained an 800-foot-long, thirty-six-foot-wide, thirty-six-foot-high iron-and-wood coal bunker for unloading incoming coal shipments. Five rail-mounted cranes could unload coal from ships to the bunker, which had featured four compartments and fifty-one chutes through which the coal could be dumped into railcars on trucks beneath the bunker.

In 1893, Huntington gave the wharf its official name: Port Los Angeles. It was a clever move. Since the wharf was two miles north of the City of Santa Monica, Huntington reasoned, an entirely new town would soon form around the enterprise. That town would need a name and a post office and that name would be Port Los Angeles. The name was also calculated to encourage the people of Los Angeles to identify with the new port.

The first vessel to call at the new wharf was the *San Mateo* on May 11, 1893, with 4,200 tons of coal. Since the coal bunker was still under construction, the coal had to be discharged manually. About 1,000 people showed up to witness the event with music provided by the Santa Monica Municipal Band. Other ships followed, and so did other visitors – especially key politicians who would be given a tour of the facility and encouraged to support the Santa Monica site rather than San Pedro.

Huntington even dropped in unannounced at the Los Angeles Chamber in 1894 and asked for a conference with Chamber officials on harbor issues. According to reports, Huntington did most of the talking. He bluntly told the Chamber officials that they were making a big mistake in backing San Pedro. He said he planned to oppose all such efforts and reminded them of how much political influence he wielded in Washington, D.C.

"Well, I don't know for sure that I can get this money for Santa Monica," he is quoted as saying. "I think I can. But I know damned well that you shall never get a cent for that other place."

Despite the bluntness of his comments, he maintained a friendly composure, even inviting members of the Chamber board to take a trip the following day to the Port Los Angeles site on Huntington's private railcar. About a dozen of the Chamber directors took him up on his offer, traveled to the site, and then had refreshments at the Arcadia Hotel. The trip did not succeed in changing the Chamber position on the issue, but it almost certainly softened it to some extent.

In any case, Huntington's prolonged campaign for his own site began to gradually erode support for San Pedro. In 1894, a little after Huntington's surprise visit, the Los Angeles Chamber was once again considering sending a representative to Washington to seek an appropriation for San Pedro. This time, however, the issue prompted some heated debate with some of the members speaking in favor of Santa Monica rather than San Pedro. When the debate was finally finished, the members voted 328-to-131 in favor of San Pedro. It was an important vote – if far from unanimous. If the influential Chamber had voted in favor of Santa Monica, the possibilities of San Pedro Bay being the site of a major port would have been considerably diminished and perhaps even ended.

When the Senate Commerce Committee met again in June, Los Angeles again made its argument for the harbor at San Pedro. But Huntington did more than just state an argument for his harbor project, he asked for a $4 million appropriation. An engineer from Southern Pacific explained at length the details of how rocks would be brought by rail from inland quarries to build the Santa Monica breakwater as opposed to transporting them by sea for a breakwater in San Pedro, and why that gave an edge to Santa Monica over San Pedro.

While some of the national press noted that Huntington and his associates – including Senator Jones – owned the property surrounding the Santa Monica project, which would give the Southern Pacific exclusive control over the harbor, Huntington was busy working the halls of Congress, talking to senators and seeking their support.

The question of where to build a harbor for Southern California, and the politics, influence, and money connected to that effort were gaining national recognition. The Commerce Committee was divided. Senators William Frye of Maine, John Jones of Nevada, Joseph Dolph of Oregon and Matt Ransom of North Carolina favored Santa Monica. Senators Stephen M. White of California, Shelby Cullom of Illinois, and James Berry of Arkansas favored San Pedro. On Frye's motion, the committee deferred any decision on the matter until the members could visit both sites and see for themselves which was better. No date was set for the visit, however, and no money was budgeted for the trip.

The Free Harbor League

The Los Angeles Chamber of Commerce had led the fight for a harbor in San Pedro, but by 1895 the Chamber had a plate full of other issues to deal with. It could no longer devote the kind of time and energy needed to advocate for the San Pedro site. A new group – the Free Harbor League – was formed with 400 members to focus on one thing: Get an appropriation to build a breakwater and develop a deep-water harbor at San Pedro.

The name said it all. The choice to be made was between a harbor at Santa Monica that would be a monopoly for one railroad or a free harbor at San Pedro that would be open to any railroad that desired to serve it or any business that wanted to use it. In 1896, the Free Harbor League sent a four-person delegation to Washington to request a $392,000 appropriation from the House Committee on Rivers and Harbors to improve San Pedro's inner harbor. The Committee took the request under advisement.

Huntington, however, went back to the Senate Commerce Committee with a request for $3,098,000 to build a breakwater for Santa Monica. The Free Harbor delegation was shocked. It had been assured by friendly sources that because the government was in a financial crunch and cutting expenditures, no large appropriations would be passed. The League's strategy had been to seek the smaller expenditure with the idea that the more money the government invested in San Pedro, the more support that site would gain. But now, Huntington was asking for a large expenditure to build the breakwater that would ensure him a deep-water harbor in Santa Monica.

The draft report of the Committee for Rivers and Harbors to the full House of Representatives – leaked to the San Francisco Chronicle – recommended approval of both appropriations, $392,000 for San Pedro and $3,098,000 for Santa Monica. The people of Los Angeles and Southern California were outraged. They buried Congress in thousands of letters and telegrams, expressing their displeasure. In response, the Committee pulled its recommendation of both appropriations. There was nothing for San Pedro or Santa Monica.

When the House bill – now stripped of any appropriation for either harbor – reached the Senate Commerce Committee, the $3,098,000 appropriation for Santa Monica was restored, but not the money for San Pedro. Although two separate engineering panels had unanimously agreed that San Pedro was the better site, the Senate appeared to be on the verge of passing an appropriation for a monopoly port at Santa Monica. The advocates for San Pedro needed a champion, and they got one.

Senator Stephen M. White, a Los Angeles resident and former district attorney, struck hard. During deliberations on the bill on the Senate floor, he proposed an amendment saying that the $3,098,000 appropriation should be approved, but that it go to either Santa Monica or San Pedro. The final destination would be decided by a third special board of engineers – this one consisting of a Navy engineer to be appointed by the Secretary of the Navy, an Army engineer to be appointed by the Secretary of War, and a member of the Coast and Geodetic Survey to be appointed by the superintendent of that agency. The amendment also stipulated that if Santa Monica were to win the appropriation, the Southern Pacific would have to agree to let other railroads use its tracks for an appropriate cost.

As might be expected from a skilled attorney, he laid the groundwork for his argument before the Senate as though he was addressing a jury. He reviewed the history of the Free Harbor fight. He used maps and photographs of the sites as exhibits. He introduced testimony from mariners about the advantages of San Pedro and related the problems any other railroad might expect in gaining access to the Southern Pacific wharf in Santa Monica.

White's presentation before the Senate went on for two full days. He was followed by Senator Frye, who took another day presenting the case for Santa Monica, conferring frequently with Huntington during his presentation. Huntington took his case directly to White to convince him to change his stand, but White would not.

In the end, White's amendment was passed by the Senate. The final amendment called for a five-member engineering board – one from the Navy, one from the Coast and Geodetic Survey, and three civilians to be named by the president. It also included the original $392,000 for the San Pedro inner harbor. President Cleveland vetoed the bill, citing the government's diminished resources and the need to cut back, but his veto was overridden by the Legislature. The bill became law in 1896.

It marked more than a victory for San Pedro. It was a resounding defeat for the Southern Pacific Railroad and a clear indication that the era of corporate dominance in the economic and political life of America was coming to an end. The Free Harbor issue had drawn the interest of the entire nation. Long Beach had even approved an appropriation to be used by San Pedro in support of its efforts to locate the port there – five short miles from Long Beach.

Only One Deep Water Port

But the battle was not over. The new five-member board of engineers – headed by Rear Admiral John C. Walker – still had to do its own study of the situation and determine which site was better suited for a deep-water harbor. Its investigation was thorough. New undersea borings were made, new charts drawn up, seven days of hearings were held, and many onsite visits were conducted.

The Walker Board filed its decision on March 1, 1897. The best location for the new port was San Pedro.

> *It is the judgment of this board that the best public policy in the interest of economy and for the attainment of a deep water harbor for commerce and refuge, demands the concentration of expenditures at one point with corresponding cumulative excellence of results, rather than dispersion and weakening of results by divided expenditure at two locations. This conclusion is strengthened by the fact that the selection of San Pedro undoubtedly involves materially less ultimate expenditure than is certain to be incurred by the maintenance of two harbors. The preponderance of physical advantages leads to the selection of San Pedro as in line with the requirements of the best public policy.*

The decision this time was not unanimous. One of the civilian engineers, Richard P. Morgan, said he needed more time before he was willing to concur in the majority opinion. Two weeks later, Morgan filed a minority report, saying he favored Southern Pacific's site in Santa Monica.

Senator White dismissed Morgan's opinion as "not important."

"His (Morgan's) appointment as an expert by the California Railroad Commission, notoriously subservient to corporate interests, and the subsequent employment of his son as an engineer by that corporation induced me to protest against his selection," White said. "The results justify every position which I have taken."

The Walker Board's report settled the issue, once and for all. There would be only one deep-water port in Southern California, and that would be at San Pedro, not Santa Monica.

The decision was celebrated as soon as it was announced. Prominent businessmen and residents joined in an impromptu parade headed by the Seventh Regiment Band through downtown Los Angeles that afternoon, waving American flags. T.E. Gibbon, vice president of the Los Angeles Terminal Railroad, which had broken the Southern Pacific Railroad's monopoly in San Pedro, was carried on the shoulders of the happy crowd.

In San Pedro and Long Beach the news was greeted with horns and whistles from factories and vessels. The whistle from the afternoon train headed toward the harbor could be heard for miles before it arrived. Long Beach joined in San Pedro's good fortune. A harbor in San Pedro translated to prosperity for Long Beach. Many of the workers at that harbor could be expected to live in Long Beach and contribute to the local economy there.

Delays and Dirty Tricks

But the long wait wasn't quite over yet. After the Walker Board announced its decision, people expected work on the new breakwater to begin within a few months. It would not take long to draw up the specification and advertise for bids. The man responsible for implementing the board decision and getting work started on the federal breakwater at San Pedro was Secretary of War Russell A. Alger.

Alger had been a Union general during the Civil War, serving with Sheridan. He was later successful in the lumber business in Michigan and served as governor of that state from 1885 to 1887. He was appointed Secretary of War by President William McKinley on March 5, 1897 – two days after the Walker Board decided for San Pedro. He was not a disinterested party. He was a friend of Collis Huntington and had associated with him in the lumber business in the Pacific Northwest. During the dispute over which harbor was better, Alger had visited the Santa Monica site and expressed his preference for it.

Secretary of War Alger stalled, apparently in hopes of getting the issue back before Congress, so what had been done could be undone. He responded to protests by claiming that the Walker Board's report – the third such report to conclude that San Pedro was the superior site – was vague. Additional study was needed, he claimed. When Senator White asked the Senate to intervene, and the Senate asked Alger what was taking so long, he sent back a report listing multiple reasons why he wasn't moving forward on the project.

Alger reported that it wasn't clear what the legislators' intentions were in making the appropriation, saying there wasn't enough money for both a breakwater and other needed harbor improvements. The building of wharves and bulkheads, for instance, would require much more than had been allotted, he said. The question that needed to be answered, he said, was whether he should commence building the breakwater and then wait for more appropriations for improvements to the rest of the harbor.

The reaction to his reply was outrage and derision. In an article dripping with sarcasm, the Los Angeles Times accused Alger of putting up a "man of straw for the purpose of fighting him."

> *It was never contemplated that the Federal government would build bulkheads for wharves or wharves any more than it would construct a tourist hotel, or saloons for sailors, or a statue of Liberty Enlightening the War Department. It was understood that wharves, and everything pertaining to them, would be built by private enterprise of corporations, who would be benefited by the protection offered by the government breakwater.*

The Senate responded by passing a resolution ordering Alger to immediately advertise for bids. He defied the Senate resolution, claiming it had no legitimacy since it had not been passed by the House of Representatives as well. San Pedro advocates wrote President McKinley asking that he take action. He referred the matter to the attorney general, who ruled there was no legal reason that Alger should not advertise for bids. Still Alger delayed.

On September 29, 1897, Senator White wrote to Alger, noting the attorney general's opinion, expressing his frustration, and asking when steps would be

FREE HARBOR FIGHTER: *A statue in San Pedro commemorates Senator Stephen M. White, who led the fight in Washington for appropriations for a San Pedro Bay port. White overcame lobbying and stalling tactics by supporters of Collis Huntington and secured the federal funds to build the first breakwater in the bay. He died at age 48 in 1901.*

taken to advertise for bids. Ten days later, Alger wrote back, assuring White that he would be ready to advertise for bids in November. By late October, however, Alger was telling legislators that he couldn't advertise for bids because no direct appropriation had been voted yet. When it was pointed out that no appropriation was necessary to advertise for bids, Alger said there was no money available for such advertising. The Los Angeles Chamber of Commerce offered to pick up the tab for all advertising expenses, but Alger said that would not be dignified.

Then, for no known reason, Alger said he must seek a ruling from Judge Advocate General McKenna, whose counsel was sought more appropriately for military matters. McKenna replied that there was in fact $50,000 available for advertising. A short time later, however, McKenna was appointed to the Supreme Court, and Alger decided he should resubmit his question to John W. Griggs, the new judge advocate general. By this time, the frustrated representatives of Los Angeles had taken their case straight to President McKinley, who ordered Alger to proceed immediately with the project.

The Secretary of War seemed to have run out of delaying tactics. However, Collis Huntington was not through yet.

San Pedro may have been seen as the logical choice by three separate engineering boards – the last one with the power to decide which port would get the nod – but Huntington was not a man to accept defeat. On January 27, 1898, Huntington himself visited the Capitol in an attempt to head off funding for San Pedro. Congressman Joseph Gurney Cannon of Illinois, one of the many allies of Huntington, was chairman of the House Appropriations Committee. Cannon reportedly planned to omit the San Pedro breakwater from the appropriations bill for the next fiscal year.

White was ready. He said if the House left it out, the Senate would put it in, and he was ready to take off the gloves and fight for the measure. He apparently was not above using a little blackmail if necessary to secure the appropriation. He warned the Huntington forces that if they pushed the matter, some unpublished facts might be brought to light that could put them in an undesirable position.

Bids for the project were opened in February 1898, just shy of a year since the Walker Board had made its decision that San Pedro would be the site of the new deep-water harbor. The Secretary of War did not get around to approving the winning bid and preparing a contract until July 21. The contract went to the low bidder, the Chicago-based contracting firm of Heldmaier & Neu.

A Cornerstone of Progress

Work on the project got off to a rocky start. It was April 26, more than nine months after the contract was approved, before the first load of Santa Catalina Island rocks to build the breakwater was dumped into San Pedro Bay amidst great pomp and down-home hoopla. Politicians and other dignitaries from across the state, including California Governor Henry Gage, showed up and gave speeches. More than 20,000 people in Los Angeles jammed aboard forty trains to make the trip south for the event.

People were more tolerant of oratory then than now, but the number of speeches delivered that day was exhausting. The giant crowd heard speeches by Governor Gage, who called the harbor a "cornerstone of progress"; by ex-U.S. Senator White, who had challenged the Huntington political machine and won; by U.S. Senator George C. Perkins, who talked about the promise posed by the new Panama Canal that would enable trade to flow to and from Europe and the cities of the East Coast; by former Congressman S.O. Houghton, who talked about the history of the San Pedro Bay; by George S. Patton, whose son and namesake was destined to win fame as a World War II general; by Colonel George H. Mendell, who had headed the first engineering board to choose San Pedro as the best site for a port; and by Captain J.J. Myler, who would oversee construction of the breakwater. Other speakers included Attorney Will A. Harris, Congressman James G. Maguire, Mayor James Phelan of San Francisco, Congressman R.J. Waters, attorney T.E. Gibbon of the Los Angeles Terminal Railroad, and California Attorney General Tirey L. Ford.

Following the speeches, the public was invited to a barbecue of 15,000 pounds of roast beef at Fourth and San Pedro streets, about a mile from the speakers' stand. There was some confusion, since the visitors from Los Angeles had no idea where Fourth and San Pedro streets might be.

Plans called for President William McKinley to push a button in the Library of the White House that would signal the dumping of the first rocks into the water that morning. The signal from the White House worked fine, but when it came time to dump the rocks from the barge, the rocks didn't want to go.

The new barge, specially built for the task, was designed to dump the rocks by flooding compartments on one side of the barge. This was supposed to cause the barge to list at an angle and the rocks to slide off. At least that was the plan. As everybody waited with a battery of photographers ready to trip their shutters, the barge began to slowly list to one side. Minutes went by until finally – on the low side – four or five feet of the barge deck was underwater. Still the rocks held firm. Finally, when spectators were starting to think the rocks were not going to slide off the barge, about one hundred tons of them slid, tumbling and splashing into the bay. People started cheering and clapping, and harbor vessels began blowing their horns.

Unfortunately, with the rocks on the low side gone, the remaining rocks weighted down the high side of the barge, restored equilibrium and caused it to stop listing. Workers were called in to attempt to manually remove the rest of the rocks. With pry bars and muscle they were able to wrestle some of the boulders to the low side of the barge, causing the barge to once again tilt up, but the remaining rocks remained stubbornly in place. The tug *Hercules*, which had towed the barge to the site from Catalina, sprayed the deck with a stream of water in order to make it slippery so the rest of the rocks would slide down. That didn't work. Then a heavy hemp line was attached from the top rock to the tug to see if the tug could pull it down and cause the entire load to slide. That didn't work either. In the end, the workers toiled into the night, joined by Ernst Heldmaier himself, to jettison the remaining rocks from the barge.

It was an early omen of how construction of the breakwater would proceed. Work on the project lagged, despite repeated warnings from Captain J.J. Myler to pick up the pace. The Heldmaier & Neu bid had raised eyebrows from the beginning because it was so much lower than those from competitors. There were even rumors that the company would forfeit its $300,000 bond and attempt to wriggle out of the contract – rumors hotly denied by the company.

Early on in the project, junior partner Peter W. Neu, who was to oversee the job, was riding in a Tally Ho carriage with about a dozen other people, including Hancock Banning, when, at the corner of Grand Avenue and Washington Street, the front axle broke, causing the carriage to lurch violently to the left spilling out the passengers, who were seated eight feet above the ground. All escaped serious injury except the 260-pound Neu, whose head smashed into an electric pole. He died at the scene.

Heldmaier was not able to remain in Los Angeles to oversee the job himself, so that role was delegated to others. In March of 1900, Captain Myler announced that the contract with the firm of Heldmaier & Neu was annulled, and new bids would be sought. It had been almost ten years since the breakwater project was first proposed. Observers of the project had come to expect double-dealing and back-room politics as part of the process. There was much speculation that Heldmaier & Neu were in cahoots with Collis Huntington and delaying the project on purpose. Heldmaier denied such allegations in an interview with the Los Angeles Herald. The delays and final annulment of the contract were due to the company underestimating the cost of the rock for the breakwater, and stormy weather that frequently shut down the job.

Advertisements for new bids went out one month after the annulment, and a contract to finish the job that Heldmaier & Neu had started was awarded to the California Construction Co.

The End of a 'Strenuous Life'

The significance of the Free Harbor fight was manifold. It marked the end of an age in which corporate power dominated politics and the economy. It designated San Pedro as the chosen harbor for Southern California, led to unfettered competition in the transport of goods coming through the port, helped make Southern California an international hub of commerce, and opened the door for Long Beach to eventually take on its own harbor project next door.

Secretary of War Russell A. Alger resigned at the request of President William McKinley on August 1, 1899. He returned to Michigan and on September 27, 1902, was appointed to fill the unexpired term of Senator James McMillan. He served as a U.S. senator until his death in 1907.

Collis Potter Huntington died slightly before midnight on August 13, 1900, at his Pine Knot Lodge in the Adirondack Mountains. He was 78 years old. Cause of his death was attributed to a "weak heart." It was an ironic diagnosis for a man who was anything but weak-hearted. He had made his fortune during the California gold rush as a merchant, not a prospector. He later became part of the "Big Four" – Huntington, Leland Stanford, Mark Hopkins and Charles Crocker – who pushed through construction of the western portion of the Transcontinental Rail connection. Of the four, Huntington was considered the most ruthless, hardest working, and the most resolute.

If nothing else, Huntington was a man of his time. But the time for men like Huntington had passed. He had been a builder, a dealmaker, and a conniver. He had gotten his own way and he had gotten things done. He had helped connect the nation, developed grand projects, determined public policy, and amassed great wealth. In the process, he had stepped on a lot of toes and used his influence and power to advance his own agenda.

Yet, even among his enemies he was acknowledged as a giant – a man who was willing to do whatever it took to meet his goals. The Los Angeles Times, which had been strident in attacking him during the Free Harbor fight, eulogized him in death.

Huntington was a lover of "the strenuous life," and was never so happy as when embroiled in the bloodless but terrific battles of business.

The San Pedro breakwater was completed in 1910. The total length was 9,250 feet. The contract had called for an 8,500-foot breakwater, but when that goal was reached, there were enough funds left over to extend it another 750 feet. It was twenty feet wide at the top and an average 200 feet wide at the bottom – depending on the depth of the water. The following year, the U.S. government filed a $1.2 million breach-of-contract suit against Heldmaier & Neu.

Chapter Nine:
Birth of a Port

It was the beginning of a new century, and the country was being defined as much by burgeoning industry and an expanding middle class as it was by the inventions that enhanced peoples' lives and the new products that lined the grocery market shelves.

In 1902, the first movie theater in the United States opened in Los Angeles. In 1906, an earthquake struck San Francisco, killing almost 3,000 people. In 1908, William Howard Taft was elected president, and in 1911, the U.S. Supreme Court ruled that Standard Oil was an unreasonable monopoly and ordered it to dissolve under the Sherman Antitrust Act.

Few places had more potential to get in on the action of the new century than Long Beach, California. The city was attracting a new generation of leadership – men of vision and action who would guide it forward in the coming years; men who saw the potential of the small city by the sea and were eager to become a part of that community.

William Willmore, the man who founded what was to be Long Beach, but was forced to abandon his dream after he was unable to meet his financial obligations, had returned to Southern California only to end up in the county poor farm in Downey. In 1899, knowing that he was ill and near death, Willmore walked out of the poor farm and headed for the town he had founded – Willmore City when he left, Long Beach when he returned. Ida Crowe, a woman with a kind heart and seven children, discovered Willmore in the First Baptist Church, trying to keep warm. He had been living in a tent with only the clothes on his back and five cents in his pocket. Crowe invited him to move in with her family. Other friends set him up in a small fruit stand on Pine Avenue. But Willmore soon failed at that business as well, and once again took to wandering the streets, bitter and angry, telling anybody who would listen how he had been conspired against. He died penniless in the Crowe home on January 16, 1901, and was buried in an unmarked grave at the Long Beach Municipal Cemetery. By the time a marker was placed on his grave twelve years later by the Signal Hill Civic League, newcomers with big ideas were already pouring into the city, ready to turn Willmore's dream into their own reality.

New Long Beach Leadership
Stephen Townsend had moved to Long Beach from Pasadena in 1894. He was 46 years old and looking for a new opportunity after selling his share of a mule-drawn

street car line he had founded in Pasadena. The Pasadena Street Railroad was the first such line in the city, and when it opened on June 30, 1886, an enthusiastic crowd of people lined up to congratulate Townsend on his new venture. But that first day was the highpoint of the enterprise. Once the novelty wore off, the line drew few passengers. The fares collected didn't even cover the feed for the mules and horses that pulled the carriages. The first-year gross receipts from the line were only $2,470. Despite the disappointing reception, the line struggled along for eight years before it sold its franchise, equipment and mules to the Pasadena and Los Angeles Electric System – later Pacific Electric – for $14,000. It was not a success story. Although he made local history with his failed horse-drawn railroad, like many entrepreneurs of his time, Townsend was involved in more than one business. One of those was the Pasadena Warehouse and Milling Co. – a venture that was a success. After he settled in Long Beach, Townsend got involved in real estate sales, development, and politics. He was a principal in a couple of real estate firms, including the Townsend-Dayman Investment Company in partnership with Bromell P. Dayman. He served as Long Beach mayor from 1903 to 1905 and founded the American National Bank of Long Beach in 1903 with $50,000 capitalization. American National merged with the First National Bank of Long Beach the following year.

• • •

C.J. Walker was born in New York state in 1869, the youngest son of a furniture manufacturer. He moved to California's Central Valley in 1889, locating in Tulare County where he got a job in a large real estate company. In 1895, he came to Long Beach and went into the real estate business. He also got involved in insurance and in banking, becoming one of the leading businessmen in a town full of ambitious and resourceful business people.

• • •

Philander Ellsworth Hatch was born in New Preston, Connecticut, in 1861. At 16 years old he started as a clerk at the Sargent & Co. hardware manufacturing business in New Haven. Four years later, he took a job with Peck and Bishop Baggage Express and Transfer Agency, then became a bookkeeper and cashier for the H.B. Armstrong & Co. wholesale and retail furniture business. He came to Long Beach in 1894, and in 1896, along with Jotham Bixby, organized the first bank in town – the Bank of Long Beach. In 1903, the name of the bank was changed to the National Bank of Long Beach.

• • •

Bromell P. Dayman was born in 1857 in Ontario, Canada, the son of a farmer. He went to school in Toronto, moved to Detroit, and at 24 years old, he went to North Dakota where he became a farmer. In 1889, he moved to Pasadena where he got involved in the real estate business and later moved to the Central Valley of California. He was an associate of Stephen Townsend both in Pasadena and in the Central Valley and remained so after he moved to Long Beach in 1900. He and Townsend later formed the real estate firm of Townsend-Dayman Inc., which developed several housing tracts in the city.

• • •

Charles Henderson Windham was born in 1871 near McMinnville, Tennessee. When he arrived in Long Beach in 1902, he was a man of the world who was used to taking bold action. As a young man, he had worked as a blacksmith helper and bridge carpenter on the Oregon and California Railroad. He worked his way up in the railroad industry, eventually moving to Central America to work on a canal that the U.S. planned to build across Nicaragua. When the Nicaragua plan was abandoned, Windham moved to Costa Rica, where he became a trainmaster on the Costa Rica Railway Ltd., which was owned by controversial United Fruit Co. founder Minor C. Keith. Seven years later, he resigned from the railroad and purchased a sugar and coffee plantation. By 1902, Windham and his wife, Angelica, moved back to the United States to secure a better education for their children. In 1904 Windham and T.M. Todd formed a realty company that subdivided and sold land east of Bixby Park. He became a member of the Long Beach Elks Lodge 888, to which many of the prominent men in the community belonged.

• • •

Colonel Charles River Drake was a wealthy businessman from Arizona who had retired to Long Beach. Drake represented a syndicate headed by Collis Huntington's nephew Henry Huntington, whose goal was to get the city to request bidders for rail service from Los Angeles to Long Beach. The city put out the request; Huntington's Pacific Electric Co. won the franchise, and Red Car service began on July 4, 1902. The day the Red Cars first rolled on their new route a reported 60,000 visitors flooded the city. The population of Long Beach at the time was somewhere between 3,000 and 4,000 people. The beginning of the Pacific Electric service to Long Beach was good for the community and good for Colonel Drake personally. Long Beach had become a tourist mecca for inland residents, which created jobs and fed the local economy. Drake, who owned almost all of the downtown beachfront property, proceeded to develop it to serve the burgeoning market. Drake then organized the Seaside Water Co., which bought the Long Beach Development Co., much of the stock and holdings of the Bouton Water Co., and the water distribution system of the Banning Co. in San Pedro in 1901. The purchase included 1,600 acres of land, thirteen blocks, 632 unsold lots, and all of the beachfront in the original town site. He developed the beachfront with businesses, linking the Bath House, the Hotel Virginia and the Pike. He also developed the famous Walk of 1,000 Lights. Drake spent the next three decades developing Long Beach.

• • •

Charles A. Buffum was born in 1870 in Lafayette, Illinois, and spent his younger years working in the retail business. He came to Long Beach in 1904 and purchased the Mercantile Company with his brother Edwin E. Buffum. It would eventually grow into the well-known and once-popular department store Buffum's.

• • •

Joseph Young arrived in Long Beach in 1902, the same year that Charles Windham came on the scene. Young wasn't as big a player in Long Beach history as Windham, but he was an interesting character who ran a successful real estate business in Long Beach, earned a fortune, and later used the development of Long Beach as a model for development of his own city, Hollywood, Florida.

A Port Plan for Long Beach

Long Beach Mayor Stephen Townsend had a sharp eye for a good opportunity, and he saw potential in the open and soggy wetlands that bordered the city of Long Beach. Where most people saw only a worthless bog, Townsend saw a property that could be upgraded into something special for the city – and for himself. In January 1905, a syndicate headed by Townsend bought an option on 800 acres of

PORT PARENT: *Charles Henderson Windham, seen in later years when he was Long Beach's city manager, is known as the "Father of the Port of Long Beach." Arriving in Long Beach in 1902 after working in Nicaragua and Costa Rica, Windham rapidly became indispensable to Long Beach's and the port's development. In October 1905, he was on the executive committee of the Los Angeles Dock and Terminal Co. when it purchased 802 acres of tidal mudflats that would soon become the Port of Long Beach.*

saltwater marshland west of the city from the Seaside Water Co. Townsend's idea was to dredge a ship canal across the Cerritos Slough from Wilmington to Long Beach and then to get the Santa Fe Railroad to come in and help market the site to industrial interests. Townsend and his associates went the entire length of the slough in small boats testing the water depths and found the slough was from nine to fifteen feet deep.

The local geography during that period – especially when it came to rivers – can be confusing. It was not then as we know it today. The rivers that crisscrossed Los Angeles County at the time were tramps, often changing their courses during floods, merging with one another, and sometimes finding new routes to the ocean. The river that entered the sea on the west side of Long Beach at the time was called the San Gabriel River. Today it is known as the Los Angeles River.

The location of today's Los Angeles River has also changed over time. Back in the early 1900s, the river entered the ocean through the marshy area that Townsend planned to develop as the Long Beach Harbor and emptied out to the ocean between Long Beach and Terminal Island. That river was later straightened and diverted to its present, more easterly position by the Los Angeles County Flood Control District. Since the river no longer flows through the harbor area, silt being washed downstream during the rainy season no longer clogs the channels. But in 1905, all that was still far in the future.

In March of 1905, Townsend's syndicate advertised to sell $100 shares in order to raise $250,000 to buy the property and develop it. The resulting corporation was called the Long Beach Land and Navigation Co. Townsend and C.J. Walker were the principal owners. Other directors of the company were Townsend's real estate associate, B.P. Dayman, S.F. Easterbrook of the Walker Real Estate Co., Long Beach attorney John E. Daly, and Los Angeles businessman J.O. Downing. The company offered inducements to lure manufacturers to the site. Pacific Electric Rail Line was promised private right of way through the tract. A site along the water was donated to the YWCA for a boathouse. The property was named the Riverside Tract, and in May it was opened to the public for inspection and possible investment. The women of the YWCA served refreshments from their boathouse and their boat, the *Twilight*, was launched when the tide came in. Opening day sales of shares raised $25,000.

In July 1905, real estate developers Dana Burks and Henry Parkhurst Barbour came forward with an even more ambitious plan. Burks was the mayor of the newly incorporated city of Ocean Park, south of Santa Monica, and publisher of the Los Angeles City Directory. Burks was also in real estate and had worked with tobacco millionaire Abbot Kinney in developing the Venice area of Ocean Park with canals and bridges. Kinney was known as the "Doge of Venice." Burks was known as the "Duke."

Fifty-year-old Henry Parkhurst Barbour was always on the move and always looking for opportunities. He had worked as an attorney in Boston, then in the magazine business and then in real estate. He worked in the railroad business in Minnesota, as a real estate developer in Washington state and in California, and in the mining business in Minnesota, Colorado, and Arizona. Along the way, he had bought 1,000 acres around the mouth of Ballona Creek, south of Santa Monica, and named it Playa del Rey – Beach of the Kings. In 1902, he teamed up with a small group of investors, formed the Beach Land Co., and announced plans to develop the marshy area into a Venetian-style resort. The plan included a beachfront bathing pavilion, a luxury hotel high atop the bluffs, and Venetian style bridges and structures. The development fell short of its goal, but that didn't discourage Barbour. He was a person who had his fingers in many projects, including the selling of oceanfront lots in Long Beach. He was known for his charisma, his snap decisions, and his reputation for plunging boldly ahead on every project in which he was involved.

Burks and Barbour, acting as the Dana Burks Syndicate, offered to purchase the Long Beach property from Townsend with the plan to develop it with an east-west channel from Wilmington to Long Beach and a north-south channel out to the ocean. Among the ideas they considered was to develop the wetland area with lagoons and canals as had been done in the Venice area, even though a similar development was already under way in the Naples area east of Long Beach. There was some thought given to turning the entire city of Long Beach into an island by digging a huge canal from the west side of Long Beach, north and east around Signal Hill, then back to the sea at Alamitos Bay east of the city. That ambitious and expensive plan would have given Long Beach nine more miles of waterfront, turned the city as it then existed into an island, and shifted the industrial area of town to the north, but it never got past the talking stage.

When it was finally unveiled, the development plan was much as had been first conceived. On September 9, 1905, the Long Beach real estate men held a Harbor Day celebration in which they boarded ten small launches for a tour of the site and from there on to the South Coast Yacht Club on Terminal Island, where the plans were discussed. The San Gabriel River (today the Los Angeles River) would be dredged to thirty feet deep and 300 feet wide for about five miles, and the Cerritos Slough would be deepened and turned into a ship channel. Slips would be developed along each side of the new channels for docking vessels.

A week later, the syndicate announced the formation of the Los Angeles Dock and Terminal Co. The president was Dana Burks, and the chairman was Henry Barbour. Clinton James Curtis, a prominent Redlands orange grower, owner of the West American Fruit Co., and a director in Redlands National Bank, was named the first vice president. David Evans of Salt Lake City, who was active in land development in Ocean Park, was named second vice president; C.C. Ames, the cashier for Redlands National Bank, was named the treasurer; and attorney Walter M. Campbell of Redlands was named secretary. Barbour, Burks, and Long Beach real estate broker Charles Henderson Windham made up the executive committee. Much of the money for the project was provided by investors from Redlands – including Dock and Terminal Co. directors C.J. Curtis, C.C. Ames, and Walter M. Campbell. Both Long Beach and Redlands were about the same size at the time, and both towns were booming.

In Long Beach the big money was in local tourism and real estate; in Redlands it was in real estate and citrus. There was a lot of money to be made, and both cities had plenty of entrepreneurs looking for ways to make it. Redlands was the center of the foremost navel orange growing area in the world, producing more than 1 million boxes of fruit in 1904. The businessmen of Redlands were not just in the business of growing oranges, they were also in the business of finding markets for their product and ways to ship it to its final destination. Their interest in logistics, plus their money, made them a good match for Long Beach's port project.

In October, the purchase of the land was completed, and the Los Angeles Dock and Terminal Co. became the owner of 802 prime acres of tidal mudflats, which would one day become the Port of Long Beach.

The Battle of the Bridges

The newly created Los Angeles Dock and Terminal Co. was determined to move ahead as quickly as possible. On December 1, 1905, the North American Dredging Co.'s big suction dredger arrived in Southern California from San Francisco to start deepening the Cerritos Slough between Wilmington and Long Beach. But there were problems. As it neared the area where it was going to start dredging, it ran aground in shallow water south of Wilmington. A week later, it was towed nearer to the dredging site at high tide, but then it had to wait because the channel was blocked by a bridge used for a spur line of the San Pedro, Los Angeles and Salt Lake Railroad. The Salt Lake Railroad, as it was commonly called, was the line that had merged with, and then absorbed, the Los Angeles Terminal Line built in 1891 between Terminal Island – known prior to that year as Rattlesnake Island – and Los Angeles.

That wasn't the only bridge the port developers had to worry about. The bridge across the Cerritos Slough was just a spur line that connected the mainland to the San Pedro Salt Works, which operated in the marshy waters of the Wilmington Lagoon. The Salt Lake's mainline bridge – another fixed-in-place trestle – crossed the mouth of the river between Long Beach and Terminal Island at about the same place the Gerald Desmond Bridge does now. Both bridges would have to be dealt with if the harbor plan was to be realized. The Dock and Terminal Co. asked the Salt Lake Railroad to remove enough of the Cerritos Slough bridge to permit passage of the first dredger, and the railroad agreed. But after the dredge had passed and the rail workers prepared to put the bridge back in place, the railroad was hit with a court order.

H.S. Carver, the owner of Western Boat Works on the Cerritos Slough, had also wanted the bridge across the Cerritos Slough removed. The bridge restricted the size of boats he could deliver to buyers. If the railroad trestle was replaced with a drawbridge, however, he would be able to build and sell larger boats. He had complained to Long Beach attorney Stephen G. Long about his dilemma, and Long had advised him to wait for the temporary removal of the bridge. Then, in anticipation of the bridge being taken down to allow the dredge to pass, Long prepared all the legal documents needed to seek an injunction against its replacement. As soon as the bridge came down, Long filed his action.

U.S. Circuit Judge Olin Wellborn issued a temporary restraining order against putting the bridge back in place until the case could be decided. After Long filed his action against the railroad, the Dock and Terminal Co. took the opportunity to join the case. Although the bridge over the Cerritos Slough was only a spur line, what the judge ruled in that case would also likely determine the fate of the bridge on the railroad's main line, the one that blocked access from the planned Long Beach inner harbor down the river channel to the ocean.

The Dock and Terminal Co.'s argument about the Salt Lake's main bridge was that the river was a natural and navigable waterway within the meaning of the Rivers and Harbors Appropriation Act of 1899. Section 10 of that Act barred obstruction of navigable waters by bridges or other structures such as dams, without approval of the government through the U.S. Army Corps of Engineers.

The Act was interpreted to say that if the Dock and Terminal Co. wanted the bridge removed, and if the railroad wished to maintain the line, it should be required to replace the wooden trestle with a drawbridge that would allow passage of ships. The request for an injunction by Carver was postponed with a compromise agreement between parties that allowed the railroad to temporarily put the Cerritos Slough bridge back in service. Meanwhile, work on the harbor project proceeded.

In January 1906, the U.S. Army Corps of Engineers reported that the San Gabriel entrance to the harbor was both feasible and advisable. The Dock and Terminal Co. immediately asked the War Department for permission to dredge a 4,000-foot river channel from the planned inner harbor to the sea.

Meanwhile, Henry P. Barbour was busy promoting the possibilities. In December 1905, as the court battle over the railroad bridges got underway, Barbour was promising a grand future for the project in an address to the Board of Realty at a luncheon in the Del Monte Tavern in downtown Los Angeles. His address, as reported in the Los Angeles Herald, offers a clear display of his talent for oratory and salesmanship:

> Los Angeles is a great city and is becoming greater. The farm, the hamlet and the workshop of the East are sending the people here. They are coming in tens, hundreds and thousands and all bids fair to a population of a million people. Our probabilities are commercial supremacy of the South Pacific and control of the Orient, but, to make these probabilities certainties, we must protect and control our water frontage. Our harbor must be protected, our facilities increased. Add to the seven miles of frontage reported by Captain (J.J. Meyler of the Army Corps of Engineers), six miles more of probable development in the neighborhood of Long Beach and we have a greater harbor than San Francisco and are in a position to handle the products of the south and receive from and ship to the Orient the great commerce of the coming century. The public is aroused. It is beginning to know, as you gentlemen know, the true condition of affairs.

He was impassioned and persuasive, but Henry Parkhurst Barbour's involvement with the project was almost over. The "true conditions of affairs" was that his past was about to catch up with him. On February 1, 1906, he was quietly asked by the other directors of the Dock and Terminal Co. – the company he helped to found – to resign as vice president, chairman of the board, and member of the executive committee. When he refused to do so, he was dismissed and replaced by C.J. Lewis of Redlands. Dock and Terminal President Dana Burks later said that although he felt sorry for Barbour, the company had little choice in the matter.

"Barbour has not defrauded the Dock and Terminal Company out of a dollar, to my knowledge, but his 'boomer' methods are objectionable and not in keeping with the policy of this company. He is a man that does not know the value of money and who has not been wise in its expenditure," Burks told the Los Angeles Times.

When Barbour had helped found the Dock and Terminal Co., he had been a major investor, owning one-quarter of the stock, worth more than $350,000. He had been forced to sell off much of his holdings to satisfy his debts. At the time of his dismissal, he owned only 200 shares.

Dock and Terminal Co. Treasurer C.C. Ames affirmed that Barbour had not misappropriated any money from the company, but added that the company had not been satisfied with the "degree of business competency" shown by Barbour. The dismissal of Barbour from the Dock and Terminal Co. board was supposed to have been a secret, but word got out, and suddenly all the people to whom he owed money – about a quarter of a million dollars by press accounts – began demanding repayment. Rumors began to circulate that Barbour had fled to Canada, Mexico, or Europe. A reporter found him four days after his resignation still in Los Angeles, still exuding the same confidence he had earlier.

He laughed at some of the rumors that were being spread about him and said that the situation was under control and that he was just taking a break from all the controversy. Within days, however, several women came forward accusing Barbour of defrauding them in real estate speculations. The district attorney was reported to be considering criminal charges against Barbour for embezzlement and fraud.

Barbour disappeared, only to turn up a few days later in Ensenada, where he had been hiding out at the Bay View Hotel under the unlikely, but ironic, name of Captain Barrow. Meanwhile, his wife Florence was holed up in a hotel in Southern California refusing to talk to anybody about her husband's financial situation.

In June, when attorney Walter Desmond and real estate developer H.B. Shaffer, both of Long Beach, went to visit Barbour in Ensenada, they found him as confident and boisterous as ever. He had been raising capital for a new resort to be built on the bay in Ensenada – a resort that he predicted would be one of the show places of the Pacific Coast. He apparently hoped to make enough money on the hotel scheme to cover the money he owed.

Back in Southern California, a meeting at the Los Angeles Chamber of Commerce headquarters was held that June by a joint harbor committee from Los Angeles and Long Beach. Their charge was to endorse the report by the government engineers that had found the San Pedro Bay harbor to be a feasible port site. That was also the month that the Long Beach City Council passed a resolution declaring all sloughs and channels within the city to be navigable waters.

On June 25, 1906, Judge Wellborn rendered a sweeping decision in the Carver case, ruling that the Cerritos Slough was a navigable stream and directing the Salt Lake Railroad to remove the bridge. Captain Amos Fries of the Army Corps of Engineers agreed with Long Beach's assertion that the Salt Lake trestle across the river entrance was also a temporary structure to be removed at the War Department's request. Fries gave the railroad thirty days to take it down. The court decided in the meantime that the bridge could be restored for two days a week so rail traffic to Terminal Island could continue.

The Great Salt Standoff

The next challenge came from the San Pedro Salt Works, which operated a manufacturing plant on the saltwater flats. The Salt Works claimed it had a leasehold on the property that the Dock and Terminal Company was planning to dredge up. The lease was with the Seaside Water Co., which had sold the property to the Long Beach Land and Navigation Co., which in turn had sold

VITAL LINK: *The Salt Lake Railroad's bascule or "jack-knife" drawbridge opens to allow a ship's passage sometime in the early 1910s. The rail bridge connected Terminal Island with Long Beach at a time when San Pedro and Long Beach were wrapping up a bitter annexation battle over the island. Over the years, the infamous pontoon bridge and the later Gerald Desmond Bridge have occupied the space.*

it to the Dock and Terminal Co. The Salt Works had reportedly abandoned the property in question two years earlier and had not continued to pay rent on the land, nor had it raised the question of title to the property since the Dock and Terminal Co. had bought it. Although the Land and Navigation Co.'s title had been cleared, the Dunn family, which owned the Salt Works, clearly disagreed. With the harbor improvement project underway, the family wanted to reinstate its claim.

On Friday, July 20, 1906, the Salt Works sent a gang of workers to build a flume – a raised water chute – across an arm of the Cerritos Slough on property claimed by the Dock and Terminal Co. On Saturday afternoon, Dock and Terminal Co. manager C.J. Curtis showed up with his own workers and dismantled the flume. The following day, the Salt Works crew was back on site, rebuilding it. The salt company executives vowed to have the people responsible for demolishing the flume arrested. Attorney W.E. Dunn of the Salt Works called destruction of the flume an outrage, estimated the damages at $1,000 and said his company had a lease on the land good through 1911.

The dispute quickly grew physical. A Dock and Terminal Co. employee digging post holes on the property was ordered to desist. When he refused, he was roughly removed from the site. The Dock and Terminal Co. vowed to seek police protection. When crews started grading Wilmington Boulevard across disputed territory on Wednesday morning, they were met by Salt Works President Irwin Dunn and ordered to leave. The city sent a marshal to investigate the matter. He was met by Dunn, who claimed title to the property and vowed to continue in his claim until ousted by due process of law.

Long Beach City Attorney John E. Daly – an original director of the Land and Navigation Company – said that if Dock and Terminal manager Curtis wanted to swear out a trespass complaint, an arrest warrant would be issued. Otherwise, the city should not at that time get involved.

Two weeks later, on August 11, 1906, as the Dock and Terminal dredge prepared to invade the contested land, the Dunn family showed up at the site with Winchester rifles to block the work. When they were threatened with arrest, they shouldered their weapons and prepared for a fight. Their wives rushed to the scene to cheer them on.

The Dunns later surrendered and were arrested without bloodshed. Dock and Terminal President Dana Burks then offered to meet with the Dunns to discuss their differences and work things out. Although the Dock and Terminal Co. seemed to have a clear title to the property, it could not afford to get dragged into a lengthy legal battle over the question. The dispute ended when banker C.J. Walker – a principal in the Long Beach Land and Navigation Co. – bought a controlling interest in the salt manufacturing company, which he expanded and ran for many years afterward. Walker and former Long Beach Mayor Stephen Townsend, who was also a Land and Navigation Co. principal, joined the Dunns as officers of the company. Townsend's associate B.P. Dayman and Townsend's son Vinton Ray Townsend became directors in the company.

That August the War Department granted the Dock and Terminal Co. permission to deepen and straighten the river for one mile, including dredging of channels and a turning basin. The permit included a map showing a channel one mile long, 300 feet wide, and thirty feet deep, with a drawbridge replacing the wooden trestle.

In September 1906, the Salt Lake Railroad applied to replace the spur line trestle across the Cerritos Slough with a drawbridge. Captain Fries gave the railroad until August 1907 to remove the existing bridge which was blocking river access to the ocean.

Former Dock and Terminal Co. Chairman Henry P. Barbour returned from Ensenada to his home in Long Beach that same month, unabashed and as enthusiastic about the Long Beach Harbor as when he left seven months earlier. He announced that he had settled most of his debts with less than $20,000 outstanding and was ready to move on. And he did. He declared bankruptcy, showing $85,841 in assets, and $91,942 in liabilities. Although he had attempted to negotiate repayment with his creditors, there were a few who refused to work with him, he said in a written statement. The only way to ensure that all of his creditors were treated equally was through bankruptcy.

The man who had spent much of his life moving from one location to another chasing his dream had finally found his home. By 1911 he was a director in the Long Beach Chamber of Commerce and president of the Long Beach Realty Board. He remained a popular and respected figure in the business community, and when he died in 1927 of a massive cerebral hemorrhage, throngs showed up at his funeral to mourn his passing.

The War Over Territory and Property Rights

While private parties were busy developing the Long Beach Harbor, a war had erupted between public agencies over boundaries and jurisdictions. The political and business interests of Los Angeles County were in empire-building frames of mind and nobody was in the mood to back down from a fight. The result was an ongoing conflict – fought at the ballot box, at the courthouse, and before the state Legislature – that would do much to define both the city and the Port of Long Beach.

There had been talk for some time that Long Beach could dredge a channel from Wilmington to Long Beach, giving it an end-of-the-line foothold on the inner harbor of San Pedro Bay. In January 1903, Long Beach printer William Galer said he had a better idea. Galer said the city should simply annex Terminal Island. Such a move would extend the city boundary right up to the Salt Lake Railroad wharf across the channel from San Pedro and give Long Beach a waterfront close to the open ocean without having to dredge across the salt marsh to Wilmington. He also advised the city to deepen the channel of the river all the way in from the sea to permit barges and small craft to come up to the southwest corner of the current city limits. He said that channel could be dredged, and the material from the dredging could be used to build up the surrounding low-lying marsh for construction of lumber yards and warehouses.

It was a good idea, even a visionary idea, but like many good ideas it was only a dream unless there were the political and financial will to implement it.

It wasn't until July 1905 – about the same time that Dana Burks and Henry P. Barbour were laying out their port development plans – that a delegation of residents from Terminal Island and Wilmington showed up at the Long Beach Board of Trade asking to be annexed to the city.

The east side of Terminal Island – formerly Rattlesnake Island – was at the time the site of a community called Brighton Beach, a fashionable resort of homes, taverns, bathhouses, and hotels. The Salt Lake Railroad tracks ran down the island between the beachfront properties on one side and the salt marsh on the other. At the end of the line on the eastern end of Terminal Island was the Salt Lake wharf – and an industrial area known as East San Pedro.

The annexation of Terminal Island and the salt marsh east and south of Wilmington would provide Long Beach with potentially more harbor frontage than San Pedro, a possibility with immediate appeal to the business community – both those who were based in Long Beach and those who did business at the port.

Meanwhile, the City of San Pedro was planning to do the same thing from the other end – that is annex Terminal Island and extend San Pedro's boundaries all the way over to Long Beach. When San Pedro found out about Long Beach's interest in Terminal Island, it began to speed up its own process to annex the land for itself.

On July 17, Long Beach discovered that San Pedro was racing to beat Long Beach to a vote on the subject, and that San Pedro planned to, at its council meeting the very next day, schedule a special election to annex the island. Since the law required that there be at least thirty days between when an election was scheduled and when it could be held, Long Beach figured that if it could hold a meeting that same night to schedule a Long Beach election date, it could beat San Pedro out by one day – making any effort by San Pedro to set an election date moot.

The problem was that the Long Beach Trustees – they were not officially called councilmembers until 1908 – were in Los Angeles that day to testify as witnesses in a lawsuit involving the city marshal. So one of the trustees, R.S. Oakford, asked to be excused from his courtroom duties long enough to scoot down to Long Beach and schedule a Trustees' meeting for that very evening. Once their legal duties had been discharged, Mayor Rufus A. Eno and the trustees hurried straight from Los Angeles to Long Beach City Hall, where they found pro-annexationists from both Long Beach and Terminal Island waiting. The Trustee meeting began at 7:30 p.m. City Attorney F.A. Knight verified that the annexation petition from Long Beach had been signed by 20 percent of the qualified voters – many of the signatures gathered that very day when it became apparent that immediate action was imperative. Only one person spoke. A Mr. Lanning, who represented the Salt Lake Railroad and other large concerns on Terminal Island, said that they all wished to be annexed to Long Beach.

Mayor Eno said the whole thing had come up so suddenly that he didn't really feel able to vote intelligently on the matter. Nevertheless, he and the other four Trustees did vote to approve the election and set the date for August 16 – exactly thirty days hence.

When San Pedro civic leaders discovered what Long Beach had done, they were outraged. The City of San Pedro went to court to seek an injunction against the Long Beach annexation election. San Pedro argued that a petition for annexation of Terminal Island had been presented to San Pedro first. It wanted Long Beach to hold off on any annexation plan until San Pedro could hold its own election to annex Terminal Island. But Superior Court Judge D.K. Trask sided with Long Beach, and the go-ahead was given for the election to be held as scheduled. All San Pedro could do was to prepare its own paperwork in preparation for annexing Terminal Island if the Long Beach annexation attempt failed, which it was expected to do.

Meanwhile, Long Beach promised Terminal Island residents police and fire protection, school privileges, and better sanitary services. To help promote the annexation, more than one hundred prominent Long Beach leaders – including Mayor Eno, ex-mayor Stephen Townsend, City Trustee Oakford, and City Attorney Knight – went out to the island with the Marine Band to get acquainted with the residents, tout the benefits of annexation, and hold a rally.

The following month, when the ballots were counted, it appeared that Long Beach had annexed all of Terminal Island, including the breakwater that connected Terminal Island to Deadman's Island, and Deadman's Island itself, most of the tidelands, including Mormon Island – a low-lying property in what was known as the Wilmington Lagoon – and pieces of the unincorporated area known as Wilmington. That land on the east side of the San Pedro harbor main channel – called East San Pedro – officially became part of Long Beach.

There was a celebration in the streets of Long Beach. A brass band staged a parade, boat and factory whistles blew, and people congratulated each other on the election victory. The vote had been a landslide in Long Beach, where annexation of Terminal Island was approved, 200-6. Terminal Island and affected voters in Wilmington had also approved it, but only by a one-vote margin, 73 to 72.

The civic leaders in San Pedro cried fraud. They claimed that five of the votes in Terminal Island for annexation were illegal since they were not properly marked. Without those five votes, the annexation measure would have failed, San Pedro contended. In addition, they claimed there also were sixteen residents of Los Angeles and Pasadena who had transferred their residences to Terminal Island in order to vote in favor of the annexation.

Following the election, San Pedro sent its city attorney, Frank Kerr, and several other representatives to Long Beach to protest the vote. But Long Beach was not in a mood to back down from its victory. The Long Beach Trustees passed a resolution making Trustee Oakford a deputy city clerk, after which he excused himself and left the room. A few hours later, Kerr served a writ on Long Beach City Clerk Will B. Julian, prohibiting him from certifying the annexation election with the secretary of state. But the writ arrived too late. Oakford, in his new role as deputy city clerk, had departed earlier that evening for Sacramento and filed the document the following morning.

The City of San Pedro hired attorney John S. Chapman to aid the city attorney in mounting a legal challenge to the Long Beach victory. San Pedro also set a September 18 date for an election so San Pedro could annex Terminal Island itself after the Long Beach election was overturned. Another election had already been set for August 30 for San Pedro to annex the industrial area known as East San Pedro, which was part of the area that Long Beach already claimed. Long Beach wanted the court to enjoin San Pedro from holding an election for territory that Long Beach had already annexed.

The case was argued before Superior Court Judge Walter Bordwell, who ruled that San Pedro could hold its election, although Long Beach would maintain jurisdiction of the territory. But he also ruled that anybody in the disputed territory could bring quo warranto proceedings if Long Beach attempted to enforce its jurisdiction against them. Quo warranto proceedings would require that the city prove in each case that it had proper jurisdiction.

Judge Bordwell's non-decision decision confused the situation even more than it already had been. The August 30 election on San Pedro annexing East San Pedro ended up an overwhelming vote in favor – 54 to 4 in East San Pedro and 241 to 4 in San Pedro.

By this time, both San Pedro and Long Beach had annexation elections scheduled for Terminal Island – Long Beach to restake its claim, San Pedro to stake a claim on territory to which it felt it was rightfully entitled. Long Beach's election was set for September 16; San Pedro's was for September 18. Both elections were subsequently called off when Wilmington filed its intention to incorporate as its own city. Although Long Beach was not opposed to Wilmington incorporating as a city, it claimed that some of the territory being claimed by Wilmington – namely Mormon Island – was already part of Long Beach. The initial Wilmington incorporation effort was rejected over a legal technicality concerning requirements for advertising the intent to incorporate, but the court battle over the Wilmington incorporation effort continued.

The Long Beach Trustee Board in November 1905 called for another special annexation vote to take place on December 23, in another attempt to bring the Wilmington waterfront into Long Beach. The annexation vote, which succeeded, was a tactical effort by Long Beach to block San Pedro from taking the land in case the Wilmington incorporation effort failed.

In early 1906, Superior Court Judge Waldo M. York ruled that the Wilmington incorporation was in fact legal and that the city organization of 1891 was valid by default. The judge rendered the Long Beach annexation of the Wilmington areas and the shoreline of the inner harbor null and void. The ruling deprived Long Beach of about half of the territory it had annexed, but not Terminal Island or Mormon Island. A few weeks later in a separate case challenging the Wilmington incorporation, Appellate Court Judge N.P. Conrey ruled that the incorporation of Wilmington was not legal and that the territory that had been stripped from Long Beach in Judge York's decision was once again part of Long Beach. Since two judges had ruled in two different ways, the case headed to the California Supreme Court.

Meanwhile, Long Beach moved ahead as though its claim to Terminal Island was undisputed. The Long Beach School Board took over the Terminal Island schools, a police presence was established on Terminal Island, and plans were made to repair the boardwalk there. People in Long Beach began referring to East San Pedro as West Long Beach. But the battle between San Pedro and Long Beach was far from settled. People on Terminal Island began to complain that the improvements promised by Long Beach – such as a garbage wagon and better lighting and walkways – had not taken place, even though the city was leasing wharf space on the island.

Long Beach's claim to the territory was once again challenged when several businessmen in East San Pedro/West Long Beach were arrested after refusing to pay the Long Beach business tax. San Pedro City Clerk Henry Steiglitz was instructed by city trustees to check it out. When he was unable to find Long Beach's original petitions for holding the annexation election filed at the County Court House, he requested that Long Beach produce the documents. Long Beach City Clerk Fred Baldwin, aided by R.H. Jackson, spent the entire day searching the Los Angeles courthouse for the records to no avail. There was a record that the petitions had been filed by Long Beach, but the petitions themselves were mysteriously missing. There was talk by some that the documents had been stolen from the files – a belief that was not entirely without substance. As the Los Angeles Times noted in its September 1, 1906, edition:

The sudden activity of San Pedro in the matter leads to the suspicion that some new scheme has been hatched to defeat the jurisdiction of Long Beach over East San Pedro and Terminal Island.

City Clerk Steiglitz – who was also an attorney and supposedly acting outside his official capacity – volunteered to defend the businessmen who had refused to pay their taxes to Long Beach. He declared that the missing documents rendered Long Beach's annexation of Terminal Island and the other tidelands illegal. Steiglitz filed a quo warranto action against the city, claiming the city had no right to collect taxes from the merchants because the area wasn't legally part of Long Beach.

Squatter Rights

As Long Beach and San Pedro continued to squabble, another land dispute came to the fore. Beginning in the 1870s, squatters – mostly fishermen plying their trade – began to build crude dwellings along both sides of the channel leading into the harbor. It was a time when the West was still being settled, the pioneer spirit was still strong, and nobody paid much heed to folks staking out their own claims on the sand and moving in. Over the years the squatter community grew from a few single fishermen to a small community of families with cottages and shacks that were passed down from one generation to another. After years of living along the shores, the resident squatters took their ownership of the property for granted, although there were often bitter struggles among themselves over where one property ended and the other began. But as long as nobody had any more lucrative plans for the property, the government left the squatters to themselves and they were simply regarded as being among the many colorful characters who inhabited the harbor area at the time.

When Long Beach annexed Terminal Island in 1905, there were more than 150 long-time squatter households living on both sides of a narrow roadway they had dubbed United States Avenue. Long Beach leased about eight acres to the Salt Lake Railroad in the vicinity of that company's station. The company sent out a notice to the squatters demanding that they vacate the property. The squatters angrily refused. There were also squatters living in houseboats and dwellings along the marshy side of Terminal Island, blocking roads that had originally run all the way down to the water. Long Beach was determined to reopen those streets for public use as landings and docks for small boats.

There was much public sympathy for the plight of the squatters. Political sentiment at the time held that corporations had grown too powerful, too rich, and too greedy. The stories of squatters who had lived peacefully on their property for years resonated with many people. Had in fact the squatters over the years acquired legal rights to the property by simply moving onto the site and living there unmolested? That was a question to be decided in a court of law, but in the meantime the railroad and other entities were quietly attempting to buy up the holdings in order to avoid such legal entanglements.

The Los Angeles Herald in its April 3, 1906, edition referred to a mysterious "Mrs. Hamilton," who was said to be buying up squatter properties on behalf of the Crescent Wharf Co. – a subsidiary of the Salt Lake Railroad. When reporters tracked down Mrs. Hamilton in Los Angeles, she refused to confirm any relationship with the company, claiming she was merely buying the homes for herself as an investment. Her statement may have been true; she well may have been amassing properties so she could negotiate to sell them at a higher price to the railroad. On May 11, the Bouton Water Co. suddenly cut off water to nineteen cottages on Terminal Island owned by Mrs. M.D. Hamilton. She said she planned to seek legal redress. Other squatters similarly affected said they would appeal to the city to turn their water back on.

Management vs. Unions

Although the cities of Long Beach and San Pedro were at bitter odds with one another during this period, there were some issues that could bring them together – issues such as helping harbor businesses resist union inroads. The sailors' union was involved in a strike aimed at forcing all ships to use union crews. The union already represented crews on the dwindling number of sailing ships still transporting cargo between ports, but it wanted to organize union crews on the steam-powered ships as well.

Seeing an opportunity to gain union dominance in the entire harbor, the Longshoremen's Union Local No. 3 of the Pacific Coast Federation of Longshoremen sent out a letter to waterfront employers demanding that all union dockworkers be paid at least forty cents per hour regular time, time-and-a-half for overtime, and double time for Sundays and holidays. In addition, the union served notice that no member of the union would work with a non-union worker or move any cargo on the waterfront "as long as there is a non-union vessel in this port..." The letter was signed by union secretary Steve May.

The employers – mostly lumber companies, wharf owners, and railroads – held a meeting to discuss strategy. Banning Co. head Captain William Banning – one of Phineas Banning's sons by Rebecca – was chosen by unanimous vote to head up a committee that would take charge of all vessels coming into port and help secure protection and labor to work them. When the steam schooner *Coronado* showed up at the Salt Lake Railroad wharf on August 17, 1906, with a load of lumber from Aberdeen, Washington, the wharf manager called Long Beach Mayor Frank H. Downs and told the mayor that he expected trouble with the union. Within a short time, twenty-five police officers arrived on a special Salt Lake train. Hearing that the police had been summoned, about thirty union workers in San Pedro took the ferry across the channel to confront them.

The union workers from the various companies were ordered to begin unloading the *Coronado*. They refused and were immediately fired. They were then ordered to leave the company property and after some stubborn resistance, they were herded off the grounds by the Long Beach officers. Foremen with the Crescent Wharf Co. began manning the docks and the non-union sailors joined in. Mayor Downs and Long Beach Trustees S.L. Lent and G.S. Benson were at the scene to observe the dockside drama as was Dana Burks from the Los Angeles Dock and Terminal Co., who peeled off his coat and offered to pitch in unloading the vessel.

Mayor Downs later called San Pedro Mayor James Weir and asked him to close the saloons in San Pedro to keep the union workers from getting drunk and making trouble, an arrangement to which Weir agreed. The saloons were ordered to move last call to 7 p.m. or risk losing their liquor licenses.

Non-union workers were hired and transported to the site to work the ships at dock with city and private police on hand to guard both the workers and the property. Attempts by the union men to talk to the non-union workers were blocked by guards. Both the Southern Pacific and the Salt Lake railroads were running special trains, transporting non-union replacement workers to the job site. Extra fire extinguishers were put in place around the job sites to fight any union-started blazes. The lumber unloaded from the ships in port was immediately transported north to Los Angeles in order to avoid stockpiling it on the docks.

"As far as the Banning Company is concerned, it never has, and never will, recognize a labor union, even though its boats should rot at the docks," vowed Captain Banning.

Many of the newspapers of the day made little effort to conceal their anti-union bias. The Los Angeles Times, which was experiencing its own labor issues, referred to the union men as "totemites" and "dupes." One of the Times articles explained the importance of liquor to the union movement and noted the rage felt by the union members when San Pedro closed the saloons.

> *"The town is going to the dogs," many unionists declared.*
> *"They are shutting the saloons thinking they can drive us out that way," said one labor union straw boss, "but we will fool them. We will bring plenty of joy water down from Los Angeles and hand it out free at headquarters. We will fix them, all right."*

As unlikely as that quote seems, it was standard fare in coverage of the labor action. The labor movement was largely regarded by the press and by much of the respectable citizenry as a hotbed of radicalism and troublemakers.

Although the strike lingered on until late in the year, in December union leaders finally agreed to let their members return to work after employers voluntarily raised their rates from thirty cents an hour to a range of thirty to thirty-five cents an hour to be determined according to how efficiently each man worked. It marked a humiliating defeat for the union.

Fire in Stingaree Town

Meanwhile, the still unresolved squatter issue was further exacerbated when a fire swept through a neighborhood on the afternoon of September 19, 1906, destroying six businesses and about two dozen shacks in "Stingaree Town." The fire apparently started when a gasoline stove overturned in one of the shacks. The blaze quickly leapt from one building to the next. The lumber schooner *Frances Leggett*, at berth on the other side of the bay, came across when the fire started and used its pumps to direct four three-inch streams of water on the blaze. The quick action of the captain was credited with heading off what could have been an even greater catastrophe. At one point at the peak of the fire, a small launch tied up beneath the Salt Lake Railroad wharf caught fire and exploded, wrecking several feet of the dock.

News of the fire was received in Long Beach about twenty minutes after it started. Less than half an hour later, a fire engine, about fifty volunteer firefighters, and 1,000 feet of hose had been loaded onto Salt Lake Railroad flat cars and were on their way to the scene. The railroad bridge was the fire department's only access to the scene, and by the time they arrived, the fire had almost burned itself out. Long Beach police officers stationed on Terminal Island were instrumental in fighting the blaze. Officer Ralph Powell led a group of volunteers who began demolishing the old Newland Dance Hall and Saloon to stop the spread of the fire down the waterfront. Officer Fred Phillips stationed himself along with others by the Salt Lake pumping plant until driven off by the flames. Total damage was estimated at $40,000. The squatters who lost their homes spent the night camping out a short distance south of their former neighborhood. The captain of the *Frances Leggett* filed a $2,000 salvage claim with Long Beach after the fire was extinguished.

The following night, Salt Lake Railroad workers erected a wire fence around the burned out area in an apparent attempt to head off any idea of rebuilding in the area. Later that same night, police arrested John Wray and charged him with malicious mischief for attempting to tear down the fence. Wray, a former newspaper correspondent and San Pedro public official, denied he was tearing it down. He said he was merely lifting a couple of strands so he could crawl under it. The displaced squatters, who had vowed to fight any attempt to evict them, suddenly found themselves fenced off from their claims. The railroad's position was that if the squatters had any valid claims at all, it was to ownership of the dwellings they had built, not to the land. Now that the buildings had burned down, the railroad was free to develop the land it had leased from the city.

The squatters appealed to the San Pedro police for help. Although Terminal Island was under Long Beach's jurisdiction, San Pedro officials still felt that Terminal Island – at least the East San Pedro portion of it – was rightfully part of their town. The night following the erection of the fence by the railroad, there was a mass meeting held in San Pedro to protest the action. Following the meeting, about 200 men led by John Wray took the ferry to Terminal Island, tore down the fence, and occupied the burned out area. Twenty Long Beach police officers who were guarding the site retreated in the face of the 10-to-1 onslaught. The following morning, every charred timber left standing in the burned out area sported an American flag. A few squatters, a small contingent of San Pedro deputies, and several dogs remained in possession of the property.

A contingent of Long Beach police officers soon returned to the scene to face a contingent of San Pedro officers, who remained there as a demonstration of San Pedro's position that the area was rightfully its territory. Long Beach officials took the case to court to ask that San Pedro be restrained from interfering in the affairs of Long Beach on Terminal Island or elsewhere. Superior Court Judge D.K. Trask agreed. He granted Long Beach's request for a temporary restraining order that prohibited the squatters from occupying the property or harassing the Long Beach guards and that also forbade San Pedro city officials from meddling in the dispute until the case was settled in court. Squatters who later attempted to rebuild in the area were arrested for not obtaining building permits – permits which required compliance with municipal building codes.

The feelings of bitterness and betrayal are apparent in an article written for the Los Angeles Herald by squatter Lilian Banes Long. She referred to the Salt Lake Railroad as the "Octopus" and accused the city of Long Beach of playing "catspaw" for the railroad. She indicated her suspicions about the origin of the fire "supposed by outsiders to have been caused by a gasoline stove" and of the arrival of the Long Beach Fire Department on the scene after the fire had burned itself out.

The Long Beach annexation election had lumped together the Brighton Beach resort area with the East San Pedro industrialized area, two communities with few common interests, she noted. Brighton Beach generally favored joining Long Beach; East San Pedro did not. Adding insult to injury, she wrote, Long Beach had begun calling East San Pedro West Long Beach – "all of which, if amusing, is yet gall and wormwood."

"The squatter community is made up of hard-working people," she wrote. "mechanics, longshoremen, boat builders, shop keepers, machinists, artists, clam diggers, fishermen, and a stray scientist or two."

> *The nucleus of our settlement was made before the Salt Lake came, when the trestlework of the old breakwater was new, a quarter of a century ago.*
>
> *Our children have been born here, and old folk have died. The old breakwater is the place where we earn our livelihood. Many of us would be hard pressed to have to establish ourselves anywhere else. We have an odd liking for the place. It is our home. We feel like we have a right to be ousted, at least fairly, when our time comes to go.*

The plea for justice by squatters such as Lilian Banes Long resonated with a lot of people, and it would take several years to finally eject the seaside settlers from their claims. But the pressure to develop the property for more lucrative uses grew stronger by the day. The days of the squatters on Terminal Island were clearly numbered.

The war between cities over territory, however, was still to be resolved.

The Banning Family and the Tidelands

Further complicating matters over control and ownership of property was the Banning family's claim to Mormon Island as part of its tidelands property. The Bannings had long claimed the property as part of their holdings and had received a state land patent to the land in 1902 from California Governor Henry T. Gage. The family wanted to enforce that patent as soon as possible by having the dredging of the turning basin proceed so the spoils could connect Mormon Island to the mainland. But there were problems. The Banning family, Southern Pacific Railroad, and other corporations owned much of the tidelands in the inner harbor, and as landowners they felt that they were in the position to call the shots when it came to planning and developing the new harbor. Tidelands property is above water during low tides, but below water during high tides. The Bannings wanted the Army Corps of Engineers to survey the property so it could be developed the way the family saw fit.

But Captain Amos Fries, the Army Corps man in charge of rivers and harbors for the Los Angeles District, recommended instead that the state reclaim the privately owned property. Progressive political elements in the community – which included both activists and some businessmen – rallied to the cause. The progressives saw a government taking title to the tidelands as a blow for the common good against selfish corporate and private interests. Banning and the other tidelands owners saw it as a simple land grab by the government. The Banning Company even went so far as to fence off the part of the tidelands that it had claimed for itself – a move that made the community more determined than ever that the property belonged in the public domain.

By 1907, the harbor committee of the Los Angeles Chamber of Commerce came out in favor of government ownership of the tidelands and development of the harbor. In 1908, the full Chamber called for public development, saying that was the only way to ensure implementation of a "comprehensive plan." In 1909, the state government took the Bannings and others with tidelands claims to court to secure title to the property. It would be almost a decade before the legal dust settled. During that time the ownership of the property and the liability of agencies and private concerns developing and leasing the property were in legal limbo. When the State Supreme Court made its final ruling in 1915, it would serve as a touchstone for all of the issues of tidelands ownership and control from then until present day. But back in the bold and heady first decade of the 20th century, when fortunes were being made and ambitious people were busy changing the world, unsettled legal questions did little to inhibit the pursuit of those goals.

Scandal and Opportunity

The first decade of the 20th century was marked in Southern California by turbulent politics, and Long Beach was no exception. The little boomtown by the sea was linked in 1902 to Henry Huntington's Pacific Electric rail line – the famous Red Car line that once connected communities to one another in Los Angeles and Orange counties. People from inland communities across Southern California would head for Long Beach on weekends to swim, listen to concerts, fish from the pier, and enjoy the ocean breezes. The city still maintained a strong prohibitionist culture – serving wine with meals at the local hotels was a hot topic of debate – and the beachside attractions were aimed at good, clean family fun, not sin and debauchery.

And yet, there were stories of crime and scandal in the news during that period – especially during the critical years of 1905 and 1906 when the city was attempting to annex outlying territories. Although the events had no direct connection to either development of the port or annexation of new territory, the headlines – "Reign of Terror in Long Beach," screamed one front page headline in the August 13, 1905, Herald – tarnished the city's clean-living image at a critical time.

In the early morning hours of August 10 of that year, someone or some people bombed the home of City Marshal J.J. Conklin and then attempted to burn down the home of Mayor Rufus Eno. Those events had followed several other incidents including the setting of a fire at the municipal Pavilion, the robbery of the Post Office, an attempted arson at the Casa Palma rooming house, the vandalizing of City Trustee Cate's home with red paint, and anonymous letters to the mayor threatening death and dismemberment.

Conklin had earlier been accused by a police officer of collecting money for business licenses and selling unclaimed bicycles at auction, then pocketing the proceeds, a charge that he denied. He vowed to track down the person who bombed his home and to bring him to justice. The mayor blamed the attempted arson of his home on his "political enemies" and rejected suggestions by friends that he should resign.

"I have two excellent revolvers at home and keep them at my bedside and shall not hesitate to kill any person who appears around my house after nightfall," he told the press.

Four months later, Eno and Trustee J.B. Losee were arrested and charged with accepting bribes for contracts to rebuild the city Pavilion, which had burned down the previous January. The mayor again blamed the accusations on "political enemies" and vowed to fight the charges, as did Losee. Eno reluctantly stepped down in February; Losee followed suit a few days later, weeping as he tendered his resignation. Losee went to trial first, ended up with a hung jury, and pleaded guilty to avoid a second trial. The charges were eventually dropped against the mayor. The sordid events – the bombings, the arson, and the allegations of graft – did nothing to make Long Beach seem like the kind of place to do business or raise a family.

The Shipyard
Although the harbor work was far from finished, the plans for an inner harbor got a huge boost in 1907 when the Craig Shipyard decided to relocate its operation from Toledo, Ohio, where the company had been building ships for almost twenty years, to Southern California. Long Beach was not high on the company's list of cities to be considered for a new home.

Craig Shipbuilding had been founded by John Craig, whose father, George Craig, emigrated from the fishing village of Eyemouth, Scotland, to Quebec in 1827. It was a typical immigrant story that continues to be repeated up through modern times. George Craig got a job, saved some money, and over the next few years sent for the rest of his family – his parents, two brothers, and three sisters. Reunited, the family moved across the border to the United States in the early 1830s, where they settled in New York City. Both of George's parents died in the cholera epidemic of 1834 that killed hundreds of people in the city. His son, John Craig, was born four years later – on Christmas Eve 1838.

John Craig grew up around the waterfront of New York, watching ships come from, and depart to, ports all over the world. He became a lifelong member of the Republican Party after hearing Lincoln speak in 1860 and was an outspoken opponent of slavery. During the Civil War, he worked in a shipyard helping to construct twenty-three vessels for Union service. After the war, Craig joined Robert Linn – a shirt-tail relative loosely connected to Craig by marriage and family ties – as partner in Linn & Craig, a shipyard on Lake Erie in Gibraltar, Michigan. The partnership was not a happy one. The two men, according to Craig, could barely speak "without almost fighting," and their wives hated each other even more. The partnership dissolved in 1878, and Craig set up his own shipyard in Gibraltar. Four years later, he moved to Trenton, New Jersey, and five years after that to an eighteen-acre site he had purchased in Toledo. Production at the Toledo yard began in 1888. Over the next nineteen years, the Toledo yard built more than sixty vessels, including tugs, freighters, lakers (bulk carriers), passenger ships, rail ferries, and yachts – making Craig both wealthy and prominent.

By 1904, Craig was 65 years old and ready to retire. He turned the business over to his 38-year-old son, John Franklyn Craig. Like his father, John F. Craig was a smart businessman, but he was not in the best of health. His doctors had advised him to move to a milder climate. Besides, the Toledo yard was proving too small to remain competitive. He decided to relocate the company to a new site on the then-booming west coast of California. When John F. Craig arrived in California to scout out a new site, he was courted by a number of cities eager for the jobs and the economic benefits that the establishment of a shipyard would offer. San Pedro seemed to be the logical site, but an appropriate location didn't seem to be available, and freight rates in San Pedro were $2 a ton more than in San Diego. The ideal location was on the waterfront near Deadman's Island, but San Pedro had already granted a franchise for that property to Lewis Blankenhorn and D.P. Hatch for $500. The leaseholders were willing to sell the franchise, but they wanted $800,000 – a 105,000 percent markup. San Diego, on the other hand, offered a free site for the company to operate the shipyard. Long Beach City Attorney J.E. Daly noted, however, that the property would still belong to the City of San Diego.

Long Beach was considered, but the problem in Long Beach was that the Dock and Terminal Co. was still in the middle of constructing the harbor and had no specific site set aside for a shipyard. Craig wanted to get started in business as soon as possible. He needed forty acres with 2,000 feet of water frontage. The Dock and Terminal Co. assured Craig that it was willing to update its plans and have such a site ready as soon as Craig wanted. Once the War Department ordered the removal of the Salt Lake Railroad trestle in 1906, the future of the harbor was secured, and Craig was ready to make his move. The Dock and Terminal Co. valued the shipyard site at $400,000, but was ready to hand over the deed to Craig at no cost to him if the people of Long Beach would raise $100,000 to pay for the property.

A campaign was begun throughout the city to raise the money. Many businesses, realizing the benefits of a major industry coming to town, contributed to the cause. The business community organized an all-day drive on January 15, 1907, utilizing a motorized force of one hundred cars decorated in flags, flowers, and banners that gathered along Ocean Boulevard before spreading out across the city to solicit additional funds. A meeting had been scheduled in the Municipal Auditorium at 4 p.m. as part of the fundraising drive. By the time the meeting opened, there had been $86,000 pledged to the cause – leaving only $14,000 to go. An estimated 5,000 people showed up to listen to patriotic music played by the Royal Italian Band and to support the cause, according to an article the following day in the Los Angeles Herald.

When the total pledges reached $92,000, Adelaide Tichenor, the former president of the Ebell Club, pledged another $1,000, with the provision that it be the last thousand to be contributed. The other $7,000 would have to be raised first. Her contribution struck a chord with the audience. Reverend J.W. Spears, who chaired the meeting, urged anybody who wanted to make a $100 contribution to the cause to come to the front of the auditorium. Within minutes there were a dozen men standing in front of the crowd, some of them carried forward on the shoulders of their friends, each pledging $100. That number soon swelled to about forty, including two women. By the end of the meeting more than $100,000 had been contributed, and the contract was assured. In exchange, Craig committed to spending $100,000 in the community within twelve months and to employing several hundred workers at the shipyard site.

Craig reportedly said that he passed up the offers of sites in San Pedro and San Diego because he wanted to work with the "energetic, up-to-date men of affairs" in Long Beach. That may have been simple and expedient flattery when he said it, but it turned out to be exactly what he got.

By March of 1907, Craig was giving speeches at civic events and being recognized as an important and prominent member of the community. By May he had a contract with the Dock and Terminal Co. to clear away debris and brush from around the river's mouth to make way for the dredge and to build twin jetties extending on each side from the mouth of the river out to sea. Craig personally supervised the work in those early days, at one point jumping in when the land

EARLY INDUSTRY: *Workers pause for a break and a photograph at Craig Shipbuilding circa 1915; John Franklyn Craig brought the family business to Long Beach from Toledo, Ohio, in 1907. Craig was smart enough to get members of the community to put up the $100,000 for the shipyard site, purchased from the Los Angeles Dock and Terminal Co. In addition to running the industry that put the port on the map, Craig contributed to dredging and developing the inner harbor and served as a harbor commissioner in the '30s. He died in 1952.*

scraper they were using unearthed a nest of a half-dozen, four-foot rattlesnakes and killing one of the snakes himself.

By fall of 1907, C.H. Windham and T.M. Todd had dissolved their partnership in the Todd and Windham real estate firm. Windham had signed a contract with the Los Angeles Dock and Terminal Co. to manage the dredging operation of the inner harbor and planned to focus his energies there. It was a mutual decision. Both men planned to continue to be active in real estate as time permitted. That was typical of the time and place – a target-rich environment for entrepreneurs. If you were one of the movers and shakers in Long Beach in 1907, you were likely pursuing several opportunities at once, and Windham was definitely one of the movers and shakers.

The Craig Shipyard site by that time was about forty acres, filled in to twelve-to-fourteen feet above the mean low tide line. It stretched a half-mile along Channel 3 on the inner harbor and was 800 feet wide. After allowing time for the filled-in property to settle, Craig began preliminary construction of the shipyard in October of that year, using day labor and sending back to Toledo for skilled shipyard labor and their families. He transported thirty-seven families by train from Ohio to Southern California, arriving on November 1. The following month, John F. Craig bought an eleven-room residence at Ninth Street and Atlantic Avenue in Long Beach, the former residence of the E.E. Buffum family, before departing to Toledo to spend the holidays with family. The move from the Midwest to the West Coast was complete.

From Tragedy to Triumph

In 1905, Colonel Drake organized the Long Beach Hotel Co. along with some of the town's leading citizens, including the Bixby family members. The hotel was to be named The Bixby after the first family of Long Beach, and the cornerstone was laid on June 20, 1906. Four and a half months later, the mid-section collapsed during construction, killing thirteen workers and injuring many more.

The Bixbys withdrew their name from the project because of the tragedy, so the hotel was renamed The Virginia. In 1908, the Virginia Hotel opened its doors with a dinner and ball for 700 guests. It was a grand hotel, and served as a focal place for both business and social ceremony and celebration. In the early 20th century, golf had become the big craze in the East and Midwest, and Colonel Charles Drake suggested to his friends that they should start a country club for themselves and the hotel guests. In 1909, the Virginia Country Club was formed with 119 charter members. Drake kept fifteen memberships for hotel guests. When the country club later opened on November 3, 1909, Dock and Terminal Co. president, C.J. Curtis was elected the first president. The golf course was located in what became Recreation Park.

Up from the Mud

Although the men who built the harbor in Long Beach had vision, realizing that vision was hardly easy. The tenacity of the people involved in developing the port is undeniable, and often the setbacks seemed to outnumber the successes. As work progressed on the shipyard and harbor in 1907, Dock and Terminal Co. co-founder Dana Burks was facing both political and legal problems in his Ocean Park home town, where he was mayor. He had worked with Abbot Kinney to help develop the Venice neighborhood with its canals and bridges, but now the two men – the Duke and the Doge of Venice – were at odds. The Ocean Park Trustees had voted in May 1907 to close saloons and discount houses in Venice and to shut down dancehalls on Sundays over reports of immoral activities. Burks denied charges that the Ocean Park Trustees had taken the action to retaliate against Kinney because of differences between the two men. He said the businesses had violated standards set by the city and had been given numerous warnings that were disregarded. Although he and Kinney had their differences, Burks denied any hostility toward the man.

"Abbot Kinney has played fast and loose with the board, has not kept his promises to us or to the public, and generally has shown his incompetency to run a high-class resort," Burks charged.

By September, Burks himself was under scrutiny after former Venice policemen signed affidavits about gambling and vice in Venice being sanctioned by a "man higher up." The district attorney brought Burks and the Trustees before a grand jury to get to truth of the charges. Burks was furious. He said Kinney – in order to get back at him – had collected the affidavits from disgruntled policemen who had been fired. He said he had no knowledge of crooked gambling halls, and if any protection was offered, it must have been from a previous chief of police who now worked for Kinney. He said Kinney had forced the removal of former Police Chief Charles Foster because of the chief's efforts to crack down on vice in the Venice area and that Kinney had encouraged vice and immorality to flourish in the area. The following week, during a meeting aimed at fighting a movement by Kinney to disincorporate the city, Burks denounced former policeman C.C. Cannon, who had testified before the grand jury against him. Burks said Cannon lied during his testimony and called the former cop a "sneak" and a "cur." When Cannon found out from friends what Burks was saying, he rushed to the meeting, arriving just as it was breaking up.

"What do you mean by calling me names?" Cannon demanded as Burks was leaving the room. Burks answered by punching Cannon in the face. The police grabbed Cannon and held him back as Burks and his party walked away.

As Burks started to get entangled in the bitter politics of Ocean Park, he stepped down as president of the Dock and Terminal Co. and was replaced by George Bixby. Bixby noted that the volume of work on the harbor was increasing and said that the company required the authority of a president "upon the ground." Meanwhile, Dock and Terminal Co. board member C.J. Curtis, who had made his mark in Redlands as a banker and the owner of West American Fruit Co., remained as manager.

Although it drew little public attention at the time, the Dock and Terminal Co. struggled through some tight financial times as the cost for dredging and jetties mounted. In January 1906, the directors had voted to levy a $14-per-share assessment on its capital stock. Raising enough cash to pay the bills was sometimes a struggle. Curtis, who had his own company to run, had not planned to take an active role in the Long Beach project, but because of his success in getting the Dock and Terminal Co. through some of its financial challenges, he was urged to step up as the executive officer. A friend from back East had been trying to convince him to sell a half-interest in the Redlands citrus business. Curtis telegraphed the friend with an offer to sell the entire business, and the offer was accepted. Curtis continued in the role of president and chief executive officer for many years afterward. He would later recall how stressful the job had been.

"I sweated blood in the old days, particularly during the panicky year of 1907, trying to get enough money to meet the bills," he said. "I don't believe I could live through three weeks of such strain, nowadays." He gave credit to Long Beach banker P.E. Hatch for his support and friendship during those years.

"Among the numerous instances when the Dock and Terminal Co. had to battle against threatening conditions and circumstances, a memorable one was the time during a storm when the ocean threatened to open an entirely new channel and to leave our expensive jetties – the rocks which cost us $14 apiece – standing off to one side, 'protecting' an abandoned entranceway," Curtis recalled.

The cause of the Long Beach Harbor received a big boost in December 1907, when C.H. Windham – an advocate of the port and a contractor on it – was elected mayor.

"The close relationship between the private and public sectors was strengthened by the fact that one of [the Los Angeles Dock and Terminal Co.'s] directors, Charles Windham, served as Long Beach's mayor from 1908 to 1912," says Professor Steven Erie of the University of California, San Diego, in his book, *Globalizing L.A.* In other words, Windham was able to work both sides of the fence. As a private businessman he helped close deals and put together partnerships. He was a director in the Los Angeles Dock and Terminal Co., a contractor in charge of the dredging operation, and instrumental in putting together the various deals that drove the process forward. As a public official, he helped foster a pro-business agenda and push through voter approval of a $250,000 port bond issue by the city.

The day after winning the election as part of the Charter Faction's ticket, Windham issued the following statement:

"The Charter ticket was elected upon the platform of businessmen for business. We have promised a business administration and it is now up to the administration to make good. I am sure that every man on the ticket feels this responsibility. The administration will make good."

The way city officials operated in those early days could be seen as a conflict of interest, but at the time it was not that uncommon and few if any raised the question – at least not publicly. Even so, Windham did step down as a director of the Dock and Terminal Co.

Meanwhile, local business leaders who were staunch supporters and often investors in the harbor project founded a company known as Western Dredging and Marine Construction. Craig Shipyard President John F. Craig was named president of Western Dredging, and Mayor Windham was named vice president. The Los Angeles Dock and Terminal Co. made a deal with Western Dredging to finish dredging the inner harbor, a job that had been started by other contractors. Both Windham, who was by then a former director of the Dock and Terminal Co., and C.J. Curtis, president of the company, denied that Craig had any stock in Western Dredging despite the fact that he was on the board of directors.

The following month, the Western Dredging board elected new officers. The board voted Craig as president, Benjamin F. Pearson as vice president, and Mayor Windham as general manager. In March, the final $600,000 deal was signed for Western Dredging to complete the rest of the harbor. As part of the deal, Craig sold the first vessel constructed at the Long Beach yard – a $65,000 dredger – to the new company.

Construction of the shipyard went quickly. Craig erected an office building, a machine shop, a foundry, and a power plant. Still to come was a huge floating dry dock that would be supported by seven 100-by-40-foot pontoons.

However, construction delays in getting the Salt Lake drawbridge built began to have an impact on the harbor development and the shipyard. In March 1908, John F. Craig had to lay off half of his carpenters. He gave seniority job rights to the men who had moved with their families from Ohio to join him at the Long Beach yard.

Despite such setbacks, the old Salt Lake Railroad trestle across the mouth of the river was finally removed in April, and the dredging proceeded to move past that point. The replacement, a $250,000 double-track, steel bascule bridge design, was the work of Joseph Baermann Strauss, the same man who would later design the Golden Gate Bridge. The new bridge soon became a local icon and a "must see" for every important person who visited the city.

The building of the harbor was beginning to attract international attention. On September 7, 1908, the Los Angeles Herald reported that Windham and Craig had hosted Señor Luis Martinez de Castro of Sinaloa, Mexico, and Mr. and Mrs. L.E. Thompson of Los Angeles on a tour of the harbor and the shipyard. That evening the visitors were treated to dinner at the Hotel Virginia as the guests of Mr. and Mrs. Stephen Townsend, Mr. and Mrs. B.P. Dayman, and Mrs. D.F. Van de Water.

In September of that year, John F. Craig also announced the contract for the first oceangoing boat to be built at the new yard – a 125-foot, $100,000 tugboat for the Western Pacific Railroad Co., for use at the railroad's operation in Oakland.

The first vessel to be launched at the Craig yard was the dredger that the Western Dredging Co. had ordered. On September 14, 1908, 1,500 people showed up at the Craig Shipyard to witness the launch of the first steel vessel built on the West Coast south of San Francisco. The vessel was christened by little Miss Marta Windham, daughter of Mayor C.H. Windham, who was also general manager of Western Dredging. What Windham didn't know until the ceremony, was that the dredge was named after him. He was reported to have been "astounded."

The *Charles H. Windham* – 110 feet long and thirty-five feet wide with a seven-and-a-half-foot draft – was christened with a bottle of champagne, a fact that some onlookers in pro-prohibitionist Long Beach found slightly scandalous. Many had assumed a bottle of water would be used for the ceremony. That point of view was immediately rejected by one of the Craig executives, according to a story in the Herald.

"We've never used water at the christening of a vessel, and we don't propose to here," he is quoted as saying.

The launch of the dredger cleared the way for construction of the Western Pacific tug, the *Virgil Bogue*.

In January 1909, two large boilers for the Western Pacific tug, plus 250,000 board feet of lumber for building the tug and a dry dock, arrived at the Salt Lake Railroad's wharf in East San Pedro on the steamship *Claremont*. The shipyard was in business, but Craig wanted to make sure there was enough business coming in the door to sustain the operation. He made a trip to Portland, Oregon, that same month to seek a contract for two oceangoing tugs and a steamer to be built for the Port of Portland. Two months later, he got his answer. Although he had submitted the lowest bid by $10,000, the Portland port commission had rejected all bids.

According to Craig Shipbuilding executives, the Portland commission was under pressure not to award the contract to an out-of-town firm. The only way to cut Craig out of the deal was to reject all bids. The port commission advertised for bids again, and received two – one from Craig and the other from the Willamette Iron Works of Portland. Again both bids were rejected. The process was so clearly biased in favor of the hometown firms that the Portland port engineer, who had recommended that Craig be awarded the contract, resigned in frustration. The Craig bid was $6,570 less than the one submitted by Willamette Iron Works.

The Border Wars
While Long Beach and San Pedro were engaged in their bitter dispute over who owned Terminal Island, Los Angeles was moving ahead with a much more ambitious plan. Officials and businessmen there saw no reason why the city should not expand to absorb all the small surrounding communities, including San Pedro, Wilmington, and Long Beach. Long Beach for the most part was not in favor of becoming part of Los Angeles, although that sentiment was far from unanimous. If anything, the visionary thinkers of Long Beach favored a plan that would create a separate city out of Long Beach, Wilmington and San Pedro – a city of impressive size that would have its own harbor. The Long Beach Telegram, in an editorial in its January 4, 1906, edition, called for a merging of the three cities to block off advances by Los Angeles. The choice was to be a great city with a port or to be simply a feeder for Los Angeles.

"Lay the foundation for the Empire City of the South by lining up with San Pedro and Wilmington," the editorial urged.

Los Angeles turned to the state Legislature in order to scoop up reluctant communities. One of the measures it proposed was to change the law governing annexation from requiring separate, affirmative votes in both the annexing city and the community to be annexed, to merely requiring one vote that would lump together voters in both communities. Since Los Angeles was so much more populous than the other communities, its voters would dominate such an election and force any outlying community into being part of the city whether that community liked it or not.

Long Beach fought the measure and won when California Governor George Pardee turned down the proposition. But the victory was only temporary. In November 1906, Los Angeles annexed a "shoestring strip" of land half-a-mile wide and ten miles long that brought its borders all the way down to the corner of the harbor, with San Pedro to the south and Wilmington to the east. Los Angeles voters approved the annexation 6,539-915. Voters in the sparsely settled shoestring strip voted 208-202 for the measure. With a foothold in the harbor area, Los Angeles planned to annex both San Pedro and Wilmington. It then began a campaign for consolidation to convince officials and voters in all three harbor communities – San Pedro, Wilmington, and Long Beach – to become a part of Los Angeles. At a mass meeting held on December 7, 1906, about 500 people gathered in Long Beach to hear arguments on both sides of the issue.

C.L. Hoge, a director for the Los Angeles Dock and Terminal Co. and a former real estate associate of C.H. Windham and T.M. Todd, made a strong argument for becoming part of Los Angeles. Hoge drew applause when he noted the efforts of Los Angeles to secure a free port in San Pedro despite opposition from Collis Huntington and the Southern Pacific Railroad. He said that becoming part of Los

Angeles would be an advantage in gaining future improvements to the harbor as well as other regional infrastructure projects.

Others charged that Long Beach would quickly lose its identity and local control once it was gobbled up by Los Angeles. Taxes would probably be higher as Long Beach would be expected to contribute to Los Angeles' efforts to build an aqueduct that would bring water down from the Owens Valley. Opponents of consolidation said Long Beach had sufficient water supplies of its own. In the end, a committee of nine Long Beach businessmen – dominated by opponents of consolidation – was appointed to meet with Los Angeles to hear that city's offer.

One week later a delegation of five Long Beach residents, including Mayor Downs and L.A. Perce of the Chamber of Commerce, had dinner in San Pedro with some of the prominent people of that town to discuss consolidation of Long Beach, San Pedro, and Wilmington into a separate city. It was an interesting proposition that never made it past the talking stage. The acrimonious court struggle over Terminal Island, and on the land between San Pedro and Long Beach, almost certainly made such a strategy politically impossible. Whether it would have changed things for the better or the worse is impossible to know. It may have turned out to be an intermediate step that would have ended up with Los Angeles eventually annexing the combined port cities. The only thing for sure is that if such a plan had been adopted, the history of the harbor area would have turned out much differently.

Los Angeles proceeded with confidence in its plan to become one huge metropolis that would stretch "from the mountains to the sea." Although there was some opposition in San Pedro, a petition to be annexed by Los Angeles was signed by fully half of the voters in that town. Both major newspapers – the Los Angeles Times and the Los Angeles Herald – committed to push the plan. S.A. Butler, president of the Los Angeles Consolidation Commission, said that the overwhelming response in San Pedro meant that annexation there was assured.

> *Consolidation with San Pedro will ensure us ocean frontage and a free harbor within our city. Wilmington, we feel certain, will follow the lead of San Pedro.*
>
> *Under the proposed borough system, the city of San Pedro will not lose its identity, and in a great measure, it will be self-governing, but at the same time it will have back of it and its great institution, the harbor of San Pedro, the prestige and support of the great city of Los Angeles, and of which it will be an integral part.*
>
> *With this prestige and support there can be procured for San Pedro harbor, both outer and inner, all reasonable appropriations demanded of the government in the name of the city of Los Angeles.*
>
> *San Pedro will lose none of her glory as being the harbor city, as she will retain her name, although included within the limits of Greater Los Angeles. In this respect, San Pedro will occupy the same position relative to Los Angeles that Brooklyn has to New York. Brooklyn now is a borough of Greater New York, but the city has retained its name and individuality.*

Eleven days later, when Butler and other members of the Consolidation Commission came south to tour the harbor area, including Long Beach, they were appropriately greeted by Dock and Terminal Co. manager C.J. Curtis, company directors C.H. Windham, Chamber President L.A. Perce, T.M. Todd, C.H. Hoge, C.A. Buffum, and others. Butler toured the area and said he was highly impressed with what he saw. The inner harbor, he predicted, would soon be jam-packed with factories and other industrial institutions.

"I am more convinced than ever that San Pedro, Wilmington, and Long Beach need the assistance of Los Angeles in developing this great project and that Los Angeles requires possession in conjunction with these cities of the harbor," Butler said. "The future of Los Angeles and the harbor cities depends upon concerted action, and such action can be obtained only by consolidation."

Although sentiment in Long Beach seemed to be against consolidation with Los Angeles, Commission members said they expected that to change as leaders of the local consolidation movement explained the benefits of becoming part of the larger city. Noting that Long Beach was going to vote on a new charter the following month, they predicted that charter proposition would be defeated at the polls and that the way would be cleared for consolidation with Los Angeles. Three weeks later, Long Beach residents voted on the new charter. The election revolved around the issue of independence versus consolidation with Los Angeles. Long Beach voters approved the new charter, 1,237 to 161.

If Long Beach was a hard nut to crack, the leaders of the Los Angeles consolidation movement were not deterred. Their campaign to annex San Pedro and Wilmington was proceeding very well. One of the problems they faced in the annexation attempt, however, was Long Beach's claim on Terminal Island, which was still being battled out in court. How could San Pedro vote on annexation if they didn't know if the people in East San Pedro were legally part of San Pedro or Long Beach?

Although the city limits at the time only stretched to the corner of the harbor, the Los Angeles Chamber urged the mayor to appoint a commission to oversee harbor affairs. Mayor Arthur C. Harper responded on December 9, 1907, by appointing as chairman George H. Stewart, a Chamber of Commerce director; T.E. Gibbon, president and managing editor of the Los Angeles Herald; and F.W. Braun, founder of a company that produced industrial chemicals and mining equipment.

On October 3, 1907, Appellate Court Judge N.P. Conrey ruled that illegal votes had been cast in Long Beach's original Terminal Island annexation election. Although Long Beach had assumed jurisdiction over Terminal Island more than two years prior, that legal jurisdiction was once again in question. Long Beach city officials had argued that when the new City Charter was passed by voters earlier that year and approved by the state Legislature, it certified the city boundaries to include Terminal Island. Long Beach vowed to appeal Conrey's ruling.

On June 11, 1909 – almost four years after Long Beach voted to annex Terminal Island – the state Supreme Court ruled that the election – carried by only one vote – was not valid. There were instances of at least two voters, one from Los Angeles and one from Pasadena – who maintained summer homes on Terminal Island. Neither of them planned to make Terminal Island their primary residence; they just happened to be in residence when the election was held. That did not qualify them to take part in the annexation election, the court ruled. In addition, the judges unanimously rejected the Long Beach claim that the inclusion of Terminal Island within its boundary in its new state-certified charter made Terminal Island part of the city. The purpose of a city charter, the judges ruled, was to give the residents of the city the ability to frame their own laws and control their municipal affairs as they saw fit. That did not include unilaterally deciding what areas were in the city and what areas were not.

It was finally official. Long Beach had no claim to the inner harbor territory. The only exceptions were the basin in front of Wilmington and the channel on the west side of Mormon Island. The decision gave San Pedro jurisdiction over the west end of Terminal Island, the so-called East San Pedro harbor area. Mayor Windham of Long Beach telephoned San Pedro Mayor J. W. Walton acknowledging the court's decision and promising to surrender its Terminal Island jurisdiction as soon as San Pedro was ready. With the election to consolidate San Pedro with Los Angeles scheduled for August 12, 1909 – a consolidation almost certain to be approved – the San Pedro City Council was not in any hurry to negotiate with Long Beach on the details of the turnover. That could wait until Los Angeles took over.

In the meantime, Long Beach acted quickly to annex the east end of Terminal island and the inner harbor lands it had been denied in court. The annexation vote on Terminal Island was unanimous. Only six ballots were cast, five for the annexation and one blank.

The court's decision was greeted with joy and jubilation within the squatter community on Terminal Island. They had waited years for a glimmer of hope that they would be able to keep their homes. They were no longer under Long Beach rule, and San Pedro had always had a more tolerant attitude toward their existence. Through the years, the squatters had battled the railroads, the wharf owners, and the city to little avail. Sometimes the bitterest battles were between the squatters themselves.

Almost by definition, the property lines claimed by squatters were ill-defined. In one case reported in the Los Angeles Times, a woman squatter named A.V. Annabel, who ran a small store on her property before it was destroyed by fire, moved to Lankershim after the blaze. When she returned to Terminal Island, she said she discovered that C. L. Radcliff and his wife, Sadie, had jumped her claim and were building a two-story house on the property. Annabel entered the premises and confronted the Radcliffs, according to the story.

When the Radcliffs ordered her to leave, and she refused, the husband and wife "kicked her out of the house, threw her down, dragged her along the sand and pounded her severely," she said. She even alleged that Radcliff had pulled a gun and threatened to kill her if she ever came back, the Times reported.

> *Radcliff states that he obtained the property by purchase from a man known as "Scar-faced Charley." Neighbors allege that the aforesaid "Scar-faced Charley" had no title to the property and since the fire has been in the habit of selling property in "No Man's Land" in which he had no right or interest.*

With consolidation right around the corner, the San Pedro City Trustees on July 27, 1909, heard arguments by attorney George W. Knox, who represented the squatters. Knox argued that if the city of Long Beach could lease property upon which many of the squatters lived to the Salt Lake Railroad, why couldn't the City of San Pedro lease the property to the hard-working people who had lived on the land for so long? The San Pedro trustees apparently agreed. They instructed the city clerk to give a fifty-year lease to each of about one hundred squatters for the parcel of land upon which he or she resided at a rent of $1 per year. While the action made the squatters happy, it turned out that the San Pedro Trustees had acted hastily in promising something they could not deliver. The whole plan began to fall apart four days later when it turned out that two names weren't on the list of squatters to be leased land – William Newland and the late Paul Le Marr. The San Pedro city attorney urged the Trustees to immediately include the two names on the list to head off any plans by the railroad to enforce its lease from Long Beach. That drew allegations from the squatters in attendance, who claimed that Newland had already sold his claim to the railroad and that the Le Marr estate was ready to make the same deal. One of the squatters accused the city attorney of being in cahoots with the railroad, and then other squatters who had been left off the list began complaining that they wanted on. Other attorneys who represented squatters advised that if they accepted the leases from the city, they would leave themselves open if the leases were challenged in the future. The only good news for the San Pedro Trustees was that soon it would not be their problem. When Los Angeles took over, the San Pedro Board of Trustees would cease to exist.

The Wilmington annexation election was first. On August 4, the annexation of Wilmington to Los Angeles was approved by voters in the two cities – 107-61 in Wilmington, 18,661-221 in Los Angeles. One week later, Los Angeles and San Pedro voters were back at the polls to decide on the annexation of San Pedro. That measure passed 726-227 in San Pedro, 11,592-109 in Los Angeles.

The result of the two votes was the cause of great celebration. Hundreds of people gathered at San Pedro City Hall to listen to the returns and hail the victory. Backers of the consolidation movement gave speeches, and when the band showed up, there was a short, but enthusiastic parade around downtown San Pedro with the band playing songs such as "A Hot Time in the Old Town Tonight" and "Marching through Georgia."

By August 1909, the cities of San Pedro and Wilmington were both officially out of business, and the City of Los Angeles had its port. There was still Long Beach out there, hanging tough despite losing the battle for Terminal Island in court, but the feeling in Los Angeles during that time of victory was that Long Beach would fall in line soon enough. It was just a matter of time. Local newspapers made no pretense of being impartial. Opponents of consolidation were often described in unflattering terms and the benefits of consolidation were trumpeted. In fact, after the election, the Los Angeles Herald ran stories about the compliments it had received both from regular folks and political leaders for helping to lead the fight for consolidation.

At the same time that Los Angeles wanted to annex Long Beach, Long Beach was busy attempting to annex territory to the east of town, causing Los Angeles to explore the possibility of moving in and cutting off the expansion of Long Beach to the east. Los Angeles found little interest. The people who lived in the area – now known as Belmont Heights – realized that taxes in Los Angeles would be higher than in Long Beach. After some back and forth among themselves, during which time they incorporated as their own city, the Belmont Heights folks finally decided to become part of Long Beach in 1909.

In the fall of 1910, Los Angeles once again began courting Long Beach. If Long Beach joined Los Angeles, the larger city could help the smaller city develop its own harbor and it could also share in the water Los Angeles was bringing down from the Owens River by aqueduct. In fact, city officials were said to be putting out feelers to other smaller communities in the area, touting the advantages of being part of Los Angeles. Few people in Long Beach or many of the other communities were interested. People in communities such as Artesia, Norwalk, Downey, Cerritos, La Mirada, Alamitos, and Naples liked things just the way they were.

The threat by the City of Los Angeles to gobble up the communities along the southeast border of the county sparked an exploration of the possibilities of those cities seceding from Los Angeles County and becoming part of Orange County, which had separated from Los Angeles County in 1889. A delegation from Orange County met with officials in the cities targeted by Los Angeles to offer their blessing if Long Beach and any of the other cities wanted to flee from Los Angeles County to Orange. The county secession idea, though not successful, was a clear demonstration of Long Beach's determination to be an independent entity.

An even clearer indication came on January 10, 1911, when Long Beach annexed three square miles of territory to the north of the city, which included a 100-foot-wide strip running east all the way to the Orange County line from what is now the Long Beach-Compton border. The city annexed the strip after word leaked out that Los Angeles was planning to annex its own strip of land over from Wilmington and to snatch up Signal Hill and the water-bearing lands north of the hill as its own. With those water-bearing lands part of Los Angeles, Long Beach would be at the mercy of the bigger city. The Long Beach strip shut out Los Angeles from expanding to the hill and from there on to Alamitos Bay and Naples. The idea of the strip drew support from large rural landowners south of the strip – including the Bixby family and the Montana Land Co. – which wanted to avoid the higher taxes of Los Angeles. The Montana Land Co., controlled by Senator William A. Clark of the Salt Lake Railroad, had more than 8,000 acres of farmland acquired from Jotham Bixby. In years to come, that property would be developed into the city of Lakewood.

No Help for the Squatters

The change in city administration that came when Los Angeles annexed San Pedro ended up meaning little for the squatters. The leases so freely promised by the San Pedro Board of Trustees never materialized, although the squatters attempted on several occasions to make payments in order to validate their claims. On November 11, 1909, Appellate Judge N.P. Conrey ruled that the lease granted to the Salt Lake Railroad by the City of Long Beach was valid since the city was at the time exercising jurisdiction over Terminal Island – a fatal blow to the squatter claims on the property in question.

On July 27, 1910 – one year after the City of San Pedro had granted the squatters fifty-year leases – W.D. Hipple, president of the squatters association, showed up at the Los Angeles City Clerk's office with attorney D.A. Gardner and $103 in gold for rent on 103 squatter claims. On the advice of the city attorney, the payment was refused.

"We were promised a fair deal if we came into Los Angeles, and we want to get it," Hipple told a reporter.

There were many deals being made at the time, but none of them involved the squatters. By the following year, many squatters began to literally lose their property as the dredge deepening the channel one hundred feet off their shore began to suck their property into the sea. By early 1912, the battle was all but over for the squatters. The city and the private businesses to which it leased property were busy developing a world-class port in Los Angeles, and the plan didn't include a bunch of shacks. The squatters would continue to attempt to pay their $1 yearly rents to enforce their claims, but the money was always refused.

The Great White Fleet
One of the events that helped put Long Beach on the map during this period and stressed the importance of Long Beach as a harbor town – even though it did not yet have a deep-water harbor – was the visit to San Pedro Bay in April 1908 of the Great White Fleet. The fleet consisted of sixteen battleships plus accompanying vessels all painted in peace-time white, manned by 14,000 sailors and Marines. With the ships' coal-fired engines pumping huge plumes of black smoke from their stacks, the fleet was a wonder to behold.

President Theodore Roosevelt sent the Great White Fleet on an unannounced voyage around the world on December 16, 1907. In typical Roosevelt fashion, the voyage was a goodwill trip, a show of American naval power, and a demonstration of the president's philosophy of "big-stick diplomacy." It wasn't until the fleet was underway that the men aboard learned they were going to circle the globe. The fourteen-month, six-day voyage was more than just a demonstration of power. It also was a test of how prepared the Navy was for war.

"I want all failures, blunders, and shortcomings to be made apparent in time of peace and not in time of war," Roosevelt said before the fleet departed from Hampton Roads, Virginia.

Perhaps the most important purpose of the voyage was to inspire the American people with the power and scope of their Navy in order to win public support for the funding of four additional battleships.

After traveling around the horn of South America, stopping at ports along the way, the fleet reached San Pedro Bay on Saturday afternoon, April 18, 1908, the day before Easter Sunday. Long Beach and the other communities up and down the coast were prepared. An estimated 200,000 people – many of them from inland communities such as Riverside and San Bernardino – showed up to see the spectacle. The smoke from the ships was visible on the horizon well before the vessels could be seen. Then the ships came into view, traveling in a file more than three miles long. Some of the fleet anchored in San Pedro Bay, others went around the Palos Verdes Peninsula to anchor off Redondo Beach.

Long Beach was thronged with 50,000 visitors. The grand Hotel Virginia, which had opened on April 1 of that year, and where Governor James Gillett was ensconced, was the center of the celebration. Long Beach had the best view of the fleet, and the beaches, bluffs, and rooftops there were lined with people – both residents and visitors – wanting to see the arrival of the great fleet. A committee from the Ebell Club had gathered 6,000 Easter lilies, divided them into four lots of 1,500 each, and sent them tied in white satin ribbons to various ships in the fleet on Easter Sunday. A delegation of four ladies from the Ebell Club delivered one batch of the lilies to Captain Henry McCrea on the battleship *New Jersey*, flagship of the Second Division. The ladies were then escorted to Admiral William Emory's quarters where they joined the admiral, the captains from the four ships in the Second Division, and Mayor Windham and his wife, Angelica. Everybody went ashore in the admiral's boat, met with the governor and other officials at the Hotel Virginia, and then went to the mayor's house for lunch.

The visit by Theodore Roosevelt's Great White Fleet was Long Beach's first formal introduction to the Navy – the first step in a courtship that in the future would shape both the city and the port and become part of their rich history.

In an ironic twist of history, after the fleet left Long Beach, it steamed on to San Francisco and Seattle, before heading across the Pacific to Asia and through the Suez Canal to the Mediterranean. While taking on coal at Port Said, Egypt, Rear Admiral Charles Sperry received notification that a massive earthquake had struck the city of Messina in Sicily. The fleet finished coaling up, then steamed full speed to Sicily, where it rendered aid to the citizens there. It was a mission of Navy mercy that would be repeated, a lot closer to home, almost twenty-five years later.

Down to Business

Through all the territorial drama and politics taking place during the first decade of the 20th century, the development of the harbor proceeded as planned. The Long Beach business community was eager to see the harbor and the shipyard succeed and both were already attracting new industry and new money to the city. The shipyard had brought jobs to the community, and the willingness of the Craigs to invest in Long Beach encouraged other businesses to do the same.

The harbor project also offered opportunity for the local business community to directly share in the benefits of the harbor and shipyard projects. In the spring of 1909, a group of San Francisco investors proposed joining with investors in Long Beach to build a $195,000 steamship. The San Francisco people would put up $100,000, and lenders were willing to put up $50,000 to be paid back a year after completion of the vessel. If the Long Beach folks could come up with $45,000, the deal could be consummated. The 260-foot ship would be able to carry 250 passengers and 2,500 tons of cargo.

Incorporation papers for the Western Steam Navigation Co. were filed on October 9, 1909. Directors included four San Francisco men and three from Long Beach – George H. Bixby, J.F. Craig, and Stephen Townsend.

Two months later, Craig announced a second contract, this one with the Hammond Lumber Co. of San Francisco for a $225,000 ship. Work on both the Western Steam Navigation Co. ship and the Hammond Lumber ship were to proceed at the same time. There was also a third – smaller – order, this one to provide machinery for a large wooden steamer. All told, Craig had a half-million dollars in orders to fulfill, and he needed more workers. To get them, he had to hire skilled shipbuilders from Seattle, San Francisco, and Toledo, where the company's former shipyard was located, and bring them to Long Beach.

The Western Steam Navigation ship *Navajo* was to be used in passenger and freight service between San Diego and Portland. The Hammond Lumber ship *General Hubbard* would transport lumber from the forests of the Pacific Northwest to California, where it would be used to build housing and commercial structures to service the burgeoning population. And a new venture – the Long Beach Steamship Co. – was incorporated with the intent to order a $200,000 steamship from the shipyard.

Although the channels from the shipyard out to sea were not yet deep enough to accommodate the new ships, work on the vessels commenced with the confidence that by the time the ships were complete, the channels would be dredged and the ships would be able to reach the open ocean. That was not as big a gamble as it may sound. Work on the harbor project was proceeding steadily despite some bumps along the way. The harbor was seen as a magnet for new industry.

The city already had a number of industrial facilities in town, including a brickyard north of the city, lumber yards and lumber mills near residential areas, fishing and cannery businesses, and an Edison Electric Light Co. with its buildings and gas tanks. The Salt Lake Railroad, which serviced many of those businesses, was building new spur lines throughout the city to be used to pick up and deliver freight at the various locations. People complained about the noise and the smells that accompanied those businesses, many of which were considered eyesores in a city that saw itself as a seaside resort. It's a battle that would plague Long Beach for years.

The harbor was seen as the ideal place for new industry to locate and for established industries to relocate. Soon after development of the harbor got underway, the City Trustees passed an ordinance prohibiting industries located in the central area of town from improving or expanding their facilities at their current locations. Other industrial zones were set aside north of the city and in the Zaferia District – near what is now Redondo Avenue and Anaheim Street – but which at the time were not part of the city proper.

On July 1, 1909, the dredge opened a channel from the harbor to the sea. It was a milestone for the project, but it almost proved fatal for Dana Burks, the entrepreneur who planned the harbor project and raised the cash to develop it. Burks wanted to be the first to use the new channel at night, and he wanted to check the water depths, so he secured a boat and hired two workers to handle it and set out at around 10 p.m. The current was so strong that it swept the boat into the nearby breakers and flipped Burks and the others out. Fortunately, Mayor Windham, who was working near the dredger, saw the accident and immediately sent a launch out to rescue the men. All survived.

For the harbor to succeed and attract business, it would have to offer more than just a place for ships to unload. It would have to provide a way for the cargo to be delivered to and from the waterfront. In July 1910, the Dock and Terminal Co. signed a deal for the Pacific Electric Railway to own and operate a beltline railway that would give all three railroads – the Southern Pacific, the Salt Lake, and the Santa Fe – access to the harbor. For a "nominal fee," the port transferred right of way for the Pacific Electric to build and operate the line. The Pacific Electric agreed to build a track to anywhere in the harbor where freight was offered in carload lots. The total right of way included about ten miles of trackage and a switching yard 200 feet wide and 4,000 feet long. There would also be public roadways provided for the movement of freight. The idea was that no one railroad would dominate the harbor, as had been common at other ports.

"We decided to have a harbor that's free to everybody," Dock and Terminal President C.J. Curtis told a luncheon meeting of the Realty Board at the Hotel Julian. "A man can drive his wagon up to our harbor and have the same hauling privileges as a corporation."

With completion of the harbor all but assured, Long Beach residents prepared to vote on a proposed forty-year, $245,000 harbor bond that would finance a municipal wharf in the new inner harbor. The city would pay the Los Angeles Dock and Terminal Co. $200,000 for 2,100 feet of water frontage. Construction of the wharf would cost $45,000. The vote was set for September 3, 1909.

On August 30, a committee of real estate men, bankers, and merchants began a four-day "educational campaign" to get the measure approved. Skeptics were treated to a tour of the inner harbor to show the work that had been done and the site where the municipal dock would be located. There was no organized opposition to the measure. The bonds passed easily – 1,235 to 278 – but they were not without controversy.

The bonds were bought by the National Bank of Long Beach through bank President P.E. Hatch, who, according to the Long Beach Press, "bucked" a proposed combination of eastern bond buyers to make the deal and who helped preserve the credit of Long Beach in financial circles. Interest on the bonds would be 4½ percent. The Dock and Terminal Co. deal provided that the city wouldn't hand over the final $50,000 payment for the property until the channels were twenty feet deep at low tide. The National Bank promised to hold that amount out of the bond issue until the time came. If that took a year, it would save the city $2,250.

But not everybody thought it was that great a deal.

A few weeks later when Mayor Windham was running for re-election, his opponent, H.S. Callahan, questioned the award of the bonds to the National Bank of Long Beach. The Windham supporters claimed that awarding the bonds to the local bank saved taxpayers thousands of dollars, but the actual deal tells another story, Callahan said. The whole bond issue was sold on the first bid offered, he noted, adding that the mayor did not demand second bids.

"Possibly the 'special privileges' in this case went where they could do the most good – to the cause of Windham," he said.

Callahan's suspicions carried little weight with the voters. Windham was a popular and charismatic mayor. He won re-election by a 56 percent majority – 1,556 to 1,232.

Despite the political good will enjoyed by the mayor and his pro-business colleagues on the City Council and in other municipal offices, not everybody was happy with the way things were. It was a time of great opportunity, and many businessmen were building wealth, but some working folks felt that they were getting less than their share of the general prosperity. On June 1, 1910, numerous metal workers across Southern California walked off the job at five or six large companies and forty to fifty smaller ones. The Metal Trades Council estimated that 1,000 workers in all had joined in the strike, crippling the metal working industry. The employers maintained that a few more than 200 people had left and that the strike had little noticeable effect.

One of those larger employers was the Craig Shipbuilding Co. at the Long Beach Harbor. Craig was about halfway along with construction of the Hammond Lumber Co.'s *General Hubbard* lumber ship. Construction of the *Navajo* for the Western Steam Navigation Co. was also well along, and that company was considering ordering a second ship. Business was good. But the workers had given shipyard President John F. Craig an ultimatum. Give the workers an average fifteen cent-per-hour raise and a reduction in the work day from ten to eight hours by June 1, 1910, or else. Craig was not a man who responded well to ultimatums. When the day came without a raise or reduction in hours, seventy-five union machinists, pattern makers, fitters, molders, and riveters walked off the job. The union would later put the number of striking workers at 136.

In any case, Craig refused to meet with the strikers, telling the press that the strike had not seriously affected production and vowing to "let the plant rot" before letting it become a union shop. Three days after the strike, Craig received a petition from his loyal workers asking for Saturday afternoon off without a reduction in pay. He agreed to allow the half-day off, but refused to pay the men for their time off, adding that he was paying workers 20 percent more than workers at shipyards in the East. He also reported a plot by striking workers to dynamite the nearby bunk houses of Japanese laborers employed at the plant. Police posted guards at the lodgings, but no evidence of such a plot was found. Although the use of explosives in labor disputes may seem strange, at the time in the labor movement, it was not unheard of. The strikers were indignant in their denials of any such plot, voicing suspicions that such rumors were simply an attempt by anti-union forces to smear the strikers' cause.

For the city, the issue went beyond a labor dispute at one local business. This was a time when manufacturers from across the country were looking at Long Beach as a possible site for opening plants. How the community addressed the issue of an open shop was being closely watched. The Chamber of Commerce on July 21, 1910, voted 19 to 3 by secret ballot to back Craig's stand. Its resolution read in part:

> *Whereas inquiries have come to members of the Chamber of Commerce from manufacturers who are contemplating the establishment of factories in this city as to the attitude this city takes on questions of the open shop, be it,*
>
> *Resolved by the Long Beach Chamber of Commerce that this body places itself squarely on record as unalterably in favor of the principles of the 'open shop' and pledges its unswerving loyalty to the same.*

A week later, at Craig's behest, the City Council tentatively passed an anti-picketing ordinance after a meeting in which union supporters argued their case. Final passage of the law was postponed one week so the union members could bring an attorney in to plead their case. Attorneys for Craig Shipbuilding and the Los Angeles Employers Association also presented their arguments.

The final ordinance, as passed by the Council on July 29, barred strikers from displaying banners, using loud or boisterous language, interfering with people going to work or attempting to stop people from purchasing goods from the business being struck. Picketing was forbidden in the vicinity of the shipyard. City Attorney Stephen G. Long said "in the vicinity" meant within two or three blocks. The councilmen refused a suggestion by Craig's attorney that they sit as an arbitration board to settle the strike. Craig said he was willing to meet with the Council to give his side of the dispute, but he flatly refused to meet with the union.

On August 2, the day the ordinance took effect, the city arrested union members picketing the shipyard and jailed them. More strikers picketed, and more were arrested – with more than forty reportedly being arrested on August 8 alone. The Long Beach jail had capacity for only about ten prisoners, so almost all of the picketers arrested that day were released on their own recognizance. In addition to the aggressive enforcement of the anti-picketing law, Judge Water

CIVIC MILESTONE: *Long Beach luminaries gather for the christening of the* General Hubbard, *the first steel full-size ship built in Southern California, on December 3, 1910. John Craig stands toward the center-left, front row with his hands in his pockets, flanked by the elderly Jotham Bixby and a heavily mustachioed Charles Windham, then Long Beach's mayor. The* Hubbard's *launch came shortly after a nasty strike at the shipyard, with workers achieving little, although labor would gain influence in years to come.*

Bordwell issued an injunction mandating contempt of court charges if any striker or his agent or attorney stopped a worker, intimidated a worker, or talked to a worker or even to a worker's family.

Mayor Windham on August 16 delivered a communication from the strikers to Craig, demanding that their original demands be met, plus additional concessions, including replacement of all Japanese laborers with white men within thirty days, the reinstatement of all former employees, and a new arrangement for piece workers. Craig was unmoved. Despite his continued refusal of striker demands and his denial that the strike had any impact on production, Craig was critical of the city for not prosecuting strikers more vigorously. The problem was that it turned out to be difficult to get convictions, possibly because of how aggressively the city had been enforcing the law.

In one case, striker Norman McLeod was acquitted of picketing charges when the jury concluded after deliberating for thirty minutes that there was absolutely no evidence that the defendant had done anything more than walk along the street. This despite the fact that City Attorney Long was assisted in the prosecution by attorney Jetson, who worked for Craig. Among the jurors in the case were Lewellyn Bixby and C.A. Buffum, both prominent businessmen.

In the end, the city began to feel the pinch, even after capacity to hold prisoners was increased. It cost the city about $18 a day to feed and house each of the incarcerated strikers. With about thirty strikers spending several weeks in jail, the city began to feel the impact on the municipal pocketbook. The fines owed by the strikers were eventually paid by the Metal Trades Council of Los Angeles.

On December 3, 1910, the *General Hubbard* was built and ready to launch. The spectacle drew 10,000 people to the harbor area to see the first Southern California-built, full-sized steel ship slip down into the water. Spectators lined the shore, and others waited aboard about forty rowboats, sailboats and launches for the big event. The stands were filled with executives from companies that did business with the shipyard, board members of the Dock and Terminal Co., railroad people, city officials, and other dignitaries and their families.

John F. Craig, always the hands-on manager, spent the pre-launch time under and around the ship, dressed in a gray working suit and sweater vest, mingling with the workers and personally making sure that all was in order for the launch. He then joined the rest of his family on the dais for the actual event. His son, John Craig Jr., had chosen to observe the launch from onboard the ship with some of the senior shipyard staff and a few of his chums.

The ship was christened by John F. Craig's daughter, Ruth. "I christen thee *General Hubbard*," she said, swinging a bottle of champagne, suspended by a weave of red, white, and blue ribbons, against the bow. At that instant, Craig waved his hat, signaling workmen to cut the cables holding the ship in place, and the *General Hubbard* slid sideways into the water. The impact of the 266-foot ship splashing sideways into the harbor almost cost some of the spectators an unexpected drenching. The small boats rocked violently in the series of waves from the ship hitting the water as people on board held on for dear life. When the waves hit the opposite side of the channel, people had to run in order not to be doused. One woman, standing on a pontoon near the shore, was not only drenched but had to be saved from falling into the water by a quick-thinking bystander. The launch of the ship, and the excitement that followed as boaters were tossed around and the shoreline was splattered, brought a huge cheer from the crowd. It was a milestone, both for the shipyard and the city.

By the time the next ship was launched almost four months later, the shipyard's reputation for building big ships had been established. This time, the honors were done by Margaret Bixby, the 14-year-old daughter of Mr. and Mrs. George H. Bixby and granddaughter of Long Beach pioneer Jotham Bixby. George Bixby was the vice president of Western Steam Navigation Co., which owned the ship. On hand for the launch were hundreds of invited guests and about 500 high school students. The 226-foot-long, forty-two-foot-wide vessel slid into the water without incident. By the time the launch took place, the ship had already been leased to Bates & Chesebrough for a service between San Francisco and Panama, and the cargo for its first voyage booked.

Long Beach was rapidly becoming a port town. Some people were already exploring the possibility of the city buying out the Dock and Terminal Co. and taking over the port, although such discussions were still in the exploratory stages. The city had been approached by S.J.E. Taylor and Associates about the possibility of leasing a portion of the new city wharf for coal bunkers and a storage warehouse, but that deal was squelched by the city attorney.

The city's purchase of property from the Dock and Terminal Co. contained no restrictions on how the city would use the wharf, but a report by an ad hoc commission made before the purchase of the property had recommended that if the city bought the land, it must make provisions to keep the proposed facility free from the dominion and control of all private interests. That was the understanding that the people had when they voted for the bonds to build the wharf, ruled the city attorney, and the city must abide by that understanding.

On June 2, 1911, the steam schooner *Iaqua* arrived in port with a load of redwood for the Long Beach Improvement Co. It would get credit for being the first cargo ship to call at the new port – but if the port was open for business, and it was – the *Iaqua* only marked the soft opening. It wasn't until June 24 that the official grand opening took place with speeches, music, a parade, and ceremony to welcome the lumber steamer *Santa Barbara* with a load of pine for the same company. The lumber would be used by the Long Beach Improvement Co. – a venture directed by Mayor Windham and other leading citizens – to build the housing and other structures necessary to fulfill the needs of a growing population.

From the time that the Dana Burks Syndicate stated its intent to develop the wetlands west of the city until the time the port was officially opened was five years, ten months, three weeks, and four days – including acquisition, design, and execution. It was a very short time for such a big task, but things were simpler in those days. The people who developed the port were working with a blank canvas. There were few bureaucratic hoops to jump through or troublesome regulations to slow down the dream. That changed in the future as it had to. The city was growing larger and more complex. The culture was changing. People were becoming more aware of the environmental costs of unrestricted development and of the basic inequities in social, political, and economic society. But that doesn't make the achievement of the people who built the port any less impressive – the visionaries such as Charles H. Windham, Stephen Townsend, and Dana Burks; the finance people from Redlands, Long Beach, and elsewhere who risked their own money; the project administrators such as C.J. Curtis who kept the dream alive when outgo was exceeding income and unexpected obstacles threatened to delay progress on the project.

In October of 1911, President William Howard Taft visited Long Beach as part of a forty-six-day tour of the nation. Mayor Windham and other Long Beach business and city leaders escorted the president down from the University of Southern California, where he made a brief morning address to students. Children were assembled from Long Beach schools to sing for the president when he arrived, to scatter flowers at his feet and to wave flags. The president proceeded to Pacific Park, where a crowd of thousands had gathered to hear him speak. He spoke about Long Beach, recognizing it as a port city, promised federal money to help it develop further, talked about the importance of the soon-to-open Panama Canal, and the need to combat the guerrillas and revolutionaries of Central America. The president took a rest at the Hotel Virginia following his speech, and then departed Long Beach by train shortly after noon.

Long Beach had its port. The port would forever after help define the city, just as it would always be defined by the city. It had been paid for and developed by private businessmen who saw an opportunity and who were willing to risk their wealth to make the port a reality.

Charles H. Windham, the man who would later be credited as the father of the Port of Long Beach, announced that after four years in office, he would not seek re-election. The Progressive League held a "valedictory" banquet in his honor at the Municipal Auditorium on October 20, 1911. Toasts to the outgoing mayor were offered by M.B. Irvine, president of the Progressive League, Fanny Bixby, who would one day become president of the Women Voters' League, and C.E. Jarvis, president of the local City Club.

TRAVELING IN STYLE: *Charles Windham's successor as mayor, Ira Hatch, gets a lift aboard the* Santa Clara *in early 1912. The* Santa Clara *offered, for a short time, passenger service to San Francisco, but the venture was not successful. Openings and new beginnings were always good photo opportunities at the Port, but hoisting the mayor with a crane was unique.*

PART TWO:
THE EARLY YEARS

Chapter Ten:
The Port and the City

Ten years into the 20th century, the days of laissez-faire capitalism were numbered in a progressive new era that valued community over individual ambition and order over chaos. In the summer of 1910, former President Theodore Roosevelt had called for a "New Nationalism" in a speech he made in Osawatomie, Kansas. In his speech, he advocated for a strong federal government, regulation of business, worker rights, a graduated income tax, an end to corporate domination of the government, and government programs to provide for those unable to provide for themselves. It was in direct opposition to the excess of the Gilded Age, and it was his declaration that human rights were more important than property rights.

> *For every special interest is entitled to justice, but not one is entitled to a vote in Congress, to a voice on the bench, or to representation in any public office. The Constitution guarantees protections to property, and we must make that promise good. But it does not give the right of suffrage to any corporation. The true friend of property, the true conservative, is he who insists that property shall be the servant and not the master of the commonwealth; who insists that the creature of man's making shall be the servant and not the master of the man who made it. The citizens of the United States must effectively control the mighty commercial forces which they have themselves called into being.*

Roosevelt's speech was his most radical. And while it reflected the frustrations felt by some in the working class, it did not necessarily reflect the reality of the day. It was an open rejection of the conservative wing of the Republican Party and of President William Howard Taft, Roosevelt's former protégé. Roosevelt later challenged Taft for the 1912 Republican nomination for president, and when it became apparent that he would not win, he formed a separate Progressive Party, commonly called the Bull Moose Party. In doing so, Roosevelt split the Republican vote, resulting in the presidential election going to Democrat Woodrow Wilson who garnered only 42 percent of the popular vote.

While the mainstream may have balked at Roosevelt's call for reform, there is no doubt that a new age had dawned. Labor unions were on the rise. Women were demanding the right to vote. A national movement was underway to ban liquor, and some people – today we would call them domestic terrorists – were using dynamite to express their frustrations with the American social order.

The Industrial Workers of the World union was organized in 1905 by radical leaders in the labor movement who were exasperated with the slow progress being made by the more moderate American Federation of Labor. At a time when government regularly restricted the rights of union members to public assembly and free speech and used police and company strikebreakers to attack union troublemakers, some of the more militant people in the movement began expressing themselves with violent actions instead of just words. In 1906, the Iron Workers Union planned a covert bombing campaign aimed at convincing employers to recognize and negotiate with the union. Over the next four years, more than 200 construction and plant sites were bombed around the nation.

On October 1, 1910, a bomb planted alongside the Los Angeles Times building exploded, killing twenty-one men, injuring almost 100 more, and gutting the building in the subsequent fire. The Times had been targeted because of its open hostility toward unions and the campaign by its publisher to keep them out of California. Two brothers, members of the Iron Workers Union, were arrested, tried, and sentenced to jail. They were represented by famed attorney Clarence Darrow. It appears the bombing was intended as a crime against property, not against the workers themselves, but the timing device, which had been set for a time that the building was supposedly vacant, malfunctioned, and the bomb exploded when the building was full of people. Further, the bomb had unwittingly been placed near a natural gas line which ruptured and resulted in the catastrophic fire. Unexploded bombs were found the next day at the homes of Times publisher Harrison Gray Otis and Merchants and Manufacturers Association Secretary F.J. Zeehandelaar, as well as at a non-union construction site, making it seem likely that these bombers were more mal-intentioned than those who bombed the Times building.

The bombing of the Times building was condemned by organized labor, including the Iron Workers, and many expressed doubts that any unionist would do such a thing. In the end, it was clearly proven that the union officials had been behind the act, and the bombing actually set back the union cause. But the days of business as usual were over. The battle lines had been drawn. The days of unconditional support for the captains of industry were clearly coming to an end.

It was a time when big things were happening – including big disasters.

In Mexico, a revolution broke out in late 1910 as liberal and radical leaders joined forces to overthrow the administration of Mexican President Porfirio Díaz. There is no accurate account of how many Mexicans lost their lives in that internal strife, but the numbers are figured in the hundreds of thousands and perhaps even millions. As the carnage raged in Mexico, a flood of refugees fled north into the United States, many of them settling in Southern California.

In 1912, the *Titanic* sank on its maiden voyage; Zane Grey's novel *Riders of the Purple Sage* was published, and the Oreo cookie was introduced. In 1913, the Owens Valley Aqueduct began to quench Los Angeles' thirst for water, the 16th Amendment to the Constitution was passed providing for a graduated income tax, and California Governor Hiram Johnson signed a bill prohibiting Japanese-Americans from owning land in the state.

By 1914, the Panama Canal connected the Atlantic to the Pacific, the first traffic light was installed, and World War I had broken out in Europe. A year later, the British ocean liner *RMS Lusitania* was sunk by a German submarine, killing

1,198 people; the San Francisco World's Fair hosted more than 13 million visitors, and Germany used poison gas for the first time as a weapon.

President Woodrow Wilson won re-election in 1916, campaigning with the slogan, "He kept us out of war." It was only a year later that Wilson asked Congress for a declaration of war, after the interception of a German missive urging Mexico to declare war on the United States and indicating Germany would help Mexico take back California, Texas and the other territory it had lost sixty-eight years previously.

World War I was called the "War to End All Wars," but that turned out to be a wildly optimistic fantasy. Even so, the war turned out to be far from the deadliest disaster of the time. The death toll from World War I, which ended in 1918, has been estimated at 16 million people. The worldwide influenza pandemic of 1918-19 killed an estimated 30 million to 50 million people across the globe – 675,000 of them in the United States. Although it draws scant attention in most history texts, that pandemic remains the most lethal event of its kind in history.

The 1910s were indeed tumultuous years for the world, and for the emerging port town tucked into San Pedro Bay.

The Port, the Community, and the Local Economy

In 1910, Long Beach was the fastest growing city in the United States with 17,800 residents and more moving in every day. It was no longer the sleepy little village by the sea. There was a mix of residents, businesses, and industries that were sometimes a little too close for comfort. The city had already passed an ordinance barring industries in close proximity to residential areas from expanding their operations at their current locations. The opening of the Long Beach Harbor and the privately owned area surrounding it provided the city an industrial area that could generate jobs and ensure economic health without the growing conflict caused by industrial businesses operating adjacent to residential areas. The presence and success of the Craig Shipbuilding yard helped convince more industries to take a look at locating facilities in the harbor.

When the Southern California Edison Co. announced in 1910 that it planned to build a huge electrical generating plant at the new Long Beach Harbor – the biggest steam power plant west of Chicago – it was an added incentive to the capitalists of the day who were looking for a new site. Edison already had a building and gas tanks on a downtown bluff in Long Beach, but those had drawn complaints because they blocked the view and smelled bad. The plant on the west side of the entrance to the harbor would be well-removed from the homes along Ocean Boulevard.

The Edison Co. began building its $2 million power plant in 1911 and started producing electricity with one oil-fired steam generator the following year. Two more were added over the next two years. Having a close source of electrical power also encouraged new industry. In 1910 the Pacific Electric Co. laid track throughout the harbor. Two 250-foot-tall high-tension transmission towers were installed by Edison in 1912 near what today is the Cerritos Channel. The towers were designed so they would clear the masts of sailing ships, and they remained in service well into the 21st century.

Lumber to provide housing for a growing population, as well as for commercial uses, remained the major commodity moving through the harbor.

The Long Beach Port continued to grow – mostly by meeting the demand for building and household supplies for the burgeoning population. The presence of the nearby port helped the surrounding communities fulfill their residents' desires for consumer goods. In 1911, the State of California approved a tidelands grant for the City of Long Beach to administer the port area. A similar grant was provided for Los Angeles to administer its harbor area.

The Long Beach Tidelands Grant provided that the city held all the rights, title, and interests in all the tidelands and submerged lands – filled or unfilled – within the city boundaries. The granted rights were to be "forever held" by the city – but there were strings attached. The lands had to be used only for the "promotion and accommodation of commerce and navigation." The grant also provided that the people of California would have "the absolute right to fish in the waters of said harbor, with the right of convenient access to said waters over said lands for said purpose." That Tidelands Grant and the extent of the city's rights to the land would be both challenged and amended over the years, but the philosophy behind it would remain much the same as it had been when it was originally made. The city had ownership and control over the land, but only for certain specified purposes.

In 1912, the Star Drilling Machine Co. of Akron, Ohio, set up a three-acre site in Long Beach Harbor and started shipping drilling and hydraulic equipment abroad. The company claimed Star rigs were used in 95 percent of the oil drilling in the world that was done with portable rigs. Whether that was true or just company hyperbole isn't really known, but one thing is certain. Star Drilling held the record for producing the largest number of a particular kind of drill used in construction of the Panama Canal, which opened in 1914. The company supplied 214 machines that were used for drilling blast holes and other canal work. Those machines permitted the rapid removal of tons of rock and earth that obstructed construction of the canal.

The harbor industrial zone continued to grow. The Western Boat Works and the Long Beach Salt Co. were already established in the area. Other companies began to locate in the harbor, including the California Glass Insulator factory, the American Potash Co., two fish canneries, the Union Oil refinery, the Long Beach Iron Works, the Salmarine Soap Co., the California Woolen Mills Manufacturing Co., the Looff Amusement Device factory, and several lumber yards and planing mills.

The California Glass Insulator factory – reportedly the only glass plant on the Pacific Coast – opened for business on a ten-acre site on Anaheim Street in the harbor area, using silica sand from the Bixby Ranch. It started out with eight months' worth of orders for glass insulators that were used in power and telegraph lines and a plan to branch out into other glassware items as soon as possible. Within three months of beginning operation, the company had shipped its first order of glass bottles. By January 1913, the company announced a five-year order from Pacific States Electric Co. of San Francisco for its entire output of glass insulators. Eighteen months later, California Glass merged with the Bloom Jar Co. of San Francisco. Bloom Jar, a major supplier for the H.J. Heinz Co. of Pittsburgh, had a patent for a hermetically sealed glass bottle, suitable as a sanitary container for milk and other such contamination-prone products. The merger put Bloom Jar in a good position to take advantage of the all-water connection to the East Coast when the Panama Canal opened the following year. It also would allow the company to manufacture the bottles themselves on the West Coast, rather than ship them to California from plants in the East.

"It's a plain, simple business proposition," Bloom Jar President Dave Bloom told the Los Angeles Times. "At present, 600 carloads of soda bottles, 300 carloads of beer bottles, and a similar number of carloads of milk bottles are used yearly in Southern California. To ship these bottles here from Illinois and other producing centers costs about $500 a carload. We hope eventually to supply the Southern California market with homemade goods that will not only cost the consumers less, but will be of higher quality." Bloom and his family moved to Southern California where he opened a distribution office to handle the local glass business and to oversee the relationship with companies in Japan that manufactured porcelain containers with the Bloom Jar cap.

The Kelp Cutters

California Glass wasn't the only business that found new opportunities in the harbor area, although not all of the ventures ended so happily. In February of 1913, the American Potash Co. began moving into a ten-acre site it bought on the upper end of Channel Three in the Long Beach Harbor. The company needed a waterfront location because it planned to manufacture potash by harvesting the undersea forests of giant kelp present off the California coast.

Potash refers to potassium compounds used to make fertilizers, various medical compounds, soaps, bleaching powders, explosives, and a variety of other industrial products. It has been around almost as long as civilization itself, and was originally made by using a pot to leech potassium salts from the ashes of burned plants. In fact, the name of the element potassium was derived from the word potash. Today most potash is mined as a mineral, but in 1913, American Potash had plans to turn the millions of tons of what was then seen as useless kelp into a cash crop. There was an inexhaustible supply of the undersea weed right off Point Fermin and the Palos Verdes Peninsula, the company claimed, and it planned to harvest and process 2,000 tons per day. In addition to potassium, the kelp contained sodium, chlorides, nitrogen, calcium, and magnesium – all of which could be refined and sold. A side benefit of the planned harvest was that the company's small fleet of boats would be clearing away the kelp from the entrances to the harbors.

American Potash was the pioneer in the kelp-harvesting field. At the time, the method of gathering the kelp involved pulling the kelp onboard from skiffs or small barges and cutting it by hand into six-inch segments. It would then be transported to shore where it would be fed by conveyer belt into a rotary drier fueled by crude oil. Some of the dried kelp was sold in that state for fertilizer, the rest was burned and the ashes processed as potash. Unfortunately, the final product could not compete with the lower-cost potash that was then being imported. But the world and the marketplace were rapidly changing. Germany had been the dominant international supplier of potash, but with war about to break out in Europe, Germany had declared an embargo on all potash exports, both so it would have enough to supply its own needs for munitions and to deny such supplies to its enemies, both actual and potential. The time seemed ripe to exploit the fresh new source of potash on the West Coast.

In 1913, Pacific Kelp Mulch Co. built the first successful mechanical kelp harvester, which featured an underwater cutting blade in front and a conveyor belt that extended about four feet underwater. The blade would cut the kelp, and the belt would lift it up onto the barge and into a gasoline-powered hopper where it was chopped up. Turning kelp into potash was an expensive business, and what worked on a small scale didn't necessarily translate to a large-scale commercial operation.

In October of 1915, American Potash was purchased by George H. Simmons of the St. Louis-based Simmons Hardware Co. Simmons Hardware, which had outlets throughout the Midwest, manufactured a variety of items ranging from children's wagons and ice skates to pocket knives and shotguns, and George Simmons had been a major financial backer of American Potash. With the purchase made, the name American Potash was changed to American Products Co., the plant was expanded, new equipment was installed, and a spur line from the Salt Lake Railroad was laid.

Other companies also began entering the kelp business. By 1916, there were eleven companies in the Southern California kelp-harvesting business, including six major players. In addition to American Products, there were the National Kelp Potash Co. and the Sea Products Co. in Long Beach, Swift & Co. in San Diego, Diamond Match Co. in the Los Angeles Harbor, and the Hercules Powder Co. in Chula Vista. Of all the plants, the Hercules Powder Co. was the largest, with most of its production going to wartime munitions.

With harbor shipbuilding companies building new kelp-harvesting boats and numerous companies producing potash along the coast, the inexhaustible supply of kelp turned out to be somewhat more exhaustible than first assumed. In order to protect the kelp beds for future harvesting, the Los Angeles County Board of Supervisors in 1916 passed an ordinance banning the cutting of kelp deeper than six feet below the surface. In July of 1916, six local companies in the kelp industry – American Products, Sea Products, National Products, Pacific Coast Products, Diamond Match Co., and Oceanic Corp. – formed the Pacific Kelp Manufacturers' Association to conserve the kelp supply. The plant and assets for American Products were sold the following month to a new company, Lorned Manufacturing. George Simmons was president of the new firm, which was also a subsidiary of Simmons Hardware. Even with the conservation efforts begun, by the following spring the kelp beds off Point Fermin and White's Point along the Palos Verdes Peninsula and Point Dume north of Malibu had been stripped. It was expected to take an extended period in order for the kelp in those locations to recover to a level suitable for further harvesting, and the kelp companies began scouting new kelp beds to exploit, some as far away as Santa Cruz.

The rise of competition and the corresponding decline of the available kelp resources wasn't the only problem facing the new companies. In April 1917, arsonists hit two of the potash plants in Long Beach, igniting a fire at the Lorned Manufacturing plant in Long Beach on April 24 and hitting the nearby National Kelp and Potash Co. the following day. The Lorned fire only destroyed the incinerator tower and ash bin, but the National Kelp fire gutted the building. The fires were believed to have been set by German agent-saboteurs to help stem the production of potash that could be used for war munitions. Harbor manufacturers hired the William Burns Detective Agency to investigate who was responsible, and the California Shipbuilding Co., working both day and night shifts on government contracts, hired extra guards. National Kelp went out of business after the fire, and Lorned Manufacturing moved its plant from Long

Beach to Summerland, south of Santa Barbara. Reasons for the move were the fierce competition for kelp in the Long Beach area, the availability of kelp stands in the Santa Barbara Channel, and difficulties with harbor facilities at the Long Beach site.

During the war, the California kelp industry was the second-largest provider of potash in the United States, surpassed only by the mining of potassium salts from lake beds. But at the end of the war, despite the high hopes and the best efforts of the companies involved, the industry collapsed. American potash buyers signed contracts with the German Kali Syndikat to supply 75 percent of the U.S. demand. The French got the other 25 percent of the U.S. market. In January 1919, Lorned Manufacturing – the company that had started the commercial production of potash from kelp as American Potash Co. in Long Beach Harbor – shut the doors of its Summerland plant. The foreign producers, it was said, deliberately undercut the market in order to destroy the fledgling American industry. The potash industry had a spectacular rise with an abrupt and sorry end. It had lasted five years, provided the nation with a vital resource from an overlooked source, and when it was over, it was over for good.

Chicken of the Sea

Fish canneries were also becoming big business in Southern California during the early years of the Port of Long Beach. The first cannery, the California Fish Co. in East San Pedro, was founded in 1893 by Alfred P. Halfhill, a wholesale grocer from Mankato, Minnesota, who had moved to California for his wife's health, and his partner, Robert David Wade, a local merchant. The company began canning sardines and mackerel, which the company's one fishing boat, the *Alpha*, scooped with nets out of San Pedro Bay. The cans were cut by hand from tin sheets and soldered; the sardines were sold through local merchants.

When the sardine population declined in 1902, Halfhill looked around for other fish to can. The answer was tuna – typically known as tunny fish in England. Tuna had been eaten for centuries in Italy and Japan, but it was not considered a food fish in the United States, where it was a popular game fish because of the battle it would wage after it was hooked. Halfhill changed that by using Japanese fishermen to catch tuna using lines attached to bamboo poles, thus avoiding the blood spots caused by the fish struggling to escape the net. He also started marketing the product across the nation, advertising that it was free of bones and skin with a flavor that "slightly resembles the white meat of chicken…" In 1908, California Fish Co. branded its new product as "Blue Sea Brand Tuna" and purchased automated can-making equipment. By 1910, the company packed 6,000 cases of albacore and began advertising directly to the public. The following year they packed 14,000 cases, and more companies began getting into the tuna business.

The South Coast Canning Co. built a plant in the Long Beach Harbor in 1910 and began selling Avalon Brand Tuna. White Star Tuna opened in San Pedro calling itself "The Home of Chicken of the Sea." Other new canneries opened in San Pedro, Wilmington, San Diego, and even in the Pacific Northwest – all playing on the similarity between steamed canned tuna and chicken. South Coast Canning claimed in its advertising that "Avalon Brand Tuna is so delicately flavored – so white and tender that there is little to choose between this 'chicken of the sea' and the two-legged kind." By 1912, California tuna canneries produced

80,000 cases, and the tuna boom was on. The Los Angeles Tuna Canning Co. in Long Beach soon joined the pack with its Panama Brand Tuna. By 1913, there were nine companies that produced a total of 128,000 cases of tuna, and people who had established themselves as dealers were making big money. By the end of the decade, there would be six canneries in Long Beach, fifteen in San Pedro and Wilmington, and nine in San Diego.

Music, Glamor, and Tragedy

The port wasn't the only big business booming in Long Beach. More than a port city, Long Beach was known to the public as a tourist mecca. Visitors from both faraway and nearby inland cities would flock to Long Beach to enjoy the waves, the family entertainment, and the cool sea breezes. There was the Pike amusement park, the pleasure pier, and the bathhouses lined along the oceanfront. Unlike some seaside venues – such as Venice – that attracted visitors interested in drinking, gambling, and other "sinful pleasures," Long Beach was the place where people could bring the whole family for some good, clean fun. And the people who lived in Long Beach were determined to keep things that way.

In 1908, the residents of Long Beach voted down a small tax to fund a municipal band. Such a band already existed – an Italian band led by Nicola Donatelli – but it was sponsored by local subscribers, which had proved to be an unreliable funding source. The time seemed right for the city to pick up the costs. The election results, however, had less to do with the idea of a city-sponsored municipal band than what kind of band it would be. The Los Angeles Herald reported the defeat in its September 8 edition:

> *Those who voted against the proposition today did so because the municipal band is an Italian organization, and it was believed that if the vote carried, the city would employ Italians instead of Americans. It is probable that now the city will not have any band at all. There is great disappointment among progressive citizens and lovers of music, as the band has always proved a big drawing card for Long Beach.*

But the musical setback was only temporary. The city did get its municipal band, led by a good American bandleader named Harry Wiley, who was quick to fill in the gap with his own band, supplementing what he earned in the city with out-of-town gigs. The Wiley municipal band proved to be very popular with residents, and in 1911 city voters finally approved a municipal tax to guarantee the band's continued performance. Long Beach had become the first city in the nation to support a year-round municipal band – one led by and staffed with American musicians.

That Long Beach Midwest attitude toward what was – and what was not – appropriate sometimes resulted in the city turning its back on opportunities. An example is the movie studios. Long Beach was the center of filmmaking long before Los Angeles lured away the business. Based in Long Beach, the Balboa Amusements Producing Co., one of the biggest movie studios in the world at the time, required all its employees to live in Long Beach, even the stars. The silent stars of the movies from 1910 to 1920 were familiar sights on the streets of Long Beach. But, the moral values of the theatrical set offended many people in the city who looked askance at these new residents who were fond of drinking, dancing, and staying up late into the night. The movie folks felt the same way about Long Beach. They weren't happy about the fact that they had to drive out of town if they wanted to throw a party and have a drink. In the end, the movie studios were not a good fit for the town, and they departed for a less hostile environment.

Through it all, the city continued to prosper and be a weekend destination for visitors, especially during the summer when between 50,000 and 75,000 people would head to Long Beach to beat the heat and enjoy a day at the beach. The good times turned to tragedy, however, on May 24, 1913, when thousands gathered in Long Beach to celebrate the British Empire and what would have been the 96th birthday of the late Queen Victoria. As the Long Beach Municipal Band played, residents and visitors alike sang along and marched in place on the elevated gangway approach to the Municipal Auditorium from the beach. At 11:33 a.m. the gangway collapsed, dropping at least 250 people to the beach below. Thirty-six died immediately, and another fourteen died later from their injuries.

If the disaster was profound, so was the response. City officials, police officers, and civilians immediately jumped into action to recover the dead and save the injured who had been dropped one atop the other in what was later dubbed the "death pit." A makeshift system of pulleys and ropes belonging to an electrical contractor was hooked to an automobile, which would drive up the hill, pulling timbers and flooring off the people who had fallen. Some of the injured were carried out by volunteers, some lifted by rope strung around their bodies to get to a place where they could be helped. It took forty-five minutes to recover all the victims. Long Beach policeman T.A. Combs, who broke two of his ribs trying to rescue the injured buried underneath bodies and debris, stayed on the job until all had been recovered. Doctors and nurses rushed to the scene to administer to the wounded at a makeshift hospital on the sand. A train arrived from Los Angeles with fifty additional policemen and more doctors and nurses. Also attending to the wounded and making coffee for volunteers were Iola Hatch, wife of Mayor Ira Hatch, and Augusta Callahan, wife of local businessman Henry S. Callahan. Both women worked into the night. Former Mayor Charles H. Windham lowered two flags in front of City Hall to half-staff – the first was the American flag and the second was the British flag that was on display for the Empire Day celebration. It was the worst disaster for the city of Long Beach up to that point – a day full of tears and panic. But it was also a day of heroism and compassion, a day when the Long Beach community was confronted with tragic circumstance and responded with brave compassion and grim determination.

But the pain of that day would not soon be forgotten. Although city attorneys advised that the city was not legally liable in the disaster, voters approved a one-time tax levy to provide for a $60,000 relief fund. The Relief Committee estimated the direct costs of the disaster at $15,000 for undertaking and funeral expenses, $35,000 in medical care for the injured, and $10,000 in aid to the dependent families. In the aftermath, voters would turn down a series of bond issues aimed at rebuilding the old auditorium. It would be fifteen years before Long Beach was ready to approve such a project.

The Problem with Silt

Turning a mudflat into a harbor was only the first challenge for entrepreneurs determined to build a port for Long Beach. After completing the Long Beach

Harbor project, the Los Angeles Dock and Terminal Co. had to operate what it had built and improve upon it. But there were problems. When the idea for dredging a harbor was conceived, engineers were not that concerned about silt washing down the Los Angeles River during the rainy season. The river was dry during most of the year because the water was siphoned off to supply the city and for farm irrigation. Even in the rainy season, the amount of silt deposited in the harbor was expected to be slight. But that optimistic assessment was flawed. The "tramp rivers" of Los Angeles County were notorious for their unpredictability. The Los Angeles River before 1825 – as far back as the historical records go – used to empty into the Pacific Ocean near the later communities of Playa del Rey and Marina del Rey. Then, during a flood year, it changed course and emptied into San Pedro Bay. Before 1867, the San Gabriel River to the east also emptied into San Pedro Bay. In the winter of 1867-68 – another flood year – the San Gabriel changed course and emptied into Alamitos Bay instead.

The rainfall during the winter of 1910-11 was not unusually heavy, but it resulted in flooding and some loss of property along the San Gabriel River, which by then emptied into Alamitos Bay. During that flood, the river cut a new channel, sending much of the flood water west where it joined the Los Angeles River about five miles north of the harbor. The resulting flow carried an estimated 350,000 cubic yards of mud downstream into the harbor area, undoing dredging work that had already been completed. The amount of rainfall isn't the only factor that contributes to flooding. Other factors include how much rain falls over a short period, what kind of land exists along the river bank, and whether the ground is too saturated to soak up the excess water. By the early 20th century, the natural circumstances had been exacerbated by the mass migration of new residents to Southern California, and the increase in population and industry had changed the flood dynamic. All those rooftops and paved roads reduced the amount of land available for soaking up the water, and the riparian benefits for property owners along the river for irrigation and exploitation of the river's wealth led them to take action that impacted their neighbors downstream.

Consulting engineer Frank H. Olmsted, in a report to the Board of Supervisors in October 1913, noted the fickle nature of the various rivers that carried storm flows to the sea in Los Angeles County. During the five previous years, the extraction of rocks and gravel by "rock crusher outfits near Duarte" had tended to shift the course of the river toward the west, he said.

Property owners along the banks of the San Gabriel River and the new channel that had redirected the flow toward the ports had also begun to take action to protect their land from erosion and flooding by erecting structures to divert and control the flow. While those steps served to protect the interest of the people upstream, they had consequences downstream. By 1913, more than nine-tenths of the flow from the San Gabriel River was emptying into the San Pedro Bay through the Long Beach and Los Angeles harbors. Although the buildup of silt during the 1910-11 rainy season had caused problems in the harbor area, such instances should only occur perhaps once a decade and were not so severe that they couldn't be handled by periodic dredging. Or so people thought.

Money for the Port
Even before the Long Beach Harbor officially opened, the business community had been lobbying the federal government for the kind of harbor improvements

that were being provided for the Port of Los Angeles next door. In September of 1910, Mayor Charles Windham, John F. Craig of Craig Shipbuilding, C.J. Curtis of the Los Angeles Dock and Terminal Co., and an assortment of business leaders and city officials met over lunch with U.S. Army Engineer Captain W.P. Stokey at the Hotel Virginia to tell him about the Long Beach Harbor project and to make a pitch for government improvements. Long Beach wanted the government to deepen the channel from the ocean to the turning basin to thirty feet and perhaps also to finish the dredging of the turning basin. The city leaders also wanted to dredge the Cerritos Slough into a shipping channel capable of accommodating seagoing vessels that would provide an inner-harbor connection between the Long Beach and Los Angeles ports. Such a channel, it was reasoned, would be beneficial to both ports, since it would provide access to the Los Angeles inner harbor in case the main channel happened to be blocked by a vessel that sank or some other obstruction. Provision for a survey of both Southern California ports was included in the Rivers and Harbors Act of 1912.

The preliminary survey by Los Angeles District Engineer Lieutenant Colonel C.H. McKinstry was completed on January 3, 1913, and the final survey was submitted on December 26 of that same year. McKinstry's report noted that the financial commitment of more than $1.5 million made by the Los Angeles Dock and Terminal Co. in developing the harbor, the $245,000 bond issue that had been passed in 1909 to build a municipal wharf with rail connections, and the raising of $100,000 by private citizens to purchase a forty-acre site in the harbor, were inducements for Craig Shipbuilding Co. to locate in Long Beach.

Since then, the shipyard had built two dredges, a tug, and three steamships, and was in the process of building four more steamships. In addition, the Craig shipyard had docked fifty-five vessels in its floating dry dock for repairs or maintenance. The Western Steam Navigation Co., with about half the stock owned by Long Beach residents, owned two steamships – the *Navajo* and the *Camino* – that had been built at the Craig shipyard. The Long Beach Steamship Co., almost wholly owned by Long Beach residents, had purchased one steamship from the Craig yard – the *Paraiso* – and had placed an order for another. Meanwhile, the Dock and Terminal Co. had continued to dredge the harbor, clearing the silt that came downstream during the previous year and filling in new land.

Establishment of the Long Beach municipal wharf had resulted in a reduction of about $5 per thousand feet in the price of lumber and twenty cents per barrel of cement. A considerable quantity of cement manufactured in Riverside had been shipped out from Long Beach, and lumber landed at the port had been sent by rail to inland destinations. Long Beach was clearly a city that was willing to invest in its own future, and if the harbor were deepened and more wharves provided, there would be an increase in cargo moving through the harbor.

On the other hand, McKinstry pointed out that the federal government had already invested a sizable amount in increasing the capacity of the Los Angeles port, and that port had a surplus of unused potential. It made little difference to the general public whether their freight came through one port or the other. If the government were to invest a large amount of money in Long Beach, it "would only be entering into competition with itself to provide another thirty-foot harbor four miles away."

Long Beach was not to be dissuaded by such an argument. On January 15, 1914, the people of Long Beach voted nearly 6-to-1 to approve the issuance of $650,000 in harbor bonds, which in addition to the $245,000 bonds approved in 1909 was a demonstration of the city's ongoing willingness to share in the cost of any harbor improvements. The approval came with the condition that the city funds must be matched by an equal amount of federal funding. In order to encourage support for the harbor, the business community provided hundreds of cars to carry voters to the polls, despite heavy rains.

Hearings had been held before the Army Board of Engineers on June 16, 1913, on the subject, and again on January 28, March 25, and April 7, 1914. The case for each port was argued by representatives of the cities, businesses, and elected officials. Senator John D. Works, along with Congressmen William D. Stephens of Los Angeles and Charles W. Bell of Pasadena, spoke on behalf of the ports. Works urged the Army engineers to include Long Beach in the harbor improvements on the grounds that the two ports were destined to become one.

"One mistake is to talk of the Los Angeles Harbor and the Long Beach Harbor. They are practically one harbor," Works told the board. "While we are talking about the growth of Los Angeles, we don't want to overlook Long Beach. I don't know whether our Long Beach friends will like for me to say it, but it will not be very long before all that section will be part of the City of Los Angeles. We are entitled to those improvements and we are helping liberally to make one of the great harbors of this country at that point."

There is no record of how the Long Beach Harbor advocates may have felt about Works' assumption on the inevitability of the Los Angeles-Long Beach merger, but it didn't really matter. On April 8, 1914, Army Chief of Engineers Dan C. Kingman announced the final recommendation of the Army Corps of Engineers. In his review, Kingman recommended $626,000 in improvements for the Port of Los Angeles.

> *In view of the large development of commerce in the past, the increasing population of Southern California, and the building of the Panama Canal, the district officer believes that the commerce of Los Angeles will continue to increase and that ships of greater draft will desire to use the harbor. He expresses the opinion that the locality is worthy of further improvement.*

Long Beach was a different story.

> *There is not sufficient local or general commerce at Long Beach to warrant the large expenditure by the United States as proposed by the district officer to improve this locality, and it is therefore unable to recommend the desired participation by the United States in the development of Long Beach Harbor, either in deepening and protecting the entrance channel or in dredging an interior channel to connect this harbor with the harbor of Los Angeles.*

The decision was a tough one for Long Beach. The city government, its business community, and its residents had strongly supported the harbor improvements, but any chance for the kind of government funding recommended for Los Angeles seemed lost. F.C. Roberts and Y.K. Prisk, who had gone to Washington to press the city's case, reported back to Mayor Louis N. Whealton that there was no hope of federal funding for the Long Beach Harbor, at least not in the foreseeable future. They proposed three options. The city could appeal to the War Department to set aside the findings of the Army Corps of Engineers. It could go around the Army's decision and attempt to get an amendment to the harbor bill introduced in the Senate, or it could proceed with development of the harbor through local bond issues. The third choice was the option recommended by Roberts and Prisk.

The Chamber of Commerce responded by calling for another election that would allow the bonds to be issued with or without federal funding and the money to be used for harbor improvements. The cutting off of the Long Beach Harbor from federal money threatened the existence of a port that had brought both new companies and jobs to the city. The one bright spot was that it appeared that the city's request for a new harbor survey and reconsideration of federal funding was about to be approved.

Late that summer, Colonel William Murray Black, the chairman of the Board of Engineers for Rivers and Harbors, visited Southern California and toured the ports. He talked about the bright future for the Port of Los Angeles, especially with the recent opening of the Panama Canal. He cautioned harbor interests, however, not to expect the canal to have a sudden and dramatic impact. The railroads connecting east and west could be expected to lower their freight rates in order to compete with cargo coming through the ports from the East, and the higher rail rate from west to east would result in many inland points preferring to get their goods shipped from the East Coast rather than the West. Black also met with Long Beach city and business leaders, including Councilman A.L. Parmley, former Mayor Charles H. Windham, Chamber President R.A. Rominger, John F. Craig, George Bixby, J.E. Monroe, and P.E. Hatch, for a tour of the city followed by lunch at the Virginia Hotel. His message for Long Beach was short and sweet. If Long Beach wanted federal assistance in improving its harbor, it had to start thinking of its harbor as a part of the Port of Los Angeles.

"If you set your harbor up as a rival to that of Los Angeles, your chances of government support is small," Black warned the Long Beach delegation.

Return of the Silt

One of the problems with dredging deep channels at the Long Beach Harbor was the inevitable necessity of re-dredging them every time silt came flooding downstream, as it had done during the 1910-11 rainy season. The obvious solution seemed to be to undertake a project that would block the San Gabriel River so as to confine its flow toward Alamitos Bay instead of silting up the harbors. But even if that wasn't possible, the 1910-11 flooding was seen as an extreme – the worst flood in twenty years. It was an infrequent enough event, said the common wisdom, that it could be handled by maintenance dredging of the harbor if, and when, it occurred.

That analysis turned out to be faulty. The rains returned in January 1914, heavier than in 1911 and creating far more damage both inland and at the harbors. Infrequent flooding had always been a part of living in Southern California, but as the region grew and became more populated, the floods began taking a high toll in both property damage and lives. People who had bought property – unaware that it was in a flood plain – were sometimes shocked to find that their land

CLEAR CHANNELS: *Workers dredge and lift silt from the harbor floor. In 1914, yearly Los Angeles River flooding was worse than normal and more than a million cubic yards of silt washed into the harbor, making deep channels shallow. Eventually the river was diverted east of the port, but dredging to maintain harbor channels is an ongoing part of port maintenance.*

was suddenly under water and in some cases, that it had been washed away and become part of a river. The floods of 1914 washed more than a million cubic yards of silt into the harbor, making deep channels shallow and raising concerns about the long-term implications of harbor channels being periodically plugged up by mud. It was a wake-up call, not only for the ports, but for the entire region. Prior to that time, Southern California had tended to consider flooding as a natural part of life in the area. Residents reacted to floods rather than prepared for them. After a flood, people would clean up the mud and move on with their lives. But those were the old days. By the second decade of the 20th century, the population had grown to the point where the propensity for flooding in the region had increased, and the losses wrought by such floods were much higher than they had been before. People were no longer content to suffer floods; they began to focus on new ways to control the flooding.

On July 1, 1914, the County Board of Supervisors held a meeting in Los Angeles to talk about ways to control the damaging floods. The meeting at Blanchard Hall – a music store at 233 S. Broadway with an art gallery and two larger concert auditoriums – drew 250 representatives of cities, businesses, civic organizations, and drainage districts. The result was the establishment of a permanent flood control agency, approval of a $9.5 million flood control plan that had been recommended by an advisory commission of engineers, and a ten-cent per $100 property tax to help pay the cost.

The meeting and the action taken marked a realization that flood control was a regional problem, not a local one. If a local agency blocked flood waters, those waters were merely diverted to someplace downstream, and the farther downstream one went, the worse the problem grew. The cost of the program in the dollars of the time may have been high, but the damage caused by the flood just a few months earlier had been estimated at about $7 million. The new tax was expected to raise $675,000 a year, and the city planned to seek additional state and federal funding to help pay for the program.

The situation was urgent, and the new agency – the Los Angeles County Flood Control Association – jumped into action. State legislation would be needed to allow the county to condemn private property in order to construct a flood control system that would change the hydrology of the entire region. The Flood Control Association called for the Supervisors to appoint a Committee on Legislation and State and National Aid to advocate for flood control. Rather than going to work immediately to remedy localized problems, committee members decided to first put together a detailed plan for the system. Spending money to solve specific local problems before a plan was developed for the entire system would offer only temporary relief at best, they said.

Work on a comprehensive solution was begun. A definitive plan was put together for protecting the entire region from flooding, but the price of such a vast enterprise was more than the $9.5 million first estimated. The new price tag for the project came in at $16.5 million. Late in the summer of 1915, legislation was passed replacing the Los Angeles Flood Control Association with the Los Angeles Flood Control District and giving the district the authority to implement the project.

The 1914-15 rainy season was not as extreme as the previous year, and the floods were not as damaging, but there was an urgency to get the project underway before further flooding occurred. The Army Board of Engineers for Rivers and

Harbors, however, refused to be rushed into funding a project designed to control intermittent flooding. The next major flood could be years in the future, and there were still too many unknowns, the engineers contended.

The first step of the plan was to block the silt coming downstream to the harbor area by building a diversion dam that would shunt the waters off to Alamitos Bay on the east side of the city. Cost of the dam and the new channel was estimated at $1.7 million. Major R.R. Raymond, the Army engineer for the harbor area, noted that "one big flood would probably do more damage to the harbor area than the diversion work would cost." The Army Board remained unconvinced.

The cost of right-of-way would very likely be more expensive than estimated, the engineers on the board reasoned. Attempts to control flooding would help some areas at the expense of others, making the federal government vulnerable to legal liability should the work be undertaken. There had only been one flood that had caused a major silting problem in the harbor and that was the flood in early 1914. Although it was estimated that such a flood might recur at an average interval of five years, the engineers didn't buy into that logic. In August of 1915, the County assumed legal liability for the flood control work – clearing the way for federal funding – and appointed engineer James Reagan as the Flood Control District chief.

Panama Canal Letdown

The Panama Canal had opened for business in 1914 as promised, but the impact on trade for West Coast ports was less than expected. There was a war raging in Europe, and although the U.S. was not yet involved, the conflict had impacted commercial trade between nations. Most of the trade being conducted was on the Atlantic side with little connection to the Pacific. And although the canal was officially open, it was plagued with problems, including the need for further dredging to deepen the channels, more work to be done to finish the locks, ancillary construction of related facilities, a problem with strikes by employees from the West Indies, and a series of landslides that closed the canal for much of 1915 and 1916, and then again occasionally in the four years to follow. The closures of the canal proved a windfall for the railroads, which profited from the extra freight that had been expected to transit the canal. The increase in water trade between the East and West coasts that had been expected to take place with the opening of the canal didn't actually materialize until the 1920s.

Long Beach Stuck in the Mud

Although the county was moving forward quickly on a flood control program, the future of the Long Beach Harbor remained at risk. Not only had the federal government rejected funding for improvements in Long Beach, but the winter rains of 1913-14 had flushed a huge amount of silt down into the harbor, and the Dock and Terminal Co. was hard-pressed to pay for the required dredging. By April 1914, Craig Shipbuilding was considering moving its yard from Long Beach to Los Angeles because the clogged channels were threatening to block the movement of ships into and out of the yard. Up until then, development of the harbor had resulted in a spate of new companies and jobs moving to Long Beach, but the federal government's rejection of improvements for the harbor and the loss of the harbor's biggest business would spell the end to all that. The mud wasn't John F. Craig's only concern. He also was irked by what he considered to be the overly high taxes levied against the shipyard by the city along with the city's tepid response to earlier union problems at the plant.

The possibility of losing its most important industry got an immediate response from city officials. Mayor Whealton determined that $125,000 of the harbor bond issue approved by the voters was not encumbered by the restriction that it could only be spent if an equal amount came from the federal government. He proposed that $25,000 of that amount be used to dredge the channels and that the rest of the funds be placed in an account for future improvements. But there were political challenges. Whealton was not a popular mayor. His opponents – led by former Mayor Charles H. Windham – claimed that Whealton's free-spending policies threatened to bankrupt the city and that he had staffed City Hall with his own cronies. One of reasons that the young city full of hard-working settlers had been so successful in the first place was the ability of its leaders to implement their agendas, and those powerful men who had been first on the scene weren't happy with the way Whealton was handling things. Further exacerbating the harbor's problems was the fact that not everybody in town welcomed the coming of industry to Long Beach. There were elements within Long Beach who wanted to eliminate heavy industry from the city, which before the development of the port had depended on sand, surf, and inland visitors to fuel its economy.

Both nature and politics seemed to be conspiring against Long Beach's pro-business, pro-growth philosophy. The problem wasn't only the annual cost of re-dredging the channels in the two ports each year – although that was considerable, estimated by the Army Corps of Engineers at an average of $80,000 a year. It was also the cost of lost business due to clogged channels when major flooding occurred. To make matters worse, solving the port's problems could exacerbate water problems elsewhere. Diverting the Los Angeles River flow and the silt that came with it eastward to the San Gabriel River where it would flow into Alamitos Bay was opposed by property owners around the bay. Especially hard hit would be the Naples Island community, where it was feared that the accumulation of silt would clog the canals that gave Naples its unique character. A memorandum from D.E. Hughes, an assistant engineer working on the Army's silt investigation, expressed sympathy for the residents of the area, which would see their access to the ocean diminished. But that was not a good enough reason "to deter one when planning public works for the benefit of the public at large," Hughes said.

> *The highlands would not be flooded nor otherwise damaged. A real estate map indicates a pretentious town named Naples within the bay. Several years ago some real estate firm entered the salt marsh and tide lands, dug canals, built temporary bulkheads, filled in the land, built a half dozen buildings – mostly now unoccupied – and sold some lots. But the river diversion would not damage the lots nor the bulkheads, but only the canals, which, on their construction, became public waters like the natural sloughs, on which no compensation for damages would be due to any individual.*

Other interests opposed to the Army's plan included the Compton Chamber of Commerce, which maintained that the plan could lead to flooding in portions of that community, and the Palos Verdes Syndicate, a property development venture headed by New York banker Frank Vanderlip. The Palos Verdes Syndicate argued that the flood diversion plan would diminish the flow of underground water needed for irrigation and household purposes in that area. It was clear that whatever was done to solve the flood problem in the region, there would be people in some locations who would be against it. But it was also clear that something had to be done.

Dock and Terminal Co. Overwhelmed

The two San Pedro Bay ports faced much the same problem, but the attitude by the federal government and by the older and larger Port of Los Angeles remained somewhat dismissive. On November 24, 1915, Long Beach city officials and business leaders turned out for a "Twin Harbor Day" banquet, hoping to find common ground with the older and larger port. Nobody from the Port of Los Angeles attended. Toward the end of the banquet, toastmaster Walter Desmond asked that if there was anybody from Los Angeles in attendance, would he please make his presence known. There was dead silence. Except for a couple of members of the Los Angeles Chamber of Commerce, Los Angeles was absent. The only bright spot came when a discouraged Charles H. Windham returned home to find a letter that had arrived after 6 p.m. that evening from Los Angeles Harbor Commission President Frederick T. Woodman. The letter pledged the support of Los Angeles in the dredging of a channel that would connect the two ports. It was a welcome message for Long Beach, which had been so publicly snubbed earlier that evening.

In January 1916, the Army Corps of Engineers approved a plan to build a dam upstream along the Los Angeles River and divert the flow eastward to Alamitos Bay. The County Flood Control District agreed that the first step to the regional flood control plan would be protection of the harbors from the annual deluge of silt. But the future of the Long Beach Harbor was far from assured. By mid-month the rains and the silt were back – greater in volume than during the 1914 flood – and they were devastating to Southern California and the harbor area. This time the floods dumped about 1 million cubic yards of silt in the harbor, overwhelming the financial ability of the privately held Dock and Terminal Co. to dredge the harbor clear. By the end of January, the water off the municipal wharf was only seven feet deep. Anaheim Road, connecting Wilmington to Long Beach, was under water and had to be closed to traffic. The rains let up, then returned, flooding homes in Long Beach and Compton. Part of a fertilizer plant collapsed into the channel at the Long Beach Harbor, and the lumber ship *Newberg*, which drew sixteen feet of water, was unable to call at the port because of the mud. A large vessel coming in for repairs at the shipyard also had to turn back.

The Merchants and Manufacturers' Association in March 1916 called for a mass meeting in Long Beach to talk about how to head off economic disaster. Because of the shallow waters, many of the harbor businesses had been forced to suspend their operations, resulting in financial loss and the layoffs of hundreds of workers. It wasn't just the shipyards that were impacted. The clogged waterway was costing American Products Co. $1,000 a day in lost productivity in the gathering and processing of kelp. By April, American Products principal George Simmons announced that he had been offered suitable property for his kelp processing plant in the less mud-clogged Port of Los Angeles. The only thing keeping him in Long Beach was the loss of the thousands of dollars he had invested in the Long Beach facility. The makeshift dredging along with the other steps taken to co-exist with the silt were taking their toll on other companies as well – both financially and personally. In May, two young workers at the Western Dredging Co. were killed when a rubber sleeve connecting two sections of pipe burst. The sudden and violent explosion of mud blew the two into the harbor, where they either drowned or were suffocated in mud.

While some businesses that had invested in the harbor were threatening to leave unless they could have access to the sea, many had to shut their doors because they were unable to operate or receive needed materials. The business community wanted the city to release $50,000 of the $125,000 fund that Mayor Whealton had earlier identified to pay for dredging the harbor, and businesses began a campaign to "save the payrolls of the hundreds of men and women employed in the industrial district."

The Dock and Terminal Co., unable to keep the harbor waterways clear, offered to provide the city with $50,000 worth of harbor land in exchange for $50,000 worth of dredging, and although the proposition won favor with most attendees at a mass meeting, little progress was made in the ensuing weeks. An opinion by a consulting bond attorney from the Los Angeles firm of O'Melveny, Stevens and Millikan found that the entire $650,000 bond issue voted in by the people two years earlier was invalid due to a legal technicality. A portion of that money was what would have been used to dredge the harbor under the Dock and Terminal land proposal. If the city wanted to proceed to clear the harbor, it would need a new bond election by the residents, O'Melveny, Stevens advised. The mayor appointed a sixteen-member committee of local business leaders to lay down a strategy for moving forward. The committee was a roster of some of the most prominent men in town, including Job Barnett, S.W. Alexander, George Bixby, C.J. Walker, Philander E. Hatch, William F. Prisk, George M. Spicer, E.J. Starr, L.W. Shuman, F.C. Roberts, D.M. Shreve, and former mayors Charles H. Windham and Louis N. Whealton. While the debate continued over how to pay for the necessary dredging, hydraulic pumps were used as a temporary measure to blow away the muck from around some of the kelp plants so that boats could access the docks. Some of the shipyards along the channel began dredging enough so they could continue to do business.

Meanwhile, the harbor and the harbor businesses remained mired in their own muck. Los Angeles was willing to join with Long Beach in dredging a channel to connect the two harbors, but that would require Long Beach to come up with its share of the costs. An election was set for October 11, 1916, to vote on three separate bond issues – $300,000 for harbor improvements, $500,000 to build a horseshoe pier, and $50,000 for a municipal hospital.

The road to a functioning harbor was sometimes as muddy as the harbor itself. In August, the City Council rejected the Dock and Terminal Co.'s offer of land in exchange for dredging money. The council members were dissatisfied with the property being offered by the company and countered with an offer for a different parcel that had better water frontage than that offered by the company. In response to the demand, the Dock and Terminal Co. withdrew its offer, but it was hardly in the financial situation to drive a hard bargain over which properties it was willing to exchange.

Despite widespread sentiment among voters that it was critical to save the jobs and businesses in the harbor industrial zone, there was some opposition from the "spotless" faction, which wanted Long Beach to reject industry in favor of tourism. Members of the newly organized Property Owners League declared that Long Beach should remain unsullied by factories and other industry. The beaches and the neighborhoods of Long Beach were greater assets than the harbor, they maintained. Members of the league on the west side of Long Beach didn't want to live next to the harbor industrial zone, while members of the east side of the city feared that plans to divert the silt to Alamitos Bay would ruin the beaches there and the ocean views of the residents. An article in the September 30, 1916, pro-industry Los Angeles Times described the issue between two opposing philosophies.

> *The "spotless town" advocates declare that they do not want the class of citizens attracted by a factory town: that they want the air, the streets, and the beach chaste and immaculate, free from cinders which lodge in the eye or smoke which gums up the clothes on the line in the back yard.*
>
> *The liberal element, and the great majority of business men, however, are body and soul for the bonds and will work for them tooth and nail. They point out that Long Beach's growth depends upon its harbor and the expansion of its industries. The harbor is now filled up with silt and almost useless. The bonds must either be sanctioned, or the harbor will go into decay, they declare.*

Although the majority of Long Beach voters seemed to support saving the harbor, a two-thirds vote was necessary to pass new bonds. That meant that even a minority faction had to be taken seriously. While the battle for the hearts and minds of the voters raged, the industries in the harbor existed in an ongoing state of limbo, many plugging along at an extreme disadvantage and losing business because of the mud-clogged channels. On October 4, with the election a week away, a group of harbor industries, headed by Lorned Manufacturing – the successor to American Products Co. – served notice on the Chamber of Commerce that if the bonds did not carry, they would move their business out of Long Beach.

One of the issues being raised during the debate over the bonds was that as tidelands, most of the property owned by the Dock and Terminal Co. legally belonged to the city. City Engineer Albert de Ruiz was ordered to investigate the claim. He presented his findings on October 6, five days before the election. He found that the city, under its tidelands grant, had claim to about 200 acres – most of it in the channels themselves. The approximately twenty-one acres that were on filled land above water consisted of irregular narrow strips and patches here and there over which it would be difficult to establish legal authority, the city attorney advised.

On October 11, 1916, the people of Long Beach voted. The harbor bonds won easily, 6,051 to 1,671, or 78 percent for the measure. The pier bonds and the hospital bonds both failed to achieve the two-thirds margin required to pass. The people had spoken, and the City of Long Beach responded by taking charge of its own harbor. The financially devastated Dock and Terminal Co. still owned industrial property in the harbor area, but it no longer operated the harbor.

The Long Beach Harbor – now popularly known as the Port of Long Beach – had become a municipal asset. The Long Beach City Council on June 29, 1917, created a three-member Board of Harbor Commissioners consisting of Mayor William T. Lisenby, Public Safety Commissioner James R. Williams, and Public Works Commissioner C.J. Hargis. The silt problem would not immediately be solved, and the harbor would continue to be plagued by incoming mud for several more years. But the port was clearly under new management.

The Cage Submarine
Charles H. Windham would come over the years to be known as the father of the Port of Long Beach, but John F. Craig, the bold and stubborn shipbuilder who demonstrated his commitment to the harbor with the money he invested there and the vessels that he built and repaired, also deserves acclaim for his contribution to the port's success. Craig's willingness to invest in the young port served as an incentive for others to do the same. Even before merchant ships were calling at the port, Craig Shipbuilding was constructing vessels that would soon be calling at Long Beach. His success and example convinced investors in the local community to organize their own shipping lines and to order ships from the Craig shipyard. But the shipbuilder with a vision of what would someday be could also be bullheaded in both large and small ways. He flatly refused to negotiate with the union when it attempted to organize his shipyard. He railed against the high taxes placed on his business by the city. And when he launched the first vessel at his new yard – a dredge named *C.H. Windham* – he caused a buzz in teetotaling Long Beach by using real champagne instead of cold water to christen the vessel.

During the 1910s Craig would build more vessels, merge his business with others, fight in the ongoing battle against silt, start new ventures, build ships for the Navy, be tried on felony charges of violating the Neutrality Act, and suffer a great personal loss. It was that kind of a decade.

Craig had spent most of his working life – both in Long Beach and on the Great Lakes – building freighters, dredges, tugboats, and passenger ships. But the world of shipbuilding was changing. War was brewing in Europe, and different kinds of vessels were in demand – some of them experimental. In May of 1911, several weeks before the Long Beach Harbor officially opened, Craig had begun building a new kind of submarine, designed by a 25-year-old Long Beach inventor named John M. Cage. The Cage submarine looked more like a fish than the typical submarine. Instead of propellers in the rear, the Cage submarine propellers hung alongside each side of the bow in cylinder-like nacelles – pulling the vessel along rather than pushing it. Unlike most submarines of the day, which ran on battery power while submerged, the Cage submarine was designed to use a gasoline engine both on the surface and beneath it.

Oxygen for the engines would be provided from tanks of compressed air, and the exhaust from the submerged engine would be disposed of away from the crew. The Cage Submarine project was bankrolled by J.E. Meyer Co. and operated under the corporate name of the Los Angeles Submarine Boat Co. Craig was so impressed with the idea that he invested in the company and became its marine architect. The prototype submarine being built at the shipyard was seventy feet long and divided into three compartments, the middle of which was designed to be occupied by a four-man crew. The company hoped to launch the submarine in October 1911.

By December 1911, with the frame of the submarine still on the timbers at the Craig yard, the Los Angeles Submarine Boat Co. ran a full-page ad in the Los Angeles Times seeking more funding. The submarine now had a name, the *Peace Maker*. The *Peace Maker* would have commercial applications as well as military, the company promised in the ad. It also could be used for undersea scientific investigation, for recovering sunken treasure, or "just for a 'joy ride.'" If investors bought stock in the company before midnight on December 20, it would be $1.50 per share. After that time, the price per share would increase to $2. Craig by that time was a major investor in the project and vice president of the company. Launch date for the sub was set for no later than April 1, 1912.

April 1 came and went. In September, U.S. Navy Captain Charles Fremont Pond, commandant of the Twelfth Naval District in San Francisco, was in Long Beach to inspect the Cage submarine, which was still in the shipyard "nearing completion," according to press reports.

Despite the company's ongoing problems and the fact that it had yet to launch its prototype submarine, it submitted a bid in December 1912 to build eight new submarines for the Navy. Getting the Navy's approval for at least one of the eight new subs was crucial to the company, which had invested a lot of money in an untested concept. When the bids were opened and the Navy contracts awarded later that month, the Cage submarine did not make the cut, although the company submitted the lowest bid. It was the first of several setbacks.

Manufacturing delays were not the only problem. The company had become embroiled in a bitter legal battle between Cage and his father-in-law, James C. Harvey, over stock ownership and control of the company. Harvey claimed that he and Cage worked together to design the boat, which is why he was awarded 200,000 shares of stock. Cage alleged his father-in-law was awarded the shares on the promise that Harvey would obtain needed financing for the company. During a proxy fight at the company's annual meeting in January 1913, Harvey was removed from the board, but the family feud between Cage and his father-in-law was hardly over. Ongoing litigation continued to impede the company as it attempted to establish credibility for its new vessel.

Finally, on January 18, 1913, it was time to prove that the new Cage submarine could deliver on its promise. With the timing chosen in order to catch the high tide, 500 invited guests gathered at the Craig shipyard two hours before dawn, standing around a bonfire, waiting in the morning chill to witness the launch of the new submarine. At the appointed time, the sub slid down the greased ways and rolled sideways into the harbor waters. Unfortunately, 700 pounds of unsecured lead ballast shifted when the submarine hit the water, causing the vessel to list to starboard. A launch took the sub in tow in an effort to put it alongside a nearby barge, but the action was in vain. The sub drifted into a mud bank, hung for a few minutes in the mud, then broke free, filled with water through an open hatchway, and sank to the bottom. It was an inglorious beginning for a vessel that needed badly to prove itself worthy of consideration.

Attempts to free the sunken submarine by pumping it full of air the next day failed after it was discovered that the hatchway on the vessel had been sprung, letting the air escape. Four days later, the submarine was finally plucked from the mud by chaining it tightly to four barges at low tide. As the incoming tide raised the barges, the sub was pulled loose, and then dragged 200 feet toward her slip where the water was pumped from inside the engine room. Although the submarine required only minor repairs and cleaning, the fiasco was a disaster for the company. By March 11, 1913, John Cage was running a series of classified ads trying to convince stockholders not to dump their shares. The ads smacked of desperation.

> *The Submarine Boat which was launched January 18, 1913, sank on that date because the vents from the ballast compartments were inadvertently left open. These vents being open made it very difficult to raise the boat to the surface again. On January 24 the boat was raised to the surface by means of barges and compressed air.*
>
> *Since that date we have been rushing the repair work as fast as possible, and in a few days the boat will be demonstrating that the L.A. Submarine Boat Co.'s stock is really worth what we claim for it – $100 per share.*
>
> *All I ask is an opportunity to show you and then if you care to sell your stock I will buy it and I will make you a better offer than you can get from anyone else.*
>
> *See others, but before you sell, see me.*
> *JOHN M. CAGE*

Repairing the submarine had been easy. Now the company needed desperately to repair its reputation. Starting in March, the company recorded a series of successful tests, beginning with five-minute descents to the bottom of the harbor with a crew – including Cage – onboard. By the end of May, the submarine was operating under its own power, and staying down with seven people onboard for two hours and six minutes. The company also pulled off some publicity stunts in a successful effort to gain press recognition. One was a twenty-minute trip to the bottom of the harbor with six women onboard – the first women to descend in a submarine. One of the women was John Cage's wife. In a tongue-in-cheek effort to dispel any thoughts that the submarine might be jinxed – and to get some press – Cage and his crew descended in the submarine for thirteen minutes, with thirteen passengers on board, at 1300 hours (1 p.m.), on Friday, June 13, 1913.

Cage's most successful demonstration of the submarine's capability, however, came on June 10, when he and five of his crew submerged in the harbor at 5 a.m. and didn't surface until 5 p.m. the following day – thirty-six hours later. The event – covered by newspapers and motion picture cameras – broke the 1907 record set by the U.S. Navy submarine *Octopus*, which had remained submerged for twenty-four hours. While submerged, the crew played cards, smoked cigarettes, did experiments, and sent underwater telegraph messages through a special wire to various people of influence – including the secretary of the Navy, President Woodrow Wilson, other politicians, the press – and to their wives. The event drew positive notice from both local and eastern press as well as a full-page feature in *Scientific American*. Cage and the others emerged from the sub on the afternoon of the following day after Mayor Ira Hatch cut a ceremonial seal, greeted everybody, and explained to the world the wonders of Cage's invention. The thirty-six-hour endurance record won easy acclaim from the media, but it did little to enhance the Los Angeles Submarine Boat Co.'s bottom line. In December, less than six months after the Cage submarine's record-setting descent, the vessel was sold at a sheriff's auction for $400. It was bought by the W.L. Cleveland Co. The buyer, which had supplied mechanical equipment for the boat, also assumed payment of about $5,000 in claims against the boat for crew wages, materials, and court judgments against the vessel.

It's not clear just how much money John F. Craig and other investors in the project lost, but it had to have been considerable. Whether the Cage submarine was just a good idea before its time or a bad idea that fell apart under its own weight, it failed spectacularly. From launch to sheriff's auction was less than twelve months. By November 1915, Cage was in London, trying to interest people in his plans for an even better submarine. In January 1916, the Markham Iron Works sought permission to dock the Cage submarine – by then wholly inoperable – at the Long Beach municipal wharf to be overhauled. The company was turned down by the city wharfinger, C.A. Wallace, who declared that the wharf was for cargo ships. A few days later, the submarine struck a concrete wharf in San Pedro, springing its seams. It was returned to Long Beach where it soon sank near the edge of the turning basin, and silt flowing into the harbor from that year's floods immediately began to cover it. It was so badly damaged that repairs were not feasible, and the only salvageable remnants of the vessel were the two engines that had been removed shortly before the submarine sank. They were installed in a new Catalina Island ferry later that year.

The Trials and Tribulations of John F. Craig

The second decade of the 20th century was a busy one for John F. Craig, and a stressful one as well. The Cage submarine fiasco was just the first on a long list of problems for the shipbuilder. Since the Craig shipyard had launched its first vessel – the dredger *C.H. Windham* – in 1908, it had established a reputation as a reliable shipbuilding operation, and additional orders came pouring in. In June 1912, while it was busy building the Cage submarine, Craig Shipbuilding also launched the 308-foot-long *Camino* for Western Steam Navigation. Four months later it launched the 225-foot-long *Pariaso* for the Long Beach Steamship Co., whose president was former Mayor Charles H. Windham. Windham's 15-year-old daughter, Clara – who arrived on the scene late and out of breath – did the christening honors.

And the orders kept on coming – for both passenger and cargo ships. In March 1914, three months after the Cage submarine was sold at auction, the 224-foot-long, oil and lumber freighter *Alvarado* was launched at the shipyard for the Long Beach Steamship Co. This time 13-year-old Eleanor Hatch, daughter of Long Beach Steamship corporate secretary P.E. Hatch, did the honors.

After the *Alvarado* cleared, Craig prepared to lay the keel for two submarines which had been part of the eight-sub Navy order that the Los Angeles Submarine Boat Co. had failed to get for its Cage submarine. The contract for five of those vessels had gone to the Electric Boat Co. Another eight went to the Lake Torpedo Boat Co., with two of the Lake submarines to be built at the Craig shipyard.

With orders continuing to pour in, Craig – along with the leaders of other harbor industries – found himself in a fight to keep his operation moving forward as the huge loads of mud clogged the channel during the floods of 1914. Finally, the shipbuilder's threats to relocate his shipyard to the less-clogged waterways at the Port of Los Angeles unless a way was found to maintain his access to the sea, spurred the city to action. But finding the money to clear the channels was easier said than done.

By 1915, with war raging in Europe, Craig decided to join a new corporation – California Shipbuilding Co. – that planned to take over several West Coast shipyards and manufacture submarines and other war ships for the government. Officers of the new company were President George H. Bixby and Treasurer P.E. Hatch, both Long Beach businessmen, and Vice President and General Manager W.C. Foley, who formerly headed the Lake Torpedo Boat Co. In October 1915, California Shipbuilding won a contract to build three Navy submarines. The final deal merging Craig Shipbuilding into the new company was signed on December 31. The Navy submarine contracts provided plenty of work to keep the shipyard busy, but there was still the problem of silt. And the mud that caked the channels was to prove a major embarrassment for both the shipyard and the city.

Shortly before midnight on August 31, 1916, the shipyard workers prepared to launch the submarine *L-6* – the first of the two-sub deal that Lake Torpedo Boat Co. had subcontracted to Craig. Although thousands showed up to witness the event, security was tight with police patrolling the harbor to make sure none of the spectators took pictures of the launch. At the appointed time, the ropes holding the sub in place were cut, the wife of Navy Lieutenant W.R. Munroe broke a bottle of California champagne over the bow, and the *L-6* slid into the harbor, hit a mud bank, rolled partway onto its side, and stuck there. The whole operation, from christening to being stuck in the mud, was 3.4 seconds, according to the company timekeeper with a stop watch. Damage to the *L-6* was negligible, and the submarine was refloated the following evening. But it was not the kind of performance that inspired confidence in the Long Beach Harbor – or in the companies that did business there.

The Navy contracts, although welcome, came with strings attached. The company had promised the government that the shipyard would remain open for construction of warships during the pre-war era of preparedness. The yard had room to build ten submarines at once. With three under construction at the California Shipbuilding yard, and a lighthouse tender about to be launched, there was surplus room at the site, but the company had to turn down orders for civilian merchant ships in order to keep its commitment to the Navy. To take advantage of the demand for merchant ships, Craig set up a separate operation adjacent to the California Shipbuilding yard.

In those tense days prior to America's joining the war in Europe, some radical isolationists were setting off bombs to protest any United States military involvement. A Preparedness Day Parade had been held in San Francisco on July 22, 1916. It was to be the biggest parade ever held in the city, with fifty-two bands and 51,000 marchers. On the day of the parade, as thousands watched from the curb, a bomb in a suitcase exploded, killing ten onlookers and injuring forty more. That bombing triggered the arrest of two radical labor leaders, one of whom ended up being sentenced to hang. Both men were later pardoned after details about tainted evidence came to light.

On December 29, 1916, the terrorists targeted Craig. His 20-year-old son, James Craig, got a box of cigars in the mail as a Christmas gift. He had read about others being injured after receiving such gifts with no return addresses, so he laid the box on the fireplace grate, lit it, and stepped back several feet to see what happened. After smoldering a few seconds, the box exploded, spraying young Craig's arms and face with copper shrapnel. His wounds were minor, but it could have been much worse. The senior Craig said the cigars were probably sent to his son by mistake since they shared the same initials.

Through it all, the mud continued to flow into the harbor. A second submarine became mired in the muck in January 1917. With the shipyard losing business because of the shallow channel and the extra work needed to launch vessels, other ports began to try to lure the business away from Long Beach. San Diego promised the company suitable property with channels free from mud. Although the offer was seriously considered, the city of Long Beach had finally started to clear away some of the inner-harbor silt by using boat propellers to blow it out to sea.

On April 2, 1917, the United States declared war on Germany, citing, among other offenses, the German practice of unrestricted submarine warfare in the North Atlantic. The U.S. Shipping Board was established within weeks to provide military logistics for the nation. In June, the new Craig shipyard began preparations for two merchant ships – the *Silverado* and the *Eldorado* – to be built for the U.S. Shipping Board. Craig Shipbuilding Co., with son James Craig as president, began ironing out the final details of the contract.

In August 1917, California Shipbuilding received a contract from the United States Emergency Fleet Corporation to build three 345-foot freighters. A week later, the federal government commandeered both the California Shipbuilding and Craig Shipbuilding yards, taking over operations at both sites. It was part of the government's plan to build a robust merchant fleet for the U.S., to be used during both war and peace. Government control wasn't distressing news for the shipbuilders. It meant that the government was going to be their partner, rather than their competitor.

"There is no secret, I take it, in the fact that the government has abandoned the proposed plan of opening its own shipyards," California Shipbuilding President George H. Bixby told the Los Angeles Times. "The policy of commandeering the present ship plants of the nation and working them to the limit of their capacity has been adopted instead. The government will look after all problems of labor and steel shipments."

In fact, the company began looking for additional nearby sites in which to expand its operation with Bixby predicting that the company's existing 450-man workforce could be expanded to as many as 1,500. In December 1917, the California Shipbuilding Co., along with its contracts, was resold to Craig, who consolidated the operations under a single name – the Long Beach Shipbuilding Co.

Although Craig's government contracts put him right in the middle of the war effort, that didn't prevent him from being charged with violating the Neutrality Act. In May of 1917, he had been indicted in federal court for being part of an international conspiracy by German agents, Hindu revolutionaries, and American businessmen to overthrow British colonial rule in India. The plot was part of the strategy employed by notorious German State Secretary for Foreign Affairs Arthur Zimmermann to foment rebellion against Germany's real and potential enemies. It was Zimmermann who had earlier sent an intercepted telegram to Mexico, promising German support if Mexico were to attempt to take back the southwestern states it had lost in 1848 during the Mexican-American War.

Craig's alleged connection to the plot was through the steamship *Maverick*, which was to be used to smuggle arms and ammunition to the rebels in India. In 1915, he had bought the *Maverick* from Standard Oil for $45,000, repaired and overhauled it at his shipyard, and made $27,000 for the work when he then sold the ship to the conspirators. The deal was set up by Fred Jebsen, known as the "The Big Swede" to people on the waterfront, but who was actually a German citizen who oversaw operations at the German Consulate in San Francisco. Jebsen organized the Maverick Steamship Co., with the names of janitors and other low-level employees at the consulate as the incorporators. The company leased the ship on a time-charter to the fictional American-Asiatic Oil Co., the name under which it was to have been used to run guns to India. Although the *Maverick* failed in that mission, it was due to incompetence, not intent.

Craig dismissed the indictment as a grandstand play by the U.S. attorney. His only involvement in the events described was as an innocent and peripheral businessman, he said. He had bought, overhauled, and resold the vessel, and he had no interest in the company. Once he sold the vessel, he had no further dealings with it. That was Craig's story and he stuck to it through the next nine months of accusations, trial, testimony, and verdicts. The trial in U.S. District Court in San Francisco ended dramatically on April 23, 1918 – shortly after U.S. Attorney John Preston had concluded his closing argument to the jury and Judge William C. Van Fleet ordered the noon recess. One of the Hindu defendants, Ram Singh, suddenly pulled a smuggled pistol from his clothes and shot Hindu ringleader Ram Chandra three times. Federal Marshal James B. Holohan, a tall man seated near the jury box, jumped to his feet, raised his own pistol high above his head, and fired one shot over the heads of the people between him and Singh. Holohan's bullet hit Singh in the neck, severed his spinal cord, and killed him instantly. Singh apparently had been feuding with Chandra over money he had given Chandra for the cause, but which he felt Chandra had used for his own gain.

The following day, with the bloodstains still on the carpet, the jury returned with a verdict. Twenty-nine defendants were found guilty. Only one defendant was acquitted, and that was John F. Craig. It had undoubtedly been a tough nine months for a proud and independent man such as Craig. But through it all he continued to build ships, conduct business, and maintain his innocence.

Despite Craig's confidence and success in moving his business agenda forward in the face of his indictment, there was a tragedy for which there was no answer, no matter how disciplined he was, how hard he worked, or how successful he became. On August 21, 1918, Craig's 6-year-old daughter, Eleanor, was killed when she ran into the street by the family home at the corner of Eighth Street and Daisy Avenue, and was hit by an automobile. She was the youngest of Craig's six children.

Later that same month, Long Beach Shipbuilding got a new contract, this one for four 8,800-ton freighters at the cost of $2.69 million apiece. Craig continued to do business in his assertive and sometimes stubborn style. In October, when workers at his shipyard were having problems finding places to live due to a wartime ban on building, he traveled to Washington in an attempt to get the ban lifted. When the Metal Trades Union called a strike against his Long Beach shipyard and the Southwestern shipyard in Los Angeles, he vowed to remain open and did as he promised. Through it all, he launched ship after ship after ship, some for the government and some for private interests.

The war ended on November 11, 1918, with the surrender of the German Army. It had been a time of testing and tragedy for the nation. It had been much the same for John F. Craig.

Moving a River

Although the city had taken over harbor operation in 1916 and began using dredges to maintain the channel, the silt continued to flood into the harbor and disrupt operations. But political opposition to a plan that would divert the silt to Alamitos Bay was impossible to ignore. After passage of the harbor bonds in October 1916, a group of anti-port residents attempted to get the election overturned in court, claiming that the city had no authority to issue bonds and that the harbor was a private business venture that did not qualify for city support. The December rains of 1916 brought new flooding and more silt, shutting down the harbor once again. There were some who felt the dredging should wait until spring, since any dredging before that time could be undone by further downpours, but industries along the waterfront demanded immediate action. The City Council agreed to a plan in late December in which the city would quickly dredge a narrow fifty-foot-wide channel that would allow harbor businesses to continue operations until the channel could be widened.

Because the harbor bonds had yet to be cleared by the court, the city established a program for the industries to pick up the bill for dredging the temporary channel, which was expected to take ten days and cost about $3,500. The dredging commenced in February 1917. Later that same month, the Army engineers approved a new route for the flood control channel that would divert the silt from the harbor without incurring the wrath of residents around Alamitos Bay by sending it there. The new north-south channel would divert the river straight down to the ocean, running between the city on the east and the harbor industrial area on the west. The decision cleared the way for a project that would make both ports nearly silt free.

All that was needed was voter approval of $4.45 million in county flood control bonds. Despite the dire situation with flooding, approval of the measure was far from certain. Some worried that the county would be liable should the channel overflow and damage high-priced property. The plan, declared one editorial writer, opens the gate to a "financial deluge." People who lived on hills and other high ground felt they were being unfairly taxed to save the property of people who resided in the flood plain. Others were critical of the plan outlined by Flood Control District engineer James Reagan, who was accused of favoring channels to flush the water to the sea over large dams with reservoirs and low restraining dams at intervals that would dampen the peaks and valleys of the flow and allow the water to percolate down to the water table.

The debate over the flood control bonds was heated and passionate, but on February 20, 1917, voters approved the bonds by such a narrow margin that the final victory was not certain for several days. Once the bond approval vote was completed, however, there was no turning back. The harbor was saved from its annual mud bath from upstream, but the controversy over flood control planning and the proper practice of urban hydrology continues.

There still remained the question of the other bonds – the $300,000 in Long Beach Harbor improvement bonds that voters had approved in October 1916. On June 26, 1917, the California Supreme Court finally ruled that the Long Beach Harbor bonds were legally valid and that the city was free to sell the bonds and begin dredging out the harbor mud.

In January 1918, the city of Long Beach gave its final approval to the new flood control channel route that would carry the river flow and the silt to the sea. Although the new 750-foot-wide, four-mile-long channel would solve the harbor silting problem, it also would cut through some of the city's prime industrial areas. The project would partially or wholly displace the Fairchild-Gilmore-Wilton contracting company, the Star Drilling Co., a Southern California Edison storehouse, the Union Oil Co., the Long Beach Sash and Door Co., a laundry, two clothes-dyeing establishments, and several houses. Many of the properties were sold voluntarily, but in some cases, the city had to seek federal condemnation to clear the land.

With construction of the channel not ready to begin for at least a year, county supervisors agreed in July to a modified emergency plan that would head off much of the silt that would otherwise flow into the harbor during the coming winter rains. The plan was to dig a 150-foot-wide channel from between Fourth and Fifth streets south to the ocean. It would serve as the first leg of the wider and longer federal channel that was to be built later, and it would divert much of the silt past the harbors. The channel was expected to cost $30,000. The Long Beach Shipbuilding Co. had already pledged $10,000 to the project. The rest would be contributed by other harbor industries.

The silt problem wasn't over, but it was definitely on the way to being solved. The first half of the decade was a time of attracting industry to the harbor area. The second half was a fight to keep industry from leaving.

Two Harbors, One Channel

Although the federal government at every opportunity urged the Los Angeles and Long Beach ports to merge into one, the recommendation was always resisted by Long Beach. But the two harbors did have some interests in common. One was in an inner harbor channel that would connect the two ports physically, if not politically. Los Angeles had agreed back in 1915 to work with Long Beach to dredge the channel, but money, as always, had been a problem. But in 1918, the two ports working together finally sold the idea of a connecting channel as an emergency war measure. It was vital for Long Beach to have access to the ocean for its shipbuilding operations in case the main entrance to the harbor became blocked. The federal government finally agreed that year to help fund such a connection if the two cities would contribute appropriate funding toward the project.

Approval for the project did hit a snag in Congress when critics noted the political pressure brought by the local boosters to secure the financing and discounted the rationale for the project being an emergency war measure. But such objections were overcome and the project proceeded with an award of contract to the Los Angeles Dredging Co. The City of Long Beach's share of the job was $240,000. Work on the Cerritos Channel began in February 1919, and it was officially opened on October 16, 1919.

The opening ceremony began in mid-channel with two boats – one from Long Beach and one from San Pedro – meeting midway to note completion of the project. There was an exchange of ceremonial pleasantries by dignitaries from both cities, after which the parties departed for San Pedro for a military parade, the dedication of a new Chief Petty Officers Club, speeches, an official luncheon, a street carnival, a tour of battleships for the public, a pageant depicting the visit by Juan Rodríguez Cabrillo to San Pedro Bay, a civilian parade, a dinner with speeches, a procession of 500 illuminated boats after nightfall, a mock battle between the Fort MacArthur Army Base and submarines and surface ships, and a brilliant display of fireworks.

It was quite a big deal at the time, but the rationale for the Cerritos Channel as a wartime emergency measure was no longer invoked. The war was over, and the two ports were connected by an inner harbor channel. More important than the channel itself, was the demonstration that when there was common interest involved, the rival ports could work together. It marked the first time for such cooperation, but it was certainly not the last.

The Long Beach Navy Connection

The other milestone event of 1919 was the coming of the Navy to Long Beach and San Pedro Bay. It was the start of a relationship that would both define and profit the city and its port for more than seventy years. It wasn't official. The Navy had established a submarine base in San Pedro in 1917 after Los Angeles deeded the government 177 acres in the outer harbor for the facility. But it wasn't until 1919 that the Pacific Fleet arrived in Southern California amid much pomp and ceremony. While there was no official recognition of Long Beach as home port for the fleet, the Navy in effect used the two ports as its center of operations. There were several advantages. The waters were deeper than those of San Diego Bay and therefore accessible to the Navy's fleet of battleships. There were facilities available for much of the Navy's maintenance and repair needs and a ready supply of available fuel in the area. The weather was consistently good, and the offshore waters somewhat protected by Santa Catalina Island, resulting in a ready-made training area and anchorage. And the local community was eager to welcome the sailors – and their money – to town.

Some officers and their families moved to homes in Long Beach. Other housing was developed to cater to the needs of Navy personnel and their families. The Navy fleet anchored off shore became a common sight, and high-ranking Navy officers were often asked to speak at luncheons and made to feel like part of the community. The Navy was also welcomed across the bay at the Port of Los Angeles, but there was a difference. Downtown Los Angeles was twenty miles inland, connected to the harbor by a narrow strip of annexed land. Long Beach was a waterfront town with the Pacific Ocean for its front porch. It was accessible, it was welcoming, and it represented a partnership that would last forever – or at least for a long, long time.

Long Beach Temperance Goes Nationwide

Perhaps the most auspicious victory of the time for straight-laced Long Beach came on January 16, 1919, when Congress ratified the 18th Amendment to the Constitution, outlawing the manufacture, transportation, and sale of alcoholic beverages. It wouldn't take effect for one more year, but the celebration of the victory was immediate. An estimated 2,000 people showed up at the First Methodist Church for a jubilee organized by the Long Beach Ministerial Association. Leaders of the temperance crusade talked about the long struggle to rid the country of alcoholic beverages. Marie C. Brehm talked about the role that women played in getting Prohibition passed, and prohibitionist Charles J. Hall drew long applause when he declared that getting Prohibition passed was just the first step in getting alcohol banned worldwide.

Long Beach, which had no saloons and whose people took pride in their rejection of alcohol, had proved itself to be a leader once more.

Chapter Eleven:
Oil, Prosperity, and the Navy

The Great War was over and peace had returned to America. It was a time that would come to be known as the Roaring Twenties, or as the Jazz Age, terms that referred both to a changing world and changing values. Radical workers, inspired by the 1917 revolution in Russia, called a general strike in Seattle in 1919. It started at the shipyards, but spread through the city, involving 65,000 workers from more than 100 union locals, bringing the city to a standstill. The strike collapsed after only five days, but it helped to bring about the "red scare," a response by the government and business to stamp out Bolshevism and other "un-American" philosophies.

The strike did little to gain the support of the public at large. People were tired of hearing about reform and radical politics. It was a time for fun, a time to make money, a time of excess. For the first time, according to the 1920 census, the United States was more urban than rural. "Urban" was defined as any town with more than 2,500 residents.

President Woodrow Wilson suffered a stroke in October 1919 that left him mostly ineffective for the last eighteen months of his term. He was followed by President Warren G. Harding, a Republican whose promise of a "return to normalcy" was endorsed by more than 60 percent of voters in 1920. The political and philosophical outlook of the nation had changed, but not for everybody. Socialist Eugene Debs, who had to campaign from prison where he had been incarcerated for urging resistance to the military draft, earned more than 900,000 votes in that same election.

One of Wilson's legacies was the League of Nations. In January 1919, he traveled to Paris – the only sitting president up to that time to ever visit Europe – for a conference to establish the League, to impose reparations for the war on the German people, and to reorganize the national boundaries and administration of the various nations involved. It was the only official American participation in the League of Nations. U.S. membership was never approved by the Senate.

America would change during the 1920s in other ways as well. The soldiers who fought in World War I came home to a nation where having a drink was against the law. Passed in 1919, the 18th Amendment – better known as Prohibition – would result in widespread disrespect for the law, the rise of organized crime, extensive corruption within law enforcement agencies, and overloading both the court and prison systems. The 19th Amendment, giving women the right to vote, passed in 1920. Women in California had been granted voting rights through state law in 1911, and in some states they had been voting much longer than that, but by 1920, women all across the country could vote.

The culture was changing as well. A generation that had grown up with electricity, telephones, and the imposition of 19th century values had come of age. Short skirts, speakeasies, and wild, unchaperoned dancing had become the way of life for the young and affluent people of the day.

The falling prices of motor cars and the widespread ownership of them had freed people from the tyranny imposed by distance and geography, but demanded a metamorphosis in both the highway system and how building roads would be financed. Roads designed for horse and buggy were no longer suitable for the kind of wear imposed by automobiles and trucks. Building roadways had once been the province of local government, but people were straying farther from home, and the need for roads became more of a state and federal issue.

Technology also was changing the way of life and entertainment in America. Radio broadcasting became common in the '20s, and the first talking movie, *The Jazz Singer* with Al Jolson, revolutionized the motion picture industry. Mickey Mouse made his cartoon debut in "Steamboat Willie," actress Mae West was arrested on obscenity charges for corrupting the morals of youth, and the first Academy Awards ceremony and dinner was held at the Hollywood Roosevelt Hotel. Tickets were $5. Former Long Beach resident and actor-comedian Roscoe "Fatty" Arbuckle was arrested, tried three times, and finally acquitted in the death of 26-year-old Virginia Rappe, whom he was accused of raping and inadvertently killing during a drunken party.

Insulin and penicillin were developed during the 1920s, and insecticides were used for the first time on crops. The lie detector was invented, lending one more tool to lawmen across the nation. Bubble gum made its first appearance, and sliced bread became commonly available. In Tennessee, substitute high school teacher John Scopes was arrested and jailed for teaching the concept of evolution, leading to a historic legal battle between William Jennings Bryan for the prosecution and Clarence Darrow for the defense. Scopes was ultimately found guilty and fined $100, although the verdict was later overturned on a technicality.

Crime and punishment had always been part of the American fabric, but the '20s were known for the sensational nature of its unlawful endeavors. Organized crime blossomed during the era with gangland killings and bootleg liquor becoming part of the news of the day. That culminated with the infamous St. Valentine's Day Massacre in Chicago, in which seven members of Bugs Moran's North Side Irish gang were lined up and gunned down in a garage by Al Capone's South Side Italian gang.

Self-proclaimed anarchists Nicola Sacco and Bartolomeo Vanzetti were arrested and convicted of murder during the robbery of a shoe factory in Massachusetts. Their case and their alleged innocence became an international cause célèbre among artists, intellectuals, and academics, who believed they were convicted because of anti-Italian sentiment and the two men's radical politics. Despite the protests, the two were executed in the electric chair in 1927. Nathan Leopold and Richard Loeb, two wealthy law students at the University of Chicago, gained equal notoriety, but little public support, after they murdered 13-year-old Bobby Franks just to see if they could get away with it. They couldn't. The two were apprehended and sentenced to life in prison where Loeb was killed by a fellow prisoner in 1936. Leopold was paroled in 1958.

Aviator Charles Lindbergh became a hero when he flew solo across the Atlantic in 1927. Amelia Earhart, who took her first airplane ride in Long Beach in 1920, flew across the Atlantic a year after Lindbergh, becoming the first woman to cross the ocean by air, not as the pilot, but as part of a three-person crew. She and her companions received a ticker-tape parade in New York for their feat.

In order to protect American culture, Congress in 1921 passed the Emergency Immigration Act. The Act limited the number of people allowed to immigrate to the United States from a specific county to 3 percent of the number of residents from that country living in the United States in 1910. That Act was replaced by the Immigration Act of 1924, which limited immigration to 2 percent of the number of residents from any specific country living in the United States in 1890. The effect of the Act was to favor immigrants from Western and Northern Europe, limit Jews and other immigrants from Southern and Eastern Europe, and to exclude as much as possible, people from Asia, Arabia, and the South Pacific.

Mexican bandit-turned-revolutionary Pancho Villa retired from the fray in 1920, only to be assassinated three years later. Russian intellectual-turned-revolutionary Vladimir Lenin became the first leader of the Russian Communist state, and later of the Soviet Union. He died in 1924 at age 53, apparently from a stroke. Mohandas Gandhi organized the Indian people to confront and defy British authority in India, while Kemal Atatürk was working hard to bring Turkey into the modern world. Germany struggled under crushing reparations, steering it inevitably toward World War II. Meanwhile, young Adolf Hitler led the failed Nazi putsch in Munich and was thrown in jail, where he wrote *Mein Kampf.*

President Harding, the first of three Republican presidents to serve during the decade, died at the Palace Hotel in San Francisco during a 1923 visit to California. Vice President Calvin Coolidge took over the rest of Harding's term and for one term to follow. The Harding administration would be forever afterward marred by the Teapot Dome scandal, although news of the scandal would not emerge until after Harding's death. The Teapot Dome referred to an oil reserve beneath a teapot-shaped rock formation in Wyoming. Albert Fall, Harding's secretary of the interior, was later convicted and jailed for taking money in exchange for awarding private oil companies drilling rights to the Teapot Dome and other government oil reserves.

Coolidge was a popular president, an opponent of big government, and a man who did much to restore the battered public perception of the White House after the scandals of the previous administration. He was followed by fellow Republican Herbert Hoover, who won election with the Republican slogan of "a chicken in every pot and a car in every garage" – a line that would come back to haunt him when the stock market crashed less than eight months into his administration, sending the nation reeling into the Great Depression.

Long Beach, as always, was a reflection of what was happening in the rest of the world. Fortune smiled on the city by the sea during the 1920s, especially when something unexpected and spectacular happened, something that would forever change the port town with the astute business sense. It was something that had its own dark legacy.

Flood Control, Local Power, and Money

Even before completion of the entire five-mile-long flood control channel that diverted the Los Angeles River eastward between the harbor and the city, a temporary partial canal diverted the flow and the silt away from the harbor. It was imperative that the silt problem be solved if the port was going to function, but if the port was going to be successful, further improvements were also essential. Port infrastructure was expensive, and that was a problem.

By 1920, Long Beach had a population of 55,593 – quite a large city for one so new – but still less than one-tenth the size of Los Angeles with its 576,673 residents. Passing harbor improvement bonds in Los Angeles and spreading the cost among a larger number of taxpayers was much easier in Los Angeles than in Long Beach, which had fewer taxpayers to carry the load. The federal government regarded Long Beach as a minor upstart in the port business. It was still just the port next door to the main gateway, and the Army engineers were reluctant to spend the nation's limited resources on a small port next door to a large port that still had unused capacity. With two harbors each seeking separate improvements, the federal engineers were in the position of weighing one port's needs against the other – not a comfortable political situation to deal with.

"Don't think of Los Angeles and Long Beach harbors as separate entities but in terms of one greater harbor," advised Brigadier General Harry Taylor, senior member of the Board of Engineers for Harbors and Rivers, during a visit to the ports. Taylor went on to note the problems encountered in New York, where various sections of the harbor were developed as separate enterprises. The result was that the needs of the various segments were often in conflict, which led to confusion and difficulty in planning and financing any improvements, he said.

"Now if you people here go ahead on the same lines of developing individual sections, I'm afraid you'll end up in the same kind of a snarl," he warned.

The obvious solution would have been for Long Beach to join Los Angeles with its superior financial resources, and everybody who understood port development and finance assumed that sooner or later the two harbors would become one. Los Angeles had never entirely given up the idea of becoming one huge city, running from the mountains to the sea, including the coastal plain and the interior valleys. Advocates of that plan had always pointed to the efficiencies of scale that would be achieved with one large city instead of the scores of smaller ones that surrounded Los Angeles.

"Local communities waste taxpayers' money on an enormous scale through their cumbersome machinery of government and especially on account of their needless duplication of governing agencies," said a 200-page treatise on the subject by the Tax Payers Association of California.

Los Angeles had been relentless in pushing its agenda. And always, whether it was a question of becoming part of the larger city, or merely merging its harbor into Los Angeles' harbor, Long Beach had resisted. The debate was never about efficiency. It was about the power to control one's own local jurisdiction rather than have it controlled by a larger, more distant organization – even if it was more efficient, which in itself was open to debate.

Early on, Long Beach had toyed with the idea of joining Orange County to escape Los Angeles' relentless pursuit. Then it explored the idea of being its own county, of becoming the City and County of Long Beach. In the end, it merely resisted Los Angeles' advances by growing larger itself, both by attracting new residents and annexing new territory.

In 1920, Long Beach was already the fastest growing city in the nation, with ten new homes being built per day. The population was exploding. American

Contractors magazine ranked Long Beach as having the most housing starts of any city of its size in the country and put it in the top fifteen cities for housing starts for any city regardless of population. Property values soared along with the population. Real estate ads invited speculators to buy property in the city as an investment with promises of making a healthy return in a short amount of time.

The Long Beach population was also being boosted by the annexation of nearby neighborhoods. The annexation strategy was used both to increase the size of the city and as a barrier to intrusion into the Long Beach sphere by Los Angeles. In 1911, Long Beach had annexed three square miles on the northeast side of the city which featured a 100-foot-wide strip running all the way to the Orange County border. Since annexations had to be of contiguous territory, that long, narrow east-west strip sealed off everything south of the strip – including water-rich lands that Long Beach relied upon for its water supply – from takeover by Los Angeles. Twelve years later, Long Beach would repeat the same tactic, this time farther north.

In July 1923, Long Beach annexed the Belmont District north of 11th Street between Temple and California avenues, adding about 10,000 new residents. In November, it annexed Alamitos Bay, Belmont Shore, Naples, and the land eastward to the Orange County line, bringing in about 2,500 new residents. In December, the city initiated an annexation election for the Virginia City area, including a 100-foot-wide shoestring strip along the Orange County line on the east and Artesia Boulevard and the Compton border on the north. That move would add another 15,000 people to Long Beach's population and effectively block Los Angeles from annexing any of the property south of Artesia Boulevard.

Los Angeles business interests sought an injunction to stop the Virginia City annexation election. When that didn't work, and voters approved the annexation, the Los Angeles businessmen filed to get the Long Beach annexation of the Virginia City area overturned, claiming it was an attempt to deny people south of the strip the choice of joining other cities. The Los Angeles Times accused Long Beach of not being a team player. Long Beach annexation advocates strongly denied that the purpose of the annexed strip was to deny residents inside the strip future choices; they claimed they were merely setting the area aside for industrial development as a sort of backlands for the harbor. Such disingenuous assertions did little to fool anybody, but that didn't matter. The court upheld the annexation. Unless Long Beach chose to voluntarily join the bigger city, it was at last out of Los Angeles' grasp. By 1924, the population of Long Beach was estimated at about 135,000, more than double the 55,593 residents counted in the 1920 census.

Still, there was some concern that brusquely slamming the door on the grand Los Angeles expansion plan would negatively impact federal funding for the harbor area. Since the federal government wanted the harbor area developed as one whole, rather than as two separate entities, would the feds see the confrontation between the two cities as a harbinger of political strife?

A meeting was called between Long Beach city officials and concerned parties from the Los Angeles harbor. Both sides agreed it was in their best interests to work together on development of both harbors. The two sides vowed cooperation. Not much had been resolved, but it was a demonstration that the rival harbors could get along when the situation called for it. The October 1920 dredging of the Cerritos Channel which connected the two harbors had been a demonstration of that.

From Small Town Politics to City Manager

Long Beach was growing, and its way of life was changing – both because of the thousands of new residents joining the city and because a new generation was slowly taking the reins of government. As always in such situations, the old guard fought to hold on to what once was, while the new people begin to slowly, forcefully assert themselves.

In 1914, Long Beach residents had voted to adopt a city commission form of government, which replaced the City Council members with five city commissioners. As a group, the commissioners were the legislative body. In addition, each commissioner was the executive head of one of the city's five administrative departments: public affairs, public property, finance and accounting, public safety, and public works. The five commissioners would elect one of their own as the mayor. The commissioners, city auditor, city attorney, police judge, and the board of education were elected posts. The city clerk, tax and license collector, engineer, health officer, police chief, fire chief, and librarian were all appointed positions.

Commissioner of Public Safety William M. Peek was part of the old guard. He was born in Missouri, grew up in Iowa, worked as a school teacher and principal, and moved to Long Beach in 1911 when he was 52 years old. By 1920, he was a Long Beach grocer and president of the Brotherhood of the First Methodist Church who had been elected to office although he apparently never campaigned for the job. Peek's term in office was marked by dissension and turmoil and inadvertently made the case to transition Long Beach from the small town commission-style government to a more formal government style that included a city manager.

Within months of his election, Peek had fired both the police chief and the fire chief and appointed fellow church member Ralph A. Newell as the new police chief. Newell was a 39-year-old law student and a chief deputy constable in a local justice court. He passed the bar less than four months later, set up his own law practice in the First National Bank Building on Pine Avenue, and resigned as police chief. Peek then appointed Police Sergeant James L. Butterfield as the new chief. Seven months later, Peek suspended Butterfield and named Sergeant James S. Yancy as the new interim chief. Peek promised a thorough cleanup of the department, saying he would take drastic action to remove disrupting elements. The problem was that some people in town were beginning to think that after three police chiefs in fifteen months, the biggest disrupting element in the Police Department was Peek himself.

The Police and Fire departments weren't the only city services that Peek meddled in. As public safety commissioner, he was responsible for overseeing the lifeguards, which brought to Peek's attention the fact that some women on the beach had begun wearing bathing suits that he thought were less than modest. So, he wrote an ordinance that defined what was, and was not, suitable beach wear and that further required that lounging robes be worn by those sunning themselves on the sand. Peek's proposed ordinance has become part of Long Beach lore – as much because of its incomprehensibility as its priggishness.

> *No person over the age of 6 shall appear on any highway or public place or on the sand of beach or in the Pacific Ocean in Long Beach clothed in a bathing suit which does not completely conceal from view all that portion of the trunk of the body of such person below a line around*

the body even with the upper part of the arm pits, except a circular hole for each arm, with the maximum diameter not longer than twice the distance from the upper part of the arm pit to the top of the shoulder, and which does not completely conceal from each view each leg from the hip joint to a line around the leg one-third of the way to the knee joint and without such bathing suit having attached a skirt made of opaque material completely surrounding the person and hanging loosely from the waistline to the bottom of such suit.

Both Peek and the city were lampooned in the press for the new ordinance. The Los Angeles Times ran a story complete with side-by-side cartoons comparing modern swimwear with that from the previous century.

"The trouble in Long Beach began, according to the factions, when the town selected its Commissioner of Public Safety. Not only was he formerly from Iowa, but his name was Peek, W.M. Peek. Mr. Peek became extremely piqued when he took a peek at the sights along the beach…" Long Beach merchants, who stood to lose earnings if out-of-towners stopped coming to the beach, thought it might be cheaper to "buy a pair of blinders for Mr. Peek," the story said.

In little more than thirty years, Long Beach had exploded into a relatively large city. It was time, some people felt, for it to be administered by a professional manager – not a grocer and church elder who somehow won the most votes. Some Long Beach residents also were saying there should be a separation of the church and community politics.

One result of the new thinking was a move to recall Peek as public safety commissioner. The recall faction accused Peek of proving himself incompetent during his eighteen months in office. He had failed to run his department in an efficient and businesslike manner, resulting in widespread strife and discord in the Police and Fire departments, the recall petition said. Peek responded by appointing yet another new police chief – the fourth in sixteen months. He was supported by an ad hoc organization composed of church and business leaders, calling itself the Peek Morals Enforcement League. The recall election was held on March 15, 1921, but it failed to pass. Peek retained his office.

The second – more important – movement was a campaign to pass a new City Charter, one that would establish a city manager form of government. Under such a structure, the City Council would set policy and a hired professional would administer the bureaucracy. There were doubts about such a course. Under the new City Charter, the mayor became merely the first among equals. He would preside over the council, greet visiting dignitaries, and represent the city at ceremonial events, but he would have very little to do with the everyday running of the city. The city manager, who would serve at the pleasure of the City Council, would run the city, and if he proved ineffective, he would be replaced. Such a form of government might be more efficient, but there was a worry that it would also place a wedge between the voters and the person responsible for running things. Despite such misgivings, the new City Charter was passed, and a new City Council was elected. The Council's first order of business was to hire a professional manager to run things. The man they chose from a list of fifty applicants was 38-year-old Charles Hewes, the city manager of Alameda and the president of the League of California Municipalities. Hewes was young, but he had experience. He had been appointed as city engineer in Alhambra in 1914, became the city manager in 1915, and was hired as city manager by Alameda in 1917. As Long Beach city manager, he would be paid $7,500 a year.

Hewes was the honored guest at a luncheon of the Progressive Business Men's Club on July 1, 1921, just two days after his selection. He told the businessmen that although he had been familiar with Long Beach when he was with the city of Alhambra, the progress the city had made since then had been astounding. He said that after meeting the new City Council he was optimistic that "we should be able to do big things in this city." Mayor Charles Buffum, who also was in attendance, praised the new city manager as a product of California.

"He is a man who has made good, and I have no hesitancy of saying that with the proper support he will make good here."

And so the honeymoon began.

Death of a Champion

Charles F. Van de Water was one of Long Beach's leading businessmen, and besides Charles Windham, was the biggest champion of the Long Beach Port. He came to Long Beach in 1904, became involved in both the insurance business as the Charles F. Van de Water Co. and in real estate development with former Mayor Stephen Townsend. When the United States entered World War I in 1917, he attempted to enlist, but was turned down because of his age. He was twice elected president of the Long Beach Chamber of Commerce and paid his own expenses to travel to Washington, D.C., to lobby for appropriations to help improve the Long Beach Harbor. The appropriation was approved. Van de Water was a strong advocate for the harbor and for any other cause that would benefit his adopted city. It was that reputation and his quiet, non-assuming manner that helped get him elected to Congress with 65 percent of the vote on November 2, 1920. He never took office.

Seventeen days after the election, he and his wife, Edith, attended a Republican banquet in Pomona to celebrate his victory. They were accompanied by his secretary, Janice Luebben, and a friend, Mrs. E.H. Jackson of the Long Beach Ebell Society. Driving home that evening along a dark road cloaked in a layer of thick fog, Van de Water ran into a truck trailer left standing on one side of the highway with no lights. Luebben, a 19-year-old honor graduate of Polytechnic High School, was killed instantly. Van de Water, who suffered a head injury, died within two minutes of arriving at the Pomona Valley Hospital. His wife, found walking around in a daze at the crash scene, was cut by flying glass, and Jackson suffered a sprained arm.

The congressman-elect's death sent a shock wave through Long Beach. Flags were lowered to half-staff, and city officials and residents openly mourned their much-admired friend. The driver of the truck was arrested and charged with manslaughter. He told police he had burned out a wheel bearing, but had not pulled all the way off the road because he was worried about the trailer becoming mired in the mud. As it turned out, the trailer's tail lights were broken.

Walter F. Lineberger, a friend and supporter, was later elected to Congress to serve the term that Van de Water had been unable to fill.

Subterranean Riches

About the same time that the members of the new Long Beach City Council were deciding to appoint Charles Hewes as their first city manager, something happened a few miles north and east of downtown that would forever leave its mark on the city.

At 9:30 p.m. on Friday, June 23, 1921, an oil well being drilled on Signal Hill near the intersection of Temple Avenue and Hill Street suddenly erupted in a gusher that spewed crude oil more than 100 feet into the air, raining the black stinking goo down on nearby homes and roadways. Workers on Shell Oil Well Alamitos No. 1 had been drilling for three months with mixed, but ultimately favorable, results. The crew drilling the well had hit an area of standing oil at a little over 2,800 feet into the ground on May 24, but it resulted in no stream of oil to the surface. It did, however, attract widespread interest in both the community and the industry. Others started setting up derricks on the hill and drilling their own wells. The drilling of Alamitos No. 1 continued, tapping deeper and deeper into the earth until at 3,114 feet below the surface, it hit a pocket of oil under such pressure that it blew up and out through the hole and high into the sky. Four separate times the oil spewed upward into the air, dying back between eruptions.

The Long Beach field turned out to be one of the largest oil fields ever discovered in California and one of the most productive fields per acre in the entire world. But it didn't start out that way. Union Oil had drilled for oil on the hill four years earlier and ended up with a dry hole – a "duster" as they called it in the industry. There was little reason for Shell Oil to believe that Alamitos No. 1 would be any different, but two persistent company geologists, Alvin Theodore Schwennesen and Frank Hayes, were convinced that there was oil beneath the hill. Previous attempts simply had not gone deep enough, they argued. Shell set up operations on Signal Hill under the guidance of drilling superintendent O.P. "Happy" Yowells.

California had been an oil-producing state for many years before the Signal Hill discovery. There was a time when the supply of oil was so great and the demand for it so low that it was considered a low-value commodity – dipping down as low as ten cents a barrel – and treated as such. When they ran out of redwood barrels to store the oil in, oilmen would sometimes store the excess crude in open reservoirs. If it rained, the oil would float to the top, overrun the banks, and spill out into the streets. So much oil had run into Echo Park Lake in Los Angeles, that in 1907 the lake caught fire and burned for three days. There was a glut of oil and only a limited number of uses. And if it spilled and soaked into the ground, nobody really cared. There was plenty more where that came from.

But attitudes changed when people began using oil for heating instead of coal – which had to be transported from back East. Railroads started using cheap oil instead of wood and coal to power their locomotives. Ships that once ran on coal began running on oil. Coal had to be hand-shoveled into the furnaces that fired the boilers, and when a ship refueled, seamen with shovels worked in the bunkers to distribute the coal – a lengthy process that tied the ship up in port. Oil simplified the logistics of refueling and feeding the boilers and produced more energy per pound than coal.

Around the same time, California had become the land of opportunity, and new residents were pouring in. Automobiles were getting cheaper and more affordable to the common man. Between 1915 and 1920, the number of automobiles in California jumped from 150,000 to 500,000 – which also raised the demand for fuel.

OIL!: *Wells and derricks dot the harbor landscape in the 1930s, a decade-and-a-half after oil was first discovered on Signal Hill in June 1921. The oil boom that started in the 1920s brought riches to the Long Beach area but also proved to be a near disaster for the port in coming years.*

Soon, not only had the demand for oil caught up with the supply, it had surpassed it. Motorists in 1919 experienced the first gas shortage, and for the first time, California had to import its gasoline by rail from other states. By 1921, California was producing only 90 percent of the oil it consumed, and experts were warning that the state was rapidly running out of its finite resources. Union Oil had three tankers under construction to transport oil up from Mexico. A 1921 New Year's Day editorial in the Los Angeles Times warned that conservation of oil was a necessity and that the nation needed to turn to hydroelectric power for its energy needs.

> *If we destroy the forests, we can replant and in time reforestation can replace them, but once we have drained our oil fields of their wealth, that wealth is gone forever and, therefore, on our use or misuse of this vanishing asset, depends our custodianship of the future.*

It was amidst this feeling of shortage and despair that Shell Oil's Alamitos Well No. 1 tapped into what was up to that time the largest oil field in the state. Thousands of people drove to the area to see the derrick and rigging dripping in oil. It took four days, but Shell finally got Alamitos No. 1 under control, capping the well at 500 barrels per day, down from the 3,000 barrels a day it had been producing before it was capped with a half-inch nozzle. Storage was a problem. When the company first hit oil, it had installed four nearby tanks connected by pipeline to the well with a total capacity of 6,000 barrels, plus an open sump hole that could hold thousands of barrels more. It was clearly not enough. Shell made a deal to run a pipeline to a nearby Union Oil line, but that would take several weeks to complete. Until then, it sold the excess oil to other companies and went to work spudding five new wells. The news of Alamitos No. 1 set off a rush of excitement not unlike the discovery of gold seventy-three years before.

Signal Hill, at 365 feet high, offered the best views of the city and the blue Pacific beyond. It was the place that city leaders would invariably take important guests – from presidents to foreign dignitaries – as part of their introduction to Long Beach tour. It was also a place that was rapidly being developed with high-priced homes and even some mansions, built for people who wanted to enjoy that same view.

The discovery of oil on Signal Hill changed all that, and it changed Long Beach too. Within days after Shell hit the first oil and weeks before the gusher, people began buying oil leases in the area and spudding new wells. Long Beach Consolidated Oil, a company incorporated by Long Beach businessmen and headed by former Mayor Charles H. Windham, signed an oil lease for an acre of land adjoining the Shell property with plans to sink two wells. Many would-be residents who had bought lots but not yet built on them, decided to sink wells on their property rather than live on it. Within days after Alamitos No. 1 broke loose, there were eleven additional derricks being installed around the hill. New oil companies were being formed, and residents on the hill were signing deals to have companies set up derricks in their back yards for a percentage of the take.

For the oil companies and the men who worked the rigs, the risks were great. Huge sums were being invested, and the work was dangerous. Around midnight on September 1, a gas fire broke out on the Shell rig known as Mesa No. 1, with flames shooting hundreds of feet into the air. The fire burned for thirty-six hours before it was brought under control. No lives were lost, but the derrick, the engine house, and all the equipment was destroyed. In an attempt to reduce the blaze, steam from eight three-inch pipes was sprayed for hours on the fire. Once the blaze had died down somewhat, it was smothered beneath a flood of soft mud pumped in through three large pipes.

Although it was the discovery well, Alamitos No. 1 had problems. Four months after it hit oil, workers on the rig were still struggling to control the high-pressure pocket of gas. On October 21, the well erupted several times over twenty-four hours, with oil spouting fifty feet into the air and bathing the rig and the surrounding area with thick layers of crude. Such incidents did little to stifle enthusiasm about the oil beneath the hill. In fact, it was seen as a sign of the potential richness of the discovery. Other companies were busy seeking to carve out their share of the underground treasure, while freelance solicitors were busy hawking oil properties to would-be investors. Some were legitimate deals, others less so. A few of the companies involved in the early drilling on Signal Hill, such as Standard Oil and Shell, are well known today. Most are not – companies such as Long Beach Consolidated Oil Co., San Martenas Oil Co., Crest Long Beach Consolidated Co., Sandburg Petroleum, the Dabny Oil Syndicate, the Signal Hill Syndicate, the Ramsey Brothers, the California Mexico Petroleum Syndicate, the Walker-Western, the Coast States, the Mike Michaels, the Guarantee, and the Spaulding Oil and Gas Co. Everybody wanted to get in on the ground floor of a sure thing.

Alamitos No. 1 had hit oil at just more than 3,100 feet deep. Shell's Horsch No. 1 hit pay dirt at just over 2,700 feet, and its Bab-Tucker well hit at 3,225 feet. Oil tycoon E.J. Miley brought in a well at 8,860 feet; San Martenas Oil brought in one at 3,540 feet, and Sandburg Petroleum hit oil at 3,045 feet. Standard Oil abandoned its Bixby No. 1 well at 5,540 feet after failing to see any indication of oil. The Signal Hill drillers were hitting oil at different depths, an indication that the oil field was fractured with the oil in some areas much deeper than in others. Punching through the dirt and rock to the oil was more difficult in some places than in others, but that was just part of the business. Standard Oil may have given up on its well, but it did not give up on Signal Hill. Even Union Oil Co., which had walked away from Signal Hill after drilling a duster in 1917, came back now, ready to go a little deeper and tap into the bonanza uncovered by Shell.

There was a problem with gas trapped in pockets beneath the ground. On November 16, 1921, Shell Oil's Martin No. 1 well tapped into one such pocket at 2,500 feet deep, sending a jet of gas rushing up the casing and into the air at the rate of 100 million cubic feet per day. The gas went out through a side casing of the well, causing the ground beneath the derrick to cave in. Shell officials said there was little they could do to contain the flow of gas and that it would have to just "blow itself out."

That night the gas ignited, sending a huge pillar of fire into the air for the second time in two-and-a-half months. Shell put in a call for Ford Alexander, a "well-shooter" from the oil town of Taft in southwestern Kern County. Alexander and his team put on asbestos clothing, placed eighty pounds of gelatin dynamite – wrapped in asbestos to avoid premature detonation – on a chair, pulled the chair by wires to the fire, and detonated the dynamite. The dynamite put out the column of fire and extinguished the blaze, and then the company pumped mud into the well to block the upward flow of gas. But it was a battle more than a process, with the gas sometimes regurgitating the mud back 100 to 200 feet into the air. Nobody was hurt in the entire process, although Shell Superintendent W.C. McDuffle and Long Beach Press reporter Max A. Morrison were almost swallowed up by the ground when it caved in beneath their feet as they scrambled to safety.

The gushers, the fires, and the explosions were all rapidly becoming part of life in the area north of downtown Long Beach, and the economy of the city was booming because of it. Oil workers flooded the city, spending their paychecks on goods and services. And if they weren't always the kind of God-fearing, sober-living folks the good residents of Long Beach liked, at least their money was always welcome.

Long Beach also was profiting directly from the boom. Although Signal Hill was not part of Long Beach, it was assumed that it someday would be. Long Beach had earlier acquired 200 acres for a grand park on the west side of Cherry Avenue in Signal Hill. Plans for the park, laid out by landscape architect Charles Deusner, called for drives, walks, golf links, tennis courts, bowling greens, an amphitheater, a stadium, and a lake. It was going to be "the Golden Gate Park of Southern California." But with the huge oil discovery beneath the surface, it made no sense to build a park on property that had suddenly become so very valuable.

Long Beach's first well, Ramsey Municipal No. 1, hit oil on November 27, and the city – which had signed a fifty-fifty deal with the Ramsey Brothers – was in the oil business. The California Mexico Petroleum Co. also signed a lease with the city to develop the property. It was a heady time for Long Beach. There was even talk about being the first tax-free city in the nation. With that kind of oil money rolling in, who needed taxes?

In December 1921, there was another fire, the third in three-and-a-half months. Once again Shell sent for Ford Alexander, who prepared a 100-pound charge, guided it with cable, and detonated it over the hole. It worked like a charm, although the blast shook the community for miles around and broke numerous windows in nearby residences. There was only one injury. Mrs. W.B. Nicholson was sitting in a chair in the bedroom of her home on Cherry Avenue when the charge was ignited. The concussion threw her from her chair, and she suffered a sprained back.

By the end of the year, slightly more than six months after Alamitos No. 1 electrified the oil industry with its fountain of crude, there were six producing wells on Signal Hill and seventy-five derricks erected to bring more oil to the surface.

The new gold rush was on – this time for black gold, the kind of gold that powers a nation, the kind of gold that grows more valuable as it grows more scarce, the kind of gold that is quickly consumed and can only be replenished by tapping into new sources.

It would make Long Beach rich – and also cost the city dearly – in the future.

Recalling Charles Hewes

Charles E. Hewes, Long Beach's first city manager, had a stellar first year in office, or so it seemed. He took over the reins of government, reorganized departments, gave out pay hikes, and negotiated oil leases on city land. He retained Ben W. McLendon, the last police chief appointed by Peek, as the head of the city's dysfunctional police force. He asked for the resignation of building inspector Joseph Raycraft, although Raycraft was a personal friend of some of the council members. He also vowed to enforce the unpopular swimsuit ordinance drawn up by Peek. If people thought it was ridiculous, he said, they should change the law. When people wanted him to fire Chief McLendon on allegations that the chief had stolen a bicycle seat and allowed cussing at the police station, Hewes called the charges ridiculous and the result of "petty jealousies" inside the Police Department. In December 1921, the first money from the city's new oil leases began rolling in, and in June 1922 – one year after he was hired – the City Council praised Hewes' work and extended his contract for another year. The following month, he estimated that in the coming budget year, the city would earn an estimated $600,000 in oil money.

Shortly after that, things began to sour. The city auditor, a feisty woman named Myrtelle L. Gunsul, crossed swords with the city manager in July 1922, when it came time to move from the old two-story City Hall on Pacific Avenue and Broadway into the new eight-story City Hall next door. The new City Hall had a switchboard through which all calls were to be routed. Auditor Gunsul, first elected to office in 1919, didn't like the idea of anybody being able to listen in on her line. She wanted a private phone in her office. Hewes said no. As an elected official, she didn't think Hewes had the authority to dictate what kind of phone she had. She went ahead and ordered a private line. She also wasn't happy with the amount of office space she had been assigned by Hewes in the new building. It wasn't big enough. So the night before the move-in, she and her staff moved some of their office furnishings into her assigned space and the rest of it into an adjacent space that had been assigned to the City Water Department. When Hewes showed up for work at the new City Hall on Monday morning, he discovered the city auditor's takeover and found himself locked out of the city auditor's office. He was irate.

"We will have to fight it out to find out whether the Council or Miss Gunsul is running the city," he declared to a local newspaper reporter. Of course, her action and his reaction sparked a feeding frenzy in the press, which saw Auditor Gunsul's acts of defiance as high comedy. On Tuesday, Hewes persuaded council members to request that Gunsul give up her stolen territory. They knocked on her door, but she said she was too busy to talk to them and suggested they come back later. On Wednesday, he sent a trio of police officers to take over the space, but the door was locked, and they decided to retreat rather than break it down. The following day, the police were back, this time with the chief. Gunsul was out of the office on business, and her staff refused to open the door. This time, however, one of the officers used the butt of his revolver to break a window, slip the catch, and enter the room. The police quickly carried the auditor's furnishings and equipment out into the hall, replaced them with furnishings for the Water Department, and evicted the auditor's staff from the misappropriated territory.

In the end, Hewes had won the battle of the office space, but it came at the price of his dignity. In the press, the dispute came off as a rollicking good feud between the "battling city auditor of Long Beach" and the rather stuffy city manager.

"Four of Long Beach's bravest coppers under the doughty leadership of Sergeant Llewellyn marched upon City Hall today to dispossess Miss Myrtelle L. Gunsul and retreated in dismay, thwarted by an array of locked windows and doors," crowed the July 27 story in the Los Angeles Times, which ran with a picture of cartoon police knocking at her door. When Hewes and a squad of "burly policemen" finally took the space back the following day, the headline read: "Fort Gunsul is Captured, Bitter City Hall Battle is Expected to Resume when Woman Auditor Returns to Fray."

A more serious challenge came the following month, when a delegation of residents – some of them the same people who the previous year had demanded that Hewes fire Police Chief McLendon – showed up at City Hall. This time they demanded that the City Council fire Hewes. Their complaints against Hewes were of a general nature. They claimed Hewes was unqualified to be city manager and too extravagant in conducting city business. The city budget had gone up $150,000 during Hewes' tenure, they noted. They also accused him of violating the City Charter by hiring outside investigators to look into problems at the Police Department. On top of it all, he was an outsider, brought down from the Bay Area to run their city. Hewes had to go, and he had to be replaced by somebody from Long Beach. If the City Council would not fire Hewes, the protesters promised to mount a recall against the city manager and let the voters decide.

Hewes defended his record in a letter to the Council. He noted that the real motivation behind the demand for his termination had been his refusal a year earlier to fire Police Chief McLendon. As city manager, he represented the City Council, not individual citizens or groups that may have their own priorities, he said. As long as he held the position, he planned to be city manager in fact, as well as in name. The City Council agreed. If the anti-Hewes coalition wanted to get rid of him, they would have to organize a recall and convince the voters that he needed to go.

Two months later, Hewes was dealing with another controversy, this one concerning Police Chief Ben McLendon and two former Long Beach police chiefs whom McLendon had arrested. The former chiefs, C.C. Cole and James L. Butterfield, had been taken into custody along with Steven Mitchell, the alleged kleagle for the Long Beach chapter of the Ku Klux Klan. A kleagle is a Klan officer in charge of recruiting new members. The three were accused of creating a disturbance at a campaign speech by District Attorney Thomas Lee Woolwine, who was running for governor.

While the idea of the two former chiefs being part of the Ku Klux Klan may seem shocking, there was a resurgence of the Klan during the 1920s. Membership in the Klan was not as scandalous then; during its peak, the Klan claimed more than 4 million members. That may have been an exaggeration, but there is little doubt that Klan membership was widespread. The Orange County Klan was so prevalent that Anaheim – where it was most dominant – earned the nickname "Klanaheim."

The arrested chiefs claimed that McLendon had arrested them because of a personal enmity toward them. Hewes suspended McLendon while he investigated the claim, but reinstated him a week later, with a rebuke for arresting the former chiefs at District Attorney Woolwine's request. Woolwine was making a speech in his role as a political candidate, Hewes noted in his report, not as an officer of the court. But McLendon had had enough. He accepted his reinstatement, but immediately resigned and went back to being a detective. The scandal was resolved, but it did little to endear Hewes to the voters.

In the end, Hewes' unpopularity as city manager wasn't a question of how he administered city affairs as much as it was an issue of being an outsider who came in and took over operations at City Hall. Despite support of Hewes by the

Chamber of Commerce and other business groups, the residents of Long Beach voted on November 29 to fire the man that the City Council wouldn't fire. Hewes had served as city manager for almost eighteen months, and the Council was happy with the job he had done, but the people had spoken. By popular vote, Hewes had been fired.

The Port, the Navy, and Public Pushback
During the same years that the city's political structure was evolving, the physical infrastructure of the port also was facing new challenges. The new flood control channel that cut through Long Beach between downtown and the harbor did solve the problem of silt flooding the harbor after every rainy season. During the rains of 1920, with the new countywide system still unfinished, flooding was kept to a minimum, and the annual deluge of mud was avoided, although there was still dredging to be done to restore past damage.

A vast migration of people leaving their homes in the East and Midwest to move to California was underway, and Long Beach was at the cutting edge of that relocation. In twenty years, the city had grown from about 2,000 people to more than 55,000 and clearly was headed for more than 100,000. With the new people came new attitudes and new priorities. The old-time confederation of the business community and local government – with business leaders active on both sides of the line – had achieved much progress during the years, but it no longer could act without challenge from other factions.

The two ports had worked together with the federal government on dredging the Cerritos Channel to link their harbors and celebrated it with pomp and ceremony when the harbors met. When Los Angeles annexed San Pedro and Wilmington in 1909, part of the deal had been that Los Angeles would spend $10 million over the next ten years on harbor improvements. By 1919, $5.5 million of that amount had been spent. On May 6, 1919, Los Angeles voters approved the issuance of bonds to finance the remaining $4.5 million. That provided Los Angeles with the blessing of deep pockets, and the city continued to aggressively develop its harbor. Long Beach, which lacked the financial resources of the larger city, lagged behind. Like any venture, the establishment of a port – especially man-made harbors such as in Long Beach and Los Angeles – takes a huge investment. That investment had already paid off in jobs and a boost to the local economy, but the port was hardly self-sufficient, and more development would be needed before it could become so.

The shipbuilding industry, which had boomed during World War I, quickly collapsed with the return of peace. During the war, the U.S. Shipping Board had built up a government-owned merchant fleet to support the war effort. By the war's end, the United States had the world's largest merchant fleet, but most of it was owned by the government, which had no desire or mandate to be in the commercial shipping business.

In an effort to address that issue, Congress passed the Merchant Marine Act of 1920, more commonly known as the Jones Act, after Senator Wesley Jones of Washington state, who introduced it. The aim of the act was to transfer the government's fleet of merchant ships to the private sector and to set up a regulatory system that would allow that fleet to operate profitably. One of the ways the act sought to do that was to limit trade between American ports to American-owned vessels, sailed by American crews and built in American shipyards.

The problem was that with such a surplus of ships in the American merchant fleet, there was little demand for new ships. The once-booming Long Beach shipbuilding industry, which had employed thousands of workers, had become idle. An accounting of vessels built and launched by the Long Beach Shipbuilding Co. – formerly Craig Shipbuilding Co. – shows the rapid fall-off after the end of the war in 1918, as the yard filled its existing government orders.

In 1918, the shipyard built four cargo ships and three submarines. In 1919, six cargo ships were built, and in 1920, five cargo ships and one yacht were built. In 1921, two cargo ships and one yacht were built; in 1923, one cargo ship and one tug were built. One yacht was built in 1925 and another in 1930. In 1931, two yachts were built. Always far-sighted when it came to business, Long Beach Shipbuilding Co. President John F. Craig had seen the writing on the wall by 1921 and had started looking for a buyer to take over all or part of his facility.

The everyday business of the port continued, but little was being done to develop the harbor infrastructure. Then a series of calamities hit that diverted attention and resources. A mysterious explosion and fire at the Long Beach Fisheries Co. on the afternoon of December 13, 1920, spread quickly to the Halfhill Tuna Co. and the Los Angeles Tuna Packing Co., causing $250,000 in total damage to the three plants. The Long Beach channels still needed dredging from earlier deposits of silt that had come downstream before construction of the flood control channel. A fire in April 1921 destroyed the Golden State Woolen Mills plant with damages reported at $500,000. The following month, a fire at the Colonial Chocolate Co. on West Broadway and an adjacent building supply outlet operated by W.L. Lynds caused an estimated $225,000 in damage. Golden State Mills subsequently rebuilt its plant, which re-opened in May 1922.

Los Angeles, on the other hand, was busy developing its harbor. The channels were dredged, the city had built a giant terminal in the outer harbor with a five-story warehouse and a 2,600-foot wharf called Municipal Dock No. 1, and tonnage moving through the harbor – which lagged during the war years – was spurting upward with a 70 percent increase from the 1918-19 fiscal year to 1919-20. By 1921, there were forty distinct shipping lines calling at the Los Angeles Port. The next project on the books was construction of a bridge across the Cerritos Channel to connect the mainland to Terminal Island.

The Los Angeles Harbor Commission, confident that it was only a matter of time before Long Beach would have to merge its harbor with Los Angeles, announced a plan in October 1921 in which the breakwater would be extended all the way to just west of the flood control channel in Long Beach. Thus sheltered from the open sea, the south shore of Terminal Island could be developed with multiple slips for loading and unloading ships.

Long Beach had been under pressure for years from both Los Angeles and from the federal government to merge the two harbors into one – especially if it wanted the federal government's financial help. Charles Windham and other Long Beach Harbor advocates had recommended in 1919 that the two ports be linked together – in name only – when applying for federal grants as the Los Angeles-Long Beach Harbor. But Long Beach had stubbornly refused any suggestion that the two harbors become one.

But by 1920, development of the Long Beach Harbor was stalled. The city may have overseen the port and the channels in the port, but the Los Angeles Dock and Terminal Co. still owned and controlled much of the property along those channels. In order to further develop the harbor, the city needed money. In December 1920, a syndicate with prominent Los Angeles attorney Isidore B. Dockweiler as trustee agreed to purchase an option to buy 244 acres of harbor property for $2 million from the Los Angeles Dock and Terminal Co. As part of the deal, the property had to be first offered to the city at the agreed upon price. Few expected Long Beach to purchase the property – it had already turned down such opportunities. This time, however, the city put a $2.5 million bond issue on the ballot – $2 million for the property and $500,000 for other needed harbor improvements.

The campaign to pass the harbor bonds was fierce and often acrimonious. The Long Beach Chamber of Commerce, the Rotary Club and the Kiwanis campaigned hard and vigorously for passage, noting that the bonds were sorely needed to develop the port into a vital and sustainable operation. The Chamber bought full-page and half-page newspaper ads urging voters to approve the bond issue, conducted a canvass of voters to determine their feelings on the subject, and held a mass meeting in the Municipal Auditorium to promote passage of the bonds. Opponents of the measure were characterized as "reactionaries." The Chamber didn't need to just convince most of the voters; it needed to convince a full two-thirds majority to win passage.

Opponents – some of them also members of the Chamber – were equally committed to defeating the measure. They zeroed in on the claim that the $2 million would be spent to the benefit of one company, the Los Angeles Dock and Terminal Co. Those opposition members – who had dubbed themselves the "Anti-Gold Brick Association" – published a pamphlet calling Chamber members, the newspapers, ministers, and other pro-bond people "paid gum-shoers" for the company.

On April 18, 1921, the people of Long Beach voted to reject the bond measure. There were repercussions. Chamber members who had opposed the bonds demanded that the Chamber provide an accounting of just how much money had been spent to push the measure. Among them were Farmers and Merchants Bank President C.J. Walker, Alexander Hotel owner Scott Alexander, furniture store owner H.S. Callahan, and other downtown property owners. When the Chamber later revealed it had spent more than $10,000 to promote the issue, it drew fire from critics for attempting to locate undesirable industries close to residential areas. City Council member Frank Downs, who represented Westside city residents, skewered the Chamber for attempting to force industries on the area, which would make it "an undesirable place in which to live."

In the early days when Long Beach was more of a village than a city, there was plenty of open space and people eagerly sought investment in the community. A new factory smokestack in town with black smoke pouring from the top was seen as jobs and prosperity, but by the early 1920s, the city had grown up and the contradictions between industry and lifestyle were beginning to emerge.

In July 1922, Long Beach demanded that Union Oil pay damages for a pipeline spill that had resulted in a heavy coating of oil spreading into the ocean off Long Beach, resulting in thousands of tourists cancelling their trips to the beach. The oil coated bathers' swimsuits, stained the white hulls of yachts moored nearby, caused downtown merchants to lose money, and damaged the city's reputation as a pleasant place to visit. It turned out not to be just Union Oil to blame for the oil sheen that polluted the ocean and drove swimmers elsewhere.

Oil was flowing into the ocean from the operations of other oil companies as well, although it was difficult to pinpoint the source of each instance. And it wasn't just the oil companies that were discharging black goo into the ocean. Although it was illegal under federal law to discharge oil from vessels into a harbor or bay, some freighters were doing just that under the cover of darkness, an act that in the aftermath was almost impossible to detect and prosecute.

Both the harbor and the oil fields provided payrolls and purchases that profited local businesses and residents, but at what cost? And was it possible to maximize the benefits while minimizing the social costs? It was a question that would not go away, not then and not later.

New Role for Charles Windham

Although the idea for the port didn't begin with Charles H. Windham, he was a key player in the development of it and in the later promotion, funding, and survival of it. He invested in the port, he promoted it, he served as mayor during much of the building of it, and during the dark days when it appeared as though the whole project was going to sink beneath a sea of mud, he was an advocate for it. It was Windham who would testify before the Board of Engineers, who would travel back to Washington, D.C. to generate support among elected officials, and who would work at home to campaign for the passage of harbor improvement bonds. As a businessman and as a public servant, Windham was deeply involved in both the development of the city and of the port.

Like many of the ambitious businessmen of his time, he followed opportunity. As a young man, he had worked on the Oregon and California Railroad. In Nicaragua, he had worked on the canal project until it was canceled. In Costa Rica, where he had worked for the United Fruit Co., he had managed Puerto Limon, the largest fruit shipping port in Central America. He had worked for the Costa Rica Railroad. He had bought and run his own coffee and sugar plantation, and when he arrived in Long Beach from Costa Rica after an attack of malaria, he had become a real estate broker and developer. He was a key member of the Los Angeles Dock and Terminal Co. in developing the harbor, later taking over management of the dredging operation. Windham was president of the Long Beach Steamship Co. and secretary to the Western Steam Navigation Co., both of which built freighters at the Craig shipyard and leased them to steamship operators. Through it all, he never gave up his real estate interests. In 1920, he joined with other Long Beach investors to form the Long Beach Consolidated Oil Co., of which he was president. The company pumped liquid asphaltum from a well it operated in the Newport Oil Field and was one of the first companies to secure a lease on Signal Hill after the oil discovery there.

Despite his busy life pursuing business opportunities, Windham continued his involvement in civic affairs – although not in any official capacity. In March 1922, that changed when Windham, a staunch Republican, was named by President Warren Harding to be Long Beach postmaster, replacing Walter Desmond, a Democrat, who had been appointed by President Woodrow Wilson in 1913. It was a friendly takeover. Windham was president of Long Beach Consolidated Oil; Desmond was a director and attorney for the firm.

Windham's appointment as postmaster turned out to be a short one. After Long Beach City Manager Charles Hewes was recalled by voters, the City Council needed to find a replacement quickly. It had to be somebody who knew how to manage an organization, who was reliable, and who was – and this was very important – a longtime resident of the city. The City Council turned to the one man whom everybody turned to when they needed competent and steadfast assistance. On December 9, 1922, the Council appointed C.H. Windham as the new Long Beach city manager. His salary was the same as had been earned by Hewes – $7,500 a year. Within half-an-hour of being notified of his appointment, he telegraphed his resignation as postmaster to Washington, D.C., and assumed the professional administration of Long Beach.

As city manager, Charles H. Windham fit all the requirements. He was competent, politically knowledgeable, charismatic, and most of all, he was a long-time Long Beach resident, with a record of public service both as mayor and as a leader of the business community. Three days after his appointment, Windham sat down with a group of reporters to talk about his intention to run the city in a businesslike manner.

"The manager form of government is based upon the general principles of a railroad corporation, the citizens being the stockholders, the City Council being the board of directors, and the manager the executive head to carry out the work authorized by the council," he explained. "The head of each department of city government will continue to be the head as long as he remains in that position. No removals or changes will be made until I have had time to check up on the efficiency of each department. No changes will ever be made for political reasons." He said he expected "efficiency of the highest grade" from every person on the city payroll from director to ditch digger.

Although Windham believed that City Hall affairs should be businesslike, that didn't mean he always sided with businesses. Although he served as the president of a steamship line and also as the president of an oil company, he was adamant that business had a responsibility to the community.

About a month after he assumed office, Windham extracted a promise from Los Angeles county supervisors that they would crack down on oil operators on Signal Hill who permitted oil from their sumps to spill onto city streets and run down the hill. Signal Hill at the time was an unincorporated county area, over which Long Beach had no legislative or police authority, even though Long Beach did suffer from the sometimes casual working attitudes of the oil men there. Later that year, after a continuing problem with oil washing up on the beach, Windham fired off telegrams to federal and state authorities demanding that more be done to enforce the law forbidding ships from emptying their oily bilge tanks into the harbor. He also strongly reminded company executives who operated oil tankers that dumped their bilge water close to shore that they were in violation of the law.

The businessman had once again become a city official. But as always, Windham was a man who would not let a good opportunity slip by, not for himself and not for his city.

The Rejuvenation of the Long Beach Harbor

One of the most important items on Charles Windham's agenda as city manager was the harbor. Windham had been involved in the harbor from the time it was a vision in the minds of a group of investors from Long Beach, Ocean Park, Playa del Rey, and Redlands. He had invested in the project, worked on the building of it, pushed through the first bonds for the municipal dock, and lobbied for federal funding. By the early 1920s, all that investment in money and labor was languishing.

In January 1923, County Flood Control Chief Engineer James W. Reagan urged Long Beach to pass bonds in order to improve the harbor. Reagan – whose son had married Windham's daughter three years earlier – submitted a plan to the City Council suggesting the city put a $3 million bond package on the ballot. The money would be turned over to the federal government to be Long Beach's share of the breakwater extension. The following day, Congressman Walter Lineberger, a longtime associate of Windham and a former Long Beach harbor commissioner, made the same suggestion. Funding for an extended breakwater that would protect the Long Beach main channel to the sea would more likely be passed if Long Beach showed it was willing to pick up some of the cost, he said.

In March, Long Beach Councilman Alexander Beck accompanied a delegation of forty U.S. senators, congressmen and their wives on a tour of the harbor. The following day, he proposed a ballot measure for a $5 million harbor improvement bond. He noted that the city of Los Angeles was proposing to pass a $15 million harbor bond issue and said Long Beach needed to follow that example. One of the members of that congressional party was Senator George Norris of Nebraska, who was staying in Long Beach for a few extra days to visit at the Ocean Boulevard home of his daughter, Maria Nelson. Beck also urged the city to develop the harbor. Although Long Beach voters had turned down a smaller harbor improvement bond less than a year before, attitudes against passage of such a bond had softened. This time the bond money would pay for improvements to the harbor, not to buy land from the Los Angeles Dock and Terminal Co. It was clear that if the Long Beach Harbor was going to thrive as a municipal asset, the city was going to have to come up with some money.

Los Angeles, with its larger base of taxpayers, had been pouring money into its port and supplementing that investment with federal funds – and it was paying off. Tons of cargo were coming through the port, well above earlier expectations. Harbor executives had estimated in 1919 that the Los Angeles port would have to handle 8.5 million tons of cargo in 1925. In 1922, Los Angeles saw 9.7 million tons move across the docks. More than 4,200 vessels called at the L.A. port that year. The port had built and extended wharves, built warehouses, dredged channels, and built roadways, and it was making money from the fees and rents it charged steamship lines that called there. New wharves and transit sheds were on the drawing boards for the west end of Terminal Island along with a drawbridge across the Cerritos Channel that would link Terminal Island to the mainland. But despite all of that, the Los Angeles port was rapidly running out of space.

Representatives of the Long Beach and Los Angeles harbors and the businessmen who depended on the ports to earn their money, met in January 1923 with Major Edward D. Ardery of the Army Corps of Engineers to make the case for more federal funding. The harbor people wanted federal help to widen and deepen the main channels in both ports to thirty-seven feet, to deepen the Cerritos Channel between Wilmington and Long Beach to thirty feet, and to extend the breakwater four-and-a-half miles to a point between the flood control diversion channel and the main entrance to the Long Beach Harbor. Ardery took their suggestions under advisement.

On June 5, 1923, Los Angeles city voters approved $15 million in harbor bonds by more than a 4-to-1 margin. It was a victory for the Los Angeles Port, but it was also seen as a victory for the smaller Port of Long Beach. Windham said approval of the Los Angeles bonds would give an impetus to the program for developing and improving the Long Beach Harbor as well. Deepening the Long Beach channels to a uniform depth of thirty feet would attract industries to the harbor, which would expand the city tax base sufficiently to offset the cost of the improvements, he said.

In fact, industry was attracted to the Long Beach Harbor by the promise of deeper channels. A month after the Los Angeles vote, it was announced that a newly formed company was interested in building a $15 million steel rolling mill on a 200-acre portion of the property that the city had earlier proposed to buy from the Los Angeles Dock and Terminal Co. That deal fell through a year earlier when Long Beach voters defeated the $2.5 million harbor bond issue that would have financed the purchase. But in 1923, the newly created Pacific Coast Steel Corp. bought the Long Beach property and planned to build the largest steel mill of its kind in the Western United States on it. As a condition of moving to Long Beach, the company wanted the city to dredge the inner harbor to a uniform depth of thirty feet, and it wanted that depth to be maintained in proportion to the channel depth at the Port of Los Angeles so that large ships could access the port to transport company products. The company also wanted Channel One to be abandoned and filled in so as to connect its property and the wharves for easy discharge and loading of cargo. Negotiations for building the plant in Long Beach had been going on for several weeks before the announcement, but not everybody was enthusiastic about the possibilities. There was a faction that wanted to make sure that Long Beach remained a residential city, rather than an industrial center. Those people discouraged the steel mill project, noting concerns that the company would bring an undesirable element to the community.

City Manager Windham and Mayor Charles Buffum had done everything in their power to bring the Pacific Coast Steel project to the city. Buffum dismissed the opposition by some citizens, saying the majority of the people of Long Beach seemed to be in favor of the project, which would boost the city's economy and tax base. It was time to either improve the harbor or just fill it up, he boldly declared.

"It is possible, however, that objections to deepening the harbor will develop," Buffum said. "If this idea should be carried out in every public and private enterprise, nothing would ever be done …"

The City Council voted to proceed with the deal, although there were several steps remaining before it would be concluded.

A couple of weeks later, word came back from Washington that the Board of Engineers for Rivers and Harbors had agreed to conduct a survey on the merits of dredging the Los Angeles Harbor channels, reclaiming government land at Deadman's Island, and deepening and enlarging the Cerritos Channel between Los Angeles and Long Beach. Major Ardery said that the Board did not plan to consider the proposed extension of the breakwater. Further, he said that the breakwater would be very expensive and that the Board doubted whether the breakwater would reduce long ocean swells unless the openings from the sea to the harbor were made narrow. Reducing the size of the passages from ocean to harbor would result in strong currents through those passages.

In addition, the Board found that any waterfront development in Long Beach was problematic. The Long Beach inner harbor had limited area for rail yards, warehouses, and other auxiliary uses. It made more sense to focus on further development of outer harbor deep water areas at the Port of Los Angeles rather than on improvements in Long Beach. Once again, the Army Corps of Engineers had dismissed the importance of the smaller harbor next door to Los Angeles. It was not entirely without cause.

Long Beach was used to playing second fiddle to Los Angeles when it came to federal funding, and so Windham and the City Council forged ahead with their own plan to develop the Long Beach Harbor. On December 3, 1923, Windham met in San Francisco with executives from the Dollar Steamship Co. to talk about the line calling at the Port of Long Beach. At the time, Dollar Line was one of the main steamship lines in the Asian trade. Robert Dollar, the 79-year-old president and founder, was a native of Scotland who had made his fortune in the timber business. In 1895, frustrated with the service he was getting from the shipping lines that transported his lumber, he bought his first steamship, the *Newsboy*. Within a few years, Dollar had a fleet of ships hauling lumber up and down the coast and had incorporated his shipping business. His was one of the first lines to establish ongoing trade with Asia. The line already called at the Port of Los Angeles, but Windham wanted to convince Dollar to establish a terminal on Channel No. 3, opposite the Craig shipyard site. Windham talked about the plans of Pacific Coast Steel to build a steel mill in the harbor – a project that would generate a good deal of ocean freight business – and of plans by the various railroads to establish links at the Long Beach Harbor.

Three months later, Los Angeles Dock and Terminal Co. officials confirmed that Southern Pacific Railroad had agreed to pay $1 million for a fifty-five-acre property between Channels Two and Three. The railroad planned to use the land to develop a huge terminal for the Dollar Steamship line that would be Dollar's Southern California terminal. It marked one of the first instances of Long Beach trying to steal one of Los Angeles' customers. But it would not be the last.

Things were looking up for the Port of Long Beach. There were rumors that another steamship line – part of the United Fruit Co. – was thinking about opening a terminal inland from the Long Beach turning basin. Windham, of course, had worked for United Fruit Co. (now known as Chiquita Brands International) during his years in Costa Rica and was acquainted with Minor Cooper Keith – one of the company's controversial founders. In March 1924, Windham disclosed that the Merritt-Chapman-Scott Corporation, one of the largest marine salvage and wrecking companies, had paid $250,000 for ten acres on the Long Beach waterfront where it planned to base its fleet of salvage and wrecking vessels. The parcel was part of the Pacific Coast Steel property. The following day, the Long Beach City Council voted to place a $5 million harbor improvement bond on the ballot.

A week later, the five-member Army Board of Engineers for Rivers and Harbors arrived in Southern California to tour the two ports and hold a hearing on possible harbor improvements. On their first day in town, the engineers toured the industrial areas of both Long Beach and Los Angeles, visited the oil fields on Signal Hill, and took a look at how far the harbor extended inland. There were no figures or proposals presented during the tour; the engineers just got a picture of the place that was going to be discussed in the hearing the following day. The board members were guests for lunch at the Virginia Hotel with Brigadier General Harry Taylor, the Board's senior officer, seated between congressmen Walter Lineberger and John Fredericks. A tour of the breakwater had to be canceled because of heavy seas after a 50-mph southwesterly gale resulted in small craft warnings. Dinner that night was at the City Club in Los Angeles.

BREAKWATER GROUNDBREAKING: *City Manager Charles Windham, top, helps lay the first rock of the new Long Beach breakwater in 1925. The previous year, voters had passed a landmark $5 million harbor bond, of which $2 million would go toward extending the breakwater.*

The hearing held on the following day ended with several questions resolved, and one big one left outstanding. After hearing all the evidence, the Board approved a recommendation to dredge the Los Angeles inner harbor channel including the turning basin, to dredge the West Basin, and to deepen the Cerritos Channel between Los Angeles and Long Beach. That came after Windham announced that Long Beach had already signed a contract with the San Francisco Bridge Co. to dredge the Long Beach portion of the channel to 200 feet wide and thirty feet deep. Mud dredged from the harbor bottom would be used to build up port property owned by the Union Pacific Railroad.

General Taylor also had some strong advice for the local harbor boosters, interrupting speakers on several occasions to stress the importance of his observations. One topic on which he had particularly pointed commentary was the industrialization of harbor property.

"There seems to me a tendency here toward overstressing the industrial development of the harbor area," he told the gathering. "You can't locate your harbor anywhere but on the ocean. You can locate your industries, or most of them, anywhere in Los Angeles County."

The other topic, on which he shared his opinion several times during his stay in Los Angeles, was unification of the harbor area. The entire harbor area should be under one port authority, he lectured. The two cities needed to find a way to share authority over the harbor area.

When it came to the breakwater, however, the Board of Engineers was not convinced. They ordered Major Ardery, the district engineer, to conduct an immediate cost survey of the breakwater project and report his findings. Since the Board had the previous year rejected such a survey, authorizing the survey was a step toward possible approval of the project. In April, Major Ardery completed his survey and concluded that a recommendation to extend the breakwater be approved. The Board of Engineers agreed. The following month, the Board said it would support extension of the breakwater if Long Beach voters approved a $5 million bond issue in the upcoming election. The Board wanted $4 million from the two cities to go toward the breakwater project – an even split of $2 million each. Without the Long Beach bond approval, the Board would not back the breakwater project.

On May 8, 1924, the citizens of Long Beach met that essential requirement when they voted, by an 18-to-1 margin, to approve the $5 million harbor bond. Of that amount, $2 million would go toward extending the breakwater. The rest was earmarked for dredging and other harbor improvements. It marked a turning point for the Long Beach Harbor. After years of struggle, tons of mud, and public pushback from some residents who feared their seaside village would be forever ruined, the port seemed to finally be taking off. The channels would be dredged, the breakwater would allow development of Terminal Island, and there were industries eager to establish themselves as part of the community. The Pacific Coast Steel mill, the joint Southern Pacific-Dollar Line terminal, a planned Union Pacific railroad-steamship facility on Terminal Island, and the coming operations hub for the Chapman and Scott Marine Salvage and Wrecking Co. all promised a bright future both for the port and the city. The Long Beach Harbor was at last on its way to being a contender.

All five of the City Council members that were up for re-election retained their seats in the election, but they were all surprised the following week when

City Manager Charles H. Windham announced he would resign as of July 1. The port was finally on the right track, and Windham, who was always a man with an eye for opportunity, was interested in getting back into the private sector – perhaps in the shipbuilding business.

"In leaving the position, I do not intend to sever my interest here," he said. "I will at all times work for the good of Long Beach and be ready at all times to cooperate in every way for its welfare."

Windham's resignation sent a shockwave through City Hall and the community. Windham had guided the city through some sticky issues, and not only with the harbor. The Chamber of Commerce and other civic organizations sent committees to meet with him and ask him not to leave. The City Council formally asked him to reconsider. More than 2,000 Long Beach residents showed up at a mass meeting in the Municipal Auditorium where a resolution was passed asking that he remain in office. In the end, Windham relented and agreed to stick around until various planned city improvements were completed, but he was clearly torn. He was first and foremost a businessman. There were opportunities to pursue and money to be made. But he was also a committed member of the community, ready to pitch in when his knowledge and skills were needed. And there were still many challenges ahead for his city.

In June, the House Rivers and Harbors Committee began hearings on the Long Beach and Los Angeles improvements. The final legislation had authorized not only an extension of the breakwater, but also a second arm of the breakwater to extend seaward from Long Beach. More importantly, however, the federal money came with several conditions, two of which would prove to be particularly troublesome.

First was that Los Angeles and Long Beach would be required to establish one port authority for the entire harbor area. They could share authority or they could include outside authority, but there had to be one agency handling all port business. There also would have to be a publicly owned belt line railroad that would handle all rail operations within the harbor and serve without discrimination all railroads and all shipping terminals. The engineering report delivered to Congress also noted the importance of developing port land for maritime uses.

"Ample room exists for miles to the north of the harbor, for industrial expansion; and while it may be to the interest of some concerns to locate on the waterfront, it is to the interest of the public, in view of the small area available to retain such waterfront under its own control," the report said. "If Long Beach and Los Angeles desire to make their own harbor a world port, they must meet the first requisite of reserving all land necessary for port purposes."

Long Beach had never sought to merge its port with Los Angeles and had actively discouraged all proposals to become part of the larger city or to turn over its territory to outside governance. It had also actively encouraged non-maritime industries to come to the port and set up operations. Construction of the breakwater would help establish the port as a viable gateway, but it would be at the cost of local control. It was a question that would consume much time and energy in the years to come.

The Signal Hill Dilemma

Long Beach was getting rich on oil revenues. The oil was being pumped from beneath the ground, and the money kept flowing into the city coffers and into the pockets of a lot of Long Beach and Signal Hill property owners. With so many small parcels of land located over a large oil field, the derricks were so close together that they formed a forest of towers on the hill, some of them with their legs crossing over one another. Even the dead were getting rich – or at least their families were. Survivors of folks buried in Sunnyside Cemetery on Willow Street were receiving royalty checks for oil pumped from beneath their family plots. Residents became outraged at one point when they found that a portion of Sunnyside Cemetery, which had ostensibly been sold as a site for a mausoleum, had really been leased to an oil company to drill a well.

By 1923 – a peak year for the Long Beach (Signal Hill) Field – 259,000 barrels of oil were being pumped every day from almost 300 wells. That year California was the source of nearly one-quarter of the world's entire output. Year-end figures for the entire area showed 85 million barrels and 850 derricks, with five miles of derricks going across Signal Hill and beyond. But there were problems.

Although almost everybody loved the money that the oil boom brought to the city, the pollution it created was a different matter. The problem was that in many cases oil wells were right next door to homes. Gushers would drench whole neighborhoods with crude oil and sometimes shale. There were fires with flames shooting more than 100 feet into the air, and sometimes firefighters had to use dynamite to extinguish the blazes. Then there was the disposal of waste – sewage, garbage, oil, and dirty water that would overflow from the wells, puddle in sumps, and ultimately flow into the ocean.

Even before Charles Windham became city manager, residents had started complaining about the blight and the obvious dangers that accompanied the oil industry, especially in residential areas. The City Council cracked down on the oil industry, restricting waste disposal and requiring sprinkler systems to guard against fires. It may have been one of the first instances of environmental concerns impinging on business interests in the city. It was difficult, however, in the case of Signal Hill. Signal Hill was not part of Long Beach, even though Long Beach schools educated Signal Hill children, Long Beach firemen responded to Signal Hill fires, and the Long Beach Water Department supplied Signal Hill residents and businesses with water.

In February 1923, city officials met with oil industry leaders to talk about the possibility of annexing the Signal Hill area to Long Beach. Although Long Beach supplied water and fire protection to the hill area, the roads were primitive and fire hydrants non-existent. Once Signal Hill became part of Long Beach, the city would improve the roads, build a fire station, and make other necessary improvements.

A campaign to bring Signal Hill into Long Beach was announced in November 1923, but not everybody was happy about the prospect. Becoming part of Long Beach would mean being subject to Long Beach's oil tax and its zoning restrictions – which could apply to oil operations. Opponents filed a court action, seeking an injunction on the annexation election over technical questions on the annexation petitions. Judge Franklin Cole granted the injunction, ruling that the petitions calling for the election were incomplete.

While annexation advocates attempted to reprise their petitions, opponents proceeded on their own drive to incorporate Signal Hill as a city. The Los Angeles County Supervisors, on January 28, 1924, heard the argument for Signal Hill incorporation by the people trying to avoid being annexed by Long Beach. The timing was somewhat ironic.

Long Beach had been going to great lengths to avoid being annexed by Los Angeles, even protecting itself with a 100-foot-wide "shoestring strip" designed to stop encroachment by the larger city. The smaller city had even threatened to form its own county in order to protect itself from Los Angeles. Now Signal Hill had turned the tables on Long Beach. The L.A. County Supervisors agreed for Signal Hill to hold an election on incorporating itself as a separate city, and a vote was set for April 7, 1924.

Long Beach had assumed that Signal Hill would become part of Long Beach, but that was no longer the case. When I.W. Fuqua, president of the Petroleum Midway Co., wrote a letter to his employees urging them to vote for incorporation, Long Beach City Manager Windham delivered an ultimatum. Any oil company getting involved in the campaign to incorporate Signal Hill would have to look elsewhere for its water supply. Long Beach controlled the water, and it had the right to shut off both industrial and domestic water service after reasonable notice, Windham warned. The same thing held true for fire protection. Once Signal Hill became a city, Long Beach would no longer be offering it fire protection.

Despite the dire warning, Signal Hill voters decided to become an independent city, surrounded by a bigger city. It elected the only female mayor in California at the time – a widow, Jessie Nelson – who was a long-time Signal Hill resident and former correspondent for the Long Beach Telegram. Signal Hill would no longer be under Long Beach's thumb. At Windham's request, county supervisors that same month ordered the county counsel to draw up a new ordinance increasing the penalty against oil operators who allowed oil, water or silt from their wells to flow into roads, a drainage system, or flood control channels. Windham had complained that the flood control channel that came through Long Beach was full of oil and silt from the Signal Hill wells.

Windham's threat to deny Signal Hill fire protection and water turned out to be little more than tough talk. On April 21, two weeks after the Signal Hill vote, a huge fire broke out at the Golden State Refinery Co. on East Hill Street in Signal Hill. Long Beach firemen spent hours at the scene battling the blaze. To get water to the location, they had to lay down several blocks worth of fire hoses from the nearest hydrant. On July 15, a fire that began at the Walter-Fisher Well at 8:30 in the morning spread quickly to other nearby wells. Again Long Beach firemen responded, laying down 5,000 feet of hose to reach the scene. A 2,000-barrel oil tank exploded during the battle, and then a second tank exploded. Fearing that other tanks might rupture and send a river of burning oil racing through downhill neighborhoods, tractors were brought to the scene to construct a makeshift dike. The firemen, aided by 350 oil workers, fought the blaze until 8 o'clock that night before bringing it under control. Signal Hill's water was also not turned off as Windham had threatened. Five years later, Signal Hill agreed to purchase the Long Beach water system and property that lay within Signal Hill.

But there were still more oil problems to come. Oil also had been discovered in Seal Beach and derricks began springing up on the Long Beach side of the border, causing residents in the affluent neighborhood of Belmont Heights and the Naples area to become concerned that their neighborhoods were about to become part of an oil field. The residents – with the help of City Attorney Bruce Mason – got an initiative on the ballot to prohibit any new derricks inside the Long Beach city limits. Voters passed the initiative by more than a 2-to-1 margin.

The discovery of oil in California also encouraged development of tankers to transport oil and other petroleum products. Because California was so far from the population and industrial centers to the east, the best way to transport oil was by tanker. Before tankers, oil was carried in barrels on board general cargo vessels or in onboard tanks. One of the first modern oil tankers was built in 1894 as a joint venture by Union Oil Co. and Pacific Coast Oil Co. That tanker, the *George Loomis*, launched a new era in January 1896 when it left Ventura on its maiden voyage. With so much oil being produced in California, development of the tanker technology advanced rapidly. The development of tanker ships also opened up foreign markets for oil.

The California oil boom was also a boom in oil exports – both to the East Coast through the Panama Canal and to foreign customers. Pipelines were laid to transport the oil from the oil fields to the port, and tankers began to arrive regularly at the harbor to load up. The bulk of that activity was going on in Los Angeles, not Long Beach, which was still struggling to emerge from the shadow of the port next door.

Two Independent Ports

The handwriting was on the wall. The federal legislation approving construction of a breakwater that would protect both Long Beach and Los Angeles harbors required that the two become one. Los Angeles, which was already a busy port with a need to expand, was willing – at least on its own terms. Long Beach, which had always steered an independent course, was willing on paper if not in fact. The Board of Engineers report recommending approval of the breakwater had cautioned that if the Long Beach and Los Angeles harbors ever aspired to be world-class ports, they would have to reserve harbor lands for strictly maritime uses – not factories or other enterprises that could be carried on at inland locations. Long Beach had been very successful in inducing factories and other industries to locate at the harbor, and it had no plans to stop or even slow down its plan for harbor improvements.

On the evening of August 26, 1924, a banquet for 300 guests – including city officials, civic and industrial leaders, Army engineers, and politicians – was held in the Long Beach Municipal Auditorium to launch the city's port development program. Most of the speakers talked about the bright future they saw. Major H.A. Finch, district engineer for the Army, stressed the need to move forward as one united port. Six make-believe pirates put on a skit, admonishing the gathering that it was folly to think anybody could build a port out of a mudflat. They were routed by another actor dressed as Uncle Sam, who chased them from the room. At the end of the evening all the guests were presented small souvenir bottles containing muddy water dredged from the harbor channels. The party was over; it was time for the work to begin.

The following month, the city announced that the Cerritos Channel all the way from Los Angeles to Long Beach had been dredged to a minimum of eighteen feet deep and was ready at last to receive coastal traffic. The mud-choked Long Beach Harbor was still a long way from being a deep-water port, but the $5 million bond issue passed by voters was a demonstration of the city's commitment to its harbor. Although most of the work still remained to be done, that commitment was enough to draw industry interest in locating within the Long Beach Harbor area.

The final plan was to dredge the channels to forty feet, and for Long Beach to build two moles, extending from the shoreline 2,000 feet out into the ocean. One mole, on the west side of the flood control channel, would be 340 feet wide. The other, on the east side of the ocean entrance to the harbor, would be 450 feet wide. The moles were to be used for the Wilmington Transportation Co.'s line of Catalina Island steamers as well as for Navy boats and ocean-going vessels. The space between the two moles would eventually be filled in as part of the port's outer harbor. It would be the beginning of Pier A.

Complicating the situation was the fact that when the flood control channel had been completed three years earlier, there were no jetties built to direct the flow of sediment out into deep water. A small river delta began to form at the mouth of the channel, an area of shallow water extending in a triangle shape out into the ocean. The mole would protect the harbor entrance channel from that flow of mud.

The Long Beach Harbor may have been going through a period of resurgence during the mid-1920s, but it clearly remained dwarfed by the Port of Los Angeles next door. That didn't mean it was ready to give up its independence. Port of Los Angeles representatives were willing to merge the ports, but only if Los Angeles kept control. After all, the Port of Los Angeles port was bigger, and Los Angeles taxpayers had invested more toward making their port successful. Any possibility of equally sharing control of a unified port with the smaller city was out of the question.

The Los Angeles Chamber of Commerce Greater Harbor Committee of 200 drew up a joint port bill in March 1925 and had it introduced in the state Legislature. The bill called for a joint commission consisting of five members – two from Los Angeles, two from Long Beach, and a fifth to be chosen by the other four. The four could choose anybody that they all could agree on as long as he was from Los Angeles. The bill would not take effect unless it was approved by the voters in both cities. Even though it came up with the bill, the Greater Harbor Committee expressed reservation about it in its report to the Los Angeles Council.

> *We are not entirely satisfied with the provision which allows the City of Long Beach a representation upon the Board of Port Commissioners, which we think is too large when considered from either the relative extent of the interest of Los Angeles and Long Beach in the harbor or upon the basis of population or assessed valuation or upon any other proper basis.*
>
> *We feel, however, that particularly in view of the attitude of the United States government, which insists that the entire harbor should be considered as a unit, under a single management, before any appropriation is made for the construction of the large breakwater, that we should approve of the present measure in the interest of the harbor and an early accomplishment of this all important improvement.*
>
> *We are more willing to do this because we feel that when we actually join operations of the port, and a single unit has become a fact the tremendous benefits resulting therefrom will be so apparent to everyone that all sectional feeling will be eliminated, to the great advantage of all interests in all parts of the harbor.*

As requested by the Greater Harbor Committee, the Los Angeles City Council endorsed the joint port bill. On that same day, Long Beach City Manager Charles Windham told his City Council that the legislation was a "joke." It would give Los Angeles control over the harbor built by Long Beach. The idea of the fifth commissioner being picked by everybody was merely "camouflage." He would still represent Los Angeles.

Both arguments were legitimate. Los Angeles was looking at Long Beach as a mud-clogged backwater whose cooperation was needed to gain federal funding vital for Los Angeles' grand harbor plan. Los Angeles was a major deep-water gateway. Long Beach was not. On the other hand, Long Beach – which was still toying with the idea of becoming its own county – wanted the federal breakwater, but was not so desperate for it that it was willing to give up local control.

The two cities continued to work together on a plan for a unified harbor district that would work as a whole. Long Beach officials maintained that they had no problem with one unified port; their only concern was with governance. On April 8, 1925, Long Beach voters went to the polls and approved a City Charter amendment that, among other things, provided for creation of a Long Beach Harbor Department that would be overseen by five appointed harbor commissioners. In December of that year, City Attorney Bruce Mason drew up an ordinance giving the Harbor Commission jurisdiction over all that part of Long Beach lying south of Anaheim Street and west of the flood control channel – an area including the Long Beach industrial district as well as the harbor itself.

Despite the conflict over merging the two ports, harbor development in Long Beach seemed finally to be on track. There were, however, some internal bumps along the way. Like his predecessor, Windham ran afoul of the city auditor, Myrtelle L. Gunsul, who had a reputation of holding city business hostage over perceived technical violations of how the city conducted its financial affairs. On several occasions, city employees went home empty-handed on pay day, even though the city had plenty of money, because she disagreed with how such money could be transferred between accounts. Despite that reputation, she won a tough re-election campaign in which her opponent, Alfred A. Williams, ran a campaign based on a return to "harmony." Apparently, voters preferred Gunsul's prickly approach to the more harmonious relationship promised by Williams.

In August of 1925, the harbor improvement program was temporarily derailed when Gunsul refused to honor a $250,000 warrant to the federal government for dredging work on the Cerritos Channel. The warrant was a loan from the city to the federal government. The city wanted the entire channel dredged as soon as possible, but the federal appropriation for dredging the Los Angeles end of the channel would not be available until the following year. In order to speed things along, Long Beach had agreed to loan the federal government the money for the dredging, to be paid back when the appropriation became available. Gunsul claimed that the warrant had been illegally signed by one of her deputies, Terry Carpenter, while she was out of town. Carpenter claimed that as her deputy, he had the right to sign in her stead. She not only disagreed, but she fired Carpenter and tried unsuccessfully to have him arrested. City Attorney Mason ruled that Carpenter did have signing authority in Gunsul's absence.

Meanwhile the bank said it would have to return the warrant to the federal government within twenty-four hours marked "payment refused" unless the mess could be resolved. The city clerk went to Gunsul's home to try to get her cooperation, but found the door locked with a note from her doctor on it saying she was ill and not available to callers. City officials were also unable to reach her by phone. She later said she had injured herself while taking a bath. Several days later, a new warrant was issued, which Gunsul was legally directed to sign, despite her protests. Three days later, the City Council appointed Terry Carpenter, the deputy she fired, to be the new city accountant.

The work continued. At the end of August, city officials, contractors, and civic leaders assembled on the shore to give speeches and watch as the first train loads of rocks from quarries in Riverside were dumped into the ocean to form the moles that would be the beginning of the outer harbor development. Richfield Oil Terminal began preliminary work for an oil terminal on Channel No. 3 in the inner harbor. And then, the man most responsible for moving the harbor forward announced he was leaving, and this time he meant it.

On January 19, 1926, Long Beach City Manager Charles Windham told the City Council that he would resign effective April 1, or sooner if possible. It should have come as no surprise. When Windham quit as city manager twenty months earlier and then relented, he only agreed to remain in the job until a few important outstanding city projects were well established. Windham's reputation as a man of substance had grown. He had been offered harbor construction positions in the Bay Area and in Florida. The man who was drawn to new opportunity and challenge had found a new role. The council members all expressed regret over his decision to leave, and Councilman John Arnold said he would not hesitate to step down if it meant Windham would remain.

The city honored Windham's request for an early release. On January 26, it named former Chamber of Commerce President Charles S. Henderson as the new city manager, sparking a near riot in the Council Chamber from people unhappy with the choice. More than 300 people, most of whom wanted G.L. Buck to be named to the post, reacted angrily at the council's choice. G.L. Buck had been Windham's right-hand man and confidential aide. At one point during the brouhaha, Councilman Fillmore Condit called protester Cora Morgan a liar during a particularly heated exchange and about fifty men rose to their feet and threatened to throw him out a window. Condit later apologized for his language, but the City Council stuck with its decision.

On February 28, more than 500 men and women gathered at the Hotel Virginia to wish the Windham family farewell. It was the last in a string of farewell dinners honoring the twenty-four-year city resident. Long Beach Press-Telegram publisher William F. Prisk was toastmaster. Windham, not known as a sentimental man, was unable to conceal his emotions as he told his friends and associates that he would always consider Long Beach his home. Near the end of the evening, Edith William Van de Water – widow of the congressman-elect who had died in a car crash in 1920 before he could take office – presented Windham with a hand-embellished scroll, signed by hundreds of everyday Long Beach folks wishing him well. Windham said it would be one of his priceless possessions.

Windham and his wife Angelica were headed to Hollywood-by-the-Sea, Florida – a new town being developed fifteen miles north of Miami by former Long Beach real estate man Joseph Young. Windham had a three-year, $50,000-a-year contract to be city manager of Hollywood-by-the-Sea and to develop its port – five times the $10,000-a-year salary he was earning in Long Beach. Windham, who had spent years in Costa Rica and met and married his wife there, recognized the new port's opportunities for trade with South and Central America. The port he developed in Hollywood is now known as Port Everglades, arguably making him the father of two major U.S. ports.

Meanwhile, when Charles S. Henderson took over as Long Beach city manager on March 2, he had to establish his credibility in light of the angry protests that had accompanied his appointment. The former sheriff of Silver Bow County in Montana, Henderson declared in no uncertain terms that he would not abide the kind of "bolshevism" and mob rule that had been demonstrated in the past. In the future, the City Council would be allowed to conduct the business of the city without the heckling by groups of residents. Two weeks later, he selected G.L Buck – Windham's former senior clerk – as assistant city manager.

Things were going well for Long Beach. In June 1926, the Ford Motor Co. purchased a forty-acre property on the Cerritos Channel, just east of Badger Avenue, from the Union Pacific. Ford's decision to move to Long Beach started with a conversation between Ford District Manager Byron Graves and his old college friend Lynn W. Ballard. Graves was looking for a property in Southern California to build a Ford plant. Ballard, a leader in the Long Beach Chamber, suggested the Union Pacific property, resulting in two years of negotiations between Ford, Union Pacific, and the city, starting with City Manager Windham. Long Beach offered many advantages for the company. The weather was mild, there was easy rail and ocean access, and there was also readily available electrical power for the factory – the Edison power plant on Terminal Island had added extra capacity that same year, making it the largest such plant west of the Mississippi River. It is probably only coincidental that two close friends, Henry Ford and Thomas Edison, both chose Long Beach as a site to do business.

Ford planned to use the factory to produce his new "X car," which when it began production in 1927 was known simply as the Model A. It was to replace the old Model T that Ford had been building since 1914. He wanted a site from which he could ship Model A's across the Southwest, as well as south to Mexico and west to Asia. But only twelve of the forty acres Ford had purchased were in Long Beach, and although the entire waterfront was part of Long Beach, the other twenty-eight acres were across the city line in Los Angeles. As part of the deal, Long Beach had agreed to dredge the channel along the 1,300-foot Ford frontage to 600 feet wide, to deposit the dredging spoils on site to elevate the property, and to guarantee the maintenance of at least a thirty-foot deep channel from the plant to the open sea. Ford promised to employ approximately 1,200 men at the new plant.

In July 1926, one month after the Ford agreement, the Navy announced that it was choosing Long Beach as the principal landing site for the Navy fleet. In return, the city promised to spend $12,000 to build an adequate and safe Navy landing facility at the harbor. The Navy also planned to move the anchorage for its battle fleet to off the coast of Long Beach due to the heavy commercial vessel traffic coming and going from the Port of Los Angeles. Long Beach had long been the shore home to ranking officers in the fleet and to hundreds of enlisted men as well. The Navy landing would make their arrival home both safer and more convenient. Once the landing was built, the city could count on more Navy personnel choosing to live – and spend their money – in Long Beach. For the city economy, it was said to be the equivalent of an industry employing 10,000 workers.

But always looming in the background was the question of consolidation of the two ports, required by the federal government as a condition of extending

MAJOR INDUSTRY: *The Ford Motor Co. plant at the Port of Long Beach is ready to turn out Model A's in this early '30s photo. The plant, situated at the western edge of the port, produced cars until the late 1950s and was torn down in 1990. Behind it on Terminal Island are the smokestacks of the Edison power plant built in the late 1910s, the port's oldest extant building.*

MAMMOTH FESTIVAL: *Buildings of the Pacific Southwest Exposition decorate the Seventh Street Peninsula in the summer of 1928. The World's Fair-type event, which featured pavilions from other nations, exhibitions of arts and manufactured goods, and an amusement zone, drew more than a million people to the port during its roughly six-week run. The space was later occupied by Procter & Gamble, Hanjin, and still later became the Matson terminal on Pier C.*

the breakwater. Long Beach in July of 1926 had asked city voters whether they would favor the idea of consolidating the Long Beach Port with Los Angeles. It was merely a straw vote – just a testing of the political waters – but the final vote showed slightly more voters, 7,884-to-7,869, in favor of consolidation.

Although the future looked bright for the Long Beach Port, not everything worked out as planned. The Southern Pacific Railroad and the Dollar Steamship Line never opened their terminal in Long Beach. In April of 1926, rumors had begun to circulate that Dollar Line was planning to shift much of its Pacific service to Los Angeles from San Francisco. A month later, Dollar noted that his company had made a sizable investment in Long Beach, and there was a strong possibility that the Dollar ships would be calling there, not in Los Angeles. Los Angeles and Long Beach would all be one port in the future anyway, he said.

City Manager Henderson traveled to San Francisco in July and returned with the news that both Dollar Line and the Southern Pacific planned to start preparing the Long Beach site later that month for construction of their joint terminal. When he talked to executives at the Pacific Coast Steel Co., he was told that work on a plant for making steel tubing and pipe would begin on their site soon. But it never happened.

Three-and-a-half years after a representative of steel interests had signed a contract with the port promising to build a huge steel mill in Long Beach if the port dredged deep channels, nothing had been constructed. There was talk that United States Steel was interested in taking over the Pacific Coast Steel deal, but nothing came of it.

In November of that year, Dollar Line committed to call in Los Angeles. News of the Dollar decision was greeted with great fervor in Los Angeles. L.A. Chamber President Arthur Samuel Bent, president of Bent Bros. Construction Co., who had participated in the campaign to bring Dollar Line to Los Angeles, called it "the most important shipping development that has taken place in the maritime history" of the city. The Chamber of Commerce in December announced plans for a Foreign Trade Week to be held in January 1927. The event would begin with a Chamber luncheon at the Biltmore Hotel, honoring Dollar Line President Robert Dollar and his son, Stanley. It was the first of what was to become an annual event, although it would later be known as World Trade Week and be held in May.

Although the Southern Pacific-Dollar Line Terminal plan and the Pacific Coast Steel Co.-promised facility failed to materialize, the port had stuck to its side of the bargain and dredged its channels and made other promised improvements. By the summer of 1926, Long Beach had become a deep-sea port with forty-foot-deep channels going from the ocean throughout the inner harbor. Construction of the west mole at the channel entrance was almost complete, and work on the east mole by the mouth of the flood control channel was well underway, protecting the harbor entrance from silt. The next step would be a breakwater extending south 4,000 feet into the ocean and then 3,000 feet southwesterly. Plans also were being laid for construction of bulkheads, additional municipal wharves, and both public and private docks. Along the way, Long Beach had acquired the entire oceanfront of Terminal Island within its city limits.

In February of 1927, Los Angeles Mayor George E. Cryer brought up the 1926 Long Beach straw vote in his annual message to his City Council. Voters in both cities were in favor of merging the ports, he told the council. It was the time for the two cities to work out a mutually acceptable system for administering the combined ports or risk losing the federal money promised for construction of the breakwater, he said. He noted that Los Angeles had invested about seven times as much in its harbor as Long Beach had, and that Los Angeles was an operating harbor with miles of publicly owned waterfront while Long Beach was mostly privately owned and was still a work in progress. The benefits of the port were in the money it brought to the local economy, the industry and jobs it attracted to the Southern California region, and easy access to goods that came through the port. Those benefits would remain no matter how the port authority was organized, he said. Yes, it was time for Los Angeles and Long Beach to thrash out their differences and put the two harbors under one port authority.

With Mayor Cryer's admonishment in mind, a new proposal for organizing the joint port authority was drawn up. Under the new plan, both cities would retain their own harbor commissions to administer day-to-day functions. There would be a joint authority formed to administer common issues involving both ports, which would include the harbor commission president from each city and the president of the Chamber of Commerce from each city. The fifth member of the board would be the United States district engineer. Such a port district board would fulfill the federal requirement for a united port so that work could get started on constructing the breakwater. In May 1927, Cryer appointed a seven-man committee to help sell the city of Long Beach on the concept. Two months later, the Army Board of Engineers for Rivers and Harbors met to reconsider requirements that had been place on funding the extended breakwater. The original plan called for one gap in the breakwater to admit vessels bound for each port – Long Beach desired two gaps.

In October, the Navy raised its own objections to the breakwater plan, claiming it was located so close to the shoreline that it would destroy the harbor area's value as a naval operating base by forcing half of the fleet to anchor outside the sheltered area. The Navy wanted the breakwater to be moved out into deeper water.

The Army Board of Engineers sent out questionnaires to the two cities and to the Greater Harbor Committee in March of 1928, seeking information on matters of policy and engineering. A board of three Army engineers came to Los Angeles in June 1928 to discuss the issues involved in the breakwater project. Long Beach – which a month earlier had passed another harbor improvement bond, this one for $2.7 million – laid it on the line. Colonel E.N. Johnson, chief consulting engineer for the Long Beach Harbor, attacked the terms of the breakwater deal. He said that Congress and the Army Corps of Engineers had exceeded their authority when they demanded that the local communities "change their form of government." The much-alluded-to election in which Long Beach voters approved the joint-port concept by a narrow margin was only a "straw vote," he pointed out, declaring that the city had not changed its mind. Long Beach had never agreed to join Los Angeles as one unified port district, he said.

Navy Captain A.W. Marshall, commander of the *U.S.S. Lexington*, attacked the Army's plan to build the breakwater in forty-two-foot-deep waters. The breakwater needed to be moved out to the forty-eight-foot mark in order to provide ample anchorage for the naval fleet, he said.

The Army engineers had heard enough. On November 28, 1928, they made their report. They recommended that plans to construct the breakwater extension to protect the two harbors be dropped since the two cities seemed unable to agree on setting up a unified port authority. The cities of Long Beach and Los Angeles had been talking about a unified port district for more than four years and seemed to be no closer to an agreement than when they began. The engineers also rejected the idea of maintaining separate ports with a joint authority to handle issues of concern to both ports as merely a confederation plan that failed to meet the federal stipulation for a single port authority.

The idea of losing the breakwater project jolted both Los Angeles and Long Beach into action. An extension to the April 1929 hearing scheduled before the Board of Engineers for Rivers and Harbors was delayed until November in order to give the two cities time to work out a plan. A joint port unification committee with representatives from both cities held their first meeting in September 1929 to forge a plan for a joint port authority. After more than a month of talks, the only thing the two cities agreed upon was that they disagreed. Long Beach wanted equal representation on any port authority; Los Angeles was not willing to concede to that demand.

On November 26, 1929, representatives from the two cities appeared before the Board of Engineers as a united front with a bold proposal. The federal government should leave the issue of how the two cities would manage the harbor area to be worked out at some future date. Since the breakwater offered national benefits for shipping and defense, the federal government should pay for the entire project – a 12,500-foot-long breakwater to be built at the forty-eight-foot depth to accommodate the Navy, with the east end left open to accommodate Long Beach. The delegation also asked that the government drop its plan to fill in a portion of the Cerritos Channel at some future date in order to provide access to Terminal Island. The benefits of the Cerritos Channel as a connection between the two ports should not be compromised.

Construction of the breakwater was too important from both a regional and national standpoint to be held up indefinitely because their two local communities couldn't agree, the Los Angeles and Long Beach representatives argued. The merger of the two ports as one was inevitable at some time in the future, said Clarence Matson of the Los Angeles Chamber of Commerce.

The argument was well received. The Board agreed with the recommendation and so did Congress. The problem of unification of the two harbors was no longer an issue. At least not for the time being.

Changing Times

During those wild years of the 1920s, Long Beach had become a rich and successful city, and that prosperity generated a sense of euphoria among many of the residents – a sense that this was the way life was now and would always be. Oil money fed the economy, and people were more willing than ever to spend – whether it was to invest in new business, spend on personal pursuits, or to pass expensive infrastructure projects.

New buildings became part of the city's skyline. The Pacific Coast Club and the Breakers Hotel both opened in 1926. In 1928, the Cooper Arms building – the city's first high-rise residential building – opened at Ocean and Linden Avenue. The following year, the Ocean Center Building and the Villa Riviera joined the landmarks.

The city also was changing culturally. A new generation was coming up, and new residents were becoming part of the city – either through annexation or migration from other parts of the country. The city had become intoxicated with the riches laid on its doorstep by the discovery of black gold in its backyard.

The Long Beach get-up-early, work-hard-all-day and go-to-bed-early ethic also had begun to fade during the decade. Prohibition had shut down legitimate bars, and the public responded with a general disrespect for the new law. It was a time of social rebellion. The harbor became a center for smuggled booze. Girls were showing more skin on the beach and on the street. In 1925, the Long Beach Amusement League announced plans for a bathing beauty contest and parade. Despite protests from some church folks, the City Council voted to allow the event, featuring 350 girls prancing in front of an audience wearing what were then considered to be skimpy bathing suits.

In the midst of all that prosperity, Long Beach spent $650,000 to build a Tunisian city on sixty acres of harbor property at the west end of Seventh Street, facing the turning basin. The Pacific Southwest Exposition opened in the harbor at the west end of Seventh Street on July 27, 1928, with California Governor C.C. Young giving the opening address and actress Gloria Swanson throwing the switch that turned on the lights. More than a million people visited the exhibition during the five-and-a-half weeks that it was open.

The Ford Motor Co. was busy building its new harbor plant out by the Badger Avenue Bridge, and another big corporation, the Procter & Gamble Co., of Cincinnati, announced in 1929 that it had bought a site in the harbor area from Southern Pacific Railroad and the Dollar Steamship Co. – the site between channels No. 2 and 3 that the railroad and shipping line had planned for a joint shipping terminal. It was partially on the same site that had been used for the Pacific Southwest Exposition. The company planned to use the site for manufacturing soap and other Procter & Gamble products, such as cooking fats, oils, and glycerin. The harbor location would allow the company to service its markets in Asia, Mexico, and the Philippines.

And then in the fourth quarter of 1929, the good times were suddenly over. The stock market crashed, and the nation was plunged into the Great Depression. The 1920s may have been a roaring good time, but those times had come to a shocking end. Suddenly, there were big changes on the horizon, and it was time for the bustling town nestled near San Pedro Bay to figure out how to weather that storm.

Chapter Twelve:
Big Crash, Big Quake, and Big Labor

If the 1920s represented America's decade of prosperity and partying, the 1930s were the hangover that followed. The collapse of the stock market and banking system left the nation's economy in shambles. People lost their jobs, their savings, and their hope for the future. More than 9,000 banks closed between 1930 and 1933, costing customers $1.4 billion in lost deposits. It was an age of despair, but also of anger. The working men and women of the country bore the brunt of the nationwide economic catastrophe. But as always is the case, life went on.

President Herbert Hoover, who presided over the fall, offered moral support and advice. He did not believe it was the federal government's role to get involved in fixing the free-market economy. He implored big business to do its part by keeping Americans working at fair wages. He asked unions not to demand more money during such a period, and he urged state governments to begin investing in public works in order to generate jobs for the unemployed. It was a well-meaning but uninspired reaction to the financial devastation being faced by millions of Americans.

Franklin Delano Roosevelt was elected in 1932 to replace Hoover. Roosevelt was charismatic and decisive – and he had a plan to correct the problems in the economic system. He was elected in a landslide. What followed was a flurry of activity ranging from the end of Prohibition to the establishment of an alphabet soup of regulatory agencies, all aimed at getting the country back to work. A few of Roosevelt's plans were blocked by a coalition of Republicans and conservative Democrats, and some were overturned or eviscerated by the courts. But many – such as the Security and Exchange Commission, Social Security, and the minimum wage law – are with us still today. Whether such efforts helped or merely prolonged the agony continues to be debated. In either case the Depression continued throughout the decade, ended only by the economic stimulus provided by World War II.

But the 1930s weren't just about soup lines and unemployment. The decade saw construction of the Empire State Building in New York and the Golden Gate Bridge in San Francisco. Boulder Dam, started during the Hoover administration, was completed in 1935 and dedicated by the new president. The much-vilified Hoover was not invited to the ceremony, nor was his name mentioned during it. Twelve years later, the dam would be renamed for him.

Pluto was discovered by astronomer Clyde W. Tombaugh in 1930, and for 76 years, schoolchildren would be taught that Pluto was the ninth planet in the solar system, until it was later demoted by astronomers from planet to "dwarf planet." Two years after the discovery of Pluto, two young English scientists, Ernest Walton and John Cockcroft, built a particle acceleration machine and succeeded in splitting the nucleus of an atom. It was a feat that helped prove Albert Einstein's theory of relativity, and Einstein himself called to congratulate them. The two would later share the Nobel Prize for physics.

The 1930s also saw the sale of the first frozen vegetables from Clarence Birdseye, the first air conditioners, Zippo lighters, helicopters, and a new meaty treat called the cheeseburger. The first photo of the alleged Loch Ness monster was taken in 1933. Nicknamed Nessie, the monster is a huge mythical beast that some still believe lives below the surface of the placid and frigid loch in the Scottish Highlands.

Adolf Hitler was appointed chancellor of Germany in 1933 by German President Paul von Hindenburg. The idea was to keep Hitler and his Nazi Party in check by giving them a seat at the table. It quickly turned into a disaster for Germany and the world. In less than two years, Hitler had gained control of the country and had no political opposition. Political enemies were either shot or consigned to concentration camps. In less than five years, Hitler, who believed that both capitalism and communism were part of an international Jewish conspiracy, would lead Germany into World War II. Perhaps the leading villain of all history, he would bear responsibility for the deaths of millions.

The violence that marked the 20th century was well underway by the 1930s. It was a time of civil war in Spain, naked aggression by Japan in Asia, a purge of political rivals in the Soviet Union, and the rise of Communist leader Mao Zedong in China.

In Britain, King Edward VIII ascended the throne in January 1936, then abdicated it 326 days later to marry his lover, twice-divorced American socialite Wallis Simpson. It was hailed by romantics as a story of true love, although later disclosures about the former king's pro-Nazi, anti-Semitic attitudes took much of the shine off that story.

The series of dust storms that started in 1933 and swept across the Great Plains resulted in the ruination of farms and farmers. The choking swirls of windblown soil became known as black blizzards, which would often reduce visibility to less than a yard. It was an ecological disaster caused by a combination of factors, including severe drought, high winds, widespread use of mechanized farm equipment, deep plowing that displaced natural grasses, and poor farming practices. The so-called Dust Bowl resulted in one of the largest migrations of people over such a short time in American history, as farmers in the Plains states saw their lands go barren and their farms foreclosed upon. In little more than a year, 86,000 people fled to California. Although they came from various states, they were lumped together in the popular jargon of the day as "Okies."

Although the Great Depression may have limited opportunities for people to make honest livings, it also did little to curb crime and the fight against it. Gangland kingpin Al Capone, notorious leader of the Chicago Outfit, was finally sent to Alcatraz in 1931, not for murder and mayhem, of which he was clearly guilty, but for income tax evasion. Charles Lindbergh, who won fame in 1927 as the first person to fly solo across the Atlantic, was back in the news in 1932 when his 20-month-old son, Charles Jr., was kidnapped from his bedroom. Despite the family receiving numerous demands for ransom in exchange for the boy's safe return, the child's decomposing body was later discovered in a shallow grave less than five miles from the Lindbergh home. A German illegal immigrant, Bruno Richard Hauptmann, was later arrested, tried, and executed for the crime.

Exploits of some of the criminals of the 1930s and their subsequent downfalls have become part of the American mythos. Bonnie Parker, Clyde Champion Barrow, and their criminal associates made the news during their extended cross-country crime sprees. They were suspected of murdering thirteen people – including nine police officers – plus numerous robberies, burglaries, and auto thefts. They were ambushed and gunned down along a rural Louisiana road in 1934 by a posse of FBI agents and lawmen from Texas and Louisiana. Bonnie was 23; Clyde was 25.

Famed aviatrix Amelia Earhart won further recognition in 1932 when she became the first woman to fly solo across the Atlantic. Five years later, she would become an aviation legend when she disappeared on a flight around the world. A different kind of aviation legend was born when Douglas Corrigan flew from Long Beach to Brooklyn, where he filed a flight plan for a return trip to Long Beach. Instead, he took off and flew to Ireland, a trip the Bureau of Air Commerce had refused to permit. His explanation – a navigation error – earned him the nickname "Wrong Way Corrigan." He later wrote a book called, *That's My Story*, starred as himself in a movie, *The Flying Irishman*, and endorsed a string of Wrong Way products, including a watch that ran backwards.

Despite the hard times, Americans survived the Great Depression with humor, grit, and an eternal optimism that better days lay ahead. With the clouds of war gathering over both Europe and Asia, that innate hope for the future was about to be tested.

Long Beach and the Great Depression

During the 1920s, Long Beach had grown fat on oil money and the good life. It must have seemed as though the times of easy money and happy choices would never end. And then, they did. At the end of the decade the stock market crashed, sending the U.S. economy into a tailspin. Long Beach was in better shape than most cities to survive the economic depression that followed. The oil money continued to accrue to the city, although at a lower rate than it had in the early days of the Long Beach Field. In those days Long Beach dreamed of being a "tax-free city," although that never happened. Instead, Long Beach had wisely invested its oil wealth in infrastructure and improvements.

Construction continued at the Long Beach Harbor. The two moles were extended out from the west end of the flood control channel and from the shore, east of the entrance channel. The flood control mole had a breakwater extending south 4,300 feet out to sea and then to the southwest toward San Pedro for another 3,000 feet to shelter the harbor entrance. The area between the moles was filled in, and a wharf and landing were built on the site, later part of Pier E. It was the beginning of the port's outer harbor. The once mud-choked harbor was open to freighters and coastal passenger services, starting with a Long Beach-to-San Francisco run.

The original municipal wharf first opened in 1911 – on what would later become the Foss Maritime site on Pier D – had been demolished and reconstructed with a new timber wharf, bulkhead, fill, utilities, rail lines, and paving. By 1929, port cargo tonnage had risen to more than 2.5 million tons, still well short of the 26 million tons flowing through the Los Angeles port, but a vast achievement for what had been a degraded and largely dormant harbor. Long Beach still had only one transit shed, so imported cargo consisted mainly of pipe, steel, and lumber. Oil tankers carried the biggest exports by weight. Most of the inner harbor, with the exception of the municipal wharf property, was privately owned at the time, but the newly created outer harbor would belong to the city. Unlike Los Angeles, until the government funded the breakwater – a job completed in 1937 – the Long Beach Port was either privately financed or paid for by the people of Long Beach through bond measures.

By the 1930s, the Port of Long Beach had achieved a sense of independence. With the influx of oil money into the city's coffers, Long Beach no longer had to rely on taxpayers approving general obligation bond measures to finance port improvements. In the early days of both the Long Beach and Los Angeles ports, the benefits were chiefly seen in the prosperity and jobs the harbors brought to the region. If the ports were able to do enough business to cover their operating costs, taxpayers could be tapped for the capital to expand facilities. The economic depression squeezing America during the '30s changed all that and made passage of such bond measures unlikely. So the rates charged to shipping lines had to increase, and the ports had to become self-sufficient.

If the port was going to be run as a business responsible for earning its own keep, there needed to be some changes made. In 1931, Long Beach voters approved a City Charter amendment that gave new authority to the Harbor Department, making it a semi-autonomous body and freeing the board members from the short-term political forces that often buffeted the City Council. Under the charter, the Board of Harbor Commissioners was given the right to enter into contracts and other agreements, take legal actions in any matter within its jurisdiction, exercise eminent domain, make and enforce rules and regulations throughout the harbor district, and fix and collect all charges for the use and occupation of the public facilities at the port. In short, the Harbor Department would act as a proprietary department on behalf of the city. The only power reserved for the mayor and City Council was approval of revenue bonds issued by the port and the annual port budget. The members of the Harbor Commission would be nominated by the mayor and confirmed by the Council to fixed, staggered terms.

Five new harbor commissioners were named to the newly empowered board – union leader Harvey C. Fremming, Broadlind Hotel owner Glen L. Clark, Long Beach Chamber of Commerce President Irwin M. Stevens, engineer James F. Collins, and shipbuilder John F. Craig. Craig, whose shipyard more than twenty years earlier had given Long Beach its foothold as a harbor, was elected the first president of the new commission. Collins would later become Long Beach Harbor manager.

Having its own harbor put Long Beach in a better position than other, less-fortunate municipalities, but it wasn't the only cushion against the economic malaise facing the rest of the nation. The Pacific Fleet remained anchored off the coast with 8,500 Navy personnel. A Navy landing had been built between the two moles to ferry officers and men between ship and shore. Some of the Navy people lived in Long Beach with their families; some just came to visit and spend their money. Bonds for the new Municipal Auditorium and Rainbow Pier had been passed in 1928, although the $960,000 structure wasn't completed until after the market crash. The 3,800-foot-long Rainbow Pier extended in a giant arc that stretched into the ocean from Linden Avenue on the east to Pine Avenue on the west. The new city auditorium was built on eight acres of fill land jutting out from the shore at the center of the arc of the Rainbow Lagoon.

Even after the crash, industry continued to move to the city. Despite the fact that the Depression meant fewer people could afford new cars, the Ford Motor Factory opened in the harbor on April 21, 1930. It soon employed 2,000 people – 67 percent more workers than the 1,200 promised by Henry Ford when he decided to come to the city – who worked turning out 300 cars per day.

Two months after the Ford plant opened, Procter & Gamble broke ground for its new $5 million waterfront plant on West 7th Street – the property which was once earmarked as a terminal for Dollar Line and Southern Pacific and later the site of the Pacific Southwest Exposition. During the opening ceremonies, Harriet Hauge, the 21-year-old daughter of Long Beach Mayor Oscar Hauge, broke a bottle of artesian water across the bow of a four-foot-long boat molded out of Ivory Soap. The Ivory Soap advertising slogans of the day said that the soap was $99^{44}/_{100}$ percent pure and that it floated. As advertised, the ceremonial boat slid into the channel and sailed atop the water. The plant opened in stages, producing edible products first and then soap the following year.

In a ten-year stretch beginning around 1926, the port added numerous industries to its portfolio, including a Richfield Oil terminal on what was later the Tesoro terminal on Pier B; the J.H. Baxter Co. wood treatment plant on what would become the backlands of Pier B; the Standard Gypsum Co. on what was later the National Gypsum Co. property on the Pier B waterfront; the Rio Grande Oil Co. and Monarch Oil Co. terminals on what was later Pier C; and the Spencer Kellogg & Son terminal and mill on Terminal Island, near the Badger Avenue Bridge, where the company imported dried coconut meat from Asia and the Philippines and extracted oil from it.

Even though oil, industry, and the Navy cushioned the blow for Long Beach during the Great Depression, the city was not immune. Tourism dropped off, and not every landmark business survived the crash. The Virginia Hotel, which had hosted presidents, admirals, generals, and governors within its walls and dining hall, saw its business decline. The 24-year-old grand hotel of Long Beach closed its doors on October 1, 1932, and never reopened.

A Different City

Long Beach in the 1930s was a different city from what it had been ten years earlier. The 1920 census showed the population as 55,593. By 1930, it was 142,032. Long Beach not only had more people, its population was more diverse. Before, the city and its culture had been dominated by Midwestern people who had left their homes behind, but not their values. In 1930, there was a mix of people from all over the nation – sailors, oil workers, stevedores, aviators, bootleggers, auto assemblers, soap makers, and others. Some residents, who had fled Mexico during the years of the revolution, had settled in Long Beach, had children, and had been joined by friends and families from south of the border. All those new people – those new voters – had their own way of looking at things. That diversity of opinion was reflected in both the city and its port.

99 & 44/100 PERCENT PURE: *Harriet Hauge, daughter of Long Beach Mayor Oscar Hauge, prepares to christen one of the more unusual vessels to be launched at the port. The four-foot-long boat made of Ivory Soap commemorated the 1930 opening of a Procter & Gamble plant, which turned out its last box of Tide in 1988.*

The Return of Charles Windham

Charles H. Windham, the acknowledged father of the Port of Long Beach, quietly returned to Long Beach in 1928 after he had completed his work in Florida. The 1930 census shows him and his wife, Angelica, living in the Lafayette Hotel at 140 Linden Avenue in Long Beach with their 26-year-old daughter, Margarita, and 24-year-old son, James. The 1931 city directory shows the Windham family residing at 2828 E. Third Street with Windham working as a manager for the Montana Land Co., the owner of a vast tract north of the city.

As always, Windham had an eye out for opportunity and something new to build. This time it was the development of an artificial lake and golf course on 5,000 acres east of Cherry Avenue and north of Carson Street. In addition to being a representative of the Montana Land Co., the aging entrepreneur had also started his own venture, C.H. Windham Development Co. The plan was for the golf course to be surrounded by a high-class residential neighborhood – an area later known as the Lakewood Country Club neighborhood.

On April 11, 1932, Windham died in his Long Beach home of heart failure after a lingering two-month battle with influenza. He was 67 years old. The entire community noted the loss. The flags at City Hall were lowered to half-staff and on the day of his funeral, City Hall was temporarily shut down so city workers could attend. The Municipal Band, which included a number of Windham's personal friends among its members, supplied the music, playing "What a Friend We Have in Jesus," "Abide with Me," and "Lead, Kindly Light." Pallbearers included former Mayor Charles Buffum, founder of the Buffum's Department Store chain; Press-Telegram Publisher William F. Prisk; Wilmington Transportation Co. Vice President David P. Fleming; banker and son of shipbuilder John F. Craig, George L. Craig; and real estate developer L. Roy Myers.

Dr. Ohl Mason, founder of the Calvary Presbyterian Church, officiated at the funeral. Myers, who had been close to Windham and had visited him on his deathbed, also spoke. "Nobody dared to offer him a bribe, nobody doubted his word," he declared to the friends, family, and associates who had come to pay their respects.

Among the floral wreaths on display was one from J.W. Young and family. Young, a former Long Beach real estate man, was the founder of Hollywood, Florida; he had recruited Windham to help develop what was to become Port Everglades. The Harbor Traffic Club, which represented steamship lines, railroads, and stevedoring and trucking companies, passed a resolution declaring Windham's death to be a distinct loss to the harbor district.

Windham had been a key figure in the development of the harbor – as a director, investor, and mayor – and he also had been the one man most responsible for the rehabilitation and rebirth of the harbor, as both a private advocate and as the city manager. But his legacy extended beyond the port. Fluent in Spanish after his years in Costa Rica and his marriage to a Latina, he had over the years become the important community leader to whom those in the Hispanic community would turn for advice and help in dealing with an unfamiliar American establishment. His had been a life well lived. He had been a grower, a land developer, an oil man, a railroad worker, a bureaucrat, a politician, and a father. He had counted as personal friends the late Thomas Edison, the late Minor Cooper Keith of United Fruit Co., former President Herbert Hoover, Southern Pacific Railroad President Paul Shoup, Dollar

Steamship Co. President Stanley Dollar, "wheat king" and agricultural adviser Thomas Campbell, and political writer Sam Blythe, among others.

He was survived by his widow, three daughters, and two sons.

Earthquake!

At 5:54 p.m. on March 10, 1933, a 6.4-magnitude earthquake rocked Long Beach, destroying buildings and killing and injuring people. The tremor lasted only ten or eleven seconds and was by earthquake standards only of moderate size. But it killed between forty-nine and fifty-two people within the city itself and a total of 115 to 120 throughout the area. The exact number was never confirmed. It remains the second-deadliest earthquake in California history, surpassed only by the 1906 San Francisco earthquake that claimed up to 3,000 lives.

Despite the obvious tragedy, the quake triggered one of Long Beach's finest hours as residents and visitors pulled together to help victims of the quake and repair the damage to their town. It was one time of many when Long Beach reaped the benefits of its role as a Navy town. Within fifteen minutes of the disaster, Admiral R. H. Leigh, commander of the Pacific Fleet, offered the Navy's help. Two thousand Navy officers and sailors were stationed around Long Beach, helping the police secure the city. Within ninety minutes of the quake, 95 percent of off-duty police and firemen had reported for duty without being summoned. The National Guard set up field kitchens in parks and began serving breakfast to displaced residents the following day. The American Legion volunteered 2,200 ex-servicemen for duty.

The off-shore gambling ship, the *Monte Carlo*, set up a kitchen to feed 4,500 people a day, and a bootlegger even got involved. As doctors ran out of alcohol to sterilize their instruments, the bootlegger arrived with a truck load of five-gallon jugs of moonshine. The only compensation he asked was amnesty for the delivery and to get his truck back.

Damage at the port and in the oil fields on and around Signal Hill was minimal. In fact, the newly restored, three-masted frigate *USS Constitution*, better known as "Old Ironsides," had arrived in the Port of Long Beach just hours before the earthquake struck. The ship, named by George Washington and launched in 1797, was on a three-year tour of U.S. ports. The ship was not damaged, although the thousands of visitors that had been expected to board and tour the ship during its stay failed to show up. The *Constitution* departed after ten days for points north, but was back in port later that month on its way south to the Panama Canal; it received a much warmer reception from visitors on that second visit.

The price paid by the city was high in both lives and property lost during the quake, but the lessons learned proved valuable. About two-thirds of the people killed were those who ran outside during the temblor and were hit by falling bricks, cornices, and ornamental building debris. The physical damage was due mostly to unreinforced brick construction and the fact that much of the Long Beach area was located on the alluvial remains of a river delta – loose rock, gravel and sand, which is not the most stable of land during an earthquake.

It could have been worse. According to the California Office of the State Architect, 300 schools in Long Beach and the area beyond experienced minor damage; 120 received major damage, and seventy were destroyed. If the earthquake had struck two or three hours earlier, the death toll would have been in the thousands, and most of the victims would have been schoolchildren.

Those buildings located on alluvial soil or on landfill were mostly complete losses. Within a month, the state Legislature had passed a bill introduced by Assemblyman Charles L. Field of San Francisco, mandating seismic standards for school construction. The Field Act established the office of the state architect and required that all plans for new school construction be submitted to the state for review and oversight.

Although the quake did widespread damage to the city, public and private disaster relief money helped create jobs and pay for rebuilding the city. The city adopted a local worker policy in order to ensure that the creation of those jobs benefitted local residents.

Repeal of Prohibition

Long Beach had always been a dry town, but by the 1930s, the city had grown up. It was no longer the little village by the sea that banned the sale, possession, and use of all strong drink within the city boundaries. Even when the 18th Amendment to the Constitution went into effect in 1920, banning alcohol-use nationwide, it did little to stop the flow of liquor. In Long Beach, which had outlawed liquor more than twenty years earlier, it may have been even harder to stop drinkers from imbibing. Long Beach drinkers had a lot of experience in breaking the law. So the liquor continued to flow – from homemade stills to imported illegal booze through the port and into the country.

Prohibition had never really worked out – not for the nation and not for Long Beach. It had led to the rise of organized crime, civic and police corruption, widespread disrespect for authority, and a polarization of public opinion. By the time the stock market collapsed at the end of 1929 and the Great Depression had spread hardship and financial ruin across the country, Prohibition didn't seem like the great moral issue it had seemed ten years earlier. But it continued to be an economic issue.

The passage of Prohibition had put an entire industry out of business. The closure of distilleries, breweries, and saloons put thousands of workers – from barrel makers to bartenders – out on the street. Those lost businesses represented lost taxes and added to the cost of trying to enforce an unpopular law that more and more people seemed willing to flout. Prohibition is estimated to have cost the federal government $11 billion in lost tax revenues, plus another $300 million to fight smugglers, bootleggers, and moonshiners. The cost to state and local governments was also substantial.

The "noble experiment" had failed. In Long Beach – no longer a town of predominantly transplanted Midwest folks – residents voted 22,465-to-13,505 to approve the 21st Amendment, which repealed Prohibition. The end came on December 5, 1933, at 2:32 p.m., Pacific Time, when President Franklin Delano Roosevelt proclaimed that the 21st Amendment had passed and Prohibition was officially over. Five minutes after Roosevelt proclaimed the end of the era, the first load of liquor was cleared through the Port of Long Beach. The French Line freighter *San Francisco* delivered 1,000 cases of champagne and 280 cases of foreign wine and liqueurs. For most of the country, Prohibition lasted thirteen years. In Long Beach, the end of Prohibition marked the first time in thirty-three years that one could legally buy a drink.

Despite some predictions of wild parties in the streets, the end of Prohibition came quietly. Although liquor and beer were suddenly available, there was no rush to consume or raucous celebrations. There were reports of toasts being offered at clubs and restaurants and private gatherings, but the observances were low-key. Prohibition was over, but many of the problems spawned by it remained. Criminal organizations, looking for new opportunities, shifted their focus to gambling, prostitution, and drugs. The idealism of the Prohibitionists – however misguided – had been replaced with a cynicism about politics and government. And although it did put some people back to work, it had only a slight effect on the overall economic stagnation gripping the country. Prohibition had provided a classic example of unintended consequences, and it was finally over. For most people, that was enough.

Long Beach, Los Angeles, and Longshore Labor

Working on the docks was a hard way to make a living in the early days of the port. Loading and unloading cargo on a ship was a physically demanding and dangerous livelihood, and most workers either had no union or had to belong to a company union – a union that answered to the company – in order to work. Early attempts to unionize the waterfront had always been blocked by management with the aid of local government. An attempt by the Industrial Workers of the World, the so-called Wobblies, to unionize the Los Angeles waterfront in 1923 was smashed. Police arrested people for handing out IWW brochures, picketing employers, and encouraging workers to walk off the job. Socialist author Upton Sinclair was arrested at the IWW headquarters on Liberty Hill in San Pedro after he attempted to read the Constitution. A restaurant owner was arrested and put in jail on charges of "prolonging the strike," for feeding strikers. IWW leaders were arrested and jailed on charges of "criminal syndicalism" – a law existing in several states that made it illegal to establish, defend, or advocate for any organization that was committed to "crime, sabotage, violence, or other unlawful methods of terrorism as a means of accomplishing industrial or political reform."

The IWW demanded that such "political prisoners" be released and that criminal syndicalism laws be repealed. The power of the IWW peaked in 1923, and then sharply declined. The decline was partly because of the more respectable alternative offered by the American Federation of Labor, and partly because many of their members had been jailed, but perhaps mostly because of the quest for ideological purity among the IWW members, who were unable to accept the pragmatic compromises necessary to achieve and build upon their victories in the workplace. In 1924, the IWW splintered over the vision of its members for the future.

The success of the IWW was mostly among disenfranchised and semi-skilled and non-skilled workers – the easiest folks for employers to exploit and replace if the need arose. Workers along the waterfront fit that description. Merchant seamen were among the most exploited and abused workers in the world – paid and fed poorly, often subject to physical punishment at the discretion of the captain, and exploited while in port by businesses designed to separate them from their money. They were rootless workers, often single, alienated from the norms of society, but with a cosmopolitan world view gleaned by engaging with people of other cultures and beliefs. Longshoremen – many of them former sailors who had come ashore and settled down – had a similar perspective. The nature of the job was to work long, often odd, hours and engage with foreign cultures, all further separating the longshoremen from mainstream society. As such, they were open to new and sometimes radical ideas.

The stories of the early years on the docks have become legend. There was the so-called "shape up" in which workers would gather outside the employer's office, rain or shine, to be selected for jobs aboard ships. Sometimes they would stand around for hours, only to be passed over. Other times, they would be chosen but expected to kick back part of their pay to the hiring boss for the privilege. Some jobs were short, just a few hours at this dock or that. In such cases, the worker might have to go from dock to dock at the end of the week to collect his wages. In Southern California the average longshoreman earned about $10.45 per week. During those early years, much of the cargo was hand-lifted and carried. There are stories of a "speedup" system. Since employers were free to dismiss any worker they deemed was not working fast enough, longshoremen were sometimes ordered to run back for their next load, rather than walk, leaving them at the end of the day in a state of complete exhaustion. Heart attacks were not uncommon, and safety standards were ignored in the name of efficiency.

That these practices existed is indisputable. How common they were may be open to debate, but suffice it to say that even in a workforce that was accustomed to a relatively high level of abuse, there simmered a great resentment.

"Among maritime workers, the tendencies toward spontaneous radicalism inherent in their subculture were like parched grasslands waiting for a spark to ignite them," says Bruce Nelson in his book *Workers on the Waterfront*. That spark came in the 1930s.

Working Class Hero

There were a number of reasons for the resurgence of labor on the waterfront. One was the economic crash, which some saw as the death knell for a capitalist system that had simply collapsed under its own weight. There were the perceived successes of the Soviet Union in changing the world order to one in which workers were esteemed, and the growing influence of the Communist Party in the United States. There was the optimism expressed by the New Deal and its promise to improve the life of the working class, and there was an overall sense that the world was changing.

One of the figures to emerge during this period was a young Australian longshoreman named Alfred Renton Bridges. Bridges was not born into the working class. His father was a businessman and property owner who sent Bridges around to collect rents from the poor people who lived in the housing he owned. Young Bridges hated it. He ended up taking money from those that could pay and lending it to those who could not. His next job was in a stationery store, an occupation that bored him to distraction. He preferred the company of his liberally minded uncles, especially his Uncle Harry, a socialist. Bridges stopped calling himself Alfred and took the name Harry in honor of that uncle.

A second influence in his life was socialist writer Jack London, whose books inspired Bridges at age 15 to join the Australian Sailors Union and become a seafarer. It was a job that opened Bridges' eyes to the world and convinced him that the picture of the world painted by polite society had little to do with reality.

"I took a trip that gave me a look at India and another at Suez, and what I saw there didn't seem to line up with what my father had told me about the dear old British," Bridges would later tell a New York Times reporter. "Then I got

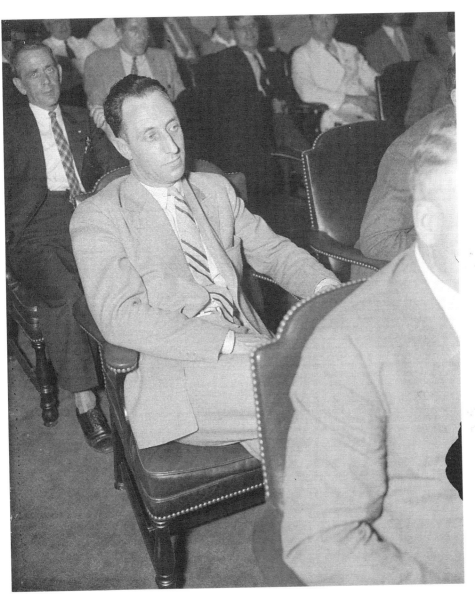

WORKERS' RIGHTS: *Harry Bridges, seen here at a meeting of labor leaders in Washington, D.C., in July 1937, was a militant union leader for decades. After he helped form the International Longshoremen's and Warehousemen's Union, he faced years of court proceedings to attempt to deport him to his native Australia.*

'home' and saw London. It was the filthiest, most unhealthy place I had ever seen ... I kept traveling around, and the more I saw the more I knew that there was something wrong with the system."

Fellow seamen – IWW Wobblies with experience in strikes and labor disputes – introduced him to the struggle between the working classes and the capitalist employers. It was an education, and perhaps indoctrination, in the principles behind the labor movement of the day. Bridges arrived in San Francisco in 1920, at age 18. He went ashore and one week later transferred his membership from the Australian Seaman's Union to the Sailors Union of the Pacific, part of the American Federation of Labor (AFL). The Sailors Union was broken during a strike the following year, and Bridges felt that the AFL had sold the union out. After his experience with the AFL, he associated with the Wobblies for a short period, but was quickly disillusioned, despite the tales he had been told by his fellow seamen. He would later testify at a 1939 hearing to determine whether to deport him, that while the IWW was good at disruption, they bogged down the advance of labor.

> *We believe in strikes, and we believe in direct action under the proper circumstances and at the proper time when it is the best thing to do. But there comes a time that you can go a little too far with direct action. The IWW philosophy was never to sign an agreement, for example; never to arbitrate, never to mediate, never to consolidate...*

In 1922, Bridges met his first wife, left the seafaring life, and became a longshoreman. He was 21 years old. In order to work on the San Francisco waterfront, longshoremen were expected to join the company-run "Blue Book" union. If you wanted to work on the docks, you had to be a member of the Blue Book. The union didn't really represent its members, rather, the union was a device of the employers for blocking legitimate unions from gaining a foothold on the waterfront and for weeding out and blacklisting radicals. There was a similar company union for longshoremen in the Long Beach and San Pedro ports called the Marine Service Bureau.

Bridges resisted joining the Blue Book union as long as he could, getting jobs from Japanese lines that were not part of the Blue Book system. Even after he joined the Blue Book Union, he got a reputation as a troublemaker. And after he marched in a Labor Day parade in 1924, at a time when the International Longshoremen's Association – also part of the American Federation of Labor – was once again trying to organize the San Francisco waterfront, he was blacklisted. But through it all, he was gaining a reputation on the waterfront for his vision of militant, even radical, unionism expressed in plain language that anybody could understand.

During the years that followed, as the ILA attempted to represent longshoremen in the area, Bridges became active in a group called the Albion Hall faction, named after the place in which they congregated. This group included members of the Communist Party, a fact that would be used against Bridges in years to come. Bridges never denied knowing and associating with party members to advance the case of workers. But he maintained that he did not agree with their overall political philosophy and was not a member of the party himself. The resurrection of the ILA on the West Coast was a grassroots attempt among local workers to get representation. Those attempts, however, were often frustrated by what many West Coast workers saw as the ILA's willingness to capitulate to employers' demands in the name of being reasonable. The Albion Hall faction was an expression of that dissatisfaction.

In 1933, President Roosevelt signed into law the National Industrial Recovery Act, which created the National Recovery Administration. The goal of the NRA was to eliminate "cut-throat competition" by bringing industry, labor, and government together to create codes of "fair practices" and set prices. But the Act also guaranteed employees the right to organize and bargain collectively through representatives of their own choosing and to be free from restraint or coercion from employers. For the longshore workers, that meant an end to the hated company union, or so they surmised. The ILA, although seen by many as weak, was the obvious choice. The only question was under what leadership? The Albion Hall faction, with Bridges as the leader, offered a strategy based on asserting its position with militant action. After waiting for the ILA to hold meetings and rally the workers, Bridges and the other Albion Hall representatives began taking their own actions. When a worker felt as though he had been treated unfairly, for instance, the other longshoremen on the job would work more slowly.

A hearing was scheduled in Washington for November 1933 in which the ILA would present its proposal for workers under an industrial code to be considered by the NRA. The union spent more than two months before the hearing holding meetings up and down the coast, recruiting new members, promoting the idea of a coastwide contract, and soliciting ideas for the proposed labor code. The proposal called for the ILA to be the exclusive bargaining agent for Pacific Coast dockworkers. It further said that the contract should be coastwide instead of port-by-port, that only full-time workers should be employed, that when employers needed workers they would hire them through the ILA hiring halls, that there should be a six-hour workday and thirty-hour week, and that pay should be $1 an hour with time-and-a half for overtime.

General Hugh Johnson, the NRA national administrator, approved the code, but Roosevelt refused to sanction it, supposedly because of conflicts with trade treaties between the United States and foreign countries. It was a defeat for the ILA, but the rejected proposal became the list of union objectives. The next setback came when ILA local leader Lee Holman complained to local NRA administrators that waterfront employers were discriminating against ILA members. The employers claimed the ILA was using intimidation tactics to get workers to quit the Blue Book Union and join the ILA. The local NRA board ruled that the Blue Book Union was a legitimate union, although it did urge the employers not to discriminate against ILA members.

For Bridges it was a demonstration that waiting for the government to get him and other longshore workers a union was a lost cause. If the workers wanted their own union, they would have to create it on their own. During a leadership election held shortly before the NRA board decision, Bridges and his Albion Hall associates won a majority of seats on the thirty-five-member executive board. Two of the three business agents elected were also Albion Hall members.

Although not the president of the union, Bridges was ready to demonstrate his belief in direct action. The long simmering resentment by longshore workers came to a head about two weeks after the NRA board's decision. Workers were loading a Matson Navigation Co. ship at the waterfront, when a representative of the Blue Book union came by to check each worker's Blue Book and make sure they were paid up. One after another, the workers refused to show their books, and one-by-one they were ordered off the ship. For many of them, it was the last straw.

According to the story, one of the discharged workers shouted, "Let's make a bonfire out of these goddamn books," and pretty soon there was a pile of the hated union books burning on the ground in a vacant lot across from the Matson pier in San Francisco. It was only a matter of minutes before a Matson foreman came out asking for men to work the ship. Forget the Blue Books, he told them, we need to finish loading the ship. It was a small victory of sorts, but two weeks later, Matson struck back, firing four workers for wearing ILA buttons. It was a minor incident, but it was the kind of minor incident in a tense environment that can spark a major confrontation.

The NRA refused to take any action in the matter. So did the local ILA president, Lee Holman, who reportedly told the men the union didn't want to cause any trouble at that particular point. Attempts by Bridges to convince the union to take action against the company were voted down, so Bridges and his Albion Hall associates took matters into their own hands. They showed up at the Matson pier and convinced workers not to take jobs there. When the company went to skid row and recruited unemployed men to work the ship, the union men convinced many of them to withhold their labor as well. The strike lasted for five days. It was denounced as a wildcat strike by Holman, who warned the strikers that they were acting without sanction of the ILA. He also appealed to ILA headquarters in New York to file a complaint with the NRA about the four fired workers. In the end, the company was ordered to fire all the replacement workers it had brought on and hire back the four workers it had dismissed.

The union had won a victory and established its credibility among waterfront workers, thanks to Bridges and his Albion Hall associates, but it had also ignited a suspicion about Bridges that would follow him for the rest of his life. A federal conciliator who had been tracking union activities in the Bay Area saw Bridges' willingness to step outside the prescribed protocol for settling labor disputes as a sign of possible communist influence, and he reported his suspicions to his superiors.

Although some government officials seemed sympathetic to the plight of the dock workers, some of their proposed solutions were unacceptable, such as the plan proposed by Labor Department economist Boris Stern that would establish a network of government-operated hiring halls. A spokesman for ILA International President Joe Ryan spoke in favor of it at a coastwide union convention in Portland. He was the only one. Everybody else who addressed the subject thought it was a terrible idea.

After the employers refused to bargain with the union on a coastwide basis, the union held a strike vote on March 7, 1934, with a two-week window for the employers to reconsider. That was not going to happen. If the union wanted a showdown, the employers were ready. Both sides were adamant. If it was going to be war, so be it.

First Blood
Labor disputes in the 1930s were not as they are in modern times. There had been recessions before and financial panics, but never anything like the Great

Depression. The world was changing and so were the relationships between those who owned the means of production and those who labored for them. Author Charles P. Larrowe notes the nature of such disputes in his biography of Harry Bridges.

> *In the thirties, strikes were sometimes more like civil war than labor disputes. It was a decade which, for wholesale violence and the use of armed force, was without precedent in United States labor history. This was the decade that produced the armed ambushes and guerrilla warfare in Harlan County, the Memorial Day Massacre, the Flint sit-down strike, the Mohawk Valley Formula, the massive use of labor spies, strikebreakers, industrial munitions and, sometimes with fatal results, the National Guard. The West Coast maritime strike was that kind of a strike. For it was not merely an argument over a few cents more or less on the wage rate. It was, on both sides, a matter of principle.*

The International Longshoremen's Association strike, set for March 24, 1934, was opposed by Holman, the local union president, who reported to the International Union in New York that the strike was being forced by a minority of radicals within the union. To get around Holman, Bridges organized a "Strike Committee" from the rank and file to take the decision out of Holman's hands. Bridges' idea of union democracy was that the rank and file would have to approve any contract that was negotiated by union leaders.

The strike was called off at the last minute, however, when President Roosevelt asked the ILA to postpone their walkout so he could appoint an impartial committee to look into the situation. The ILA leadership agreed. The rank-and-file Strike Committee established by Bridges did not. In San Francisco, 400 longshore workers who had planned to strike the next morning protested the postponement by the ILA headquarters, giving angry speeches and planning a waterfront demonstration for the next day. The "Waterfront Workers," a worker publication put out by the Albion Hall group, urged the workers to strike anyway, "despite the advice of a couple of weak-kneed brothers."

The inspiration and driving force for the revolution about to take place on the waterfront was centered in San Francisco, not at the Long Beach and Los Angeles ports. But the same resentments and anger among rank-and-file workers existed in both places. On the same day that the strike was postponed, the L.A. Times – which made no secret of its anti-union feelings – warned that many of the labor problems being experienced in various Southern California industries were the result of communist agitators.

"The longshoremen and stevedores strike, originally set for this morning, is another example," said an article in the March 23 edition of the paper. "Although the American Federation of Labor still is in control of the situation and the workers at the harbor apparently are resentful of any expressed suspicion of Communist affiliation, reports from Seattle and San Francisco indicate that the 'Red' influence is very considerable and is trying to block attempts to reach a solution of the difficulties."

The situation had changed. Waterfront management had been used to operating with company unions or negotiating with established AFL unions led by reasonable men who would sign a contract on behalf of their members, and then announce the results to them. They were not used to a rank-and-file union in which the union membership would vote whether to ratify whatever contract had been negotiated by their leaders.

The shipping lines and waterfront business owners were understandably reluctant to give up any control to the people whom they hired. They were the ones who had invested their money; they were the ones who would lose their investment if the business was poorly managed. And they were men who were capable of doing whatever was necessary to preserve control over their ventures.

In San Francisco, local union President Holman warned the rank and file that the union could not win a strike and that he was not in favor of walking off the job. The local's executive board accused him of violating the confidence placed in him by union members and suspended him from holding union office for a period of one year. When ILA District President W.J. Lewis attempted to explain to the union members the "gentlemen's agreement" that he had brokered with ship owners, Bridges tore the proposed deal apart in an impassioned critique. During one such meeting, Lewis leaped to his feet in a rage, declaring that communist activity on the waterfront must end.

A new coastwide strike date was set for May 9, 1934, and when that date arrived, both sides had declared their positions and were ready to do battle. Nonetheless, there was a somewhat feeble attempt made in Southern California to bring the two sides into agreement. Two committees – one of employers and one of union leaders – arranged to meet in order to see if some common ground could be reached. The employers group consisted of eight shipping executives with Phineas Banning's grandson, Joseph B. Banning Jr., as chairman. The ILA delegation was led by local President W.R. Patterson.

On May 9, the strike finally began. It would turn out to be a bloody and lengthy battle, waged with rocks, clubs, guns, knives, tear gas, and fists. The blood was essential. The differences between the strikers and the employers were not such that they could be negotiated away at a bargaining table. Both sides knew it, and both sides were prepared to both spill blood and shed it.

The politicians, the police, the press, and the chambers of commerce backed the employers. The rank and file of other unions tended to support the strike, although many labor leaders saw the strike as a threat to their power as well. Communists, socialists, and other political radicals mainly supported the strike, in which they saw the seeds of a new economic order. The federal agencies – many of them sympathetic to the cause – were concerned that their influence as conciliators and mediators had become superfluous.

The mood on the waterfront was tense. In an action totally unrelated to the longshore strike, about 200 cannery workers and fishermen ended up in a pitched battle with police during a protest over the hiring of non-union men on the Alaska Packers' Association freighter. Bricks were thrown, shots were fired into the air, and both officers and workers were treated for bruises and lacerations.

With management and workers committed to their own courses, the strike by the longshore workers began despite last-minute efforts to head it off. An organization calling itself the Longshoremen's Mutual Protective Association claimed it had 300 replacement workers ready to man the docks. Eugene A. Mills, president of the Crescent Wharf and Warehouse Co. and chairman of the Marine Service Bureau, predicted cargo handling at the port would be back to normal by the end of the week.

Approximately 1,300 union longshoremen went out on strike, but by noon the first day, there were 100 non-union replacements working six ships, according to the Los Angeles Times, not the most reliable of sources when it came to labor news. By nightfall, the number had grown to 225, and employers were claiming they would have 500 on the waterfront by the following day. Police and private guards hired by management watched as union members engaged in peaceful picketing. There was no reported violence or attempts to intimidate either replacement workers or strikers. But all of that was about to change.

The San Pedro union workers were being chided by union locals in other ports, which had brought their ports to a standstill. In the San Francisco and Pacific Northwest ports, strikers were attacking replacement workers, fighting their way onto ships, battling police and private security, and bringing business to a standstill. In San Francisco and the Pacific Northwest, there was war in the streets. In Long Beach and Los Angeles, there had been little or no violent actions and no real disruption besides peaceful picketing. Each day, more workers were found to replace the ones who had walked out, and each day, employers predicted that the strike would soon end, and even if it didn't, the ports could continue to operate at full strength.

On May 14, five days after the strike began, things exploded. Frustrated San Pedro union longshoremen had apparently heard that a decision had been made to attack the compound where the replacement workers were housed, according to labor historian Art A. Almeida. The replacement workers, labeled "scabs" by the union men, were using two old sailing ships at dock in the West Basin for sleeping quarters and a mess hall. The compound itself was surrounded by barricades and under police and private guard. At 11:30 that night, while most of the town was asleep, about 300 union men attacked the camp. Within minutes, the charge turned into a melee of gunfire, tear gas, rocks, and clubs as the two sides battled.

First to die was 20-year-old union member Richard "Dickie" Parker, a graduate of San Pedro High School, who was shot in the chest. The second was 45-year-old longie John Knudson, who was shot in the abdomen and died at Seaside Hospital in Long Beach two weeks later. Three others were shot, one had a fractured skull and many more on both sides of the battle suffered less serious injuries. Fires ignited during the fighting resulted in much of the camp burning down.

More police were sent to the harbor area, bringing the total number of police officers on strike duty to more than 300, plus scores of private security men. Two union men were later arrested on suspicion of arson and assault with a deadly weapon, and four others were arrested on suspicion of inciting a riot. Plans for an upcoming Harbor Day Celebration were temporarily canceled.

Parker and Knudson would not be the only ones to die. Two more workers would later die in Seattle and two in San Francisco. Hundreds would suffer injuries, but for the strikers, there was no turning back.

In the San Pedro ports, union truckers supported the strike by refusing to deliver cargo to the harbors. Some of the San Francisco strikers – wise in the ways of the kind of guerrilla warfare practiced by the northern union locals – were reportedly sent to town to lend their experience to their Southern California brothers. Strikers began following replacement workers when they left the port, ambushing them, and delivering beatings that sent the strikebreakers to the hospital. In Long Beach, striking workers reportedly tried to kidnap one of the private guards off a street corner. In another case, two replacement workers approached a policeman, saying they were being followed by strikers. As the policeman listened to their story, a carload of strikers jumped out and attacked all three.

When the government began supplying the hungry families of strikers with food, it sparked an outrage among many law-abiding citizens who had been shocked by the tales of violence and communist influence that they had read in the newspapers. Despite the anti-labor stance of most of the press, the stories of intimidation and violence used by union strikers are not for the most part in dispute.

The ports of Los Angeles and Long Beach were struggling, but they were the only major West Coast ports still in operation. Employers reported that more than a thousand replacement workers were on the job, guarded by a cadre of police and private security. Police were escorting convoys of trucks, driven by non-union drivers, down Alameda Street to the ports.

On June 10, about 300 strikers attacked a Panama Pacific Line yard on Terminal Island after coming across the Los Angeles main channel by ferry. Police had responded to a false alarm at the Dollar Line Terminal, far away from the Pan Pacific Dock, at the time the attack occurred. The attack came during a shift change on the union picket line, so twice as many strikers were present than usual. The strikers commandeered two trucks, busted through the gate, and attacked workers with clubs and iron pipes. In a battle that raged for almost an hour, non-union workers were overwhelmed and beaten. An attempt to board the vessel was turned back by ship officers and guards armed with shotguns. When police finally arrived, the injured were taken to the hospital, and the supposed leaders of the attack were arrested.

On July 5, 1934, San Francisco authorities had had enough. Continued disruptions by the union were not to be tolerated. Police and strikers had clashed that morning, with the police using tear gas, mounted officers, and guns to break up the crowd. The battle continued that afternoon outside the union strike kitchen. During that fracas, police shot into the crowd of strikers and strike sympathizers, killing two men and injuring one. That evening, the National Guard began patrolling the waterfront, and federal troops at the Presidio were put on alert. The day was dubbed Bloody Thursday by the union. Casualties among the protesters included two dead, thirty shot, and forty-three clubbed, gassed, and stoned.

The following Sunday, a general strike of all unions was declared by the San Francisco and Alameda County labor councils. For the next four days, workers in the city stopped working, bringing business to a near standstill. When the general strike ended, the Labor Councils' general strike committee called for submitting the issues in dispute to arbitration. That suggestion was taken up by the government, which set up a coastwide vote on the matter by striking longshoremen. The longshore locals, with the exception of the Port of Everett in Washington, voted to approve.

The strike had lasted for eighty-three days, and when it was over, the waterfront was a different world than it had been. The final arbitration provided for a hiring hall to be financially supported and run jointly by the employers and the union with no favoritism or discrimination due to union membership. A list of registered longshore workers would be maintained, and no worker not on the list would be dispatched to a job as long as there was a registered worker available. A registered worker who was not a member of the union would have to pay a portion of his earnings to cover his share of the cost of running the hall. The dispatchers would be elected by the union. In addition, the union got a six-hour day, a thirty-hour week, and a raise to 95 cents an hour – only a nickel short of what they had originally requested. They did not get the union hiring hall they had fought for, but that would come later.

The agreement provided a new way of life for the dockworkers. They no longer had to mill around outside the docks waiting to be picked or turned away without work. There was no blacklist, no speedups, and no kickbacks. It had been a long battle, paid for in blood, but the waterfront would never be the same again. A decent wage and a secure future meant that longshoremen could provide for their families and plan for the future. Their higher salaries and more stable existence enriched the local economies of the cities and towns in which they lived. The economic benefits of the ports were not in the amount of cargo that passed through the harbor communities, but in the amount of money that stayed there.

Charles Larrowe relates in his Bridges biography a conversation Bridges had in 1950, talking to a friend about how hard he had worked to convince the longshore workers – who were widely treated with contempt by society in general – that they were just as good as anybody else and that they could become respectable members of the community.

"They started to win better wages and conditions," Bridges said. "They started to buy homes and then property, apartment houses especially. I kept telling them they could be respectable. And now, they've become too Goddamned respectable for me. Now they're starting to worry if I'm respectable enough for them!"

There were more battles to come. In 1937, the Bridges' longshore followers would leave the International Longshoreman's Union and the American Federation of Labor and form their own union – the International Longshoremen's and Warehousemen's Union. It wasn't unanimous. Three locals in the Pacific Northwest decided to remain part of the ILA for many years afterward.

Bloody Thursday – that terrible day in San Francisco – would remain a touchstone for the union – a reminder of the price paid by those early longshore workers, who like their adversaries, were willing to do whatever it took to win their victory, even if it meant breaking the law and even if it meant dying. Every year, on the July 5 anniversary of that day, all the ports on the West Coast shut down, and the longshore workers take the day to hold picnics, listen to speeches, and pay homage to their past.

It's not the same union today as it was back then. The members drive late-model cars, live in nice neighborhoods, pay their taxes, and send their kids to college. All that good living has moved them a few steps away from the labor wars of the 1930s, and that has given the union leadership a vested interest in celebrating Bloody Thursday and the glory days of the dockworkers. Every step further away that today's rank and file moves from the union history is a step further away from the militancy and commitment that gives the ILWU its power on the waterfront.

The Discovery of Oil in the Harbor

It was oil that had made it possible for Long Beach to invest in its harbor and other municipal improvements, such as parks, golf courses, piers, and auditoriums. And in 1936 – fifteen years after oil was first discovered on Signal Hill – a new rich reservoir of the valuable commodity was discovered beneath the city. But this time the city would have to fight for the wealth that came shooting out of the ground.

The Wilmington Oil Field was first tapped into in 1932 by Rogers Petroleum Corporation's Watson No. 2 well, but the extent of the field it had tapped into wasn't recognized until 1936. That's the year that General Petroleum drilled its exploratory well, Terminal No. 1, in Wilmington, just west of the Henry Ford plant. Long Beach had given General Petroleum permission to conduct a seismic survey on Terminal Island, looking for indications of oil. The survey was encouraging, but Long Beach at the time didn't allow new drilling inside the city limits – even in the industrial Terminal Island area – because of citizen complaints. So General Petroleum sank its well on 456 acres of land in Wilmington leased from the Los Angeles Harbor Department. The field it tapped into was known thereafter as the Wilmington Field.

The Long Beach City Council, recognizing the potential riches beneath the ground, was quick to lift the citywide ban on new derricks to exclude the harbor area, but stipulated that only one well per acre would be allowed. The Council also amended the City Charter, authorizing the Board of Harbor Commissioners to pump oil from any place in the harbor, provided that the particular parcel would not be required for commerce, navigation, or fishing for the next twenty-five years. Under the amendment, the Harbor Department would be required to spend the proceeds from the oil to pay off harbor bonds and for improvements in the city's tideland area. The Legislature approved the amendment on May 14, 1937.

It was the second time that an oil bonanza would enrich the city. But, before that happened, Long Beach would be forced to defend its rights to the riches beneath its harbor. The State of California challenged Long Beach's right to the tidelands oil. The state contended that when it had granted the city rights to the tidelands, it had been to operate a port, not to drill for oil. The city might own the port, but the state owned the oil beneath it, the state claimed. In order to clear up the challenge, the city and Harbor Department in 1938 sought a writ of mandate against Port Manager D.A. Marshall that would order him to seek bids for contracts to drill for oil on behalf of the city. State Attorney General Ulysses S. Webb intervened on behalf of the state, saying that when the state had approved the tidelands grant, it had no way of knowing there was oil beneath the surface. In July 1938, the Supreme Court backed the city and ordered Marshall to go ahead and arrange a deal with private operators.

Judge William Langdon, who wrote the opinion, rejected Webb's argument that the tidelands grant merely gave the city the right to administer what the state owned. The wording of the tidelands grant made it clear that the state was granting title of the property to the city for the use of commerce, navigation, and fishing. If they didn't want the city to drill for oil on the property, they should have exempted that use. The fact that the Legislature had approved the 1937 charter amendment allowing drilling on the site was evidence that the state was well aware of the oil reserves at that time.

The city for the time being had won the right to the oil beneath the harbor, but Langdon's opinion was hardly the last word on the subject. The issue would come back again and again in a series of court cases. The question of who actually owns the port and what rights they may possess to what was once considered a worthless mud flat was a subject of legal debate and wrangling for the next fifty years.

After long discussion, the city decided to lease the land to independent drillers and negotiate the best contract they could with the companies. The result was a contract that called for an 85-15 split of profits from the field, with the city getting the 85 percent share. The first well on the Long Beach side of the line started pumping in 1938.

The state was not the only entity claiming rights to the Long Beach tidelands oil. The federal government also asserted its claim on the oil. In 1937, Secretary of the Interior Harold Ickes convinced North Dakota Senator Gerald P. Nye to introduce a resolution authorizing the U.S. attorney general to file a lawsuit claiming the tidelands oil on behalf of the federal government. Ickes and Nye believed the tidelands were part of the public domain, with their riches to be shared by the entire country, not just the coastal states. They wanted the California tidelands oil to be included as part of the Naval oil reserve. In August of that year, the Senate passed Nye's resolution. The Senate action didn't stop Long Beach from profiting from its oil field, but the federal claim would in years to come turn out to be one more issue in which the city and its port would have to defend their claim to the oil.

The Navy Connection

There was no Navy base in Long Beach during the 1930s, but Long Beach was a Navy town nonetheless. Naval officers and sailors were a constant presence in the city, in the businesses downtown, and in residential areas around town. Although Los Angeles officials talked about that city as hosting the Pacific Fleet, Long Beach was home to the Navy personnel – both figuratively and in reality. The Navy paychecks were spent in Long Beach; the Navy did business in Long Beach, and most of the Navy families lived in Long Beach.

Almost from the beginning, the Navy was more drawn to Long Beach, perhaps because the city had a history of welcoming out-of-town visitors. From the time the Navy arrived, Long Beach outshined San Pedro in hospitality, whether it was helping arrange sporting events or setting up dances. So when the Navy was looking for a principal landing for its men, it chose Long Beach because that's where most of them chose to live. By 1932, when Los Angeles needed to upgrade its Navy landing in San Pedro, the Harbor Department dithered so long that the Chamber of Commerce a year-and-a-half later finally chided the port about the lack of progress – pointing out that Long Beach had accomplished much more in less time.

By 1933 Long Beach was shore home to 70 percent of the Navy's commissioned officers in the area. Many of the senior officers lived in the Villa Riviera – a posh twelve-story apartment building on Ocean Boulevard at Alamitos Avenue. Lower-ranking officers and enlisted men lived in other housing in the area. The naval shore community enjoyed a busy social life with wives arranging teas and receptions, and various ceremonies and celebrations being held at local hotels, golf course country clubs, and restaurants. Long Beach welcomed the Navy, and those steady Navy paychecks made a big difference to the local economy during the Depression years.

The focus for U.S. sea power shifted after World War I from the Atlantic to the Pacific, as a counterforce to the Japanese Imperial Fleet, which was dominant in the western Pacific. Naval headquarters might still be on the East Coast, but the center of naval power for the United States was in San Pedro Bay. In March 1932, shortly after the Navy first arrived, hundreds of people from Long Beach and inland communities got up before dawn to witness the power and fury of a Navy night battle practice, to hear the roar of the guns and see exploding shells lighting up the sky. By November of that year, the Navy agreed to go at least twenty-four miles offshore to conduct such practice after complaints by Long Beach residents that the concussion from the guns was disturbing their sleep, cracking window panes, and frightening chickens and other livestock.

Air power was also becoming an important part of the naval equation, and the harbor area was often the target during war games between various forces. During one such game in February 1933, the Black attacking forces staged carrier-based air raids on the San Francisco and San Pedro Bay ports, while the Blue defending forces tried to respond to the threat. In a grim forecast of what would come, an analysis of the battle found that coastal cities were extremely vulnerable to carrier-based attacks. The calculated damage that would have been wrought in a real attack was extreme. The ease with which the Black forces were able to elude the Blue defenses was an indication of how important the role of air power had become.

Although the Navy had made its presence felt in the local community, it needed an official onshore base as well. It needed its own place for training, maintenance, repairs, warehousing, and resupply of food, ammunition, and fuel. And it needed a fleet air facility from which it could fly both conventional, float, and amphibian aircraft. In August of 1935, it signed a thirty-year lease with the Port of Los Angeles for Reeves Field on Terminal Island – 250 acres of land and fifty acres of shallow water – with a promise to develop the field with hangars, maintenance, and repair equipment, an administration building, and barracks. Two years and almost $1 million later, the Navy commissioned the field as an official airfield. In May 1938, the Navy finally moved in with aircraft and personnel to fly and maintain them.

The problem was that the Navy was spending a lot of money to develop an airfield on the site – by 1939 more than $3 million – and it wanted title to the land, not just a leasehold. There was some urgency, because wars were being fought in both Europe and Asia, and the Navy had to be ready to respond. A vote of Los Angeles residents had approved granting the land to the Navy, but left the particulars of the transfer up to the mayor and City Council. Los Angeles Mayor Fletcher Bowron and the Harbor Commission felt that the transfer should be subjected to a fair cash payment, reservation of oil drilling and pier construction rights, and a reversion of title after two years of disuse. The Los Angeles and San Pedro Chambers of Commerce urged the mayor to back down, since expanding the Navy presence would benefit the city much greater than trying to get the best deal for the property. Despite such pressure, the Harbor Commission held firm while the Navy brass seethed.

It was an example of the difference in attitude between Los Angeles and Long Beach. Long Beach saw itself as a Navy town and saw the Navy people as part of the community. They lived in town, and they socialized at the same places as the civilian population. Los Angeles – a major city by any standard, with City Hall twenty miles from the port – had a more detached view of its Navy relationship. Los Angeles did business with the Navy; Long Beach made the Navy part of its family.

By 1938 – Long Beach's 50th anniversary year if you don't count the fifteen months Long Beach ceased being a city – the federal breakwater had been extended and 50,000 Navy personnel and forty-three ships were homeported in

NAVY TOWN: *The port's Navy Landing welcomes vessels in 1936. Although there was no Navy base in Long Beach in the '30s, the Navy presence was increasing in the years leading up to World War II. The landing was built as part of Pier A, a landfill project that was later renamed Pier F and connected to container terminals on Piers G and J.*

AFTERMATH: *Sailors help provide security following the Long Beach earthquake of March 10, 1933. The* USS Constitution, *"Old Ironsides," was at the Port of Long Beach during the quake but was undamaged.*

Long Beach. If Long Beach had been good to the Navy, the Navy had been good to Long Beach as well.

Harbor Life

Because of the discovery of oil – first on Signal Hill in 1921, then under the harbor in 1936 – Long Beach was able to invest in its port and the infrastructure needed to make it profitable, even in the middle of the Depression. The city had filled in land, built new terminals, and built a second transit shed at the municipal dock. It had negotiated the removal of railroad tracks on Ocean Boulevard and the removal of the Union Pacific bascule drawbridge that had been built across the port's channel in 1910, allowing it to widen the channel from 180 feet to 300 feet. If the money from oil had boosted Long Beach, it had also provided a nice, unexpected bonus for private property owners in the port area, such as the Ford Motor Co. and Procter & Gamble.

Japanese tankers continued to call regularly at both ports, buying all the California oil they could and shipping it back to the homeland for use by the Imperial Navy. Long Beach also ended up doing a brisk business in the export of scrap steel to Japan. Imports included copra, which produced coconut oil, Japanese silk, and hardwoods from Asia. Long Beach became the leading lumber port on the West Coast.

The silt that had once clogged the harbor every rainy season had finally been confined to the flood control channel. Completed in 1929, the breakwater resulted in shoaling in the entrance approach to the harbor, but a delta of material carried down the flood control channel began to form down coast and out to sea. Much of that material would later be used to help fill in the Long Beach outer harbor.

The 1930s were marked by labor strife and social discord. It wasn't just the longshore workers. It was also the truck drivers, fishermen, shipyard workers, and railroad men. There was a sense that the system was failing, that the old ways no longer worked. There was a yearning for something better – something that would allow regular folks to work hard, make a living, and be respected for what they did. The harbor changed in some fundamental ways during the 1930s, and for better and worse, it would never go back to the way it had been before.

Former mayor and department store founder Charles Buffum – one of the Long Beach leaders who helped raise the port from the mud for the second time – died in 1936. The Harbor Department remembered its history, and in 1937 approved a bronze plaque, honoring Charles H. Windham as father of the port. The original idea was to place the plaque on the breakwater, but that was not practical. It was mounted on a large slab of granite and placed in front of the port headquarters.

There was a change in management in 1939 for both the city of Long Beach and its harbor. Voters on June 6 of that year had replaced all but one of the seven incumbent councilmen running for re-election. The only surviving incumbent was Councilman Carl Fletcher with 52 percent of the vote. The new Council, eager to clean house, hired a new city manager and city clerk and appointed five new members to the Harbor Commission. It was one of only two times in Long Beach history that the entire Commission was replaced in one sweep. The other time was in 1931, when a City Charter amendment boosted the board's authority.

One of the new commissioners, W.R. "Frosty" Martin, would become one of the longest serving harbor commissioners in port history – serving from

September 1, 1939, until his death in 1955. Martin had grown up and made his fortune in the oil business. He was the founder of Martin-Loomis Co., which manufactured oil drilling instruments and later became the Martin-Decker Corp. He was one of the original owners of the Long Beach Independent newspaper, an avid aviator who owned his own plane, and an inventor with more than forty patents. He would play a dominant role in the expansion of the port in the years to come.

The Great Depression had squeezed Long Beach hard, but the city had been lucky and its leadership had been smart. The port town not only survived, but actually grew stronger during the decade that wreaked havoc on the world. But new developments were brewing that would change life in the harbor and in the city. The Great Depression was coming to an end, but a bloodbath was about to begin.

Chapter Thirteen:
The War Years

As if the worldwide economic devastation of the 1930s hadn't delivered a big enough blow, the end of the decade saw new trouble spread across the globe as nations struggling to extricate themselves from the financial wreckage began turning on each other. By 1937, the Empire of Japan – which was seeking to dominate all of Asia – had engaged in full-blown war with the Republic of China. Two years later on September 1, 1939, World War II officially began as the German Army marched into Poland, causing the United Kingdom and France to join together as the Allies and declare war on the Nazis. The United Kingdom launched a naval blockade of Germany that lasted the entire war. Germany, meanwhile, formed the Axis with Italy and other fascist countries as part of its drive to conquer Western Europe and entered into a 1939 non-aggression pact with the Soviet Union that included a plan on how to divvy up Europe between the two countries. When France fell in 1940, the United Kingdom was forced to use an armada of small craft to evacuate its troops from the continent, leaving the island nation stranded, drained of resources, and with little hope of launching an invasion on its own. Germany's non-aggression pact with the Soviet Union fell apart by June 1941 when the Axis invaded the Soviet Union. By December of that year, the fighting had spread throughout Northern Africa and the Horn of Africa.

During the early years of World War II, the United States had maintained a non-interventionist policy bolstered by a series of Neutrality Acts signed throughout the 1930s. The Neutrality Act of 1939 allowed for arms trade with France and Great Britain at the same time that the U.S. was still selling oil and scrap steel to Japan. The Act also barred American ships from entering designated war sites.

While war raged in Europe and the Pacific, life went on pretty close to normal in the United States. Hollywood held its 12th Annual Academy Awards ceremony in 1940, and *Gone with the Wind* was nominated for thirteen Academy Awards; it became the first movie to win ten. Hattie McDaniel, who played Scarlett O'Hara's mammy in the movie, became the first black actor to win an Oscar when she beat out Olivia de Havilland for best supporting actress. McDaniel gave a glowing acceptance speech, and then returned to the segregated table for two where she and her escort were required to sit – apart from her *Gone with the Wind* colleagues and the rest of the white attendees. Later criticized as an "Uncle Tom" for her role in the movie, McDaniel responded, asking "Why should I complain about making $700 a week playing a maid? If I didn't, I'd be making $7 a week being one."

Glamour girls such as Kate Hepburn, Ava Gardner and Betty Grable fascinated the nation with flashy styles that included tight sweaters and tighter skirts, high-waisted trousers, cropped, midriff-baring tops, peplum waists, platform heels, wide-brimmed hats, and tailored suits with big shoulder pads. Chemical company DuPont began marketing nylon stockings to women in 1939, and in 1940 made a record by selling 4 million pairs in one day. Glenn Miller's orchestra wowed the country with hits such as "Moonlight Serenade" and "In the Mood." Mount Rushmore was completed, and the Jeep was invented.

U.S. neutrality wavered a bit when the Lend-Lease Act, which allowed the U.S. to give or sell materiel to nations it wanted to support, was signed in March 1941 and over time, the U.S. eventually provided $50.1 billion in materiel to the Allied Nations.

Then on December 7, 1941, Pearl Harbor was bombed by Japanese aircraft, war was declared, and America became part of what would be the biggest, most horrific war the world has ever known. By the time it ended, it had directly involved 100 million people in thirty countries. The art of war had met the age of industry. Never before or since have death and destruction been experienced on such a scale. World War II would engulf the entire economic, industrial, and scientific capabilities of the major participants, and in the end between 50 million and 85 million people had died – the uncertain range of the estimate an indication as tragic as the huge numbers themselves.

The war would be the curtain behind which the extermination of 6 million Jews would be hidden and the launching ground for new technologies that ranged from ballpoint pens to development of the atomic bomb. It would alter the political alignment of the world, promote the creation of the United Nations, usher in the beginning of the decolonization of Asia and Africa, lead to the creation of the State of Israel, and sow the seeds of conflict in the Middle East.

As American GIs fought in Europe and the Pacific, those left behind changed their lives to support the war effort. It became a time of war bonds, ration stamps, and women acting as the heads of families. One hundred ten thousand Japanese living in the U.S., including 75,000 American citizens, were taken from their homes and relocated to inland camps to ensure they wouldn't help the Japanese war effort. More than one woman sent her soldier off to war with the Mills Brothers singing "Till Then" on the phonograph, and 6 million Americans bought the group's 78-rpm version of "I'll Be Around" so they could get the "B" side song, "Paper Doll."

As the country moved into a time of "total mobilization," gasoline, rubber, and other critical materials were rationed. When government advertisements prodded, "If you can operate an electric mixer, then you can operate a drill," women responded by putting on slacks and heading to the assembly line to spend their days making munitions and war supplies. If working on the assembly line changed women, women changed the workplace as well. Companies opened onsite banking and shopping facilities, and the federal government established nursery schools and extended day care centers. While much of that reverted after the war, some women stayed in the workplace – and ladies' slacks became commonplace.

Assembly lines focused almost entirely on the war effort. Not one consumer automobile was manufactured between 1942 and 1945, and the nation's automakers started producing armaments, aircraft, and military vehicles. The auto factories produced 5.9 million weapons, 2.8 million tanks and trucks, and 27,000 aircraft.

With food in short supply because of the war effort, ration booklets were issued. Butter, a particularly scarce commodity, was replaced by oleomargarine, which was packaged with a packet of yellow dye that consumers stirred into the stark white product to make it look more appetizing. American families produced 40 percent of all the produce they consumed during the war in "victory gardens" where they planted fruits, vegetables, and herbs in their backyards, on apartment building rooftops and in neighborhood parks and vacant lots. Personal products also became scarce. During the war, DuPont turned its nylon stocking production line to the production of parachutes, airplane cords and rope instead, causing nylon stockings to become a black market item.

In 1945, when the war finally ended, America and the world had changed. The countries that had fought so long and hard were bloodied and exhausted, and ensuring a new and lasting peace was paramount. The United Nations was formed to promote international cooperation among nations and the "great powers," the victors of the war – the United States, the Soviet Union, China, the United Kingdom and France – became permanent members of the United Nations Security Council. The United States and the Soviet Union soon became rival superpowers and launched forty-six years of Cold War. DuPont went back to making stockings, which had by then become so coveted that the nylon stocking riots of 1945 occurred, the worst of which was in Pennsylvania, where fights broke out when 40,000 women lined up to buy 13,000 pairs of nylons.

Through it all – the support of Europe before America entered the fight, the four bloody years of death and destruction, the rationing, the women on assembly lines, and the heady time after the war – the Port of Long Beach played its part.

Preparing for War

It was 1939 and the flames of war were raging across both Europe and Asia. The United States was not at war, but it was coming. You could see it at the port, where ships from warring nations were loaded up with vital supplies, especially those from Japan – tankers taking on oil and freighters loading up with scrap steel. The naval presence in Long Beach continued to grow with Navy men and their families becoming an integral – if somewhat transient – part of the community.

The Navy was preparing for battle and spending great amounts of money to do so. Time mattered, and the Navy wanted possession of the Reeves Field from the Port of Los Angeles, but the two sides couldn't agree to a deal. The Los Angeles mayor and Harbor Commission wanted $10 million and for the Navy to meet other strict conditions before it would turn over title to the property. The business community and the press urged the port to just give the property to the Navy so it could start the massive development that needed to be done. The property itself hadn't existed until the federal government dredged the channel and filled in the land with the spoils. The investment that the Navy was getting ready to make in infrastructure and payroll that would be spent in the community would benefit the city and local economy well beyond the $10 million the port was demanding. Admirals and congressmen attempted to negotiate an end to the deadlock, but they got nowhere.

Eloi J. Amar, general manager of the Port of Long Beach, accused Los Angeles of having a "Navy-be-damned" attitude. L.A.'s insistence on payment had "created an antagonism in Washington that undoubtedly has harmed Long Beach and the state as a whole," he told a civic group gathering at the Pacific Coast Club.

Long Beach, in the meantime, was already working to improve a forty-acre plot adjacent to Reeves Field on the Long Beach side of the line, for use by the Navy. It was to be used as an athletic field for sailors in the fleet with the idea that at some point after the Navy obtained title to the airfield, it would become an addition to that facility.

To be fair, the controversy was about more than just patriotism and real estate. There was also the question of oil and ownership – a question that would be raised and debated many times in the years to come. The Senate's Nye Resolution in 1937 had directed the U.S. attorney general to take action to legally establish federal ownership of the tidelands and the oil beneath them. The Department of the Navy in February 1939 had asked Congress to ban the drilling and extraction of tidelands and offshore oil in California. The legal dilemma was how to give the property to the Navy without setting a precedent that the federal government owned the land – and the oil beneath it.

In July of 1940, the Navy, stymied in its attempts to get title to Reeves Field, ordered the filing of condemnation proceedings against the cities of Long Beach and Los Angeles for a large portion of Terminal Island. The property in question would run from the western boundary of Reeves Field along Ferry Street, east almost to the entrance channel for the Port of Long Beach between Seaside Boulevard (later Ocean Boulevard) and the Pacific Ocean. The total property sought was 14,000 feet long and from 1,000 to 4,000 feet wide – 228 acres from Los Angeles, 105 acres from Long Beach. The condemnation was for surface rights only, not for the oil beneath the surface. Payment for the Los Angeles property would be decided by legal action brought in August of 1940, but Long Beach would be paid only $1 for its property, as specified in an agreement already negotiated between the Navy and the city.

War was becoming more certain by the day and the Navy had big plans for the area. It needed to separate the question of inherent legal ownership of the tidelands and its oil from the Navy's need to gain title to the property to prepare for the conflict ahead. Long Beach didn't donate the land to the Navy; it sold it for $1. And although the city lost the right to drill on the property, it did not lose the right to the oil beneath it. All that would have to be settled on a future date in a different venue.

Navy plans for the Long Beach property included building a dry dock and associated facilities at the east end for ship repairs; Congress had already allocated $19.75 million for that project. Other projects, including dredging a forty-five-foot-deep channel big enough to allow battleships to land at the facility and construction of a supply depot, would require additional allocations. In addition to the Terminal Island improvements, the Navy planned to extend the existing breakwater that protected the Long Beach and Los Angeles ports and then add an 11,000-foot detached breakwater that would extend eastward off the downtown and residential coast of Long Beach. The plans called for an 1,800-foot gap between the expanded breakwater and the new breakwater to allow passage for ships. Once complete, the chain of breakwaters would reach almost all the way to Orange County and provide the Navy with miles of protected anchorage. The Navy would also dredge away some of the silt deposited at the mouth of the flood control channel, and the spoils from that dredging would be used to restore beachfront that had been badly eroded during the previous several years.

The Long Beach Harbor Department had been working on its own improvements for some time, including plans for filling in and developing its outer harbor with terminals and landings for freight and passengers – the beginnings of what became Piers D and E. In May of 1940, the port had unveiled its fifty-year plan for developing a streamlined harbor, drawn up by two prominent port engineers, George F. Nicholson and James F. Collins. First there would be construction of the area just west and south of the flood control breakwater, but east of the entrance to the inner harbor – an area labeled the East Basin. A huge West Basin facility would be filled in and developed west of the entrance channel all the way up to the Los Angeles city line with seventy ship berths. The plan included two underwater tubes connecting the mainland to Terminal Island – one under the Cerritos Channel and one under the entrance to the Long Beach inner harbor. The funds to develop the future harbor would come from oil revenues. Of course, the plan as submitted was in complete conflict with the Navy's plan to develop a major naval base on Terminal Island – the same area Long Beach was proposing as the port's West Basin.

As with many such plans for the future, the reality turned out to be much different from the vision, but there is always value in taking the time to look at the possibilities and to set a course, even if it has to be adapted as new circumstances arise. Much of what was proposed in the Long Beach plan, in fact, did come to pass – just not in exactly the same way it was planned.

What had earlier allowed the port to progress as rapidly as it did was the money it received from its 85 percent share of the tidelands oil profits – well over $1 million a year. Since that money was earmarked for tidelands improvements, it had been used to pay off outstanding harbor bonds, resulting in a tax cut to Long Beach property owners. But by early 1940, those oil revenues were at risk. Just because the Navy had agreed to seek only the surface rights to the tidelands property did not mean the Justice Department was willing to waive what it considered federal rights to the tidelands and the oil. Long Beach was cautious.

In April, it had been disclosed that the Justice Department had sent a memorandum to President Roosevelt proposing that the federal government file suit against the State of California and other interests, both public and private, asking for a declaratory judgment over who owned the tidelands. Among the probable additional entities to be named in the suit would be the cities of Long Beach and Los Angeles, the County of Los Angeles, and private owners of property in the tidelands area, including Standard Oil, the Southern Pacific and Union Pacific railroads, Southern California Edison, and the Ford Motor Co. The memorandum was the result of a year-and-a-half investigation by the Justice Department. At risk were not only $2 billion worth of tidelands and offshore oil, but also title to port lands that had been mostly developed and paid for – especially in the case of Long Beach – by private industry and local taxpayers.

But that would be a battle for the future. The more immediate concern and opportunity was in the war fever sweeping the harbor area. In May 1940, President Roosevelt ordered creation of a defense zone stretching from Point Fermin to Sunset Beach in Orange County and set parallel to, and 18,000 feet out to sea, from the existing breakwater. The area was to be known as the "Los Angeles-Long Beach Harbor naval defensive sea area." The president's order, dated May 7, 1940, said in part:

> *At no time shall any vessel or other craft ... be anchored within the defense area above defined unless authorized by the Secretary of the Navy. Merchant vessels and small craft may anchor in the defensive sea area during a thick fog or in an emergency of such nature as to require anchoring therein to prevent serious damage. Such merchant vessels and small craft shall leave the area on or before the passing of the fog or emergency, provided, however, that, in the discretion of the Secretary of the Navy, any such merchant vessel or small craft may be required to leave or to be towed out, immediately or at any time, without expense to the United States ...*

United States and State of California vessels were exempt from the requirement. Creation of a defensive zone wasn't unprecedented. Eleven months earlier, the president had ordered that a similar zone be established around Pearl Harbor in Hawaii. And Congress in 1938 had passed the Espionage and Sabotage Act, which barred photographing, sketching, or otherwise obtaining information on military or naval reservations, or in any established defensive sea area.

The president's order did not inhibit traffic at the port, just the anchoring of vessels offshore. It was thought to have been precipitated by reports of Japanese merchant ships anchoring just beyond the breakwater, but close enough to monitor the Navy battle fleet at anchor and the movements of the Navy vessels.

But Roosevelt was not finished. On June 2, 1940, Congress approved an act "to expedite the strengthening of the national defense."

The new law gave the president authority "to prohibit or curtail the exportation of any military equipment or munitions, or component parts thereof, or machinery, tools, or material or supplies necessary for the manufacture, servicing or operation thereof, he may by proclamation prohibit or curtail such exportation, except under such rules and regulations as he shall prescribe ..."

The act included a sunset clause that would terminate such executive authority two years and twenty-eight days later, unless Congress voted to extend it.

The same day that Congress passed the law, the president issued a proclamation declaring that, in the interest of national defense, certain items could not be exported unless a license was first acquired from the office of the U.S. secretary of state. Requiring a license would allow the administration to pick and choose who got what. Friendly nations, such as England and Australia, might be allowed to obtain critical items from the U.S. that unfriendly nations, such as Germany, Italy, and Japan, might be denied.

Included on a list of restricted items were arms, ammunition, and implements of war. The list also restricted material or products containing rubber, silk, wool, tin and tungsten, along with a whole list of other materials and chemicals. Specific products requiring a license included aircraft parts and accessories, armor plate, bulletproof glass, clear plastics, optical elements for fire control and aircraft instruments and metal working machinery for melting and casting, pressing into forms, cutting and grinding, and welding. It was a long list and a nightmare of paperwork for exporters. On July 26, 1940, the president added license requirements for shipments of petroleum and scrap metal – two leading exports for the Long Beach and Los Angeles ports. The previous year, more than $36 million worth of petroleum and scrap metal had moved through the two ports, much of it to Japan.

The export restrictions didn't bar such exports, but it did give the president and his administration a key card to play in negotiations with foreign countries. Exports of oil and scrap metal to Japan continued, but the threat to cut off Japan from such resources was a powerful one. Japan was poor in natural resources, which was one of the reasons the island nation was so intent on bringing the rest of Asia – with its vast resources – under Japanese control. The United States had been supplying 85 percent of Japan's petroleum, most of it exported through the Long Beach and Los Angeles ports.

The threat to restrict exports to Japan didn't only threaten Japan. It also meant reduced earnings for the U.S. businesses that dealt in those products. Petroleum and scrap metal exports to Japan continued, but not for very long. In August 1940, the United States cut off export to Japan of aviation gasoline and most kinds of machine tools. In September, a ban on scrap steel exports was announced, due to take effect in October. On September 27, Germany, Italy, and Japan announced the Tripartite Pact, a treaty of alliance. The main objective was to dissuade the United States from coming to the aid of its allies. On October 16, as scheduled, the embargo on scrap steel went into effect.

In the week before the embargo began, the harbor area was jammed with Japanese ships, its crewmen rushing to load cargo while they still had time. They didn't get it all. In Long Beach there remained 500 tons of scrap metal, intended for export to Japan before the embargo was ordered. It was exported instead by rail to the Columbia Steel plant a few miles away in Torrance.

Things were moving rapidly. Exports through the two ports fell, while imports rose. The loss of trade with Japan was partially offset with an increase in trade with the Soviet Union, through the port of Vladivostok. The Navy announced it planned to build a 400-house community in Long Beach for Navy personnel and their families.

Meanwhile, one harbor industry was preparing to make a significant comeback. During World War I, shipbuilding had been a thriving business in the ports of Long Beach and Los Angeles. When the war ended, the outstanding orders were fulfilled, putting a glut of ships on the market in the 1920s. Ships that cost $1.9 million to build were being sold for $25,000 to $100,000 with 2.5 percent down and the rest on credit. Established shipyards went dormant. An industry that once employed thousands of craftsmen was reduced to doing repair work and building yachts for rich people.

Eighteen years later, as the next big war approached, the shipyards were once again tooling up to build vessels. The Maritime Commission, an agency created in 1936 to replace the United States Shipping Board, had instituted a program to build 500 new merchant ships that would replace the World War I-era vessels that made up the bulk of the merchant marine fleet at the time. The plan was to order ships and sell or lease them to commercial shipping lines, but to make sure they were available for military service if the need arose. A subsidy would cover the difference in cost between building the ships in the United States or foreign country, which would cost less.

Modern warfare was about logistics. The battleships and destroyers might be the stars, but those ships needed fuel, ammunition, maintenance and repair supplies, and food and water for the crew to fulfill their missions. The merchant ships supported the supply chain for the warships, and it was estimated that it took twenty merchant ships to support one battleship. The first series of ships

AIR POWER: *A Navy pilot trains over the Port in 1940. The Navy had leased Reeves Field on Terminal Island from the Port of Los Angeles for use as an official airfield.*

LONG BEACH AT WAR: *Scores of naval vessels are protected from rough water by the Navy Mole in the early 1940s. The city sold the Navy the land for its station and shipyard for $1.*

ordered by the Maritime Commission was the C-1 freighter. The C-1 was a small ship – 412 feet long with a draft of 23.5 feet – that cruised at fourteen knots. It was meant to be used on short routes where neither speed nor capacity was a priority.

The Maritime Commission had awarded a $7.56 million order in 1939 to Consolidated Steel Corp. for four C-1 freighters. It was the first shipbuilding order in the local harbor area since the 1920s. The company planned to fabricate the sections of the ships at its plant in Maywood and then bring them to the Craig Shipyard facility, which it had leased.

Other shipyards in the harbor area also were coming alive at the prospect of new business. The Los Angeles Shipbuilding and Dry Dock Co. in the Los Angeles West Basin got a contract to build a Navy repair ship worth $16 million, and the Bethlehem Steel yard on Terminal Island, which hadn't built a ship in twenty years, was awarded a contract to build six destroyers costing more than $8 million each. Everybody wanted in on the bonanza. California Shipbuilding Co. set up shop along the Cerritos Channel on Terminal Island in Los Angeles, and Craig Shipbuilding remained active, although on a smaller scale – retrofitting yachts for wartime duty as coastal patrol boats.

On November 14, 1940, Consolidated Steel launched the new age of shipbuilding in the Southern California harbors when the *Cape Mendocino* slid down the ways into the waters of the Long Beach Harbor. It would be the first of many vessels – both large and small – to be launched at the two ports in the next several years.

By the middle of 1941, there were 6,800 workers employed at the port, either building ships or constructing yards in which to build ships. Consolidated Steel had a new contract, this time for twenty-six new freighters to be built at its second shipyard on the north end of the West Basin in Los Angeles.

The Great Depression was over, at least in Southern California, but then there was a new problem in the harbor area. All those workers trying to get to their jobs were creating massive traffic jams, especially on Terminal Island where the Navy was busy building a major shipyard and Navy base. Terminal Island was only connected to the mainland by one three-lane bridge – a bridge that had to open for every significant vessel that traversed the Cerritos Channel as it moved between the two ports. When that happened, the line of traffic with people trying to get to work would back up to Anaheim Street. The problem would get much worse when the Navy shipyard and other facilities opened.

One suggested solution was to build underwater tubes connecting Long Beach or Los Angeles with the island. That would be a major undertaking that would take too long to solve the immediate problem. A ferry might work, but shuttling people and vehicles back and forth on a ferry would not be efficient. In the end, Long Beach Port engineer Robert Shoemaker came up with the solution that was adopted by the Navy. It involved construction of a swing bridge near the Ford plant – an eighty-foot-long, four-lane highway – anchored to the shore on one side with the other end floating on a scow. When a vessel needed to pass, the bridge would swing open like a gate, and then swing back after the vessel had passed. It was makeshift and it was temporary, but it helped solve the traffic problem for the next three years.

The Trials and Tribulations of Harry Bridges

During the 1930s, there had been a growing militancy among labor unions, spurred both by friendlier government policies and the economic squeeze being experienced by the working classes. Unions had gained experience during those years to leverage their power in order to get what they wanted. But there was one union leader who was targeted by both Democrats and Republicans – Harry Bridges, president of the newly formed International Longshoremen's and Warehousemen's Union and a director of the Congress of Industrial Organizations, rival of the American Federation of Labor.

Even some pro-labor New Deal Democrats resented Bridges' lack of cooperation with their efforts to negotiate better pay and working conditions for labor. Bridges was not interested in attempts by the government to speak for workers. He believed workers were better served by taking militant actions to gain their own deal. He had enemies within the labor movement as well, especially among the old guard union leaders. He had clashed with Joe Ryan, president of the International Longshoremen's Association, and had founded the ILWU as a West Coast alternative to the ILA. He had also crossed swords with Dave Beck of the Teamsters Union when he attempted to organize truck drivers in the Long Beach and Los Angeles harbor areas.

Through it all, the accusation that had dogged Bridges since the days of the 1934 waterfront strike – that he was a radical communist whose aim was to overthrow the government – would not go away. And since Bridges was not yet a U.S. citizen, there was a campaign by his enemies to deport him to Australia. In 1938, Bridges was hit with a warrant from the Labor Department, charging him with belonging to an organization that advocated the overthrow of the government by force and violence and which circulated radical literature.

The hearing went on for eleven weeks in San Francisco in front of Harvard Law School Dean James M. Landis, who was acting as a special examiner for the Labor Department. Numerous witnesses testified to seeing Bridges associating with known communists and said that he had sympathetic views on some communist issues. Bridges conceded in his testimony that he knew communists and that he had worked with many of them on union matters, but he denied that he was a party member. He also denied advocating the violent overthrow of the government.

Landis handed down his final ruling on December 29, 1938, which found that Bridges was not a member of the Communist Party nor was he affiliated with it. It was a victory for Bridges, but it didn't last long. The law under which Bridges was tried – a leftover from the Red Scare years following World War I – required that the defendant had to be a member of the party at the time he was charged. Having past membership in the party was not enough to have someone deported. So, Congress passed a new federal law, one just for Bridges. Under the new law, an alien could be deported if he had *ever* been a member of the Communist Party. In August 1940, FBI Director J. Edgar Hoover announced that he was assigning a squad of specially chosen FBI agents to investigate Bridges. Three months later, he submitted a 2,500-page report on Bridges to the Justice Department to help determine whether further action against the union leader was necessary.

A new trial was ordered in February 1941 in an attempt to deport Bridges under the new law. Although the Justice Department said that the FBI report on Bridges did not include any recommendations, Hoover said he personally thought there was ample evidence available to oust Bridges from the country.

In the second trial, special Justice Department Examiner Charles B. Sears reached the opposite conclusion from that reached two years earlier by Examiner James Landis. Sears ruled that Bridges was both a member of, and affiliated with, the Communist Party and that he should be deported under the 1940 Alien Registration Act. Although no one incident proved Bridges' communist affiliation, the pattern established over time left little doubt, Sears said.

The Los Angeles Times, in an editorial the next day titled "Good Riddance – If We Get It," praised the Sears' decision, but lamented that Harry Bridges would probably appeal and delay his final ouster.

> *It probably will be time enough for the United States to congratulate itself on the prospective deportation of Harry Bridges when the recommendation, made public yesterday, of ex-Judge Charles B. Sears is carried out and this alien radical and long-time disturber of the industrial peace is – actually on his way back to his native Australia.*

The editorial went on to detail all the ways that Bridges could fight his actual deportation. The Times was right. Bridges did not get meekly on the boat and return to Australia. He did fight, and he did stay, and he continued to lead the union he had helped found.

Five days after the decision, Bridges received a standing ovation that went on for several minutes as he prepared to address the California state conference of the Congress for Industrial Organizations. He called on union workers to dedicate themselves to the defeat of fascism and urged those working in defense industries to avoid strikes which would help the enemy. When they encountered disputes with management, they should use arbitration and avail themselves of government aid in resolving such issues, he told them.

Whether or not Bridges was ever a member of the Communist Party in the perspective of modern day seems almost to be irrelevant. It is true he was sympathetic and perhaps even naïve as to what was going on in the Soviet Union at the time – as were many intellectuals of the day. But the union he led had become a power on the waterfront – a partner in the process that management had no choice but to acknowledge. And through it all, the people who mattered to Bridges, the men and women in the ILWU, never lost their faith in him.

Long Beach vs. Los Angeles

The struggling little port that had been so easily dismissed for its lofty pretensions in the early days had finally grown up. It was a contender, and the rivalry between the Port of Long Beach and the still-larger Port of Los Angeles next door grew, despite frequent attempts by both sides to work together.

The ports had their own personalities and their own cultures. In Long Beach, the port was snuggled up against downtown and the seat of local government. In Los Angeles, the port in San Pedro and Wilmington was twenty miles away, an adjunct to the rest of the city, connected by a long and narrow strip of land whose only purpose was to physically link one area to the other. Los Angeles was a sprawling mess of a city, a cobbling together of diverse areas spread over hundreds of square miles. Although Long Beach by the 1940s had grown to be the second-largest city in the county with 164,271 residents, it was more compact in scale and much more of a large town than a city.

Geography matters. In Long Beach, the port was isolated from the residential neighborhoods by the commercial area of downtown and the industrial area north of the port. In San Pedro, the residential neighborhoods were on hills overlooking the port, and in Wilmington, the residents lived in close proximity to the industrial components that fed off the port. But the power was in Los Angeles, not in the local communities.

Long Beach and Los Angeles may have been next-door neighbors in the harbor area, but they were neighbors forever separated by culture and interest. The differences soon became glaringly apparent, and the comparison tended to cast Los Angeles as the villain and Long Beach as the contender – still number two, but more user-friendly and more willing to accommodate.

Nowhere was this more apparent than in the differences between how Long Beach answered the Navy's need for land and how Los Angeles had approached the matter. Long Beach had long recognized the economic benefits in having the Navy presence, and so it had crafted a deal that would protect its oil interest – at least in the short term – but also clear the way for the Navy to invest in the area. Los Angeles had stubbornly refused to hand over Reeves Field to the Navy unless the Navy met the city's price and list of conditions.

Faced with Los Angeles' intransigence, the federal government finally filed a lawsuit in August 1940 to secure the needed parcel. Los Angeles continued to fight bitterly to protect its rights. Six months after the Long Beach-Navy deal was closed and construction had begun, Los Angeles was still demanding $22 million in claims for the value of the land plus severance of the airfield from the harbor area. In addition, the State of California wanted the federal government to pay it $228,600 for the state's interest in Reeves Field and $105,000 for its interest in the property that Long Beach had already sold to the Navy for $1. The basis of the Los Angeles claims was that federal government ownership of the property would impair the commercial expansion of the port in the future.

"The real issue is whether our harbor is to be hereafter a naval base or a world port ... If the Navy, which is to protect commerce, must displace commerce itself in taking over this area, we believe it only fair that the city be paid sufficient to approximately replace the facilities disarranged by acquisition, providing that just compensation guaranteed by the United States Constitution, under which we are proceeding," argued Los Angeles City Attorney Ray L. Chesebro. The argument may have been logical, but with the nation teetering on the brink of all-out war, the timing was terrible.

And whenever such disputes arose, Los Angeles was again reminded of the example set by Long Beach, with its $1 sale to the Navy.

It was a comparison that also had been raised months earlier when Los Angeles ran afoul of the U.S. Maritime Commission over California Shipbuilding Corp.'s attempt to secure a lease for a shipyard to build vessels needed for the war effort. The federal officials accused Los Angeles of "profiteering" and having a "bargain-counter" attitude toward a $48 million contract for construction of thirty military cargo ships to be built by the company at the site. The shipyard was expected to employ from 6,000 to 7,000 workers with an annual payroll of more than $7 million a year. The Los Angeles port was demanding a $35,000 annual rent for the property plus one-half of 1 percent of the gross income. At that price, it would be cheaper to move construction of the ships to some other locale, warned federal officials. Other ports were charging from $1,500 to $2,500 for such property.

The federal government made no secret that they were fed up with what they saw as Los Angeles' attempts to squeeze every dollar out of the need to beef up the nation's defense posture. Nor were federal officials shy about indicating to reporters that Los Angeles' "hold-up" reputation would be remembered in the future when the government was determining where to award contracts.

On July 25, 1941, Secretary of the Navy Frank Knox – the Republican vice presidential candidate in 1936 – approved construction of a $2.5 million naval hospital on eighty to 100 acres owned by Fred H. Bixby on the east end of Seventh Street in Long Beach. The original site chosen by the Navy had been in the Palos Verdes hills of San Pedro.

In late 1941, as the nation edged ever closer to its bloody destiny, the animosity between the two cities sharing the San Pedro harbor reached new levels of pettiness when the Los Angeles City Council voted down a contract for the city to handle the Navy base's sewage at the Los Angeles Harbor treatment plant. The Navy base was in Long Beach, not Los Angeles, noted Councilman Wilder Hartley.

"Why don't they use the Long Beach sewage system?" Hartley asked. "We are always being hurried into a deal that winds up with Los Angeles footing Long Beach's bills. Right now we are paying $40,000 a year for operating expenses of a bridge that is being used by the people of Long Beach."

Los Angeles' irritation with Long Beach was clear. But the dismissive attitude it had earlier displayed in its dealings with the smaller city was beginning to change.

Losing Elevation
There was one worrisome event that happened on Terminal Island in 1941 as the Navy worked to prepare its new base. For some reason, the elevation of the ground seemed to be dropping – not by much, just one to three inches – but enough to cause concern. The ground also seemed to be sinking by the Edison plant and in the Union Pacific oil field across Seaside Boulevard from the Navy property. Geologists thought it may have resulted from nearby dredging tapping into a subterranean stream and relieving the pressure underground. The decision was made to pump water and sand back into the tapped area to see if that solved the problem.

The Missing Fleet
The one element missing during much of the military buildup in the harbor area was the Navy fleet itself. There were numerous advantages for the Navy to homeport its ships in Long Beach. The weather was good, there were nearby naval gunnery ranges on San Clemente and Santa Rosa islands, fuel was plentiful, and there were convenient ship repair facilities. The down side had been that when the Santa Ana winds blew from the inland desert areas, the ships would sometimes pitch at anchor, although that problem had been mitigated somewhat by the extension of the breakwater. A bigger concern, however, was that since many of the sailors onboard those vessels were able to go home every night, they were getting soft. If they were going to be ready for battle, they needed to spend more time at sea.

In April 1940, wives and girlfriends were kissed goodbye and the fleet sailed for seven weeks of war games in the mid-Pacific. It was due to return on May 17. But that didn't happen. On May 7, it was announced that the fleet would remain in Pearl Harbor for an indefinite period. That indefinite period stretched into more than a year-and-a half. The deployment of the Pacific Fleet to Hawaii was not a sudden decision. President Roosevelt had wanted a show of force closer to the action. It was a message aimed at Japan about the seriousness of U.S. resolve.

The relationship between the two nations had been unraveling since the declaration of the oil embargo. Japan's situation was hopeless. It was dependent on U.S. oil to power its military machinery, and its stockpiles were being steadily depleted. The only rational choice it had was to back off its dream of conquest and the building of an Asian empire under Japanese control. Or so some thought.

Long Beach at War

At 7:48 on Sunday morning, December 7, 1941, Japanese planes launched from six aircraft carriers swept down from the sky and began bombing the Navy fleet at anchor in Pearl Harbor and the nearby airfields on shore. The United States was totally unprepared. Many of the guns protecting the harbor were unmanned, and ammunition had been stashed off-site. The planes parked at the airfield were placed wing-to-wing to make them easier to protect from saboteurs, but also easier to destroy in an attack by air. The Japanese planes attacked in two waves – 353 fighters, bombers, and torpedo planes in all. They were backed up by five two-man mini-submarines, each armed with two torpedoes. The attack damaged all eight battleships in the fleet, sinking four of them. Because the waters of Pearl Harbor were relatively shallow, three of the battleships that had been sunk were raised, repaired, and returned to service. Only the *Arizona* remained on the bottom. Also damaged or sunk were three destroyers, three cruisers, one minelayer, and an anti-aircraft training ship. The U.S. lost 188 aircraft, most of them destroyed on the ground. The Japanese lost twenty-nine planes and all five of its mini-subs.

Fortunately, the United States' only aircraft carriers – the *Lexington*, the *Saratoga*, and the *Enterprise* – were at sea at the time of the attack. Their absence helped dissuade Japanese Admiral Chuichi Nagumo from sending in a third wave of aircraft to hit the fuel storage tanks, shipyard, and power stations. By that time, the element of surprise was gone. The Americans had rapidly responded and were on alert and ready to fight. Two-thirds of the Japanese losses had occurred during the second strafe. With the weather worsening and the possibility of American carriers somewhere in the area, Nagumo reasoned that it was time for the Japanese fleet to leave.

The human toll for the United States included 2,403 Americans killed and 1,178 wounded. Probably no one city in the nation was hit harder by the news than Long Beach, where the war was personal right from the start. Overnight the attack resulted in 160 Navy war widows and 125 fatherless children living in Long Beach, mourning their husbands and fathers and trying to figure out what to do next. The men who had been killed had been members of the community. They shopped at local stores, ate at local diners, and attended local churches. The wives, who had spent long months waiting for their husbands to return home, now spent anxious days waiting to see if their loved one was alive or dead. It took a while to sort things out. The telegrams began arriving around Christmas. And even for the families whose husbands and fathers had survived, there was the knowledge that their loved ones were now in harm's way.

The survivors of the men killed in Pearl Harbor were treated with kindness by the community. The civilian population responded with donations of food and delayed the payments for rents and other obligations. But mostly it was up to the wives themselves – the ones who had been widowed and the ones who had not – to fend for themselves. There were no Navy death benefits at the time – a small pension would later be established by Congress – and any back pay owed to their husbands was tied up in Navy red tape. As always happens in such cases, the survivors pooled their resources, and they survived. The aircraft companies in Long Beach and other nearby communities gave employment priority to military widows, and many of the women were soon learning new skills and drawing regular paychecks for the first time in their lives.

The casualties of war continued to mount. The United States was at war, and people were being added to the long list of Long Beach dead. On the night of January 16, 1942, fifteen Long Beach-based Army Ferry Command pilots died in an airliner crash in Nevada. Four more died that month in other incidents.

The Naval Affairs Committee in Long Beach held a memorial service for the war dead on February 22 in the Municipal Auditorium. The auditorium was jammed to capacity with 4,500 people coming to pay their respects, including 1,000 families of the dead, and hundreds of others who were turned away at the door.

Mayor Francis Gentry opened the ceremony; Rabbi L. Elliot Grafman delivered the invocation, and a boys' choir sang. California Governor Culbert Olson spoke of sacrifice and heroism. Admiral Ralston S. Holmes promised everybody that the "Navy would not forget Pearl Harbor." Navy Chaplain John E. Johnson read a brief burial service, after which four servicemen, representing each branch of the service, laid floral wreaths. Sobs were heard throughout the audience as a Navy bugler played taps, and singer Jeanette MacDonald sang the hymn "Face to Face" and then, "The Star-Spangled Banner."

Long Beach was at war.

Attacks Real and Imagined

In the frenzy following Pearl Harbor and the declaration of war, it was feared that Long Beach could be the target of enemy saboteurs or even a Japanese attack on the mainland. The Navy took over operational control of both harbors, with a port director – Richard M. Coffman, assistant commandant of the 11th Naval District, overseeing all shipping operations, including the movement of commercial freighters. Anti-submarine nets were stretched across all openings between the breakwater and the harbor, including one from the end of the breakwater to the Rainbow Pier in Long Beach. The nets were lowered to permit the passage of friendly vessels.

Helmets and gas masks were shipped to the city by the Office of Civil Defense, and armed soldiers guarded the bridges over the Cerritos Channel. Nightly blackouts were imposed for the first four days following Pearl Harbor, which resulted in a rash of traffic accidents that killed at least two pedestrians in downtown Long Beach and injured several more. Armed guards were posted at strategic spots around the harbor area, patrolling shipyards, oil refineries, tank farms, wharves, and warehouses. Gasoline, solvents, oil, lumber, and other flammable materials were moved away from the waterfront.

The federal government took over the Long Beach Ford plant on Terminal Island for the Army to use as a supply depot. The manufacturing of cars ended, and the auto parts at the plant were moved to the Ford facility in Richmond, California. Anti-aircraft guns were mounted on the roof next to the Ford sign, and a cluster of barrage balloons, anchored to the ground by cable, was raised west of the plant to protect the harbor from aerial attack. Some of the employees stayed on to work for the Army; others found work at the nearby shipyards or defense plants.

Anti-aircraft guns were mounted on the roof of the Procter & Gamble plant on West Seventh Street and the plant began turning out cans of Crisco for military kitchens. To save tin for the war effort, in 1943 the plant stopped putting the Crisco shortening in cans and began packing it in glass jars. The following year, the plant began turning out salt-water soap for the Navy. After the war, the plant once again focused its efforts on housewives and families instead of soldiers and sailors.

At the California Shipbuilding Corp. yard on Terminal Island, welders who had walked off the job before the attack on Pearl Harbor were given twenty-four hours to return to work or be dismissed. The names of the fired workers would be turned over to the Selective Service Board – the agency in charge of the military draft. The message was clear: work or fight.

On Terminal Island, military and customs officials cordoned off the areas in which 3,000 Japanese-Americans lived and worked at Fish Harbor. Navy gunboats turned back Japanese fishing boats as they tried to depart the harbor and ordered them to return to the docks, where the fishing fleet was quarantined and placed under armed guard. None were permitted to leave the area, and only those who had been away during the sealing off of the area were permitted to return home. Several Japanese business owners were detained for questioning.

There were, in fact, Japanese submarines off the coast, and two American vessels came under attack. On Christmas Eve 1941, the Japanese submarine *I-19*, with Lieutenant Commander Narahara Shogo in command, fired a torpedo at the lumber schooner *Barbara Olson* as it steamed along the Long Beach coast headed for San Diego. The torpedo fortunately went under the ship, then exploded on the other side, spraying water about 300 feet into the air. The Navy sub-chaser *USS Amethyst*, on patrol outside the harbor entrance, saw the explosion, sounded general quarters, and responded to the location. The *Amethyst*, however, was unable to locate the enemy sub.

Four hours later, *I-19* had a new target off the Palos Verdes Peninsula – the McCormick Steamship Co.'s freighter the *Absaroka*, also headed south to San Diego with a load of lumber. This time *I-19* had better luck. It fired two torpedoes at the 23-year-old freighter. One went wide, but the other struck on the starboard side, about fifty feet aft of the beam. Three of the four men on deck were thrown into the sea. The fourth, Joseph Ryan, managed to stay aboard and immediately began trying to help his fellow crewmen out of the water. The blast had caused the *Absaroka* to roll so far over that a portion of the deck was underwater. As the ship righted itself, one of the crewmen was able to grab on and climb back aboard. Ryan tossed a line to another shipmate, whose leg had been injured in the explosion, and began pulling him aboard. It was his final act. The explosion also had snapped the lashings that secured a ten-foot high stack of lumber to the deck. The lumber stack suddenly collapsed, crushing Ryan's head and tumbling him overboard.

The *Amethyst* and several military aircraft spent the rest of the morning dropping depth charges in the area, attempting to destroy *I-19*, but with little success. The *Absaroka* crew abandoned ship, but several of them came back aboard when it became apparent that the ship was not about to sink. A tug towed it into harbor and beached it on a sandy strip below Fort MacArthur.

In an era of global warfare, the attack on the *Absaroka* was hardly a major event, although a man had been killed saving his fellow shipmates. But it wasn't the intensity of the battle or the loss of life. It had happened right off the coast of the United States – about a mile from the Point Fermin lighthouse – as hundreds of witnesses watched from the shore. The war was no longer something that people just read about. This time it happened right before their eyes, right in their own backyard.

On February 23, 1942, a Japanese sub surfaced off Goleta to shell an oil field just up the coast from Santa Barbara. The sub fired shells from its deck gun toward an oil field onshore for almost half-an-hour. There were no casualties and little damage, but it did raise an already heightened level of concern. And then, two days later, with everybody on alert and tensions high, the inevitable happened – the infamous and slightly ridiculous Japanese "air raid" on Southern California.

In the early morning hours of February 25, anti-aircraft batteries blasted away at reported enemy planes, with spent shell fragments falling to earth and peppering Long Beach streets and rooftops. A blackout was declared from the Mexican border to the Central Valley, and anti-aircraft spotlights around the Los Angeles basin pierced the skies in an attempt to find the enemy. Numerous witnesses – including Long Beach Police Chief James McClelland, who watched the battle unfold along with a Navy observer from atop City Hall, swore that they saw nine "silvery looking" aircraft flying across the night sky. The guns blasted away for five and one half hours before the sun came up and a cease-fire was declared.

Afterward, there was some dispute about what had just happened. The Navy announced within hours that the whole thing was a false alarm brought on by jittery nerves. The Army kept insisting that the raid was real and the result of unidentified aircraft flying over the area. Thousands of residents claimed that they had seen the planes and were convinced that they had lived through an actual air raid. Los Angeles County Sheriff Eugene W. Biscailuz said it was possible the planes had flown up from Mexico to stage the attack. He noted that there were also vast uninhabited areas in San Bernardino, Inyo, and Mono counties and in the states of Nevada and Arizona where the planes could be launched from camouflaged bases. Even after attempts to find evidence of enemy planes ended in failure, officials tried to find a silver lining to the tale.

"It should give the public a feeling of confidence to know, as the tremendous barrage established beyond a doubt, that the Army is here in force and it ready to do its job, too," said Los Angeles Mayor Fletcher Bowron.

Despite the absence of an actual air raid, there was some damage inflicted during the incident. What goes up has to come down, and all those shells exploding in the sky rained shrapnel down all over town. And the duds, the shells that did not explode in the air, did explode when they came back down. One Long Beach man suffered an eight-inch gash to his head when a shell hit the sidewalk in front of the Bank of America and exploded. Two others narrowly escaped injury when shells pierced the roofs of their homes and exploded inside. Automobiles parked outside were dented and pierced by falling shrapnel.

At least five people were killed in auto accidents during the blackout – including 55-year-old Long Beach Police Sergeant Engebert Larson, whose car collided head-on with another auto while he was rushing to the police station for emergency duty, and Navy Captain Irwin Keeney, who died on his way to the Navy Landing. Others suffered heart attacks, broken limbs, and concussions while fumbling around in the dark. In the end, it turned out there were no enemy aircraft, just a lot of nervous military folks with itchy trigger fingers.

Deportation of Japanese to Inland Camps

By the time the U.S. had entered World War II, the Japanese-American population had been a visible and significant part of Southern California for years. Many owned truck farms throughout the region, and there was a Japanese fishing community on the Los Angeles side of Terminal Island numbering about 3,000 people. An estimated 2,200 were citizens; the rest were not. Some of those who were citizens were second-generation Americans born in the United States. Although all Japanese were being viewed as potential spies, the fishing village was especially troublesome to the government because it was adjacent to both the Reeves Field Navy airbase in the Port of Los Angeles and the new Navy resupply base and shipyard being constructed at the Port of Long Beach. Even before the U.S. entered the war, the Navy had been concerned that some residents of the Terminal Island community might be transmitting messages about ship movements and shore defenses to the Japanese government.

The Japanese village on Terminal Island was somewhat fractured. The Immigration Act of 1924 had banned Japanese from entering the country, which made pretty much every Japanese person who came into the community after 1924 an American citizen because he or she had been born here. Although Southern California was well-populated by 1941, the island community was separated from the mainstream, and the people living in the village kept many of the old ways and customs from back home. There was a Shinto shrine; judo and kendo lessons were held at the Fisherman's Hall, and much of the business along Tuna Street – the main street – was conducted in a dialect unique to the village – part English and part Japanese. As the American-born second generation grew up and began attending high school on the mainland, they brought home American ways. Baseball games became weekly events, and the villagers began celebrating typically American holidays.

Before the war began, the FBI had spent months compiling a list of Japanese that they determined were suspicious – both citizens and non-citizens. The day Pearl Harbor was bombed, federal agents sprang into action, hunting down the people on the list. Within forty-eight hours of the attack, the FBI had taken 500 non-citizen Japanese into custody across Southern California.

The Japanese attack on Pearl Harbor had taken a huge emotional toll in Southern California, and people began to call for "something to be done" about the Japanese living in the state. Japanese people found themselves targets of that anger. Even on Terminal Island in the fish canneries where the Japanese had long worked along with other immigrant groups, there were problems. The Filipinos, angry about the invasion of their homeland, would clash with the Japanese, and sometimes fists would fly.

As the American involvement in the war grew, and the losses suffered became more personal, people grew even more resentful. The anti-Japanese fever was fed by the news that some Japanese had been arrested for leaving their lights on during the blackout or for shining flashlights into the air. The governor's office was deluged with angry telegrams asking that all Japanese be exiled from the state.

On February 2, 1942, federal agents raided the Terminal Island fishing village shortly after dawn and arrested 336 non-citizen Japanese residents. Japanese people had been legally barred from becoming naturalized citizens under a 1922 Supreme Court decision, and now they were seen as more likely to be loyal to Japan. Accompanied by the police, federal agents went to the homes of those targeted, knocked on their doors, and told them they were under arrest. Some of the arrestees were still in their bed clothes or eating breakfast when the authorities arrived. Others had heard the raid was planned and were sitting up with their bags packed, ready to go.

Life went on in the village, but not for long. On February 19, President Roosevelt signed Executive Order 9066. Although the presidential order did not single out Japanese people, it did authorize the military to take whatever action was necessary to exclude "any and all persons" from the right "to enter, remain in, or leave a designated military area."

It meant the end of the Japanese fishing village on Terminal Island. On February 25, the Navy began posting flyers in the area, giving residents forty-eight hours to take whatever possessions they could and leave the island. By the morning of February 28, the once-bustling community was a ghost town. Piles of household items and broken furniture were left behind along with stray dogs and cats. Sentries stood guard outside the area. A few of the former residents were allowed to re-enter the area briefly to complete the removal of their belongings, but that was all. The electricity and gas were turned off shortly after dawn, and the city humane department came later that day and rounded up the abandoned family pets. The Navy later bulldozed homes and shops in the 200-acre area and commandeered abandoned boats.

The Terminal Island residents moved temporarily to other California communities, but often found themselves unwelcome there as well. On March 27, Lieutenant General John L. DeWitt, head of the Western Command, ordered all Japanese living in Military Area No. 1 – virtually every place within 100 miles of the coast – to report for assignment to inland relocation camps. Most of the Terminal Islanders were later interned in the Manzanar Camp on the east side of the Sierra Nevada Mountains.

DeWitt was quite open in his disdain for the Japanese people. When testifying before the House Naval Affairs Committee on April 13, 1943, he told the congressmen: "A Jap's a Jap, it makes no difference whether he's an American citizen or not." It was a remark that got him into hot water with the top brass. In a telephone conversation the next day with Assistant Secretary of War John J. McCloy, he confirmed that he had indeed made the statement, to which McCloy icily informed the general: "When we have taken them into the Army and put the United States uniform on them, we don't say a Jap is a Jap."

Despite the rebuke, the Japanese remained in camps, enclosed by barbed wire and surrounded by armed sentries, until almost the end of the war. General DeWitt was not censured for his remarks. He was later assigned as commandant of the Army and Navy Staff College.

Arsenal of Democracy

The U.S. had been edging toward becoming part of the war effort – if not joining it outright – prior to the attack on Pearl Harbor, and the twin ports in Southern California were the perfect gateway to bring materials in and products out to the Pacific. To take advantage of the ports of Long Beach and Los Angeles, defense manufacturers started building assembly plants in the area. It was a war-time buildup that would create a large and lucrative aircraft industry in Southern California. In 1940, Donald Douglas acquired 200 acres of property north of Daugherty Field, south of Carson Street, and east of Cherry Avenue. It was close to the harbor and ready to be built upon, and on November 22, 1940, Douglas broke ground for an aircraft plant. Production began on August 13, 1941, and on December 23, just sixteen days after the attack on Pearl Harbor, the first C-47 Skytrain rolled off the assembly line with 4,284 more to follow. On the following day, Christmas Eve, the first of 999 A-20 Havocs rolled off the Douglas line. The C-47 was a military version of Douglas' DC-3 and would be nicknamed the Gooney Bird by the pilots who flew it. The Douglas plant also built 3,000 B-17s and 1,156 A-26 Invaders. During the peak production year of 1943, Douglas employed 43,000 workers – more than half of them women. The average wage was sixty cents an hour.

After the war began, the Army Air Corps took over Daugherty Field and gave it a new name – the Long Beach Army Airfield. It became the headquarters for the Air Transport Command's Ferry Division with pilots – many of them women – flying new planes to duty stations all over the world.

In 1941, the Navy, which had used Daugherty Field as a Reserve Navy aviation base, had bought 480 acres in Orange County from Suzanna Bixby Bryant, the daughter of John and Susan Bixby. The property was used to construct a new Navy Reserve base, known as the Naval Reserve Aviation Base at Los Alamitos.

Back at the harbor, the ports became a whirlwind of shipbuilding and construction of new facilities. The Navy finally settled its court battle with the city of Los Angeles in May 1942, when it agreed to lease surface rights to the property until 1970. The Navy agreed to give the city $50,000 to cover litigation costs in the case, and the city agreed not to commence drilling for oil in an area from 1,000 to 2,000 feet from the edge of the field until six months after the war was over.

On the Long Beach side, work continued through 1941 on the Terminal Island Naval Station and shipyard. The Navy dredged a harbor for its ships, using the spoils to fill in and elevate the original 105 acres and to add an additional 100 acres to the site. A mole was constructed from the west end of the base adjacent to Reeves Field, extending southward and curling to the east to protect the harbor. The shipyard construction was on the east side of the property, the administration and recreation facilities to the west. An additional forty acres were purchased on the south side of Seaside Boulevard.

Allied Engineers Inc. of Los Angeles, won the contract to build the Fleet Operating Base. Adrian Wilson was the chief architect; Paul R. Williams, the associate architect; Donald R. Warren, the chief engineer; S.B. Barnes, the structural engineer; and E.L Ellingwood, the mechanical engineer. Both Wilson and Williams were experienced and nationally recognized, but Williams had the added distinction of being black – a rarity in the world of professional architecture at the time. Williams' reputation would grow even larger, and years later, his participation in the project would become part of a vehement battle over what to do with the base after the Navy left town.

The buildings were secured atop pilings driven into the ground with steel-reinforced walls made of poured-in-place concrete. The base was named Roosevelt Base in honor of the president, and commissioned on September 1, 1942. Construction of a gymnasium, swimming pools, officers' club, bowling alley, additional housing, and mess halls came later.

Meanwhile, shipbuilding in the area exploded after the U.S. joined the world's hostilities. Warships were needed to fight, and cargo ships were required to supply food, equipment, fuel, and armaments to remote combat zones. All kinds of crafts, large and small, were being built on both sides of the San Pedro Bay. Even the smallest boatyards that had been building yachts, sailboats, fishing boats, and other civilian craft found themselves busy turning out military vessels and helping win the war.

Liberty ships, Victory ships, smaller cargo ships, destroyers, destroyer escorts, minesweepers, crash boats for rescuing downed airmen, Coast Guard cutters, landing craft, tugs, barges, lifeboats, tankers, sub-chasers, fireboats, PT boats, target boats for gunnery practice, frigates, cruisers, and repair ships were all produced or repaired in the harbor area.

Consolidated Steel Corp. was building cargo ships for the Navy on land it had leased from Craig Shipbuilding in Long Beach and at an additional shipyard on the Los Angeles West Basin. Consolidated also used its plant in Maywood – thirty miles inland – to manufacture anti-aircraft guns to be mounted on Navy ships and mechanized landing craft that would be launched in a test pool before being trucked to the harbor. California Shipbuilding, on Terminal Island, managed by American industrialist Henry Kaiser and his associates and better known as CalShip, employed 40,000 men and women – only 1 percent of whom had any previous shipbuilding experience. Kaiser is well known for his association with Kaiser Aluminum, Kaiser Steel and for the health-care system he organized for his workers and their families called Kaiser Permanente. He also made cars and dabbled in real estate.

Western Pipe and Steel Co. built destroyer escorts and landing craft for the Navy and icebreakers for the Coast Guard at its yard in the Los Angeles harbor. Meanwhile, forty-five miles inland, the United Concrete Pipe Corp. of Baldwin Park was busy building sections that would be trucked to the Long Beach Harbor to be assembled into 175-foot, steel freight-passenger ships for the Army.

The Hodgson-Greene-Haldeman boatyard on the west end of Seventh Street in Long Beach kept busy during the war years, turning out sixty-five tugboats for the Army. It also built two patrol boats for the Navy and ten barges. With steel in short supply and the bigger shipyards at full capacity, Hodgson-Greene-Haldeman was one of the yards that had contracts to use wood. Half of the barges – Redwood 1 through Redwood 5 – turned out during the time were built from wood. Across the bay in San Pedro, Standard Shipbuilding Co. built eight wooden tugs during the war years, all of which were sent to Britain.

The U.S. Naval Dry Docks at Roosevelt Base, which opened in 1943 at the east end of the Navy complex, employed more than 16,000 people at its wartime peak. The Dry Docks facility had five industrial piers and three dry docks. The largest one – Dry Dock No. 1 – could contain a dozen vessels at one time. During the war, Naval Dry Dock workers repaired 635 damaged vessels and returned them to combat. The name was changed to the Terminal Island Naval Shipyard at the end of the war in 1945 and to the Long Beach Naval Shipyard in 1948.

Fighting and winning a war depends as much on logistics as it does on strategy and tactics – especially when the supply chain is stretched. One of the strategies employed by the Germans, in particular, was to "win the tonnage war" in the Atlantic – simply put, to sink cargo ships carrying supplies to the front lines faster than new ships could be built to replace them. America's response was the

Liberty Ship. Of all the Navy cargo ships built during the war, the best known were the Liberty Ships and later the Victory Ships. Neither were particularly pretty or elegant. They were built of a basic British design that was cheap, fast to build, and expendable. Rivets were replaced by welding – cutting labor costs by up to one-third. The Liberty Ships were 441 feet 6 inches long, 57 feet wide, and designed to last five years and carry 10,000 tons. Many of them lasted much longer, and during wartime they often carried much more weight.

American shipyards built 2,710 Liberty Ships during the war, the largest number of ships ever produced from a single design. That feat remains one of the legends of American industrial might during an era rife with such examples.

Much of the workforce recruited to build the Liberty Ships, many of them women, had never done anything remotely like it before. They learned on the job. The first ships off the line averaged about 230 days to build, but as the shipyard workers gained experience, that number dropped to about forty-two days. The ships tended to be named in honor of deceased people – any group that raised $2 million in war bonds could propose a name. One such ship was the *SS Charles H. Windham*, named after the "father" of the Port of Long Beach and built at the California Shipbuilding yard on Terminal Island. The keel was laid on March 15, 1943, and the *Windham* slid down the ways and into the Cerritos Channel twenty-six days later. It was used as a grain ship from 1954 through 1958 and sold for scrap to Bethlehem Steel Co. in 1959. The cost to build it was $70,200.

Later in the war, as the United States began to gain the upper hand, the Liberty Ships were replaced by Victory Ships. The Victory Ship was a Liberty Ship derivative that was fourteen feet longer, five feet wider, and four to six knots faster due to a larger engine and redesigned bow and stern. American shipyards built 531 Victory Ships by the end of the war.

Not all of the casualties of World War II came through combat. Shipyard workers in the harbor area and at other ports were exposed during the course of their workday to asbestos dust used for insulation in the ships. The danger was not immediately obvious, but in the years to come, many of those workers experienced such ailments as lung cancer and mesothelioma. Although both cancers are asbestos-related, they manifest themselves in different ways. The health consequences experienced by those workers would lead in the future to strict regulation of exposure to asbestos.

Port Infrastructure
Even though the Navy was in operational command during the war, the Long Beach Port continued to improve and grow, sometimes through projects it initiated itself and sometimes because of the Navy's need for more facilities. Despite the Navy taking over port operations, the Harbor Department was still flush with oil money from more than 100 city-owned wells pumping oil from beneath the harbor, and the demands for shipment of military cargo kept the port busy.

The port continued to improve the area around the East Basin, located west of the flood control channel and east of the entrance to the inner harbor. New timber wharves were built along the east side of the entrance channel south of Ocean Boulevard and on the south side of Pier D. New land continued to be filled in. Improvements to the wharves and facilities also were made in the inner harbor at the east end of Channel 3.

On October 14, 1943, Long Beach finally got its own 24-hour downtown connection to Terminal Island when a new four-lane pontoon bridge connecting Ocean Boulevard to the island opened to cars and trucks. The bridge, which went up and down with the tide, was for cars only, but for the ceremonial opening, Long Beach Mayor Clarence Wagner and Police Chief Walter Lentz walked to the middle from one direction while Commodore Schuyler F. Heim and other naval officers walked from the other. Although the bridge served its purpose, whenever a ship or any other vessel needed to pass, the traffic had to stop, and the bridge was floated off to one side until the channel was clear.

That same year, the Navy began development of twenty-eight acres of what would be known as Victory Pier in the outer harbor – along the 7,300-foot dogleg breakwater built in 1929 that extended south from the western side of the flood control channel, then southwest to protect the entrance to the harbor. The site was leased to the Navy for $1 a year with the condition that the port would be able to buy the finished site when the Navy no longer needed it. The Navy later added a mole 1,988 feet long and seventy-eight feet wide to protect the Navy wharves from southeasterly storms. That mole later became the site for Pierpoint Landing, a popular sportfishing, eating, and entertainment complex.

In 1943 and 1944 the port built another breakwater – this one 3,500 feet long – from the west side of the flood control channel in a long-radius curve from south to east, basically directing the flow from the channel down-coast. In 1944, a fire in the inner harbor destroyed many of the improvements that had been made two years earlier to the east end of Channel 3.

The Navy started construction of the breakwater that was going to extend along the residential coast of Long Beach and extend the Navy's protected anchorage, but that was discontinued in 1943 because of the shortage of materials; it was not finished until after the war. When that breakwater was finished, Long Beach was protected from the ravages of the sea, but it had lost something along the way. Long Beach no longer had a surf.

Financing the War
One of the ways the government helped finance the war was through the sale of war bonds. It was relatively easy because people working in the defense plants, the shipyards, and other war-related occupations were making good money, but there were not a lot of places to spend it. No new cars were on the market and even if there were, gasoline was rationed. Buying war bonds was a way that ordinary people could lend money to help finance the battle and support the troops.

The government took the promotion of war bonds very seriously. On the Fourth of July 1945, folks who bought a $100 bond got a ticket to tour the Navy Dry Docks on Terminal Island to see the damaged ships that were being repaired. The following week the legendary – and controversial – General George S. Patton Jr. and Army Air Corps Lieutenant General James H. Doolittle, who led the famous B-25 raid on Tokyo in 1942, appeared at the Long Beach Municipal Auditorium to help launch a bond drive. General Patton – called "Old Blood and Guts" by his men – raffled off a set of his campaign ribbons to a lucky bond buyer.

For Patton it was a homecoming of sorts. He had been born in San Gabriel, California. His father, George S. Patton Sr., had been a Los Angeles County district attorney and one of the leaders in the Free Port Fight to locate the harbor on San Pedro Bay instead of in Santa Monica. His mother, Ruth, was the daughter of Benjamin Wilson, former Los Angeles mayor and a business partner of Phineas Banning. General Patton's wife, Beatrice Banning Ayer of Boston, was Phineas Banning's first cousin. Coming back to California was a return to the general's historic roots, but it would be his last visit. Five months later he died following a traffic accident in Heidelberg, Germany.

Peace at Last

For America, the war raged on for the better part of four years. Four hundred seven thousand American soldiers lost their lives in Europe and the Pacific. And then it was over. The Western Allies and the Soviet Union invaded Germany. Soviet and Polish troops captured Berlin. United States aircraft dropped atomic bombs on Hiroshima and Nagasaki. The Nazis agreed to unconditional surrender on May 8, 1945; the Japanese did the same on August 15, 1945. The end of the war was the beginning of what has been called Pax Americana – a long period of peace among the great nations of the world.

For America, the time after the war was one of optimism and innovation. The Depression was over, the war was over, and people were ready to get back to the business of life – of building families and a new lifestyle that saw more people in their own homes, more people going to college, and more consumer goods flying off the shelves.

But of course, nothing is ever as good or as bad as it first seems.

PART THREE:
THE POSTWAR YEARS

Chapter Fourteen:
Swords into Plowshares

The war was over and peace had descended upon the land. But it was not the same land that it had been five years earlier. The global bloodshed had changed things in America. It had changed attitudes and expectations and the way people thought about themselves and others. Tens of thousands of soldiers, sailors, airmen, and Marines were coming home to familiar ground, many to sweethearts that they had married in a fever of wartime passion, sweethearts that in many cases they hardly knew.

Adolf Hitler and Eva Braun – married less than two days before their deaths in a bunker deep below the city of Berlin – spent their last hours without ever glimpsing sun or sky, or feeling the spring breeze upon their faces. Afterward, their bodies were carried to the surface, doused with gasoline, and burned. It marked the end of a personal legacy of hatred and death that Hitler ended with his own hand.

Benito Mussolini and his mistress, Clara Petacci, were captured by Italian partisans, executed, and taken to Milan. Their corpses were kicked, spat upon, and shot before being hung upside down on meat hooks from the roof of an Esso gas station, where their bodies were ridiculed and suffered further abuse.

Japan, which less than four years earlier had chosen to attack the most powerful manufacturing power on the planet, was in ruins – its once formidable military defeated, its cities destroyed, the corpses of its people uncounted. The terms of surrender were unconditional, the documents signed on the deck of the battleship *USS Missouri* as the world looked on.

The war had ended with an unexpected suddenness, hastened to its conclusion in an explosive fury that was staggering in its potential for destruction. Two Japanese cities were instantly reduced to rubble, hundreds of thousands were dead, others lingered in a haze of radiation sickness.

President Franklin Delano Roosevelt had suffered a stroke and died on April 12, 1945, at the "Little White House" in Warm Springs, Georgia, eighteen days before the suicide of Hitler and three weeks and four days before the unconditional surrender of Germany. His successor, Vice President Harry S. Truman – a failed haberdasher and a protégé of the infamous Kansas City political boss Thomas J. Pendergast – assumed the office of commander-in-chief.

On July 16, 1945, a test atomic bomb was detonated at Alamogordo, New Mexico. Four days later, Truman ordered that an atomic bomb be used against the Japanese, then went to bed and slept soundly, confident that he had made the right choice, the only choice in the circumstances. Dubbed "Little Boy," the device was detonated over Hiroshima, Japan, on August 6, destroying the city and immediately killing between 90,000 and 100,000 people. Three days later, an even bigger bomb – "Fat Man" – was detonated over Nagasaki, immediately killing another 40,000 people. The two bombs remain at this printing the only atomic bombs ever used against cities and people. Radiation sickness and bomb-induced cancers killed many thousands more during the next five years. The estimates of deaths vary, mostly according to the political slant of the estimators, but suffice it to say that the two bombings marked a new high in the ability to efficiently kill great numbers of people in a single act.

The reaction in America was joy at the end of the war and the vanquishing of the enemy. But, as always happens, one problem had been solved, and a new one had arisen. Over the days and years to follow, that initial elation was slowly replaced by a growing horror of the act and the realization that a new era had been born in which the unthinkable had become reality. Within a decade, schoolchildren would practice how to hide under their desks in case such devastation was brought down upon America. Although the wisdom of Truman's decision is still debated, his was an era in which war was taken seriously and pursued ruthlessly. From Pearl Harbor to the formal Japanese surrender on September 2, 1945, had only been three years, eight months, and twenty-six days.

The generation that grew up in the Great Depression and then fought in a war halfway around the world – the people called the "Greatest Generation" – was home again, home to a country that had changed and people who had changed the way they thought about themselves. The times were uncertain, but there was an optimism about the future. The industrial power and political will of America during the conflict had been an example of what could be accomplished by a united people when they put their minds to it. People were eager to put the same energy and drive into buying homes and starting families that they had exhibited vanquishing the nation's enemies and building the ships and planes that made that victory possible.

The other side of that yearning to make up for lost time was the fear that the country might slip back into economic depression, with the stimulus provided by the war at an end and the men who had served so gallantly looking for work. There were hard times following the war, but there had also been steps taken that mitigated those hardships.

One was the Servicemen's Readjustment Act of 1944 – commonly called the GI Bill of Rights – which provided returning veterans with educational subsidies, unemployment benefits, and no-down-payment, low-interest home mortgages. The intent had been to provide a cushion for the returning warriors and to avoid the veteran discontent that had followed World War I. The reality was a boom in new housing and a core of educated college and trade school graduates ready to move into the job market.

The federal government's decision to build an interstate highway system physically united the nation, encouraged the migration of people from rural states to urban ones, and helped make feasible the development of suburban communities from which residents could commute to jobs.

There were other changes after the war as well. During the war, everybody was needed – whether on the front lines or on the factory floor – and everybody pitched in, no matter what the color of their skin or their ethnic origin. Japanese-

American soldiers fought in the military, even as many of their families resided behind barbed wire and gates in relocation facilities. That hardly meant that racial prejudice disappeared during the war, but it was balanced somewhat by need and the ability to get the job done. That brief taste of respect and freedom would be difficult to put back in the jar once the war was over. Sitting in the back of the bus, or sending one's children to second-rate schools, or being excluded from union brotherhood, was no longer acceptable in America. There were still struggles to come, but the demands of fighting a world war would forever change the way minority citizens were viewed in this country. Racism would not be abolished, but it would come to be an attitude regarded as both shameful and ignorant. President Harry Truman ended segregation in the armed services in 1948, and the U.S. Supreme Court ended school segregation with its 1954 landmark *Brown v. Board of Education* ruling.

World War II had ended, but something else had taken its place – the Cold War, a battle of conflicting ideologies and proxy police actions between the Soviet Union and the United States that played out in places such as Korea. World War II had been clear-cut. The new wars in which Americans fought and died to block the advance of Communism, measured victories in a cold-blooded analysis of strategic advantages won or lost.

The colonial system, already beginning to break down before the war, quickly fell apart afterwards. One by one, colonies and territories became independent countries – India, Pakistan, Burma, Ceylon, Indonesia, Libya, Algeria, Egypt, Morocco, and the Philippines.

Indian independence leader Mahatma Gandhi was assassinated in 1948 by a Hindu extremist. King George VI of Britain, a heavy smoker who suffered from both heart problems and lung cancer, died in 1952, and his 25-year-old daughter, Elizabeth, ascended to the throne. Soviet strongman Josef Stalin died in 1953, and in the ensuing struggle for power was denounced for his practice of doing away with everyone he suspected of questioning his authority.

On November 1, 1950, two Puerto Rican nationalists attempted to assassinate President Truman. One White House police guard was killed in the shootout, and two officers were wounded. One of the would-be assassins was killed, the other, Oscar Collazo, was sentenced to death. In 1952 Truman commuted the sentence to life in prison. Exactly three years and four months after the Truman assassination attempt, Puerto Rican nationalists opened fire from the spectators' gallery at the U.S. Capitol, hitting five congressmen, all of whom recovered from their wounds.

The insurgent Viet Minh defeated the French colonial powers in 1954 in a fierce two-month-long battle at Dien Bien Phu in French Indochina. That defeat led to the French withdrawal from all of its Indochina colonies and the temporary division of Vietnam into the Democratic Republic of Vietnam in the north and the State of Vietnam in the south. The U.S. would later get involved in the hostilities between north and south in what would become known as the Vietnam War.

General Dwight D. Eisenhower, who oversaw the Normandy invasion and the subsequent defeat of Hitler and the liberation of the European continent, was elected president in 1952. His vice president was a 39-year-old California senator, Richard M. Nixon, who would later become president himself.

In 1957, after Arkansas Governor Orval Faubus called out the National Guard to block nine black children from attending the all-white Little Rock Central

High School, Eisenhower sent troops from the 101st Airborne Division to Little Rock to replace the National Guard, protect young black students from angry mobs, and to make clear to the world that the ruling by the Supreme Court was not to be ignored.

Life continued. U.S. Air Force pilot Chuck Yeager became the first person to break the sound barrier in the X-1 rocket plane in 1947. Captain James Gallagher completed the first around-the-world, non-stop flight in the B-50 Lucky Lady in 1949, taking off from Carlswell Air Force Base in Fort Worth, Texas, on February 26, refueling four times in flight, and landing at the same airfield ninety-four hours and one minute later.

A new toy called a Slinky hit the stores in 1945, and a two-piece swimsuit called a bikini came out a year later. The first Frisbee was flung in 1948, marketed under the name "Flyin' Saucer." Velcro was invented in 1948, but not perfected and marketed until almost ten years later. Legos replaced Tinker Toys and Erector Sets as the favorite toy for junior engineers, and by the end of the 1950s young girls across the nation would twist and gyrate to keep their hula hoops from spiraling down around their knees. A new brand of plastic, seal-tight containers called Tupperware was introduced in 1948 and direct-marketed to housewives at home Tupperware parties.

The postwar period saw an end to poliomyelitis, the nightmare disease that crippled and sometimes killed. A vaccine virtually eliminated it in the developed world. Ongoing research showing a link between smoking and lung cancer prompted tobacco companies to launch an advertising campaign in 1954 assuring smokers that their cigarettes were safe and pledging to fund impartial research to investigate allegations that tobacco was unhealthy.

Jet aircraft became commonplace after the war. The Soviet Union ushered in the space age with the launching of Sputnik, and the nuclear standoff began with the United States and the Soviet Union developing their arsenals of intercontinental nuclear-tipped ballistic missiles aimed at each other.

The first Playboy magazine – featuring Marilyn Monroe on the cover and as the first centerfold – was published in 1953. It cost fifty cents. Runner Roger Bannister broke the four-minute mile, actor James Dean died when he crashed his Porsche, actress Grace Kelly married Prince Rainier III of Monaco, and the age of rock 'n' roll became official when Elvis Presley appeared on the Ed Sullivan TV show in 1956.

It was a new America that had emerged from the ashes of the war with both new possibilities and new problems. Social critics of the time would come to denigrate postwar American culture for its blandness and public conformity. There may be truth in that view, but it was also a time of healing, renewal, and of feeling good about being an American.

End of War, End of Jobs

The transition from war to peace was both thrilling and jarring in Long Beach and at its port. Long Beach was the staging area and logistics center for much of the Pacific campaign. Long Beach was where ships were built and sent to the combat theater. It was where the fuel and ammo and supplies were dispatched, where new warriors were sent into battle to replace and reinforce the ones already there. It was where the wounded returned and the war-damaged ships were repaired. It was where new planes – bombers, attack aircraft, and transports were built. If there was a front line for the home front, it was Long Beach. It was the link that connected the industrial power of America to the vanquishing of the Japanese empire.

At the peak of wartime production in 1944, workers at four harbor-area shipyards – Consolidated Steel, California Shipbuilding, Bethlehem Steel, and Western Pipe & Steel – were putting in ten-hour shifts, six days a week. At the Navy Dry Docks – where war-damaged ships were patched up for return to combat – the shifts were nine hours long, with men working twelve days out of every fourteen, and women working eleven days out of fourteen. When the allies stormed the beaches at Normandy on June 6, 1944, the news was announced over the public address systems to the graveyard shifts at shipyards and aircraft plants. Employees took less than a minute to absorb the news before they went back to work.

In early 1945, with both Germany and Japan in retreat, the Navy announced that shipyards would shift their priority from building new ships to repairing damaged ones. But the work went on. When Germany finally surrendered in May 1945, the reaction again was one of satisfaction, not celebration. The job was only half-finished, especially on the West Coast, where men and materiel for the Pacific campaign were being dispatched to the front lines. Estimates of casualties in the invasion of Japan were expected to run as high as a million. The soldiers who had spent the war fighting across the deserts of North Africa and the farmland and forests of Europe were headed for more combat and more killing in Asia.

And then the dropping of two nuclear bombs brought Japan to its knees. The Japanese surrendered and the war was over. This time the announcement of the news at the shipyards and war plants was greeted with cheers, tears, and the sound of tools being banged together. At the ports, the air was filled with the sound of ship horns and sirens. Workers at the California Shipbuilding yard on Terminal Island had just launched their 459th ship, the *SS Hattiesburg Victory*, when the news of victory was announced. Sailors and soldiers getting ready to ship back out to the Pacific war zone cheered, tossed their hats in the air, and fired guns in celebration. Fireboats blasted streams of water high into the air in the shape of V for victory.

This time it was not back to work after hearing the news. Civilian workers at the Navy Dry Docks were given a two-day holiday starting immediately. Many other plants shut down to give the workers a break. Two days later, there was a second announcement – the cancellation of millions of dollars in military contracts and the layoff of thousands of war workers. At the Douglas Aircraft Plant in Long Beach, 11,900 employees lost their jobs. At the California Shipbuilding Yard, 3,500 workers were notified that their services were no longer needed. Employees who had been working seventy hours a week were suddenly cut back to forty hours if they were lucky, and zero if they were not.

Four days after that, the Maritime Commission announced cancellation of $425 million in contracts for 135 new ships. The workers who survived the layoffs were put to work finishing up ships that were partially built and repairing those that had been damaged.

In the weeks and months following the end of hostilities, tens of thousands of Pacific veterans began returning home, jammed aboard both cargo and war ships, sharing bunks and sleeping in shifts, eager to get back home. For months, the Long Beach waterfront was a place of both cheers and tears – exuberant homecoming celebrations and tearful dockside reunions.

The exclusion of Japanese-American citizens had ended in January 1945, more than six months before the end of the war, at a time when the winds of war had shifted and both Germany and Japan had been driven back. But for the Japanese who had lived on Terminal Island in the Port of Los Angeles, there was no home to which they could return. Their homes had been bulldozed by the Navy when they left. Most of the Japanese had ended up in the Manzanar camp on the eastern side of the Sierra Mountains. Upon release, they were each given $25 and a train ticket to their former home town. But the lives they had when they left were gone. Their belongings were scattered or had been commandeered and used by others who in their absence had also taken their jobs.

Despite the elation at war's end, it was understood that there were big challenges in peace as well as war. The war workers who had lost their jobs and the returning warriors who were looking for jobs represented a surplus of labor, at least in the short term. As the economy shifted from production of war supplies to production of consumer goods, there would be a period of adjustment. The challenge was to make that period as brief and painless as possible.

Some of the problems were close to home. A 1943 federal report by the House Naval Affairs subcommittee talked about the congestion problems in Southern California due to the massive migration of war workers and military men to the area. Among the issues raised were the need for sewage disposal, a shortage of public transit, access to gasoline for cars, the need for more schools, and racial problems resulting from an influx of black people from the South seeking work. Many of those people who had migrated to Long Beach to work in the war plants and shipyards decided to stay after the war was over. So did many of the veterans, who had been stationed in the area or who had passed through Long Beach on their way to the war zone. The weather was good, the pay was good, and the possibilities seemed endless.

At the same time that the government was slashing its wartime budget, the need for new infrastructure had become critical – especially in Southern California. The military had invested in some projects during the war, such as improving and widening Alameda Boulevard – dubbed the "Direct Road to Tokyo" because of all the war supplies that moved along it on the way to the harbor. But many of the improvements had been only temporary, such as the floating gate bridge across the Cerritos Channel and the pontoon bridge across the entrance to the Long Beach inner harbor. When the war ended, Secretary of the Navy James Forrestal canceled plans to build a permanent bridge near the Ford plant, connecting Terminal Island to the mainland. Navy Base commander Commodore Schuyler F. Heim immediately called a meeting of state and city officials to see if there were local funds available to build the span. In less than a month, federal funding for the bridge was reinstated.

Meanwhile, the state was moving forward with plans to improve its highway system. In 1947, the Collier-Burns highway bill was signed by Governor Earl Warren, raising the gas tax from 3 cents to 4.5 cents a gallon. In Southern California a system of parkways – soon to become freeways – was drawn up to connect one part of the region to another. Both parkways and freeways were limited-access roadways with grade-separated cross streets. The main difference was that the former emphasized beauty and a pleasant drive, while the later emphasized speed.

During the war there had been little to spend money on, so at war's end there was a pent-up demand for consumer goods and housing. The freeway system allowed development of low-density housing tracts at a distance from where people worked. It also cut communities in two, encouraged urban sprawl, and pushed the development of shopping centers that slowly began to displace downtowns as economic retail hubs.

A side effect of the spike in population, traffic congestion, and the growing reliance on cars, was something called smog – a word combining smoke and fog. Air pollution was a problem that would plague Southern California for decades to come. The severe, choking, eye-burning smog of the early postwar period would be greatly reduced, although not eliminated, in the decades to follow.

The enemy had been vanquished and peace had descended upon the land, but as is always the case, new problems were on the horizon.

Labor Struggles

The labor movement had for the most part – especially in the defense industries – cooperated with management during the war, arbitrating its grievances rather than going on strike. When the war ended, there was a return to the adversarial relationship between the two competing perspectives. Within a month after the war's end, more than half-a-million workers nationwide – including coal miners, steel workers, oil workers, factory workers, lumber workers, telephone workers, New York longshoremen, and truck and bus drivers – had walked off their jobs.

The militant International Longshoremen's and Warehousemen's Union headed by Harry Bridges was quite aware that the wartime truce between labor and management had ended. Even as the war was winding down, Bridges warned that Pacific Coast employers should not attempt to reverse union benefits when peace returned. Postwar labor conflicts will make past conflicts "look like peanuts," he said. Bridges noted that the relationship between the union and the employers was pretty well-stabilized for the time being, and said that he hoped it stayed that way.

An outspoken enemy of fascism as well as an admirer of the Soviet Union, Bridges had adopted a no-strike attitude during the war. He had even been commended in 1944 by U.S. Attorney General Francis Biddle for his efforts in support of the war, although that did little to help Bridges in his citizenship battles. Bridges may have been doing "an excellent war job on the waterfront," Biddle said, but that didn't mean he wasn't a communist. In fact, Biddle was convinced that Bridges was a communist.

Three years earlier, the Board of Immigration Appeals had recommended that Bridges be deported. Although that decision had been overturned due to "unreliable witnesses," the attorney general had overruled the BIA and ordered that Bridges be deported. Bridges appealed, but lost. The matter went to the Supreme Court, and Biddle declared that if the Court finally ruled against Bridges, the labor leader would be deported "as a routine matter, just like anybody else."

But the Supreme Court did not rule the way Biddle expected. In a 5-3 split decision, the court majority on June 18, 1945, found that Bridges was not a communist and canceled the government order to deport him to his native Australia. Justice Frank Murphy said that even if Bridges had been a communist, "not the slightest evidence was introduced to show that either Bridges or the Communist Party seriously and imminently threatens to uproot the government by force or violence." The three dissenting justices held that Bridges was a member of the Communist Party and that there was sufficient evidence to deport him.

Bridges greeted the decision as a triumph for democratic values and announced that he planned to immediately move forward to become an American citizen – a process that had been held up since 1939. "Naturally I welcome the decision because American citizenship is a priceless possession," he declared at a press conference in San Francisco.

On September 17, 1945, Bridges finally became a citizen, appearing before Federal Examiner Lloyd Garner in San Francisco with a class of twenty-five applicants and accompanied by his 21-year-old daughter, Jacqueline. Like much of his life, it was a day of drama and confrontation. His ex-wife, Agnes, with whom he had been through a bitter divorce trial the previous month, also showed up, interrupting the proceeding to declare that Bridges had indeed been a communist under an assumed name and had hidden a "Communist book underneath the linoleum under the bathtub" of their home. When asked by Garner if the allegations were true, Bridges simply smiled and said no. In an ironic twist, it was Bridges' marriage to an American citizen that allowed him to short-cut the naturalization process and quickly establish his own citizenship.

Being a citizen did little to change Bridges' militant and adversarial approach to the relationship between workers and management. It was an approach that didn't endear him to employers, government bureaucrats, or even to other union leaders. The employers' contract with the International Longshoremen's and Warehousemen's Union had expired on September 30, 1945. Under that contract, longshoremen were being paid $1.10 an hour and $1.65 an hour for overtime. The following month, the ILWU demanded an immediate 25-cent-an-hour pay hike and a 37.5 percent overtime pay hike until the new contract could be reached.

Meanwhile, some government officials were blaming labor problems at the port for delays in transporting returning troops back home. Bridges rejected that allegation, claiming that the government was reassigning many of its cargo ships to private service instead of using them as troop transports. On November 26, Bridges announced that beginning December 1, the ILWU would cease loading all ships capable of "transporting American troops for demobilization." On December 3, port unions across the nation staged a twenty-four-hour work stoppage to support efforts to bring the troops home as quickly as possible. Bridges was once again alienating important people. The Los Angeles Times accused him of setting himself up as a "dictator of public policy" and dismissed it as a "grandstand play for veteran sympathy."

In January 1946, Bridges announced that he had sent a telegram to President Truman, asking him to intervene in order to get employers to pay $8 million in retroactive pay for wage hikes that had been ordered by the War Labor Board in 1944. The Waterfront Employers of the Pacific, which represented waterfront companies, said the pay was being held up by a muddle of details that might require several additional months to work out. The following month, ILWU longshoremen voted 13,979 to 1,120 to authorize a strike if negotiations for a new contract failed to meet union demands. This did result in federal mediators getting involved in an attempt to head off such an event.

By June, the union was ready to back up their demands with action. A strike was set to begin at midnight on June 14. At the Long Beach and Los Angeles harbors – which shared the same ILWU Locals – it began at 2 p.m. with a mass meeting at the Wilmington Bowl, an arena at the intersection of Anaheim Street and Alameda Boulevard that could hold 3,300 people. The strikers had received confirmation from dockworkers in Mexico, Chile, France, and Australia that they would not work ships loaded by non-union replacement workers.

The ILWU was not the only union negotiating a new contract. It was one of seven maritime unions in the Congress of Industrial Organizations – better known as the CIO – negotiating contracts with employers. The seven unions had agreed that no one union would settle unless all seven settled. By the day of the strike, the ILWU was the only holdout – a situation that reportedly led to blows being exchanged between union leaders, a not uncommon occurrence among the headstrong union men of the day.

That morning Bridges had addressed ILWU union members by telephone from Washington, D.C., saying that it looked like a settlement might be reached with employers, but there was no effort to cancel the strike. He complained about the government's role in the negotiations. "There are no friends of labor in this government, in this administration," he said. "If there are, they are certainly not in the high circles of Washington."

The federal government made no secret of what it planned to do in case the strike tied up ports. President Truman had vowed to use Army and Navy personnel to operate the ships if it became necessary.

Although a proposed agreement was reached late that night, the strike went on as scheduled. The West Coast ports were shut down, with the exception of Tacoma, which had voted to remain part of the International Longshoremen's Association, a member of the American Federation of Labor (AFL). As expected, the new contract was ratified, the employers promised to pay the retroactive wages by the end of October, and the union workers returned to the docks and the ships.

But the labor problems weren't over, and it wasn't always labor versus management. Sometimes it was labor versus labor. One ongoing feud was between the unions affiliated with the AFL and those affiliated with the CIO. The International Longshoremen's Association – an AFL union – had represented West Coast dockworkers during the landmark waterfront strike of 1934, until Bridges defied the ILA leaders, hijacked the process by going straight to the rank and file, and later founded the ILWU and then affiliated with the CIO.

Harry Lundeberg, the leader of the Sailors Union of the Pacific, had a long-running feud with Bridges, although the two men had once been allies. Lundeberg had been planning to affiliate his sailors' union with the CIO, but when he was passed over for the job of West Coast CIO director in favor of Bridges, he decided to remain with the AFL. And, he remained convinced that Bridges and his CIO associates were a bunch of communists. In 1937, dissident members of Lundeberg's sailors' union left to form the National Maritime Union, taking about 30,000 of Lundeberg's members with them. The NMU became a member of the CIO.

The personal animosity between the two men and their unions would continue over the years. In July of 1946, ILWU longshoremen refused to work ships manned by Sailors' Union of the Pacific crews, over jurisdictional issues. Four days later, AFL union members in New York shut down six Staten Island piers as "a warning to Harry Bridges and the Communist-dominated Committee for Maritime Unity to stop raiding our ships." Paul Hall, a charter member of the Seafarers International Union and a hard-nosed union activist from Jefferson, Alabama, vowed to tie up every ship at an East Coast port that was manned by CIO union members, unless Bridges changed his ways.

While the feud between unions played out, the ILWU foremen also voted in July to go on strike unless they were granted pay raises. Although the foremen got more money when the longshoremen signed an agreement with employers the previous month, they did not get the same percentage of increase received by their longshore brothers. Some longshoremen that same month began slowing down the rate at which they handled cargo in order to pressure employers to pay them their retroactive pay. After 600 of the slow workers were discharged, union leaders told employers that they planned to call a stop-work meeting every day unless the employers agreed to reinstate the discharged dockworkers and come up with the back pay by August 15.

Employers noted that only the ports of Long Beach and Los Angeles were targeted by the slowdown, which came at a time when Southern California businesses were making a bid to secure new foreign markets. The labor action at the harbor was not only slowing down business at the port, it was driving business north to San Francisco and other West Coast ports. The slowdown was a threat to the prosperity of the entire region, declared Harold W. Wright of the Los Angeles Chamber of Commerce.

"Cargo is piling up on the docks," he said. "Ships are leaving without cargo. Merchandise is being diverted to other ports for shipment and may never move this way again. Shipping lines may find other ports are better places to establish permanent services. The slowdown is a threat to the $200 million harbor investment of the people of Los Angeles and Long Beach. It is a threat to the future of everyone with jobs in local business and industry."

The AFL unions, anxious to strike a blow at their CIO rivals, announced a big AFL anti-communist rally for 2 p.m., August 7, at the Wilmington Bowl. Employers were asked to close their shipyards, shops, and other businesses to enable their AFL workers to attend. Rally organizers said the harbor area, in particular, was infested with communism in the union movement and that proponents of that "alien philosophy" were out to sign up workers currently affiliated with AFL unions. The ILWU and other CIO unions issued a statement calling the rally "an adventure in fascism."

It wasn't just the ILWU and other CIO unions that were creating havoc at the harbors in 1946. On September 5, the Sailors Union of the Pacific and Sailors International Union, both led by Bridges' nemesis Harry Lundeberg, went out on strike, shutting down ports across the nation. This time the union's beef was not with the employers, but with the Wage Stabilization Board, the government agency established by President Truman at the beginning of 1946 to control wages. The employers and the union had negotiated a raise for the sailors, but the Wage Stabilization Board decided the sailors' pay hike was too much and ordered it to be reduced by 23 percent. Tankers were exempted from the strike.

Although the AFL and CIO unions were often in opposition to one another, the ILWU, as a matter of policy, refused to cross the sailors' picket lines. It didn't take long for the animosity between unions to bubble to the surface in the Long Beach and Los Angeles harbors. The CIO unions – including the longshoremen – announced plans to conduct a mass demonstration at the harbor with 5,000 pickets. The AFL sailors' union made it clear that although they appreciated the CIO unions refusing to cross the sailors' picket lines, they didn't need or want any other CIO involvement. The ILWU made it equally clear that they didn't care what the sailors' unions wanted. The longshoremen and other CIO maritime unions were also out of work while the strike went on, and they did not plan to sit on the sidelines while the sailors' unions "muddled along," said CIO official L.B. Thomas. "We want it settled, and we'll form our own picket lines, supporting AFL lines, and we'll close up the port solid," he said. And they did. The following day, hundreds of CIO pickets showed up to help build pressure for a settlement.

It took just over a week for the sailors' union to settle their issues with the government. But the strike continued as it had been; only the reason for striking changed. This time the sailors were striking in protest against the CIO unions attempting to raid their jurisdiction on some of the ships. And the CIO unions were picketing to resolve about 100 grievances of various kinds against ship owners. By the end of the month talks between ship owners and both the CIO's Marine Engineers Beneficial Association and the AFL's Masters, Mates, and Pilots union had deadlocked over union demands for preferential hiring for union members, and a new strike was underway. At the same time, ILWU Local 13 began a strike to enforce its demands for higher wages and better working conditions. The strikes shut down most commerce at the local harbors through November 21, 1946, when outstanding issues were settled and the ports were back in business.

Uncounted millions of dollars had been lost due to the long series of strikes and labor problems that had plagued the harbors from June through November. It wasn't just the ship owners, traders, and other businesses that depended on the ports who suffered losses. It was also the union members themselves, who had been out of work for weeks. As a demonstration of union strength, it was an unmitigated success. The unions were no longer a junior partner – an assumed participant – in harbor operations. But there were consequences.

In 1946, more Americans went on strike and more industries were hit by strikes than any year before or since. The wave of strikes that swept the country began in 1945, shortly after the atomic bomb was dropped on Hiroshima, and culminated the following year. One reason was the buildup of grievances that had accumulated during the war years when many unions had pledged not to strike. Another was that union membership during the war had doubled from what it had been when war broke out.

In some cases, the strikes bordered on insurrection, as in Oakland, where workers took over several square blocks and cordoned off the area. Anyone could leave, but only card-carrying union members could enter. The whole affair lasted only two days, and little was accomplished. But in those heady days after the war, workers were loudly proclaiming their contribution to society and demanding a voice in the way things were run.

The strikes may have been mainly focused on business, but many regular folks with no direct connection to either side found themselves inconvenienced or cut off from wanted goods by the flood of labor disputes. It was one of the reasons that Republicans were able to seize control of the House of Representatives in the 1946 mid-term elections and pass the Taft-Hartley Labor Act – overriding a presidential veto – the following year. The Act, sponsored by senators Robert Taft of Ohio and Fred Hartley of New Jersey, prohibited such actions as boycotts of businesses not directly involved in a specific dispute, sympathy strikes or boycotts of businesses on behalf of other unions, closed shops, union-versus-union jurisdictional strikes, and monetary donations by unions to federal political campaigns. It also required that every union officer submit an affidavit once a year to the National Labor

Relations Board swearing that he was not a communist or affiliated with the Communist Party.

Meanwhile, the local waterfront continued to struggle with labor problems in the months and years to follow. In 1947, there was a dispute over whether the ILWU could represent the foremen, commonly called "walking bosses," as members of the union. The employers said the walking bosses, who supervised work on the docks, were part of management and not eligible for union membership. The union disagreed. When the walking bosses targeted individual companies and put up picket lines, the longshoremen refused to cross. In the end, the Long Beach and Los Angeles harbors were shut down for more than a week in October when employers locked out the union. The impasse was broken by Arthur C. Miller, the new chairman of the joint union-management Coast Labor Relations Committee.

Despite such altercations, the waterfront in 1947 was mostly peaceful. That changed in 1948. The political backlash against unions made labor relations on the waterfront particularly contentious. ILWU leader Harry Bridges remained outspoken on both his union and political views, even if it often offended management, other unions, and his own allies within the CIO. In January 1948, he launched a campaign for dockworkers around the world to refuse to load weapons that would be used against workers in other countries. He was also openly contemptuous of President Truman, the government labor agencies, and the new Taft-Hartley Act.

The members of his union were fiercely loyal to Bridges and his ideas on militant action. The marine clerks – who were called checkers at the time and handled the paperwork involved in moving cargo – decided they wanted to be dispatched from their own hiring hall, rather than be employed directly by the shipping company. They began quickie strikes around the harbor, crippling the movement of cargo by establishing picket lines at various terminals, which their union brothers refused to cross. Talks by the union over a new contract were stalemated over the validity of union hiring halls under the Taft-Hartley Act. The employers maintained that it would be impossible to have an open shop if all longshore workers were to be dispatched through the hiring hall. That was unacceptable to the union. The hiring hall concept was a sacred issue for the union – the result of a bitter lesson learned from the years in which workers were forced to gather in a group to be picked over by bosses for work. With little progress being made at the bargaining table, the union scheduled a strike to begin on June 16, 1948.

Under the Taft-Hartley Act, the president was empowered to appoint a fact-finding board when he believed that a threatened strike might endanger national health or safety. After the board reported its findings, the president could then order the attorney general to seek an injunction to impose an eighty-day cooling-off period in an attempt to settle differences between the parties. Truman got his injunction, the order coming down on June 14, less than two days before the union was to strike.

Bridges flew down to Los Angeles from San Francisco to address a mass meeting of union workers at the Wilmington Bowl. He told the union members that the eighty days for cooling off would be "just enough time for us to warm up."

"We will not openly defy the injunction at this time, but if the ship owners or the president of the United States think we are going to take this lying down they are going to be wrong, and I am sure there is going to be a strike. I can't say when, but it can come September 5 just as well as June 15."

As predicted, the cooling-off period did little to cool things down.

The longshoremen continued to work the docks, but they worked them at a much more leisurely pace than they had been working, while getting paid the same amount of money. By the time the cooling-off period ended, all parties were ready for the strike to begin. The final step was to be a poll of the union members by the NLRB. If the majority voted to accept the employers' offer, the contract would be signed. If the majority voted no on the contract, the strike could begin.

A week before the strike deadline, the union held a six-hour meeting of its members. They voted to reject the employers' offer of a five-cent-an-hour pay hike, with the employers taking over control of the hiring hall. The union also voted to boycott the NLRB election poll and turn all government ballots mailed to the members over to the union. When the NLRB released the official ballot count, it showed 26,695 employees eligible to vote, but zero ballots cast.

Both sides were adamant in their positions, and both sides demanded control of the hiring hall. The employers demanded that all union officials take loyalty oaths as required in the Taft-Hartley Act; the union refused. At 12:01 a.m. on September 2, the strike began. Two days later, the first blood was shed when sailors on the lumber ship *Rolando* attempted to unload the cargo themselves. The sailors, members of the Sailors Union of the Pacific, had been ordered to unload the lumber by SUP president and Bridges' adversary Harry Lundeberg.

The order was a direct challenge to the ILWU, and it was certain to draw a violent response. It didn't take long. The *Rolando* had barely reached the dock at the Consolidated Lumber Co. yard in Wilmington, when the battle began. There were about 150 union men on each side. Dozens were reported to have been clubbed to the ground or cut and stabbed with knives. An unemployed AFL seaman was arrested after he fired four shots – two in the air and two into the ground – when some CIO unionists came at him with knives. A dozen sailors ended up in nearby hospitals. Longshoremen injured in the battle were whisked away to private doctors, an arrangement that appeared to have been prearranged by the union.

Five days later, the ship returned to dock and was unloaded by the sailors as 500 Los Angeles police officers stood guard. The ILWU posted only a token picket at the site and did not interfere. ILWU spokesman L.B. Thomas said his union didn't bother to try to stop the unloading. "We'll let the police-protected AFL scab on us for one day," he told reporters.

AFL Central Labor Council President Bud Satre summed up the event somewhat differently. "No commies are going to run us off the docks," he told reporters. "This is not a labor dispute. This is a battle inspired by communists to disorganize the port and create confusion."

In the end, the only point really made that day was that companies could unload their cargo during a strike if they had 500 policemen standing guard at the dock. The strike went on, but it wasn't just the Sailors Union that was questioning Bridges' motives. It was also government officials, the media, and even other leaders in the CIO. When President Truman began using government workers to load military cargo in the Bay Area, Bridges warned him to back off if he had any hope of getting reelected. Bridges was one of the most charismatic labor leaders in the nation, but the more he pushed, the more enemies he made.

The notoriously anti-union Los Angeles Times published an editorial entitled "Happy Days Are Here Again – In the Kremlin," in which it accused Bridges of advancing the Soviet agenda.

Bridges' fall from grace in the CIO began as early as 1939 when, as West Coast director of the labor federation, he attacked President Roosevelt for being a warmonger and an enemy of labor. CIO Chief John L. Lewis responded by eliminating the position of West Coast director, reducing Bridges' territory to California alone. Bridges' continued attacks on the president even alienated some of his own members within the ILWU.

The 1948 strike lasted ninety-five days, and in the end a three-year contract gave the union most of what it had demanded. The employers had relented on many positions after a rebellion against the hardliners within their own ranks. The union kept control of the hiring hall, and nobody had to swear that they were not communists. It was important because it established the union's position on the waterfront. There would be no going back to the old days. Few decisions would be made on the waterfront without taking into consideration the union's position on the issue. Settlement of the strike ushered in several years of relative peace, and there would not be another major strike for twenty-three years. Most disputes were settled quickly, and if not always to everybody's liking, at least without the disruption of a long strike.

The losses were estimated at half-a-million dollars a day, but there were other losses that were more long-lasting. U.S. ship operators, who had leased their vessels from the Maritime Commission, turned seventy-six of those vessels – representing 3,200 seafaring jobs – back into the Maritime Commission rather than operate at a loss.

The One and Only Spruce Goose
In June 1945, just before the Japanese surrender ended World War II, Howard Hughes unveiled his newest and most controversial project – a gigantic flying boat made of wood. The airplane, larger than any aircraft built up to that time, had a wing span of 320 feet, eight huge engines, and the ability to fly 750 fully armed soldiers nonstop from Honolulu to Tokyo. It would have a top speed of 218 miles an hour and cruise at 175 miles an hour. It could carry tanks or it could serve as a flying hospital with room for 350 patients, plus doctors, nurses, and a surgical facility. At least that was the claim.

The plane was officially named the Hughes Hercules H-4, but it wasn't long before the media had given it a new name, one by which it would become widely known – the "Spruce Goose." The H-4 may have been almost entirely made of birch – not spruce – but that was just a niggling detail to the press. The Spruce Goose was what it was called. Hughes hated the name, but that didn't matter either. The Hercules H-4 became little more than a footnote in history as the official name for the Spruce Goose.

There were several problems with the Spruce Goose. First, the war was all but over, metal was no longer in short supply, and there was no more need for wooden airplanes or for airplanes of such a size. Redesigning it in metal would be too expensive. The Spruce Goose, as magnificent as it was, would be one of a kind. No more would be built.

The second problem was how to get the huge 400,000-pound flying boat from the Hughes Aircraft plant in Culver City, at Jefferson Boulevard and Centinela

Avenue, to the port in Long Beach where it would be launched into the harbor. A lease had been signed with the Port of Long Beach for a four-acre parcel on Pier E (later Pier T) in the outer harbor with 350 feet of waterfront. The plan was for the hull, wings, tail section, engines, and other parts to travel in three separate segments along a twenty-eight-mile route to the harbor, where the entire plane would be reassembled. Star House Movers, the company contracted for the journey, would move or cut 2,300 telephone and power lines, and Army guards would rope off intersections to hold back curious onlookers as the giant plane passed by. The move would take three days and cost an estimated $2 million. Hughes promised it would be the biggest overland moving job ever attempted.

The third problem was Howard Hughes himself. The multi-millionaire movie producer, airplane manufacturer, test pilot, and industrialist was a proud and eccentric man. The idea for the aircraft had come from Henry J. Kaiser – the same man who built hundreds of Liberty Ships at his California Shipyard – but he finally dropped out of the project because it was moving too slowly. Hughes was a perfectionist, and in wartime that was a liability. At a time when planes went from the drawing board to the skies in a matter of months, development of the Hughes flying boat had taken years. Hughes had gotten the contract in 1942; the Spruce Goose was not ready to fly until long after the war was over.

And then there were the congressional hearings into possible wrongdoing in the award of contracts to the Hughes Aircraft Corporation for the Spruce Goose and the XF-11 wooden reconnaissance plane. But the hearings would come later, after Hughes had already moved the huge plane and its parts down Santa Fe Avenue, across the pontoon bridge that connected downtown Long Beach to Terminal Island, and to the dry dock at the water's edge for final assembly. The hearings also came after Hughes – who was not only the owner of the company, but also the test pilot – crashed the XF-11 into a Beverly Hills neighborhood and nearly killed himself on its maiden flight.

The hearings, held in 1947, focused on testimony about how Hughes Aircraft had wined and dined government VIPs at parties with Hollywood royalty, how President Roosevelt's son Colonel Elliott Roosevelt was a guest at those parties, how he had pushed to have a contract awarded to Hughes and Kaiser for the Spruce Goose and XF-11, and how the contract was approved despite the fact that most military leaders didn't think it was a good idea.

But the senators also heard Hughes testify about how the committee chairman, Senator Owen Brewster, in a private conversation, had offered to cancel the hearings if Hughes would agree to merge Hughes' airline, TWA, with Pan American Airways, which was controlled by its founder Juan Trippe. Merger of the two lines would have guaranteed Pan American a U.S. monopoly in foreign flights. In retaliation for Hughes rejecting the Trippe deal, the hearings were launched, Hughes claimed. Brewster admitted that he had met with Hughes, but claimed that the alleged conversation never took place.

Hughes defended the Spruce Goose during his testimony, calling it a monumental undertaking and vowing that if the plane turned out to be a failure, "I probably will leave this country and never come back." It wasn't just the airplane or the money. Hughes felt his reputation was at stake.

During a recess in the hearings, Hughes headed back to California with a quest to prove the viability of the Hercules H-4. That proof came less than two months later in Long Beach. On November 2, 1947, taxi tests began for the Spruce

MASSIVE MOVE: *The Hercules H-4 Flying Boat, nearly universally known as the Spruce Goose, is trucked in pieces along Seaside Boulevard in 1946. Apart from its only test flight the following year, the plane remained in its Berth 120 hangar for more than 30 years.*

THANK YOU: *Howard Hughes' note to Port of Long Beach General Manager Eloi J. Amar following the Spruce Goose's only flight on November 2, 1947.*

Goose with Howard Hughes at the controls along with mechanics, technicians, pilots, reporters, and others – all in all, thirty-six people – on board. An estimated 15,000 people gathered on nearby beaches and piers to watch the tests. A Coast Guard cutter patrolled the bay, making sure all other traffic was clear. Two pilot boats, one with Long Beach Port Pilot J.A. Jacobsen on board and the other with Los Angeles Port Warden Frank D. Higbee on board, followed the plane during its runs.

With winds gusting from ten to twenty knots and a four-foot choppy sea, Hughes began the first run from east to west at about 40 mph. On the downwind run, west to east, Hughes pushed the plane up to 90 mph, raising it up onto its step – a state in which a seaplane is skimming across the water. On the third run, back toward San Pedro and upwind, Hughes unexpectedly lifted off and flew across San Pedro Bay. It wasn't much of a flight. It was only about a mile long, lasted less than a minute, and reached an altitude of about seventy feet. But Hughes felt vindicated.

"When I got up to 95 mph, I lowered the flaps to take-off position and it felt so good, I just took it off," he told the press. After that flight, the Spruce Goose was returned to its onshore roost, where a hangar was built around it. The hangar door was locked, and the big wooden plane never flew again. In fact, it was never taken out of its hangar or seen in public until well after Hughes' death in 1976.

Hughes did not forget the part that Long Beach played in providing a home port for his Hughes Hercules H-4 flying boat. He gave a signed photograph of the giant airplane's first and only flight to Long Beach Harbor General Manager Eloi J. Amar. The message on the photo read:

> *Your past kindness and cooperation is truly appreciated. I hope that someday Long Beach will regard this plane with a certain amount of pride.*
> *Howard Hughes*

The Spruce Goose may have been built in Culver City, but its brief moment of glory took place in the waters of the Port of Long Beach. It was a part of Long Beach history and a reclusive resident of the city for more than thirty years. It was there, and then it was gone, but its legacy remains.

The Problem with Oil

Oil made the Port of Long Beach, and oil almost destroyed it. It was oil – and more specifically, the revenue from oil – that allowed the port to grow into a major international gateway and full-fledged rival to its older sister in Los Angeles. But from the beginning it was a battle. First the state tried to claim that the oil beneath the tidelands belonged to the state, but Long Beach challenged that in court and won. The state had given the city title to the land in 1911 when it approved the tidelands grant. As long as revenues from the oil were used for the purposes of the grant – commerce, navigation, and fisheries – the oil belonged to the city.

Then in the late 1930s, the federal government claimed that it owned state tidelands and the oil beneath them. That position was challenged by the state and the city, but the challenge was temporarily put aside during the war years and not resolved. After the war ended, however, the federal government began pressing the issue once more. The federal position was that the tidelands belonged to all

Americans and so did the oil beneath them. California's position, as well as that of other coastal oil states, was that the states are sovereign entities with absolute authority over all lands within their borders – including the tidelands. That included the property that the state had granted to the city of Long Beach in its 1911 Tidelands Trust.

In June 1945, two months before the end of the war, the federal government filed a test case against one oil company, Pacific Western Oil Corp., which was operating under a state permit to drill oil from beneath the waters off Santa Barbara. Although the state was not named in the suit, the implication was clear. California State Attorney General Robert W. Kenny told a joint session of the House Judiciary Committee and a subcommittee of the Senate Judiciary Committee that the suit would stifle postwar development not only in California, but in every coastal state from Maine to Washington. He was one of forty-six state attorneys general to protest the suit. He noted that six major California ports – Long Beach, Los Angeles, Oakland, San Francisco, San Diego, and Stockton – were built on fill land. If the federal government owned the tidelands, it would then own the ports as well – ports that had been paid for and developed over the years by private businessmen and California taxpayers.

Four months later, the U.S. attorney general dropped its suit against Pacific Western Oil Corp. and filed suit against the state of California, seeking federal mineral rights to the state's submerged lands. The suit did not challenge submerged oil fields off Texas, Louisiana, or any other state. By singling out California, the federal suit was seen as a way to diffuse congressional support of legislation that would protect state ownership of tidelands. It also allowed the federal government to take the case directly to the U.S. Supreme Court. Usually, the Supreme Court acts as an appellate body, the final arbitrator of a case that already has been through the district and appellate courts. But Article III, Section 2 of the U.S. Constitution provides that:

> *In all cases affecting ambassadors, other public ministers, and consuls, and those in which a state shall be party, the Supreme Court shall have original jurisdiction.*

Suing the state and going straight to the U.S. Supreme Court enabled the federal government to avoid months, and perhaps years, of testimony, argument, and debate in lower courts over the issues. A decision in the case could be rendered in a relatively short period – too short according to some, who claimed the states never were able to fully develop their arguments against what was considered by the state to be nothing less than a "land grab."

The action may have been against the state, but the implications for Long Beach were huge. The port earned $6 million annually from its tidelands oil interests; loss of those earnings, past and present, would be devastating. As long as the question of who actually owned the oil was in dispute, the leaseholds of companies that had entered into contracts with the state and with local cities such as Long Beach were in question. Should those companies continue to pump and sell oil or should they cease operations?

Long Beach City Attorney Irving M. Smith pledged his full cooperation in protecting California's – and Long Beach's – rights to both the tidelands and the oil beneath them. Smith, who would lead the legal battle for the city, saw the federal action as part of a tidelands oil racket. When the federal government first advanced the idea that the federal government owned tidelands mineral rights, some oil speculators had applied for federal leases for offshore oil plots already leased by others on the chance the federal government would prevail. If it turned out that the federal government actually owned the land and were to approve the speculators' applications, the speculators could become rich overnight.

The battle wasn't just about oil. Many saw the action as an attempt to diminish the sovereign rights of states, to make them merely divisions of the federal government instead of separate entities in a federalized system. If the federal government could seize oil land in California, why couldn't it seize coal mines in West Virginia or copper mines in Montana or even corn fields in Kansas?

In case Long Beach needed a reminder of what was at stake, Julius Albert Krug, U.S. secretary of the interior, toured the port in February 1947 to inspect the oil operations there.

"I just wanted to see something of the actual operations in order that I might have a basis for planning if the government gets control of the tidelands," he said. He later added that he felt sure that if the federal government prevailed, it would treat Long Beach fairly. "After all, they did not come into the property as poachers," he said. "I would assume that Congress will be sympathetic with the municipalities. However, the question now is who owns the tidelands, the federal government or the municipalities."

California fought back, both in court and in Congress. In order to head off the federal suit, California convinced Congress to pass a bill that would legally clear coastal states' ownership of their tidelands. The bill was vetoed by President Truman, who claimed that it would not be right to sign such a bill while the Supreme Court was considering the case.

On the legal front, state Attorney General Kenny filed an 822-page answer with the Supreme Court over legal ownership of 65,000 miles of tidal and submerged lands along the coast of the United States. The interests of all the coastal states, not just California, were imperiled by the federal action, he argued. The federal brief claimed that no state – including the thirteen original states – had ever had title to their submerged or reclaimed coastal land.

U.S. Attorney General Tom Clark promised that the federal government would not bill California and its local entities for the oil they had already taken from the ground. That debt would be forgiven by the president, Clark promised. The problem was that it was a promise that neither Clark nor the president could guarantee. There would be future attorneys general and presidents who might feel differently.

In the end, California's arguments failed to sway the Supreme Court, which on June 23, 1947, ruled 6-2 that the state was not entitled to the three-mile-wide seabed along its coast or the oil beneath it. That submerged property belonged to the federal government and always had, the court decided. The majority opinion noted that California's location immediately adjacent to the ocean also made the issue one of national security. The Supreme Court's decision stunned California officials, as well as the oil industry. The decision could result in the federal government taking possession of the Long Beach and Los Angeles ports and presenting the cities with bills for all the oil they had previously authorized to be pumped from federal property – despite assurances to the contrary.

GRATEFUL PORT: *President Dwight Eisenhower accepts the Port of Long Beach's inaugural Honorary Port Pilot Award in 1954 from Congressman Craig Hosmer for his efforts to restore control of tidelands (and their revenue) to California and Long Beach. The award is given on an occasional basis for contributions to the maritime industry.*

Over the coming month, the federal government, along with state and local officials, hammered out an interim agreement that called for oil royalties to be put into escrow accounts until a final plan could be developed for the takeover. It was an agreement that would keep the oil wells producing during an interim period, but the cloud over the oil leaseholds remained.

The uneasy truce between the two sides remained in effect as the months wore on. California continued to try to push another bill through Congress to have the submerged property quit-claimed to the states. Although the federal government had always indicated that the suit against California was just about one state, in December 1948, the Justice Department asked the Supreme Court to rule on ownership of Texas and Louisiana tidelands. Texas argued that it had been an independent republic for nine years before joining the United States, and as such it retained its sovereignty over its coast.

The Supreme Court disagreed. Relying heavily on its earlier decision in the California case, the court ruled in June 1950 that Texas had given up that sovereignty when it joined the union and "ceased to be an independent nation. She then became a sister state on an equal footing with all the other states," the court ruled. The Louisiana decision was largely a reflection of the earlier California decision, the court said.

The decision against Louisiana and Texas, and rumors of possible additional federal action to come against Mississippi, Alabama, and Florida, made passage of legislation an even greater priority. That, coupled with the upcoming presidential elections in 1952, gave hope that the states could still recover that which they once had assumed was theirs – ownership of their coastal waters.

Although there were enough votes to pass a bill to return the coastal lands to the states in both the House and the Senate, it was not clear there would be enough support in the Senate to override a presidential veto. Despite that, a bill was passed in May 1952 returning the tidelands to the states. It was vetoed two weeks later by the president.

In his veto message, Truman said that the Supreme Court decision did not take possession of the tidelands away from the states and give it to the federal government. Rather, the federal government had always owned the tidelands. The issue never came up before because the submerged property was not deemed important. The discovery of oil, however, changed that situation, he said. Since the tidelands belonged to the federal government, the oil riches beneath the tidelands should be shared with the entire nation, not just the states that happened to border the sea.

Congress never voted to attempt to override the presidential veto. It didn't have to. In 1952 former General Dwight D. Eisenhower ran for president against Adlai Stevenson. One of the major campaign issues was state ownership of their coastal waters. Eisenhower favored it. He saw federal takeover of the tidelands as a trend toward centralized ownership and control of the nation, to which he was bitterly opposed. Stevenson favored federal ownership.

In November 1952, Eisenhower won the election. On May 22, 1953, he signed a bill into law returning the ownership and control of adjacent undersea lands to all twenty-one coastal states. A year later, the Port of Long Beach honored the president with its first Port Pilot Award, recognizing his role in restoring the tidelands to California and Long Beach. The award became an annual event at the port as a way to honor individuals for their leadership and achievements in international trade.

Long Beach had its tidelands and coastal waters back, but the city's problems with oil were not over. Not by a long shot.

The Other Problem with Oil

Long Beach had another big problem with oil, one that couldn't be settled by lawyers or politicians. This problem would have to be solved by geologists. The entire port was sinking – just a little bit at first, hardly enough to worry about. Then a little more, and a little more, until it became a full-fledged crisis that set back the plans for the city by years. The problem was called subsidence.

The first signs of it were in 1941, almost four months before Pearl Harbor, when a one-to three-inch drop in elevation was noticed in the area around the Southern California Edison Plant and the adjacent Union Pacific oil field. The theory was that the sinking was caused by nearby dredging operations for the Navy Dry Docks.

Three years later, U.S. Grant, a professor of geology at UCLA, confirmed that the harbor area was indeed sinking. Grant had been hired as a consultant by the Long Beach Harbor Commission to figure out why the port seemed to be declining in elevation. He found the subsidence was caused by deep-well operations necessary for construction of the dry docks. There were layers of water-tight strata trapped under pressure beneath the surface. When that water was drawn off, it caused the overlying beds to settle, Grant explained.

But when the pumping ended, the sinking went on. By May 1945 the problem was getting serious. Over an eight-year period, parts of the east end of Terminal Island had settled three and a half feet and were continuing to subside. Even the Long Beach breakwater was two feet lower than when it was built. The Navy was concerned about its investment, and so was the port. A team of geologists working under the direction of Professor Grant was hired to figure out what was going on.

A year later the worst of the subsidence showed that a four-foot drop had occurred since 1937. There was still some dispute over what the cause was, but the majority view was that the 450 Terminal Island wells pumping oil from the ground were responsible for the surface settling. With the oil gone, the earth began collapsing in upon itself, slowly at first, then faster as more oil was removed. The good news was that the rate of subsidence would begin to decrease, and the total subsidence would be limited to about seven feet, or so the geologists said. Instead it accelerated.

By 1947 the geologists had revised their estimates of total subsidence from seven feet to twenty-two feet by 1964, which would put a large part of Terminal Island below sea level. By 1948, some parts of the island had sunk as much as seven feet, and the Navy was looking at its options. The $75 million it had invested in the Navy Station and Dry Docks was too big to just walk away, but further development could not be justified unless the problem could be solved. If the Navy was forced to curtail activities, some of the ongoing functions would probably have to have been shifted to San Diego, San Francisco, or Seattle. That was not good news for Long Beach, which had grown used to the Navy being one of the economic mainstays of the local economy. It seemed as though the port, which early in its life had threatened to be overrun by mud, was – thirty years later – in danger of sinking back down into the mud.

By this time, ownership of the land and the oil beneath it had become a source of contention between the federal government and the state. One option explored by the Navy was to see if the federal government could order a halt to extraction of the petroleum beneath the surface – one of the richest oil fields operating in the nation at the time.

But Long Beach had a plan. Port Chief Engineer Robert R. Shoemaker told a committee of oil operators that water could be pumped under pressure into the oil field to replace the oil being pumped out. He estimated the cost at $5 million, a fraction of the more than $100 million in oil being pumped out of the field each year. If the subsidence was not stemmed, the consequences could be huge overall – and not just for the Navy. A number of industries – such as Ford, Procter & Gamble, and Spencer Kellogg & Son – had located in the harbor area, and their land was sinking as well.

Figuring out a plan is not the same thing as implementing it. Not everybody was convinced that extraction of the oil was the cause of the subsidence, plus it wasn't just the port's decision about drilling in the harbor. Many private owners were also extracting oil from the area, and it was hard to begin solving the problem when the ownership of the oil was unclear. The Supreme Court had ruled that the oil was owned by the federal government, but the oil fields were still being operated by the port and private operators. As the land kept sinking, the political battles over ownership kept raging.

Rear Admiral John J. Manning, head of the Navy's Bureau of Yards and Docks, was pessimistic about the situation when he talked to harbor officials and civic leaders at the Lafayette Hotel in November 1948. The Navy wanted to continue to operate its Long Beach facilities, but the ground level at the Navy Dry Docks – which that year had been renamed the Long Beach Naval Shipyard – was dropping about fifteen inches per year, he said. The major concern was that the subsidence was not uniform – one end of the 1,200-foot-long dry dock was settling faster than the other end. Building dikes to hold back the sea could extend the use of the facility for a few years, but that would only be a temporary solution.

The admiral's pessimism was soon borne out by the facts. By March of 1949, subterranean earth movements more than 1,600 feet below the surface began crushing casings on between thirty-five and fifty Terminal Island oil wells, a clear indication that not all of the earth movements were just up and down. In June, the port was stacking sandbags along the waterfront and manning pumps along low spots when the highest high tide of the year sent water lapping onto port property. That same month, Long Beach Congressman Clyde Doyle flew back to Washington to counter rumors that the Naval Shipyard might be closed. In August, the Department of Defense announced budget cuts. Among the facilities on the list to be cut were the Long Beach Naval Shipyard and the adjacent Long Beach Naval Station. One of the main reasons was subsidence. Almost 6,000 civilian employees were expected to be laid off at the shipyard. Some Navy ships were to be reassigned to other ports.

Loss of the $31 million civilian payroll and the $127 million military payroll would be devastating for Long Beach. And it wasn't just the Navy and the Navy jobs that were at risk. As the harbor continued to sink, the problems for the port grew worse, and predictions of future subsidence became more dire. The subsidence occurred in an elliptical bowl, centered just north of the Terminal Island Edison plant. As the center of the bowl sank, the land at the edges was drawn in toward the center, leaving some property owners with a slight stretching of their property at the expense of others, whose property was contracting. Other problems included

BELOW SEA LEVEL: *A ship docked at Pier C sometime in the '50s looms over the Port Administration Building, thanks to subsidence caused by oil drilling that caused the building to sink.*

UNDER WATER: *A wider view of Port HQ shows the dikes needed to keep water out of the sunken building; flooding here means that wasn't always effective. Subsidence was one reason the port moved to new headquarters at the end of the decade.*

cast iron water pipes fracturing below the surface, railroad tracks buckling, gravity-fed sewer lines backing up, and gutters becoming separated from roadways.

By 1950, the subsidence had widened all the way into the downtown area – stretching about five miles out from either side of the Edison plant. The intersection of Chestnut Avenue and Seventh Street – two blocks west of Long Beach's downtown main street, Pine Avenue – had already dropped almost two feet. Many of the businesses in the harbor had sunk below sea level. The Ford assembly plant, which had sunk about seven and a half feet, spent $1 million on a sheet-pile dike and a system of pumps in order to continue operations. The Union Pacific oil field on Terminal Island was surrounded by fifty-foot-wide earthen dikes protecting it and the nearby Edison plant. The Navy had spent $1.5 million for new bulkheads and was planning to spend $4 million more. The port itself had spent $4 million raising the elevation of its piers and bulkheads in order to stay ahead of the subsidence.

Through it all, the port continued to operate and develop new facilities at the same time it was restoring old ones. Although much of the port's revenues were in an escrow account awaiting final decision on the transfer of mineral rights to the federal government, what funds were available were used to maintain and expand port infrastructure, including development of the East Basin around what was later known as Pier E and Pier F – the Navy's former Victory Pier and its attached mole. The port had bought the Victory Pier from the government for $1 million in 1947. The main pier was operated as a cargo terminal, but the mole had been turned into a recreational area named Pierpoint Landing, complete with restaurants, kiddie rides, a seal tank, and fishing opportunities. Long Beach remained a smaller port than Los Angeles, but for four months in 1949, cargo moving across Long Beach docks had actually exceeded that moving through Los Angeles.

Despite the fact that the port was literally sinking into the sea, an air of optimism – real or affected – continued. So did the subsidence. Damage to oil wells from earth movements continued, with some of the wells having to be re-drilled. Even small earthquakes resulted in unexpected and magnified consequences beneath the oil field. In July 1951 record high tides backed up through the storm drains and flooded a neighborhood of 100 homes on six square blocks south of Ocean Boulevard, bordering on the inner harbor channel – an area later known as Pier D. At the time it was a mixed area containing small homes, oil properties, and motels.

A joint meeting of the City Council and the Harbor Commission was called to discuss the issue. Port Engineer Robert Shoemaker reported that there was a triangle of land about ten blocks on each side that was seven feet below the high-tide mark. Although dikes were by that time protecting the area, with subsidence expected to total more than sixteen feet, those barriers would be insufficient to protect the property. There were other subsidence problems to be dealt with as well, reported Port General Manager Eloi Amar. Subsidence had lowered the Los Angeles River flood control channel and the bridges across it. The levees on both sides needed to be raised, and the Broadway Bridge across the channel would have to be rebuilt. It had sunk to the point that in a severe flood year, it would function as a dam, rather than as a bridge across the channel.

Later that year, subsidence closed off auto traffic on the pontoon bridge, which connected downtown to Terminal Island. Large vessel traffic on the Cerritos

Channel beneath the Heim Bridge was also blocked in order to repair damage to the bridge caused by sinking ground. Meanwhile, geologists were again revising their estimates on the limit of subsidence that could be expected. The center of the subsidence bowl – by then down fifteen feet from its original height – could be expected to sink to twenty-five feet, according to a report by scientists from the California Institute of Technology. The Municipal Auditorium, south of Ocean Boulevard at American Avenue (later Long Beach Boulevard), had already sunk two feet and could be expected to sink another six.

In 1952, the West Coast Packing Corp., which had been in the port area since 1914, shut down its plant on Water Street south of Channel No. 3, and moved the operations to other sites. The company's port property had sunk fifteen feet, and the surrounding water was only three feet from the top of the retaining wall, company manager Albert Vignolo Jr. told reporters.

It was hard to find a bright spot in the continued descent, but people did. In addition to lowering the height of the property along the port channels, subsidence had also lowered the depth of the channels themselves, turning twenty-foot-deep channels into thirty-five-foot channels and making them accessible to larger ships without having to dredge. Early attempts at re-pressurizing the oil fields by pumping seawater into the field had unexpectedly succeeded in squeezing extra oil out of the ground, raising the yield of the wells. When wells had to be re-drilled, the new practice was to drill them on slants from one central location, rather than scatter them across a large area. The subsidence disaster had also forced the port and port businesses to invest in new and improved infrastructure at an earlier date than they otherwise would have done.

Attempts to put a positive spin on what was happening, however, seemed to be a combination of wishful thinking and out-and-out denial. Subsidence, by almost any standard, was calamitous for the port and the city – a disaster in slow motion, as the Milwaukee Journal characterized it. By 1956, subsidence covered a twenty-square-mile area. The Edison plant at the center of the subsidence pit had already sunk twenty-two feet, and the ground was continuing to drop. By mid-1957, City Hall and the library had dropped three and a half feet, and Polytechnic High School, north of downtown, had dropped two feet.

The situation was growing desperate. The port and a large part of the city were slowly, but steadily descending. The estimates of how low the area would sink in the future were varied, but few were optimistic. There was a proposed solution, but efforts to implement such a solution were stymied by the large number of independent oil producers involved in taking product from the field. Attempts to set up a voluntary program to re-pressurize the field seemed doomed to failure.

Ford's Flight to Higher Ground

In July 1957, Ford Motor Co. announced it was shutting down its Long Beach plant on Terminal Island and consolidating operations in Pico Rivera. It was a devastating blow to Long Beach, but not a surprising one. The Ford plant was near the center of the subsidence bowl. From the time the plant opened in 1930, the property had sunk between fourteen and eighteen feet, putting it well below sea level.

The plant had experienced its first major problem with subsidence during a high tide in July 1947, when water backed up through drains, flooding the floor up to eleven inches deep with a combination of seawater and sewage. Measurements disclosed that the property had sunk three to four inches over the previous six-month period. At the time, the worst-case estimate of total subsidence for the property was 10.9 feet, so the company built a new bulkhead, using steel pilings and concrete to erect a wall between the plant and the Cerritos Channel that was more than seventeen feet above sea level. That would be enough to protect the plant even if an extreme high tide, storm, and wind chop occurred at the same time. An elevated pump house was constructed on the property, with three 7,500-gallon-a-minute pumps to remove any storm water that might gather on the property.

But the projected total of worst-case subsidence turned out to have been wrong. By July 1951, the port informed the company that the ground had already settled eight feet and could be expected to settle an additional eight to nine feet. The company took additional measures in order to protect its investment.

Aside from the problems with subsidence, the Ford plant was doing well. A trend in America toward two-car families was underway, and the Long Beach plant was helping meet that demand. Business was good. Cars were being manufactured on one side of the property, and oil wells were pumping crude from the ground on the other. In fact, during its last years in Long Beach, the plant – by then below sea level – set production records. But the ground kept sinking. It wasn't just the sea that was the threat. Doing business in a low land meant the plant was vulnerable to flooding from inland as well.

During heavy rains in January 1956, the Dominguez Slough, which emptied into the Port of Los Angeles, broke through its rain-weakened levee about half-a-mile west of the Ford plant, flooding adjacent oil fields. The water and oil sludge rushed along railroad rights-of-way into the plant. The entire property was flooded, including offices, assembly areas, the paint ovens, and the convoy yard where new cars were parked, awaiting delivery. When the flood poured through a tunnel that connected the main plant to the oil storage area, it caused the tanks to float free, breaking their connecting pipes, and releasing 30,000 gallons of gas, oil, and paint thinner. The water also shorted out a transformer, sparking a massive explosion. The blast sent burning oil spreading across the grounds and out onto the waters of the nearby Cerritos Channel. Three Ford employees were in a rowboat at the time, about twelve feet off the Ford dike, inspecting for any leakage when the explosion occurred. They jumped overboard, swimming for their lives under the blazing oil. Fireboats from both Long Beach and Los Angeles responded to the blaze, as did land-based firefighters. It took them five hours to bring the flames under control.

Ford cleaned up the plant, repaired the damage, and went back to making cars. The plant set new production records that year and was recognized for manufacturing the one-millionth 1956 Ford nationwide – a two-door Fairlane Victoria. Then, the following year, Ford packed up and left. A company statement explained that the 28-year-old Long Beach plant had "become inadequate for modern automobile assembly operations." Ford executives denied the move had anything to do with subsidence.

Few believed it. The city had lost one of its leading industries. Ford sold its eastern acreage and oil rights to the Mobil Oil Corp. and put the building and twenty-two and a half acres on the market for $1.25 million. The Port of Long Beach considered buying the property, but the cost of protecting the area from flooding was too high, and the city was reluctant to take the property off the tax

FORD FIRE: *Flooding made worse by continuing subsidence causes a fire in January 1956 at the Ford plant, adjacent to the Industrial Freeway (later State Route 47). Although the plant resumed operations, a year later, Ford pulled out and sold the site.*

rolls. Potential purchasers all had the same questions – could the property be protected from flooding, and how much would insurance cost?

The site was finally sold in 1960 to the Dallas and Mavis Forwarding Co., of South Bend, Indiana – parent company to Robertson Truck-A-Ways, which planned to use the site to import foreign cars and prepare them for sale. The old Ford oil house was turned into the Red Witch Café, which operated for a number of years before closing in the 1980s.

The Navy Ultimatum

As the ground beneath its base continued to sink, the Navy also was looking at its options. Despite early budget cuts, it was reluctant to abandon a base in which it had so much invested, and in which it continued to invest in order to hold off subsidence. But putting more money into a facility that might have to be abandoned met opposition in Congress. In the summer of 1957, members of a congressional subcommittee came to Long Beach, held hearings, and toured the port.

Their findings were to the point. The Naval Shipyard was vital to the Navy's defense effort, and the $100 million-plus annual shipyard payroll was vital to the community. Although oil production had caused the land to sink, the federal government received no money from that oil. Congress should not have to tax all the citizens of the United States to correct subsidence problems, while the cause of those problems was something that was enriching both the city and private operators.

City efforts to get legislation passed at the state level that would force oil operators to take steps to stop subsidence were opposed by the oil industry, which claimed there was no proof that pumping water into the oil field would stop the sinking. The legislation lagged.

Navy Base commander Admiral Robert L. Campbell told an Assembly subcommittee that 80 percent of the Naval Shipyard was below the high-tide level.

"An uncontrolled break in the dike's wall on Terminal Island at high tide would flood the shipyard ten feet deep," Campbell testified. "Such a break during working hours would certainly be accompanied by hundreds of drownings."

Stopping subsidence was only a part of the solution. Getting all the various interests to agree to a united program was the harder part. Oil doesn't respect property lines. When an oil field is re-pressurized, additional oil is squeezed out of the field, increasing the yield. But sometimes re-pressurizing squeezes the oil onto adjacent properties – especially if the operators of those properties are not re-pressurizing – thus enriching one property at the expense of another. On April 16, 1958, the governor signed the requested legislation. The final plan provided that all operators inject water proportional to their holdings.

In less than two months, Long Beach had joined with Union Pacific, Southern California Edison, General Petroleum, and the Long Beach Oil Development Co. in a crash program to stop subsidence at the very heart of the problem. There were already twelve water-injection wells at the site that were pumping 22,000 barrels a day into the ground. The program added forty new injection wells and converted an additional forty-four oil wells into water-injection wells. The additional wells raised the amount of water being pumped underground to 390,000 barrels a day.

If a city sinking slowly into the ground was not incentive enough, more incentive came in August 1958, when the U.S. Justice Department filed a suit against the state of California, the city of Long Beach, and almost 400 private oil operators demanding $170 million in damages and that immediate steps be taken to stop the subsidence. It also asked for an injunction to stop all oil production in the Wilmington field until the problem was solved.

Faced with the possible loss of the Naval Shipyard and the jobs it provided, the port in February 1959 ordered its engineers to implement a water-injection program at the shipyard to stop any further sinking. Later that month, the port announced a $60 million emergency effort using 259 water-injection wells and a giant pipeline network to flood the oil field with sea water.

It was not only necessary; it was long overdue. The Southern California Edison plant had sunk more than twenty-five feet. City Hall, two-and-a-half miles to the east, had sunk four feet, and the Villa Riviera apartment building at the edge of the subsidence bowl was down two feet from when it had been built.

By March, the water-injection program implemented by the port was showing results, and the federal lawyers agreed to drop the request for an injunction from their suit, on the condition that the fight to stop subsidence continued to show progress. There were some setbacks, but the water injection not only stopped the subsidence, it also increased the yield of the field. By the end of the year, it was clear that the battle had been won. The victory did not reverse subsidence, however. What had been lost was lost, and it wasn't only land and money.

The city's reputation as a sinking metropolis and its frantic efforts to stop the sinking, had made headlines around the world. The little town that once had no difficulty attracting new business had become a city with a huge image problem. John Mansell – the former city auditor who became city manager in 1961 – would later estimate that subsidence had cost the city $90 million to stop the sinking, and twenty-five years of lost industrial and commercial growth.

The Third Oil Problem

In addition to the subsidence problem and attempts by the federal government to claim coastal oil rights, Long Beach faced a third problem with oil during the 1950s – an embarrassment of riches. The city was bringing in millions of dollars from its tidelands oil operation, but questions remained as to where and how the money could be spent. In 1946, voters had approved an amendment to the City Charter that would allow the city to take a portion of the tidelands oil money and spend it outside the harbor district, and in 1951, the state adopted a bill drafted by Long Beach to allow the city to spend half of the tidelands oil money citywide.

That legislative authority, however, was somewhat moot since the U.S. Supreme Court by that time had ruled that the federal government owned the tidelands and its oil, not the state and not Long Beach. But in 1953, after President Eisenhower was elected and promised to approve legislation to return the tidelands to the states, the way seemed clear for that money to be spent on projects across the city. The city was flush with cash – $61,187,000 that had been impounded in an escrow account since 1948.

The city's plans for the money were challenged on April 1, 1953, when Long Beach resident Felix Mallon filed a lawsuit against the city challenging expenditure of tidelands oil revenue outside the harbor district. Legislation notwithstanding, under the city's 1911 Tidelands Trust, such money could only be spent on commerce, navigation, and fisheries, the suit claimed. It asked for a writ of mandate that would compel the city to return the funds set aside for inland projects to the tidelands fund. Mallon's suit was filed two days before an election in which Long Beach voters approved spending $39 million of the money on park improvements, an airport terminal, hospitals, highways, storm drains, incinerators, libraries, and other "upland" projects.

Mallon, an oil well supply dealer, said his suit was not filed with malicious intent. He brought the suit expecting it to lose. He said he was merely seeking legal acknowledgement of Long Beach's right to spend the oil money outside the harbor area as a safeguard before the city actually spent revenue to which it might not be entitled.

Meanwhile, the city was looking at new ways to cash in on its tidelands ownership victory afforded by the Eisenhower promise. The harbor district wasn't the only place with oil beneath the surface. The oceanfront east of downtown was also seen as a cash bonanza waiting to be tapped. The field, an extension of the Wilmington Field, was estimated to hold 1.3 billion barrels of recoverable crude, worth as much as $4 billion. The plan was to construct three or four steel and concrete islands – each more than six acres in area – at strategic spots offshore. Each island could accommodate up to 400 wells. Since much of the field was beneath downtown and easterly residential areas, a plan for unitization – how to equitably share the oil among the 115 well operators of the field – would be necessary. But none of that could happen until a determination was made of the city's legal authority to put the plan into action.

The city scored its first victory in December 1953, when Long Beach Superior Court Judge Paul Nourse ruled that the state had granted the city proprietary rights to the oil in its 1911 tidelands grant. Although that grant limited expenditures to harbor area improvements, the 1951 state legislation granting the city the right to spend the money anywhere in the city had removed that condition, the judge said. The city had contended at the time that it was impossible to spend all that money in just the harbor. "Not even if we gold-plated all door knobs and railroad tracks could we spend the money," City Attorney Irving Smith had argued. Although the city had won its case in Superior Court, Mallon launched an appeal.

The voters, who had expected an oil money windfall for projects across town, were frustrated. On May 11, 1954 – almost a year after voters had approved numerous projects to be paid for with oil money – they voted City Attorney Irving M. Smith out of office. The main issue in the election was Smith's handling of the city's effort to redirect half of the tidelands money to inland projects. The new city attorney, Henry D. Lawrence, had made his first run against Smith and lost in 1939, when Lawrence was an assistant city attorney. He later left office and went into private practice.

Smith had been city attorney for fifteen years and devoted much of his public career to defending the city's oil rights. He had led the city's fight against a federal takeover of the tidelands oil rights, represented the city in testimony before Congress, and been a vigorous advocate of the city's interest at various venues. But in the middle of the fight over oil, the city was about to change its legal representation, once by choice and once by circumstance.

On December 30, 1952, following the election of Dwight D. Eisenhower as president, Smith had advised the City Council that the city was free to spend half of the tidelands oil money outside the harbor district. He warned at the time, however, that the only way to be sure the expenditures were absolutely legal was to have a California Supreme Court ruling. He said he would not recommend that the city file a test case in the matter, but if a private citizen did so, the issue could be clarified.

That is exactly what Felix Mallon had done. But while that case progressed, the money remained unavailable. The feeling among many in the city was that it was time for a change. Smith, who was running for reelection in May 1954, had made many enemies during his public career defending city interests, including the harbor commissioners, whom he had accused just nineteen months earlier of mismanaging tariff charges and concession leases. A number of city commissioners were backing Smith's opponent in the upcoming race – Henry D. Lawrence.

The Independent, Press-Telegram said in an editorial that Smith had served the city well, but that he should have gone straight to the State Supreme Court himself and gotten a decision instead of waiting for a private citizen to sue in order to get a ruling. Besides which, the editorial said, Smith was grumpy.

> *Many of the people in City Hall who must deal with the City Attorney report that they find him testy and difficult to get along with. These matters of temperament are important because friendly, co-operative relationships in the official family are essential to the smooth, efficient operation of the city government.*

On June 26, a little over a month after being elected as the new city attorney, Henry D. Lawrence died after suffering a heart attack while working in his garden. His wife Esther returned from the market to find him sprawled on the front lawn of the home they had recently purchased. He was replaced as city attorney by Wahlfred Jacobson.

Three months later, on September 28, Irving Smith's wife, Mabel, returned to the Smith home on Ocean Boulevard at about 6 p.m. and found her husband dead in their bedroom, a pistol by his side. Smith had left three suicide notes – all apologizing for what he had done and saying "there was no other way out." His widow told police that Smith had been despondent since losing the election.

On April 5, 1955, the California Supreme Court handed down a ruling in the case that stunned Long Beach and forced a radical change in the way the city and port operated. The court denied the city the right to use tidelands oil funds for any purpose other than harbor development. By the time of the ruling, the city had $75 million stockpiled in an account, waiting to be spent on city projects. It also had projected an additional $24 million a year in future earnings.

City Hall officials began referring to April 5, the date of the court decision, as "Black Friday." Felix Mallon, who had brought the suit, was as stunned as everybody else. He never expected the city to lose, he said. He just wanted to clear up the matter before the city spent the money on projects, and then had to return it.

Long Beach didn't give up all that money without a fight. Vice Mayor Gerald Desmond led a delegation of city officials to Sacramento, where he met with legislators from Southern California. Desmond told the legislators that Long Beach did not plan to just turn over the money. It would be put in a special trust until the matter was officially settled, even if it meant going all the way to the U.S. Supreme Court. The litigation could take years.

Despite the brave talk, Long Beach's effort to keep the tidelands oil revenues in house was a lost cause. In the summer of 1955, Attorney General Edmund Gerald "Pat" Brown sued the city of Long Beach to force it to turn over the disputed oil money to the state. Brown would later become governor of California as would his son, Edmund Gerald "Jerry" Brown, Jr.

A compromise was reached between the state and the city in May 1956. Under the terms of the compromise, Long Beach agreed to give to the state $120 million in tidelands oil trust funds, 50 percent of all future tidelands revenue, and all of the dry gas revenues from the field. (Dry gas is basic methane gas as opposed to wet gas, which also contains other compounds that can be processed and sold separately.) The city would be allowed to spend tidelands money on construction of a marina at Alamitos Bay, on reconstruction of the Ninth Street and Ocean Boulevard bridges over the Los Angeles River Flood Control Channel, and on subsidence repair.

It was not the outcome that Long Beach had hoped for, but the matter of what agencies were entitled to profit from the tidelands oil revenues was finally settled.

Citizen Bridges
Although the 1948 waterfront strike set the stage for more than two decades of waterfront peace and established the ILWU as a full-fledged partner on the waterfront, ILWU President Harry Bridges' problems were not over. Top officials in the Congress of Industrial Organizations (CIO) were tired of Bridges' independent attitude and his willingness to lead his union down its own path, whether it met with CIO approval or not. Bridges himself was getting tired of the constant questioning by other CIO officials of his loyalty. He complained to his ILWU followers that whenever he questioned or criticized CIO policies, the answer would always be: "Have you ever criticized the Soviet Union?"

"When I asked why the CIO doesn't put out a financial statement, what the hell difference does it make what I think about Russia?" he asked a meeting of the rank-and-file members. He told his union brothers that the ILWU was a left-wing union, and that it should continue on that path, but that it had "no revolutionary plots and was not dedicated to communism."

Within months after the end of the 1948 strike, a federal grand jury in San Francisco had begun looking into whether Bridges had committed perjury back in September 1945 when he stated that he was not a communist and had become a U.S. citizen. Although the Supreme Court had found that Bridges was not a communist a mere three months before he became a citizen, Bridges and two of his associates were indicted on May 25, 1949, and charged with conspiracy to defraud the United States. Bridges and two other men, J.R. Robinson and Henry Schmidt, had testified during the naturalization process that Bridges was not a communist. Now all three faced prison time, and in Bridges' case loss of his American citizenship as well.

On June 6, less than two weeks after his indictment, Bridges was re-elected to his sixth consecutive two-year term as international president of the ILWU. His own union may have been loyal to Bridges, but the CIO was not. In July, after an ILWU regional director asked that the CIO oppose the indictment, CIO leaders flatly refused.

"There is no issue of civil liberties involved in a charge of this kind," the CIO said in a prepared statement. "Perjury is perjury, whether it be for the purpose of falsely obtaining an automobile license or falsely obtaining U.S. citizenship."

Bridges' attorney in the case, Vincent Hallinan, was a colorful figure with a reputation for defending political radicals and left-wing causes. He was known for his witty sarcasm, his withering cross-examinations, and his willingness to duke it out with opposing lawyers – settling it out of court, he called it. But even he wasn't prepared for the prosecution of Harry Bridges. Bridges had a lot of enemies in high places.

The trial went on for weeks, and time after time the judge turned back objections raised by Hallinan and the other defense attorneys. On April 4, 1950, the jury came back with its verdict. Bridges, Robinson, and Schmidt were all guilty. The verdict stripped Bridges of his citizenship. The government's repeated cases to get rid of the troublesome labor leader had spanned eleven years, but it finally seemed to be over.

Hallinan said he would launch an immediate appeal and made a motion for a new trial. The judge agreed to hear the motion and to sentence the defendants on the following Monday, April 10. But there was one more item to be taken care of that day – sentencing two of the defense attorneys for contempt of court for their conduct during the trial. Hallinan was sentenced to six months in jail, co-defense counsel James MacInnis to three months.

During the trial, old friends and one-time allies of Bridges had testified against him, and some shipping line executives and officials in the Pacific Maritime Association – which had supplanted the old Waterfront Employers Association – had testified on his behalf. Former California Attorney General Robert W. Kenny attested to Bridges' honesty and integrity. Bridges spent ten days on the stand, denying he had ever been a communist and sometimes lambasting other union leaders, calling Teamster chief Dave Beck an out-and-out "gangster."

At the April 10 sentencing hearing, Bridges was sentenced to five years in prison for his part in defrauding the government. Robinson and Schmidt each received two-year sentences. They were all released on bail, pending their appeal.

The ILWU stood by their chief throughout, vowing to raise money for his legal battle. But in August, after Bridges spoke out against the Korean War, the court revoked Bridges' bail and sent him to jail as a threat to national security. Nineteen days later, an appellate court reinstated his bond and released him, noting he had done nothing more than express his opinion and had not advocated sabotage or attempted to stop the shipment of war supplies.

Bridges was again a free man, but if his appeal failed, he would be back in prison. Five days after his bond was reinstated, the CIO expelled the ILWU from the labor organization for being pro-communism. Nine days later, the members of the ILWU Local 13 – the local union for the Long Beach and Los Angeles ports – gave Bridges a loud and long ovation during his visit there.

The '50s may have been a time of union peace, but peace is relative. The union often closed down the port for short periods over everything from jurisdictional disputes with the Sailors Union to beefs with management. Management charged the union with featherbedding practices and refusing to supply enough manpower to work ships quickly. The cost of moving cargo at the ports of Long Beach and Los Angeles was significantly higher than at other ILWU ports, causing diversion of cargo from the local area, employers charged.

On June 15, 1953, Harry Bridges finally got the answer for which he was waiting. The U.S. Supreme Court dismissed the case against him without going into the validity of the charges. The government had waited too long to bring the charges, the justices ruled. The statute of limitations for perjury was three years.

The government waited four years from the time of the alleged offense – lying to obtain citizenship – before indicting the defendants.

Harry Bridges was a free man, a U.S. citizen, and one of the most powerful and controversial labor leaders in the nation. Some of his rivals in the labor movement didn't fare quite so well.

Joseph P. Ryan, the International Longshoremen's Association president for life, from whom Bridges had hijacked the 1934 strike before founding the ILWU, resigned as union president in 1953 after disclosure of ties to organized crime. The following year, he was convicted of taking payoffs from employers. Teamster chief Dave Beck, whom Bridges had charged with being a gangster, turned out to be just that. Beck was prosecuted for embezzlement and labor racketeering in 1959 and convicted. The early reputation and culture of both the ILA and the Teamsters would remain.

The ILWU, on the other hand, remains Harry Bridges' left-wing union – sometimes involving itself in political actions that seemingly have little to do with its relationship to management. Its members have a reputation for defiant obstinacy – not wholly undeserved – that often infuriates management. But ILWU ties to organized crime are not part of that culture.

Another Rejected Proposal
Although labor, oil, and subsidence dominated much of the news at the port during the postwar years, the port continued to develop during the period, and trade through the port continued to grow as well. At the same time, some old ideas suddenly became new again.

In 1945, a little more than three months after the end of World War II, Assemblyman Vincent Thomas of San Pedro proposed that all California ports, including Long Beach and Los Angeles, be merged under a state port authority. The Port of San Francisco was already run by the state. Long Beach, Los Angeles, San Diego, and Oakland were administered by their cities. Under the plan advanced by Thomas, a three-man board, appointed by the governor, would oversee the statewide authority.

Thomas – the Americanized version of Tomasevich – was born to Croatian immigrant parents in Biloxi, Mississippi, in 1907. The family came to San Pedro in 1919, where his father died shortly after arriving – a victim of the Spanish flu epidemic. Thomas learned to use his fists early, first on the street defending his turf from rival newsboys, and then in the ring as a boxer. Along the way he earned a bachelor's degree from the Jesuit University of Santa Clara and a law degree from Loyola Law School. He was elected to the state Assembly in 1940.

The plan for a state port authority never got off the ground, but Thomas had other issues as well. In 1947, he introduced a bill that would allow San Pedro to secede from Los Angeles. Annexation of the cities of San Pedro and Wilmington to Los Angeles had occurred in 1909 at a time when Los Angeles was on a campaign to annex the entire basin from the mountains to the sea. Long Beach had fought back and remained an independent city. Almost forty years later, the Port of Los Angeles, which had become so important to the economy of San Pedro and Wilmington, was controlled by a City Hall twenty miles away. Harbor commissioners often had few ties to the local community.

Thomas withdrew his bill in the face of political opposition, but he had made his point. The City of Los Angeles had made certain economic promises to San

SPOILS OF WAR: *The massive "Herman the German" floating crane at work. Eventually painted red, white, and blue, the crane was a familiar part of the Long Beach skyline for decades. The crane was later sold and renamed "La Titan," and used for maintenance work on the Panama Canal.*

DEDICATION: *The Robert R. Shoemaker Bridge, named after the port's chief harbor engineer, who had died in 1958, opens the following year to typical '50s fanfare. The bridge connects the Long Beach Freeway to downtown. Shoemaker was instrumental in reversing the subsidence in the harbor.*

Pedro and Wilmington at the time of annexation – among them construction of a fishermen's wharf and expenditure within San Pedro of an amount equal to the taxes collected there – that it had failed to provide. Unless the city addressed those issues, Thomas would reintroduce his measure.

In 1949, Thomas was back with a bill to merge the Long Beach and Los Angeles harbors into one big port – a familiar scheme that always had been rejected by Long Beach. Under the Thomas plan, the new port would be governed by a nine-member port authority – three appointed by the Long Beach City Council, three by the Los Angeles City Council, and three by the governor. The plan, Thomas said, would benefit taxpayers by removing competition between the two ports and benefit customers by having standardized harbor practices. He was backing a similar plan for the ports of San Francisco and Oakland. That bill also failed to gain support.

In 1956, Thomas introduced a new plan to merge the two ports – this time with an eye to gaining some of the Port of Long Beach tidelands oil money for the Port of Los Angeles. The California Supreme Court had ruled that if Long Beach was unable to spend more than 50 percent of its oil money in the harbor district, it should be returned to the state. Thomas figured that even if the Port of Long Beach found it impossible to use all of its tidelands oil money on harbor projects, the two ports merged together should have no problem using all of the funds. It was a long shot, and once again it failed, but the idea of consolidating the two ports into one lived on. Los Angeles has always been the suitor. Long Beach has always declined the proposal.

Building and Changing

The Long Beach harbor district got a new landmark during the postwar years – a landmark that was immune to subsidence, since it wasn't on land at all. The YD-171 was a huge 375-foot-tall floating crane – one of the largest in the world – built along with two others by the Germans in 1941 and seized as a war prize by the allies after the German surrender. One of the cranes went to the British, who lost it during the channel crossing. One went to the Soviets, who transported it back to their homeland, although what the Soviets did with it there is unknown. The third was dismantled by the U.S. Navy, transported through the Panama Canal, and reassembled in its new home at the Long Beach Naval Shipyard in 1948 at a cost of $350,000. Along with a new home, the YD-171 got a new name – Herman the German. It went into operation at the shipyard in 1949.

Herman was a marvel of engineering. It was powered by three 750-horsepower diesel engines. It had more than two miles of cable (11,681 feet) and a lift capacity of 386 tons, although tests later pushed that limit to 425 tons. At 100 percent load, the engines used 144 gallons of fuel per hour.

For forty-eight years, Herman the German's superstructure would dominate the harbor skyline, and the story of how Long Beach got one of the world's three biggest floating cranes would be told and retold to successive generations.

The times were changing, and so were the people. Clinton J. Curtis, the Redlands citrus grower who came to Long Beach in 1905 to help build a new port as head of the L.A. Dock and Terminal Co., died in 1948 at his home near Rancho Santa Fe, about ten miles northeast of Del Mar in San Diego County. He was 78.

John F. Craig, whose decision to locate his shipyard in Long Beach invested the yet-to-be-built port with needed credibility, died in 1952 at his home on Atlantic

Avenue. A conservative, anti-union, hard-nosed businessman, Craig played a huge part in making the harbor what it was, both as a shipbuilder and as a harbor commissioner. He served on the board from 1931 to 1938.

W.R. "Frosty" Martin, another influential harbor commissioner, died in 1955. Martin was a former oil pioneer, inventor, and newspaper publisher, who played a large role both in the city and at the port. He had been largely responsible for bringing Douglas Aircraft Co. to Long Beach and played a significant role in the development of the Navy Base on Terminal Island. He served on the harbor board from 1939 until his death.

Robert R. Shoemaker, who left the Port of Los Angeles in 1940 to take a job as chief engineer for the Port of Long Beach, died of a heart attack at his home in 1958. He had helped guide the port through the war years and helped lead the battle to stem subsidence in the harbor. The following year, the Ninth Street Bridge, connecting the Long Beach Freeway with the downtown area, was dedicated as the Robert R. Shoemaker Bridge.

Long Beach Assistant General Manager Charles L. Vickers – brother of Long Beach City Manager Samuel E. Vickers – replaced Eloi "Frenchy" Amar as general manager of the port in the summer of 1958. Amar, who retired after eighteen years in the top job, was a former member of the Los Angeles Harbor Commission. Charles Vickers, 56 at the time, was a longtime port employee and engineer who first joined the city as a surveyor in 1925.

Los Angeles remained the dominant port in the area, but Long Beach – boosted by oil revenues and a governance system that somewhat insulated it from political whim – was catching up. Tonnage moving through the port was growing, and despite subsidence, new harbor-related businesses were choosing to locate in Long Beach.

In fiscal year 1949-50, Long Beach had moved 6.3 million tons of cargo across its docks, while Los Angeles moved 22.7 million tons. Ten years later, Long Beach tonnage had increased to 10.3 million tons, and Los Angeles had increased to 24.1 million tons. Long Beach was still moving significantly less cargo than its big sister across the bay, but the little port was steadily closing the gap.

Although much of the port's development during the 1950s was devoted to building dikes and filling in land lost to subsidence – a task comparable to building a new port on top of the old one – there were also new facilities being developed. The first radar system for guiding ships into a harbor was installed in 1949 at the Jacobsen Pilot Station on Pier A, the former Navy Victory Pier, later designated as Pier F. Modern transit sheds were constructed at numerous piers to handle general cargo. While much of the port may have been sinking away, new channels were being dredged, and new land was being filled in to expand port acreage. The port added 138 acres of landfill to the Pier A Victory Pier property. Pier E was created on new filled land on the west side of the entrance channel, adjacent to the Naval Shipyard in 1952.

In 1950, the port bought thirty-six acres in the north harbor area, filled it in and leased eighteen acres to the Atlantic Richfield oil company for a tank farm. The sunken town lot of small houses and motels south of Ocean Boulevard – where floods had driven people from their homes in 1951 – was purchased by the port in 1956, razed, and covered with eighteen to twenty-two feet of imported fill dirt to bring it up to grade. And in 1958, the port purchased about ninety-six acres of property in the north harbor from Pacific Dock and Terminal Co.

– the property on which the Pacific Coast Steel Corp. had thirty-five years earlier planned to build a steel mill. The steel mill plan had never come to fruition, but the property was finally owned by the port.

The Long Beach Freeway provided a high-speed link north for both commuters and cargo. In 1953, the port completed the Anaheim Street Bridge across the flood control channel and the freeway. Both the Robert R. Shoemaker Bridge and Ocean Boulevard Bridge opened in 1959.

Five miles east of the Port of Long Beach, development of another harbor was begun in the mid-1950s – this one a marina for yachts and smaller pleasure boats. A flood control channel had diverted the San Gabriel River eastward from Alamitos Bay, clearing the way for the bay to be dredged and turned into a massive marina capable of berthing 1,800 boats. It entailed the construction of twin parallel jetties stretching 3,500 feet out from the marina to the sea, the removal of a bridge that connected Seal Beach to Ocean Boulevard at the tip of the Long Beach peninsula – a move opposed by some Seal Beach owners who thought it would impact their businesses – and building a new bridge across the Los Cerritos Channel at Second Street.

The Seal Beach Council approved removal of the bridge in an agreement in 1954 that included using the spoils from the marina dredging to replenish the eroded beach south of the Seal Beach Pier. The idea was that construction of the new Second Street bridge connecting Naples Island to Pacific Coast Highway would provide a convenient, if slightly longer, link to Seal Beach.

Although the new bridge was built in 1956, it did not open until 1959. The city did not own the property at each end of the span, and so the completed bridge spanned the channel for three years and four months before opening to traffic, while the city negotiated to purchase the property at each end. During that period, it earned the dubious title of "the bridge from nowhere to nowhere." Its official name is the John H. Davies Bridge, after a prominent and civic-minded Long Beach engineer. Despite the criticism over the delay, city officials defended building the bridge when they did. If the city had waited for the legal questions at each end of the bridge to be settled, construction of the $1.5 million bridge would have cost at least $600,000 more, they claimed.

Although the price tag for the finished marina would grow from $10 million when first proposed to $14 million when finished, it would become one of the premier small boat harbors in California. The marina was not part of the Port of Long Beach, but since it was included in the 1911 Tidelands Trust, it did qualify for funding from harbor oil revenue.

The Coming of the Box

All the while that the Port of Long Beach was fighting subsidence, filling in new land, and building transit sheds, on the other side of the country a North Carolina trucking company owner named Malcom Purcell McLean was busy developing an idea that would change the way things were done at the Port of Long Beach – and at every port around the world.

In short, McLean's idea was to put cargo in big boxes that would fit on the chassis of a truck trailer, use a crane to take it off the truck and load it onto a ship, unload it at its destination, stick it on another truck, and drive it to its final destination. McLean was not in the maritime business, and the idea of containers was not new. People had been talking about putting cargo into containers for a long time. In fact, the military was already using small steel containers called Conex boxes – short for Container Express – to ship household goods and personal belongings for military families being stationed abroad. The idea of wide-scale containerization of cargo, however, had never quite worked out.

But McLean was a businessman. The 1950s was a time of strict regulation of transportation, ostensibly done in the name of efficiency and fairness, but by its very nature a barrier to innovation. What McLean had that others did not, was a business plan. He knew what he wanted to do, and he knew how he wanted to do it.

And so he did, and the world changed forever.

People lost their jobs, and new jobs were created. Many American workers would find themselves in direct competition with low-paid workers in other countries. Consumers would be able to afford well-made foreign products at a low price, economic barriers that once separated nations would start to come down, and the leaders of industry would began to realize that if they wanted to stay in business, they had to understand logistics.

The world was moving toward a global economy, and Long Beach was in a perfect place to profit from it.

Chapter Fifteen:
A New Beginning for Old-Style Ports

America got a new flag in 1960 – one with fifty stars to signify the addition the previous year of two new states, Alaska and Hawaii. The census that year showed a nationwide population of 179,323,175, up 18.5 percent from ten years earlier. The nation had gone through a growth spurt and not just because of the two new states. The warriors of World War II had returned home eager to make up for lost time. They got jobs, bought houses, and began having children. There was a deluge of babies as the new generation was born, a generation aptly called the "baby boomers." The boomers were a restless generation that for the most part had never experienced economic depression or been called upon to routinely sacrifice for others. They were a generation of vague and shrouded discontent. By the time the boomers came of age, they had become a generation that yearned for change, a generation of rebels in search of a cause, a generation that would change the world – sometimes for the better; sometimes not.

The decade in which this new generation began to reach adulthood would be marked by assassinations, riots, war, a changing moral code, great leaps in technology, scandal, silliness, and bitter politics. A great civil rights struggle would be waged by marginalized citizens seeking what was rightfully theirs. The decade would begin with men wedged into claustrophobic capsules being hurled at high speed for short hops into space, and end with men walking on the moon and planting the Stars and Stripes on its barren surface. Two superpowers would walk up to the brink of nuclear holocaust and stare into that dark abyss until one of them finally backed down.

It was a time of freedom riders pushing the limits of Southern intolerance, of sit-ins at lunch counters, of stubborn refusal to sit in the back of the bus, of murder, fire hoses used as weapons, and dogs unleashed on people who refused to take the place others assigned them. In 1963, the Reverend Martin Luther King Jr. spoke to millions when he said he had a dream. In 1968, he was dead, gunned down at a Memphis motel. But the dream refused to die. King believed in nonviolence, but change in a society long-accustomed to a rigid assumption of white superiority would not come without bloodshed. There were riots in the streets, first in Harlem in 1964, then Rochester and Philadelphia. The black Los Angeles neighborhood of Watts exploded in 1965. There were riots in Cleveland, Omaha, and Newark and Plainfield, New Jersey. The list goes on – Detroit, Minneapolis-St. Paul, Chicago, Baltimore, Glenville, Ohio, and Washington, D.C.

The stubborn non-violence of King began to give way to the anger of Stokely Carmichael and the revolutionary zeal of the Black Panthers. King saw nonviolence as a principle; to Carmichael it was merely a tactic. The Black Panthers saw violence as the real tool for bringing about change. Malcolm X – a one-time leader of the Nation of Islam who later publicly rejected their teachings – was shot to death in 1965 by three Nation of Islam gunmen as he prepared to speak at a banquet hall in New York.

The first televised presidential debate was in 1960; the election of John F. Kennedy came later that year. Kennedy inherited the Bay of Pigs from Eisenhower, stood toe-to-toe with the Soviet Union over Cuba, founded the Peace Corps, and promised to send men to the moon within a decade. He was assassinated in 1963 as he rode through the streets of Dallas in a crime that has been debated ever since. The President's younger brother, Robert F. Kennedy, was shot and killed less than five years later in the kitchen of the Ambassador Hotel in Los Angeles as he campaigned for president.

The Kennedy decade ended in scandal after Senator Edward Moore "Ted" Kennedy, the youngest of the brothers, drove his car off a bridge late at night on Chappaquiddick Island with 28-year-old Mary Jo Kopechne in the passenger seat. Kennedy managed to swim free; Kopechne did not. Kennedy did not report the accident to police. The car was discovered the next morning by two fishermen. One week later, Kennedy pleaded guilty to leaving the scene of an accident after causing injury and received a suspended sentence. He remained in the Senate, but any ambition for the presidency died that night with Mary Jo Kopechne.

On the day of his death, John F. Kennedy was replaced by Vice President Lyndon Baines Johnson. Kennedy had sent advisers to South Vietnam; Johnson sent combat troops. Johnson would later beat Barry Goldwater to claim the seat as his own in 1964. In 1968, as thousands protested the war, Johnson opted not to run for re-election. The Democratic Convention was held in Chicago that year as anti-war protesters engaged in bloody combat with police on the streets outside. Richard M. Nixon, who had lost to Kennedy eight years earlier, beat his Democratic opponent, Vice President Hubert H. Humphrey. Johnson died of a massive heart attack in 1973, four years after he left office. One of his last official appearances was at the funeral of former President Harry S. Truman four weeks earlier.

Besides Vietnam, which dominated much of the international news during the decade, the 1960s also saw the downing of the U-2 spy plane over Russia in 1960 and the arrest, trial, and imprisonment of pilot Francis Gary Powers, a member of the Central Intelligence Agency. Powers was freed in an exchange of spies in 1962. He ended up as the Telecopter pilot for KNBC-Channel 4 News in Los Angeles and died in 1977 in a crash at the Sepulveda Dam Recreation Area.

It was a decade in which Soviet Premier Nikita Khrushchev pounded his shoe on his desk during an angry exchange at the United Nations, Israel tried and hanged war criminal Adolf Eichmann, East Germany erected the Berlin Wall in 1961 to keep its citizens from fleeing to the West, and Nelson Mandela was arrested and jailed in 1964 for conspiring to overthrow the government of South Africa. It was also the decade of the Six Day War between Israel and its Arab neighbors in 1967, the death of revolutionary Che Guevara in the jungles of Bolivia, and the seizure of the *USS Pueblo* intelligence-gathering ship by the North Koreans in 1968.

Prayer was banned in public schools in 1962. Medicare and Medicaid began in 1965, and the Department of Housing and Urban Development and the Department of Transportation were organized as cabinet-level departments in 1966. Police began advising suspects of their rights after a Supreme Court ruling in the case of *Miranda v. Arizona* that same year. The National Organization for Women was founded in 1967, and gay people rioted on the streets of New York after a police raid at the Stonewall Inn in Greenwich Village, a gay bar owned by the Genovese crime family.

The first laser – light amplification by stimulated emission of radiation – was introduced in 1960. The birth control pill became widely available that same year, providing women with sexual freedom without the fear of pregnancy. In 1964, the U.S. Surgeon General issued a landmark report linking smoking to lung cancer and heart disease. Bulletproof vests made of a new material called Kevlar came out in 1966. Japan's first bullet train was introduced in 1964, and the first heart transplant was performed in 1967. A 1968 nerve gas leak at the Army's Dugway Proving Ground in Utah resulted in the death of 6,000 sheep on nearby ranches.

By 1962, ABC was offering three- to- five hours per week of color telecasts. Pull tabs on soda and beer cans were introduced that year and so was Diet-Rite, a low-calorie soda; Coca Cola's Tab soda came out the following year. The U.S. Postal Service introduced ZIP codes in 1963. The GI Joe action figure debuted in 1964; miniskirts became the rage in 1965, and not surprisingly, pantyhose were introduced shortly thereafter.

Caryl Chessman, a convicted rapist and robber who had pleaded his case in books written from behind bars, was executed in the gas chamber at San Quentin prison in 1960. A last-minute stay of execution arrived seconds too late when a secretary dialed the wrong number the first time. Three convicts escaped from the federal penitentiary on Alcatraz Island in 1962, using an inflatable raft they assembled from glued-together raincoats. They were assumed to have died in the waters of San Francisco Bay, but no bodies were ever recovered. Alcatraz was closed the following year, not because of the escape, but because of decaying infrastructure, high operating costs, and complaints about the sewage being released into the Bay from the 250 prisoners and sixty prison personnel and their families.

Albert DeSalvo, better known as the Boston Strangler, was sentenced to life in prison in 1967 and would be stabbed to death there six years later. The Zodiac killer began his murder spree in the Bay Area in 1968, sending letters to the press describing his crimes. He was never caught. In 1969, members of the Manson family – a hippie cult led by Charles Manson – murdered actress Sharon Tate and four friends in her home in the Hollywood Hills. The next night they killed Leno and Rosemary LaBianca at the couple's home in the Los Feliz area of Los Angeles. Manson and his family members were later arrested, tried, and sentenced to death, but were spared execution after the California Supreme Court ruled in 1972 that capital punishment was unconstitutional under the law as it then existed.

The 1960s were the years when rock 'n' roll king Elvis Presley became a GI, did his duty, and returned to a career in movies and records. Brash young boxer Cassius Clay captivated Americans when he beat heavyweight champion Sonny Liston for the title, but got into trouble after he changed his name to Muhammad Ali and refused to go to war. Although his conviction on draft evasion charges was later overturned, he lost four prime years of his boxing career. The Flintstones became America's favorite cartoon family in 1960. Barbie, a new kind of doll with a grownup figure, acquired boyfriend Ken in 1961. The first James Bond movie, *Dr. No*, came out in 1962, the same year that pop artist Andy Warhol displayed his painting of a can of Campbell Soup as art.

Rachel Carson's book *The Silent Spring* warned Americans in 1962 of the environmental dangers posed by pesticides and other toxic chemicals. Michael Harrington's 1962 book, *The Other America*, related the problems of poverty within the United States, a book thought to have influenced President Johnson to launch his War on Poverty. And Betty Friedan's 1963 book, *The Feminine Mystique*, woke up a generation of women looking for an alternative to living in a male-dominated world. Johnny Carson took over *The Tonight Show* in 1962. Marilyn Monroe overdosed in the bedroom of her Brentwood home that same year, and singer Patsy Cline died in a plane crash in 1963.

The Beatles appeared on *The Ed Sullivan Show* in 1964. Captain Kirk and Mr. Spock began their *Star Trek* adventures in 1966. The Summer of Love in San Francisco brought young and restless youth from across the nation to the Bay Area in 1967, the same year the Doors released their first album. The musical *Hair* shocked the nation when it opened in 1968 on Broadway, featuring a mixed-race cast and a scene including full-frontal nudity. The Woodstock concert brought a message of peace and love to America in 1969, the same year that *The Brady Bunch* and *Sesame Street* began on TV.

The lifestyle and culture of the nation was evolving at fast-forward speed during the 1960s. By the end of the decade, the excesses of the age resulted in a sharp rebuke from voters across the nation. It was time for the disaffected and alienated youth who had played such a starring role in the social turmoil to ease off. The middle-class – the "silent majority" of regular Americans – was fed up with the war, the rioting, the drugs, the wild music, and the disregard for long-established moral and religious standards.

The 1960s came to an end, and it seemed the nation breathed a sigh of relief. And as always, the mood of America was reflected in the City of Long Beach and at its port.

Back to Business as Usual

After a decade of legal battles over oil, geological and political battles to stop the port from sinking beneath the water, and the everyday struggle to keep customers happy and attract new business, the port seemed by 1960 to be getting back to normal.

Subsidence had been brought under control. The Navy decided in March 1960 to retain its Long Beach Naval Shipyard, although the facility was badly in need of repair from the damage done by subsidence. Retaining the shipyard – and the 6,500 jobs of the people who worked there – was a huge victory in Long Beach's battle against subsidence. The port had spent considerable energy and money refilling sunken areas and rebuilding damaged infrastructure, but it had been worth it. At the center of the subsidence bowl near the Southern California Edison plant, the land dropped twenty-seven feet before it was all over. With minor and insignificant exceptions, the sunken land never rebounded, but it did at least stop sinking.

Throughout the subsidence experience, the port had managed to hold on to business and even expand its property. The official end to the outstanding litigation over subsidence came in October 1963, when the federal government settled its damage suit against the city, state, and private defendants for $6 million and the purchase of 1,039 acres of property adjacent to the Shipyard and Navy Base for $1. The city and the state each paid $1.2 million for damages with the private defendants paying the additional $3.6 million.

The port had broken ground in June 1958 for a new seven-story administration building on a ten-acre campus in the outer harbor, with a view of both the city skyline and the ocean. The two-story Mediterranean-style headquarters building on El Embarcadero – which the port had moved into eighteen years earlier – had become too small to accommodate the port's expanded operations. Moreover, by 1958, the land underneath the building had sunk more than fourteen feet and was surrounded by twenty-three to twenty-eight-foot-high earthen dikes to hold back the sea.

Both the groundbreaking and the dedication of the new $2 million port headquarters were accompanied by the pomp and ceremony common to that era. For all such events of the kind – be it the opening of an administration building or of a transit shed – there were beauty queens or similar fresh young female faces standing by to cut ribbons and pose with public officials.

The city that had once passed a bathing suit ordinance that was so complicated nobody could figure out what it said, by the 1950s and 1960s was celebrating the female form at every possible occasion. Pacific Mills, maker of Catalina Swimwear, was a sponsor of the Miss America pageant until Yolande Betbeze, Miss America 1951, refused to do publicity shots wearing the company's swimsuit. The company pulled its sponsorship and started its own Miss USA and Miss Universe contests the following year with Long Beach as the host city. The last Miss Universe contest in Long Beach was in 1959. A dispute over the amount of money being demanded by Pacific Mills to hold the contest in the city, and over moving up the time of the event so East Coast TV viewers could watch it live, ended with the Miss Universe Contest moving to Miami Beach.

Long Beach started its own pageant – the International Beauty Congress – with the city and the port each picking up half the cost. Around this time, the city began calling itself the International City, and the contest was touted at every occasion by the port. Each year the contestants would tour the port, engage in a ceremony in front of the administration building, and help promote the port image. Promoting commerce through the port was an allowable expenditure of harbor revenue under the city's 1911 Tidelands Grant, and in the 1950s, hosting beauty pageants was seen as a great way to promote the port.

More than 200 port and city officials, shipping line executives, harbor employees, and representatives of the harbor oil contractor turned out to celebrate the administration building groundbreaking with Harbor Commission President William A. Harrington presiding. Harrington took over the controls of a pile driver, and with the help of 1958's Miss Long Beach, 19-year-old Sally Cannon, swung the first piling for the new building into place.

At the dedication ceremony of the building less than two years later, thirty-one girls participated in a scripted ritual called a "wedding of the waters." Each girl represented a foreign or U.S. port, each was dressed in the fashion of the harbor she represented, and each carried a container of water from that harbor. At the designated time, the young women emptied their waters – foreign and domestic – into the reflecting pool in front of the new building.

PHOTO OPPORTUNITIES: *In the 1950s and '60s, it was common for the port to create a sense of occasion at milestone moments (for better or for worse) by including attractive young women to pose in commemorative photos. Two of the wilder examples: Above, TV's Art Linkletter, left, and Harbor Commissioner Joseph Bishop pose with a "real-life" mermaid, Van Camp Sea Food executives, and an enormous can of Chicken of the Sea during the dedication of the firm's administrative offices next to Port HQ in 1959. Below, Assistant Port General Manager Thomas Thorley, left, and Koppel Bulk Terminals President Irving Koppel admire model Marianne Miller, along with the grain that would be brought to the harbor in the new Koppel terminal that opened in 1961.*

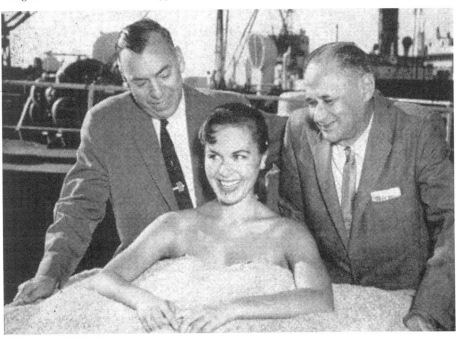

The volume of cargo coming through the Long Beach and Los Angeles ports continued to grow, with economists predicting that it would double or even triple by 1980. The Long Beach port moved aggressively forward, sometimes stepping on local toes.

The Van Camp Sea Food Co. signed a twenty-five-year lease with the Port of Long Beach in 1958 in which the port agreed to build a $576,000 corporate headquarters for the company on Pier A in the outer harbor. The Van Camps had been in the seafood business since 1914, but their recent adoption of a mermaid mascot and the catchy jingle – "Ask any mermaid you happen to see, 'What's the best tuna?' Chicken of the Sea" – had made the brand a household name. The company's lease with the port, however, raised the hackles of commercial building operators in the city, which claimed the agreement put the port in direct competition with private industry.

The new Van Camp headquarters office building opened in 1959 with a ceremony that included TV personality Art Linkletter arriving by helicopter with a pretty young woman dressed as a mermaid. She was greeted by corporate President Gilbert Van Camp Jr., who posed her on the label of a giant tuna can. She presented him with a golden can of tuna representing the 3 billionth can of tuna that Van Camp Sea Food had produced. It was packed with tuna caught off the coast of South Africa. Since the early days of fishing local waters for tuna, the industry had evolved into fleets of large refrigerated fishing boats that scoured the globe for fish. The company employed about 175 administrative executives and workers at its Long Beach site, and its cannery on the Los Angeles side of Terminal Island remained in operation.

In 1961, a 216-foot-high grain elevator opened near Pierpoint Landing. It became one of Southern California's tallest structures of its day – exceeded only by three buildings in downtown Los Angeles: the Los Angeles City Hall at 450 feet, the Wilshire Tishman office building at 285 feet, and the California Bank at 257 feet. The grain facility was built by the port and operated by Koppel Bulk Terminals under a forty-year lease agreement with the port. Plans for the grain terminal had been promoted in the typical fashion of the day – by photographing Assistant Port General Manager Thomas Thorley and Koppel President Irving Koppel with a young, bare-shouldered model buried up to her armpits in grain as though she were taking a bath.

The finished terminal included thirty silos, each more than 120 feet high, and a towering workhouse from which the loading and unloading of ships, railcars, and trucks was controlled. Storage capacity was 810,000 bushels of grain, and ships could be loaded at a 43,000 bushel-per-hour rate. Exports passing through the terminal included wheat, safflower seed, sorghum grains, and animal feed. Copra and barley were imported.

Construction of the reinforced concrete silos was challenging. Each silo had to be formed in one continuous pour to eliminate any weak spots where set concrete met wet concrete. That required sixty-two concrete trucks and shifts of 150 workers operating around the clock. The concrete was continuously poured into a cylindrical slip form, which was slowly jacked up at the rate of fifteen feet per day as the concrete was poured and set. Three years later, the storage capacity at the terminal was expanded to 2 million bushels, more than double its original volume.

The Richfield Oil Supertanker Terminal on Pier E – later Pier T – was also dedicated in 1961 with the tanker *Princess Sophie* at dockside, ready to discharge its 506,000 barrels of oil – the largest shipment ever offloaded in either the Long Beach or Los Angeles ports. The nineteen-acre terminal featured dockside water depths of fifty-two feet, 1,225 feet of water frontage, and was one of the few in the world able to take the largest oil tankers of that time. Richfield Vice President David E. Day was the main speaker at the dedication ceremonies, which were attended by several hundred people. Day, who had negotiated the first oil terminal in the harbor for his company in 1924, talked about the long-term relationship between Richfield and the port, both as oil terminal operators and as drillers of oil. After his talk, Day participated in a symbolic turning of the valve to officially open the terminal for business. He was aided by Mayor Edwin Wade, Harbor Commission President John P. Davis, and 1961 Miss Long Beach Sandi Jenkins.

Richfield Oil would merge five years later with Atlantic Refining to become Atlantic Richfield Co., better known as ARCO. In 2000, ARCO would become a subsidiary of BP (British Petroleum), which would later sell it to Tesoro Corp.

In 1962, Mitsubishi Shipping Co.'s *Santa Isabel Maru*, the world's largest ocean-going ore ship, was the first to call at the port's new iron ore export terminal on Pier G. The ship took on 57,000 tons of iron ore from the Kaiser Steel's Eagle Mountain Mine, east of Indio, California. The shipment was the first of many under a contract between Kaiser and Mitsubishi for 1 million tons of iron ore per year to be exported through the port. The ore was transported from the mine to the port by a 100-car shuttle train. Metropolitan Stevedore Co., the operator of the new terminal, was able to load the shipment in twenty-four hours. Additional products handled at the terminal included potash, petroleum coke, and other ores.

In October of 1962, the first shipment of industrial salt arrived in Long Beach from the Black Warrior Lagoon halfway down the West Coast of the Baja California Peninsula in Mexico. The salt was being imported and refined by Ocean Salt Co. on what what became Pier G, next door to the grain elevators.

Harbor Banana Distributors, located just west of the salt terminal, discharged ships arriving with bananas from Central America, stored the bananas temporarily in a refrigerated ripening room, and then shipped them from Long Beach to buyers in the Western U.S. and Canada.

The port got its second gypsum plant in 1965, when National Gypsum Co. completed its new terminal and processing plant in the inner harbor. The company imported gypsum from Mexico and processed it into drywall for construction. Kaiser Gypsum Co. had been doing business in the inner harbor for years.

Long Beach was growing and business was good, but the port in those days was not just about moving cargo. It was also about recreation.

By 1960, more than 100,000 visitors were arriving at the port each year on Orient and Pacific Lines passenger ships, and a quarter-million people were going by boat or amphibian airplane to and from Catalina Island. The ocean liners of the time were not cruise ships offering three-day or week-long round trips to Mexico. When P&O Orient Lines' *S.S. Oriana* called on its maiden voyage in February 1961 with 1,719 passengers on board, it was coming from England via the Suez Canal, and that was where it was bound when it left. The 1960s were the twilight days for the big ocean liners, and soon they would fade into history to be replaced by faster and cheaper airliners. But while they still sailed the sea, the Port of Long Beach provided them a welcome berth.

The Harbor Commission in 1957 also approved a 1.5-acre outer harbor lease with a restaurant group headed by Long Beach businessman David Tallichet. The group opened the Reef Restaurant the following year with a South Sea décor and a view looking back at the Long Beach skyline.

Long Beach hit a noteworthy milestone in 1961, when the port celebrated fifty years of struggle and triumph from that day in 1911 when the lumber ship *Santa Barbara* arrived with 350,000 feet of Oregon pine to help build the growing community. To mark the occasion, the port hosted a birthday party at Pier 1, the location where the port first began. Harbor Commission President John P. Davis announced that the board had approved development of Pier J – a 270-acre site on the south side of the outer harbor. The climax of the party was the arrival of a sea-going birthday-cake barge – 110 feet long and thirty feet wide – "tastefully decorated" with fifty young women in swimsuits and high heels, lining the edges. The women represented the fifty years of port history. The arrival of the giant birthday cake was heralded by a Marine honor guard from the Long Beach Naval Station firing a fifty-gun salute as helicopters circled in the sky.

That same year saw the end of an era as the famous Red Car rail line went out of business. The line had begun as the Pacific Electric Railroad, a venture of railroad man Henry E. Huntington and banker and real estate investor Isaias W. Hellman. The electric railway's first route started running from Los Angeles to Long Beach in 1902. Fifty-nine years later, that same route was the last one to close.

The early Pacific Electric Railroad was as much about electricity and real estate as it was about transportation. Developers and communities anxious to get an electric connection and a transportation link to their areas were often ready to provide real estate opportunities in exchange for service. The passenger service provided by the line was mostly a loss leader for the Pacific Electric. Carrying freight was where the profit lay.

An early agreement with the Los Angeles Dock and Terminal Co., which had developed the Port of Long Beach, gave Pacific Electric rights to service the local docks. Both Huntington and the Hellman group later sold their shares to Southern Pacific, and in 1910, Southern Pacific took over operation of port rail traffic under the Pacific Electric name. There were forty-three miles of rail line in the port by the early 1960s, with about twenty-five miles of it owned by the port itself. The rail lines stretched from transit sheds along the docks to a switching yard where the various cars were sorted. The cargo would be moved between ship and transit sheds on the dockside and moved onto trains or trucks on the opposite side.

Although Southern Pacific still moved the port cargo, by the time the Red Car passenger service completely shut down in 1961, it was a publicly owned line. Much has been made of the alleged conspiracy by General Motors and others to buy up street car lines and then shut them down to be replaced by buses. But there were many other factors in play over the years as well. The decline of the Pacific Electric line began as early as the 1920s when less profitable routes started being converted to cheaper and more flexible bus service. Freeways, increased private ownership of cars, and government regulation all played a role in the demise of the system too.

The last Red Cars remaining in service were rundown and dilapidated. Maintenance was mostly confined to critical components – undercarriage, brakes, and motors – not the passenger compartments, where paint was peeling, windows were cracked, seats were worn, and metal parts were corroded. As the system shut down during the 1950s and early 1960s, the old red cars were stacked four-high on Terminal Island, waiting to be scrapped. The impact of the passing may have been a blow to the fond memories held by people who had grown up riding the Red Cars, but even most of those folks did not ride them anymore, and the impact to the transportation system was minimal.

The Mechanization and Modernization Agreement

The waterfront experienced great change in the 1950s. The cost of moving cargo was rising, and shippers – the people who owned the cargo – were putting pressure on ship owners and stevedore companies to reduce those costs. The only way to do that was to move ships in and out of port more quickly and speed the cargo to its final destination. Unloading a ship was extremely labor intensive. Longshoremen worked down in the holds of ships, using cargo hooks and their bare hands to move the cargo out of the hold and onto the dock. The heat was often stifling, the work dangerous, and the time needed to unload a ship measured in days. But employers had begun using new practices and devices, all aimed at smoothing out the flow of cargo. Ships were being redesigned to make them easier to load and unload. Lumber was being strapped together and lifted by crane rather than carried off by hand. The same situation worked with bags of sugar. Rolls of newsprint, previously taken off the ship one roll at a time by a team of six to eight longshoremen, were being lifted off eight at a time by one man operating a mechanical hook. Forklifts carried pallets of goods from the dock to transit sheds, and scrap steel was cut into small pieces and loaded into bulk carriers by conveyor belt. The biggest change of all was containerization, which required large cranes to lift the cargo directly out of the ship and onto trucks.

The machines presented the International Longshoremen's and Warehousemen's Union with a dilemma. The easier and faster it was to unload a ship, the fewer longshoremen were needed. Some wanted to resist automation of the waterfront, not only because it meant fewer jobs, but for cultural reasons as well. People, longshoremen included, don't like change.

Former longshoreman Stan Weir, author of *Singlejack Solidarity*, lamented the esoteric connection that was being lost between longshoremen from around the globe. Weir was a critic of Harry Bridges and seen by Bridges and the ruling majority as a troublemaker. He was later discharged from the union. He was also an outspoken opponent of the changes taking place on the waterfront. His critique of mechanization was almost poetic in its condemnation of the new ways.

> *The old ships which carried break-bulk cargoes provided hold and dock longshoremen around the world with physically identical work environments. The workplaces traveled the globe and were the same. What changed in each ship as it went from port to port was the cargo and the nationality of the men who worked on it. As each longshore gang boarded a ship and uncovered the hatches, they found each other's city and union newspapers, cargo hand hooks lost or left behind, and evidences of secret feasts made possible by edible or imbibable articles in the cargo. This very special form of international communication is becoming extinct. More and more, longshoremen work exclusively on the dock in the shadow of the ships, but not inside them.*

There were two ways for union members to respond to the mechanization of the waterfront. One was to hold it off as long as possible, and if they could not head off the inevitable, they could at least slow it down. The other approach was to find a way to live with it. The ILWU did both.

In the early to mid-1950s, the ILWU held tightly to the old ways – forcing employers to hire more men than was needed to do the job. There was the four-on, four-off feather-bedding system in which four members of an eight-member longshore gang would work, while the other four sat around drinking coffee and playing cards. After a while, the two foursomes would switch.

By the end of the 1950s, the waterfront calm that had existed since 1948 was beginning to fray around the edges. For a decade, employers had been willing to give in to union demands rather than face the consequences of a strike, but they were under pressure from their customers – the ones who paid for that indulgence – to get their house in order.

ILWU President Harry Bridges was a militant left-wing union man – a working-class hero to most of his followers – but he understood that mechanization of the waterfront was going to happen with or without the union. Instead of waiting for the inevitable showdown, which the union would most certainly lose, Bridges wanted to negotiate a new contract that would avoid a strike and win new benefits for union members. Early in his labor career he had broken with the Wobblies because they would strike, but not consolidate the gains they had won. Bridges was a pragmatist. He understood that changing times required changing tactics. That concept wasn't universally shared by others in the union, who felt that any concession to mechanization was a betrayal of past battles and past sacrifice. Bridges held firm, according to author Charles P. Larrowe in his Bridges biography:

> "Those guys who think we can go on holding back mechanization are still back in the thirties, fighting the fight we won, way back then," Bridges said. In 1957, Bridges brought the subject up with the leadership of his union. They asked that he work with some of the leaders to study the idea and report back. The report that was prepared noted that mechanization of the waterfront was already under way. The question it posed was, "Do we want to stick with our present policy of guerilla resistance to the machine or do we want to adopt a more flexible policy in order to buy specific benefits in return?"

The report was made in October of 1957 with the contract due to expire the following year. In 1958, the union voted to approve a new contract with a pay raise and a controversial provision that reduced the work day from nine hours to eight in order to spread the work around. But negotiations continued on a proposed contract – dubbed the Mechanization and Modernization (M&M) Agreement – that would eventually be a turning point for the union and for the West Coast maritime industry.

In the meantime, however, the rank and file were growing restless – especially at the ports of Long Beach and Los Angeles. With available work disappearing and featherbedding being discouraged, the union was reluctant to add more workers to their rolls, which caused a problem. The union had enough registered members available to supply about 100 work gangs for the Long Beach and Los

Angeles ports. The problem was that ship arrivals came in bunches. During the spring, the heavy citrus harvest caused a logjam at the port. Winter storms would delay ships in the Atlantic, and then when the weather cleared the ships would all arrive at once. When work was slow, employers might need only seventy to eighty work gangs, and there would be too many longshoremen. When things got busy, there might be enough work for 175 gangs. During those times, ships would sometimes have to wait days to be worked. The union agreed to give the work during those times to striking workers from other industries, but that was not enough to make up the shortfall.

"The only way we can make money is to have ships call here," Port of Long Beach General Manager Charles Vickers told a reporter in 1959. "If they go elsewhere, we suffer. Over a long haul, ships bypassing Long Beach with regularity would definitely hurt our building program." But since neither the Port of Long Beach nor the Port of Los Angeles were a party to the labor contract between the ILWU and the Pacific Maritime Association, which represents terminal management, there was little they could do to speed things along.

But people tried. The Los Angeles Times in June of 1959 ran a five-part series of articles, entitled "Trouble on the Waterfront," which detailed some of the labor problems being faced by waterfront businesses. After the Times asked him for his reaction to the series, Los Angeles Mayor Norris Poulson issued an angry statement in which he blasted Harry Bridges as a power-seeking union leader.

"One thing seems to be clear in the labor picture," the mayor said. "Harry Bridges is at work to set up an enormous international labor empire. He hopes to consolidate forces with certain eastern labor leaders. And he is strengthening himself in the Hawaiian Islands, Japan, and the Philippines. When he achieves his goal he will have enormous powers over the economy of the world. By comparison, he will make James Hoffa sound like the fourth soprano in a high school choir." Poulson also condemned waterfront management for a "lack of intestinal fortitude in standing up for their rights."

During contract negotiations that year, Bridges was reported to have flown back to Washington, D.C., for a meeting with International Brotherhood of Teamsters President James "Jimmy" Hoffa to discuss Teamster support should a strike become necessary. Bridges and Hoffa had collaborated before on the possibilities of an air-sea-land transport super union. The proposal called for a merger between the Teamsters, the International Longshoremen's and Warehousemen's Union on the West Coast, the International Longshoremen's Association on the East and Gulf Coasts, and other transportation unions. The super union never happened, not only because of the clash of union cultures, but also because most of the unions, from sailors to airline pilots to railroad workers, were not willing to give up their turf. Although in the past Bridges had criticized both the Teamsters and the ILA, he also felt that the working class would benefit from one union controlling the entire transportation industry.

The final Mechanization and Modernization Agreement was reached in 1960, and it changed the waterfront forever. The Agreement provided for waterfront workers to be redefined into three groups – "A" men, who were registered longshoremen with full membership in the union with all rights and benefits; "B" men, who were registered longshoremen with partial union benefits; and "casuals," who were not official members of the union and enjoyed none of the union benefits. The "A" men would get first pick at available jobs from the dispatch hall.

Once every "A" man seeking work had been dispatched, the "B" men would be sent out. Only during the busiest of times, when the available supply of "A" men and "B" men had been dispatched to the job, would the casuals be sent out.

The agreement allowed employers to introduce labor-saving devices, but in exchange they had to guarantee job security for the "A" men. The casuals and "B" men would be the first to lose their jobs. If the workforce was still too big, the employers could institute a voluntary early retirement program for workers who were ready to leave. And if that weren't enough, they could institute a compulsory retirement plan with an enhanced retirement benefit to be negotiated. The employers also would have to share the productivity gains from the agreement with union members in the form of increased salary and benefits. As part of the agreement, the employers also established an M&M fund to which they contributed $5 million a year for five and a half years. This money was reserved for longshoremen who were fully registered union members at the time the agreement was signed.

The new agreement was passed by the rank and file, but not by a large margin. It remained unpopular among many longshoremen – especially younger ones – for years to come, and tarnished Bridges' image of a firebrand labor leader. But it worked.

The longshoremen remained a dominant force on West Coast waterfronts, and as the volume of trade increased, new jobs were created. The union turned to organizing other related – and sometimes unrelated – industries in order to build its base among workers.

Some still argue that the M&M Agreement brokered by Bridges marked a permanent change in work on the waterfront, sending some ports, such as San Francisco and Portland, into decline while others, such as Long Beach, Los Angeles, Oakland, Seattle, and Tacoma prospered. Those changes were the result of mechanization, but they were merely coincidental to the M&M Agreement, which was in itself a reaction to the reality of advances in port technology.

There were still problems fine-tuning the final agreement, finding the balance between what was written on paper and what actually worked in the real world, and parsing what the agreement actually meant in various situations. In the summer of 1960, Local 13 shut down the Long Beach and Los Angeles ports in a dispute over how many men were needed to off-load containers on the *Hawaiian Citizen*, a Matson ship that called at the Port of Los Angeles.

Harry Bridges and Pacific Maritime Association President Paul St. Sure were meeting in San Francisco with the union-management Joint Labor Relations Committee in an attempt to resolve the situation, but no easy solution was in sight. Los Angeles Mayor Poulson – who had made his feelings on Bridges clear in his statement the previous year – called for a meeting with Long Beach Mayor Edwin W. Wade and the harbor commissioners from both ports. The next day, the two port boards issued a stern warning to the ILWU and PMA to resolve their differences and get back to work.

The following week, the Long Beach and Los Angeles harbor commissions ran identical advertisements in the Long Beach Press-Telegram and the Los Angeles Times under the title of "Open Letter to the Citizen-Owners of the Port of Los Angeles and the Port of Long Beach." The letter recounted how the citizens of the two cities had spent $300 million to develop the ports, how a small group of union members in a dispute over how many men were needed to unload a container ship had decided to shut down the ports, how the ship in question had sailed to San Francisco to be unloaded while the dispute went on, how more than 100 ships had diverted to the Port of San Francisco because of the dispute, and how the extra cost of transporting those goods back down to Southern California would be paid by consumers. The cost of the shutdown to business was estimated at $6 million.

Neither Long Beach, Los Angeles, nor their citizens, were parties to the contract between the ILWU and the PMA, even though they owned the two ports, the letter pointed out. It went on to outline a plan of action.

> *Last week, we officially demanded of the presidents of the International Longshoremen's and Warehousemen's Union and the Pacific Maritime Association that cargo handling operations be resumed while negotiating their disagreement. To date, our demand has been ignored.* YOUR PORTS ARE STILL CLOSED AND NO REPLY HAS BEEN RECEIVED FROM EITHER ORGANIZATION.
>
> *We, therefore, have taken a further step to discharge our duty to you. We have directed the general managers of the two ports to secure the services of a nationally known firm of labor-management consultants to investigate and report on the deplorable union-employer situation at your harbors and make recommendations to correct the situation permanently, including:*
> 1) *Requiring the posting of bonds by the Pacific Maritime Association and the International Longshoremen's and Warehousemen's Union which would guarantee their compliance with the provisions of their contract;*
> 2) *Licensing longshoremen and stevedore companies, as done by the Waterfront Commission of New York Harbor;*
> 3) *Establishing a civil service labor force.*
>
> *This firm of experts also will be asked for their advice as to what federal, state or municipal legislation should be sought to correct conditions which have become intolerable.*

The letter was attributed to the two harbor commissions. Although the two ports were not parties to the ILWU-PMA labor agreement, they were not completely without options. Both ports were landlord ports, meaning they rented terminal space to private companies under long-term leases and made their money from lease payments and various fees. To become operating ports, on the other hand, to actually operate terminals and hire longshore labor, would open a huge can of legal and political worms, but it was an option the ports were willing to consider – or so the open letter contended.

"We are determined to put an end to the constant bickering between labor and management," Long Beach Harbor Commission President John P. Davis told reporters. "We are tired of being caught in the middle, and we are going to protect the public and the public's investment in our port."

The tough talk by the two ports did get the attention of the ILWU and PMA. The ILWU arranged a meeting in Los Angeles with the PMA and the mayors and port boards of the two cities. Both Bridges and St. Sure attempted to assure the city and port officials that the difficulties had been ironed out.

"We think we have our mutual problems here solved, but we're keeping our fingers crossed," Bridges said. "We have put together a constructive agreement that has penalties attached and arbitration built in."

"Then why have you got your fingers crossed?" interrupted Poulson. "What are you dubious about?"

"I'm not dubious," Bridges shot back. "But our boys can't be kicked around. Maybe they are SOBs, but they are our own SOBs and we've got to live with them and so do the employers."

It was not an answer that served to calm the official outrage over port shutdowns, but it was pure Harry Bridges. Many in the media and in the union thought that Bridges had mellowed, that finally in his middle years, he had succumbed to respectability and forgotten his working-class roots. But the old man obviously still had some fire left in his belly.

Winners and Losers

The one single thing that most changed life on the waterfront and resulted in some ports expanding while others withered and died was containerization. It had been pioneered on the East Coast by trucker Malcom McLean, who would later explain that he got the idea in 1937 while he was waiting in line at a Jersey City pier to unload his truck. Marc Levinson, author of *The Box*, says he is convinced the story was just that, a story of an imagined moment that never took place, an easy answer to the oft-repeated question of where McLean got the original idea.

> *Malcom McLean's real contribution to the development of containerization, in my view, had to do not with a metal box or a ship, but with a managerial insight. McLean understood that transport companies' true business was moving freight rather than operating ships or trains. That understanding helped his version of containerization succeed where so many others had failed.*

McLean was an entrepreneur and a risk taker. Once he set a course, he moved quickly to implement his idea and test it in the market place, first with a converted tanker, then with modified World War II-era freighters. He relied on people he hired to iron out the details. The idea was to modify a traditional freighter so that containers could be stacked in vertical cells below deck as well as on deck.

Heavy steel posts formed the vertical corners of each container in order to support the weight of the containers higher in the stack. Conventional rotating cranes proved too awkward to quickly lift a container out of the ship and place it on the chassis of a truck, so a shipboard gantry crane was designed – one placed forward of the wheelhouse and one aft – that spanned the deck from side to side. The crane moved forward and back on rails along the sides of the ship and from side to side on a beam. Each trolley beam could be folded out so it extended off the ship and over the wharf. Each crane operator had two lights – one red and one green. The red light signified that the other operator had moved his load over the wharf. A green light meant he had returned to the ship. It was important that both operators weren't cantilevered over the wharf with a heavy load at the same time in order to make sure the vessel didn't capsize.

A truck chassis was designed with sloping sides so the container would be guided automatically into the proper position, and a locking lug was designed that would fix a container in the stack to the one below it. The first ship to be so modified, an old C-2 freighter named the *Gateway City*, was able to load and unload its 226 thirty-five-foot containers in only eight hours.

McLean had a trucker's sense of making do with what was available. The ship owners of the time were steeped in industry tradition and knowledge, and not especially open to new ideas or to understanding their customers' need to move freight more cheaply and efficiently. McLean was not burdened by such conventional wisdom. He brought to the business a team of young and ambitious trucking executives, eager to shake up a moribund industry and leave their marks.

What McLean did on the East and Gulf coasts would be modified and repeated on the West Coast by Matson Navigation Co. for its services between California and Hawaii. But McLean's company, which would become known as Sea-Land Service, and Matson were far apart in philosophy and approach. McLean was more likely to fly by the seat of his pants, setting his course as he went along. Matson's approach was more deliberate and conventional.

Matson was a family-controlled company, established in 1882 with one ship. It had grown from that point to an extended enterprise that owned hotels, sugar plantations, passenger ships, California oil wells, tankers to ship oil to Hawaii, and tank farms to store it in. The shipping line had not been particularly profitable, but after World War II the line began to look at ways to deal with low-productivity issues and to develop tighter budgetary discipline. Unlike McLean's company, Matson was a mature organization with many interests to consider. McLean had hired people from the trucking industry, many of whom had learned by experience, to implement his plan. Matson hired Foster Weldon, a professor at Johns Hopkins University and a leading expert in the field of operations research.

Weldon did studies to determine the best container sizes, how much containers could save in labor costs, and how to deal with the imbalance of trade between the Hawaiian Islands and the mainland. As an island, Hawaii was dependent on outside sources for its consumer goods and most of its food. Each ton of cargo bound east to the West Coast of the mainland was matched by three tons headed west to the islands. That meant that many of the containers on east-bound ships would be carrying mostly empty boxes. Weldon collected volumes of data on trade between the islands and the mainland and fed it into a computer for analysis – a task which in the late 1950s involved a huge room-size computer and thousands of punch cards.

Matson introduced containerization to the West Coast in 1958, first in San Francisco, then at the Port of Los Angeles. The first ships featured containers stacked on deck, with conventional cargo stowed in the holds. The early Matson containers were twenty-four feet long, eight feet wide, and eight-and-a-half feet tall – the dimensions dictated by California trucking regulations. Unlike the shipboard crane developed by McLean's team, Matson opted for a land-based crane. The first landside gantry crane was built by Pacific Coast Engineering Co. (PACECO), which was so leery about the new design that it agreed to build it only if Matson accepted responsibility for any operational problems.

The *Hawaiian Citizen* – the same ship that caused the two-week tie-up at the Long Beach and Los Angeles ports – was launched by Matson in the spring of 1960. It was the line's first pure container ship. Despite initial labor problems, it was an immediate success. For each fifteen-day voyage, the *Hawaiian Citizen* spent twelve-and-a-half days at sea, moving cargo, and only two-and-a-half days in port, discharging and taking on cargo.

Although the savings in cargo-handling was dramatic, the idea of moving cargo in containers took a little time to catch on. Some dismissed it as an expedient that would work for special niche trade routes, but not for international trade. Others doubted that it would live up to its promise in reduced costs over the long run. Moving containers required an investment in both ships and infrastructure, and few were willing to invest in a new concept that was still seen as unproven. Like many disruptive technologies, containerization would win widespread acceptance only after a critical mass of companies had committed to it.

That day was coming.

The Urge to Merge

Although the Port of Long Beach and the Port of Los Angeles would sometimes work together on projects of common interest, they were usually more likely to be in competition, each pursuing its own objectives independent of the other. From the early years Los Angeles on numerous occasions had suggested mergers that would meld the two ports into one cohesive whole. And on each of those occasions, Long Beach chose to remain independent. The reason was clear – local control.

Long Beach is a port town. It owns its own port, and it administers its own port. San Pedro and Wilmington could have been port towns, but in 1909 the citizens of those two cities voted to be annexed to the City of Los Angeles. From the beginning, the Port of Los Angeles has been administered by a city government twenty miles to the north of where it is located. The local benefits of the port were diluted, and the needs of the people who lived nearby became less important. Long Beach was determined not to let that happen to their city or their port.

In 1961, the California Assembly Interim Committee on Transportation announced it would look at the feasibility of creating a single port authority to administer the Los Angeles and Long Beach ports. The decision to study the issue stemmed from a resolution introduced by San Pedro Assemblyman Vincent Thomas – who had been pushing for years to merge the two ports.

In his resolution, Thomas listed eleven advantages of a joint port authority, many of them redundant, some valid, and some not. In summary, the argument was that with competition between the ports removed, a united port authority would have the power to negotiate better contracts with customers. Administrative costs would be cut, project planning would be coordinated, and a united port would operate more efficiently.

What was not included in Thomas' list was any mention of local control. Long Beach was still not willing to sacrifice what San Pedro and Wilmington had given up fifty years earlier. Thomas' new effort to unite the ports – just like his earlier efforts – never got beyond the talking stage.

Three years later, Los Angeles Harbor Commission President Albert Perrish raised the question once again at a luncheon talk before the Los Angeles Transportation Club. A merger would probably be good for both ports, he said. Although his advocacy of a merger was merely his personal opinion, Los Angeles Mayor Sam Yorty told the club members that he and some of Perrish's fellow harbor commissioners informally supported the concept. He doubted that the

Port of Long Beach would favor the merger, but warned that if the ports didn't voluntarily unite, the state might force a merger upon them. Again, the merger plan turned out to be nothing more than talk before a trade group.

In 1969, the entire Los Angeles Harbor Commission officially went on record favoring a merger with its sister port next door. But nobody, including the commissioners, thought there was much of a chance that it would ever take place. Long Beach, it was pointed out, had never displayed the slightest interest in considering such an idea.

"It's like walking on water," said Commissioner William F. Quinn, "a commendable idea, but pretty hard to accomplish."

Port vs. Port
The Long Beach and Los Angeles ports were indeed sister ports, as evidenced by a simmering sibling rivalry that would sometimes erupt into full-blown, bitter quarrels between the two. In November 1960, Port of Los Angeles Real Estate Manager Leonard Doyle reported that 208 boats had moved from Los Angeles marinas to rent berths at the new Alamitos Bay marina in Long Beach. The marinas on the Los Angeles side of the bay charged $1.25 a foot for berthing a boat there; Long Beach only charged 85 cents a foot. It was an unfair competition, Doyle complained, because Long Beach had used tidelands oil money to finance the new marina.

In fact, Long Beach at that very time, was considering a motion to raise slip fees at its marina from 85 cents a foot to $1.10. That plan was immediately attacked by the members of the Marine Advisory Committee, which argued that the fee hike would come just weeks after a group of boat owners who had been waiting three years for available slips finally got them. The city decided to hold the line at 85 cents. Sometimes the sniping turned into legal challenge.

In 1962, Malcom McLean's Sea-Land Service announced it was going to begin serving West Coast ports, moving commodities from Newark, N.J., to the ports of Long Beach and Oakland. In September of that year, as the port prepared to welcome the arrival of the first Sea-Land ship, the *SS Elizabethport*, with 420 thirty-five-foot containers on board, the Los Angeles and San Francisco ports and an Oakland terminal filed papers with the Federal Maritime Commission attacking the proposed Long Beach deal with Sea-Land. The complainants argued that the lease did not include the wharfage and dockage charges levied against other shipping lines, and so it was unfair.

The following year, the Port of Los Angeles once again accused Long Beach of using its oil riches to engage in unfair competition. Los Angeles harbor board members claimed that Long Beach could afford to offer leases at lower rates than Los Angeles because Long Beach was flush with oil money. Los Angeles Commissioner Gordon MacLean, Harbor General Manager Bernard Caughlin, and Deputy City Attorney Arthur Nordstrom said they would plead their case with the State Lands Commission after first holding a strategy session with Mayor Sam Yorty.

Long Beach officials reacted to the charge with righteous indignation.

"The charges represent the greatest assortment of sour grapes since wine was invented," declared Long Beach Mayor Edwin Wade. He said the Los Angeles port representatives "didn't know which way they were going because Mayor Yorty hadn't told them yet."

The feud between the two ports flared up again in January 1964, when Los Angeles Harbor Commissioner MacLean charged in a hearing before the Senate Natural Resources Committee that Long Beach was using its oil money to lure business away from Los Angeles. If something wasn't done soon, he complained, Long Beach would "bankrupt all the other ports in California."

Long Beach officials acknowledged that their port could not have been built up in so short a time without the oil money, but they said that was preferable to taxing Long Beach citizens for the improvements. Port of Long Beach General Manager Charles Vickers, usually a soft-spoken man, bristled over the continuing complaints coming from the Los Angeles port.

"The people on the Los Angeles Harbor Commission have to live with the deals made in the past, and some of those past deals were real stupid," he said. "I'm tired of being criticized for their poor management. If they yell and scream about me long enough nobody will look at what Los Angeles is doing."

As an example, Vickers noted the construction of three passenger-cargo terminals in Los Angeles at the cost of $13.5 million. In the first ten months of operation, only 2,278 passengers were served by American President Lines at the terminal, he said. There was not enough passenger demand for the terminal to pay for it, he contended.

Vickers' counterpart at Los Angeles, Bernard Caughlin, said Los Angeles built the terminal for no other reason than to keep shipping lines from moving to Long Beach. "Even though passenger traffic is not enough to pay for the investment, the cargo coming through the terminal is," he said.

"Long Beach is scared to death that Los Angeles is going to swallow them up," Caughlin said. "But if they continue to have this oil money and continue these practices, I don't know where we're going to end up. They offer special deals that we can't make because we don't have the oil money. Their rate of growth in facilities is fantastic. It's not supported by the growth of normal business. The only way they can support it is by taking customers away from somebody, namely us."

It was true that the Port of Long Beach market share was growing. In the 1950 fiscal year, Los Angeles moved 22.7 million tons of cargo and Long Beach moved 6.3 million tons. In 1963, Los Angeles had increased its volume to 24.4 million tons, while Long Beach had increased to 11.4 million tons. Over a thirteen-year period, Long Beach had moved from 22 percent share in the cargo moving through the two ports to a 32 percent share. What distressed Los Angeles most of all was that almost all of the additional trade arriving during that period was absorbed by Long Beach.

The tables were turned in August of 1964 when the Port of Long Beach attacked plans by Los Angeles commissioners to build a bulk terminal in their harbor. Long Beach Harbor Commissioner Harry "Bud" Ridings told a Los Angeles Council committee that construction of the $4.8 million iron ore loading facility would be uneconomical and cause Long Beach and San Diego to lose substantially. The project was approved nonetheless.

The following month, Los Angeles renewed its attack on the Port of Long Beach at a hearing by a committee of the State Assembly. Assistant Los Angeles City Administrative Officer Arthur Spaulding urged the distribution of Long Beach's tidelands oil revenues to all cities holding tidelands trusts. Sharing Long Beach's oil revenues "would eliminate in the case of Los Angeles, much of the wasteful competition that currently takes place between the Port of Long Beach and the

Port of Los Angeles, and should prove of benefit to the entire state of California by the reduction of port costs and charges." But nothing came of Spaulding's suggestion, and the issues continued to simmer.

A Federal Maritime Commission examiner finally took testimony in June 1966 on allegations that the Port of Long Beach-proposed deal with Sea-Land Service was illegal. Long Beach Deputy City Attorney Leslie Still admitted that the proposed lease was different from most general cargo leases, but pointed out that Sea-Land's containerized business model was also different. "Archaic practices developed during the days of the sailing ship must not restrict progress in transportation," he said. Los Angeles argued that the lease was merely an attempt to circumvent tariff regulations and grant Sea-Land a reduced rate.

In November of that year, the Federal Maritime Commission examiner ruled in favor of Long Beach. As was the case with most of the disputes between the two ports, it was more about bluster and rant than forcing significant change. The two ports had different cultures and different perspectives. The Port of Long Beach was just blocks from its City Hall, an easy walk on a balmy day. The Port of Los Angeles was an appendage to a metropolis, hanging twenty miles below downtown attached like a pendulum by a narrow shoestring strip of land.

Geography counts.

The Bridges

Despite the rivalries between the two cities and their ports, they shared an island and a city line that zig-zagged Terminal Island north to south. But there were only three bridges connecting the island to the mainland – the Commodore Schuyler Heim Bridge at the north, just barely inside the Long Beach city line, the Henry Ford Bridge just west of the Heim Bridge, and the old Navy pontoon bridge that connected downtown Long Beach to the island. By the beginning of the 1960s, it became clear to both cities and ports that it was time to take a look at the bridges and make sure that they were both sound and efficient.

Built in 1948, the original Heim Bridge was a vertical-lift bridge with a center section that would rise vertically to let boat traffic pass while auto traffic waited. The Henry Ford Bridge, which allowed rail access to the island, employed a bascule design that rose like a drawbridge for boat traffic. And the pontoon bridge was a left-over from the war days – a temporary floating connection that would be moved to the side while auto traffic waited at each end, to allow the passage of vessels. It was dilapidated, dangerous, and often closed for repairs.

One idea considered at the time was to take down the Heim Bridge and the Henry Ford rail bridge, and move the Heim Bridge to downtown Long Beach to replace the pontoon bridge. A portion of the Cerritos Channel could then be filled in to form a causeway with an eight-lane road and rail lines connecting the mainland to Terminal Island. Moving the huge Heim Bridge would have been a challenge, but not impossible. However, the plan drew protests from the operators of work boats, barges, and pleasure boats, who didn't want the waterway that connected the two ports blocked off. In the end the cost of moving the bridge to Long Beach and altering it to fit a new site was too high to be feasible, so the plan was discarded.

San Pedro Assemblyman Vincent Thomas had been lobbying for a road link that would connect the San Pedro community to Terminal Island and replace the ferry system that ran back and forth across the Port of Los Angeles Main Channel.

Some people favored construction of an underwater tube roadway that would cross beneath the main channel, while others wanted a bridge high enough over the channel for ships to pass under. In March 1959, the California Division of Highways announced preliminary plans for a half-mile-long toll bridge with a 185-foot clearance above the water that would connect the Harbor Freeway to Terminal Island. The study and plan were prepared in response to a bill authored by Thomas. Cost of the project was estimated at $18 million to $20 million. Part of the financing plan was to seek a $1 million loan from oil-rich Long Beach to help pay for construction. Long Beach officials refused, claiming the city had already contributed $3 million toward the bridge in gasoline taxes to the county and that it had its own street construction program to pay for.

By the early 1960s, Long Beach was looking at the possibilities of its own state highway bridge that would connect the Long Beach Freeway and downtown area to Terminal Island. Cost of such a bridge was estimated at $16 million. There was some discussion about whether an underwater tube or a tunnel should be used to connect to the island, but in either case nothing could be built until the sinking of land due to subsidence came to a complete halt. Water injection wells had all but stopped the sinking by that time, but there remained places where the ground had not yet stabilized.

In January 1963, the Long Beach Harbor Commission decided that a bridge made more sense than a tunnel and ordered Port General Manager Charles Vickers to negotiate a design and feasibility study for the structure with Long Beach-based Moffatt & Nichol Engineers. A preliminary plan was drawn up for a four-lane, cantilevered, tied-arch bridge with a 160-foot clearance above the water. The plan was presented to the harbor board in September and approved.

Construction of the suspension bridge over the Los Angeles Channel was completed in November. Named for Vincent Thomas, who had championed the project for years, the bridge officially opened at noon. A bus containing Thomas and his extended family was the first to cross on November 15, 1963. The celebration continued that evening with a banquet at the Yugoslav Hall (later the Dalmatian-American Club) in San Pedro. After dinner people went down to the waterfront for one last ride aboard the ferry before it shut down. The toll to cross the new bridge in an automobile was 25 cents, in a large truck, $1.05.

On January 31, 1964, Gerald Desmond – the city councilman turned city attorney – died in Long Beach Memorial Hospital after a year-long battle with cancer. He was 48. Despite almost constant pain, he had continued to work through his illness, testifying before hostile legislators and defending the city's interests. In May of the following year, the Long Beach Harbor Commission voted to name the yet-to-be-built bridge from downtown Long Beach to Terminal Island for him.

Construction bids were received that summer, a groundbreaking was held, and work began. Four years later, on June 10, 1968, the bridge opened to traffic. It was a structure that would become a Long Beach landmark for almost fifty years. Over that time, it became a vital link, not just between downtown Long Beach and its port, but for thousands of trucks that would pass across it every day, shuttling freight between the port and the rest of the nation.

The Oil Islands

Long Beach suffered a disastrous financial blow in 1955 when it attempted to spend a portion of its tidelands oil riches on inland city projects, an idea that was

FLOATING BRIDGE: *Connecting Long Beach to Terminal Island, the Navy's pontoon bridge remains infamous to a couple of generations of Southern California drivers. Built as a temporary measure during World War II, it endured until the late '60s.*

A BETTER CONNECTION: *The Gerald Desmond Bridge towers over the pontoon bridge during its construction in 1967. The span, named for a former Long Beach councilman and city attorney, is itself slated for replacement.*

slapped down by the State Supreme Court. *Mallon v. Long Beach* ended with the city having to turn over half of such earnings to the state. Despite that setback, Long Beach was still eager to exploit a huge oil field off its residential coast, east of downtown.

The plan was to construct small ten-acre islands between the breakwater and the beach, where wells could be slant-drilled to extract oil from both under the city and under the sea. The problem was that the oil stash that lay beneath Long Beach's tidelands property, and what was seen as the city's flaunting of its wealth, had made it a target in the eyes of other tax-strapped governmental entities, including the state of California.

When Long Beach took steps to develop its offshore oil pool, it ran into a wall of opposition at the State Capitol. Legislators were tired of Long Beach dipping into its oil reserves at every opportunity, while other state and local entities were fighting to make ends meet. It wasn't fair that one city should have so much, just because it had been fortunate enough to be located on top of a rich oil field. Even though the state would receive half of all the profits from the field, that was hardly a big enough share, opponents argued.

State law required that the tidelands oil revenues be spent on commerce, navigation, and fisheries. It would be impossible for Long Beach to spend that much money on port projects without wasting it, opponents said. Soon Long Beach officials were being called before legislative hearings to explain just how they had spent their oil funds and to justify why one city should be so rich. Legislation was introduced that would strip Long Beach of all its interests in the offshore field. The proposed law said that the money would all go to the state, and if Long Beach needed funds for some special project, the city could apply to the state for a grant. That legislation was blocked by Governor Edmund "Pat" Brown, who agreed that Long Beach was getting too much, but thought that the city should retain some share in the oil revenues – just not 50 percent.

In the end, the Legislature passed a new bill, and a deal was struck. The state would get an 85 percent share of the profits, and Long Beach would get 15 percent. It wasn't much, but it was better than nothing. Although Long Beach received only a small share of the profits, it remained in charge of the operations. Long Beach brought a lot to the table. The city had years of experience in using private contractors to operate publicly held oil fields to make a profit. And Long Beach – through long and hard experience – probably knew more about how to avoid subsidence than any public agency in the world.

Five oil companies formed a syndicate called THUMS – Texaco, Humble, Union, Mobil, and Shell – to lease the majority of the field. Under the deal, they agreed to pay the state and the port 95.56 percent of the profits as a royalty. The remainder of the field went to Pauley Petroleum and Richfield/Standard.

A number of Long Beach residents were unhappy about the plan to put oil islands off the coast. THUMS agreed to beautify the islands with palm trees, gardens, waterfalls, and high-rise facades that would hide 180-foot-high derricks mounted on rails. After the deaths of astronauts Gus Grissom, Ed White, and Roger Chaffee in a launch-pad fire at Cape Kennedy in 1967, three of the four oil islands were named after them. The fourth was named in honor of Ted Freeman, an astronaut killed in a plane crash in 1964.

The Changing Scene

The Port of Long Beach continued to expand throughout the 1960s, building new terminals, planning new projects, dealing with new times and new issues.

Two new harbor commissioners from two old Long Beach families joined the port board in 1965. One was Llewellyn Bixby Jr., whose grandfather Lewellyn Bixby came to California looking for gold, only to grow wealthy as a merchant, sheep rancher, and land owner. (The elder Bixby had early on dropped an "L" from his name in order to Americanize it. Llewellyn Bixby Jr. went back to the traditional two-"L" spelling.) The other was James Craig Jr., whose grandfather John F. Craig ensured development of a port in Long Beach when he chose the city as the site to build and operate his shipyard.

In 1962, Connolly-Pacific Co. won the contract to fill in a 310-acre parcel of ocean to be called Pier J. Connolly-Pacific was a spinoff of the Rohr-Connolly Co. that had helped build the Long Beach extension of the breakwater and military installations at Pearl Harbor before the war. German-born Hans Wilhelm Rohl was president of the company and a naturalized U.S. citizen, who had lived in California since 1914. He made headlines in 1943 when he was called before the U.S. Joint Legislative Un-American Activities Committee and questioned at length about his loyalties. He later referred to the hearings as nothing more than "monkey business." Connolly-Pacific was incorporated after the war in 1946. Building the new pier, which pushed the land boundaries of the port farther out into the Pacific, required 3 million tons of rocks and thirty-three million cubic yards of fill.

Americans were buying more foreign cars and some of those cars – Volkswagens, Fiats, Renaults, Jaguars, MGs, Peugeots, Lancias, and more – were arriving at the Port of Long Beach, where they were unloaded one-at-a-time by cranes from the holds of ships. After arrival, they had to be inspected for dents, dings, and scratches encountered during the voyage, and prepared for sale. Foreign car imports through the port totaled 31,403 in fiscal year 1963, up 25 percent from the previous year, and continued to grow throughout the decade. In 1969, Long Beach scored a coup when Toyota – second only to Volkswagen in total volume of imported cars – signed a lease to transfer its import business from the Port of Los Angeles to a new location on Pier J in Long Beach.

In the mid-1960s the Vietnam War boosted both the amount of cargo coming through the port and activity at the Long Beach Naval Station. Supplies had to be shipped to the war zone. The mothballed fleet, which was moored at the Naval Station awaiting just such a moment, began to be broken out of its anti-corrosion wraps and prepared for a return to sea. With a third of the local Coast Guard fleet off to the war zone, the volunteer members of the Coast Guard Auxiliary used their private boats to help supplement search and rescue obligations. Although most of the war supplies flowed through the Bay Area, a significant amount came from the two San Pedro Bay ports – enough to boost business there.

The splitting of the atom during World War II had spawned a number of peacetime nuclear issues in the years following, and Long Beach and its port were not immune. In 1960, the city discovered that a company called Coastwise Marine Disposal Co. was storing radioactive waste in a warehouse at 2100 W. 15th Street, an industrial area in West Long Beach, only two blocks from the Eugene Field Elementary School. The low-grade nuclear waste, enclosed in concrete-encased steel drums, was trucked to the warehouse from the University of California's

Lawrence Laboratories in Livermore. Coastwise had a contract with the Atomic Energy Commission to dispose of the waste by dumping it 185 miles out to sea.

The city got involved after neighbors, who had seen the "Danger-Radioactive" placards on the trucks and at the premises, protested to the school board and the City Council. As it turned out, Robert Boswell, the 32-year-old contractor, had not yet received a business license to conduct what the city branded as a junkyard. The city demanded that Boswell cease his operation immediately, which was a problem since there were thirteen more trucks on their way to Long Beach with 728 more barrels of nuclear waste to add to the 12,000 barrels already stored at the site.

As always, there was another side to the story. Boswell had applied for a license four months earlier, described his business as handling nuclear waste, and paid a license fee. A month after that, there had been a special meeting with representatives of the port, the state, and county health departments, the Department of Fish and Game, and the Atomic Energy Commission (AEC) to discuss the process. Following that, there were repeated inspections by the Long Beach Fire Department. There had been no complaints or warnings raised during any of those events, Boswell complained. He thought his license was just being processed and would be issued in due course.

The barrels contained only items that might have been exposed to radiation during the course of research. The reason they were encased in concrete and plastered with warning labels was due to an abundance of caution. The AEC sent inspectors to the site, checked the storage area, and said the radioactive levels were what might be encountered in a typical backyard. The one barrel with the most radiation registered less than would be found on the radium dial of a watch, the AEC assured the public.

Still, the city responded quickly to shut down the operation. The incoming trucks were ordered not to unload their barrels, directed to a street in the harbor area, and placed under twenty-four-hour police guard. Boswell was taken to court and charged with operating a junk business without a license. The frustrated contractor complained that he had become a "political football" and was facing bankruptcy.

Boswell, in an attempt to comply with Long Beach's orders to get rid of the nuclear waste, took it to the Port of Los Angeles and began loading it on a barge for disposal. By the time the Los Angeles port warden – retired Coast Guard Admiral Frank Higbee – found out what was going on and ordered a halt, more than 1,000 of the 1,927 Long Beach-banned barrels had been loaded.

In the end, Boswell went out of business – either the result of nuclear hysteria or his own bad judgment to get involved in such a politically hazardous venture. The AEC, fourteen months after the controversy began, cleared the last of the waste from the warehouse, trucked it to Utah, and had it buried in the ground.

The other nuclear incident involving the port was a 1962 visit by the *NS Savannah*, the first and only nuclear-powered merchant ship at the time. The *Savannah* was a passenger-bulk cargo carrier built by the federal government as part of the Atoms for Peace initiative, and had been christened in 1959 by first lady Mamie Eisenhower. The finished ship was finally delivered to the U.S. Maritime Administration (MARAD) in 1962. It was 597 feet long, had seven cargo holds, a swimming pool, a promenade deck, a main lounge, a "veranda lounge," a bar with a glass wall overlooking the swimming pool, a lobby, an infirmary, thirty passenger cabins with private baths, and a seventy-five-seat dining hall. Unfortunately, there was only room left over for 8,500 tons of bulk cargo, and the streamlined shape of the hull made loading and unloading difficult.

The problem was that when the *Savannah* called at Long Beach in November, the engineers in charge of operating the ship reactor – members of the Marine Engineers Beneficiary Association – refused to sail until a dispute over pay could be resolved. The engineers, as nuclear technicians, didn't like their wages being pegged to the pay of other ship officers. Since it would take seventy-two hours to shut down the reactors, the engineers didn't walk off the job, but they refused to proceed. The ship later had to be towed by tugs to its next call, the Port of Los Angeles.

The *Savannah* was not an economic success. In fairness, it was never meant to be. It was a demonstration of the peaceful possibilities of nuclear power subsidized by the federal government. Even at that, it is difficult to fashion a successful perspective for the *Savannah* experiment. MARAD took her out of service in 1971, only nine years after her maiden voyage. The *Savannah* was the first of four nuclear-powered merchant ships to be built. The others were built and tested by Japan, Germany, and Russia. None proved successful, both because of the economics of building and operating the ships, and overcoming public and union opposition to nuclear-powered ships.

Long Beach became the Queen City in 1967, when it acquired an old ship that was to become a new harbor icon. Whether the purchase of the ocean liner *Queen Mary* from Cunard Lines was a good deal that gave the city a tourist attraction and a new hotel-convention center or a complete boondoggle is still debated, but the link between city and ship is undeniable. When people think of the *Queen Mary*, they think of Long Beach and vice-versa. Long Beach bought the 1,013-foot-long, 31-year-old ship at auction for $3.44 million. The idea was that the *Queen Mary* would help rejuvenate a dying downtown. The State Lands Commission approved the use of tidelands oil funds to pay for the ship after hearing city arguments that it was to be used as a museum and hotel. A recent change in legislation had cleared the way for Long Beach to use tidelands funds for a maritime museum.

In order to defray the $600,000 cost of transporting the ship from Britain to Long Beach, the city worked with the shipping line to put together one final sentimental journey aboard the aging liner for up to 1,200 passengers. Passage for the thirty-nine-day voyage would cost from $1,200 to $3,000, according to accommodations. The *Queen Mary* would depart Britain on September 14 with stops in Lisbon, the Canary Islands, Rio de Janeiro, Valparaiso, Lima, Balboa, and Acapulco on its way to Long Beach. The City Council and the Harbor Commission voted to send members on the voyage. In order to ensure a quorum to take care of city business, the Council divided the voyage into three parts – Southampton to Rio de Janeiro, Rio to Valparaiso, and Valparaiso to Long Beach. Three councilmembers would each fly to the departure point for their leg of the voyage and then fly home when they completed their portion of the trip.

The 14,455-mile voyage was not without its problems. The *Queen Mary* was an ocean liner, not a cruise ship. It was designed for quick luxury travel back and forth across the North Atlantic, not the tropics. Since it was too big to fit through the Panama Canal, it had to go around the southern tip of South America. Most parts of the old ship were not air conditioned, and the trip was long and often hot. Those who had booked passage as an adventure said they were delighted with the voyage. Those who had anticipated being pampered and entertained as they lounged around the ship were not so happy. Cunard had advised Long Beach against taking passengers on such a long voyage, but the city had wanted both the publicity and the money – 20 percent of the gross earnings – to help cover the cost of moving the ship.

Whatever problems may have been encountered en route, the *Queen Mary's* welcome to Long Beach was spectacular. While it was still off the coast of Baja, a new Douglas DC-9 jet with Douglas executives and city officials on board buzzed the ship and flower-bombed it with red and white carnations. When the *Queen Mary* approached the harbor on December 10, 1967, she was surrounded by an estimated 5,000 small craft which escorted her into her berth. Scores of private aircraft flew over, waggling their wings in welcome. People in boats pulled alongside and begged souvenirs from obliging passengers and crew members and were bombarded with a hail of objects, from pillows, towels, and blankets to soup tureens, life jackets, and silverware, until customs officials put a stop to the nonsense. After the ship was signed over, the city was able to recoup thousands of dollars from auctioning off the left-over booze and tobacco in the ship's spirits locker. The cache included 2,158 fifths of Scotch, 711 bottles of gin, 292 bottles of rum, 222 bottles of cognac, 648 bottles of assorted liqueurs, 3,220 bottles of champagne, 6,790 bottles of assorted wines, 713 bottles of vermouth, 120,497 cans of beer, 16,414 bottles of ale and stout, and a large amount of cigars, cigarettes, and tobacco.

The excitement and shine of that day wore off in the weeks and months to come. There were problems – big problems. Union workers from the AFL-CIO Maritime Trades Department picketed the ship two months after it arrived in Long Beach, demanding for themselves the work that was being done by civil service workers on the ship. The city responded that the *Queen Mary* had been decommissioned and was no longer a ship, but a building. The controversy held up plans to put the ship in the Navy Dry Dock for repairs to its hull. The red stacks on the ship were so degraded that they had to be replaced by replicas. Cost of converting the ship turned out to be significantly more than anticipated. By the regular city election in June 1969, the ship had become an issue – with some challengers charging that the purchase had been a boondoggle of monstrous proportions that was costing millions.

Meanwhile, the port had begun work on a thirty-three-acre landfill with access roads to what would be the permanent mooring for the historic and expensive ship. A bridge from downtown across the Los Angeles River flood control outlet – renamed Queensway Bay – was completed in 1970, connecting Magnolia Avenue to the port and the permanent site for the *Queen Mary*. The ship would remain controversial, but in the years to come its role as a symbol of the city would remain strong.

Not everything proposed during the 1960s worked out. For instance, in 1962 there was a plan proposed to hold a "World Peace through World Trade" World's Fair on the 311-acre landfill that would become known as Pier J. The fair, to be held in 1966-1967, was expected to draw 40 million visitors. The executive director of the exposition was former Kansas Governor Fred Hall, and Del E. Webb Corporation would oversee construction of the fair. But by the time a year had passed, the Harbor Commission had lost faith in Hall and his project. The idea was shopped around to other cities for a while, but it never went further than that.

A plan to build twin twenty-five-story towers on port property near the Port Administration building was also proposed and accepted in 1962. One of the towers would be a 600-room hotel, the other a World Trade office building. The towers were to be erected by June 1964. In the summer of 1965, with no construction yet underway, the Harbor Commission gave developer International Towers Inc. its final "put up, or shut up" lease extension. By 1966, the project was just another forgotten dream.

In 1969, there was an idea to build a regional airport on the seaward side of the breakwater. Backers of the plan said that building an airport in the ocean would largely eliminate any noise problems, but that it would still put the airport close enough to be convenient. Passengers and air cargo could be transported to the mainland over a bridge. The downside was the cost of the project and the fact that visibility and weather off the coast would be a problem. Needless to say, that never happened either.

Committing to Containers

The promise of containerization for moving cargo may have seemed immediately apparent, but that doesn't mean that everyone jumped on the idea. Sea-Land Service and Matson Navigation had led the way, building container ships and profiting from the quick turnarounds and ease of cargo handling, but most companies and some ports were not ready for that bold a commitment without somebody else testing the concept over time. Some companies stuck their toe in the water – mixing containers on deck with general cargo in the hold – to see if it was feasible. While some ports held back because of the investment containers would take in port infrastructure, the Port of Long Beach was not a part of the wait-and-see crowd. At the end of 1969, it committed itself to containers when it signed a contract with Sea-Land Service to build a $30 million, 120-acre container terminal with eight container cranes on the wharf. It also signed contracts with Transocean Gateway Corporation for a terminal that would function as the West Coast end of a railroad "land bridge" between the east and west coasts. By using trains to transport the ocean cargo across country, the company could avoid the Panama Canal and move freight more quickly to where it needed to be.

The Port of Long Beach and its Los Angeles sister were in a perfect position to profit from containerization. The two ports were located on the growing Pacific Rim of nations at a time when manufacturing was beginning to move to Asia. They had a large population of consumers and industry in relatively close proximity, which meant that when the cargo arrived, much of it would be within a few miles of its final destination. The two ports had ample rail and highway connections for the cargo that had to travel across country, and they had land on which to stage the containers for pickup and loading. Although it may seem in historical hindsight that the choice to commit to containerization was easy, at the time it required a level of political and intellectual will to take the first steps.

Containerization changed the tide for some ports. San Francisco, which at one time was by far the dominant California port, withered with the coming of containerization. It did not have the land or easy access to rail and highway connections, or even the kind of population density that Southern California had. Oakland did, and Oakland became the dominant Bay Area port, while San

Francisco reluctantly turned its back on its industrial waterfront. The Port of San Diego also lacked the kind of rail access, highway infrastructure, and population density of Long Beach or Los Angeles.

The longshoremen in Long Beach and Los Angeles had never been proponents of the Mechanization and Modernization Agreement that their international president Harry Bridges had negotiated in the early 1960s. They continued to show their displeasure through sporadic job stoppages – sometimes to support the Teamsters, and sometimes in opposition to Teamster union members doing jobs the longshoremen felt were their own.

By the end of the decade, containerization was here to stay. But not everybody was yet convinced it was a good idea.

Dirty Waters

By the late 1960s, the ports of Long Beach and Los Angeles were both under pressure to do something about the polluted water in their harbors. It was estimated that about 1 million barrels of wastewater was being dumped into the harbor every day from upstream sources and from sources in or near the harbor itself. Fish life in the harbor was almost non-existent. The oil industry was under pressure from the federal government and conservationists to control its waste. The Federal Water Pollution Control Act of 1965 required the states to file acceptable water quality standards with the federal government.

Long Beach had experienced pollution problems stretching back to the early part of the century. Ships would discharge oily waste into the water. Oil companies would store crude in open reservoirs, and when it rained the excess would spill into the street and flow into the ocean. In the ensuing years, it had only gotten worse. Enforcement of the Federal Water Pollution Act was lackluster.

The Los Angeles Regional Water Quality Control Board tried to be "practical" when it came down to enforcing water quality rules, Executive Director Raymond Hertel told a reporter in 1967.

"Our guiding legislation is not opposed to discharges per se," he said. "To many people a discharge of any type is pollution. Well, I'm a conservationist myself, but not to the point where I want to plug up the sewers or stop industry. This might end up costing the public a lot of money."

Later that year, the Los Angeles County engineer, the general manager of the County Sanitation District, and the chief engineer of the Flood Control District filed a report asserting that the water at the two ports was not polluted. The report conceded, however, that the harbor water was "obviously degraded by discharges of industrial waste."

There was a difference between polluted and degraded, the report argued. "There is little circulation of water in the inner harbor and oxygen levels there are too low to support marine life, but that's beneficial. It means wooden pilings are less likely to be eaten away by marine organisms, that the growth of barnacles on the hulls of vessels is inhibited, and that the water used for industrial purposes does not contain sea life," the report said. If the harbor waters were cleaned to the point that marine life could thrive, it "would cause private industry and public agencies to expend many millions of dollars."

In January 1968, Long Beach challenged the Water Quality Control Board to hold the Long Beach inner harbor to the higher standard expected in the outer harbor. Port General Manager Charles Vickers said he had no objections to protecting fish and wildlife in the inner harbor. This was in sharp contrast to the Port of Los Angeles, which was worried that cleaner water would result in tiny marine organisms attacking wood pilings – something that the Port of Long Beach didn't have to worry about since it had replaced almost all its wooden pilings with concrete ones when it rebuilt after subsidence.

The willingness to clean up the port environment was part of the Long Beach legacy, Perhaps that was because Long Beach had been a resort town before it was a port town. Or maybe it was the fact that Long Beach had to struggle, first with being clogged beneath a tide of mud in the early years and then with sinking below the sea during the subsidence years. Whatever the reason, the port seemed committed to attack its problems squarely and directly, whether the challenge was business or environmental.

It was part of the Long Beach culture.

Chapter Sixteen:
No Longer the Little Sister

If the 1960s had been a time of exuberance and excess, the 1970s were an era of recovery and retrenchment. During the '60s, people had heard the cries for rebellion against the establishment, for the questioning of authority, and for the joys of the communal experience. But what they had seen were riots, assassinations, more crime, and a dramatic change in the moral standards of young people. By the 1970s, flower power was out, getting a job and earning your keep was in, and the silent majority was once again in charge.

The 1970 census showed more than 200 million people living in the United States, up 13.4 percent over 1960. Of women 16 years and older, 43.3 percent were in the workforce, up from 37.7 percent ten years earlier. Unemployment was 4.9 percent and inflation was at 5.7 percent.

President Richard Milhous Nixon beat down a challenge by peace candidate Eugene McCarthy in 1972 to win a second term in one of the most lopsided presidential election victories in history. His triumph was short-lived. Vice President Spiro Agnew was forced to resign from office in 1973 as part of a plea bargain after being accused of bribery, extortion, tax fraud, and conspiracy. The Watergate scandal, the ensuing attempts at a cover-up, and the revelations about misuse of power, forced the president to also resign in 1974, less than two years after being re-elected. Nixon was succeeded by Agnew's replacement, Vice President Gerald Ford, who pardoned the president for any criminal acts he may have committed. Forty-three others convicted and jailed for their parts in the conspiracy were not so lucky. Ford was beaten in the 1976 election by the former governor of Georgia, a peanut farmer named Jimmy Carter.

It was a time when America started to clean up its environmental act. The first Earth Day was held in 1970, the Environmental Protection Agency was created by the Nixon administration that same year, and catalytic converters to reduce the emission of dangerous exhaust gases became commonplace on new cars in 1975. In 1979, a near meltdown of the nuclear power plant at Three-Mile Island doomed dreams of a using nuclear power as a clean source of energy.

The war in Vietnam had become a lengthy morass that seemed unwinnable, and an honorable peace seemed just as elusive. It was the first war to be televised on the nightly news. The U.S. bombed Hanoi, slipped over the border into Laos and Cambodia, debated the shape of the table at which peace talks were to be conducted, and split politically between hawks and doves. There were demonstrations against the war and a refusal by some to do their military duty.

On May 4, 1970, members of the Ohio National Guard gunned down unarmed students during an anti-war demonstration at Kent State University. In thirteen seconds, sixty-seven rounds were fired, leaving four students dead and nine more wounded. The war ended for the U.S. in 1973 with a pullout of forces, but no victory. The military draft was ended that year as well. Two years later, Saigon fell as Americans watched on their television screens. Americans were not used to losing, and the trauma weighed heavily on the national psyche for years to come.

Terrorists representing causes rather than governments began exerting their deadly influence during the period. The Popular Front for the Liberation of Palestine hijacked five jetliners one day in 1970. During the 1972 Olympic Games in Munich, the terror group Black September captured and killed eleven members of the Israeli Olympic team. Five of the eight terrorists plus one German policeman were killed during an unsuccessful attempt to rescue the hostages. Mossad, the Israeli intelligence agency, later tracked down and killed other members of the group.

A group of Iranian students took over the American Embassy in Tehran in 1979, capturing and holding fifty-two Americans hostage for 444 days. A mission to free the captives and return them to the United States failed when some of the helicopters required to carry out the rescue turned out not to be operational. During the course of aborting the mission, one of the helicopters and a transport plane collided, killing eight servicemen. In the wake of Vietnam, it further damaged U.S. prestige and President Carter's chances for re-election.

The United States recognized Communist China; the USSR invaded Afghanistan, and India got the nuclear bomb. Pol Pot and his Khmer Rouge took over Cambodia in 1975 and implemented policies that during the next four years resulted in the death of 1 million to 3 million of his countrymen. Revolutionary Chinese Communist leader Mao Zedong – traditionally written as Mao Tse Tung – died in 1976, and Margaret "Maggie" Thatcher became the first woman Prime Minister of the United Kingdom in 1979.

President Nixon, in an attempt to control inflation, announced a wage and price freeze in 1971. The result was long lines in supermarkets and butcher shops as farmers and ranchers shut off supplies rather than operate at a loss. In 1973, the Middle East oil-producing companies announced an embargo of oil to the United States and other Western nations in retaliation for U.S. military aid to Israel during the Yom Kippur War. In the United States, long gas lines and fuel shortages were common. A national 55 mph speed limit was imposed in order to save fuel. The 1974 Daylight Saving Time change was moved up to start in January, and gas was sold only to cars with even-numbered license plates on even dates and only to cars with odd-numbered license plates on odd dates. The oil embargo ended in 1974 after a negotiated settlement in which Israel returned some taken lands.

The economy limped through the next few years with high unemployment, high inflation, and low growth – a situation that became known as stagflation. By adding high unemployment and high inflation together, economist Arthur Okun created a new economic indicator – the Misery Index – a measurement more useful for its political bite than as an economic tool.

In 1979, a second oil crisis occurred – this one under President Carter – as a revolution in Iran cut off oil supplies from that nation. The lines at the gas station were back, and so was the sense of frustration and malaise. The president summed it up in a nationally televised "Crisis of Confidence" speech, when he told the nation, "We've always had faith that the days of our children would be better than our own. Our people are losing that faith, not only in government itself but in the ability as citizens to serve as the ultimate rulers and shapers of our democracy."

The first man walked on the moon in 1969, the 11th and last man – Eugene Cernan – in 1972. We went, we looked around, we picked up some rocks, and we never went back. The dream that had inspired a decade of scientific effort and achievement died almost as quickly as it had succeeded. Viking 1 landed on Mars in 1976, and Pioneer 11 buzzed Saturn and Jupiter and flew through the asteroid belt in 1979, but unmanned probes lack the drama and adventure of people venturing into space. The glory days of humans reaching out into the unknown quickly faded as did so much else during the decade.

America had always been about being inspired by the possibilities. The 1970s were a decade in which people were told to understand their limitations. Turn up the thermostat in the summer, turn down the heat in the winter, drive smaller cars, and take shorter showers. But despite the stagnant economy and the general sense of malaise, the groundwork was being laid for a new direction and a new age. Bill Gates and Paul Allen founded Microsoft in 1975; Steve Jobs and Steve Wozniak founded Apple Computers the following year. They, their companies, and other young nerds would change the world in the years to come.

Bar codes were introduced, floppy disks became common, and the first Cray supercomputer was installed at Los Alamos National Laboratory in New Mexico. A Georgetown University professor named Robert Ledley invented a computerized tomography scanning machine that could take three-dimensional X-ray pictures of people – a system more commonly known as a CAT scan.

The Sony Betamax gave people the power to record programs off the TV. The Sony Walkman allowed them to listen to recorded music as they went about their day. Rubik's Cubes challenged people to line up the colors, and arcade computer games introduced them to games such as Pong. A new supersonic jetliner, the Concorde, took to the sky, dramatically cutting the time for long-distance flights, but falling far short of its objectives.

Cable television expanded television choices. CNN offered around-the-clock news, and Home Box Office gave people the option of subscribing to commercial-free entertainment. ESPN began providing an entire menu of sports coverage.

America celebrated its 200th birthday in 1976 with fireworks, concerts, and by painting mailboxes and fire hydrants red, white, and blue. The event was marked by special coins, tall ships, appropriate rituals, presentations, and exhibits.

Drug guru Timothy Leary was sentenced to ten years in jail for possession of marijuana; newspaper heiress Patty Hearst was kidnapped by the National Symbionese Liberation Army, and San Francisco Mayor George Moscone and Supervisor Harvey Milk were shot and killed by former fellow Supervisor Dan White. White later received a reduced sentence after his attorney argued diminished capacity, partly the result of a fast-food binge the night before the murders. It became known as the "Twinkie Defense." U.S. Army Captain Jeffrey MacDonald, a Special Forces Army doctor, killed his pregnant wife and two small daughters at Fort Bragg, North Carolina. He later moved to Long Beach, where he worked as an emergency room physician at St. Mary Medical Center. He would finally be convicted nine years after his wife's and children's deaths, despite the fact that so many people found him charming.

Author Tom Wolfe introduced the term the "Me Decade" to describe the narcissistic and self-involved nature of the culture during the period – a period known for people yearning to find themselves as human beings, overcome their fears, and reach their full potential. Books such as *I'm OK, You're OK, To Have or to Be*, and *Jonathan Livingston Seagull* all encouraged people to look at their approach to life.

The Beatles broke up in 1970, and so did the Supremes. Rock singers Janis Joplin, Jimi Hendrix, and Jim Morrison all died of drug overdoses at age 27. Elvis Presley died in 1977, and disco became the rage.

Movies of the period included *Patton, A Clockwork Orange, The French Connection, Chinatown, The Godfather, The Towering Inferno, The Exorcist*, and *A Touch of Class*. Hank Aaron broke Babe Ruth's homerun record, and Secretariat won the Triple Crown.

The 1970s were a mixed bag for the nation. America, as much as its citizens, was seeking to find itself, to set a new course, to rejuvenate and replenish its spirit, and perhaps most of all, to move on to better days. It was not an easy decade, but few of them are.

A City and its Port

The port had left its mark on the city, just as the city had marked the port. The people of Long Beach had decided to become a port town in 1907 when 5,000 citizens turned out to raise $100,000 to purchase the property on which John F. Craig would build his shipyard. They decided again two years later, when they voted for a $240,000 bond issue to build a municipal wharf at the new harbor. Again and again over the years, the people of Long Beach would recommit their resources and their efforts to that decision. Those decisions had never been reached without opposition.

There were always people along the way who wanted Long Beach to remain the small, seaside resort city that they loved. But they were a minority. Long Beach had the right location for a port – adjacent to a wetland and to an already working port. It had ambitious leadership who had the vision to see the possibilities of progress and prosperity. There finally came a point when it no longer mattered whether the decisions had been correct or not. Long Beach was – and would remain – a port town. The lumber that built the early town came through the port. The port was an integral part of the city's economy. People worked at the port and supported their families with the wages they earned at the port.

But, as always, there was a price to pay. By the 1970s the port was a going concern, still providing jobs and prosperity for the community, and no longer dependent on taxes for support. But the California of the early days was over, and the village by the sea had become a thriving city – the sixth-largest in the state. Its downtown beach, which had once fronted the Pacific Ocean, by the 1970s looked out over Queensway Bay, a fancy name for the mouth of the Los Angeles River flood control channel. New land that was created from material dredged up from the ocean floor to expand the outer harbor sat directly across from downtown. The giant waves that once crashed against the shore from downtown to the Orange County line had been reduced to a fraction of their former grandeur by the federal breakwater, built to shelter the Navy fleet.

The decision was no longer whether the city should have a port. It had one. By the 1970s, the decision was how to manage a community asset that had been built and defended by the city and from which the city had profited. The people of Long Beach may have owned the port, but those people had changed over the years. Some had died, some had moved from Long Beach to the new tracts springing up across Los Angeles and Orange counties, and some new people had moved to Long Beach and adopted the city as their own. Although pockets of affluence remained overall, Long Beach was becoming less white, less middle-class, more blue-collar, and more bilingual.

The *Queen Mary* may have been greeted with wild acclamation when it arrived, but as the months drew on some began to see it as a larger-than-life symbol of what was wrong with Long Beach. The city bought the ship for $3.45 million in 1967 and estimated it would cost $5.5 million to convert it into a hotel-convention center-museum-tourist attraction. By 1970, the total cost had risen to $57 million. As the bills mounted and the opening date kept being pushed back, public frustration grew.

Political frustration with the legislators in Sacramento and at the Los Angeles county seat were also growing as the city poured much of its share of tidelands oil revenues into the project while the rest of the state struggled with tight budgets. The problematic process of restoring the *Queen Mary* had become a political time bomb. The longer the process went on, the more vulnerable the city was to criticism.

"Long Beach bought an old bucket, a rust bucket," Los Angeles County Supervisor Kenneth Hahn declared in 1969. "It's a monument to stupidity."

City leaders ignored the naysayers. Large corporations were interested in running the shipboard hotel, they said. Oceanographer Jacques-Yves Cousteau was going to open a Museum of the Sea within the ship. Diners would eat in the onboard restaurants, and conference attendees would use the ship's meeting facilities. Also planned was an aerial tram that would transport people from downtown Long Beach to the *Queen Mary* and back. The city expected to reap $3.5 million a year in rent and taxes from the ship. And when it was finally opened, the *Queen Mary* was expected to attract 3 million visitors a year. It was estimated that each of those visitors would spend $11, adding $33 million a year to the local economy.

That was the hope, but the promise was wearing thin. By June of 1970, the opening date had been pushed back to December. When December came, the *Queen Mary* was still at Pier E being worked on, and four of the nine city councilmen were facing a recall election. Although there were numerous issues on the table – airport expansion, fluoridation of the water, noise from speedboat races, and the presence of a napalm factory near a North Long Beach neighborhood – the *Queen Mary* was a focal point of outrage. The four targeted councilmen issued a joint statement, defending their actions regarding the *Queen Mary* and dismissing the cost overruns and delays as "temporary difficulties." The recall was rejected by voters – many of them alienated by the anti-establishment tenor of some recall leaders as much as the issues – but the political winds were clearly shifting.

The new demographics were catching up with the established order. Many of the middle-class, English-speaking residents that had dominated the community were moving away and being replaced with working-class, multilingual people. The old city leadership was finding its cozy ways of doing business being questioned, and not just by disgruntled residents.

The out-of-town media also had Long Beach in its crosshairs. In March 1971, the Los Angeles Times reported that putting a maritime museum on the ship was an afterthought – the only way that the city would be able to use tidelands

ROYAL REFIT: *After her arrival in Long Beach in 1967, the legendary ocean liner* Queen Mary *is transformed into a floating hotel and museum in a drydock at the Long Beach Naval Shipyard. Through financial ups and downs the ship has remained a symbol of the city.*

oil revenue to finance the venture. The decision to buy the ship had been a last-minute rush deal made with little due diligence or analysis, the Times reported. Neither the City Council nor the State Lands Commission, which oversees expenditure of tidelands oil money, had officially approved the deal before the bid was submitted.

The Times story was more than just about buying a ship, however. It was an examination of the power elite of businessmen and elected officials who ran the city.

Harbor Commissioner H.E. "Bud" Ridings – owner of the local Cadillac dealership – had come up with the idea of bringing the ship to Long Beach, but it wasn't clear who had made the final decision to go forward. City Manager John Mansell wasn't able to detail the circumstances of the decision, other than to say that it was a "consensus." He was part of the group that had made the decision to buy the *Queen Mary*. So were Ridings, Mayor Edwin Wade, Mansell's assistant Harry Fulton, and Sam Cameron, the general manager of the local Independent, Press-Telegram. A delegation of movers and shakers had been sent to London to bid on the ship. That delegation included Ridings and fellow Harbor Commissioner Llewellyn Bixby Jr., Vice Mayor Robert F. Crow, City Attorney Leonard Putnam, Fulton, Cameron, and Clark Heggeness, a member of the powerful Long Beach law firm of Ball, Hunt, Hart and Brown – the Brown being former Governor Edmund "Pat" Brown.

When the City Council was informed that the city had purchased the ship, some expressed surprise, although the city manager said that he had privately briefed all of the Council on the possibility. Councilman Emmet M. Sullivan, a former harbor commissioner, said he was amazed to discover the city was actually buying the *Queen Mary* and was openly critical of Mansell's handling of the purchase.

The city manager should have brought the proposal before "the entire Council to lay out the possibilities of feasibility of these things so they could be informed," Sullivan said. Councilman Paul R. Deats agreed. Nonetheless, the City Council belatedly approved the purchase the following day and authorized the city attorney to hire Ball, Hunt, Hart and Brown as special counsel for the purchase.

The Times also ran a sidebar story pointing out the various business connections between some city officials, newspaper executives, and *Queen Mary* contractors, including attorney George A. Hart, a partner in Ball, Hunt, Hart and Brown. At one point Hart was representing both the city and Diners Queen Mary Corporation, which was negotiating a master lease for concessions aboard the ship. Diners Queen Mary pulled out of the project after its parent company, Diners Club International, was sold. The new concessionaire was Specialty Restaurants Corp. Long Beach restaurateur David Tallichet, president of Specialty Restaurants, was a member of the Long Beach inner circle. Since his first restaurant, the Reef, was built on port-leased land, he had gone on to develop Ports O'Call and Whaler's Wharf shopping villages at the Port of Los Angeles, the Proud Bird Restaurant at Los Angeles International Airport, the Castaway restaurants in Burbank and Oakland, and various other theme restaurants around the country.

The local newspaper – whose top executives were among those running the city – offered a much kinder perspective on the *Queen Mary* purchase. Independent, Press-Telegram columnist Malcolm Epley commented on the matter the day following the Times' story.

> *Now nobody pretends that the QM Project was a model of management or planning. One-sided, hindsight critiques, presented in blockbuster style, may make damaging impressions as was obviously intended. But fair-minded people will realize that no project of such magnitude with city-state sponsorship could be wholly without merit, and that any coverage that pretends to tell it all, and virtually ignores the important favorable aspects, is a journalistic venture of questionable integrity. The QM project is an imaginative endeavor to lift L.B. above the crowd with a big and different attraction of world-wide interest. While the plan was pursued in good faith, there were no guidelines or precedents and it proved far more difficult, complicated and expensive than had been anticipated.*

The I,P-T also published an editorial refuting the Times story and imploring state assemblymen getting ready to look into the matter not to focus on mistakes that had been made. "To use the project's difficulties as an excuse for the state to attempt to seize Long Beach's share of tidelands oil revenue would be to pile injury on injury," the editorial said.

The Los Angeles Times stories on the social and political machinations in Long Beach continued over the months and years to come, as did the Independent, Press-Telegram's support of the local establishment. It would culminate in December of 1976 with an exposé by the Times of the I,P-T itself, entitled "Long Beach – Government by Newspaper." The article detailed the role of top executives at the newspaper as ex-officio decision makers in the affairs of the city.

In fairness, it must be noted that during most of its existence, the Los Angeles Times had been an unabashed politically biased, anti-union booster sheet – protecting the local business community and participating in its ventures in much the same way that it accused the Independent, Press-Telegram of doing. That had changed only after Otis Chandler took over the newspaper and determined to make it an objective and respected publication. Chandler, son of Norman and Dorothy Buffum Chandler, also had ties to Long Beach. His maternal grandfather was former Long Beach Mayor Charles Buffum.

It wasn't only out-of-town newspapers that were critical of Long Beach's handling of the *Queen Mary*. In 1971, State Legislative Analyst A. Alan Post called the project a "colossal mistake" based on a "capricious decision." Post claimed the city had illegally spent $6.6 million of tidelands funds on the *Queen Mary* to that date. State Lands Commission Executive Director F.J. Hortig estimated the figure closer to $8 million. Walter J. Quinn of the state auditor general's office said the city's overspending of tidelands oil revenue money on the *Queen Mary* resulted in the port having to issue $30 million in bonds to finance development of Pier J.

In May 1971, the Assembly Ways and Means Committee, chaired by Assemblyman Willie Brown, amended the state budget to send a message to the State Lands Commission and to Long Beach. If the State Lands Commission authorized any further expenditures of oil funds on the *Queen Mary* – conditionally or otherwise – the State Lands budget would be automatically cut by $500,000. In September 1974, the State Lands Commission finally reached a settlement with Long Beach on the issue of oil revenues.

Long Beach got its ship, but the political price it paid was almost as steep as the financial one.

A Major Gateway

Despite the controversy over the city's acquisition of the *Queen Mary*, the Port of Long Beach continued to gain reputation and business as a major trade gateway. Charles L. Vickers had retired in 1969 as general manager after fourteen years as the port's chief executive. He had been succeeded by Assistant General Manager Thomas J. Thorley, an engineer-turned-administrator who had joined the port in 1958.

Total tonnage moving across Long Beach docks in the 1970 fiscal year was 22,188,939 tons, up from 10,285,868 tons ten years earlier, but still less than the 25,937,196 tons moved at the Port of Los Angeles. That would soon change. By the 1973 fiscal year, Long Beach squeaked ahead of Los Angeles for the first time in history with 26,195,071 to 26,146,304 tons.

Toyota Motor Sales set a record at its Long Beach terminal in 1970, when it unloaded 2,080 Corona cars from the Toyota *Maru 10*, a new type of car carrier in which the cars are driven on and off the ship rather than lifted on and off by crane. The Toyota *Maru 10* was a "pure car carrier" – unlike the general cargo ships that had been used to transport vehicles. This was not a new concept. Ferries had been transporting people and vehicles over short distances for years. But the new ships – known as RORO ships for Roll-On, Roll Off – were transporting new cars across the ocean. The eight-ship Toyota fleet was owned and operated by the Kawasaki Kisen Kaisha, Ltd. shipping line – better known as "K" Line.

The following year, Toyota signed a contract with Long Beach-based Atlas Fabricators Inc. to manufacture, assemble, and paint truck beds for imported Toyota's Hi-Lux trucks at the company's twenty-acre plant. Atlas Fabricators had been targeted by protesters in the late 1960s and early 1970s after it leased space at its plant to American Electric Co., which manufactured napalm for the government. The napalm contract had since expired. Toyota bought Atlas in 1974 and renamed it Toyota Auto Body California – better known as TABC. It operates on Paramount Boulevard in North Long Beach.

Development at the port continued through the decade. The port broke ground on the Sea-Land Services terminal in January 1970. The eighteen-acre Pier J container terminal being used by Sea-Land was phased out and replaced by a new 100-acre facility on Pier G. Crescent Terminals Inc. signed a ten-year lease for 1,200 feet of wharf and 200,000 feet of transit sheds on Pier F to accommodate the eight-ship fleet of the Tokyo steel shipping company Toko Kaiun Kaisha. In October 1970, the six-lane Queensway Bridge, connecting downtown to the port, opened and provided direct access from downtown to the outer harbor and the *Queen Mary* site.

There had been a plan to homeport the *Queen Elizabeth* – a sister ship to the *Queen Mary* – in Long Beach as a floating international university. The Queen Corporation, organized by a group of Philadelphia businessmen, had purchased the *Queen Elizabeth* in 1968, planning to turn her into a floating hotel in Port Everglades, Florida. When that plan fell apart, Chinese shipping executive C.Y. Tung, founder of Orient Overseas Container Line (OOCL), bought the ship at auction. He signed a memorandum of understanding with Chapman College in Orange County to use the ship to expand the school's World Campus Afloat program.

BOXED TO GO: *The Pier G Sea-Land terminal moves cargo in containers shortly after its 1972 opening. Containers first came to Long Beach a decade earlier, but it took some years for standards to be established and a fully containerized terminal to be built.*

CROSS-OCEAN FERRY: *Toyotas are driven off an early RORO (Roll-On, Roll-Off) cargo vessel sometime in the '70s. The RORO ships, specialized car carriers, replaced general cargo ships for long ocean voyages.*

The ship – to be renamed the *SS Seawise University* – would be based in Long Beach, but embark on five voyages a year as part of the educational program. The ship was to be retrofitted as a school in Hong Kong before sailing to Long Beach. Unfortunately, while anchored in Victoria Harbour with the renovation almost complete, the *Queen Elizabeth* caught fire. Arson was suspected, since several blazes broke out simultaneously onboard the vessel, but nothing was ever proven. The *Queen Elizabeth* was destroyed by the blazes and the water used to fight the fire caused her to roll over on her side. The remains were later scrapped.

Meanwhile, as the Port of Long Beach worked to improve its infrastructure, there was one old relic that stood stubbornly in the way. Howard Hughes' old airplane, the H-4 Hercules Flying Boat – better known as the Spruce Goose – remained in its hangar on Pier E, where it had been locked away ever since its first and only flight in 1947. The port had been threatening to evict the plane since 1956, but the Goose remained steadfastly in place through the 1950s, the 1960s and right up into the 1970s. In February 1972, the port demanded that Hughes move the aircraft off port property by March 1973 and restore the site for development as a deep-water tanker terminal. In August 1972, the port relented and gave the Spruce Goose a lease for another two years in exchange for a rent increase from $3,000 a year to $100,000. Three years later, the Goose was once again facing eviction, and once again received a stay of eviction until July 1976. The port warned Hughes' Summa Corporation, which held the lease, that although the port had no immediate need for the site, sooner or later it would.

The Spruce Goose was more than just the biggest airplane in the world. It was Howard Hughes' obsession. Moving it from Culver City to Long Beach in 1946 had been a major production. Moving it again thirty years later would be monumental. For the time being, it remained in its solitary home on Terminal Island. Los Angeles Times reporter Don Dwiggins ventured to the edge of poetic license when he described the scene in a 1971 Spruce Goose feature story.

> Pier E in Long Beach Harbor is a lonely place. Creaking oil wells and croaking fog horns accompany a ballet of swaying gantry cranes. At night, ghostly green lights filter from a massive structure squatting on the Terminal Island waterfront. Behind a barbed-wire fence and a sign reading "Company Secret" sits a guard shack occupied by armed men who study you on closed circuit television if you come too close.

In a somewhat less dramatic fashion, the thirty-seven-year exclusive port rail contract between the port and the Southern Pacific Railroad came to an end in 1971. The end of the contract allowed the Union Pacific and Santa Fe railroads to bring their long-haul trains into the port's bulk-loading facilities. Previously the Southern Pacific provided all switching services in the port for the other two railroads.

By 1971, Long Beach was the dominant port in the nation for citrus exports – an appropriate, if unrelated, circumstance given the legacy of Redlands citrus investors in the port's formative years. Sunkist Growers doubled their exports through the port that year with a new two-ship-a-week service to Europe. The company had previously been sending its European-bound oranges and lemons across country by rail to East Coast ports for export.

The Atlantic Richfield Co. began regular service between Alaska and Long Beach in 1972 – using the *Arco Prudhoe Bay* to transport Alaskan crude oil south. It was pumped from ARCO's oil terminal in Long Beach to the company's refinery in Carson for processing into low-sulfur fuel – mostly to be used to generate electricity at Southern California Edison and Los Angeles Department of Water and Power plants. The schedule called for the *Prudhoe Bay* to deliver 550,000 barrels of low-sulfur crude to Long Beach every thirteen days.

The Soviet Union's first fully containerized vessel in the Pacific trade, the Fesco Line's *MV Alexander Fadeyev*, called in Long Beach in May 1973. It was the first of several Soviet ships to call at the port that year. In December, the first cargo ship in twenty-five years from the People's Republic of China arrived in Long Beach to take on 10,000 bales of cotton destined for Shanghai. The *MV Caspian Sea* break-bulk cargo vessel was chartered by the government-owned China Ocean Shipping Co., better known today as COSCO.

At times during the 1970s, the port became the scene of international events over which it had no control. Over the years, the fishing industry in Southern California had invested in larger and faster boats in an effort to extend their range beyond local waters. This sometimes led to conflict with foreign governments over how far their authority extended off the coast. In January 1971, the Ecuadorian government seized California tuna fishing boats for violating the 200-mile territorial limit it had established as its jurisdiction. The United States only recognizes a twelve-mile limit.

Over the next few months, when more boats were seized, held until hefty fines were paid, and then released, tensions rose. The United States cut off aid to Ecuador, but still the seizures continued. In March, about 500 protesters showed up at the Port of Long Beach and blocked the unloading of $500,000 worth of Ecuadorian bananas being imported by the Standard Fruit and Steamship Co. The ILWU longshore workers and Teamster truck drivers refused to cross the picket line, and the unloading of the perishable cargo came to a halt. The shutdown lasted only two days. The ILWU and Teamsters agreed to return to the job after the company agreed to pay their members for the time they were not on the job. The main cost to Standard Fruit was the market value of the bananas, which decreased each day they remained off supermarket shelves.

During this period, the port was not merely focused on moving cargo. It planned to develop the outer-harbor shoreline along Queensway Bay to take advantage of recreational and other business opportunities. In 1971, the Harbor Commission approved a plan in principle to develop a commercial complex along the shoreline with two major hotels, offices, shops, and restaurants. One of the hotels would be a Hilton, the other an ITT-Sheraton. The following year it granted a sixty-year lease to Feinberg Development Corporation of St. Louis for 18.8 acres to be developed with a 200-room Hilton, a seafood restaurant, and convention complex at the harbor end of the Queensway Bridge. The following month, the City Council approved the development by M.J. Brock and Sons, Inc., of a 400-room Sheraton Hotel, not in the port, but across from the *Queen Mary* on the downtown side of Queensway Bay.

While the port was making plans to welcome visitors at new upscale restaurants and shops near the *Queen Mary*, it was closing down a complex of funky and low-scale restaurants and shops on Pier F. Pierpoint Landing – which had entertained local folks since 1948 with its seal tank, kiddie rides, bars, restaurants, outside picnic tables, and charter fishing trips – was closed by the port in 1971 to make room for a Humble Oil supertanker terminal. The original plan was for land to be made available for Pierpoint tenants to relocate to the end of Channel Three, off Pico Avenue near the original municipal wharf. But, by the end of the year, Pierpoint Landing was history. The proposed supertanker terminal was never built.

Trouble in San Pedro

Even though Long Beach was battling outside forces critical of how it was spending tidelands money on the *Queen Mary* and putting down a revolt by dissident citizens, the power structure of the city remained intact during the 1960s and '70s, and the port continued to prosper and grow during the period. But, while the Port of Long Beach was setting cargo records and developing new infrastructure, its sister port across the bay in San Pedro was in the middle of a politically painful period.

Los Angeles was involved in a scandal over plans for a World Trade Center to be built on Terminal Island. The problems in Los Angeles were predominantly within the family, with the City Council on the warpath over how the mayor and port officials were conducting business.

The idea of building a high-rise World Trade Center at the L.A. port came from San Sebastian Development Co., owned by Los Angeles Human Relations Commissioner Keith Smith. In 1967, a contract to develop the World Trade Center was awarded to Smith's company without competitive bidding, and without checking the company's credit or requiring it to post a performance bond. An analysis prepared by L.A. City Administrative Officer C. Erwin Piper strongly questioned the company's financial condition and its ability to perform. That resulted in a high-level meeting attended by Piper, all five Los Angeles harbor commissioners, a deputy mayor, another aide from Mayor Sam Yorty's office, and other city officials. The delegation attacked Piper's report and pressured him to change it. He refused. When the port's real estate manager recommended that the project be subject to competitive bidding, he was demoted.

With San Sebastian Development teetering on the edge of bankruptcy, the L.A. Harbor Commission approved a reassignment of the lease to Trade Center Development – a company with no assets or liabilities, whose application before the California Corporations Commission was still pending.

After a Los Angeles Times exposé in October 1967 detailing business dealings by four of the five L.A. harbor commissioners with developer Smith, an investigation was launched by the county grand jury. The jury returned an indictment of developer Smith and three of the harbor commissioners in December of that year. The body of the fourth harbor commissioner involved in the scandal, Board President Pietro Di Carlo, was found floating in the harbor near the old ferry building three weeks after the Times story broke. Di Carlo, father-in-law of Assemblyman Vincent Thomas, had reportedly been despondent over the newspaper story. It was not clear whether his drowning had been a suicide or an accident.

The three accused harbor commissioners – George D. Watson, Karl L. Rundberg, and Robert "Nick" Starr – were later convicted on bribery charges. Watson's bribery conviction was dismissed in December 1968, although he was fined $1,000 on a conflict-of-interest charge and barred for life from holding public office in California. Rundberg, a Los Angeles councilman before being appointed to the Harbor Commission, died in April 1969 of a heart attack at his Pacific Palisades home. Starr's conviction was later reversed after the Court of Appeal found that the trial jury had been improperly instructed. The district attorney in April 1971 finally dropped the charges against Starr because of evidentiary problems, stemming in part from Rundberg's death.

The only person not convicted in the scandal was developer Keith Smith, whose Long Beach lawyer, Joseph Ball of Ball, Hunt, Hart and Brown, had gotten a change of venue for the trial to San Francisco. The prosecution of the case was weakened when the judge ruled that a tape – inadvertently made on an automatic recorder Smith had installed – was inadmissible. Smith bragged on the recording that he controlled four of the five commission votes, that the contract to build the World Trade Center was ensured because of "a political decision that emanates from the mayor's office" and referred to "cutting the pie" with city bureaucrats. An attempt by Smith after his acquittal to have his World Trade Center contract restored was later denied.

The World Trade Center scandal and other missteps by the Los Angeles Harbor Commission resulted in a feud between the City Council and the Commission. Some on the Council felt that the harbor board and its senior executives were not only inept, but also devious. The harbor board responded by demanding that the councilmembers offer proof of any wrongdoing, instead of just making general accusations. The harbor commissioners even considered a move to censure the City Council over the Council's questioning of the board's handling of harbor pollution – a somewhat unusual response since the board members are all appointed and rank lower in the political pecking order than the elected councilmembers. Councilmembers called for a change in harbor management that would start with the Commission and go down to the senior executives. The new commissioners claimed they were unfairly being lumped in with the former corrupt commissioners.

In an effort to discuss the issues in a calm and rational manner, the Harbor Commission set up a meeting with the City Council in April 1970. It was supposed to be a closed-door meeting with no press, but since the entire Harbor Commission was there along with eleven of the fifteen councilmembers, it was legally impossible to bar the media. The meeting turned out to be anything but calm and rational, turning quickly into a shouting match between the two sides. Two of the councilmembers, Ernani Bernardi and Louis Nowell, accused the commissioners of not doing more to merge the L.A. port with the Port of Long Beach next door – a move Bernardi said was necessary in order to put the Port of Los Angeles on a profitable basis.

The harbor commissioners agreed that a merger made sense for Los Angeles, but said that Long Beach was not interested and had declined to even discuss such a move. Nowell said he had heard that argument before, but that Los Angeles needed to support the passage of legislation in the state Capitol to force the merger.

Later that same year, the L.A. City Council voted to put a City Charter amendment on the ballot that would allow the city to transfer funds from the departments of Airport, Water and Power, and Harbor to the city's general fund. A thirty-page opinion by the city attorney's office concluded that moving Tidelands Trust revenues to city coffers would be both illegal and improper. Not only would such an action be opposed by the State Lands Commission, it would also threaten the harbor's ability to sell revenue bonds.

The Los Angeles family feud between the Harbor Department and its critics on the City Council simmered on through the months to come as the Port of Long Beach continued to expand its business. By 1973, Los Angeles voters were ready for a change. They elected a new mayor, retired Los Angeles cop Tom Bradley, to replace Mayor Sam Yorty in the city's top job. During his campaign, Bradley had excoriated Yorty for his frequent trade trips to foreign countries, supposedly to drum up business for the harbor. In the eleven years from 1961 to 1972, tonnage through the Port of Los Angeles had increased only 2 percent, while tonnage over Long Beach docks had risen 105 percent, Bradley noted. "The mayor," candidate Bradley declared, "should be protecting the jobs of men and women in Los Angeles, not playing footsie around the world with foreign officials who only care about selling us cheaper goods that put our manufacturers out of business because they can't compete."

A report prepared by the Los Angeles port staff revealed that Long Beach was spending less than a third as much money and man-hours on trade missions as Los Angeles. But L.A. Harbor Commission President John Kilroy said that since Long Beach had begun with lower base numbers than Los Angeles, a higher percentage increase in trade was not that significant. Other commissioners pointed out that Long Beach had more wharfage, more cargo-handling facilities, and deeper water.

The newly elected Bradley ordered a port audit after complaints by some harbor commissioners that top port executives who reported to them were both incompetent and arrogant. Those executives had failed to provide commissioners with adequate information, resulting in approval of unsuccessful projects, the commissioners said. Most of the complaints were directed against port General Manager Bernard J. Caughlin and Chief Harbor Engineer Lawrence L. Whiteneck. The port's chief executive was accused of being a one-man gang who was contemptuous of the board he served.

The common thread running through the complaints over management of the Los Angeles Harbor was the comparison of Long Beach's success to Los Angeles' failure. Return on investment at the Los Angeles Port was only 3.1 percent, less than what was needed to service the revenue bond debt. Return on investment in Long Beach was 9.1 percent. Examples of Los Angeles projects that had been bungled included building a passenger terminal promoted as the Grand Central Station of ocean travel at the same time that airplanes were replacing ships, and building a bulk-loading terminal after consultants warned that there was not enough demand to warrant it. Passenger terminals in Long Beach were used for both people and cargo. When passengers arrived, they were serenaded by the Long Beach Municipal Band. When freight arrived, owners were provided with dockworkers and facilities for discharging and loading cargo.

By the end of the year – before the L.A. port audit was made public – Bradley shook things up. General Manager Caughlin chose to retire rather than be fired. The port board had voted to extend his contract for ninety days or until a suitable replacement could be found, but Bradley vetoed that. The mayor wanted Caughlin gone immediately. Bradley said in a statement that Caughlin had given the city a "distinguished period of service," but that it was time for him to go. Port Planning Director Donald A. Walsh was named assistant general manager. He would fill in for Caughlin until a permanent general manager could be hired. Caughlin's once-heir-apparent, Chief Harbor Engineer Whiteneck, was passed over.

The city's sixty-page Port of Los Angeles audit was released in February 1974. The audit slammed prior management for its poor judgment and lack of leadership. Its main recommendation, however, was that the Port of Los Angeles and the Port of Long Beach merge into a single entity. Joining the two ports would eliminate duplication of expensive facilities, end costly competition, and streamline administration. The audit went on to detail how such a merged port might be organized.

The merger recommendation was opposed by three of the five Los Angeles harbor commissioners, who noted that Long Beach was not interested in merging and that a little friendly competition was good for both ports. However, they did favor the need for closer cooperation by the two ports in attacking common issues. Bradley eventually told the harbor commissioners to forget about a merger of the two ports.

Thinking Inside the Box
The benefits of containerization were apparent almost from the start with the exception of some naysayers, who warned that it was an untested concept that might work out in a limited way in narrowly defined coastal trade routes. But once Sea-Land Services and Matson Navigation led the way, others were quick to follow. One problem, however, was the need to standardize the containers themselves.

Sea-Land used a thirty-five-foot container because it worked for the type of cargo the company moved. Matson used a twenty-four-foot container because it worked well for delivering small shipments directly from the port to multiple locations. But that meant that Sea-Land containers could not be transported in Matson ships or unloaded by Matson cranes and vice versa. If each shipping line had its own size and type of containers, much of the advantage to be realized by shipping cargo in containers would be lost.

People in the business were talking about establishing a standard for containers as early as 1958, but it was more complicated than it seemed. It wasn't just finding the right size containers for ships. It was also finding the right size for transporting the containers by truck and train, and it was finding a standard that would be able to meet the variety of trucking regulations in each state through which the containers would be transported. Operating a shipping line is a high-asset business. To require Sea-Land and Matson – container pioneers that had already invested millions in ships and cargo handling equipment – to adopt a new standard would put them at a competitive disadvantage to those just entering the field.

Size definitely counted, but there were other things to consider. Some containers had slots in the bottom to accommodate forklifts, some were lifted by hooks attached to eyes at the top, and some had spreader bars. There had to be a standard way of stacking the containers inside the ship and locking the stacks together. The containers at the bottom of a stack had to be able to support the entire stack above them, even in rough seas when the ship might be rolling and pitching. The various companies all had patented locking devices that would attach the containers to one another and then attach them to a truck chassis, but what design should be picked as a standard, and how should the patent holder be compensated for the chosen design?

Of course, shipping lines were free to use whatever kind of containers they wanted, but it would both limit their ability to move the containers of other lines and make them ineligible for government subsidies toward building new ships. In 1965, Sea-Land's thirty-five-foot containers and Matson's twenty-four-foot containers accounted for two-thirds of all containers owned by U.S. shipping lines. Both companies wanted their size containers to be among the standard sizes finally chosen. Containerization had benefited both companies, but now they were ready to invest in new ships and new equipment, but they were reluctant to do so before a standard was established.

In 1964, the International Standards Organization adopted ten, twenty, thirty, and forty feet as the standard sizes for containers, but the debate continued. A ten-foot container proved to be too small. It took the same amount of time and work to unload one ten-foot container as one forty-footer; containers that small diluted the advantages of containerized cargo. The twenty-foot containers were too small for Matson's Hawaiian trade, and the thirty-footers were too big. Trucking companies hated the twenty-foot containers because it took one truck and one driver to move half as much freight as could be moved in a forty-foot container. Sea-Land complained that the cargo it transported in its thirty-five-foot containers tended to hit weight limits before the container was filled. Putting their typical cargo in a forty-foot container would mean its ships could carry fewer containers, and the containers it did carry would be only partially filled.

One by one the problems were hashed out, but it took time. And while the industry waited – wanting to know what the standard was before investing in new ships and equipment – the container revolution simmered. By 1970, the battle over container standards was finally winding down. Having a standard helped the industry, but the final mix of containers was set by the marketplace, not the government or some standardizing organization. Ten footers never caught on. Neither did thirty-footers. Twenty-footers won some acceptance in the marketplace for heavy cargos, but the most popular size became the forty-foot box. Containers and the ship's capacity to carry containers became measured by TEUs – twenty-foot equivalent units. A 10,000 TEU container ship could theoretically carry 10,000 twenty-foot containers or 5,000 forty-foot containers, sometimes expressed in FEUs – forty-foot equivalent units.

Nobody was 100 percent happy with the new standards, but having standards allowed shippers – the people importing and exporting the cargo – to load their freight into a container, put it on a truck or a train, transfer it to a ship, and send it anywhere in the world.

Converting fleets and terminals from general cargo-handling operations to containerized operations was expensive, but the rewards were substantial. From the 1969 fiscal year to the 1971 fiscal year, the number of containers coming through the Port of Long Beach rose from 17,000 to 50,000. The general cargo ships – some still using World War II-era designs – were facing a situation similar to that faced by sailing ships at the beginning of the era of steam-powered vessels. Shipping lines were forming joint ventures to finance construction of new all-container ships or the conversion of old ships to a hybrid mix of old and new. The company that began it all – Sea-Land Service – announced plans in 1970 for a huge container ship that would carry 1,200 containers on board. In December 1972, Zim Container Service, a one-year-old Israeli shipping line, arrived at the Port of Long Beach with the biggest single load of containers to ever call on the West Coast – 721.

For the Port of Long Beach and its Los Angeles sister, the container revolution was good news. The ports had the land area, the rail connections, the population, and a prime location on the booming Pacific Rim. The Port of San Francisco was not so fortunate. Its 6.5-mile-long waterfront was a narrow strip of land and warehouse piers bordering the downtown area. Its facilities were rotting and rusting. It did not have the land required for container yards or the easy rail and highway connections to the rest of the country. Transporting cargo from the waterfront through the narrow and hilly downtown streets posed a major dilemma. Soon ships were sailing beneath the Golden Gate, past San Francisco, to call at Oakland, across the Bay. By 1973, Oakland was handling two-thirds of the general cargo going into the Bay Area.

There were political denunciations of San Francisco port management for its poor judgment and failure to recognize the changes going on in the industry. There was even talk of merging the San Francisco and Oakland ports, but nothing ever came of it, primarily because there was nothing in it for Oakland. Much of the criticism of the San Francisco port was true – port management had been sleeping on the job – but most of the criticism and second-guessing about what would have kept San Francisco a bustling cargo port was just wishful thinking. The Port of San Francisco had a proud legacy, stretching back to before the Gold Rush, but it had been designed for sailing ships. San Francisco had history on its side, but history doesn't pay the bills. Containerization doomed San Francisco to its status as a minor West Coast port.

There were some glitches along the way to containerization, as there always are with disruptive new technology. Some California counties – Los Angeles, San Francisco, Contra Costa, Monterey, San Mateo, and Santa Barbara – began taxing containerized cargo under an 1819 U.S. Supreme Court ruling designed to protect American manufacturers.

The tax – part of the annual inventory tax – did not apply to break-bulk cargo unloaded by hand. The difference was between cargo in the original packaging, as opposed to repackaged cargo. Bottles of sake imported from Japan, for instance, would have to pay the inventory tax if the container were opened in California. The container was seen as the original packaging. Sake unloaded on a pallet, on the other hand, was not subject to the tax. In order to avoid the taxes, some California companies threatened to truck the containers to Arizona or Nevada, open them there, and then reload the goods into a truck for transport back to California. Others – including many Japanese companies faced with a choice between the Port of Seattle and the Port of Long Beach or Los Angeles – merely diverted their shipments to ports outside California. Taxing the containerized cargo was overturned in court in 1974, following an outcry from ports and importers.

There was a 1973 Federal Maritime Commission case that looked into complaints by some East Coast ports and the International Longshoremen's Association, which represented dockworkers on the Atlantic and Gulf coasts, over the rail "mini-bridge" being used to shuttle containerized cargo overland from coast to coast. Cargo from the Far East, principally Japan, destined for the eastern part of the U.S., would be offloaded at a West Coast port, and then sent by rail across country. The cost was about the same as taking it by ship through the Panama Canal, but the cargo arrived five days earlier. The same concept worked in reverse. European cargo bound for the West Coast would be discharged at an East Coast port and transported by rail to the West Coast. The problem was that the eastern part of the country was more populated than the West, and there was more cargo coming from the Pacific Rim to the East than coming from Europe to the West. The net result was that the mini-bridge service was costing Atlantic and Gulf coast ports business and costing dockworkers at those ports their jobs. The Port of Long Beach took a stand in favor of the mini-bridge; the Port of Los Angeles chose to remain neutral.

One of the arguments used by the mini-bridge opponents was that moving the cargo by ship through the Canal had less environmental impact than moving it across country by rail. Ships were cleaner than trains per ton of cargo, and trains caused cars to wait with their engines idling, burning up fuel and polluting the air at each grade crossing. Proponents of the mini-bridge reminded the FMC that its role was to regulate commerce, not environmental practices, but the agency took the environmental impact under advisement. It finally concluded in a 100-page report that the environmental differences were minimal, but it took until December 1975 to reach that decision.

In a relatively short period of time, containerization had become the preferred way of moving large quantities of cargo, and it had changed the world in the process. But clearly, not everybody was a winner.

Dissension on the Docks

The Mechanization and Modernization Agreement brokered by International Longshoremen's and Warehousemen's Union leader Harry Bridges had never been popular among longshoremen – especially those in Southern California. The waterfront had changed and many of those changes were not popular among the rank-and-file longshoreman. Some even felt that Harry Bridges had gone soft in his older years, had gotten too cozy with management, and had sold out the union members. The ILWU had always gotten what it wanted by fighting for it, not by compromising away their hard-won victories at the negotiating table. Many of the older members of the union had departed, taking their pension payoff as stipulated in the M&M agreement. The remaining younger members wanted an end to the agreement, more job security, and better pay.

As biographer Charles P. Larrowe put it, Bridges had gone from an angry labor radical to a labor statesman. The once-militant, left-wing unionist was seen by management in his later years as a stabilizing force on the West Coast waterfront. In 1970, his friend San Francisco Mayor Joseph Alioto appointed Bridges to the San Francisco Port Authority. Bridges had developed personal friendships with people he respected on the opposite side of the negotiating table. He retained a mistrust of government and an independence of thought when it came to politics, registering in turn as a Democrat, an Independent Progressive, and a Republican.

The sentiment for a strike among the rank and file was strong, with 96 percent of the workers voting to walk off the job. Although Bridges did not think striking was a good idea, there was little he could do to stop it. On July 1, 1971, the ILWU longshoremen shut down twenty-four West Coast ports, from the Mexican border to Canada. The impact of the strike was immediate. Companies that depended on the port had to lay off their own workers, and the ripple effect of those changes spread through the local economy, from fuel vendors to vehicle repair shops. The usual wharfage fees collected by the ports came to an end. Domestic car manufacturers got a slight boost because of disruption in the delivery of new foreign autos, but shippers had anticipated the strike and stockpiled extra

TRAFFIC JAM: *Ships wait to be unloaded outside the ports of Long Beach and Los Angeles during a three-month strike in the summer of 1971. By the time ILWU workers returned to the docks, 122 ships were standing by to offload cargo.*

inventory. Ships that once had called at West Coast ports diverted to ports along the Gulf Coast, to Vancouver in Canada, and to Ensenada in Mexico. Ensenada, the closest Mexican port to Southern California, welcomed the business, but it had only three berths, and one of the berths was too shallow for many of the ships.

The strike dragged on for weeks and then months. The crews on ships stranded at anchor off the coast spent restless days chipping old paint and laying down new, and watching television. Delivery of fresh water became an issue, with a refill of the ship's water tanks costing $1,000 – many times the amount usually paid for such service. The ships' garbage began to pile up with no easy way to dispose of it. A water taxi to transport crew members to town and back was $50 per round trip.

In October, President Nixon invoked the Taft-Hartley Act, ordering the strikers to return to work for an eighty-day cooling-off period. The dockworkers returned to the job with 122 ships at the Long Beach and Los Angeles ports waiting to offload or pick up cargo. Some ILWU steady men – skilled workers who are assigned to specific terminals instead of being dispatched through the union hall – quit their jobs in favor of working as regular longshoremen. Without the steady men manning the cranes and other machinery, the terminals were disabled. That raised the question of whether the steady men had a right to quit their jobs or whether it was a deliberate ruse to defy the government order – a difficult case to prove.

In the end, the steady men returned to work, and cargo continued to move through the ports, at least temporarily. In December, when the eighty-day period ended, the workers voted again on management's best offer – essentially the same offer that the union had turned down in October. Once again, the union turned it down.

On January 17, 1972, the union walked off the job again. Nixon called for Congress to enact a resolution to end the strike by binding arbitration in which the Secretary of Labor would appoint a three-man board that would hear both sides and pass down a decision. Under pressure to conclude the strike, the union returned to the bargaining table with Sam Kagel as a mediator. Kagel, a longtime arbitrator of issues between the ILWU and the employers, had in his younger days helped organize the 1934 waterfront strike in San Francisco. By February 8, the arbitration board had a tentative contract to take back to the rank and file. It was essentially the same contract that the union had turned down in October and again in December.

Despite being turned down twice, the final two-year contract offered a lot. Included was a 72-cent-an-hour raise, going up another 40 cents an hour in July 1972. The basic full-time longshoreman could earn $12,000 a year under the new contract with total medical and dental coverage for his family, and a $350-a-month pension. Even after the contract was approved by the rank and file, however, it still wasn't official. One more hurdle remained – getting approval of the government pay board. The pay board – along with a price commission and a committee on interests and dividends – had been set up by President Nixon to help control inflation.

The pay board was attempting to hold annual salary increases to no more than 5.5 percent. The wage increase in the new ILWU contract at 25.9 percent was almost five times that much. Bridges threatened to take the union back out on strike if the board cut the wage increases negotiated with the employers by as much as one cent. The union, along with other unions facing similar restrictions, took out full-page ads in major newspapers calling for approval of the ILWU's negotiated deal and noting that productivity on the docks had gone up 138 percent in the past decade, while labor costs per ton had dropped 30 percent. The pay board voted on March 17 to cut the pay hike negotiated by the union to 14.9 percent – much higher than the 5.5 percent ceiling the pay board usually imposed, but considerably lower than the union had negotiated.

Although Bridges had vowed to resume the strike if the pay board didn't approve the full amount, 135 days off the job had worn down the members. And so the strike was over. The longshoremen took what they got and went back to work.

Anchors Aweigh

The ink on the new longshore contract was barely dry in 1972, when Long Beach and its port suffered another blow. The Pentagon announced that it would lay off 875 civilian employees at the Long Beach Naval Shipyard as part of an economy and fleet-modernization program. The following year, the news was even worse. In April 1973, the Pentagon announced plans to close 274 military sites across the country, including the Long Beach Naval Station. Closure of the Naval Station meant 17,284 of 19,337 military personnel would be transferred out of the area – a huge loss to the local economy. The remaining military would consist of shipboard personnel en route to new assignments. The closure would also end 780 civilian jobs. Forty-seven ships homeported at Long Beach would be transferred to other Navy facilities.

The one bright spot was that the Long Beach Naval Shipyard – which the year before had lost 875 civilian jobs – would be hiring workers to fill 820 new positions. In addition, 220 civilian jobs at the Hunter's Point Naval Shipyard, which was also on the closure list, would be transferred from the Bay Area to Long Beach. Target date for the closures was June 30, 1974.

Long Beach's relationship with the Navy had already been changing. After President Nixon appointed Admiral Elmo "Bud" Zumwalt as Chief of Naval Operations in 1970, Zumwalt set about to make life easier for enlisted men, ease racial tensions within the service, and help boost enlistments and re-enlistments. He issued a series of policy directives, known as Z-grams, which changed long-standing Navy traditions.

Among the Z-grams was one authorizing enlisted men to keep civilian clothes on their ships. Before that, sailors had to wear their uniforms when they left the ship or the Navy station, and then rent a locker in town for their civvies. The locker clubs were a key part of the Sailors' Strip of bars, beaneries, pool halls, and porn shops that existed along Ocean Boulevard. When the sailors no longer needed a place to keep their civvies, they were free to go wherever they wanted as soon as they left the base, and the Navy-dependent businesses along the strip began to close down. In a way this was a good thing. Long Beach was desperate to improve its downtown area into a family-friendly place, something that was never going to happen as long as the Navy strip existed, but the short-term economic pain of losing all those sailor dollars was acute.

If there was a winner in the Navy's plan to close and realign its assets, it was San Diego. Thirty-one ships from Long Beach were reassigned to the Naval Station in San Diego, plus 11,000 more personnel, making it the No. 1 Navy base in the nation – a title that was once claimed by Long Beach. Those new assignments were expected to bring up to $100 million a year in paychecks to the community. Once the transfers were complete, San Diego would be home to 94,000 enlisted men and officers. San Diego Mayor Pete Wilson welcomed the news, noting that San Diego had always been receptive to the Naval community. "The people like the Navy because it has been such a good citizen," he said.

Long Beach had been a Navy town for more than six decades, but that time was coming to an end. It was a huge loss for Long Beach, but its Navy days weren't quite over yet.

Rise of Environmentalism
As a coastal city, Long Beach had always been concerned about water pollution, whether it was oil from wells spilling down streets and into the ocean or ships anchored off shore dumping oily bilge water into the sea. But as Southern California grew, more industries moved to the area, more ships called at the ports, and more trucks and trains hauled freight through the city. There were more people, driving more cars, living more miles from their jobs, and commuting through heavy traffic to work. More oil was dripped onto the streets, more industrial effluent spilled into drains, more trash was thrown in the gutter, and more exhausts were spewing lead and sulfur and soot into the air. It didn't take long until pollution of both the air and the water became intolerable.

By the late 1960s, the Los Angeles Regional Water Quality Board had set up a task force to look into what it would take to clean up the Long Beach and Los Angeles inner harbors. The task force consisted of nineteen members representing industry, government, and conservation organizations. At the time, the water in the two inner harbors was heavily polluted, fish life had all but disappeared, and even the barnacles had died off. The outer harbors were better, but only marginally. Discharge of oil and sewage from ships was prohibited, but common. Oil and toxic chemicals from ships and boat yards would run into the harbor water. Waste from the canneries would be flushed into the harbor, and upstream discharges of toxic wastes from refineries and industrial plants would flow through channels and drains down to the harbor. Identifying the problem was the easy part. Fixing it was more complicated.

In February 1970, the Los Angeles Harbor Commission asked its City Council to hold off on passage of an ordinance to bar ships from discharging wastes into the harbor, even though port executives had drafted the rule, and the board had approved it. The board had changed its mind after the Steamship Association of Southern California pointed out the problems with the proposed rule. To comply with the rule, every ship would have to install holding tanks – a process that would cost from $50,000 to $100,000 per ship and take up to two years. Alternately, the port could install sewer lines on the wharves that ships could connect to for dumping their waste – a project that would cost about $3 million. Or the ships could simply go next door to the Port of Long Beach, which had no such ordinance, or to any other port along the West Coast. It was the kind of dilemma that ports would have to deal with many times in the future as they attempted to clean up their local environments. Being the first to adopt environmental standards often put ports and their customers at a distinct competitive disadvantage.

Four-and-a-half years later, the Los Angeles City Council finally passed a tough ordinance banning the discharge of "sewage of any and all waste substances, liquid, solid or gaseous, or radioactive, associated with human habitation or from human, animal or fish origin" into the harbor. But shortly after the measure was passed, the Council got a panic call from L.A. port executives, who had been unaware that the item was on the agenda. It turned out that the port employee responsible for keeping track of Council actions was on vacation at the time, and nobody else had thought to check the agenda.

One of the reasons the ordinance had been delayed for so long was that everybody was waiting for federal regulations that would impose uniform standards for all ports. Those regulations were expected to pass within four months. If the L.A. Council could hold off, the federal rules would establish the same controls for all ports. The Council reversed itself, in effect un-passing the ordinance it had passed the day before.

Nobody was immune when it came to pollution. The state of California sued the Navy in 1970, accusing the Navy of spilling large quantities of oil off shore as well as in the waters of the Long Beach and San Diego harbors. The suit was aimed at publicly shaming the Navy into cleaning up its act, and it seemed to accomplish that end. Later that month, state authorities received an important weapon in their fight to clean up the harbor, when Federal Judge Warren J. Ferguson ruled that federal and local authorities had the right to seize foreign vessels if they polluted port waters. The case involved the *SS Bournemouth*, which had been seized by U.S. Marshals and state Fish and Game wardens after it spilled 400 gallons of bunker fuel at the Port of Long Beach.

The Port of Long Beach was taking its own steps to clean up the harbor. The port commissioned design of a special boat to clean floating trash and debris from the harbor. The Big Dipper was a $100,000 two-man, forty-foot-long catamaran with a hydraulic basket at the bow that would scoop up debris and deposit it in an on-deck bin. If the object was too heavy for the basket, a hydraulic crane would lift it out of the water. The Big Dipper was ugly, but it worked, picking up 180 cubic yards of junk from the water each month.

In 1972, California voters approved Proposition 20 – an initiative to establish a California Coastal Commission that would oversee development along a strip of land stretching 1,000 yards inland from the ocean, ensure that public access to the shoreline was preserved, and protect the marine environment. Robert F. Rooney, an economics professor at California State University, Long Beach, was elected chairman of the South Coast Regional Coastal Commission at its first meeting in 1973. Rooney, a former oil company executive, had opposed the Coastal Commission initiative as had the City of Long Beach.

The Coastal Commission went right to work. In June, the regional board approved a modernization plan for the Southern California Edison power plant on Terminal Island, but with stiff requirements attached. The plant would operate at an average capacity of 34 percent over a month unless air pollution authorities granted an exemption. The company was to conduct a study to see if freshwater cooling towers would be less environmentally damaging to marine life than the customary practice of releasing heated saltwater into the harbor.

The Supertanker Wars

By 1973 – in the midst of an oil crisis that had long lines of cars at every service station – there was pressure to build a supertanker terminal that would be able to service the largest tankers available and import large quantities of crude oil quickly. There were no ports in the nation that could handle tankers bigger than

150,000 dead weight tons. Dead weight tonnage is a measure of how much a vessel can carry, but not the ship itself. The capacity of supertankers of the time was 250,000-plus dead weight tons, so they had to enter U.S. ports partially laden.

The Army Corps of Engineers was conducting a study of the best place to put such a terminal. Possibilities included San Diego, San Clemente Island, the Long Beach and Los Angeles ports, El Segundo, Port Hueneme, and Estero Bay. It was an idea that didn't sit well with environmental groups and their allies at the state Capitol in Sacramento.

By 1975, a full-fledged war had begun over plans by Standard Oil of California to place the first supertanker terminal at Estero Bay – a scenic, unspoiled coastline along Pacific Coast Highway that includes the small town of Morro Bay. Thousands of visitors came to the area each year to relax, enjoy the views, and feel the sea breezes. The plan to build an oil terminal in such a place outraged environmentalists and offended other folks who might not have been opposed to such a project in an urban industrial area.

The plan was to build a floating platform called a mono-buoy that would be anchored offshore, and from which oil from a supertanker could be pumped through a 280-mile-long pipeline to the company refinery in Richmond, California. Standard already had a small tanker facility in the area that it had operated for forty-five years. In order to sweeten the deal, the company would agree to let Morro Bay annex a large parcel of company-owned land that would generate $174,000 a year in city taxes. The plan also included a $1 million cleanup system to deal with oil spills. The company even drafted an environmental impact report on the project – the first ever prepared for a supertanker facility. Opposition to the idea was overwhelming, and in 1975, Standard Oil quietly dropped the project.

Meanwhile, both the Port of Long Beach and the Port of Los Angeles had submitted separate proposals to Standard Oil of Ohio – known as Sohio – to develop a supertanker terminal at their own location. Neither port favored offshore mono-buoys because of the danger of spills in the open sea and the hazard they would pose to navigation. Both ports' positions were that if there were any spills, they would be much easier to isolate and control at a land-based terminal in a harbor. As might be expected, the proposals by the two ports also stirred controversy and opposition.

L.A. County Supervisor and former Long Beach Councilman James Hayes also had a seat on the Coastal Commission. He had been appointed to the Board of Supervisors in 1972 to succeed Supervisor Burton Chace, himself a former Long Beach mayor, who had been killed in a truck vs. car crash on the Long Beach Freeway. Hayes told Long Beach harbor commissioners in 1974 that he opposed dredging harbors to accommodate supertankers and urged them to reconsider an offshore buoy system. Although the Long Beach Harbor would need only minimal dredging to accommodate the supertankers, its long-range plans called for the dredging of an eighty-five-foot deep channel for future tankers that might carry as much as 400,000 dead weight tons. Hayes maintained that within forty years at the most, the world's oil resources would be exhausted, oil terminals would be rendered obsolete, and the investment in them wasted – commonly accepted environmental wisdom at the time.

The competition between the Long Beach and Los Angeles ports for the Sohio terminal went on for more than a year, but a week before Christmas in 1975, the Cleveland-based company announced that it had chosen Long Beach as its new supertanker terminal. Sohio said it chose Long Beach with its deeper channels (a side-effect of subsidence) because it wanted to minimize dredging and disposal work. The company tankers would transport crude from Valdez, Alaska, at the southern end of the Trans-Alaska pipeline – which at the time was still under construction – to the Sohio terminal in Long Beach. The company expected to ship 1.2 million barrels of oil a day through Long Beach.

The Sohio decision was expected to pay off in a big way for the Port of Long Beach and the city. The port was expected to earn $80,000 a day in tariff fees alone. The three-year construction project would provide several hundred temporary jobs, and a substantial number of permanent jobs would be created when the Sohio terminal was in operation. There would be twenty-five additional tanker calls at the port each month, and about twenty of the tanker crews would be based in Long Beach. Workers and their families would live in the area. Each crew would consist of from twenty-six to forty-two men. A tank farm to be built on Pier J would be able to store an estimated 3.6 million barrels of oil. Sohio would take about 600,000 barrels of the oil arriving each day with 400,000 of that to be shipped by pipeline to Texas. The remainder would be wholesaled to other companies. Part of the plan was to build a pipeline from Long Beach to Blythe, California, on the Arizona state line. From there it would be transported to its destination through existing pipelines.

But the battle to locate the terminal in Long Beach was not over – not by a long shot. There was much opposition to locating the terminal in an already polluted region of the state. Sohio made no secret that it was preparing a Plan B, in case the Long Beach terminal plan was blocked by environmental concerns. Plan B would involve building an offshore mono-buoy system at Avila Beach, just north of Pismo Beach on the Central Coast. The crude could be pumped by pipeline from there to Texas. Surprisingly, the Avila Beach site drew less opposition from environmentalists than the site near Morro Bay. The area was sparsely populated at the time, and the prevailing currents would make any spills easier to contain. It would take longer to develop a terminal in Avila Beach and cost slightly more than the one in Long Beach, but it was a reasonable alternative for the company.

It was not an alternative vision favored by the Port of Long Beach, however. An Avila Beach terminal would be subject to intense fog, require extensive dredging, and threaten the ecological resources of the area. A major spill would wipe out the famous Pismo Beach clams, and construction of the terminal would destroy kelp beds along the coast, port officials said. Sohio had considered and rejected the Avila Beach site in the past. The reconsideration of the site had been encouraged by California Air Resources Board Chairman Tom Quinn, an outspoken opponent of the Long Beach site.

The battle would continue over the next few years, with the port putting together plans for the new terminal, and the state Air Resources Board putting up environmental roadblocks to the project. In 1977, the agency prepared a sixty-one-page analysis of the Long Beach project in which it contended that air pollution from the project would be equivalent to the exhausts of 2.7 million automobiles. A major spill would release as much hydrocarbon into the air as that generated by all other sources in the area, the analysis warned. The chances of such a spill would be "rare," the report conceded, but if it occurred, it would cause residents in the area to experience headaches, coughing, and lingering respiratory discomfort. Some people might even die.

Despite such dire warnings, the project moved ahead, with the port working to overcome, or at least mitigate, some of the environmental objections. In November 1978, after the port and Sohio had agreed on the terms of a forty-year lease, Long Beach voters approved the Sohio project by a 61 percent majority. But still the project dragged on. In May of the following year, Sohio dropped out of the project. The decision, said Sohio Chairman Alton Whitehouse, was the result of "five years of delay which have substantially eroded the attractiveness of the project."

It was a tactic that would be employed many times in the future by environmental groups and regulatory agencies. If a project could be delayed long enough, the people who had invested in it would finally give up and go elsewhere.

The Port and the City

The Spruce Goose, sitting securely in its hangar on Pier E, was not Howard Hughes' only presence in the harbor. The mysterious Hughes Glomar Explorer was also homeported in Long Beach during the mid-1970s. The Glomar Explorer was a drill ship built in 1973-74 to mine manganese nodules from deep beneath the ocean – at least that was the cover story. The ship was actually used by the Central Intelligence Agency in a 1974 attempt to recover the Russian submarine K-129, which had been lost at sea in 1968 with nuclear missiles on board. The wreck of the K-129 was found 3.7 miles beneath the surface and 3,000 miles from Long Beach. Attempts to raise the sub were only partially successful. A portion of the bow, including the bodies of six Soviet submariners, was raised to the surface, but the main part of the vessel was not. Due to radioactive contamination, the bodies were buried at sea in a steel vault. A videotaped ceremony of the burial was given to the Soviet government.

The Queensway Hilton Hotel opened at the harbor in 1975 on 18.8 acres at the south end of Queensway Bridge. There were convention facilities for up to 600 people, 200 guest rooms arranged in four clusters with views of the downtown skyline, and Adolph's restaurant on the ground floor. The hotel, the Reef Restaurant, and the *Queen Mary* provided not only a visitor-friendly destination, but also a visually attractive buffer between the city and the industrial bustle of the port.

In 1976, the Pacific Far East Line announced that it was moving from the Port of Los Angeles to Long Beach. It was a move that provided additional ammunition to Los Angeles city critics, who felt their port was letting business slip away to the Long Beach competition.

By the mid-1970s, Port of Long Beach executives were starting to feel they were running out of space and facilities to meet the growing demands of business, and they would have to scramble if they wanted to keep up. Immediate needs included another container terminal, additional dry-bulk loading facilities for petroleum coke and chemicals, more grain elevators, and additional space to handle imported cars and trucks. Building new facilities had become more difficult. Environmental regulations and procedures had made development of necessary infrastructure a lengthy and complicated affair.

In 1977, the Regional Coastal Commission ruled that if the Port of Los Angeles wanted to fill in a section of its main channel for a container terminal, it would be required to provide an equal amount of restored wetland someplace else. The ruling set a precedent that would make future development of terminals on filled-in property much more difficult. Los Angeles was only seeking to fill in three-tenths of an acre as part of the development of the Seaside Container Terminal on the east side of the main channel, south of the Vincent Thomas Bridge. The regional commission granted permission for the project to proceed, as long as the comparable wetland area was established by the time the project was done.

In 1978, the Port of Long Beach was fighting a state Air Resources Board rule that would require ports to include all ship and train emissions resulting from any new terminal in their assessment of pollution impact. Port executives pointed out that they had no control over ships or trains. "We're being used as the patsy because the ARB can't get at the trains and ships," declared Donald B. Bright, the port commerce director. "It's not a fair price to pay."

In 1979, both ports were involved in a dispute with the South Coast Air Quality Management District over plans to jointly develop a near-dock rail yard on the north side of the port. The ports were planning to help meet the emission-reduction goals by substituting train trips for trucks. Building a rail yard near the port would eliminate the need for 300,000 truck trips a year to shuttle containers twenty-five miles up and down the freeway between the port and rail terminals to the north. That would cut air pollution by 90 percent because trains are environmentally cleaner than trucks, port officials said. The trains would also reduce freeway congestion and lower drayage rates, making the Long Beach and Los Angeles ports more competitive with other West Coast ports.

The problem was that the AQMD required the ports to find a way to eliminate the same amount of extra pollution created by the extra train traffic, and the AQMD wouldn't count the reduction in truck traffic because trucks were exempt from the agency's regulation. A new environmental awareness had taken hold, and it wasn't going to go away. Port executives may have been frustrated by the new reality they faced, but that didn't matter. Their world had changed, and they had no choice but to do the same.

Port Governance
The Long Beach Port had become a major business. Harbor commissioners wielded a huge amount of power, made decisions with far-reaching impacts, and controlled hundreds of millions of dollars. They were not elected, but they were granted a considerable amount of autonomy by the City Charter. The idea was to protect the Harbor Commission from the political whims and temporary furies that frequently buffeted the elected City Council. Perhaps in some measure it was also to protect councilmembers from sometimes having to defend necessary, but unpopular decisions. The rationale for the arrangement was that the port was a city-owned business, and the Harbor Commission needed to maintain a certain detached focus to operate that business for the benefit of the residents. But by the late 1970s, some people were beginning to think that maybe the Harbor Commission was too isolated from the everyday concerns of the citizenry.

Press-Telegram reporter John Sheehan in a February 6, 1977, story concluded that many of the port staff had an attitude that "what is good for the Port of Long Beach must, by definition, be best for the community at large." Sheehan's story reflected concerns that were held by a segment of the community who believed that the port acted as though it was not subject to the same electoral pressures as the Council.

In 1977, a task force appointed by Mayor Tom Clark urged that the City Charter be amended to provide the City Council with broad power to review and approve major harbor projects. The task force's report characterized the Harbor Department as an "independent and autonomous entity, a sovereignty within a sovereignty..." that needed to be made accountable. The charter election was not held until November 4, 1980, and the most significant change in the Harbor Department's arms-length relationship with the Council was to allow the Harbor Commission to transfer 10 percent of the port's net earnings to the city for such things as beach and marina maintenance.

Moving Forward

As required by the 1976 California Environmental Quality Act, the Port of Long Beach prepared a port master plan in 1978. Among the projects listed in the plan were a second hotel near the Queensway Hilton, a marina, bike paths, cruise ship and ferry terminals next to the *Queen Mary*, two new fireboat stations, an expansion of Pier J, warehouse improvements on Pier C in the inner harbor, and establishment of a Foreign Trade Zone.

In May 1978, the Long Beach Harbor Department took over control of the *Queen Mary* from the city – pending voter approval of a boundary shift that would expand the harbor district to include the ship-turned-hotel's anchorage. Approval came the following November. The port planned to invest $13.8 million to upgrade the ship and make it a financial success.

The eccentric and once-dashing Howard Hughes died April 6, 1977, onboard a jet plane rushing him to Houston Methodist Hospital for treatment. He was 70 years old and had spent his last years in tortured seclusion inside darkened hotel rooms, still buying and selling and moving the pieces of his empire from his lair behind closed doors. Cause of death was kidney failure, but Hughes was also suffering from malnutrition – his 6-foot-4-inch body weighed only ninety pounds. His hair, beard, fingernails, and toenails were untrimmed, and five broken-off hypodermic needles were discovered embedded in his arms. The life of the man who had made history in the Long Beach Harbor on a November afternoon in 1947, who dated and married movie stars, who founded and ran disparate businesses, who survived plane crashes and battled mental illness, had come to a sad end.

In 1979, Long Beach Port executives and representatives of Hughes' Summa Corp. announced plans to move the famous Spruce Goose flying boat from its hangar on Pier E to a new home next to the *Queen Mary* for public display. Details of the plan were still being worked out, but Hughes' Summa Corp. would handle the move and the erection of a display venue in the *Queen Mary* parking lot.

The financially ailing city turned to the port once again in 1979 to help sponsor a float in the 1980 Rose Parade on New Year's Day. The city was not able to afford a parade float, although it had entered one every year since the Rose Parade began in 1915. Although port money could be spent only on commerce, fisheries, and navigation, entering a City and Port float in the parade was considered a form of advertising port services.

A delegation of Chinese shipping authorities visited the port in 1979 and announced that Long Beach would be China's designated port of call. The delegation took a tour of the harbor and talked to port executives about port operations. Their visit followed a trip by Long Beach Port officials to China four months earlier.

The port also received approval to establish its first Foreign Trade Zone – a designation that allowed cargo to enter the country duty free and not to be subject to duty until it left the zone. Improvements made to the goods within the zone – assembling parts into a whole, for instance – would only be subjected to the original duty, not the duty for the finished products. Products that were exported from the Foreign Trade Zone would not be subject to any import duties.

Meanwhile, the port began a study on the feasibility of a high-rise World Trade Center to be built in downtown Long Beach. The idea was to attract maritime and international businesses to Long Beach from Los Angeles and San Francisco. It was another indication that the port was reaching beyond the harbor district to promote commerce and trade and to bring business to the city.

Changes

The world changed significantly in the 1970s and so did the city and the port. A new generation of leaders was taking over as stewards of Long Beach's largest asset. Port General Manager Thorley retired in 1977 after eight years in the top spot. He was replaced by James H. McJunkin.

Two harbor commissioners, descendants of historic Long Beach families, resigned from the board in January 1977. Llewellyn Bixby Jr., whose family once owned virtually all of what was to become Long Beach, and James Craig Jr., whose grandfather opened a ship-building company at the port before there were even channels dredged to the sea, had both been appointed to the commission in 1965. They decided to step down rather than comply with a new conflict-of-interest disclosure law for people in public office. Bixby, in his resignation letter, called the disclosure requirements "an unnecessary invasion of what little privacy still remains to me." Craig denied any conflict of interest, but said, "I don't believe my financial position is any business of the public." Financial privacy may have been an old-fashioned concept, but the two men clearly were not ready to give it up. They were replaced on the board by two federal employees – Reed M. Williams, an attorney with the U.S. Justice Department, and E. John Hanna, director of industrial relations at the Long Beach Naval Shipyard.

Union bad boy Harry Bridges – who had brought the San Francisco shipping establishment to its knees in 1934 – had mellowed somewhat with age. The man the U.S. government spent sixteen years attempting to deport as a subversive radical was honored in 1975 at a $50-a-plate banquet in San Francisco's Fairmont Hotel on Nob Hill. Among the 1,700 attendees were leaders in the maritime industry, many of whom had butted heads with Bridges over the years. Some thought Bridges, by that time 74 years old, might take the occasion to announce his retirement. But Bridges, who had founded the International Longshoremen's and Warehousemen's Union, and had been the only president the union had ever had, was clearly not ready to step down. At the end of the tribute, he was presented with a new Mercedes-Benz automobile and a check for $25,000. Harry Bridges – the angry young man who had become a statesman of labor – finally retired from office in 1977.

Chapter Seventeen:
Cargo, the Navy, and Mickey Mouse

It was 1980, and Americans had a new attitude. People were tired of the long lines at the gas pump and the stagnant economy that had given rise to high inflation, high interest rates, and low employment. They were tired of having people tell them to drive smaller cars, to turn the thermostat up in the summer and down in the winter, to take shorter showers, to flush their toilet less frequently, and to carpool to work.

American hostages were still being held in Iran in 1980, after a mission to rescue them fell apart when U.S. military aircraft broke down in the Iranian desert. The United States declared a grain embargo against the Soviet Union and boycotted the Olympics in Moscow over the Soviet invasion of Afghanistan. Japan passed the United States as the largest manufacturer of automobiles.

It all added up to voters who were ready for a change. In 1980, they elected former California Governor Ronald Reagan president. His campaign theme was "Make America Great Again." Reagan was sworn in on January 20, 1981. The hostages – after 444 days in captivity – were released by Iran by the end of Reagan's inaugural address. The release had been negotiated by the Carter administration, but as a final humiliation to Carter, the Iranians had delayed the actual freeing of the hostages until a new president was in office.

Iraq invaded Iran in 1980 sparking a war that lasted just short of eight years. An estimated 1 million people were killed – about half of them soldiers, the rest civilians. At the end, the borders remained where they were when the first shots were fired. Argentina invaded the Falkland Islands about 300 miles off its coast in 1982, beginning a ten-week war with Great Britain. Argentina claimed it was just reestablishing its rights to the islands, which had been under British control since the 19th century. Great Britain prevailed. Casualties included 907 deaths, 649 of them Argentine military. The United States sent troops into Grenada, where deaths on all sides totaled 113, and to Panama where they totaled about 1,000.

Benigno Aquino Jr., an outspoken opponent of Philippine dictator Ferdinand Marcos, was assassinated in 1983 at the airport in Manila. In 1984, Indian Prime Minister Indira Gandhi was shot and killed by two of her Sikh bodyguards at her home in India. In 1986, Swedish Prime Minister Olof Palme was shot and killed in Stockholm while walking home from the movies with his wife.

The first space shuttle was launched into orbit in 1981. Astronaut Sally Ride became the first American woman into space onboard the Space Shuttle Challenger in 1983. Three years later, that same shuttle would explode seventy-three seconds after liftoff, killing all seven people onboard, including schoolteacher Christa McAuliffe. Several elementary and middle schools have since been named in her honor.

A new disease, acquired immunodeficiency syndrome – better known by its acronym AIDS – was first recognized in 1981, although it was expected to have existed in West Africa as far back as the late 19th or early 20th centuries. Two years later, scientists were able to identify the human immunodeficiency virus (HIV) that caused the disease. The 1980s saw the first liposuction surgery and the first artificial heart transplant. In the Chicago area, somebody laced Tylenol capsules with potassium cyanide, leading to the death of seven people and resulting in the development of tamper-proof pill containers. An illegal drug called crack cocaine began showing up on the streets of American cities around the same time a legal drug called Prozac started showing up in medicine cabinets of American homes.

President Reagan cut taxes, appointed Sandra Day O'Connor as the first woman to the Supreme Court, and fired striking air traffic controllers. He also initiated the controversial Strategic Defense Initiative – quickly dubbed Star Wars by the press – to intercept incoming missiles before they reached their targets. The Immigration Reform and Control Act was signed into law by the president in 1986. It provided amnesty for illegal immigrants who had entered the country before 1982, had not committed any crimes, and possessed a minimal knowledge of U.S. history, government, and the English language.

Democratic presidential challenger Walter Mondale picked as his running mate Geraldine Ferraro, the first woman to run for vice president on a mainstream U.S. ticket. But the duo failed to unseat President Reagan. Angela Davis ran for vice president in both 1980 and 1984 on the Communist Party USA ticket and lost both times. The Equal Rights Amendment to make women's rights part of the Constitution, failed to win required backing from enough states and died in 1982. The third Monday of January was designated as Martin Luther King Jr. Day, an official federal holiday honoring the civil rights leader. The U.S. Senate in 1982 passed a bill that would have effectively banned school busing as a way to integrate schools, but it never made it to the House of Representatives.

The Iran-Contra scandal – a complicated secret deal in which arms were sold through Israel to Iran to secure the release of seven hostages taken by a terrorist group – shook the Reagan administration in 1986. A portion of the money for the sale was to be diverted to fund the anti-communist Contra insurgents in Nicaragua. Presidential candidate and former senator Gary Hart was caught with a girlfriend on a yacht after daring reporters to "follow him" if they thought he was having an affair. The following day, the Miami Herald ran a story about a model named Donna Rice leaving Hart's townhouse in Washington, D.C. Two days later, reporters obtained a picture of Hart wearing a T-shirt that said "Monkey Business" with Rice sitting on his lap. *Monkey Business* was the name of the yacht on which the two had spent a night in Bimini, Bahamas.

During the 1980s, we first began using Post-It Notes, camcorders, mobile phones, and disposable cameras. The IBM personal computer was introduced in 1981, the first Macintosh computer in 1985, the first version of Windows that same year, and the first IBM laptop in 1986. The first computer virus joined us one year later. The first DeLorean sports car was introduced in 1981, and the last one marketed in 1983. Work began in 1988 on a tunnel beneath the English Channel to connect Britain to France – a project that became known as the Chunnel.

On October 19, 1987, stock markets around the world crashed, starting in Hong Kong in what became known in financial circles as "Black Friday." The U.S. government instituted a $125 billion bailout of the savings and loan industry in 1989, a move some think encouraged financial institutions to engage in risky behavior once again fifteen years later. Financier Michael Milken was indicted in 1989 for racketeering and securities fraud in his development of high-yield junk bonds. He accepted a plea bargain to a lesser charge and was sentenced to ten years in prison. His sentence was later reduced to two years for testifying against former colleagues and for his good behavior while incarcerated.

John Hinckley Jr. shot President Reagan in 1981 to impress actress Jodie Foster. Six weeks later, Turkish gunman Mehmet Ali Ağca shot Pope John Paul II four times. The pope recovered and forgave him. Former Beatle John Lennon was gunned down in 1980 in front of the Dakota Apartments in New York City, where he lived with his wife, Yoko Ono. Gorilla expert Dian Fossey was killed in her bed. Singer Marvin Gaye was shot and killed by his father. And Black Panther Party co-founder Huey Newton was shot and killed in 1989 by a member of the radical Black Liberation Family.

Atlanta was shaken by the murders of young black children in 1979 and 1980. Twenty-five victims were identified – most of them children, but some adults as well – in a murder spree that ended with the arrest of 23-year-old Wayne Williams, a self-proclaimed photographer and music promoter.

Serial killer and rapist Richard Ramirez, dubbed the "Night Stalker," terrified Southern California for fifteen months that spanned 1984 and 1985. He was eventually chased down, beat up, and turned over to the police by outraged citizens after one woman recognized him from his picture in the papers. He was later convicted of thirteen murders, five attempted murders, eleven sexual assaults, and fourteen burglaries, and sentenced to death. Ramirez showed up for his first court appearance in a jacket on which he scrawled on the back "Hail Satin." It's fairly certain he actually meant "Hail Satan." He died in prison of natural causes in 2013, before he could be executed.

Subway vigilante Bernard Hugo Goetz shot four young muggers on a subway in New York, and three young robbers gunned down thirteen people at the Wah Mee illegal gambling club in Seattle's Chinatown. Deranged gunman James Huberty killed twenty-one people, including five children, and wounded nineteen others in a July 18, 1984, killing spree at a McDonald's in San Ysidro, California. His rampage ended after seventy-eight minutes when a SWAT sniper killed him with a single shot. Although the McDonald's was completely refurbished within forty-eight hours, it was torn down before the end of the month, and a permanent memorial to the victims was eventually built at the site.

Mount St. Helens erupted in Washington state in an awesome display of raw power that killed fifty-seven people and caused $1 billion in damage. More than 400,000 died as the worst famine in a century hit Ethiopia. An earthquake in Armenia killed 25,000, and a toxic gas release at the Union Carbide India Ltd. pesticide plant in Bhopal, India, killed thousands more. The official death toll was more than 3,700 after the release, although thousands more died or were permanently disabled in the days and weeks to come.

Atlanta businessman Ted Turner started the CNN all-news cable network, USA Today became a national newspaper, and MTV began putting images to the music. Reggae singer Bob Marley died. So did John Belushi, Princess

Grace, Karen Carpenter, Rock Hudson, and Lucille Ball. Prince Charles and the commoner Diana Spencer married and had two sons. Bruce Willis married Demi Moore, Arnold Schwarzenegger married Maria Shriver, Billy Joel married Christie Brinkley, and Reverend Moon of the Unification Church married more than 2,000 couples – brides and grooms chosen by the church and often of different races, nationalities, and ethnic backgrounds – in a mass ceremony in Madison Square Garden.

Pac-Man and Ms. Pac-Man became video arcade favorites; Cabbage Patch Kids became the must-have dolls, and compact discs became the preferred way of listening to music. Singer Michael Jackson caught his hair on fire during a Pepsi commercial, comedian Richard Pryor set himself on fire while freebasing cocaine, and rocker Ozzy Osbourne bit off the head of a live bat during a performance in Des Moines, Iowa.

Vanessa Williams became the first black Miss America, but had to turn in her crown early after Penthouse magazine published nude photos of her taken a year before the pageant. First lady Nancy Reagan told American kids to "just say no" to drugs, and Nike shoe company encouraged Americans to get fit by telling them to "Just Do It."

From the Queen Mary to New York's Battery Park, we held hands across America to fight homelessness and hunger, and then we listened as singers from around the globe sang "We Are the World" to fight famine in Africa.

Americans turned their noses up at New Coke, wept at the new Vietnam Veterans' Memorial Wall, and watched the first infomercials on TV. The 1989 World Series being played in the San Francisco Bay Area was interrupted by the Loma Prieta earthquake that killed sixty-three people and caused an estimated $6 billion in damage.

The beginning of the end for world communism came in 1989 with the tearing down of the Berlin Wall, which had been built to hold captive the residents of East Germany. In China, pro-democracy protesters were gunned down following huge protests in Tiananmen Square in Beijing and elsewhere in the country. The world watched as a 19-year-old student stood in the street facing a column of four tanks and refusing to move. Nicknamed "Tank Man," it's not known what finally happened to that one young man, but estimates of deaths range from hundreds to thousands of his comrades. From that point on, China gradually began to loosen the rigid controls it had held over its citizens. In Romania, the Communist government of dictator Nicolae Ceaușescu was overthrown. Nicolae and his wife, Elena, faced a firing squad only minutes following their two-hour trial. Two weeks later, the new government abolished the death penalty.

The decade was defined by wars, assassinations, scandals, crime, politics, natural disasters, advances in science, new music, crazy fads, and all the things – great and small – that distinguish one era from another.

It was the 1980s, and history was on the march – across the world, and in Long Beach.

Vincent Thomas

When people think about Vincent Thomas, they think about the bridge, not the man. But the man has his place in history too. He was an unwavering advocate for his San Pedro hometown. A Democrat, he served for thirty-eight years as the California assemblyman for the San Pedro and South Bay area before being defeated in his final bid for re-election by Republican Gerald Felando in 1978.

Thomas was the prime mover in building the bridge that bears his name. The Vincent Thomas was built after a long campaign to construct a highway connection between San Pedro and Terminal Island. Before the bridge opened, the only direct link to the island from San Pedro was a ferry. The assemblyman was also the author of the legislation that established California State University, Dominguez Hills.

One of the efforts in which Thomas was not successful, however, was his ongoing determination to merge the Port of Long Beach with the Port of Los Angeles – either as one big port authority or under a state port authority. Throughout his years in office, he had often called for a merger of the two ports, introduced legislation to force their consolidation, and argued at every possible opportunity the benefits of joining the two ports together as one. And always, his efforts were opposed and rejected by Long Beach.

In the wee hours of January 31, 1980, Vincent Thomas died after suffering a heart attack at his home in San Pedro. Although Thomas was dead, his legacy was written against the sky in steel and concrete, and his goal for consolidation of two rival ports lived on. And just as when he was alive, that idea would be opposed and defeated by the people of Long Beach time and time again.

Growing Pains

The Port of Long Beach was built in exactly the right place. Eventually, time also came to be on the port's side. By the 1980s, trade around the Pacific Rim was booming, and the port was benefiting from it. Add a large population base – much of the cargo arriving at the port was within one hundred miles of its final destination – and good rail connections to the rest of the nation, and the future was quite rosy. During the 1979-80 fiscal year, Long Beach moved 41.2 million metric revenue tons of cargo across its docks, up 86 percent from the 22.2 million metric revenue tons moved ten years earlier and slightly more than the 40.9 million metric revenue tons that moved that year through the Port of Los Angeles. (A metric revenue ton is a billing unit used in the shipping industry based on a formula that compares pounds and volume. A metric ton is a unit of weight equal to 1,000 kilograms or 2,205 pounds. A revenue metric ton equals one metric ton or one cubic meter – whichever has the highest revenue.)

By the 1980s, yearly cargo growth through both ports was solidly in the double digits. The challenge was suddenly not how to get more business, but how to keep up with the flow of cargo – inbound and outbound – arriving at the docks. Mechanization had initially cut into the number of longshore jobs in the two ports, but the rapid growth soon reversed that trend. The longshore labor situation went from not having enough jobs to go around to sometimes not having enough dockworkers to go around. By the summer of 1984, there were times when as many as eighteen ships were left waiting to be worked – an expensive proposition for ship owners who still had to pay their crews and keep a schedule, regardless of the labor problems at the San Pedro Bay ports.

By fall, the Pacific Maritime Association, representing employers, and the International Longshoremen's and Warehousemen's Union, representing workers, began soliciting applications for new dockworkers. The response was overwhelming. A one-day temporary job center was set up on September 23 at the San Pedro Drive-In Theater on Gaffey Street. The rush by jobseekers, eager to make the $15.57 hourly longshore base wage, backed up traffic for more than ten miles. By the end of the day, 20,250 applications had been turned in.

The PMA and ILWU spent the next month reviewing applications and interviewing potential workers. In the end, about 350 new longshoremen were hired, with a few hundred others standing by as temporary labor. It wasn't like the old days when unskilled labor could be hired to move cargo into and out of a hold. The new hires had to be trained on the equipment they would encounter in the terminal and on procedures and safety rules for dispatching and loading cargo. The first fifty rookie longshoremen went to work by the end of the year.

Deregulation of Trucking
When President Jimmy Carter signed the Motor Carrier Act of 1980, it was seen by conservatives and liberals alike as a welcome end to a restrictive and regulated industry that encouraged monopoly practices by trucking companies, discouraged competition, and resulted in a union stranglehold on trucking both in the ports and elsewhere. Deregulation of the industry had been encouraged by presidents Nixon, Ford, and Carter during the 1970s and finally passed into law during the last full year of the Carter administration. The Act would drastically change how the trucking business was conducted in the harbor.

Before deregulation, the Interstate Commerce Commission limited the number of trucks involved in industry, resulting in high company profits and good wages for union drivers, who were represented by the Teamsters Union. It also raised costs for shippers and consumers and made the price of entering the industry prohibitive for new companies. After deregulation, it was easy to break into the industry – all it cost was a down payment on a used truck. Trucking companies that once were heavily invested in the ownership of trucks could suddenly farm out jobs to independent contract drivers who owned their own trucks and were paid by the load. The once-powerful Teamsters Union saw the market flooded with new trucking companies using non-union contract drivers, causing a steep decline in the union's influence at U.S. ports.

The business model of the port trucking companies had been drastically altered. Trucking companies used to the old way of guaranteed rates had to change or go out of business. Many of them simply went under. Some of the new trucking companies became little more than cargo brokers, signing up customers who needed to move freight and then distributing the work to a network of drivers. Others used a combination of employee drivers and independent contractors. Efforts by the Teamsters to organize the contract drivers were not successful; as independent contractors, they were businessmen. Negotiation by employees for higher wages is called collective bargaining. Independent businessmen doing the same thing is called illegal price fixing.

As the number of independent drivers servicing the port went up, their wages and the cost of moving cargo went down. A few of the drivers were able to form their own companies. But many of them left the port drayage industry, which increasingly became dominated by immigrant drivers, willing to work long hours for low wages. Despite the drawbacks, many of those immigrant drivers had a fierce entrepreneurial spirit. They liked setting their own schedules and were free to use their trucks to haul other types of cargo during slow periods at the port.

But there were problems. Since the lowly paid owner-operators were responsible for maintenance of their trucks, they sometimes tended to cut corners, driving on bald tires or with faulty brakes. The older trucks they bought emitted higher volumes of pollutants than did newer trucks. And since they were paid by the load, they got a reputation of driving recklessly in order to move as many loads as possible each day.

Unrest among the drivers grew. The loosely organized workforce of contract drivers interfaced at the terminals with members of the ILWU, one of the most highly structured workforces in the nation. The drivers, some of them not fluent in English, struggled to make ends meet, and many felt they were treated with disrespect both by the companies that hired their services and by the well-paid unionized workers they encountered on the job.

The drivers banded together, lamenting their treatment in an industry where everybody seemed to be making good money except them. They protested in convoys of trucks, driving through the harbor area and around the civic centers in Long Beach and Los Angeles to vent their frustrations and demand that something be done. The cost of drayage had come down, but much of the savings came from the pockets of the union drivers who lost their jobs and the low-wage independent contractors who replaced them.

By the summer of 1988, many drivers had joined an ad hoc organization called the Waterfront/Rail Truckers Union and were taking to the streets. At Long Beach Container Terminal, protesting truckers were able to cut the normal flow of containers into and out of the terminal by 35 percent. Rocks were thrown through truck windows of non-striking drivers; a radiator of a parked truck was punctured, and roofing nails were thrown at the gates to puncture the tires of drivers who were willing to run the protest gauntlet. Many independent drivers refused work servicing the terminal rather than deal with the protesters.

The drivers clearly had the power to shut down the system, but while they protested, their bills were not being paid. And even if they forced concessions from a company, there was no mechanism to translate those concessions into a binding contract.

The question of the drivers' status was litigated in the courts. Were the drivers really employees, who brought their own trucks to work as a carpenter might bring his tools? Or were they actually independent businesspeople who had agreed to provide a service for a price? There were legal tests to differentiate one from the other, but as long as the companies that hired the drivers stayed on the legal side of that line, they could forestall the drivers creating a formal union.

The trucking companies also struggled. Drayage was seen as a commodity by shippers, and with the cost of entry into the marketplace so low, the competition was high. There was little room for error. Some trucking companies that signed big contracts by promising low rates, found themselves out of business if anything went amiss.

These issues emerged at the ports during the 1980s, but they continued to define the battle between management and unions, terminal operators and trucking companies, and ports and shippers for many years to come.

Investing in the Future

Both the Long Beach Port and the city were booming during the 1980s. New hotels, high-rise apartments, and shopping areas were transforming the old downtown. The port was being transformed as well. It was the beginning of a period when the port was always in a state of flux, with terminals and boundaries being altered and moved as the need arose.

The port added more fill to low-lying property at the end of the Seventh Street Peninsula, later Pier C, to raise it back up above sea level. Construction was underway on a ninety-acre parcel on Pier J that would serve as container terminals for Pacific Container Terminals, a subsidiary of Stevedoring Services of America, and for Long Beach Container Terminal, a subsidiary of Orient Overseas Container Line. The property included land that had been earmarked for development of the Sohio supertanker terminal before Sohio pulled out of the deal.

In 1981, China Ocean Shipping Co., commonly known as COSCO, inaugurated its international shipping service. Its first port of call in the United States was Pacific Container Terminals in Long Beach. The company would find itself as the focus of an intense political storm more than twenty years after that first call. OOCL's Long Beach Container Terminal would move once again in 1986, this time to a new eighty-eight-acre terminal on the old Navy Victory Pier area – then part of Pier A, later Pier F – that had been expanded with fifty acres of new fill. Several break-bulk operations also were moved to make way for the new facility.

Toyota Motor Sales had outgrown its terminal on Pier J, and a new 140-acre property was developed in the inner harbor on the north side of Channel 2 as auto import terminals for Toyota Motor Sales and Pasha Industries. The new facility provided room for a processing center to prepare newly arrived cars and trucks for sale and easy rail and freeway connections for moving the vehicles to dealers throughout the Southwest. The truck beds were manufactured at the Toyota Motor Manufacturing plant in North Long Beach.

From its very beginning, the port had fed the Southern California construction market with wood and other materials needed to erect houses and commercial buildings, and that continued. Despite a lull in the construction industry due to high interest rates in the early 1980s, the first cement import terminal on the West Coast was built for Pacific Coast Cement Corp., opening in 1981 on Pier D. Two lumber terminals in the inner harbor – a nine-acre Weyerhaeuser Co. and six-acre Forest Terminals facility – were shut down to make room for the new auto terminal. Two new lumber terminals were constructed on a thirty-two-acre parcel at the south end of Pier E, later Pier T.

The port had been trying for some time to evict Howard Hughes' old Spruce Goose flying boat, which had been sealed off in its hangar off the back channel since a few months after its one and only flight in 1947. The site was needed to build a new oil terminal for ARCO. The company's old terminal, which had opened in 1961 about 1,500 feet to the north of the Spruce Goose hangar, was outmoded, and some of the larger tankers unloading there made it a tight squeeze for other vessels trying to navigate up the channel to the inner harbor.

Even before the Spruce Goose was moved, the port had begun the environmental review process for the new ARCO terminal, with the plan that once the plane was moved from its hangar in October 1980 and the hangar was destroyed, work on the new $30 million terminal would begin. The new terminal had more pipeline capacity, which meant that tankers calling at the port could offload 40,000 to 50,000 barrels of oil per hour. The channel also was widened at the site to provide more room for passing ship traffic. The first ARCO tanker called at the new terminal in June 1983.

Making Money on Trash

One of the unique projects to be built at the port during this era had nothing to do with moving cargo, but everything to do with making money, saving energy, and getting rid of trash. The Southeast Resource Recovery Facility, usually just called the SERRF plant, was a $116.6 million trash incinerator located on a seventeen-acre site on the north side of Ocean Boulevard, just west of the Terminal Island Freeway. According to the business plan, trash would be trucked to the Terminal Island site where it would be chopped into large chunks, and the iron and steel separated out by a large magnet. A washing process would further separate out glass, aluminum, and other non-combustible items. What was left over would be chopped into small pieces and burned to generate electricity.

The 900 tons of garbage to be processed daily at the plant was expected to yield 644 tons of fuel, 170 tons of metal and glass, and eighty-six tons of ash. The electricity would be sold to Southern California Edison. The metal and glass would be sold as scrap for recycling, and about half of the ash would be used in the manufacture of cement. The other half would have to be trucked away for disposal. The city, which had been paying $36.60 a ton to truck trash to a landfill, hoped instead to net $15 per ton of garbage by burning it in the plant. Pollution-control devices would filter the emissions generated at the plant.

The project soon became entangled in a three-way battle of bureaucrats in which the state Waste Management Board refused to approve the project until Los Angeles County submitted its Waste Management Plan to the state. The county's Waste Management Plan was bogged down by a feud with the city of Los Angeles over a county plan to establish two landfill dumps in the city of Los Angeles. The dispute was overridden by the legislature, and the project went forward. Despite some glitches in the design, the SERRF plant went on line in 1989 and by the end of the decade was turning 1,200 tons of trash a day into electricity.

The Coal Boom

When the price of oil skyrocketed in 1979, long lines began appearing at local gas stations, and the energy-dependent nations of Asia began to feel the pinch. Demand for coal to fuel power plants was suddenly high, and the popular wisdom was that the market for coal – something of which the United States had plenty – would continue to boom.

After Port Executive Director James McJunkin attended a White House Energy Conference in December of 1980 where President Carter said he would encourage other countries to use U.S. coal instead of oil, McJunkin was convinced. Such a coal terminal would bring added business to the port and help mitigate the U.S. trade deficit with Asia. The port already accounted for about 54,000 tons of coal exports annually from its bulk terminal on Pier G. By expanding that terminal and adding an even bigger terminal on the north side of the Cerritos Channel, that number could be raised to 30 million tons a year by 1990, McJunkin told the press. The port began working on a proposed joint venture with Upland Industries to develop a massive new terminal that would export coal brought in by train from Arizona, Utah, Wyoming, and Colorado. Such a terminal could be up and running in four years, McJunkin predicted, giving Long Beach the jump on other West Coast ports. Upland Industries was an Omaha-based subsidiary of Union Pacific Railroad, the owner of the property on which the coal terminal would be located.

By the summer of 1981, the Port of Los Angeles had come up with its own plans for a coal export terminal that would be built on land filled in from the spoils taken during the deepening of the Los Angeles Main Channel. The two ports agreed that even with two huge coal export terminals, there was plenty of business to go around. Long Beach expected to receive ten trains a day, each of them eighty or more cars long, bringing coal from Western mines to the terminal.

But things didn't work out quite as expected. By 1982, there were twenty-six coal export terminals proposed for the West Coast alone – the biggest two at Long Beach and Los Angeles. People in the industry were beginning to realize that all the predictions about the coming boom in coal may have been overstated. In fact, early on in the 1980s, oil prices began falling rapidly as did the predictions of a runaway market for coal. Port executives in both Long Beach and Los Angeles, however, said they felt that recent studies throwing doubt on the market for coal were too conservative. The two ports continued with their plans.

Long Beach harbor commissioners voted to move ahead with expansion of the existing coal terminal on Pier G, despite complaints by residents about train traffic. Those residents didn't care about the market for coal. The Union Pacific tracks over which the coal would be transported cut right through their area of working-class neighborhoods in North Long Beach – in some cases only fifteen or twenty feet from residential property lines. Residents complained about the diesel fumes, the noise, and the danger posed by trains speeding through the neighborhoods on ill-maintained tracks.

By March of 1983, the subject of coal was once again before the port board, this time in reference to plans for a proposed $200 million joint venture with Upland Industries; Crowley Maritime Corp.; Metropolitan Stevedore Co.; and C. Itoh & Co., a Japanese trading firm, to build what had been dubbed the Long Beach International Coal Project on the north bank of the Cerritos Channel. The neighbors were better organized this time around – 200 of them jammed the hearing – and they had more political clout than they had previously. Councilman Warren Harwood, who represented the area, declared that he was not satisfied with the environmental impact report prepared by the port.

One of the residents was Gary Gabelich, who complained that he had to wash down his sidewalks to get rid of the coal dust blown by the passing trains. Gabelich was a car and boat racing celebrity, who had gained fame in 1970 when he set the world land speed record of 630 miles per hour in the rocket car Blue Flame on the Bonneville Salt Flats in Utah. He died in a motorcycle accident ten months after the port hearing on the project. His wife, Rae Gabelich, would remain active in city affairs and be elected in 2004 to a seat on the Long Beach City Council.

It wasn't the coal terminal to which the residents objected; it was the trains that would bring the coal to the port. The City Council urged the Harbor Commission to consider alternative rail routes to the port and to disapprove construction of the terminal until the train issue could be resolved to the satisfaction of residents. Lakewood Mayor Robert Wagner attended the next Harbor Commission hearing to argue that the environmental report did not deal with the issue of vibrations, pollution, and noise from the coal trains, which also came through Lakewood. Assemblyman Bruce Young from Norwalk, another city on the Union Pacific route, sent an aide to read a statement urging that a study be conducted to ensure the best route.

Plans for the coal terminal turned out to be a tipping point for many in city government, who were concerned about the attitudes of the harbor commissioners as well as their plans for a coal terminal. Planning commissioners were outraged when nobody from the port board bothered to show up to hear their concerns about what they felt was an inadequate and ambiguous environmental impact report. In the Planning Commission's first meeting on the subject, the consultant from the firm that had prepared the environmental report left before the discussion on it was over. In the second Planning Commission meeting on the subject, the port didn't even bother to send a representative.

Some councilmembers had privately been complaining about the aloof and insensitive attitude of the harbor commissioners. Those private mutterings soon became public. Councilman Harwood was on the attack. He called for the Council to take away the port's authority to approve environmental documents and to give that authority to the Planning Commission. He promised, as the chairman of the Council Finance Committee, to go over the port's proposed budget for the next year with an eye for detail.

"The Harbor Commission can make a decision that affects the entire city, and yet they are responsible to no constituency," he said. "We have many problems as a result of past Councils passing up their rights to exercise authority over the harbor."

Harwood accused some of the port board members of lobbying other councilmembers behind the scene to head off his proposal – a charge that the harbor board members admitted was true. The stakes were too high and the issues too complex to hand off to a board more attuned to dealing with conditional use permits and zoning questions, the commissioners claimed. The harbor commissioners wanted to work out a compromise that would satisfy Council complaints without inserting unnecessary steps into mundane development decisions.

Mayor Thomas Clark wanted that as well. He asked that the vote to transfer environmental authority to the Planning Commission be postponed until the two sides could talk things over. Harwood agreed. A private off-site lunch was arranged for a week later, where Clark sat down with Harwood, Councilman Edd Tuttle, Harbor Board President Richard Wilson, City Attorney Robert Parkin, and Port Executive Director James McJunkin to discuss alternatives. A proposed compromise was reached that would provide authority for the Planning Commission and City Council to review all projects that could impact the entire city – such as the coal terminal. Two weeks later, the Council approved the compromise plan.

By the summer of 1983, the controversy over coal trains was a moot point. The Harbor Commission canceled plans for the Long Beach International Coal Terminal after determining that there was not enough foreign demand for coal to justify such a project. It had been an expensive lesson for the port board. In all, about $4 million had been spent in planning for the project, $1.67 million by the port and the rest by Union Pacific, Crowley Maritime, Metropolitan Stevedore, and C. Itoh & Co. In addition, the canceled project had cost the board political capital with elected city officials, who held the ultimate power over port affairs. But most of all, it introduced the harbor commissioners to a new reality – the port was not only responsible for the pollution produced on its own real estate; it was also responsible for the pollution produced by third parties traveling to and from the port.

Inferno on Gale Avenue

Sometimes, history catches up with you. Those are the times when the consequences of past actions or inactions show up in unexpected – and often catastrophic – ways. Shortly after 6 p.m., on December 1, 1980, as many of the residents along the 2700 block of Gale Avenue were having dinner, all hell broke loose in the street outside their homes. An eight-inch pipeline carrying naphtha under 28th Street had ruptured at the intersection of Gale Avenue, creating a geyser that sprayed twenty feet into the air, and then flowed along the gutter down Gale Avenue. When it finally ignited, it was with such an explosive force that flames shot seventy feet into the air. The Gale Avenue residents, just one block west of the Long Beach Freeway, were suddenly in the middle of a nightmare of epic proportions. Naphtha is a volatile liquid used in the gasoline refining process, as a fluid for the old Zippo-style cigarette lighters, as white gasoline used for camp stoves and lanterns, and as a cleaning solvent. It is not only flammable, it is also a toxic substance that can cause dizziness, skin rashes, and respiratory problems.

Long Beach firefighters responded to the scene, laying down foam and trying to contain a blaze that for more than two hours kept being fed by a continuing flow of naphtha through the ruptured pipe. It was a major disaster. One home was destroyed, eleven were severely damaged, eleven motor vehicles destroyed, and five people were injured – one of them critically. That man, 40-year-old Robert James Davis, was outside, trying to warn neighbors about the pipeline leak when he was engulfed by flames. His wife and children came outside in time to see him catch on fire. The Gale Avenue fire was more than just a disaster; it was a public awakening to the hidden network of underground infrastructure that had been built to support the modern city of Long Beach – and the danger that lurked within that infrastructure.

After Gale Avenue, the old way of doing business was over – at least in Long Beach – although the company executives and some of the people in city government didn't seem to get that right away. Four Corners Pipe Line Co., a subsidiary of ARCO, at first vowed to have the pipeline back in operation in twenty-four hours. Company President Dick Chamberlin said there were no guarantees that such an incident wouldn't happen again, although he said the chances of that were slim. Fire Captain T.F. Stewart told the press that he saw the incident as "an act of God," as though it was something beyond the control of mortal men. Fire Department Deputy Chief Bob Guyett went on record saying his department did not enforce any safety standards for the pipelines beneath the city.

"We're not in a position to do it," he said. "We're having enough problems keeping up with our day-to-day fire problems. I don't feel there is a reason to panic. You must have concern about it, but those chemicals are part of modern society." Everybody agreed that transporting volatile liquids and gases through pipelines was much safer than transporting them through city traffic on trucks or trains. The real question was, "Is 'safer' safe enough?"

The pipeline in question was Four Corners Pipeline No. 8. Because of Long Beach's history as an oil town and a town that had encouraged industry, it had more than its share of such pipelines. In fact, Pipeline No. 8 was just one of sixteen fuel and chemical pipelines, not all of them active, running beneath the pavement at the intersection of 29th Street and Gale Avenue. Long Beach had 372 miles of such pipelines running beneath the city, a fact which most residents – and even many city officials – didn't know. That was not the case, however, with the residents of Gale Avenue. Eighty-four days earlier, on September 8, 1980, that same pipeline had ruptured just a few feet from where it exploded on December 1. During the earlier rupture, the pipeline was carrying crude oil, which poured down the street, but did not ignite. Four Corners sent out a crew that cleaned up the mess and replaced a twelve-foot length of pipe – not the whole section of pipe. It was the rest of that original section that would later rupture with such a disastrous outcome.

As it turned out, there were no Long Beach city regulations in place to ensure that the pipelines beneath its street were operated in a safe and prudent fashion. The city checked to make sure new pipelines were laid correctly, but after that, it basically trusted the companies that owned the pipelines to act in a responsible manner. There were no state pipeline regulations in place either. Los Angeles, on the other hand, had standards in place to oversee pipeline operations, but that was only because it had its own version of the Gale Avenue incident four and a half years earlier. In that case, an excavation machine digging up the median strip along Venice Boulevard hit a gasoline line, sending gasoline spraying into the air, drenching cars and pedestrians for ninety seconds before it ignited. In that incident, nine persons were killed, fourteen others were burned, and sixteen buildings were damaged or destroyed.

After Gale Avenue, Long Beach city officials, faced with an outraged constituency, moved quickly to draw up a safety ordinance to address the problem. The ordinance required pipeline owners to inspect and pressure-test their pipelines annually and to provide the city with complete inventories of their equipment. Maximum operating pressures were specified by law, and the city manager was authorized to shut down any pipeline if he deemed it necessary. Operators who violated the ordinance would be subject to fines of from $1,000 a day up to a total of $200,000.

Eight months later, the National Transportation Safety Board issued a report that showed that the Gale Avenue accident on December 1 had been almost identical in cause to the accident on September 8. The cause was pumping product through the line from one point while the valves were not open to receive the product at the other end. The pressure built up – to as much as 1,000 pounds per square inch – and the pipe ruptured. The pipe in question was put in the ground in 1947 – more than thirty-three years before it broke. To top it off, because of a postwar shortage in steel when it was laid, the pipe had previously been used. The lap-welded pipe was corroded, and the rupture in both cases was longitudinal along the seam. The dispatcher in charge of the Four Corners pipeline network that night was a newcomer to the job. His training consisted of twelve weeks of on-the-job instruction, which mainly consisted of working next to a senior dispatcher and getting familiar with all of the equipment. He had received no formal classroom training, yet he was put in charge of 1,500 miles of pipeline, ranging from four to forty-two inches in diameter, in five Western states.

The Port of Long Beach was not directly involved in the incident on Gale Avenue – the naphtha was being transported from the Marlex Refinery on Signal Hill to ARCO's Watson Refinery in Carson. But the port sat atop a maze of pipelines that connected to producing wells, oil terminals, tank farms, and other petroleum-based facilities. The problem was that the port also handled many volatile and toxic cargos, some of them contained in the 360 storage tanks that sat on port property. A pipeline fire like the one that occurred on Gale Avenue could have disastrous effects if it happened in the vicinity of some of those cargos. In the days of the oil boom, when oil was first discovered beneath the city and the port, pipelines were laid without too much concern, and records, if there ever were any, were not preserved. City Oil Properties Director Leonard Brock told reporter Robert Gore that the network of old pipes running in various directions beneath the port was a mess.

"There are a jillion old lines," he said. "In the old days, people would just run a line from point A to point B and not ask anybody."

The port had detailed records of all the pipelines laid in the port since the 1950s, but little documentation for pipelines that were laid before that time. There was no map of where those pipelines might be, who might own them, and whether they were active. It was assumed that most were not active, but there was no way to be absolutely sure. The only strategy available was for the port to keep tabs on the pipelines that it knew about, to try to identify the pipelines it didn't know about, and most of all – to hope for the best.

The Burden of Being Green

From the first Earth Day in 1970 to the 1980s was a period marked by a growing awareness of the environment and man's impact upon it. The newspapers and magazines at the time were full of dire warnings that time was quickly running out for the planet and that something must be done immediately to reverse the environmental degradation taking place. By the early 1980s, some scientists were warning of a new pending disaster, called "global warming," which was caused by the greenhouse gas effect that resulted from burning fossil fuels. New evidence suggested that the Earth was warming up at an even faster rate than had previously been suggested, the scientists said. By the end of the decade, the Earth would see the highest global temperatures ever registered on thermometers. While many of the most extreme warnings from the 1970s and 1980s seem silly in retrospect, the fact remained that until that time too little attention had been paid to short- and long-term environmental consequences. That had to change, but it wasn't going to be easy.

In 1980, Colonel Gwynn A. Teague, the district director for the Army Corps of Engineers, testified at a hearing of the House Merchant Marine Committee held in Long Beach. Colonel Teague said that environmental regulations were stifling much-needed port development. He predicted that cargo through the ports of Long Beach and Los Angeles would increase 350 percent by the year 2000. Unless the ports built for that future, the transportation system would be overtaxed, and the result would be widespread congestion, he warned. Executives from both San Pedro Bay ports, along with some labor leaders, criticized what they saw as overly zealous state and federal air pollution agencies for attempting to impose requirements on ships and for delaying critical infrastructure projects. State Air Resources Board Chairwoman Mary Nichols defended efforts of her agency to control pollution. She pointed out that while refineries and power plants had done much to control their emissions, the maritime industry had done little. She was kept at the witness table for an hour, being questioned by congressmen Glenn M. Anderson of California and John M. Murphy of New York.

Business at the ports had been booming for a while, and the people in charge were focused on preparing to meet the challenges posed by the demands of international trade around the Pacific Rim. By the 1980s, however, every decision had to be backed up with reports, documents, hearings, and seemly endless red tape.

The ports were doing things that would improve the environment, although the motives behind such efforts were subject to question. As things often work out, actions and projects that made sense for business were also good for the environment. One of those projects proposed in 1980 was development of a joint Los Angeles-Long Beach near-dock rail yard to be built on 114 acres owned by the Port of Los Angeles about four miles north of the two ports, south of the San Diego Freeway and bordering the city of Long Beach on the east side.

Most of the containers being unloaded at the two ports at that time were trucked twenty miles north on the Long Beach Freeway to railheads in East Los Angeles and the city of Commerce. It cost shippers about $100 to dray a container from the port to the distant railheads, a cost not encountered by ports in the Pacific Northwest or at Oakland where major rail yards were closer to the ports. Draying containers from the port to the proposed yard – to be called the Intermodal Container Transfer Facility (ICTF) – would reduce that cost and make the Long Beach and Los Angeles ports more competitive to their northern rivals.

The ICTF also was expected to take 24 percent of the trucks draying cargo between the port and the distant rail yards off the Long Beach Freeway. That was significant. The Long Beach Freeway was not only becoming increasingly congested, it also was getting a reputation as the most dangerous freeway in California because of all the truck traffic – which by that time constituted a quarter of all the vehicles on the freeway. The roadway was often littered with large pieces of debris ranging from packing crates and pallets to various tools and pieces of jagged metal. There were some drivers, under pressure to get in as many trips a day as they could, who sometimes pushed safe limits in order to keep their schedules. Moving traffic from trucks to trains also had important air pollution-mitigation benefits. Although each locomotive would generate much more pollution than a truck, one train could be expected to replace as many as 300 trucks on the freeway, and ton-for-ton, trains were a much cleaner way to move cargo than trucks.

The Long Beach and Los Angeles ports agreed in 1983 to build the ICTF and to split the cost, which was expected to be $60 million. The final project would be about 133 acres with about fifteen acres of land in the city of Carson still to be purchased. Development would be overseen by a five-member Joint Powers Authority composed of two members from each port and a fifth member to be selected by the other four. Since the tracks of the Southern Pacific Railroad ran adjacent to the site, that railroad would design and operate the new yard.

It seemed to be a done deal, but in 1984, as the ports began site preparations for the ICTF yard, they got pushback from the city of Carson. The city refused to issue building permits for the fifteen-acre portion of the project within its city limits until it received funding for street improvements in the area. Although it had been more than two years since the environmental impact report for the ICTF project had been done, Carson had become concerned over a new proposal to create a consolidated rail line that would directly link the ports to the distant railheads.

The new line, proposed by planners at the Southern California Association of Governments, would consolidate the traffic from the three current rail lines – operated by the Union Pacific; the Atchison, Topeka, and Santa Fe Railroad;

RAIL YARD OPENS: *The Intermodal Container Transfer Facility, or ICTF, is used to assemble long trains of containers to be sent to rail yards in Los Angeles and destinations all over the country. Opened in 1986 as a project of both the ports of Long Beach and Los Angeles, ICTF was an example of the costs and pitfalls that await the construction of any large project.*

and the Southern Pacific – into one line. The Union Pacific line meandered east through North Long Beach, Lakewood, and other communities before reaching the main rail yards. The Santa Fe went west through Lomita, Torrance, and the beach cities of the South Bay before turning back east. The consolidated line would run along the Southern Pacific right-of-way, which went straight north through a mostly industrial area parallel to Alameda Street.

The SCAG planners estimated that by consolidating the three lines into one, train noise would be reduced by 36 percent and locomotive emissions by as much as 29 percent. The Long Beach City Council endorsed the plan, at least in principle, but Carson opposed it. The new line would carry the traffic of all three of the existing lines through the eastern portion of Carson, resulting in noise, traffic congestion, and air pollution in the city's Lincoln-Dominguez neighborhood.

Before it approved building permits for the ICTF project, Carson wanted assurance of $4 million in street improvements on Sepulveda Boulevard, funding for overpasses along Del Amo Boulevard and Carson Street and sound walls along the railroad right-of-way. It only took a week to reach a deal with Carson. The ICTF Authority would provide up to $10 million for the improvements, and the city would issue the needed permits.

The Intermodal Container Transfer Facility was built and opened for business in 1986, but it served as an expensive illustration that anybody wanting to develop a major project had to consider a new and complicated reality. That reality involved not only more studies, reports, and permits, but sometimes large payments to affected cities and businesses. The problem that the ports faced then, and that they continue to face, is that developing new infrastructure and cleaning up the environment is seldom an enterprise that is fair to everybody. Taking the trucks off the freeway would be a good thing for commuters driving to work and for residents living near the freeway, but it wasn't necessarily a great deal for people who lived next to the proposed rail yard. Few of the decisions made by the port in those days – and few of them later – pleased everybody. It would remain one of the dilemmas of operating a major asset in a crowded urban environment.

The 2020 Plan

The sister ports of San Pedro Bay could be tenacious rivals. Over the years, their disputes were often bitter and public. Los Angeles was always somewhat dismissive of the little port next door, and even after that port grew up, there was little change in L.A.'s attitude. While it was true that Los Angeles often suggested that the two ports consolidate into one, it was always viewed as L.A.'s attempt to eliminate competition by absorbing it, even if it meant giving up some power. Every time the offer was made, it was rejected by Long Beach. But when the interest of the two ports coincided, both Los Angeles and Long Beach were willing to work together to achieve their common end, as evidenced by the development of the Intermodal Container Transfer Facility.

In 1982, the two ports were working together again to create a plan for the future. Trade around the Pacific Rim was exploding, and the volume of cargo coming through the two ports was growing by double digits every year. Both ports were running out of room to accommodate all the incoming business. The ports joined with the Army Corps of Engineers to come up with a "2020 plan" for expanding the available land by dredging channels as deep as eight feet and using the spoils to fill in 2,600 acres of new land. The planned expansion of the ports was expected to meet the needs of international trade in the area through the year 2020.

But as always, there were problems. No port dredging projects had been approved by Congress in seven years, so the ports might have to pay for the dredging themselves. Both state and federal wildlife agencies were concerned about the loss of marine habitat that would result from filling in the harbor. The project would disrupt or eliminate the habitat for 150 species of birds – including endangered least terns and brown pelicans – and 130 species of fish. If the area had to be filled in, the ports would be required to construct or restore wetland areas somewhere else in Southern California in order to mitigate the damage. Wildlife and conservation officials favored a plan in which the fill would be placed outside the federal breakwater, a proposal that would raise the price significantly because the water was deeper and a causeway would have to be built out to the new area.

Environmentalists and other members of the public also were concerned about increased congestion and pollution resulting from the project. Local freeways – especially the Long Beach Freeway – were already heavily impacted by trucks, and residents along rail routes were tired of trains running day and night past their homes. The ports' challenge was no longer just a matter of providing enough facilities to handle all the ships calling in the harbor. The new challenge was how to get inbound cargo through the congested urban landscape to its final destination, and outbound cargo from its source to the ports.

In 1983, Governor George Deukmejian signed a bill that exempted eight projects at the ports of Long Beach and Los Angeles from having to prepare environmental impact reports. The bill was a somewhat watered-down version of three bills introduced by Assemblyman Dave Elder of Long Beach on behalf of the California Association of Port Authorities. Elder said the bill was aimed at relieving the backlog of stalled projects at the port during a time of high unemployment. None of the projects was especially controversial; mostly they were aimed at updating and improving existing facilities.

Opposition to the ports' 2020 plan didn't just come from environmental groups. Long Beach City Planning Director Robert Paternoster warned at a 1984 Army Corps of Engineers hearing that the proposed dredge-and-fill project could alter water circulation patterns and affect water quality. The additional capacity made possible by the plan would also overload roadways and rail lines serving the harbor area. He predicted that truck traffic through the harbor would triple and that there would be an increase in harbor area train traffic from sixteen trains a day to forty-three. Paternoster, speaking on behalf of the City Council, recommended that the proposed consolidated rail line from the two ports north along what was by then being called the Alameda Corridor, be built along with a truck expressway along the same route. Further, he recommended that the 2020 plan should be linked to the needed road and rail improvements, so that the planned land expansion could not proceed without the additional improvements being made. Of the seventeen people who spoke at the hearing, only three, including Paternoster, had issues with the 2020 plan. The others, representing business, industry, and union groups, expressed strong support for the plan.

By early 1985, the Port of Long Beach was busy building and expanding the harbor to handle the future crush of business. By that summer, however, both ports withdrew their support for the 2020 dredging plan that had been drafted by the Army Corps of Engineers. Officials from both ports said they felt the plan was premature, that it didn't necessarily sync up with specific expansion plans each port had for itself, and that funding for it was uncertain. When the Army Corps had submitted the plan to the Coastal Commission the previous year, it was sharply criticized by Coastal Commission staff, which said it didn't deal adequately with the environmental consequences of the project. The plan was later withdrawn altogether.

As it turned out, Congress did pass a bill authorizing the 2020 port expansion plan, and President Reagan signed it. The 2020 plan may have been aimed at ensuring the ports would have the capacity to handle the amount of future cargo for the coming thirty-five years, but like all long-range plans it was flawed. The assumptions on cargo growth were conservative, and the plan did little to consider the kind of technical advances that would make it possible to squeeze more cargo through a limited amount of space. But it set a course for the ports to follow into the future.

Return of the Navy

The Navy left Long Beach, except for support activity and the shipyard, in the mid-1970s. But as the end of the decade approached, senior officers began to think about a return to the city. San Diego – which had acquired most of the ships and personnel that once were in Long Beach – was becoming overcrowded, and it made sense to shift some of those ships and people back to Long Beach. Although the Navy's new presence in Long Beach would not be on the same scale as it once had been, the return was greeted enthusiastically by city officials. In 1980, a new assault ship, *USS Peleliu*, arrived at the Long Beach Naval Station with 2,750 officers and men, including an 800-man Marine assault battalion. As part of a Navy program to reactivate old battleships, the 887-foot-long battleship *New Jersey* – the largest battleship ever built – arrived under tow from Bremerton, Washington, in August 1981 to be refitted at the Long Beach Naval Shipyard. Hundreds of people lined the shore to watch its arrival, and three days later, when the Navy opened the *New Jersey* for tours, more than 100,000 people jammed the harbor area to participate. At one point, the Long Beach Freeway was backed up six miles – all the way past the interchange with the San Diego Freeway.

With 30,000 naval personnel and fifty ships expected to be homeported in Long Beach, the city had to consider the need for more housing. Rental units in the city were running a low 3 percent vacancy rate, in part because of the influx of new residents from Southeast Asia following the wars in Vietnam and Cambodia. Traffic was also a concern. Many of those new Navy personnel and their families would be living off base and commuting to work. The traffic system would be stressed, and accommodations – such as banning rush-hour parking along busy arteries – would have to be made to help ease the flow of vehicles.

The Navy, in the meantime, was preparing the Naval Station for its return by upgrading the mess halls and the Navy Exchange store and building a $15 million enlisted housing complex at the base. The historic battleship *USS Missouri* – sister ship to the *New Jersey* – arrived under tow in Long Beach in 1984, twenty-nine years after it was decommissioned, for retrofitting and reactivation. The *Missouri* gained fame as the vessel aboard which the Japanese surrendered following World War II.

The return of the *Missouri* led to a three-way battle between Long Beach, San Francisco, and Honolulu over where the *Missouri* would be homeported after the retrofitting was finished. All three cities lobbied the Navy for the ship, with Long Beach stressing its historic naval connections. The competition was for more than just bragging rights. The *Missouri's* presence would bring a $25 million-a-year payroll to the local economy – an economic boost that all three cities wanted. The drawback for Long Beach was that the *USS New Jersey* was already stationed there, and it didn't seem likely that the Navy would want to station two of its battleships in the same port.

In 1985, Long Beach got its answer. It had been eliminated as the *Missouri's* home port. Four months later, the Navy announced that the *Missouri* would be homeported in San Francisco, despite widespread public opposition in that community. Many San Franciscans wanted the Navy to guarantee that the ship would not carry nuclear weapons onboard. San Francisco Mayor Dianne Feinstein, who cited the economic benefits the battleship would bring to the community, vetoed a vote by the city and county board of supervisors against the *Missouri* coming. The *Missouri* arrived in its new homeport of San Francisco and was recommissioned there in May 1986. However, the following October, Congress – at the behest of U.S. Representative Ronald Dellums of Oakland – scuttled the Navy's $22 million plan to station the *Missouri* at San Francisco's Hunters Point Naval Shipyard. Feinstein was furious.

The Navy took its ship and its payroll and returned to Long Beach. In 1989, Hawaiian Senator Daniel Inouye inserted conditions in a military construction bill for the *Missouri* to be brought to Pearl Harbor. That idea failed, however, after the federal General Accounting Office crunched the numbers in 1990 and reported that it was too expensive to move the battleship to a new home. Congress agreed, and the ship stayed in Long Beach until it was decommissioned in March 1992. It then went to Bremerton to be mothballed. In 1998, she made her last voyage – to Pearl Harbor, where she was put on display not far from the remains of the battleship *Arizona*. The *Arizona* was sunk during the attack on Pearl Harbor in 1941; the Japanese surrendered on the decks of the *Missouri* less than four years later. Together the sister ships mark the beginning and end of the Second World War for the United States.

Crime on the Waterfront

Containerization may have led to a boom in international trade and changed the way business was done at ports around the world, but it had some interesting and sometimes unexpected side effects. If containers made it easier to unload and deliver foreign goods, it also made it easier to steal them. There had always been petty pilfering of cargo moving through the ports, but the volume of cargo stolen was relatively small. Locking the goods inside a steel box cut down on the pilfering, but it also increased the ability for the bad guys to steal a whole container of goods at one time. Some of the containers with high-priced electronics or other manufactured goods inside could be worth as much as $1 million.

As cargo crime increased in the 1980s, the way in which thieves operated changed as well. Some containers were driven away from trucking company parking lots, some were hijacked by gunmen as drivers stopped on freeway offramps, and others were stolen by crooks pulling inside jobs. More than a few sophisticated thieves found a poorly paid immigrant driver who could be paid a large sum to park his truck, go for a cup of coffee, and let the truck be stolen. The truck would later turn up abandoned – the thieves didn't want the truck – and the driver would supposedly get his rig back, unless he ended up going to jail instead.

To be successful, cargo thieves needed some indication of what was in the container. Although thieves couldn't tell what was in a container by looking at it, each container had a manifest with a list of contents, and a number of people in the supply chain – including customs workers, brokers, trucking companies, and others – had access to the manifest. Electronics were expensive, but they had serial numbers that could be traced. Frozen lobsters were also expensive, but they had no serial numbers. Thieves also needed a buyer to whom they could sell the cargo quickly and with no questions asked. Pilfering on the docks was usually a matter of individuals swiping something for themselves; container theft was highly organized.

Further complicating the situation was the fact that cargo crime covered multiple jurisdictions and multiple categories. A container could be stolen in one city, unloaded in another and the goods sold in a third location. It could involve the theft of a vehicle, a chassis, the container itself, and the goods inside the container.

By the end of the decade, with container theft soaring, law enforcement agencies and the industry had formed a Cargo Theft Security Council to find ways to combat what had become a major problem. By December 1989, the Los Angeles County Sheriff's Office was talking about formation of a special team of sheriff's deputies, police officers from various departments, and the FBI that would focus on combating cargo theft. That team, which debuted in 1990, was called the Cargo Criminal Apprehension Team, which soon became known by the acronym – Cargo CATs. It was a multi-jurisdictional team that included officers from various police agencies working together to track down cargo thieves and recover stolen property. The Port of Long Beach – which had no sworn police force – was not a part of it. Although the containers being stolen came through the port, the actual stealing was done off-site – from warehouse parking lots or at gunpoint along the way.

A second criminal enterprise that benefited from containerization was the smuggling of drugs and other contraband. By the 1980s, the harbor had become a primary gateway for the importation of drugs – especially cocaine. The drugs could be secreted on a vessel and smuggled into the country by a crew member, or they could be concealed among legitimate goods inside a container destined for a company where an accomplice could retrieve it. Federal agents are primarily responsible for controlling drug smuggling.

One other problem made possible by containerization at the port was the smuggling of human beings inside containers. It was a dangerous practice that often resulted in the tragic deaths of the people trying to enter the country illegally through the ports.

The World Trade Center
Although the Port of Long Beach was a city-owned and operated asset, the benefits of the port were for the most part restricted by law to creating jobs and local commercial opportunities and helping fund tideland projects and operations, such as sea walls, piers, and marinas. The port would sometimes sponsor promotional events and opportunities – such as the Municipal Band or a float

DOWNTOWN DEVELOPMENT: *The World Trade Center under construction in the mid-1980s. The Port partnered with private developers to build the complex, aimed at revitalizing downtown Long Beach. The early '90s recession meant that the project was not as successful as hoped.*

in the Rose Parade – on the rationale that these were opportunities to promote commerce through the port. The port also accepted responsibility for the Queen Mary, hotels and restaurants, and offices for maritime-related businesses in the port district. But not all the port projects were within the port district.

By the end of the 1970s, the Port of Long Beach – anxious to cement its reputation as a primary trade gateway and to provide an anchor for the ongoing revitalization of the downtown Long Beach area – began looking at the possibility of building a World Trade Center. The Port of San Francisco's dominance as the West Coast gateway had ended with the coming of containerization. The Long Beach Harbor Commission hoped that a World Trade Center in Long Beach would lure some of the Bay Area maritime companies to relocate to Southern California. In September 1979, the commission voted to spend $350,000 on a study to see if such a project were feasible and what it might include.

Although the Port of Los Angeles' disastrous attempt to build a World Trade Center on Terminal Island in the late 1960s had ended with three harbor commissioners and the developer being indicted, Los Angeles did operate the Pacific Trade Center in San Pedro. That eleven-story office tower was not expected to offer significant competition to the World Trade Center envisioned by Long Beach, which would include exhibition space, conference rooms, a private club, and business services geared to international trade. The Long Beach Port would either build the World Trade Center itself or act as a partner with the city's community development agency.

In February 1981, the port unveiled its conceptual plan for the World Trade Center complex to an audience of city officials and the public. The plan was for the trade complex to be built on a 13.5-acre parcel between Ocean Boulevard and Broadway, just east of the Long Beach Freeway and west of Magnolia Avenue. The first building to be erected would be a thirty-story, 500,000-square-foot office tower – which would make it the tallest building between Los Angeles and San Diego. A second, twenty-five-story office tower and a third, smaller, office building would be added later. The plan called for the first phase to open in 1987.

In February 1982, as the port went about purchasing the needed properties, it drew fire from the California Department of Housing and Community Development over the port's plans for relocating the 800 residents and fifteen businesses that would be displaced by the proposed development. The port was already being sued by some of the property owners, who claimed that the port's environmental review of the project was inadequate. The criticism and litigation were not unexpected in an urban development of such scope, and they were quickly resolved.

Plans for the development moved forward. People were relocated, the property cleared, historic houses were moved, and the search was on for a private developer. That developer turned out to be a joint venture between Long Beach-based IDM Corp. and Kajima International – the U.S subsidiary of Kajima Corp., a 140-year-old Japanese construction firm. The port leased the property to the developers who designed and built the complex. Groundbreaking ceremonies were held in July 1986 with speeches by politicians, trumpets blaring in the background, sixteen hot air balloons, 5,000 small balloons, and eight confetti cannons. IDM Chairman Michael Choppin said the complex would include a 400-to 600-room hotel, just west of the main tower. A federal office building was scheduled to be built on property to the east of the World Trade Center complex. The name for the complex would be the "Greater Los Angeles World Trade Center-Long Beach."

There were some qualms. There were delays in securing the necessary building permits and easements, which pushed the project behind schedule. Although many would-be tenants had committed to leasing office space, those commitments were hard to finalize before the building was finished. Long Beach had just added a large volume of office space to the downtown area, and the rates planned for the World Trade Center were the highest in town. Shipping lines and freight forwarders may have been drawn to the harbor area, but most of them were seeking buildings with lower overhead, skeptics warned. People began to worry that the new, magnificent building being constructed as a magnet to draw new tenants might just add to a glut of downtown office space.

Building a massive World Trade Center – the largest in the country after New York – was a high-stakes gamble to be sure, but the developers and city officials remained confident that it was a gamble that would pay off. The city and the developers, whether they believed in the project or not, stayed the course. It was too late to do anything else.

The year following the World Trade Center groundbreaking, construction began on an adjacent eight-story federal office building on the corner of Ocean Boulevard and Magnolia Avenue. It was designed to complement the World Trade Center next door, and many of the government agencies represented there would be involved in maritime and international trade activity.

The first phase of the World Trade Center opened in May 1989 – two years later than the original plan. The twenty-seven-story office tower included 553,000 square feet of office and retail space. The final design featured vertical panes of blue glass intersecting horizontal bands of brown. Visible from miles away, it was a beautiful building that had a luminescent copper sheen when viewed in the proper light. But its future remained clouded.

Foreign Trade Zone Designation

The Port of Long Beach received its designation as a foreign trade zone from the Commerce Department in 1979. The Foreign Trade Zone 50 authority included Los Angeles County south of the mountains, Orange County, and the western portion of San Bernardino County. The port could also create sub-zones within its designated area. The designation allowed the port to establish an industrial zone in which businesses could avoid paying duty on imported items until the items were sold.

The way foreign trade zones work is that a manufacturer can import into the zone components necessary to create finished products, assemble the products, and then when the products are sold, pay duty only on the components, not on the finished products, which carry a higher value than the component parts. A foreign trade zone also allows businesses that want only to warehouse their goods to defer payment of duty until the goods are sold. The goal of foreign trade zones is to generate American jobs, but some critics claim it encourages companies to buy raw materials and manufactured components from foreign sources at the expense of American workers.

The port bought a ten-and-a-half-acre parcel off Dominguez Street in West Long Beach as the Foreign Trade Zone 50 site and built two warehouses surrounded by a chain-link fence at the site. The plan was that the zone would be divided up and leased out to companies wanting to establish businesses there.

But things didn't work out as expected. Administration of the trade zone was contracted out to Cal Cartage Enterprises, but it was a struggle to keep even one of the warehouses operating at capacity. The second warehouse was finally removed from the zone and used as a bonded warehouse. With its foreign trade zone struggling to stay in business, the port decided to focus on creation of subzones in the area. The first one – the 1,350-acre California Commerce Center, adjacent to Ontario International Airport – was established in 1985. A second, sixty-five-acre subzone was established in 1986 in Santa Ana.

The Queen and the Goose

The *Queen Mary* had fallen sadly short of what Long Beach had envisioned when she first arrived in the harbor in 1967. Despite all of the optimism and hoopla about the new role for the aging ship, she turned out to be more of a money pit than an asset. The ship had been expensive to retrofit and expensive to maintain. The millions of dollars spent to present her in her best light did not translate to the millions of visitors that had been expected to flock to her decks. In 1978, the city had turned the money-losing historic liner over to the port.

At the time, the port was in the process of evicting the Spruce Goose from its Terminal Island hangar to make way for construction of an oil terminal for ARCO. A tentative agreement had been reached with the plane's owner, Summa Corp., to relocate it to a new home adjacent to the *Queen Mary*, where it would be put on public exhibit. A 1980 report on the proposed move showed the port would recoup its costs in three years if 2,850,000 visitors came to view the plane at $4.50 each during that time.

It was time for harbor commissioners to make a hard decision. Since the port had taken over the *Queen Mary*, it had been losing money at a slower rate than previously, but it remained a long way from being profitable. Was it time for Long Beach to cut its losses on the ship and stop hemorrhaging cash? The port had three options: keep the ship with all the long-term losses that option could include, find a buyer for it, or sell it for scrap. An attempt to attract interest from buyers had not been successful.

The port ran the museum aboard the ship, but the hotel and the food services were operated under two separate leases – Specialty Restaurant Corp. and PSA Hotels Inc., a subsidiary of Pacific Southwest Airlines. Any buyer would have to consider the cost of buying out those leases – expected to add about $9 million to the cost – and the cost of possibly moving the ship to another location. Finally, in order to offer the ship as a complete entity, the port bought out the lessees. Further, any deal the port made to sell the *Queen* would have to be approved by the State Lands Commission since $54 million in tidelands oil revenue had been used to buy and fix up the vessel. In the meantime, the city and the port were stuck with the ship. The purchase of the *Queen Mary* had been made in haste, and undoing that impulse purchase was proving to be much more difficult and costly.

In August 1980, the port signed a sixty-six-year lease with the Wrather Corp. for an unencumbered *Queen Mary* and the Spruce Goose. The Beverly Hills-based Wrather Corp., led by Chairman Jack Wrather, had big plans for the ship – starting with a $10 million make-over of the vessel. He had budgeted another $1.5 million for advertising during the first year.

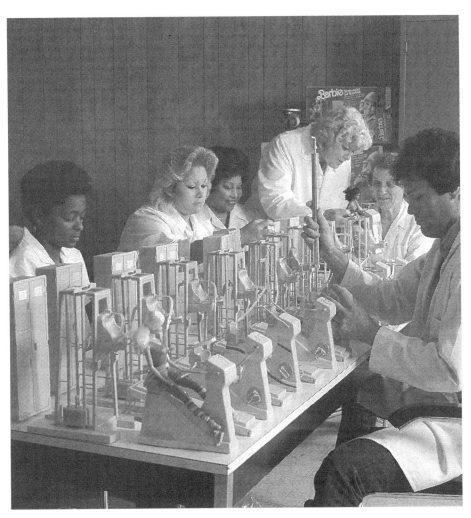

IN THE ZONE: *Mattel workers package Barbie dolls at Foreign Trade Zone 50 in the mid-'80s. A Foreign Trade Zone allows businesses to defer paying duty on imported goods until the items are sold, or, in this case, assembled and sold.*

Wrather, who owned the Disneyland Hotel in Anaheim, was a close friend and confidant of President Ronald Reagan. Heir to a rich Texas oil family, he had moved to California after the war and built an empire in the communications and entertainment business.

The Spruce Goose was floated free from its hangar in October 1980, the first time it had been exposed to daylight in more than three decades. It was then gently lifted from the water by "Herman the German" – the giant World War II crane that was taken from the Germans as a war prize – and stored under wraps a few hundred yards away. The Goose would stay there until its new nest – a giant, white geodesic dome – could be prepared.

In 1981, Wrather unveiled his grand plan for the *Queen Mary* and the surrounding property, which he called PortAdventure. Designed by Disneyland's first marketing director, Ed Ettinger, it would include an expansion of the shopping village next to the ship, which Wrather renamed LondonTowne. The plan would include two new hotels, one of them a floating structure, and a marina to be built off the ship's stern. The rock dike surrounding the *Queen Mary* would be pushed out into a large arc, forming a separate lagoon for the ship. Coca-Cola would be the official PortAdventure drink.

At the end of the first year of the lease, Wrather's plan for the aging ship was running into the same problems that had been encountered by the city. The number of visitors coming to the ship was far less than projected, and so were the revenues. Wrather admitted to making some "horseback estimates" before signing the deal that later turned out to be wrong, but predicted that it would all turn around in the months to come. By January 1982, shortly after Wrather had laid off seventy-five of the 980 shipboard employees to cut costs, he announced that he was seeking financial partners to help build a $1 billion development around the ship. The development would include three hotels with a total of 3,000 rooms, five office buildings, shops and restaurants, a 1,100-slip marina, a fishermen's wharf, an 11,000-car parking garage, and a marine research institute.

The Spruce Goose exhibit opened to the public in May 1983. The entry cost was $6 for adults and $4 for children. A long line formed on the first day to see the plane, cradled in a steel frame above a shallow pond. It had been painted a brilliant white and lit in dramatic fashion against the dark interior of the giant dome, its huge size enhanced within the confines of the structure. Many of the attendees who stood in the long line that first day were aviation or history buffs who wanted to see the great plane up close. There were videos showing the history of the plane and exterior stairways that visitors could climb up to peer into the plane's interior. A gift shop sold t-shirts, souvenir brown fedoras like the ones Hughes had worn, books, model Spruce Goose planes, tie pins, posters, glassware, ash trays, and salt and pepper shakers.

On November 12, 1984, Jack Wrather died of cancer at 66, and his widow, former actress Bonita Granville Wrather, took over as chairman of the company. The following month, Wrather Corp. withdrew its PortAdventure development plan with a promise to submit a new development proposal by the following March. That scaled-down proposal, presented to the Long Beach Harbor Commission by Wrather Port Properties President Joseph Prevratil, envisioned a 350-room hotel to be built by 1988, a large exhibit hall to follow within fifteen years, and a half-dozen office buildings to be erected at some unspecified future date. The taller

TOURIST ATTRACTION: *The Spruce Goose moves into its giant dome home adjacent to the Queen Mary. The exhibit opened to the public in May 1983. The Hughes flying boat remained in Long Beach for nearly a decade and was moved in the 1990s to an aviation museum in McMinnville, Oregon.*

buildings would be built in the background around the *Queen Mary*, presenting a backdrop to the ship as viewed from the downtown side of the Bay, Prevratil said. The port board endorsed the concept.

The Wrather Corp. – including its lease on the *Queen Mary* property – was bought in 1987 by the Walt Disney Co. and Industry Equity (Pacific) Ltd., of Hong Kong, an entity controlled by New Zealand investor Ronald A. Brierley.

In 1989, Disney secured the exclusive rights from the Long Beach Redevelopment Agency to a parcel of land on which to build an 800- to 1,200-room downtown resort hotel near Pine Avenue and Shoreline Drive. The hotel would link to a possible $1 billion Disney theme park to be built on the opposite side of Queensway Bay. Disney Chief Executive Officer Michael Eisner briefed city officials over lunch at the port administration building. The project, if it were to be built, would have an ocean theme and employ about 10,000 people. The *Queen Mary* would serve as a backdrop, but the Spruce Goose would probably have to go elsewhere.

Wrather's PortAdventure dream may have died with him, but the *Queen Mary* and the prime waterfront property by which it was moored still retained the power to inspire grand plans. But what was perhaps the grandest plan of them was still to come.

The Last Box of Tide

After fifty-six years at the Port of Long Beach, Procter & Gamble announced in June 1987 that it was going to close its plant on the West Seventh Street Peninsula within twelve to fifteen months. The plant had employed several generations of Long Beach residents during those years, churning out Ivory bath soap, several brands of laundry and dishwashing detergents, Crisco and Puritan cooking oils, and other household staples. The closure of the Long Beach plant, which employed 420 workers, was part of a worldwide restructuring aimed at making the Cincinnati-based company stronger and more competitive. Other Procter & Gamble U.S. plants to be closed were in Cincinnati, Omaha, and Green Bay.

The plant had been part of the Long Beach scene during the Great Depression, during World War II, and during the period of subsidence during which company executives had to take measures to hold back the ocean as the land on which the plant was built sank lower and lower.

The last box of Tide to be manufactured at the plant was sealed shut on September 29, 1988, and the facility's doors were shut for good on October 2. It had been a good run for the company, and for Long Beach. The company had been able to cash in on the oil found beneath the plant in the 1930s and on the importation of raw materials through the port. The city had gotten fifty-seven years of jobs, tax revenues, and other economic benefits from the company. But time was marching on, and so was Procter & Gamble.

When the company left, the port bought the plant and the property for $23.5 million in order to develop the land as a container terminal. To make way for the terminal, the 140 boats moored at the West Seventh Street Marina would also have to go, as would the Chowder Barge, a colorful, low-end restaurant on a moored barge by the plant.

Making Way for Industry

The boaters next to the Procter & Gamble plant were not the only ones to have to find new moorings. There was also a small, rundown marina on the Cerritos Channel, next to the former Ford plant, called Our Marina. It was described as "the trailer park of marinas," and the people who lived aboard old, leaky and non-working vessels in the shadow of the Commodore Heim Bridge, were mainly poor and semi-destitute. But property in the harbor was too valuable for a slum marina, and the port planned to develop the property as a shipping terminal.

The port paid $14.4 million to buy seventy-two of the acres next to the wharf and had an agreement with the marina operator, Melamed's Channel Enterprises, to clear the docks, which included giving the tenants a year's notice that they would have to move. But that didn't happen. The company continued to rent out slips in the marina. Then, on July 8, 1987, Melamed's served its tenants with thirty-day notices to vacate the marina and move elsewhere. The port, anxious to get out of the marina business and to build its terminal, moved forward. Boat slips in the harbor were at a premium, and existing marinas were expensive and had strict limits on how many "live aboards" were allowed. With terminal development looming, the tenants who had lived aboard their boats had no place to go. The result was a dispute that ended up in court, with the Long Beach Legal Aid Foundation representing the boaters. In 1988, the port agreed to a settlement in which it gave eight tenants each $3,000 as relocation benefits.

On-Dock Push Back

The port was also getting pushback on its plans to develop on-dock rail capabilities at its container terminals. The port had used on-dock rail for years to transport bulk materials such as grain or steel to and from the port, and it made sense to do the same for containers. By locating the rail yard right at the dock, there would be no need to dray many of the containers to off-site rail yards to be loaded onto trains. With the on-dock rail yards, containers headed for a common area would be loaded onto unit trains that would transport them directly from the port to their destination. On-dock rail was expected to lower the cost of moving each container by about $70 by eliminating the truck trip to the rail yard. Other containers would still have to be drayed to either the near-dock yard or more remote locations.

The problem was that while taking trucks off the freeway was a good idea for reducing pollution and highway congestion, putting the containers directly on trains would result in more trains rumbling through residential neighborhoods in North Long Beach.

The first terminal to begin on-dock rail was "K" Line's International Transportation Service (ITS) terminal on Pier J (renamed Pier G in 1986). The plan almost immediately drew opposition, not only from Northside residents, but also from Los Angeles harbor executives who claimed on-dock rail would undercut business at the near-dock International Container Transfer Facility that the ports were jointly developing. Los Angeles Port Chief Deputy Executive Director Jack Wells sent a letter to Long Beach Harbor Commission President David Hauser noting that Los Angeles had also received requests by its tenants for on-dock rail, but had turned them down. Developing on-dock rail was inconsistent with plans by the two ports to develop a near-dock rail yard, Wells wrote.

"If the ITS project is actually developed, there will be an immediate demand at both ports for similar facilities for competitive reasons," Wells warned. "Therefore it is important to view the ITS proposal not in isolation but as one of a series of other similar projects creating an accumulative impact far beyond that associated with the ITS project alone." Wells' letter also advised Long Beach to think about the time and money already invested in the near-dock project and the cooperative relationship it had developed with the Port of Los Angeles.

Long Beach Port Executive Director James McJunkin said he wasn't sure what effect on-dock rail would have on the ICTF near-dock yard and that many smaller batches of containers headed for various places would still go there. He also noted that the ICTF near-dock yard was to be a Southern Pacific operation. (The ITS on-dock yard would be operated for Union Pacific trains.) The Port of Long Beach had never intended to solicit rail business only for Southern Pacific, McJunkin said. Major ports were all looking at on-dock rail facilities, and Long Beach would be at a major disadvantage if it ignored the trend, he said.

The complaints by residents about on-dock rail were more of a concern than the issues brought forth by the Port of Los Angeles. In August 1986, Long Beach Mayor Ernie Kell had sent a letter to the port board on behalf of the City Council stating its concerns over on-dock rail and warning that the Council would take all necessary steps to prevent the development. In December, the ITS on-dock rail plan was withdrawn with the idea that an alternate plan would be proffered in the near future. The opposition by the City Council and the jettisoned plan infuriated the International Longshoremen's and Warehousemen's Union, which shut down the port in a nine-hour boycott to protest the city's position. On-dock rail meant more jobs for longshore workers. On-dock rail made a lot of sense, both for the environment and for freeway congestion, but for the people living next to the railroad tracks, it was an idea whose time should never come.

By 1988, with ITS still pressing for its on-dock rail yard and opposition to it still strong, the port was examining its options – all of which were expensive. If ITS got its rail yard, other terminals would be demanding their own on-dock rail, which would not only cost a lot of money, it would also add to the noise and congestion problems of trains running through residential neighborhoods. Building rail overpasses and underpasses across major roadways and installing sound walls along the Union Pacific route would do much to mitigate the noise, but it would be only a partial solution.

The idea of a consolidated rail line along the Alameda Corridor was a good long-term solution, but there was opposition to that as well. Southern Pacific was not happy about sharing its right-of-way with competing railroads. The railroad also felt that if the ports developed on-dock rail, they would undermine the ICTF yard in which Southern Pacific had already invested large amounts of money. Cities and residents north of the ports along the Alameda Corridor were not happy about the idea that rail traffic from all three railroads serving the ports would be coming through their areas. Then there was the question of how to pay for the consolidated rail line – expected to cost $220 million.

The Port of Long Beach did what public organizations do when confronted with a dilemma. It commissioned a study. That study, released in April 1988, concluded what everybody already knew. There was an immediate need to develop on-dock rail at four of the port's container terminals. The residential problems of such a solution could be mitigated by the construction of rail grade separations, the laying of continuous-welded rails to reduce the clatter of train traffic, and sound walls. But it would not be cheap. The cost of constructing the on-dock yards was estimated at $18 million, the cost of rail improvements and grade separations within the port up to Anaheim Street would be $48.5 million, and the cost of the sound walls and other grade separations through residential neighborhoods would be an additional $40 million to $50 million.

The on-dock rail question was far from clear-cut, and there was no correct answer. The port was a multimillion-dollar, publicly owned business, but its funds were hardly unlimited. On-dock rail would reduce pollution in the region, but not for the people who lived near the tracks. It would take trucks off the freeway, which was good for drivers, but that was also a temporary condition. The growing volume of trade would put more trucks on the freeway eventually – it was just a matter of time. Plus, local cargo still had to move by truck. No matter what the port did, there would be unhappy people. That was a reality the port would learn to live with.

Public Agency vs. Business Entity

The other reality the Harbor Commission was learning to face in the late 1980s was how to balance the needs of the city with the needs of the port as its own entity. The port might be a public agency, but it was also a business. As a business, it had to plan for the future, watch its finances, make sure it maintained enough reserves for rainy days, and reinvest in new infrastructure and services as times and technology changed. But all that money the port controlled represented a temptation to anybody in the city with a project they thought was worthy of support. Sometimes the port board was happy to fund requests – according to how much was needed and whether such support was legal under state law. A good example was the World Trade Center, which was a huge part of the downtown revitalization effort, but which was also related to international trade.

The story was different, though, when the City Council asked the port to help pay for expansion of the downtown Long Beach Convention and Entertainment Center. Port officials said no – the port's money was already committed to other projects. A citizens' committee, set up to explore Convention Center expansion, insisted the port was the best place to get money for the project. Expected to cost $59.5 million, the expansion would almost double the available exhibit space and add 25,000 square feet of meeting rooms. The argument was that the Convention Center would enhance the port's position as a trade center and thereby justify the expenditure of harbor revenues. Faced with the port's reluctance to bankroll the Convention Center expansion, plans for the facility were shelved – at least temporarily.

By May 1989, the idea of port funding for the project was once again revived. In July the Harbor Commission agreed to the idea, but it planned to seek a court ruling on whether harbor funds could legally be used to help build the center. The Steamship Association of Southern California protested any such move, because it wanted the port to keep its funds for port development. But the port wasn't just a business. Despite its relative autonomy, it was still a department of the city of Long Beach – a public agency that once again had to balance its priorities.

If there was one constant in the port, it was change – not just in infrastructure and policy, but also in people. In January 1988, Long Beach Port Executive Director James McJunkin had announced that he was leaving the job he had held since 1977. Although McJunkin was well liked and respected, the Harbor Commission had felt it was time for a change. Under the deal they offered McJunkin, he would step down from the job as executive director for which he was paid $102,500 a year, and take a job as international trade and marketing adviser at a salary of $120,000 a year. He would hold that job until April 1989, at which time he would retire.

Critics said the move was indicative of the port board becoming more politicized. A new majority – commissioners David Hauser, George Talin, and Joel Friedland – had taken over the board and were getting involved in running the port, rather than just setting policy, claimed former Harbor Commissioner James Gray in a Los Angeles Times interview. Hauser denied such allegations. He agreed that McJunkin had done a good job, but the commissioner had definite ideas about policies the port should be following. Paul Brown, the port director of administration and operations, took over as acting executive director.

The new Port of Long Beach executive director was announced in April 1988. Wrather Corp. President Joseph Prevratil, who had been overseeing the *Queen Mary*, had agreed to take the top job. Wrather by that time was owned by Disney, and Prevratil said he could have stayed with Disney at a higher salary, but that his new job with the port was too good to pass up. The harbor commissioners were just as high on their new hire. Commissioner Talin predicted that Prevratil was "going to be to the port what Babe Ruth was to baseball."

In January 1989, Prevratil reorganized top management, appointing three managing directors to oversee ten port departments. Paul Brown would head administration and maintenance, Leland Hill would be charge of planning and engineering, and Steve Dillenbeck would be managing director of commerce and development.

In May 1989, one year after he was hired, Prevratil quit his port post to take a job as a private consultant with the city, which had hired him to oversee the proposed $80 million expansion of the Long Beach Convention and Entertainment Center. Prevratil said he became interested in heading up the project when he was involved as port director in discussing how to finance it. Under his contract with the city, Prevratil would be paid $138,000 a year, plus $10,000 in expenses. And he would be free to contract with other clients as well. At the port, administration and operations director Paul Brown was once again acting executive director.

As it turned out, Prevratil and the port had not been the great match that the harbor commissioners had envisioned. The new executive director and the board often clashed over policy, and Prevratil's seeming reluctance to defer to the board's directions. It was a question of personality and philosophy rather than of competence.

There was one more controversy left at the port, and it had nothing to do with on-dock rail, trucking, trash incinerators, coal exports, underground pipelines, historic airplanes and ships, or moving cargo. In 1989, the Harbor Commission approved spending $1 million to upgrade their board room. It seemed a little steep to some people, but board members argued that it was long overdue. "A million dollars doesn't buy what a million dollars used to buy for us," explained acting Executive Director Brown. "We don't like that it's costing a million either."

Merchant Seamen

By the 1980s, the job market for U.S. merchant seamen had declined to the point of almost disappearing. There were still U.S. seamen on some ships involved in the domestic trade, protected by the requirements of the Jones Act, which limited trade between American ports to American ships. But the American-flag merchant fleet had declined from around 1,300 ships in the 1950s to fewer than

600 by the 1980s. Some 700 ships had been replaced by other ships, flying so-called "flags of convenience." Ship owners could escape U.S. taxes and restrictions by registering ships in other countries and were able to employ foreign seamen who were willing to work for less money than American seamen. There was nothing to stop Americans from seeking those jobs, but most were not willing to do so for the wages being offered.

Some blamed the maritime unions for pricing themselves out of the market. Ship owners had responded to escalating union wages by automating tasks aboard vessels in order to reduce the size of the crew and by registering their ships abroad and hiring cheaper labor. Whatever the reason for the decline, by the late 1980s sailors arriving aboard merchant ships at the Port of Long Beach were mostly foreigners. The job of the American merchant seaman had been outsourced.

Chapter Eighteen:
Cutting Through the Urban Maze

The last decade of the 20th century was remarkably the same as – and just as remarkably different from – the decades that had led up to it. It was a time of turmoil and strife, politics and scandal, music and fun. But it was also marked by a shift in power, a change in attitude, a flattening of institutional structures, and the globalization of economic and environmental philosophy. The ability to lower transportation costs made possible by containerization and other technical advances had made low-cost, foreign-made or harvested goods widely available. Fresh fruits and vegetables were on U.S. grocery store shelves year-round since the sowing season in the Northern Hemisphere was the harvesting season in the Southern Hemisphere. Barbie dolls from Asia filled Christmas stockings. Toyotas, Hondas, and Nissans from Japan were commonplace on America's highways. Furniture manufactured from tropical woods in foreign countries replaced American oak and walnut in stores. Foreign-produced shoes and clothing filled our closets. Our children rode bicycles made in China, and we crisped our bread in toasters from Taiwan. Many American workers found themselves in direct competition with workers from other countries who were willing to work harder and longer for less pay. A new word was created – outsourcing. It was a word with both a negative and positive connotation, depending on whether you were a businessman or stockholder looking for a way to compete or a working stiff who found himself "outsourced" from his job.

The population of the United States, according to the 1990 census, was 248,718,310 people – up 9.8 percent from 1980; California's population was 29,760,021, up 25.7 percent; and Long Beach's population was 429,433, up 18.8 percent. George Herbert Walker Bush was president of the United States, and Long Beach son George Deukmejian was governor of California. The Soviet Union was collapsing under its own weight and economic inefficiencies, and the Cold War between two superpowers was about to come to an end – an event that would have economic and political impacts far beyond the end of a hostile relationship.

The world was changing in large ways and small. East and West Germany were reunited after forty-five years of separation. Union leader Lech Walesa was elected the first Polish president ever. The first elections were held in Romania; Russia re-emerged as an independent country following the breakup of the Soviet Union, British Prime Minister Margaret "Maggie" Thatcher resigned, and Chilean President Augusto Pinochet left office after sixteen years as the national leader. Panamanian dictator Manuel Noriega surrendered to U.S. forces and was taken back to the United States, where he was tried, convicted, and imprisoned for drug offenses, money laundering, and racketeering. Nelson Mandela was freed from prison, apartheid ended, black people in South Africa got to vote, and Mandela was elected president.

Iraq, under Saddam Hussein, invaded Kuwait in 1990, resulting in what would become known as the first Gulf War. The following year, Operation Desert Storm, an American-led coalition of forces, defeated the Iraqi Army in forty days, freeing Kuwait and setting the stage for the next round of hostilities. In 1992, U.S. forces were again involved, this time in a war in Bosnia following the breakup of the former Yugoslavia. The war, which pitted ethnic groups against one another, was marked by massacres, mass rapes, and the introduction of an ugly new term – "ethnic cleansing." In 1993, U.S. forces were involved in a bloody battle in Somalia that came to be known as the Battle of Mogadishu. The battle, which resulted in eighteen American deaths, was immortalized in the book and subsequent movie *Black Hawk Down*. In Rwanda, a nation ethnically divided between the ruling Hutus and the disenfranchised Tutsis, a 100-day genocide in 1994 ended in the deaths of about 800,000 people.

Indian Prime Minister Rajiv Gandhi was assassinated in 1991. He had become prime minister after his mother, former Prime Minister Indira Gandhi, was assassinated in 1984. Israeli Prime Minister Yitzhak Rabin was gunned down in 1995 by Yigal Amir, a right-wing Jewish radical. The murder followed three earlier attempts that year to kill Rabin.

The fairy tale wedding in 1981 of Prince Charles and Lady Diana Spencer turned out to be not quite so romantic behind the scenes. Although the union produced two sons – princes William and Harry – the relationship between the two became strained and distant. In December 1992, they separated, and in 1996 – at the Queen's request – they divorced. Diana got a lump sum settlement of $22.5 million and a yearly allowance of about $600,000 in exchange for an agreement not to discuss the details of the marriage. Although she remained Diana, Princess of Wales, she could no longer be referred to as Her Royal Highness. Princess Diana died the following year in an auto crash, along with her boyfriend, Dodi Fayed, and his driver, as they were pursued by paparazzi through a tunnel in Paris.

It was not a good decade for royal relationships among Queen Elizabeth's children. Prince Andrew and Princess Sarah Margaret Ferguson – popularly known as Fergie – separated in 1992; they divorced in 1996. Princess Royal Anne and Mark Phillips also divorced in 1992 after more than eighteen years of marriage.

President George H.W. Bush created a stir in 1990 when he announced that he didn't like broccoli. "I haven't liked it since I was a little kid and my mother made me eat it. And I'm president of the United States, and I'm not going to eat any more broccoli!" The Americans with Disabilities Act and the Clean Air Act became law, and smoking was banned on domestic flights. President Bush vetoed the Civil Rights Act of 1990, which he said would lead to enforced racial quotas, but signed an amended Civil Rights Act of 1991.

David Dinkins became New York's first black mayor in 1990. Washington, D.C. Mayor Marion Barry, first elected in 1979, was arrested by FBI agents in 1990 after he was videotaped smoking crack cocaine. He was convicted and served six months in prison. After his release, he was elected to the City Council in 1992 and re-elected as mayor in 1994. Supreme Court nominee Clarence Thomas was accused of sexual harassment by attorney Anita Hill during his confirmation hearing in 1991. Despite the allegations, he was ultimately confirmed by the Senate.

Former Arkansas Governor William Jefferson Clinton defeated George H.W. Bush in the 1992 presidential election. A charismatic leader, Clinton's eight years in office would be marked by political successes, personal scandals, and popular support. He signed the controversial North American Free Trade Agreement – popularly known as NAFTA – with Canada and Mexico, issued a presidential directive on gay and bisexual people in the military known as "don't ask, don't tell," and approved the Family and Medical Leave Act of 1993. The Republicans took both the Senate and the House in the mid-term elections of 1994 with their "Contract with America" promise. Despite the Republicans' legislative victory, Clinton still beat back presidential bids two years later by Senator Bob Dole of Kansas and Reform Party businessman Ross Perot to win a second term. He worked with Republicans to pass a welfare reform act, a balanced budget act, and the Defense of Marriage Act that defined marriage as between a man and a woman. He had sexual relations with a White House intern, lied about it, was impeached by the House of Representatives, and ended his eight years as the president with the highest approval ratings of any president since World War II.

The Keating Five were U.S. senators – Alan Cranston, Donald Riegle, Dennis DeConcini, John Glenn and John McCain – accused of improperly intervening on behalf of Lincoln Savings and Loan Chairman Charles Keating in a federal investigation of the company. Cranston, Riegle and DeConcini were all determined to have acted improperly, but only Senator Cranston was censured. Glenn and McCain were cleared, but determined to have used poor judgment.

Former President Richard M. Nixon died in 1994. Ruth Bader Ginsburg became the second female Supreme Court judge in 1993. And Madeleine Albright became the first female secretary of state in 1997.

The Dow Jones Industrial Average suffered a mini-crash on October 27, 1997, when it dropped 554 points. On March 29, 1999, it soared past the 10,000 point mark for the first time in history. The World Wide Web was introduced in 1990, the Bank of Credit and Commerce International (BCCI) was shut down by authorities in 1991 amid allegations of large-scale money laundering and fraud, and Commodore Computers declared bankruptcy in 1994.

Mount Pinatubo erupted in the Philippines in 1991, killing 847 people. Hurricane Andrew devastated South Florida in 1992, killing forty-four. Earthquakes in Los Angeles County in 1994, Japan in 1996, and Turkey in 1999 killed seventy-two, 6,400, and 17,000 people respectively.

The U.S. Food and Drug Administration approved the contraceptive Norplant in 1990. Nicoderm, the first nicotine patch, designed as an aid to kick cigarettes, went on the market in 1992. Men began using Viagra in 1998 to enhance their sexual performance.

The Hubble Telescope was launched in 1990, but soon afterward it was discovered to have a flawed main mirror. It was repaired by astronauts in space in 1993. John Glenn, who in 1962 became the first American to orbit the earth, returned to space in 1998 at age 77 aboard the Shuttle *Discovery*, becoming the oldest American to ever orbit the earth.

Doomsday fears of a worldwide computer meltdown on December 31, 1999, sent programmers scurrying during the late 1990s, trying to fix the dreaded Y2K glitch. The scare was that since computers had been programmed to assume the 19 in the date – using 92 instead of 1992 – when the date turned to 2000, computers would get confused and shut down. Despite predictions of catastrophe, with airplanes falling from the sky and power grids shutting down, when the date arrived, Y2K ended up being much ado about very little.

Jeffrey Dahmer was arrested in Milwaukee in 1991 for the rapes, murders, dismemberment and sometimes consumption of seventeen young men and boys between 1978 and 1991. He later confessed, pleaded guilty, and was sentenced to fifteen terms of life imprisonment. He was beaten to death in 1994 by a fellow inmate.

Teenager Amy Fisher pleaded guilty in 1992 to shooting Mary Jo Buttafuoco, the wife of Fisher's 35-year-old lover, Joey Buttafuoco. Fisher served seven years in prison, wrote a book about her experiences, got married, became a mom, got a job as a porn film actress, and became a minor TV celebrity. Joey Buttafuoco pleaded guilty to statutory rape and served four months in jail. Mary Jo Buttafuoco survived her gunshot wounds, had reconstructive surgery, and eventually became an author and motivational speaker.

Lorena Bobbitt took out her frustrations with her abusive husband in 1993 by attacking him while he slept and cutting off his penis. The severed member was reattached in a nine-and-a half hour operation. She was later tried for assault and found not guilty by reason of insanity. The couple divorced in 1995. He formed a band called "The Severed Parts" and starred in two adult movies.

Nicole Brown Simpson and restaurant worker Ron Goldman were killed in a savage knife attack outside her Brentwood home in 1994. Her estranged husband, O. J. Simpson, an actor and former professional football player, was later arrested for the crime, tried, and acquitted in 1995. In 1997, Simpson lost a wrongful death suit brought by the Brown and Goldman families, and was ordered to pay $33.5 million in compensatory and punitive damages. Exactly thirteen years to the day after Simpson was acquitted of killing Nicole Simpson and Ron Goldman, he was found guilty on ten charges related to breaking into a Las Vegas hotel room. On December 15, 2008, he was sentenced to thirty-three years at Lovelock Correctional Center in Nevada.

The World Trade Center in New York was bombed by foreign terrorists in 1993. A rented truck filled with explosives parked in the garage of the north World Trade Center tower was designed to topple the north tower into the south tower, bringing them both down and killing thousands of people. That didn't happen, but six people were killed and more than a thousand injured. In 1995, the Alfred P. Murrah Federal Building in Oklahoma City was bombed by domestic terrorists, also using a rented truck, this one parked outside the building. It killed 168 people, including 19 children, and injured 680.

Theodore Kaczynski, the so-called Unabomber, who killed and maimed advocates of modern technology by sending them bombs through the mail, was arrested in 1996. Three of his victims died, and twenty-three were injured between 1978 and 1995. He was sentenced to life in federal prison.

Muppeteer Jim Henson died in 1990 of a bacterial lung infection. Professional wrestler André Roussimoff, better known as Andre the Giant, died of congestive heart failure in 1993. Former first lady Jacqueline Kennedy Onassis died in 1994 of cancer. Kurt Cobain, the 27-year-old lead singer of the rock group Nirvana, committed suicide that same year by shooting himself in the head with a shotgun. Grateful Dead lead guitarist Jerry Garcia died of a heart attack in his room at a California drug rehab center in 1995. Mexican-American singer Selena Quintanilla-Perez, better known simply as Selena, was shot and killed in 1995 by the former president of her fan club. West Coast rapper Tupac Shakur was killed in a drive-by shooting in Las Vegas in 1996, supposedly as part of an East-West rapper feud. East Coast rapper Notorious B.I.G., rumored to be involved in Shakur's murder, was murdered in a drive-by shooting in Los Angeles the following year.

Basketball legend Magic Johnson revealed he was HIV-positive in 1991, eight members of Reba McEntire's band plus the pilot and copilot were killed in a plane crash near San Diego that year, and advertising icon Joe Camel was fired after critics complained that he made kids think smoking was cool. In 1998, the movie *Titanic* became the most financially successful film up to that date, grossing $1.84 billion. A story of young romance aboard an opulent vessel headed for disaster, it seems in retrospect, was the perfect film to wrap up the 1990s.

End of a Cold War; Beginning of an Oily Mess

The Berlin Wall had been torn down by the free citizens of the city, the Soviet Union was disbanding, and the Cold War was a thing for students to learn about in history books. The blessings of peace were many, but the end of the Cold War also meant hard times for the military and the defense industries, both mainstays of the Long Beach-area economy. Politicians spoke with optimism about the coming "peace dividend," a term coined to refer to the money that would be saved by a decrease in defense spending as the U.S. stopped preparing for war. But Long Beach – the Navy town with aerospace giant McDonnell Douglas as its biggest private employer – was in the preparing-for-war business. With peace came cuts to military spending and fat aerospace contracts – cuts that made Long Beach ground zero for the economic implosion that resulted from the end of the Cold War.

At the same time, indefensible negligence by major oil companies covered in detail on television and in the press had awakened the environmental consciousness of the nation and the state. The *Exxon Valdez* – a single-hulled super tanker on its way from Valdez, Alaska, to the Port of Long Beach with its tanks full of North Slope crude – slammed into a reef in Prince William Sound in March 1989, rupturing its tanks and spilling between 260,000 and 750,000 barrels of oil into the ocean. The ship's captain had been drinking heavily and was asleep at the time of the collision. The crew was fatigued, the crewmember at the helm had not been certified to operate ships in those particular waters, and the onboard radar had been broken for a year. Night after night Americans saw oil-soaked birds and sea mammals on television as crews attempted to clean up the mess. Less than 10 percent of the oil was ever recovered. The spill killed between 100,000 and 250,000 seabirds, 247 bald eagles, more than 2,800 sea otters, twenty-two killer whales, and 300 harbor seals, plus innumerable fish.

Eleven months later, the tanker *American Trader* was getting ready to offload some Alaska crude oil at an oil mooring off Huntington Beach, California, when it ran over its own anchor and pierced its hull. It was lightering barrels of North Slope crude from the tanker *Keystone Canyon*, a very large crude carrier anchored at the Port of Long Beach. Lightering is the process of offloading crude oil from a large tanker to a smaller tanker so it can be delivered to a site too shallow to service the bigger ship. The oil was to be pumped ashore at Huntington Beach, and then sent by pipeline to a refinery in Santa Fe Springs. The resulting 10,000-barrel spill washed oil ashore along the Orange County coast from Newport Harbor to Sunset Beach. The offshore cleanup took ten days; the cleanup of the beaches lasted almost two months; and the spill killed an estimated 3,400 birds.

On the morning of April 6, 1989, while workers in jumpsuits were still sopping up oil on the beaches from the *American Trader* spill, the *Exxon Long Beach* – sister ship to the *Exxon Valdez* – got stuck in the mud inside the Long Beach federal breakwater while on its way to Pier E to offload 1.3 million barrels of North Slope crude. The ship had a draw of from fifty-four to fifty-six feet of water when fully loaded. It was only stuck for about a half-hour, and it popped free when the tide came in. No oil was spilled, and no damage done. But it was another reminder of the potential for disaster that existed when huge quantities of oil were transported across the ocean.

The actual long-term damage resulting from the *American Trader* spill was not as significant as the changes it triggered in how people thought about the threat of oil to the coastal environment, the general increased hostility they felt toward oil companies, and the political fallout that followed. Over the next few years, new regulations were passed, new standards were required for tanker safety, and new practices were implemented for the transportation of oil.

The Mickey Mouse Connection

On January 12, 1990, Walt Disney Co. chairman Michael Eisner made a proposition to Long Beach and to Anaheim in as plain language as he could. His company wanted to build a new amusement park that would generate 10,000 local jobs and attract millions of free-spending tourists to town. Disney would build the new park either in Anaheim or Long Beach, he told reporters at a press conference in Anaheim. "It depends on which community wants us more."

The question was simple. What could Long Beach offer Disney that Anaheim couldn't? The answer was just as simple. The ocean. But would that be enough? Anaheim Mayor Irv Pickler told reporters after the announcement that his city was "ready to cut any deal we have to. If we haven't given that message to Disneyland, we are going to give it to Disneyland real soon."

Long Beach Mayor Ernie Kell was more guarded. City officials had been meeting with Disney executives for months about a possible nautical theme park that would be developed around the *Queen Mary* and Spruce Goose. But Long Beach already had been through the *Queen Mary* experience – a seat-of-the-pants decision made with little analysis of what could go wrong. This time the city was determined to consider traffic, pollution, and quality-of-life issues, as well as the potential benefits or injury to the local economy.

"We will not allow ourselves to do something foolish because of what may or may not be some competitive bidding," Kell told a reporter, voicing a popular suspicion that the Long Beach plan was just Eisner's negotiating ploy to soften up Anaheim. "It has got to be a plus for us as well as Disneyland. If we end up with more traffic and more smog – those days are gone."

On August 1, 1990, Disney unveiled its concept for a $2.8 billion project dubbed Port Disney – an upgraded version of the PortAdventure once proposed by the Wrather Corp. The plan included a theme park, five luxury hotels, a cruise ship terminal, marinas, and a harbor transportation center. The project would be built on both sides of Queensway Bay and require about 250 acres of landfill. A 225-acre theme park to be called DisneySea would include a multi-story parking structure for 17,000 cars. The five luxury hotels, with a total of 3,900 rooms, would occupy 125 acres. Casualties of the development would include the Viscount (later the Maya) Hotel, the Reef and Quiet Cannon restaurants, and most likely the Spruce Goose and the dome in which it nested. A cross-channel ferry would connect downtown to the port's side of Queensway Bay, and a cruise terminal on the south side of the park would be operated by the port. Disney predicted that Port Disney would attract 13 million visitors a year to Long Beach, with nearly two-thirds arriving on the already congested Long Beach Freeway.

It was a grand plan, but if Disney expected Long Beach to go gaga over the chance to become part of Mickey Mouse's entourage, Disney was due for a rude awakening. It wasn't that Long Beach didn't need the kind of shot-in-the-arm that Disney promised to provide. The downtown area was run-down and in decline. Long Beach's Pike amusement park, long surpassed by modern theme parks such as Disneyland and Knott's Berry Farm, had been razed. Suburban malls had replaced Long Beach's once vibrant downtown shopping area. An attempt to lure that lost business back to the city with the three-block-long Long Beach Plaza shopping center had failed miserably – with boarded-up stores inside the center replacing the boarded-up stores that had been torn down to build it. And then there was the *Queen Mary* – perhaps the biggest buildup with the biggest letdown of all, a floating money pit that had been turned over to the port in order to cover its losses. Long Beach had been promised a lot, but Disney would have to do better than flash some fancy renderings to win over the community.

There was also the question of traffic. If two-thirds of the visitors arrived from the north on the Long Beach Freeway, what about the other third – the people arriving from the south and east, who would jam city streets on their way to the park? And what about all the trucks on the Long Beach Freeway – a highway that already frightened many motorists competing for space next to thirty tons of rolling steel and freight? Disney was counting on the Blue Line light rail connection that linked Long Beach to Los Angeles to bring some visitors and on the proposed development of the Alameda Corridor rail and truck artery to take many of the trucks off the Long Beach Freeway. The questions were asked not only by city officials, but also in community meetings in which Disney executives were confronted with skepticism and doubt.

The trade and transportation industry was also concerned about the effect that plunking down a major theme park in the second-largest container port in North America would have on the movement of freight. The industry was already struggling to move its cargo from the port through the urban maze that surrounded it. The idea of a theme park at the Port of Long Beach was a cause of concern from Hong Kong to Tokyo, and from Singapore to Busan. The port reassured the industry that Disney's planned development would not affect business, but most remained skeptical. The Steamship Association of Southern California, which represented multiple shipping lines, urged the port to hire an independent consultant to analyze the traffic impact posed by the Port Disney development.

During this time, the Port of Long Beach signed its biggest deal ever – a ten-year, $60 million-plus lease with the Maersk shipping line of Denmark for a 107-acre terminal on Pier J. Maersk would move to its new terminal from the fifty-four-acre terminal it had been operating at the port. The agreement followed two years of talks between the port and Maersk, before the shipping line finally signed on the dotted line. But Maersk insisted that its lease contain an escape clause. If the Disney theme park resulted in a traffic nightmare, Maersk could void the lease and go elsewhere. "K" Line's ITS terminal was also in negotiations with the port for renewal of its lease. If Maersk got an escape clause, ITS wanted one too.

The Port of Los Angeles also was concerned. The trucks that carried cargo to and from Los Angeles port terminals also used the Long Beach Freeway. Furthermore, Disney's plan for a five-berth cruise terminal in Long Beach would be in direct competition with Los Angeles' existing four-berth cruise terminal in San Pedro.

Disney also had its challenges. The cruise terminal, the marinas, and the cross-channel ferries were important parts of the Port Disney plan. To pass muster with state regulatory agencies, Disney would have to demonstrate that the project was waterfront-dependent. Just because the park had a nautical theme didn't mean it had to be built on the coast, so including waterfront-dependent uses became an important part of meeting state requirements.

There was also the question of landfill. In its original plan, Disney envisioned 250 acres of new land dredged up from the ocean floor. The company had badly misjudged the regulatory labyrinth that is California environmental law and quickly found itself bogged down in a political and bureaucratic morass. It became clear along the way that it would be impossible to get a 250-acre landfill approved to develop a theme park.

David Malmuth, a young Disney executive charged with guiding the effort, admitted later that he and his company had misjudged the Long Beach point of view. "I didn't take into consideration the sensitivity of legislators or environmentalists. I thought they would see this as truth, beauty, and the American way. We thought that once people saw the project, they would say, 'This is great. We'll help you.'"

In October 1991, the port unveiled a compromise land-use plan – designed to clearly separate cargo from tourists – with a downsized, 200-acre DisneySea theme park. The compromise plan required only fifty acres of landfill for the Disney development instead of 250. Another twenty-five acres of fill would be added by the port to expand the ITS container terminal. The port administration building would be torn down, and port headquarters would be moved to the proposed cruise terminal site. In general, the industry liked the idea, but said it did little to address the question of congestion on the Long Beach Freeway.

The other agreement between the port and Disney was that Disney would drop the name Port Disney from their project. It would be simply called DisneySea. The Port of Long Beach was the only port in town. Using the name Port Disney suggested that perhaps the Disney presence would disrupt the Port of Long Beach mission of moving maritime cargo.

Then there was the question of pollution. If Disney's projections were correct, there would be an average of 6,200 cars driving to Long Beach daily to visit DisneySea. In addition to the cars, the attraction itself – the ferry boats, the rides, the hotels, and cruise ships – would add to the pollution. Disney planners were looking for ways to mitigate those impacts, but it would probably be impossible to eliminate them completely.

In the end, it didn't matter. On December 12, 1991, Disney announced that it had decided to dump its Long Beach plan and develop its new theme park in Anaheim, next door to Disneyland. It was a huge disappointment for Long Beach, but not a big surprise. To build the Long Beach park, Disney needed to get the approval of twenty-seven local, state, and federal agencies – a process that would have taken five years and cost $70 million more than building in Anaheim. And there would be no guarantees at the end of that process. Disney's fight to build DisneySea was not lost in Long Beach, but in Sacramento. The dream of a Long Beach-Disney future was dead, suffocated in a morass of red tape and restrictions.

The Disney Aftermath

The Disney decision to withdraw from Long Beach was just one more piece of bad news. The city had built up its downtown with new office towers and hotels, but by 1991, there was a glut of empty office space on the market, and the new hotels were often only 60 percent booked. Buffum's, the department store chain begun in downtown Long Beach in 1904 by Charles and Edwin Buffum, closed its sixteen stores in Los Angeles, Orange, and San Diego counties and went out of business that year. The original downtown Long Beach store had evolved over the years to be the main anchor of the new Long Beach Plaza shopping mall. By the early 1990s, it was just one more boarded up outlet within that mall. McDonnell Douglas, the city's largest single employer, had laid off thousands of aerospace workers at its Long Beach operation. The Long Beach Naval Station and Long Beach Naval Hospital on Carson Street near the San Gabriel River Freeway were both expected to shut down and leave the city in the near future. Disney, with all its demands, would have returned some of the shine to a city that once drew thousands to the beach each weekend for a day of sand and surf. As it was, four months following the Disney decision, widespread rioting and looting broke out in Long Beach, part of six days of such riots in area communities following the acquittal of four Los Angeles police officers involved in the beating of Rodney King. It seemed as though Long Beach was fated to failure, despite all its bold attempts to rebuild itself in a new image.

Not everybody was unhappy about the Disney pullout. Environmentalists were ecstatic about their victory over the Disney behemoth. Representatives from the trade and transportation community expressed relief over the demise of a project they believed would have made the freeway congestion problem even worse than it already was.

Although DisneySea was not to be, The Walt Disney Co. still held leases on the *Queen Mary* and Spruce Goose. In March 1992, Disney dropped its second bombshell on the city when it announced that it planned to give up the leases and close down its operations there on September 30. Both the *Queen Mary* and the Spruce Goose were money losers, the company said. Disney had many better places to invest its money.

The port, which had previously taken over the *Queen Mary* at the city's request, once again began a worldwide search to find any company or person interested in buying or operating the ship. The port asked interested parties to submit proposals for taking over the *Queen* – "as is and where is." It got some responses.

While the *Queen's* fate remained uncertain, the announcement came in July 1992 that the Goose would soon be gone. The famous airplane would be moved to a new home in McMinnville, Oregon. Del Smith, owner of Evergreen International Aviation, planned to feature the plane as the centerpiece of the AirVenture Museum he was building in McMinnville. The Spruce Goose was owned by the Aero Club of Southern California, a nonprofit company that had leased the plane to Disney. Aero Club representatives said their intent was to find a place where the plane could be displayed with dignity in an appropriate setting with other vintage aircraft.

Meanwhile, a port survey of 1,100 registered Long Beach voters found the majority, 51 percent, favored getting rid of the *Queen Mary* if it was losing money. Only 43 percent favored keeping it under such circumstance. During its twenty-five years in Long Beach, the ship had cost the city an estimated $100 million. Disney reportedly lost $25 million to $30 million on the ship during the four years it held the lease. Still, not everybody wanted to see the ship gone. It had become an icon of the city, some city officials contended, and the ship should be kept in Long Beach even if it required a yearly subsidy from the port.

The port received eighteen proposals from companies and groups interested in the ship. Thirteen wanted to buy it; five wanted to operate it. The highest bid, $20.1 million, came from a Hong Kong group that planned to transport the *Queen Mary* to Hong Kong where it would be renovated as a hotel and shopping center. The next highest bid was $8 million from a Japanese group. The port quickly narrowed down the list to five finalists – four who wanted to buy the ship and take it elsewhere and one – former port Executive Director Joseph Prevratil – who wanted to lease it and operate it where it was in Long Beach. Prevratil maintained that with some improvements to the vessel, and with good promotion and pricing, he could make the ship profitable.

The fate of the *Queen* was the port board's decision, and although most of the harbor commissioners favored selling the ship, they seemed willing to defer to the city. Mayor Ernie Kell said that the ship had lost money in nine of the past ten years and that it was time to sell it. Councilman Evan Braude suggested that the port transfer the ship back to the city and let the city lease it to a new operator.

The City Council voted at the end of September on a motion by Councilman Alan Lowenthal to take control of the *Queen Mary* back from the port. Only two of the nine councilmembers voted in opposition – Jeff Kellogg and Doug Drummond. Kell, who as mayor did not have a vote in the matter, voiced his opposition to keeping the ship, and both outgoing City Auditor Robert Fronke and incoming auditor Gary Burroughs advised the Council that it should be sold.

A consulting engineer hired by the port examined the ship and reported that it was in urgent need of being put into dry dock for repairs. There were indications that rust was eating away at the hull, some of the rivets were in danger of failing, and that if a series of them were to pop loose, the *Queen* could be flooded. The city affirmed its decision to keep the ship in Long Beach and instructed the city manager to seek a second opinion. It didn't take long. Hal Johnson, a 62-year-old retired diver from Wilmington, had previously been employed as a contract diver to periodically inspect the *Queen Mary's* hull. He volunteered to dive the ship one more time. He found no evidence of rusted-out rivets or salt water leakage. The Navy did its own inspection. Although it did find some rust, it reported that there was no imminent risk of flooding and no need to dry dock the ship.

The *Queen Mary* was no longer a working ship and had not been for twenty-five years. It was not subject to the vibrations from the engines driving it forward or from the pounding of heavy seas. Repairs were needed, but not to the extent previously indicated, according to the later reports.

In the end, the City Council voted to take back the ship and lease it out to a private operator. The Harbor Commission offered to provide $4 million for needed repairs to the ship; the city had requested $5.9 million. In the end, the port gave the city the ship, eighty-seven acres of land, 244 acres of submerged land, and leases worth $840,000 a year for two restaurants, a hotel, and facilities operated by Catalina Channel Express ferry service and Island Express Helicopters.

The city later leased the *Queen Mary* to RMS Foundation Inc., a non-profit group operated by Joseph Prevratil, who took over operations of the ship. Financial backing for the deal came from Dr. Robert Gumbiner, founder and chairman of FHP Inc., one of the first and most successful health maintenance organizations. Gumbiner, a Long Beach resident, would later use his fortune to found the Museum of Latin American Art in Long Beach.

In the meantime, the Spruce Goose was taken apart, shrink-wrapped, and loaded on a barge. On October 13, 1992, the barge containing the plane and its various components sailed from the Long Beach Harbor on the first leg of its 1,055 mile trip to its new home. In Portland, Oregon, the Goose and its parts were loaded onto smaller barges for a trip up the Willamette River to the locks at Oregon City to arrive at the Yamhill River. There it was loaded on trucks for the final leg of its journey to McMinnville.

The Coming of Steve Dillenbeck

In the year that Joseph Prevratil was the Port of Long Beach executive director, he reorganized port management, creating positions for three managing directors who would report directly to him. Those three senior executives – Paul Brown, Steve Dillenbeck, and Leland Hill – would oversee the port's ten major functions. Brown was managing director of administration and maintenance; Dillenbeck was managing director of commerce and development, and Hill was managing director of planning and engineering. When Prevratil resigned after such a short tenure, harbor commissioners were not ready to immediately appoint a new executive director.

The commissioners instead appointed the three managing directors as a kind of triumvirate of directors – a move widely criticized by outside observers. Each of the three would serve in rotation for nine months as acting executive director. After all three had shown their stuff, the board would pick one as the executive director or bring in somebody from outside to take the position. Brown was first in the rotation, then Dillenbeck, and then Hill.

Only two months into Hill's term, the Harbor Commission voted 4-0 to appoint Dillenbeck as the new Port of Long Beach executive director at an annual salary of $128,000 – second in the city to City Manager James Hankla, who was earning $131,557. The only commissioner opposed to the Dillenbeck appointment was George Talin, owner of Talin Tire Inc. in Rancho Dominguez, who was absent from the commission meeting. Dillenbeck and Talin had clashed in the past over leasing policy at the port.

The port's new executive director was 50 years old, plain-spoken, 6 feet 5 inches tall, and had about him a gruff manner. Some even called him "intimidating." He did not suffer fools, and that had apparently caused him problems in the past. He had been the assistant port director at the Port of Los Angeles until 1984, when he was demoted to project manager at the port's Cabrillo Marina and exiled to a trailer office. James McJunkin, former Long Beach Port executive director, had tried for ten years to hire Dillenbeck away from Los Angeles. In 1987, McJunkin finally got his wish. That year, one day after being promoted to director of property management, Dillenbeck quit his job at the Los Angeles port, where he had worked for eighteen years, and joined the Port of Long Beach.

Four months into the top job, Dillenbeck rearranged the port management team. Paul Brown became assistant executive director; Leland Hill was let go. Hill remained on the payroll for two months, and the port agreed to hire an employment agency to help him find another job. But Hill had a different idea. Two months after being ousted, he filed a $10 million wrongful termination claim. He alleged that one of the reasons he lost his job was his opposition to a planned roadway to the DisneySea theme park. Although as a senior director, he could be fired at will, he claimed reversionary rights – an option of public executives to return to a lower-ranking civil service job if they lost their management position. So on November 11, 1991 – three-and-a-half months after being ousted – Hill returned to the port as an environmental specialist in the planning division that he had once directed. He took a $43,000-a-year pay cut. His reception was cool. Dillenbeck told the Press-Telegram he took Hill back because he didn't have a choice. Harbor Commission President Joel Friedland told the Press-Telegram he was surprised Hill returned, but that he was entitled to the job. In May 1993, a Compton Superior Court Jury awarded Hill $913,425 for being fired without good cause. In March 1995, that judgment was reversed on appeal.

Keeping Up with the Cargo

The Port of Long Beach was clearly the West Coast tonnage leader during the 1980s. Cargo moving through the port during the 1979-80 fiscal year had totaled 41.2 million metric revenue tons, just more than the Los Angeles Port, which moved 40.9 million metric revenue tons during that year. By 1989-90, however, Long Beach had pulled far ahead in the tonnage war with 94.8 million metric revenue tons, up 130 percent during the ten-year period. Although Los Angeles only moved 67.9 million metric revenue tons across its docks that year, it remained the leader when it came to the number of containers moved. Los Angeles moved the equivalent of 2.1 million twenty-foot containers, expressed as TEUs. Long Beach moved only 1.6 million TEUs.

The 1980s were years of growth and rising expectations, but by 1990 that strong economy began to falter. During the last six months of 1990, cargo volume at the Port of Long Beach was down 4.7 percent from the previous year. It marked the first slump in cargo volumes since the recession in 1982. Unemployment was up, consumer demand was down, and it was reflected in the statistics, not just at Long Beach, but at other ports as well. As the numbers rolled in for 1990, Long Beach edged out the Port of New York and New Jersey to become the No. 2 container port in the nation – second only to its big sister on the other side of the San Pedro Bay.

But overall, Long Beach cargo volumes and earnings for the 1990-91 fiscal year were not encouraging. Tonnage was down 3 percent from the year before, and net income was down 6 percent. The main losses came in bulk cargo, cement, petroleum coke, coal, and petroleum products. Container trade through the port was mostly flat. Los Angeles showed a tonnage gain of 4.4 percent, but earnings fell there too, although only by less than 1 percent.

Despite the downturn, both the Long Beach and Los Angeles ports were betting on an eventual turnaround in their fortunes and were building infrastructure to make sure they would be ready to meet that demand. It was especially important in Long Beach, which had seen layoffs in its aerospace industry and had lost the DisneySea project to Anaheim. The port was the only bright spot in the local economy. When the recession ended, it needed to be ready to meet the anticipated demand, and that meant buying new land, filling in land, and building new infrastructure.

The rundown marina by the old Ford plant on the north side of the Cerritos Channel was gone. Now the plant itself – by this time an old and empty shell – needed to be cleared away. The port had bought the plant and the surrounding property in 1977 in order to develop the land as a container terminal. Destruction of the plant that had once been a mainstay of the local economy drew little opposition. It may have been a pinnacle of industrial efficiency in 1930, but 60 years later it was an outdated relic, an asbestos-filled earthquake hazard that needed to be torn down and replaced with something better. In acknowledgment of the important economic role the Ford facility had once played in Long Beach, the port spent almost $100,000 compiling a photographic and written record of its history.

The old Procter & Gamble plant at the west end of Seventh Street had fallen to the wrecking ball in 1989. It was replaced with a fifty-five-acre container terminal for Hanjin Shipping Co., a South Korean line. A "kosa" dedication ceremony was held in May 1991 with incense, candles, white wine, and a roasted pig. Both Korean and American executives bowed their heads and knelt on mats to ensure the blessing of spirits and good fortune for the new enterprise. It was the kind of East-meets-West ritual that marked port business – an indication of the power of money and business to bring people together.

Sometimes the gains in one port come directly at the expense of another. In 1992, Hiuka America Corp. announced it was dropping plans to move its scrap metal operation at the Port of Los Angeles from San Pedro to a twelve-acre site in Wilmington. The Japanese company's attempt to consolidate and expand its operation at the Port of Los Angeles had run into a wall of protest from the Wilmington community and residents of nearby marinas. Hiuka's move to a twenty-acre site in Long Beach took with it 100 new jobs and $1.1 million a year in fees, but community activists in Wilmington were ecstatic at their victory. So was the Port of Long Beach, which signed a twenty-five-year lease with the company to operate a scrap metal export terminal on Pier T.

Hiuka's business with both ports was marked by political and legal entanglements. Los Angeles Commissioner Jun Mori, whose law firm represented Hiuka America, resigned in 1992 after opponents of the scrap steel yard began to question a possible conflict of interest. Mori denied his resignation had anything to do with the Hiuka connection, and there was nothing solid to indicate otherwise. Mori, a member of a successful law firm that had represented various port clients, had been questioned in the past over alleged conflicts of interest. After fifteen years on the port board, he may have just been tired of it.

In 1995, just fourteen months after Hiuka's new facility opened for business on Terminal Island, three of its top executives were arrested. The three were alleged to have secured loans by showing bank officials phony contracts for the sale of scrap metal. The money was used to keep the financially ailing company afloat. Hiuka declared bankruptcy the following day, and the company's assets and lease were assumed by Pacific Coast Recycling. SA Recycling bought Pacific Coast Recycling in 2008.

Long Beach had been trying for years to get American President Lines to move from its terminal in San Pedro to a new terminal to be developed in Long Beach. In July 1993, APL was ready to move – but not to Long Beach. The company signed a deal with the Port of Los Angeles to move from its 129-acre terminal in the West Basin to a 230-acre terminal on Pier 300, complete with on-dock rail. It would be the first container terminal in the nation that was more than 200 acres in size.

Pier 300 was part of the landfill dredged from the bottom of the main channel to accommodate the Los Angeles port's planned coal terminal. L.A. had used development of the coal terminal and the number of export jobs it would generate at U.S. mines as a selling point to get federal support for its channel-deepening project. Long Beach had decided in 1983 that development of a coal export terminal was unwise, but Los Angeles had continued to pursue development of its coal project. APL moved into its new terminal in 1997.

Trade with Asia began to grow again. And although both ports were building at a frantic pace to meet that demand, public opposition to unlimited expansion of the ports was growing as well. A controversial plan that called for adding 1,444 acres of landfill between Terminal Island and the breakwater was attacked by some local residents with visions of trains rumbling through their neighborhoods and by boaters who saw their access to the coast being squeezed. Federal and state environmental agencies also were critical of the plan, claiming it would have a devastating impact on marine life and air quality. Despite opposition from port neighbors and environmental agencies, the development programs at both ports drew support from a wide range of business people who saw the expansion as a boon to both the local and national economy. At a 1990 hearing into the Army Corps of Engineers' preliminary report on the plan, comments were evenly split between those who favored the plan and those opposed to it. The report concluded that the massive expansion of the harbor would produce major economic benefits for the nation that outweighed the local environmental impacts.

The Port of Long Beach quietly dropped out of the landfill expansion plan during the next year and refocused its development toward buying up privately owned, often contaminated and subsided, properties in its inner harbor, remediating the toxic soils, bringing in dirt to raise the elevation, and building terminals.

Power and Money

The Long Beach Harbor Department – commonly called the Port of Long Beach – was established as part of a City Charter amendment in 1931. The amendment provided for an appointed five-member Harbor Commission that was granted a great degree of autonomy from the rest of the city in order to conduct harbor business. The idea was to isolate the commissioners from the political whims and quirks that often buffeted the City Council. The Harbor Commission was still beholden to the elected officials, but since the port was a business whose purpose was to provide long-term economic benefit to the city, there was a degree of isolation provided that allowed the board to run the port in a businesslike manner. It was a system of governance that provided the necessary latitude for the port to prosper and make the necessary hard decisions without political interference. But like all systems, it was not without its flaws – especially when times got tough.

By state law, the port's money had to be spent for harbor purposes. But that left room for liberal interpretation. The port invested millions in buying and clearing the property for the World Trade Center, with the rationale that it promoted trade and commerce through the port. It had taken over the money-losing *Queen Mary* as an education and convention venue. But there were limits to the port's largess. Unlike many West Coast ports, both the Long Beach and Los Angeles ports were self-sustaining, not subsidized by taxpayers. That led some elected officials and others in the respective cities to view the ports as cash cows – there to be milked for the common good with little regard for the long-term business consequences.

There were some councilmembers who wanted to strip the port not only of its money, but also of its power. They felt the Harbor Commission – as part of the city – needed to be more accountable to the City Council. City Councilman Warren Harwood, in 1992, proposed a City Charter amendment that would expand the port board to seven members, four of whom also would be members of the City Council, with the other three appointed by the mayor. That was rejected by the majority of councilmembers. The port was a complex business and being on the Harbor Commission required both time and expertise that the Council didn't have. Three months later, Councilman Ray Grabinski suggested that the city manager be empowered to hire and fire the executive directors of both the Harbor Department and the Water Department. (The Water Department is also an enterprise department that operates on revenue from water rates, rather than general funds.) The commissioners would only be able to confirm or reject the city manager's choice. Once confirmed, only the city manager could fire the executive director. That suggestion drew heated protests from commissioners in both the Harbor and Water departments.

The harbor commissioners took seriously the need to prepare for the expected boom in cargo when the recession of the early 1990s ended. That took money – a lot of it. While the commissioners understood many of the city's needs, they were also attempting to balance those needs against the long-term needs of the port. Efforts to get the port involved in projects outside the port district further complicated an already complicated business.

One example was the port's World Trade Center project – designed to serve as an anchor to the revitalization of the blighted downtown area. The World Trade Center turned out to be not as successful as the Commission had hoped. The recession had resulted in a glut of downtown office space, and the World Trade Center was no exception. In 1991, the port and World Trade Center developers were locked in a $5 million squabble over empty office space.

Back when harbor commissioners were putting together the deal with developers IDM and Kajima International, and the World Trade Center building was expected to be an immediate success, the port had agreed to find tenants for three stories of the building. In 1991, the port claimed its lobbying efforts had resulted in the U.S. Customs Service and two other tenants moving into the space, but the developers refused to recognize that as fulfillment of the port's obligation. The two sides ended up settling their dispute the following year in a deal in which the port paid the developers $3.5 million, and the developers doubled their payments to the port for four nearby parcels of land that were as yet undeveloped.

With its economic base crumbling around it, the city went to the port for money to expand the Convention Center in an effort to lure people back downtown. The port agreed to put up $80 million to build a modern facility, with the Redevelopment Agency agreeing to reimburse the port $55 million from hotel bed taxes and other revenues. The expanded facility would be almost three times bigger than the existing Convention Center at the time.

Not everybody was happy about the situation. The Steamship Association of Southern California – which represented a major block of port customers – argued against the port payout and even talked about filing a lawsuit to seek an injunction on the transfer of funds. In May 1991, harbor commissioners, senior port staffers, the city manager, and the city attorney met over lunch with Steamship Association leaders at the members-only International City Club.

Industry representatives said they feared that the transfer of money for the Convention Center would set a precedent for the city to continue to dip into port coffers for every project that came along. City Manager James Hankla said the project would turn the $2-million-a-year money-losing Convention Center into a money-making enterprise. The investment "would preclude future revenue raids on the port."

The Steamship Association did not file a lawsuit, but they did threaten to take their case to the State Lands Commission in order to get the deal overturned. In the end, the Steamship Association decided not to pursue the matter.

Bids to build the expanded Convention Center were opened in January 1992. The two low bids – one for the building and one for the parking structure – totaled $79.3 million, just a $700,000 smidge under the port's $80 million cap. Unfortunately, when preparing new foundations for the project, the construction crews ran into an old seawall left over from the early days of Long Beach. There also was a rush to get the parking structure finished in time for the annual Grand Prix auto race, as well as some design mistakes that had to be corrected, and they all added to the cost. By September of 1993, the Redevelopment Agency was back with a request for an additional $10 million from the port and $3.2 million from the city Gas Department.

The city also was seeking port support for an aquarium to be built on the downtown side of Queensway Bay as part of a new tourist harbor. The plan was first suggested by consultants in 1992 as Long Beach was recovering from Disney's decision to build its new park in Anaheim instead of Long Beach. Eighteen months later the plan had evolved into a $100 million project to be financed by revenue bonds that would be paid back from aquarium admissions and concession earnings.

The final financing plan was complicated. Aquariums were not known for turning huge profits, so the city needed to ensure investors that the bonds would be safe. The city Redevelopment Agency guaranteed that if aquarium admissions and concessions were not enough to pay off the bonds, it would cover the difference from the city's hotel bed tax. However, that hotel bed tax had previously been earmarked to pay back the port for the Redevelopment Agency's share of the Convention Center expansion. The port agreed to give the aquarium bondholders first call on the bed tax if the need arose. In addition, if the earnings and the bed tax together were not enough to pay off the aquarium bonds, the port promised to provide up to 10 percent of its net revenue to make up the difference.

Meanwhile, in order to balance the budget, the state Legislature began to take property tax revenues that would have normally gone to cities. In order to offset that hit on the city budget, the Legislature passed a two-year bill to allow cities with ports to dip into port reserve funds to make up the funds that had been diverted to the state. In Long Beach's case that amounted to about $21 million over the two years.

All of the investments in city projects that were only marginally connected to port business – the World Trade Center, the Convention Center, the *Queen Mary*, and the aquarium – plus the city bailout, began to have an impact on the port's bottom line. In addition, the port paid $4 million a year for fire protection, plus provided free office space in the harbor administration building for the Fire Department headquarters. The port paid $400,000 a year for police protection – although it had its own security staff, and there was little crime in the harbor district. Those payments were a sore spot for port tenants, who felt that as taxpayers they should automatically receive police and fire protection just as any other businesses in town did. Since the port received its income from those tenants, and the port payments for police and fire protection were reflected in the rents they paid, the tenants maintained that they were in effect paying twice for the same services.

By September of 1993, the port was feeling the crunch. Net earnings had dropped by two-thirds because of both city-related projects and expenses and the port's own spending on new land and new terminals for the expected upswing in trade. In March 1994, a consultant warned the port that it was nearing its credit limit and needed to cut spending, especially on projects that were non-maritime related and offered no expectation of future revenue.

Port profits rebounded by the end of 1994 as cargo-related revenue rose and port fund transfers to the city were reduced. Its problems, however, were hardly over. In 1994, attorney Richard I. Fine filed a class-action lawsuit on behalf of Raymond Veltman, claiming that the transfer of port funds to five California port cities was illegal and that the funds should be returned. Fine was on a spree, suing various government agencies to make sure that transfers of government funds were done exactly by law, and earning a couple million dollars for himself along the way. Some had branded him a fiscal ambulance chaser, but Fine said it was the politicians' own fault for not operating in a financially responsible manner. Veltman was a retired Brentwood businessman and former Los Angeles transportation commissioner. He also had been the owner of Trojan Transportation Co., a trucking firm that moved goods to and from the Port of Long Beach. Veltman had been the plaintiff in a similar case brought by Fine against the Metropolitan Transportation Authority concerning $50 million the MTA had transferred to the Los Angeles County health care system.

Fine settled his suits against the ports of San Francisco, Oakland, and San Diego. The Port of San Francisco had transferred money to the city, but the city had given it back after the city attorney there ruled it illegal. Oakland and San Diego never transferred money to their cities. All three agreed as part of the settlement not to divert any port money in the future. The Port of Los Angeles, which turned over $69 million of port revenues to the city, settled the lawsuit in March 1995. Los Angeles agreed to return $10 million to the port, minus $300,000 for Fine. Long Beach settled in May 1995 by agreeing to return $3 million to the port over ten years. City Attorney Robert Shannon said that represented an internal shifting of money between the city and the port that had little significant impact on city or port operations. However, a share of the money would go to cover attorney fees for Fine.

Dirty Land vs. Clean Fill

With the old Ford factory out of the way, the port was ready to develop the property on the north side of the Cerritos Channel into a container terminal. The port already owned the Ford property, and in May 1993, it agreed to purchase 725 acres of additional waterfront property for $405 million. That property, an oil field owned by the Union Pacific Corp., included 289 acres north of the channel, 354 acres south of the channel, and eighty-two acres beneath the channel. The property was heavily contaminated, with much of it below sea level and protected by dikes, which meant it would take a lot of work to clean it up, bring in dirt to raise the elevation, and get it ready for development.

Purchase of the property increased the size of the port by about a third. Harbor Commission President David Hauser had spearheaded the move to buy privately owned port district property instead of relying on new landfill to expand. The transaction also included 120 idle oil wells, 180 active wells that were producing 7,000 barrels a day, and a 70 percent interest in a co-generation plant on the property. (The co-generation plant heated water into steam that was then pumped into the ground to help extract crude oil and to generate electricity that was sold to Southern California Edison. Edison operated the plant and owned 30 percent of it, as well. The plant turned a profit of about $11 million a year.) The property stretched north and west from the Edison plant on the west end of the Gerald Desmond Bridge all the way to Anaheim Street. A portion north of the Cerritos Channel extended over the city line into Los Angeles.

Although preparing the property for development would take time and money, Hauser and the other commissioners felt it would be better than the expense, uncertainty, and environmental headaches involved in dredging up new land. As part of the deal, Union Pacific agreed to share a portion of the first $150 million in cleanup costs with the port. The company would pay the first $50 million in such costs, half of the second $50 million, and a quarter of the third $50 million. Anything beyond that would be paid for entirely by the port. There was an additional aspect that sweetened the deal for the port. During a time of budget shortfalls by the state and local governments, the purchase of the property could be expected to forestall expected money grabs by state legislators. At such times, it was perhaps better to be land rich and cash poor than the other way around.

Bumps in the Road

Long Beach's purchase of the Union Pacific land drew protests from the Port of Los Angeles, which filed a lawsuit in June 1993 claiming that Long Beach had failed to comply with California environmental law in making the transaction. Los Angeles had also been talking to Union Pacific about buying a portion of the property when Long Beach made the deal. The suit contended that Long Beach should have done an environmental assessment of the property before buying it. Long Beach Executive Director Steve Dillenbeck wrote back that there was no environmental review needed until the port decided to develop the property. Nothing had changed except the ownership.

When the Port of Long Beach decided to move forward on projects for the site, it would file the necessary environmental reviews, Dillenbeck said. In fact, an environmental review had already been initiated for thirty-one acres of the site that the port planned to develop as an expansion to the Toyota auto and truck processing center. The property – which had been designated as a state Superfund toxic site back in 1983 – contained lead, cadmium, hydrocarbon compounds, vinyl chloride, PCBs, and benzene.

A week after the Port of Los Angeles sued the Port of Long Beach over the Union Pacific property, the city of Long Beach sued the Los Angeles Port over plans for a high-volume $180 million coal and coke export terminal on Terminal Island. The Los Angeles Export Terminal – dubbed LAXT – was expected to export 17.3 million tons of coal and 2.5 million tons of petroleum coke a year. The coal and coke would be stored in open piles on the old Reeves Airfield site. Long Beach wanted to make sure none of that coal or coke dust would blow into Long Beach.

The LAXT project also threatened Long Beach's own coal and coke export operation – run by Metropolitan Stevedore Co. – which stored its product under cover in sheds until it was loaded on ships. Long Beach also was preparing to expand that operation, although on a much smaller scale than the L.A. project. Dillenbeck said there was not enough of a market to warrant the kind of facility planned in Los Angeles, and predicted that Los Angeles was "throwing money down a tube."

Meanwhile, the new Maersk Terminal on Pier J, complete with on-dock rail, had opened in April 1993. A month before the opening, there was a setback when one of the new $6.2 million, 175-foot-tall hammerhead gantry cranes toppled over while being unloaded. It was an accident with international overtones. It was a Japanese-built crane, being unloaded from a Dutch ship, for a new Danish company terminal, at a U.S. port. Taking huge new cranes from ship to shore is a slow and carefully planned process as the weight of each crane is rolled from the ship onto the land.

Within three months after the terminal opened for business, a new problem was discovered. When the waves, winds, and tide came together in a particular way, an unexpected surge was created inside the basin where the ships docked – described by engineers as similar to what might happen to water disturbed inside a bathtub. Long-period waves resulted in a slow rise and fall of the water that was strong enough to break the lines that secured the ship to the wharf and to endanger longshore workers in close proximity to multi-ton cargo. Tugs had to be called in twice in July and twice in September to steady vessels alongside the wharf. Army engineers at the Waterways Experiment Station in Vicksburg, Mississippi, built a scale model of the Pier J area and found that under certain conditions, the design of the basin would amplify the energy of the waves coming in.

Among the solutions explored were to build a breakwater extending out from the entrance to the Maersk basin, or to construct a huge mechanical gate that would open to admit a vessel, and then close behind it. The solution finally chosen was to build two large rock jetties extending 600 feet eastward from each side of the entrance to the Maersk basin, then turning inward toward each other for another 800 feet. A ship turning-basin was dredged to the east of the jetties. It cost more than $30 million, but it worked.

Another problem addressed during the time was the often confusing way that piers in the harbor were designated. The growth of the harbor had not necessarily been in a linear manner, and the names of the piers did not reflect their geographic relationship to one another. In January 1993, the names of the piers were officially changed, but to keep some consistency, the numbers of the berths did not. The Seventh Street Peninsula started being called "Pier C." "Pier A" had been the designation for the area in which the harbor administration building and the old Navy Victory Pier were located. Under the new system, "Pier A" became the designation for the North Harbor area, which had formerly been occupied by the Ford Motor factory and the Union Pacific. New signs were posted and new maps printed. Apart from the brief period it took everyone to get used to the new names, there was little impact – except to confuse later attempts to reconstruct the port's past.

The Hanjin Move to Pier A

The South Korean-owned Hanjin Shipping Co. had moved into its new terminal at the west end of Seventh Street in 1991. Three-and-a-half years later, Hanjin's business at the port had grown 250 percent, and its fifty-nine-acre terminal on the newly renamed Pier C was bursting at the seams. The port had bought the old Henry Ford property and planned to develop it along with a portion of the newly purchased Union Pacific oil field to develop a 170-acre terminal – the biggest at the Port of Long Beach. Hanjin executives were not only interested, they said it was vital for the company to have more terminal space, whether it was in Long Beach or elsewhere.

In March 1995, the port agreed to build a container terminal for Hanjin on the north side of the Cerritos Channel, east of the Commodore Heim Bridge. The terminal would have an on-dock rail yard, a 3,700-foot-long wharf, and six gantry cranes big enough to service post-Panamax-sized ships – the then-new generation of vessels too large to pass through the Panama Canal. Cost of the terminal, including the environmental cleanup of the property, was expected to be about $300 million. It would be the single largest construction project in the history of Long Beach, bigger by far than either the Long Beach Aquarium of the Pacific at about $100 million, the expanded Convention Center at $110 million, or the World Trade Center at $125 million.

Since much of the property was still below sea level, plans called for more than 2.2 million cubic yards of clean dirt to be brought to the site to replace contaminated soil and to raise the elevation of the subsided property. The elevation of land on the north side of the terminal would have to be raised about three feet, and then on the south side close to the center of the subsidence bowl, it would have to be raised about twenty-two feet. The northwest corner of the terminal would extend into the city of Los Angeles. The following month the port agreed to expand the planned Pier A terminal another thirty-two acres by adding property from land being leased at the time by Toyota as part of its auto import and processing terminal. The addition of land would expand the Hanjin terminal to about 200 acres.

Groundbreaking ceremonies for the new terminal were held in July 1995. Speeches were made and gifts exchanged. Vice Mayor Doug Drummond, who years later would become a harbor commissioner, noted the economic hardships that the city had suffered during the previous few years. The project provided the city with a "brilliant burst of sunshine and a ray of hope for the future," Drummond said. Harbor Commission President Roy Hearrean called the relationship between the port and Hanjin a "marriage made in heaven." Hanjin President S.H. Cho praised the partnership between his company and port and promised that the company would "continue to work hard to contribute to the local economy."

The terminal opened in October 1997 with only three of its gantry cranes in operating condition. There had been delays in construction resulting from unexpected hazardous waste cleanup, unusually stormy weather, a contractor's lawsuit, and ongoing delivery setbacks of the Paceco-Mitsui cranes. But those problems were little more than verification that in any complicated endeavor, things will inevitably go wrong.

"We always do our projects on a fast-track schedule where we're very optimistic," said Chief Harbor Engineer E. Dan Allen. "The lesson we've learned is that things happen."

Among the things that happened was the creation of about 3,000 jobs during construction of the project and another 200 direct ongoing jobs at the terminal itself. Other indirect jobs up, down, and across the supply chain would add several-fold to that number.

The old Hanjin Terminal on Pier C was taken over by SSA Marine, first as a storage yard and then as a terminal. Matson Navigation Co. moved its operation from the Port of Los Angeles to call at SSA's Pier C terminal.

The Final Navy Farewell

The Navy had been good for Long Beach, and Long Beach had long enjoyed the benefits of the military and civilian payrolls that accompanied the Navy presence in town. But sooner or later, all good things come to an end. In January 1990, Defense Secretary Dick Cheney released a hit list of more than 100 military bases and installations targeted for possible closure. The Long Beach Naval Shipyard was on the list. Its inclusion inspired both anger and dread, not only among employees at the shipyard but among city leaders as well. The 48-year-old Naval Shipyard employed 4,100 civilian workers plus forty-two military personnel and had a total annual payroll of $220 million. It was the third-largest employer in the city, behind the McDonnell Douglas aerospace company at the airport and the city of Long Beach. The loss would be devastating. An estimated 2,000 shipyard employees staged a massive protest with management standing shoulder to shoulder with workers.

There was more bad news in April 1991, when the Defense Department announced a tentative plan to close the Long Beach Naval Station and the Long Beach Naval Hospital. The only glimmer of good news was that after an extensive lobbying effort by the city, the Naval Shipyard had been removed from the closure list. But, the closure of the station and the hospital would still be a staggering blow to the local economy – estimated at $710 million to $735 million a year by City Manager Jim Hankla.

Two months later came the second blow – the shipyard was back on the closure list. The only hope for the shipyard was to regain a small percentage of the work that was going to San Diego by subcontracting jobs assigned there. But, Navy regulations stated that short-term ship repairs had to be made within seventy-five miles of a ship's homeport, otherwise it would pose a hardship on Navy personnel who would have to commute between the homeport and the repair facility. Long Beach was outside San Diego's radius, and therefore precluded from the work. The Navy's position was reinforced by San Diego Congressman Duncan Hunter, who included language in the 1993 defense bill prohibiting the Long Beach yard

NAVY GOODBYE: *One of many buildings to be demolished following the closure of the Long Beach Naval Station. Despite a campaign by TV host Huell Howser and local heritage groups to save the buildings, it was virtually inevitable that the land would be used as a cargo terminal.*

MASSIVE OPERATION: *The Hanjin terminal on Pier T, built on the land formerly occupied by the Naval Station, became the largest cargo terminal at the Port of Long Beach.*

from working on San Diego ships. The political battle over the Naval Station and the Naval Shipyard continued for months in Washington, D.C., but Long Beach's days as a Navy town were numbered.

In 1992, 50th anniversary celebrations were held at the Long Beach Naval Station. At the Allen Center Officers Club, it was a scene of formal wear, sad speeches, a display of historic photos, toasts to the end of an era, and a band playing tunes made famous by Glenn Miller and Cole Porter. At the nearby enlisted men's club the dress tended toward jeans and cowboy boots, and the music ranged from contemporary country tunes to rap.

The Navy had closed up shop in Long Beach before, but it had left a military presence that time. And the Navy had eventually returned in force to protect and supply American troops in foreign combat zones. This time was different. On June 30, 1994, the Navy weighed anchor for the last time and departed. The final closure came on September 30, 1994, when the doors were closed and the lights turned out. The Naval Station was history.

The Long Beach Naval Shipyard limped along for another three years before it too was closed down on September 30, 1997. There had been a Navy presence in Long Beach for more than seventy-five years. Long Beach had welcomed the Navy with open arms, and the Navy had responded in kind. When the 1933 earthquake rocked the city, killing fifty people in Long Beach and causing millions of dollars in damage, Navy personnel were on the scene within the hour, helping keep the peace and setting up kitchens to feed survivors. In World War II, the ports of Long Beach and Los Angeles would together become known as the Arsenal of Democracy. But that was the past. The Navy legacy will always be part of Long Beach's story, but by 1997, it was time for the city to move on.

Scandal and Other Unpleasantness

In 1991, Long Beach Harbor Commissioner George Talin, appointed to office by Mayor Ernie Kell, got into trouble. The district attorney had been investigating the Long Beach tire dealer after complaints that he had been billing the County of Los Angeles and other customers for work that had not been done. The investigation had been instigated by a Talin employee who claimed he quit because he didn't want to work for a company that was stealing. Before the employee left, however, he photocopied some examples of how the Talin billing process worked. That led to a second employee, who had agreed to wear a wire for a conversation in which the store manager told him to take two good tires from a customer, claim they were defective, and then sell them as used tires. Investigators, armed with a search warrant, raided the Rancho Dominguez company on June 26, 1991. They seized sixty boxes of paperwork detailing Talin's business dealings with the city of Long Beach, the Long Beach Unified School District, and the Los Angeles Department of Water and Power.

An investigative article in the Long Beach Press-Telegram disclosed that Talin had voted on harbor leases for at least four of the port's seven major shipping terminals while continuing to sell them tires. One of the terminals – Sea-Land Services – spent about $90,000 a year on tires from Talin's company. During five of the six years he sat on the harbor board, Talin received an annual tire service contract for servicing the port's trucks, cars, and heavy equipment.

Talin denied he had any conflict of interest in voting on port contracts for companies to which he sold tires. His waterfront contracts, he told reporters, amounted to only about $1 million a year. That was "peanuts" compared to his company's annual revenue of about $50 million a year.

His fellow harbor commissioners, however, felt the conflict was obvious.

"Port tenants could feel they were obligated to do business with a commissioner or that if they didn't buy from him it would affect their lease or position with the city," one commissioner was quoted in the Press-Telegram.

Port staffers said Talin would ask to see all supporting documents dealing with port tire purchases. Shipping terminal executives, on the other hand, said they never felt any pressure to do business with Talin Tire.

Mayor Kell was both friends with Talin and a political ally, but in July 1991, when Talin's term on the board expired, Kell did not reappoint him to a second term. Developer Roy Hearrean was named to replace Talin, and Carmen Perez was named to replace Commissioner Robert Langslet, who had finished his second and last term.

The Harbor Commission meeting on the afternoon of July 29, 1991, would have been Talin's last board meeting before being replaced, but he was absent. It was probably just as well. The board voted 4-0 to adopt a conflict-of-interest policy for board members to make clear that conflicts such as that posed by the Talin incident would not reoccur.

Talin continued to protest his innocence, but it wasn't until three years later that the district attorney's office announced that it did not plan to bring criminal charges against him over the incident. But the district attorney did not clear Talin either. In fact, the prosecutors said they had found evidence showing that Talin had used his position as a harbor commissioner to get business from port tenants. The decision not to bring charges was based on the facts that Talin was no longer a harbor commissioner, had since retired from the company, and the statute of limitations had run out.

"We're not clearing him of anything," Deputy District Attorney Efrem Grail said. "We just declined to bring charges."

Talin wasn't the only harbor commissioner to leave the board under unpleasant circumstances. In December 1994, Harbor Commissioner Joel Friedland resigned from the harbor board under pressure from the Redevelopment Agency. The Agency was attempting to buy up property on the Westside in order to put together large tracts of land to interest potential developers. Friedland, a former paint manufacturer and exporter, owned industrial property in the area that he wanted to sell. The Redevelopment staff said Friedland needed to combine twelve small parcels into one large parcel and decontaminate existing pollution, which he did. When Friedland went back to the Agency, however, the Agency declined to buy the land.

Members of the Redevelopment Board said they didn't feel comfortable buying the property because Friedland was a harbor commissioner. Although they were advised by Deputy City Attorney Heather Mahood that there was no conflict of interest, the board members still balked at the deal because there might appear to be a conflict. Friedland had gone into debt cleaning up the property and was in a financial crunch. In order to convince the Redevelopment Agency to approve the purchase, he agreed to resign as a harbor commissioner, even though there was no conflict of interest involved.

Most people agreed that Friedland, who had served honorably on the Harbor Commission for seven years, was given a raw deal. But what was done was done. He later sued to regain his seat on the board, but that effort was not successful. When the plan to build the Aquarium of the Pacific on the downtown side of Queensway Bridge was introduced, Friedland was a vocal critic. He was also unsuccessful in changing that plan.

About the same time that Friedland was being encouraged off the harbor board by Redevelopment Agency board members, there was another sad note of interest. Congressman Glenn Anderson, a political advocate for both the Long Beach and Los Angeles ports, died at 81. Anderson grew up in Hawthorne, raced motorcycles at Ascot Speedway in Gardena, owned his own Willys dealership in the 1930s, and in 1940 was elected mayor of Hawthorne. At 27 years old, he was the youngest mayor in the country. He later became an assemblyman – taking two years out to fight in World War II – and then lieutenant governor. He was elected to Congress in 1968, where he served until his retirement in 1992. His ability to get federal dollars for local projects was legendary. Late in his career, however, he had trouble remembering names and important facts. After he retired, it was disclosed that he was suffering from Alzheimer's disease. Among his survivors were his wife, Lee Anderson, at the time a Los Angeles harbor commissioner, and stepson, Evan Braude, a former Long Beach city councilman.

The Alameda Connection

Trade with Asia was booming, and the ports of Long Beach and Los Angeles were busy trying to keep up with the demand. At the same time, the ports were drawing fire from the community because of the pollution and traffic congestion being generated by that trade boom. The public criticism was unfair in many ways. The ports were not responsible for the boom in international trade – that was driven by consumers, eager to buy good-quality, cheap, foreign-made goods. If the ports were not able to meet that demand, the local cargo would go to other ports, then be transported by truck or rail back to Southern California – causing even more congestion and pollution.

A consolidated rail and truck corridor hooking up with transcontinental rail lines north of the port would eliminate many freeway truck trips and much of the pollution caused by the three existing rail lines. The consolidated line – which was generally assumed would run along Alameda Street – would replace those three lines, which had a combined ninety miles of rail among them, with one twenty-mile-long line that would speed up slow-moving trains and eliminate traffic jams at 200 road crossings. It was expected that sometime in the early 2000s, the volume of rail traffic to and from the port would exceed ninety train trips a day. Having one straight-line rail expressway made sense for the ports, for the environment, for the railroads, and for commuters. But that didn't mean that building the expressway would be easy or cheap.

The proposed project – nicknamed the Alameda Corridor – would be built along the Southern Pacific right-of-way that ran north in a straight line from the port through a mostly industrial area. But Southern Pacific was not eager to share its rail line with its competitors, and the competitors were not eager to give up the rights-of-way for their existing lines. Although the consolidated line would reduce pollution in the region, it would also increase noise and pollution in the communities through which it passed. Instead of having the trains from one railroad passing through those communities, once the corridor was built, the trains from all three railroads would run through the communities. Ninety train trips a day would translate to an average of one every sixteen minutes. Even with grade separations at major streets, a consolidated rail line would cut cities in two – making it tougher for police and fire services to rush to emergencies.

And then there was the cost. Everybody knew that building such a project would be expensive – early estimates put the cost as high as $220 million. The cost would be paid by the two ports, along with funds from federal, state, county, and municipal grants. At least that was the plan.

In 1989, the city of Long Beach and the city of Los Angeles formed a joint powers agreement – fashioned after the joint powers agreement they had formed to build the Intermodal Container Transfer Facility that had opened three years earlier. It was to be governed by a seven-member board with two representatives from each port, one councilmember each from the cities of Long Beach and Los Angeles, and one representative from the Los Angeles County Transportation Commission. The six cities along the Alameda rail route protested that they would have no representation at all, so a plan was made to add two new members to the board – one to represent the six corridor cities and one from the State Transportation Commission. The corridor cities were still not satisfied. Each city had its own issues, they argued. One representative could not satisfactorily represent all six cities.

Led by Los Angeles City Councilwoman Joan Milke Flores, the board expanded to fourteen members – the executive director and one board member from each port, one councilmember each from Los Angeles and Long Beach, a member for the Los Angeles County Transportation Commission, a member of the Los Angeles Board of Supervisors, and one representative from each of the six corridor cities. The name of the board became the Consolidated Transportation Corridor Joint Powers Authority – CTCJPA. Both the name of the organization and the fourteen-member board were cumbersome to say the least, but with all due optimism, the fledging organization set about to bring all of the necessary players together to turn a good idea into a reality.

One of the challenges of the board was to bring various interests together to get the Corridor built. The unwieldy name did not help. In 1990, the organization rebranded itself as the Alameda Corridor Transportation Authority – ACTA – a name everybody could remember and relate to. Unfortunately, that did little to help focus the needs and desires of the fourteen board members.

In October 1991, the ACTA board members were hit with a reality check that left them stunned. The price tag for what once had been a $220 million project had risen steadily to more than $500 million, but few were prepared for the new estimate – as much as $2.2 billion.

Five of the corridor cities – Compton, Lynwood, South Gate, Huntington Park, and Vernon – had insisted that the rail line be submerged in a trench as it passed through their communities. Only Carson, which already had separated crossings, was not insistent on a trench. If the line remained at street level, without putting it in a trench through those five cities, the cost would be $1.6 billion. Either way, the cost estimate gave board members a bad case of sticker shock.

The rising price estimate was driven by inflation, the trench, the cost of more roadways passing over the tracks, and uncovering more detailed information than what had previously been available. It did not include, however, the cost of buying the ninety miles of right-of-way from the three railroads. The first reaction by board members – at least the board members from the public agencies that would foot most of the bill – was that the cost of the project was too high to be feasible. But if the ports wanted to be competitive, move landside cargo to and from the ports more efficiently, and mitigate the environmental impacts of moving that cargo, there was no other choice. They would have to find a way to make it work or let business go somewhere else and give up the jobs and other economic benefits that all that cargo brought.

Part of the plan had been for the Alameda Corridor to be both a rail and truck corridor. At least one plan called for elevated truck lanes on both side of the tracks that would eliminate those trucks from the freeway. That plan was dropped early on. First, the elevated truck lanes would add significant expense to the project. Second, the corridor cities did not want an elevated roadway and didn't want to bear the burden of both trucks and trains. And third, studies showed that the Alameda route was a less direct route to most trucking destinations than the Long Beach Freeway.

Thoughts about canceling the project or scaling back the railroad portion, however, were dropped as federal and state funding started to become available. The ports' role had always been to create economic well-being in the local region. They also had a responsibility as national gateways to facilitate commerce and trade. None of that was going to be possible without the Alameda Corridor.

One problem with the trench was that the whole thing had to be built at the same time. Overpasses across a street-level track could be constructed one at a time as money became available. A trench would have to be paid for and excavated as one unit. And a trench would significantly raise the cost of the project. But the corridor cities were adamant. The problem with overpasses was that the community would still suffer from the noise of the passing trains, and the approaches for the overpasses across the tracks would extend on either side into residential or commercial areas. With a trench, it would become feasible to have more connecting roadways across the trench so that communities would not be split in two. Unless the corridor cities got their trench as part of the deal, they threatened to sue and hold up the whole project. The trench idea was finally adopted by the ACTA board – at least for the ten miles of the corridor north of the Artesia (91) Freeway.

The other early problem was securing the rights-of-way from the railroads. Unless ACTA could secure the rail rights-of-way and get the railroads on board, there would be no Alameda Corridor project. An intense series of negotiations began in 1992. The railroads wanted the best price they could get for their property. ACTA needed to keep the cost of the project under control. The railroads would provide revenue for the project by paying a toll on every container they moved along the corridor. In exchange, they would get a shorter, quicker, and more efficient route from the port to their main lines.

The ports were to jointly represent ACTA interests in the purchase of rail rights-of-way. Negotiations were often strained. The ports, which were usually fierce competitors, were on one side of the table, and the railroads, which had always been engaged in a long-standing, three-way battle for port cargo, were on the other.

Meanwhile, until the Alameda Corridor could be built, trains would continue to carry increasing numbers of containers on rail lines over three separate routes. The most troubling of these was the Union Pacific line, which crossed residential areas in Long Beach and other communities to the north. In November 1992, the two ports reached a complicated $38.4 million agreement with Union Pacific to build sound walls through residential areas, install welded track to eliminate the clicking and clacking of passing trains, and build an underpass at South Street. The railroad would pay for the new rails; the two ports would split the cost of the sound walls with Long Beach paying two-thirds; and all three would pay for the underpass with the Port of Long Beach picking up 58 percent of the tab. In exchange, the city of Long Beach agreed not to impose restrictions on the number or length of trains using the line. A second part of the agreement covered what would happen if the Alameda Corridor project fell through. In that case three more railroad grade separations would be built, with the Port of Long Beach picking up most of the cost.

The agreement with Union Pacific was costly, but it was also important. Less than five months later, it would provide a bargaining chip to be used by Long Beach in negotiating the purchase of the Southern Pacific right-of-way. The railroad wanted to be compensated not only for the land involved, but for the competitive advantage it would lose over the other two rail lines. Long Beach shocked both the Southern Pacific and the Port of Los Angeles when it pulled out of negotiations for the property, claiming the railroad was asking too high a price. If Southern Pacific wasn't willing to come down on its price, the route could be shifted to the Union Pacific line, which the ports were already paying to soundproof and grade-separate.

Both Los Angeles and the Long Beach City Council howled in protest. The talks resumed shortly, but the Long Beach negotiators – led by Executive Director Steve Dillenbeck and Harbor Commissioner David Hauser – remained adamant. Unless Southern Pacific was willing to come down on its price, there would be no deal. As it turned out, the two ports settled on a $260 million purchase of the right-of-way in June 1993, but this time it was Los Angeles' turn to pull out of the deal.

Los Angeles Mayor Tom Bradley had retired that summer and been replaced as mayor by attorney-turned-politician Richard Riordan. Riordan had problems with the Southern Pacific purchase.

Unlike Long Beach, where harbor commissioners had more autonomy and were removed from office only for cause, Los Angeles harbor commissioners were traditionally replaced en masse when a new mayor was elected. This practice resulted in a jarring change in direction, a period of confusion as the new board members educated themselves on harbor operations, and a panel that was often little more than a rubber-stamp for the mayor. That practice made it tougher for people doing business with the port, because of uncertainty about what changes in port policy would arrive with each new mayor. And while the practice politicized the port, it also gave the mayor control over what happened at the harbor – which could either be good or bad, depending on who the mayor was.

In this case, Riordan, through his new Harbor Commission, declared that the railroad was asking too much for the property and had not sufficiently addressed environmental issues. The Port of Los Angeles canceled the deal. Long Beach had no choice but to go along, since it could not cover the cost of the project by itself and was not willing to continue on without Los Angeles as a partner.

Riordan's gambit paid off. In December 1993, a new tentative deal was struck. The two ports would pay Southern Pacific $240 million for the right-of-way – $20 million less than the old deal – with the environmental details settled. This time, however, it was Southern Pacific's turn to pull out of the deal. In order for the Alameda Corridor concept to work, all three railroads had to be willing to reroute their traffic to the new corridor and pay a toll – $15 per twenty-foot-container, $30 for a forty-footer. The Union Pacific and the Santa Fe claimed that was far too much. With no master agreement in hand, Southern Pacific withdrew from the deal.

Everybody returned to the negotiating table. The only thing that kept the whole deal from falling apart was the obvious need to build the Alameda Corridor in order for the two ports and their private-sector partners to continue the business of moving freight from the ports to the rest of the nation. The parties involved – the ports and the railroads – were in competition with one another, and nobody wanted to give away any advantage that might be had. Finally, memorandums of understanding and purchase agreements were signed on December 29, 1994, at a ceremony held in the Port of Long Beach with locomotives from all three railroads parked side-by-side. The price paid for the Southern Pacific right-of-way had come down to $235 million; the price for the Union Pacific line was $75 million, and the price for the Santa Fe line was $2 million.

There were many problems still to be ironed out and many bitter battles still to be fought, but the purchase of the railroad rights-of-way and the signing of the memorandums of understanding got the project back on track and moving forward.

The Unsettled House of Labor

The International Longshoremen's and Warehousemen's Union had a powerful presence on the waterfront, and few seemed willing to defy it. The ILWU brothers and sisters took pride in their militancy and were not shy about flexing their collective muscle. For instance, when a group opposed to U.S. policy in El Salvador threw up a picket line in 1990 at a terminal where a ship was due to unload Salvadoran coffee beans, the union refused to cross it. In the end, the longshore workers agreed to work any cargo slated for unloading except the coffee beans.

Later that same year, the union shut down the Long Beach and Los Angeles harbors for thirteen hours after two district attorney's investigators attempted to arrest a union member at the ILWU dispatch hall for non-payment of child support. The two were surrounded by 300 irate union members, who refused them passage. Fearing for their safety, the investigators retreated to an office, barricaded the door, and called for backup as the union members tried to bust inside. A union dispatcher was later arrested for allegedly inciting a riot. Few were willing, however, to publicly criticize the union. Crossing the union could translate to lots of dollars if union members decided to retaliate.

But none of that meant the union couldn't be defied – especially when the business entity involved was not a direct employer of the workers. The Southern Pacific Railroad had operated the International Container Transfer Facility north of the ports since 1986, but by the early 1990s, it had become dissatisfied with productivity at the yard. The railroad had been contracting with Pacific Rail Services, a subsidiary of Stevedoring Services of America, for its labor needs. Pacific Rail Services in turn employed ILWU members to supply that labor. In late 1991, the railroad notified SSA that it planned to operate the ICTF yard with its own employees and was canceling the Pacific Rail Services contract, effective February 17, 1992.

Southern Pacific planned to use employees from railroad unions when the Pacific Rail contract ended. That meant more than 300 ILWU workers would be out of work. The railroad said the displaced ILWU workers could apply for jobs with the new union, but that railroad workers – displaced at other sites – would be given preference. The Southern Pacific was apparently aware of the ILWU's reputation for militancy. Union members complained that armed guards wearing bulletproof vests showed up on the day of Southern Pacific's announcement to keep an eye on things. A railroad spokesman said the guards were there to protect container cargo, not to intimidate workers.

The Long Beach City Council passed a resolution of its "deep concern" over the matter after about 100 union members and their families attended a City Council meeting to ask for the Council's support. On February 11 – six days before the contract was due to be canceled – Southern Pacific unexpectedly told its ILWU workforce to go home. The workers would be paid for the last week, but their services were no longer needed. The 335 ILWU workers at the yard were replaced by 200 workers from the Transportation Communications Union. The railroad said it was contractually bound to hire rail union workers. The new workers were bused into the yard after the ILWU members left, and were even fed there because the company said it feared for the replacement workers' safety if they left the job site to eat.

A week after the ILWU departure, Southern Pacific said that the yard was getting back to normal. The railroad claimed that before they left, the ILWU members had erased vital information on 4,000 containers from company computers and had mounted 700 containers on the wrong chassis in an attempt to snarl operations. The union denied the charges, calling them railroad propaganda.

The ILWU had threatened to shut down the entire West Coast for twenty-four hours to express its outrage over the Southern Pacific action, but those plans were blocked by a temporary restraining order. Instead, the union held rallies in protest of the mass discharge of ILWU workers. Union dispatchers were ordered to send any union members who wanted to work out to the job, but most elected to take the day off. It wasn't a strike, but the action idled waterfronts from San Diego to the Canadian border.

Sporadic slowdowns in cargo-handling up and down the coast tangled operations in March. Union leaders said it was part of a program to observe enforcement of safety codes and denied it had anything to do with the ICTF incident. But the message seemed clear. The union kept the pressure on Southern Pacific for months – pointing out instances where the company was in violation of local zoning codes and threatening to file a class-action lawsuit on behalf of the displaced workers. In the end, Southern Pacific won. The loss of the ICTF jobs was a rare defeat for the ILWU and one that would be long remembered.

History, Birds, and Communist Spies

When the Navy left Long Beach, it was a huge blow to the economy, but it also represented an opportunity to gain some new economic benefits. After the Navy left, the Naval Station became a ghost town of deserted streets and weed-filled lots surrounded by oil fields, shipping terminals, and other industry. The Long Beach Naval Station was only one of a number of military installations that were being closed down with the end of the Cold War. The federal government established a program to identify the best way to reuse what was public property in a fair and rational way. It solicited proposals from public agencies with plans for the property.

Nobody in Long Beach wanted to see the Navy leave, and it wasn't just because of the economy. Long Beach had an emotional tie to the Navy. A significant number of residents had first come to Long Beach as part of the Navy. Some sailors had dated local girls, gone to social events, and even gotten married at the Naval Station. The Naval Station wasn't just part of the city's history; it was part of a lot of residents' personal histories as well. The Naval Station had wonderful old buildings, tree-lined streets, and a whole population of birds that nested there. But that was all sentiment – understandable, but not necessarily practical.

After the Navy announced it was leaving Long Beach in 1991, the port began looking at ways it could use the property. The flood of containers arriving at the port was expected to continue to increase. If the port could use the Naval Station for a terminal, it would mean that it could avoid, or at least postpone, dredging up more fill from the ocean floor. In March 1994, six months before the Navy finally shut down the Naval Station, the port had prepared a conceptual plan for a container terminal on the site. According to the plan, the port would tear down the Navy buildings, clear the land, and create a 104-acre container terminal and twenty-three-acre rail yard. It would include a mini-Naval Station for sailors whose ships were in for repairs at the Naval Shipyard next door. The terminal was expected to provide 800 jobs by the year 2000 and generate $271 million in state and local tax revenues. In economic terms, that would hardly cover the loss of the Navy, but it would help.

The Navy, however, was not quite ready to turn over the Naval Station. What it did offer was to lease the Navy mole – a 100-acre, hook-shaped breakwater that sheltered the Navy docks from open water – and a twenty-seven-acre strip of property spanning the gap between Ocean Boulevard and the mole. The plan was for the port to put a rail yard on the site with extended rail lines stretching out along the mole for making up long freight trains and elevating Ocean Boulevard in order to allow the trains to pass beneath it.

Through all the planning over reuse of the Naval Station property, the port was carefully avoiding any commentary on the fate of the Long Beach Naval Shipyard, which was still operating, but scheduled to be closed. Although convincing the federal government to keep the shipyard open was a long shot, harbor commissioners were determined not to publicly consider the more likely scenario.

By the last half of 1995, it was apparent that the Port of Long Beach was the heir apparent to the Naval Station acreage. Using the surplus military land for a terminal seemed to be the obvious solution – both to the city and the federal government. In fact, the process was so far along that the port was talking to a possible customer about leasing a terminal on the Naval Station property. China Ocean Shipping Co., more commonly known as COSCO, had been calling at the Pacific Container Terminal on Pier J since 1981. With its business growing, the Chinese-owned company wanted its own terminal and more acreage. The company was also being wooed by the Port of Los Angeles – which had the old American President Lines terminal available, as well as a new terminal to be developed on Pier 400.

Although the Navy had not yet transferred the Naval Station property, the Port of Long Beach on April 4, 1996, signed a letter of intent with COSCO for a ten-year lease on a terminal to be built after the port received the Navy property. The non-binding agreement only applied to the Naval Station, not the Naval Shipyard property next door. But by May 1996, the Naval Shipyard Reuse Committee voted to turn most of the Naval Shipyard over to the port, which had submitted a plan to develop the property as a cargo terminal, bulk storage area, and private ship repair facility.

The Port of Los Angeles tried unsuccessfully to get the committee to bar Long Beach from developing an oil terminal for ARCO at the site, since it would compete for federal dollars with a similar terminal planned in Los Angeles. Long Beach, however, brushed aside such objections.

"It's just like Ralphs and Lucky's stores competing with each other on opposite sides of an intersection," said Long Beach planning chief Geraldine Knatz. "We believe competition is good."

Los Angeles planner Dave Mathewson accused her of being too simplistic.

"I'm sorry," she shot back. "I meant to say Nordstrom and Sears."

The irony was that ten years later, Knatz would become executive director of the Port of Los Angeles.

In September 1996, Long Beach harbor commissioners approved an environmental impact report for a container terminal on the site. The reuse process was moving forward as expected, and the transfer of the property from the Navy to the city seemed to be near. What followed constitutes one of the most bizarre stories in Port of Long Beach history.

While preparations for taking over the Navy property were being made, opposition against the idea was quickly growing. It started with the historical preservationists. In January 1996, the Navy, as part of the legal process for turning over the Naval Station, distributed a Historic American Buildings Survey that detailed historically significant structures at the base. One of the architects who designed the buildings was Paul Revere Williams, a black architect at a time when that field was almost exclusively the purview of white men. In addition, the buildings on the base were part of the Navy's efforts during World War II, the Korean War, and the Vietnam War.

Distribution of the survey was seen as a formality, a routine part of the turnover process. But the survey was read by historical preservationists with great interest. Long Beach Heritage – a group devoted to preserving historical buildings – organized a tour of the base in March 1996. The event, which drew about 100 people, was reported in the Press-Telegram newspaper, arousing the interest of Huell Howser, the host of the KCET television shows *California Gold* and *Visiting* – programs that featured California history and places. Howser, a former Marine, was hooked. He visited the Naval Station, interviewed both historical preservationists and port officials, and embarked on a personal crusade to save the station from being torn down.

His reporting had a huge impact. In August, Long Beach Heritage organized a second tour of the Navy property. This time, more than 4,400 people showed up to personally meet Howser and sign petitions to save the Naval Station. The following month, when the Navy held a hearing on reuse of the former Naval Station, 1,700 people showed up at the Terrace Theater to vent their frustrations. It was not a night for rational discussion, and attempts by city and port officials to explain the reasoning behind their decision were doomed from the beginning. But, of course, they tried.

City officials and staff armed with PowerPoint presentations full of facts and figures began the meeting with lengthy explanations about how the process had proceeded, about all the points along the way that people could have provided their objections and did not, and about how every "T" had been crossed and every "I" dotted. The port, in an effort to placate the crowd, had promised earlier that day to provide $2 million toward development of a thirteen-acre park on the west side of Long Beach. That commitment was again made to the angry crowd, who saw it for what it was – an attempt to buy away their anger and frustration with what was their own public money. While the official explanations continued for more than an hour, the members of the crowd became more annoyed and irritated. They had come to give City Hall a piece of their mind, not to be lectured to by a bunch of bureaucrats.

Beverly O'Neill, one of the most popular mayors in Long Beach history, found herself being booed and heckled by the audience. It was her first experience with such hostility, and she was clearly flustered. "When you become rude, I think it's impolite," she chided the crowd, which did nothing to calm their demeanor.

Navy Captain Mike Johnson, who was running the hearing, warned the crowd on repeated occasions not to interrupt speakers.

"I realize there is a lot of emotion," he said. "Don't make me do something I don't want to do." His threat had no effect on the crowd, and whatever it was that Johnson did not want to do, he didn't do. The raucous behavior continued.

When it came time for responses from the audience, the flood of pent-up anger gushed forth in bitter allegations and recriminations, each one greeted with wild applause. TV host Howser warned city officials that the fight against destruction of the Naval Station would continue in court and at the ballot box. Some said new uses should be found for the buildings and the grounds and Navy recreation facilities should be saved as a public park. Others complained about turning the station over to a Communist-controlled Chinese company. The meeting ran well over three hours before the crowd began to run out of steam and drift away. But the message was clear. The path ahead for the port and the city was no longer clear and easy.

"Our city is crying out in economic despair," Mayor O'Neill told the crowd. The aerospace industry was in decline. Disney had chosen to take its grand plan to Anaheim. The Naval Station had shut down, and the Naval Shipyard would soon be closed as well. The port was the one remaining bright spot in the local economy. But leveraging that asset to the economic benefit of the city would not be accomplished without a fight – a battle that would end up being waged on the national stage.

The first issue was damage control. The city had signed a memorandum of intent with China Ocean Shipping Co. to lease the terminal when it was built. That agreement was now at risk. If Long Beach was unable to deliver on its promise, COSCO would go to Los Angeles, which had the choice of two terminals available – one existing and a larger one to be built. Also at risk was the port's reputation. COSCO had been calling at Long Beach for fifteen years, but because of the controversy swirling around the Naval Station property, the company was being depicted as part of an evil communist conspiracy to take over America.

In October 1996, less than a month after the hearing at the Terrace Theater, Long Beach Heritage filed suit against the port to block it from demolishing the Naval Station buildings. The suit claimed the port's legally required environmental impact report on the project did not adequately address possible alternative uses that would preserve the Naval Station complex of buildings and recreational facilities.

The city and port argued that it had considered a number of alternatives and dismissed them as either illegal under state tidelands law – which limits uses to commerce, navigation, fisheries, or recreation – or because they were impractical. If the port did not opt to use the Naval Station for a container terminal, it would become difficult, if not impossible, to later get state permission to fill in new land to meet the demand for commerce.

Meanwhile, the Navy, the port, and the historical preservationists were negotiating a possible settlement of the issues. Even though the issues were far from concluded, the port needed to stake its claim with COSCO or risk losing the company to Los Angeles. Harbor commissioners in late October approved a binding lease with COSCO for the Naval Station property. The lease agreement was contingent on the port getting title to the 145-acre property. If the port obtained the Naval Shipyard as well, the company would be able to expand by as much as another 134 acres. In case the port was unable to build a terminal for the shipping line, it committed to buy the six large container cranes that COSCO had ordered for the new terminal and to make up any other losses the company suffered.

The Coastal Commission two weeks later approved the port's plan for a terminal at the site. Although coastal commissioners were sympathetic to the preservationists, they voted unanimously to approve the project because of its economic implications and the fact that the port would then not have to use landfill in order to expand. It was a victory for the port, and the talks with the preservationists shifted from saving the Naval Station to how best to mitigate the loss of the Navy buildings. The port had offered a $3 million trust fund to be used toward the preservation of historic buildings in Long Beach. The preservationists, represented by attorney George E. Wise, wanted more.

The battle raged on. The Coastal Commission set back dredging plans for a month after environmentalists expressed worries about disposal of contaminated dredge spoils. In January 1997, TV host Howser filed a suit to stop demolition of the Navy complex on the grounds that it was a misuse of public funds. His attorney was Richard I. Fine, the same lawyer who had sued port cities seventeen months earlier in an effort to force them to return funds they had taken from their ports. Ten days later, the Audubon Society joined the Long Beach Heritage suit, claiming the project would displace birds, including a large colony of black-crowned night herons that nested at the old station and some endangered least terns.

Long Beach, facing a deadline as part of its contract with COSCO, pressed on with its plans for the terminal. The various litigants pressed on with their suit to stop the port. Negotiations over how large a trust fund it would take to mitigate the loss of the Navy buildings continued. The port had raised its offer to $4.5 million. The preservationists were asking for $20 million. Superior Court Judge Robert O'Brien, who was hearing the preservationists' case against the port, ordered the port to hold another hearing to reconsider its proposal for the container terminal. The port set a hearing for March 12, 1997.

Three days before that hearing, the Associated Press ran a story by reporter Karen Gullo that attempted to link allegations of illegal Chinese contributions to U.S. politicians to the port's plan to build a container terminal for COSCO. The story was basically a collection of unrelated events with little evidence to connect them. It was poorly researched, short of facts, and highly speculative, but it managed to tap into a deep well of paranoia among a segment of the population. Radio talk show hosts seized on the story as evidence of growing Chinese Communist influence in U.S. affairs, and what had been a local dispute blossomed into something much more.

When the day of the hearing drew close, it became apparent that the port administration building would not be big enough to accommodate the crowd. The hearing was shifted to the City Council Chambers downtown, which seated 268. Others would be able to watch the proceedings via closed-circuit TV at the city library next door. Although the hearing wasn't scheduled to start until 7:15 p.m., people began showing up at 4 p.m. to make sure they would get good seats.

The people who testified at the hearing were clearly angry and upset by the idea that the "Red Chinese" would soon have an outpost in Long Beach, even though COSCO had been calling at the port since 1981. People branded the harbor commissioners as traitors and expressed concern that COSCO would use containers to smuggle nuclear bombs, AK-47s, illegal drugs, and even enemy combatants into the country. The harbor commissioners were compared to serial killer and cannibal Jeffrey Dahmer and accused of being part of a political conspiracy with President Bill Clinton. Most seemed unaware that four of the five commissioners were Republicans.

Huell Howser told a reporter before the meeting that it was easy to tell who was for and who was against the terminal. The ones who were for it were wearing ties he said; the ones against it were not. The tie test proved to be not totally accurate, but it was close.

On March 24, the port considered all the commentary received at the hearing, discounted most of it, and voted to reapprove the COSCO lease. That wasn't good enough for Judge O'Brien, who on April 11 ordered the port to cancel its lease with COSCO and to reconsider once more its plans for a container terminal on the former Naval Station land. The following week, the port took the first action to cancel the lease. With the COSCO lease canceled, the port voted once again to build a container terminal on the property.

In May 1997, the judge ruled against the port, claiming that the port had predetermined its approval of the project when it signed a memorandum of intent with COSCO and drew up conceptual plans for the container terminal. It was too much for port officials, who had for several months endured many hours of verbal abuse and sanctimonious pronouncements. The port decided to appeal O'Brien's judgment.

It would take almost a year, but in the end the port prevailed. The appellate court overturned Judge O'Brien in almost every instance – especially his ruling that the port had predetermined its approval of the environmental impact report when it signed a memorandum of intent with COSCO. The memorandum of intent was just that – a non-binding declaration of the port's intent, the appellate judges ruled. It would have been impossible to prepare an environmental assessment unless a project had been identified for the study to assess.

In the meantime, there had been unconfirmed reports of death threats against Harbor Commission members and an Internet rumor that a COSCO ship was at anchor off the coast with 450 enemy troops ready to move in as soon as the lease was confirmed. Two lawsuits filed by Huell Howser had been dismissed, and the preservationists had settled their beef with the port for a $4.5 million preservation trust fund. The port promised to make a record of the history of the Naval Station and to relocate the black-crowned night herons to a new nesting area at the end of the Navy mole. The big outstanding question concerned the future of COSCO and whether it would relocate to Los Angeles or remain at the Port of Long Beach. The company had been insulted and attacked by people, most of whom had no idea of how a port works. But perhaps the biggest slap in its corporate face was yet to come.

The San Diego Hit Squad
Duncan Hunter and Randy Cunningham were two congressmen from San Diego, both decorated veterans of the Vietnam War and both dedicated to the fight against communism. Hunter had been an Army Ranger attached to the 173rd Airborne Brigade, which fought in the jungles of South Vietnam. Cunningham had been a Navy fighter pilot who, with his radar intercept officer, was credited with shooting down five enemy planes over North Vietnam, making them the only Navy aces in the Vietnam War.

Hunter and Cunningham had clashed with Long Beach early on, when the two had pushed for the military to close the Long Beach Naval Station and Naval Shipyard and relocate those functions to San Diego. When Long Beach attempted to save more than 4,000 civilian jobs at the Naval Station, the two pushed to get that work reassigned to private shipyards in San Diego. And when one of those private San Diego shipyards, the National Steel and Shipbuilding Co., wanted to subcontract work back to the Long Beach yard, Hunter protested the work because it would be inconvenient to Navy personnel who might have to commute 120 miles to Long Beach or temporarily relocate there while the repair work on their ship was being done.

Together Hunter and Cunningham pulled every string they could to block the former Naval Station from being leased to COSCO. They fought so hard that at times it seemed the two had a personal vendetta against Long Beach. They fretted about the national security implications of leasing the former Navy land to a Chinese company. They talked about the terminal being used to spy on America and as a place where the company could smuggle in weapons or drugs. For anybody with an inkling of how a port worked, their arguments were so preposterous that their motives had to be questioned.

If COSCO was banned from the former Navy property, it could lease a terminal at the Port of Los Angeles, only a few hundred yards away or remain in Long Beach, also a few hundred yards away. Of the 300 people employed by COSCO in Long Beach, only three were Chinese citizens. COSCO cargo was unloaded by union longshore workers, the terminal was open to inspection by a variety of federal, state, and local agencies – both law enforcement and regulatory. And if the Chinese wanted to spy, it would be easier for them to rent an office in a downtown high-rise rather than a terminal in a relatively remote area of the port.

It may have been Long Beach's lobbying efforts to save the Long Beach Naval facilities or the mayor's warm relationship with President Clinton, whose patriotism had been challenged by both men, but whatever their motivations, they were determined to stop Long Beach's plan to lease the property to COSCO.

In March 1997, the two had co-sponsored a bill that would prevent the government from conveying any portion of the former Naval Station in Long Beach to a commercial shipping company owned or controlled by a foreign country. The bill was later watered down to bar COSCO unless the president determined there was no security risk to leasing the terminal to the Chinese company. But anti-communist legislators in 1998 deleted a provision to the $250 billion defense spending bill that would have allowed COSCO to lease the terminal if the Defense Department and the FBI determined there was no security threat. Without that provision, COSCO was essentially banned from leasing the former Navy land.

Despite that final rebuke, COSCO did not go next door to the Port of Los Angeles. It would later form Pacific Maritime Services – a 51 percent COSCO-owned joint venture with SSA Marine – to operate the Pacific Container Terminal on Pier J in the Port of Long Beach. That terminal was later expanded to 256 acres with 5,700 feet of wharf.

A lease for the container terminal on the former Navy property, by then labeled as Pier T, was signed with the Hanjin Shipping Co. in 2000. The terminal opened in 2002, with operation of the terminal taken on by Total Terminals International, a Hanjin subsidiary. The former Hanjin Terminal on Pier A was leased to SSA Marine.

Duncan Hunter continued to serve as congressman for the San Diego area. He ran unsuccessfully for president in 2008, but withdrew his bid early in the race. He did not seek re-election to Congress. The seat was taken by his son, Duncan D. Hunter, a Marine Corps veteran who served in both Afghanistan and Iraq.

Randy Cunningham was arrested following a scandal over his inappropriate and financial ties to defense contractors. He later pleaded guilty to tax evasion, mail and wire fraud, and conspiracy to commit bribery. He resigned from Congress in 2005 and was sentenced to eight years and four months in prison. He was released in 2013.

The Battle for the Alameda Corridor

Once Long Beach and Los Angeles had the railroads on board for the Alameda Corridor project, the Alameda Corridor Transportation Authority had to deal with the cities along the route of the proposed consolidated rail expressway. The corridor cities – predominantly minority communities – were understandably anxious to get the best deal they could from a regional project that would direct all port rail traffic through their areas. But from the perspective of the two principal joint venture partners, the corridor cities' demands seemed more like extortion than good-faith negotiations. The corridor cities had been made voting members of the ACTA board, and now they were demanding new parks, police and fire stations, and other amenities to ensure their cooperation.

In order to keep the process moving forward, the two ports proposed an amendment that would turn all of the financial decisions on the project over to a six-member finance committee – two from each port and one each from the cities of Long Beach and Los Angeles – thereby cutting the cities along the corridor out of the loop. After bitter debate, one corridor city member was included on the finance committee to represent the six cites.

It amounted to a declaration of war, with Long Beach and Los Angeles on one side and the six corridor cities on the other. While Long Beach and Los Angeles were trying to get federal funding for the project, representatives of the cities were telling the federal government about their displeasure with the project. They even sued ACTA in an effort to ban any further development at the two

DIRECT LINE: *The Alameda Corridor stretches north toward downtown Los Angeles shortly after its opening in 2002. An unprecedented joint effort of both ports, as well as corridor cities and other government agencies, the trench allows trains to travel between the ports and rail yards without blocking street crossings.*

ports until after the Alameda Corridor was built and to get a financial voice in how the project money would be spent. It was a game of political chicken with the corridor cities threatening to derail the entire project unless they got their way.

The Port of Long Beach had had enough. At the start of the August 11, 1994, meeting of ACTA, Long Beach Harbor Commission President David Hauser and Executive Director Steve Dillenbeck announced that the Port of Long Beach was dropping out of the project and withdrawing its funding. The corridor cities would have to deal with the rail traffic on their own with no trench and no overpasses to connect the east and west sides of their communities. Without Long Beach as a joint venture partner, Los Angeles had no choice but to cut off its funding as well.

The corridor cities pursued their case in court. Long Beach, Los Angeles, the two ports, and ACTA itself were represented by attorney Lisa Beazley of Keesal, Young and Logan. She attempted to get the corridor cities' case dismissed. When the court refused to do so, she appealed that decision. It took more than a year, but a State Appellate Court panel finally heard the case and ruled that not only were the two joint venture principals entitled to make all the financial decisions, they could also reorganize the ACTA board at will. In December 1996, shortly after the ruling, Los Angeles and Long Beach amended their joint powers agreement, downsizing the fourteen-member board to seven members – two from each port, one each from the cities of Los Angeles and Long Beach, and one from the Metropolitan Transportation Commission.

Just because the small cities were no longer on the board didn't mean there wasn't plenty of opportunity for mischief or attempts to block progress on the project. Separate agreements had to be worked out with each of the corridor cities to head off future problems, and all six of the cities had to be on board before the project could move forward. The agreements called for a binding arbitration process in case of disputes. There were setbacks. There were times when one city would hold out on an issue, and the entire matrix of separate agreements would have to be renegotiated. It took scores of meetings and a willingness to compromise, but over the months and years to follow, the entire project was finally put together and constructed with a combination of funding that included grants, loans, and revenue bonds.

With contracts awarded and the job of building the project ready to begin, ACTA needed to shift its focus from planning and funding to contracting and construction. The board hired Long Beach City Manager James Hankla – who would later become a Long Beach harbor commissioner – to be chief executive officer for the project. Gill Hicks, who had been with the project from conception, was named general manager and chief operating officer. The project was being designed and built by one team. The design people stayed just ahead of the construction folks and were there to assist when problems arose. There were numerous problems, ranging from Indian remains being uncovered during the digging of the thirty-three-foot-deep, ten-mile-long trench, to environmental concerns about the quality of ground water that would be pumped from the excavation. There were disputes over the movement of underground utilities and the expense of those moves.

Construction of the Alameda Corridor was a huge task, but it wasn't an engineering challenge as much as it was a navigational journey through political and legal entanglements that popped up along the way. The Alameda Corridor opened for business in 2002. It was more than a giant transportation project; it was perhaps one of the largest and most effective environmental projects ever accomplished in the area. More than 200 rail crossings were no longer holding up street traffic while idling cars and trucks polluted the air. Trains were traveling at faster speeds and over fewer miles to make their connections, which lowered emissions. And trucks hauling trailers through stop-and-go traffic on local freeways and surface streets were being replaced with trains that burned less fuel and produced less pollution per ton of freight.

It was a massive accomplishment with an equally massive debt to be paid off from revenues collected. In the years to come, the project would be attacked by misleading press reports and economically weakened by changes in logistics practices. But the Alameda Corridor would continue to serve its purpose. Without it, the flow of cargo to and from the ports would have long since clogged the roadways and neighborhoods of cities between the ports and the open deserts to the east. But even with the Alameda Corridor, moving goods and raw materials to and from the ports to their final destination would remain a challenge.

Logjams and Other Complications
Nobody would deny that Long Beach Port Executive Director Steve Dillenbeck was a brilliant negotiator, but a skilled practitioner of the political arts, he was not. The ongoing attempts by city officials to raid port funds, and the rampant political opposition to a terminal for COSCO, made him nuts. On August 25, 1997, Dillenbeck announced that he was retiring in October. He planned to move to a ranch in Montana.

"After thirty-four years, I've had enough," he told Press-Telegram reporter Art Wong. "I'm just burned out. I'm satisfied with what I've done. It's just time for me to get out. It'll be a great relief to not have all this pressure." He admitted that he was frustrated by the COSCO controversy, but denied that was the reason he was stepping down. His wife, executive secretary to the Port of Los Angeles executive director, had retired the previous May. They planned to sell their home in San Pedro and move to the ranch. "It's got a house, pond, pastures, and trees," he said.

If he had stopped there it would have been good. In September, just weeks before he left office, he talked to Wong once again. This time he opened up about how he felt about the city using the port like a cash cow.

"The thing that hurts me most is to send money over (to City Hall) to throw down a toilet," he said. "Why don't they cut their budget? This is a state port. We're here to promote commerce, navigation, and fisheries. We're not here to build parks, run beaches, and throw our money down a ... hole."

It was an understandable attitude for somebody trying to run a business while others were finding ways to siphon money from the port coffers, but it was not politically astute. Dillenbeck was a plain-spoken man with strong opinions on subjects. And he let those opinions be known, even to his bosses on the Harbor Commission. The commissioners were mostly businessmen themselves, and they understood him and respected him even when they disagreed. But it was one thing to grouse about such matters in private and another thing to air them in public.

The City Charter provided the port with a large measure of autonomy, which was good, but charters can be changed, and not everybody on the City Council agreed that the port board should be as independent as it was. Dillenbeck's statement set back efforts by the port board to keep peace with the City Council. The board members, who were mostly politically savvy, looked for ways to use the port assets that would enrich the city, both indirectly through the creation of jobs and directly with money and projects that would benefit residents.

It was one of the dichotomies faced by every port board – the effort to balance its role as a business entity with its role as a public agency. The two roles did not always coincide, but walking that line was part of the challenge. Dillenbeck was clearly a little further over that line than the harbor board, and his exit interview with the Press-Telegram did not help restore whatever gains in trust had been made between the harbor board and the city it served.

Dillenbeck was replaced by Port of Long Beach Property Director Dick Steinke. Reporter Art Wong's lead on the December 8, 1997, Press-Telegram interview with Steinke read, "If you know former port chief Steve Dillenbeck, you know his successor Richard Steinke is no Steve Dillenbeck."

It was true. While both men had backgrounds in real estate, Steinke was soft-spoken instead of gruff. He was a consensus-builder rather than a "Lone Ranger." In the story, Captain Karsten Lemke, a vice president with Zim-American Israeli Shipping Co., summed up the differences between the two men with diplomatic precision.

> Mr. Steinke has no enemies. He is very well liked in the industry. He is not as controversial as Mr. Dillenbeck. He has a much softer approach, which may be the better approach. There are certain things you should say and certain things you shouldn't.

Steinke would be the man who would oversee the repairing of fences between the port and the City Council in the coming years and the one who would lead the port into the next century.

A more serious problem faced by both ports during the 1990s was a series of meltdowns in the ports' ability to move cargo – meltdowns that did long-term damage to the two ports' reputation.

In February 1990, the eleven harbor pilots at the Port of Los Angeles went out on strike. The Los Angeles port is unique in that its pilots, who guide ships into and out of the harbor, are city employees. The Port of Long Beach contracts with a private company – Jacobsen Pilot Service – to guide ships in and out of the harbor and was not affected by the strike. The strike lasted only two days, but the pilots local was part of the International Longshoremen's and Warehousemen's Union. The longshoremen honored the picket line, and the pilots were able to shut down the port and give management an expensive lesson in union power.

In July 1997, the Los Angeles pilots walked out again. The strike lasted four months, but this time it proved the limits of union power. Although it disrupted cargo flow through the port for several days, the city and the Pacific Maritime Association, which represents waterfront employers, took legal action to keep the terminals open and the cargo moving. Again it didn't affect the Port of Long Beach, but it did contribute to the reputation of both ports – long lumped together in people's perception – as unreliable gateways.

The ILWU was a highly paid workforce, but it wasn't the high pay that troubled people as much as the union's penchant for shutting down the workplace for what often seemed to outsiders as little more than temper tantrums. Terminals would be shut down over perceived or real violations of work rules. The issues would usually be resolved quickly through a system of arbitration that was included as part of the contract, but that didn't mean the interruption was without real costs.

There was also a political side of the ILWU and the pride its members took in their militancy and willingness to stand up for their union credo even if it sometimes meant violating the contract to which it agreed. An example would be the *Columbus Canada*, a Columbus Line ship that became stranded at the Matson Terminal in the Port of Los Angeles after ILWU members refused to touch its cargo of frozen beef and lamb from Australia. The cargo had been loaded onboard in Australia by non-union dockworkers. Although an arbitrator called to the scene found that the union was contractually obligated to unload the ship – including the non-union-loaded meat – the longshoremen refused. The union finally agreed to discharge the cargo on the ship that had not been loaded in Australia, and when the ship sailed some days later, the "scab meat" was still onboard. The load of frozen meat had little impact on the port's bottom line, but it was those kinds of instances that reflected badly on the reputations of both the Long Beach and Los Angeles ports.

The perception by some that the ILWU was a loose cannon in the supply chain was probably not as damaging to the ports' reputations as the meltdown of harbor traffic due to the merger in 1997 of the Southern Pacific railroad into the Union Pacific. Problems with merging the two companies, their work forces, and their computer systems led to chaos across the supply chain and in the ports.

Cargo due to be delivered at one destination was sometimes found sitting on a rail siding at a location miles away from where it should have been. An inability to get the Union Pacific and Southern Pacific computers to communicate with one another led to cargo sometimes being routed from one location to the next, then back again in an endless loop of round trips. Freight deliveries through the ports were taking up to four times as long as usual and ships were backed up at anchor from Los Angeles down to Newport Beach. Containers waiting for shipment were jammed up in port terminals, slowing down the process as longshore workers had to dig down into huge stacks of containers to get the one they wanted, then restack the ones that had been moved. On the docks and beyond, "Union Pacific" was being referred to as "Union Pathetic."

In addition, projections of inbound containers had been badly underestimated. The higher-than-expected cargo flow, plus the logjam of containers in terminal yards, resulted in a shortage of longshore labor. The Pacific Maritime Association rushed to get more longshore workers on the job, and workers were brought down from smaller ports in the Pacific Northwest to bolster the workforce in Southern California.

But all those explanations did nothing to help ease the pain felt by businesses across the nation that depended on the ports to process their cargo in a reliable manner. Slowly, the two railroads ironed out the kinks and freight began to flow again. But it would take the two ports and the ILWU weeks to dig out from under the backlog of cargo.

Perhaps the most stubborn problem faced at the two ports was with the small army of independent truckers – drivers, who worked long hours, were paid by the load, received no benefits, owned their own trucks, paid for their own fuel and maintenance, and were treated with general disrespect by the union workers with whom they interfaced at the ports. The independent drivers were generally poorly paid and many, if not most, were recent immigrants to the United States from Mexico and Central America. Many attempts were made to organize the independent truckers into unions, but they were legally considered independent businessmen, who have no collective bargaining rights.

Before deregulation of the industry in the early 1980s, drivers were members of the Teamsters Union, well paid, but with a reputation for lazy indifference. At that time, all trucking companies charged the same rates and competed by the services they offered. As would be expected, deregulation lowered the rate of moving freight, but it also led to the demise of Teamsters domination at the ports and made cost the predominant factor in the purchase of trucking services. It also led to the rise in the number of independent truckers who often had only one truck, which they drove themselves.

Despite their designation as independent contractors, the truckers would often stage protests and boycotts of certain trucking companies, but without a formal union, there was no binding contract to sign or enforce even if the company agreed to concessions. Since independent drivers were not paid by the hour, there was no financial incentive for terminal operators to process their loads quickly in order to keep costs down. This led to long lines at terminal gates as truckers spent hours – for which they were not being compensated – waiting to pick up their loads. Since their pay depended on how many loads they could deliver in a day, long lines cut the money they needed to support their families.

Despite efforts by unions, including the Teamsters, to make the independent drivers employees, those efforts have failed. There are some who have established themselves in niches in which they make a decent living, but many get into the business and then get out, or remain in the business and grow bitter. For the independent port truckers, there seems to be no easy answer.

A Challenging Decade

The 1990s were challenging years for Long Beach and its port. The city was not the fast-growing, affluent community it once had been. Long Beach had been blessed in many ways – in the vision of its early leaders, in their tenacity and bold plans, in the answers they found to the problems of their day. But the solutions of one generation often become the problems of the next. Oil helped define the city, but it also instilled in its citizens a sense of entitlement. The Navy was welcomed to town for its payroll and its patriotic essence, and when it left, a huge piece of the city's economy went with it.

The Port of Long Beach started out slow, then clogged with mud, then recovered, then sank, then bounced back once more. It was there in the 1990s, during the community's time of need. The relationship between the city and the port was often strained, but that relationship was almost always beneficial to both sides. The city gave the port the political space to be successful; the port provided the city with both economic and quality of life benefits – from sponsorship of Municipal Band concerts to backing the bonds needed to build the Aquarium of the Pacific.

The new century would come with some new problems, even as many of the old problems remained. That was a given. How those problems were addressed would be up to Long Beach – both the city and its port.

A NEW EXPORT: *Dignitaries gather for the 1998 opening ceremonies of Sea Launch. Based on the Navy Mole, mobile launch platform Odyssey, left, and the Sea Launch Commander sail to a site near the equator in order to send satellites into geostationary orbit, making the Long Beach the first port to export into space.*

PART FOUR:
CHALLENGES OF THE 21ST CENTURY

Chapter Nineteen:
A New Age with Some Old Problems

In every historic narrative that attempts to explain how we got to where we are, there comes a time when the storyteller approaches the present day of which he or she writes. It is a time in the story when perspective becomes less clear and when the history becomes little more than a compilation of events of uncertain importance. As one approaches that point, the narrative ceases to be history and becomes instead a short-sighted journalism.

The beginning of the 21st century defines that time in our story of the Port of Long Beach. Except on the pages of the calendar, there was no explosive change in circumstance that distinguished January 1, 2000, from December 31, 1999. But since lines at some point must be drawn to separate now from then, the beginning of the new millennium seems an appropriate, if an admittedly arbitrary, place to make the transition.

The world in the 21st century continues to change at an accelerated rate, with new ideas, new concepts, and new ways of doing things always pushing aside the old ideas, concepts, and ways. But the importance of those changes, of the reaction to those changes, and to the long-term consequences of those changes, remains uncertain. Things will become clearer in years to come, but for now, what it all means is mostly conjecture. So let us conject.

Shipyard Dreams and Wishful Thinking

In June 1999, as the 20th century drew to a close, the Port of Long Beach signed a five-year lease with AMC-Long Beach, an affiliate of Astoria Metal Corporation, to operate a ship repair and barge construction business on a thirty-three acre portion of the former Naval Shipyard property. Douglas Watson, president and CEO of Astoria, planned for the AMC shipyard to employ 500 workers and fifty managers. The planned venture would be headed by retired Navy Captain John Pickering, the respected former commander of the Naval Shipyard.

The Harbor Commission had been under a great deal of pressure from the City Council to hurry up and make the AMC deal in order to get a portion of the 4,000 workers who had lost their jobs at the Naval Shipyard back to work. The sad truth was that U.S. shipbuilding was an industry in decline. Cheap foreign labor and less stringent environmental rules in other countries made it difficult for U.S. shipyards to compete – no matter how much local politicians wanted to create jobs. To open a new, privately owned shipyard was bucking a long-term trend.

But only six months after the lease was signed, Captain Pickering withdrew from the venture "to spend more time with his family." By that time, AMC-Long Beach was $300,000 behind in its rent to the port and still had not put up the required $300,000 security deposit. More than 2,500 applicants had submitted resumes for positions at the yard.

On January 31, 2000, harbor commissioners voted unanimously to evict the company from its leasehold. Its financing had fallen through. A lot of hopes had been raised, but no workers had been hired. In six months, the company had paid the port only $100,000 for one month's rent. By the time the commissioners acted, an attempt by the company to give the port the $300,000 security deposit was refused as insufficient. The company later declared bankruptcy. Harbor Commission President Roy Hearrean said the port had been "more flexible" with AMC than it would normally be with a prospective tenant because it wanted the jobs.

It was an example of what separates the port as a business from the city as a political agency. The Long Beach Harbor Department is a part of the city, but one of the strengths of having a degree of separation from the political process is the ability to make decisions based on facts rather than on wishful thinking. In the case of AMC-Long Beach, unfortunately, wishful thinking didn't work.

Port Carnival

In the last month of 1999, a new ocean carrier came to Long Beach. It had little to do with moving cargo and everything to do with tourism. Carnival Cruise Line, which had been calling at the World Cruise Center in Los Angeles, had decided to berth its ships in Long Beach instead. The Long Beach Harbor Commission had withdrawn from the hotel and restaurant business when it turned the *Queen Mary* back over to the city several years earlier. By 1999, the port's focus was on cargo, not on tourists.

The Carnival Cruise deal was negotiated between *Queen Mary* boss Joseph Prevratil – a former Long Beach Port executive director – and the Miami-based cruise line. Carnival had first started looking at Long Beach after the Port of Los Angeles announced that it was increasing the per-passenger tariff in order to finance improvements to its cruise center. But the cruise line chose Long Beach, mainly because of the city's tourist-friendly downtown area.

Downtown Long Beach was not without its problems. But the city's revitalization efforts had paid off, and the Port of Long Beach had been a key financial player in making that happen. The World Trade Center and the expanded Convention Center had played their role in attracting business, restaurants, and entertainment to the area. The Los Angeles Cruise Center, on the other hand, was located near a blighted and crime-ridden area of San Pedro, separated by many dark and sometimes scary blocks from bars and restaurants.

A passenger-loading pier was built, a portion of the Spruce Goose dome was converted into a passenger reception area, and Long Beach became Carnival Cruise's West Coast home.

More Than a Landlord

The Port of Long Beach began as a private real estate venture with the plan to build an industrial waterfront and then sell land along that waterfront to businesses. And even after that plan became mired in mud flowing downstream from the Los

Angeles River, and the port was taken over by the city, the port remained in most ways a real estate venture. The modern Port of Long Beach evolved as a landlord port with tenants leasing terminals and paying rent. It was very straight-forward. The port provided the land and the infrastructure; private companies used the land to conduct their business.

An owner of an apartment house is probably not interested in where his tenants work or how they behave once they leave the premises. In a similar fashion, the port's interest was limited to the property it controlled – not to what happened before the inbound or outbound cargo arrived at the port or after it left. It was concerned with whether the tenants were financially able to meet their obligations and what benefits those tenants would provide to the community in the way of jobs, in the purchase of local goods and services, and in tax revenues.

The port was merely a way-stop along the supply chain that connected the seller and his goods with buyers on the other end. Over the years that model began to change, although the official recognition of the port's expanded role often lagged behind the actual changes themselves. Even though the port on many occasions reached beyond its boundaries – to restore wetlands in exchange for fill or to build sound walls next to railroad tracks – port executives would remind observers that the port's role was as a landlord, nothing more.

The change to that model evolved not by design but because of changes in circumstances and in what people valued most. It happened because people outside the port were unhappy about train traffic through their neighborhoods, congestion on the freeway, and skies that were often more brown than blue. And it happened because the tenants themselves were concerned about what happened to their cargo before and after it passed through the port.

By the end of 1999, the port still described itself as a landlord port, and that description was accurate. But the role of a landlord had by then been stretched to include being an advocate, being a good neighbor, and being a leader to the assemblage of competing tenants and vendors that depended on the port for their livelihoods.

The port developed the World Trade Center to lure the companies that managed trade from downtown Los Angeles to Long Beach and to position itself as a hub of commerce. But it also invested in the Trade Center to help revitalize a downtown area that had become blighted and depressed. The port had helped build the Convention Center as a place to lure international conferences that would benefit the port and help recapture some of the city's reputation as a place to visit. The port put sound walls along the Union Pacific tracks in the northern part of the city, and it joined with its cross-bay rival to develop the Intermodal Container Transfer Facility five miles north of the port as a near-dock rail facility. Later the Port of Long Beach and the Port of Los Angeles spent years putting together the financing and agreements that were necessary to build the Alameda Corridor, a rail line that stretched twenty miles north through six different communities.

The port's landlord business model was changing, not by choice, but by necessity.

Escalation of the Environmental Wars

Under the old landlord model, the port held that it was not to blame for the congestion, the pollution, or the other ills that people cited when they railed against the harbor. The trains that came through the port were owned by the railroad – they just happened to be heading to and from the port. The trucks congesting the freeways were owned by individuals and companies, not the port. And it was much the same with the ships.

It was a logical if somewhat limited position. The port did provide enormous positive benefits to its community, but those benefits were hard to measure. Unless a person was directly involved in moving cargo, it was sometimes difficult to see what jobs were involved in the process or what the economic benefits were. The congestion, the pollution, and the noise that went along with those jobs were easy to see.

While the port may not have been the owner or operator of the trains, trucks, and ships, it was the destination they all had in common. In 1998, the California attorney general's office, the Natural Resources Defense Council, and other environmental groups filed suit against four supermarket chains – Vons-Safeway, Lucky-Albertsons, Ralphs, and Stater Brothers – over pollution generated by trucks and other equipment at their distribution centers. The environmentalists monitored the air in nearby residential neighborhoods for several months to show that even if all the individual trucks coming to the distribution centers met legal standards, the gathering of all those vehicles in one place exceeded legal standards. The plaintiffs in the case argued that the distribution centers should be considered stationary sources of pollution – much as a refinery or electrical power plant would be, since the centers were the destination that drew the trucks to the site. The case did not go to trial. The supermarket chains agreed to replace 150 diesel trucks with alternative-fueled vehicles, to limit idling time within the distribution complex to three minutes, and to distribute 25,000 bilingual cancer warnings to residents in the area of their property.

The supermarket case was a prelude to a brilliantly executed environmental assault on port pollution. Even if the ports did not own the trucks, trains, and ships that came there, or the cranes and other equipment used to handle the cargo, it was responsible for the pollution they produced.

An Expensive Lesson

A coalition of environmental organizations and neighborhood groups led by the Natural Resources Defense Council filed suit against the Port of Los Angeles on June 14, 2001, over port plans to develop a terminal for Shanghai-based China Shipping Co. The company – not to be confused with China Ocean Shipping Co. (COSCO), which called in Long Beach – had signed a lease with the city for a 110-acre container terminal to be built on the old Todd Shipyard site near the west end of the Vincent Thomas Bridge. The lawsuit would prove to be an expensive lesson for the port, and it would provide the environmentalists with a bloody example of their power to cause financial damage to those who blatantly defied their wishes.

The Port of Los Angeles had relied on an environmental impact report it had prepared for the port's entire West Basin – the area in which the terminal was to be built – back in 1997. Another EIR was done in 2000, but that one was for deepening the channel. That wasn't good enough, the NRDC contended. Things had changed in the ensuing three years, and the environmental impact report needed to respond to the specific plans for the new terminal, not a general impact for the entire area.

In the meantime, the Port of Los Angeles continued to construct the terminal, pending the outcome of the lawsuit. In October 2002, that came to an end when a three-judge state appellate court ruling ordered the port to stop further construction and to send the workers home until an adequate environmental impact report was prepared. It was a humiliating setback for the port, but the worst was yet to come.

Los Angeles had a contractual obligation to deliver a terminal to China Shipping Co. by December 2002, but because of the environmental battles, the port did not meet that obligation. It had little choice but to reach a settlement in the case. In March 2003, the port agreed to a deal in which it would spend $50 million over five years on environmental projects, prepare new environmental impact reports on all phases of the terminal project, use alternative fuels for all container-handling equipment, create and implement a traffic mitigation plan, and install low-profile cranes if feasible. Some residents found the traditional cranes objectionable because they were "ugly" and ruined the view of the Vincent Thomas Bridge.

In addition, the Port of Los Angeles agreed to pay $1.43 million in legal fees run up by the plaintiffs in bringing the suit and to implement cold ironing of all ships calling at the terminal. (Cold ironing is the practice in which dockside electric power is provided for the ships to plug into, allowing the vessels to turn off their onboard auxiliary diesel engines.) At the time, cold ironing was a rare practice for several reasons. Ships were not equipped to plug into a dockside power source, and it was difficult to design the connection in a way that would not interfere with discharging and loading cargo.

The low-profile cranes and the demand that the port implement a system for cold ironing ships would add to the cost of the terminal in a big way. Further, the port had agreed to the settlement without consulting China Shipping – agreeing in effect that the company would have to modify its ships to be cold ironed. When China Shipping couldn't move into its new terminal on time, it had a legal claim against the port, plus the port would lose $1 million a month that the company would have been paying to lease the terminal. The contractors whose construction crews had been pulled off the job also had claims. The port paid China Shipping $22.2 million in damages due to delays in opening the terminal and the added cost of modifying company ships to be cold ironed. The first ships began calling at the terminal in June 2004.

The requirement for low-profile cranes – on which the boom would be hinged and fold down when not in use – was dropped in 2008 after a three-year, $1 million port study found the idea not to be feasible, and an arbitrator finally agreed.

While the Port of Los Angeles had to foot the bill for its environmental transgressions, the lesson learned was not lost on other ports, particularly at the Port of Long Beach next door. The big ports and their deep pockets were obvious targets for lawsuits. The environmentalists – especially the Natural Resources Defense Council – had earned a seat at the table. Few significant projects would go forward from that point without consideration of the NRDC's position on the matter.

The Maersk-Sealand Merger

A.P. Moller-Maersk Line closed a deal in July 1999 to buy Sea-Land Services from its parent company – CSX Corp. – for $800 million. The purchase included about seventy container ships, 200,000 containers, and all related terminals and leases. The new combined service was to be marketed under the name Maersk-Sealand. Both lines were based in Long Beach, but that didn't mean the combined line would stay there. The Port of Los Angeles was offering the company a terminal on Pier 400 – a landfill still in the process of being pumped up from the harbor bottom. The new terminal had the potential to be expanded to more than 600 acres just inside the Angels Gate harbor entrance with water deep enough for the largest ships.

Long Beach was offering a 500-acre terminal to be formed by the former Navy property south of Ocean Boulevard and the Pier S former Union Pacific property to the north. Ocean Boulevard would be raised to allow terminal traffic to pass underneath. The terminal would have double wharves – one on the Navy side in the outer harbor and one on the Cerritos Channel in the inner harbor.

Three months after the merger, Maersk-Sealand announced its decision. The shipping line would relocate to Pier 400 in Los Angeles. It was disappointing news for Long Beach, which had been the nation's largest container port since 1994. Together Maersk and Sea-Land moved almost 1 million TEUs across Long Beach docks each year. Those containers would be going to Los Angeles, and when they did, so would Long Beach's bragging rights as the No. 1 container port.

Although Long Beach pride was hurt by the loss, it wasn't devastating. There was high demand for container terminal space from shipping lines – demand that had been put on hold while Maersk chose between the two ports. With Maersk gone, Hanjin agreed to move once more to a bigger facility. The rapidly growing South Korean line had started in a fifty-five-acre terminal on Pier C in 1991, moved to a 170-acre terminal on Pier A in 1997, and was ready to move on again – this time to a 385-acre terminal on Pier T. The terminal opened in 2002. The plan to develop a 500-acre, Pier S-Pier T terminal with wharves on both sides was dropped.

The New Normal

Life for Americans changed abruptly on September 11, 2001, when Islamic terrorists hijacked four American airliners. Two of the planes crashed into the New York World Trade Center towers, bringing both towers crashing to the ground. Another plane crashed into the Pentagon, and the fourth crashed in an empty Pennsylvania field after passengers onboard fought against the terrorists and kept the plane from reaching the hijackers' intended target – Washington, D.C. It was a day that changed the way people conducted themselves, and the port was no exception.

Within minutes of the attack, the two ports called in extra security and took measures to guard against further attacks. Port of Long Beach executives remained in the administration building with extra security on hand. Los Angeles sent all non-essential port workers home and moved port administration into a nearby Emergency Operations Center. The Coast Guard restricted all vessel traffic within the harbor and required all incoming ships to go to anchor offshore for boarding and inspection before they could enter the port. ILWU members walked off the job shortly after the attacks and refused to return until an evacuation plan had been set up for their safety. After meeting with the Coast Guard and Pacific Maritime Association executives, they returned for the second shift.

When people talked about port security after the World Trade Center "9/11" attacks, they were talking about terrorists and acts of war – not hijacked containers with tons of frozen lobsters or high-end sneakers. That was still a problem, but of a lower priority than it had previously been.

It was the beginning of what came to be known as the "new normal." It was the new way of doing things that reflected the new reality of American life. There is no perfect security, experts in the subject pointed out. All that could be done was to remove vulnerabilities and make the ports less attractive as terrorist targets. And so they did.

The new normal took many forms. Customs computers were set up to track anomalies in inbound cargo in order to identify suspicious containers and keep an eye on them. Systems were set up to screen containers before they left foreign ports and after they arrived in the United States. When people started worrying about a "nuke in a box," radiation detectors were set up to screen all containers before they left the port. The chances of a nuclear bomb in a container were remote – a terrorist organization with access to such a device would probably not want to risk it being discovered in a container before it could accomplish its deadly mission. A more likely scenario would be a dirty bomb, a conventional explosive device wrapped in radioactive material.

Ports began using sonar to detect underwater security threats, and divers began inspecting the hulls of ships for possible explosive devices. Cruise ships were escorted by small armed Coast Guard vessels into and out of the port. And port police and security forces were on patrol, checking out suspicious parties and stopping to question photographers.

Some legislators called for all incoming containers to be opened and inspected – only 2 percent had been in the past – but such a program would bring trade to a standstill and inflict a huge economic penalty on the nation. After much bureaucratic bungling, a controversial transportation workers identification credential was developed for all workers at the port. Physical security at terminals was enhanced and closed-circuit television systems were installed to monitor suspicious people and circumstances.

Not all ports had the same conditions and issues. Some were more remote, with few points of access. Others, such as Long Beach and Los Angeles, had been built years ago with no thought toward the possibility of terrorist attacks. Public highways run through both Long Beach and Los Angeles harbors. Access to Terminal Island is possible over three large, vulnerable bridges – the loss of any of the bridges is capable of congesting the flow of freight.

The world changed on September 11, 2001, and things were probably never going to go back to the way they had been. It was the new normal.

Locked Out

In 2002, talks began between the Pacific Maritime Association and the International Longshore and Warehouse Union – the union's new non-gender name adopted in 1997 – over a new contract for 10,500 union members. The main issue was to be the use of technology. The PMA wanted less paperwork, fewer antiquated work rules, and more computers. There were also jurisdictional issues. With the rise of computerization and the Internet, documents that were once the purview of the marine clerks could be prepared anywhere in the world and submitted electronically. The world was once again changing, and it was time for the ILWU

VIRTUAL PORT: *Following 9/11, ports and other government agencies stepped up security spending. From Long Beach's Joint Command and Control Center on Pier F, members of many law-enforcement agencies can monitor the port in real time.*

CUTTING POLLUTION: *One of the centerpieces of the port's Green Port Policy, enacted in 2005, was the Clean Trucks Program, which phased out all pre-2007 trucks from working inside the port. The program cut emissions from trucks 90 percent over a few years.*

to change along with it. Union leaders understood that, but they also understood that the more efficient the waterfront became, the fewer people were needed to do the work of the waterfront.

It was an ongoing dilemma. It's what union President Harry Bridges faced when he worked out the 1960 Mechanization and Modernization contract with Pacific Maritime Association President Paul St. Shore – how to maintain the hard-fought past victories won by union members, while still retaining the union's position as a relevant waterfront work force?

By the beginning of the new century, the issues were no longer about replacing muscle with machinery. They were about replacing pens and clipboards with optical character reading software, closed-circuit TV cameras, and digital scanners.

The relationship between the PMA and the union would have to change. There had been a feeling among waterfront management that they had caved in to union demands too many times. This was seen in the series of terminal and port shutdowns over issues that had little to do with the companies involved in moving cargo and everything to do with political and labor issues beyond the scope of the contract.

In 1996, the Pacific Maritime Association had hired Joseph Miniace to replace William Coday as president. Miniace was appalled at how easily employers gave in to union demands in an effort to maintain labor peace at any cost. It was an issue of union solidarity on one side and a loose association of rival companies on the other.

Miniace was determined to build a tough unity among the employers as well. It was not an overnight process. The shipping lines were more likely to favor labor peace at any price. Containerization and the mechanization of the waterfront had made longshore labor a less expensive part of the overall formula, but with the increase in international commerce that resulted, the shutdown of ports became a much more expensive prospect. Stevedoring companies, which operated the terminals, on the other hand, were more willing to stand up to the union. From their perspective, rolling over for the union had emboldened union members to engage in illegal walkouts and slowdowns. Stevedoring was a labor-intensive business, so costs were a huge part of the formula. And it was the stevedoring companies that had to handle the daily disputes and hassles over enforcement of work rules and practices.

When the new ILWU contract came due for renewal in 2002, the PMA put the union on notice that it expected some concessions from the union on the issues of technology and productivity. In April of that year, Miniace warned the union that the PMA would no longer tolerate workplace slowdowns – a tactic sometimes used by the union to put pressure on employers. Miniace claimed that during contract negotiations in 1999, the union slowed down the flow of cargo in some places by as much as 70 percent.

Miniace, who had a plain-spoken manner, made no secret of his plan to change the relationship between management and the union. He called the Long Beach and Los Angeles ports the most expensive and inefficient in the world. While union members were still using chalk sticks to mark containers, other ports in the world were using optical sensors, databases and robots to manage the flow of freight, he said. The union members had an unwarranted sense of entitlement, he added.

"They've got a pretty good deal," he said in an Associated Press interview. "They don't work too hard and they make a lot of money."

The rise of the interconnected global economy had been good to the union. The ease with which goods could be cheaply transported over vast distances had blurred the geographic limits and led to great efficiency. "Just in time" delivery had become the catch phrase of the industry in the 1990s. Instead of building expensive warehouses and stockpiling huge amounts of inventory, businesses could order supplies, let the container be the en route warehouse, and have the goods delivered just in time for use. Ideally, the new shipment would arrive at the factory or distribution center just as the old shipment was running out.

It was a good system, but it made the supply chain vulnerable. Floods in the Midwest, train derailments in mountain passes, and strikes on the waterfront could result in economic chaos downstream.

The ILWU's ability to block the flow of commerce and its militant culture had allowed it to deal from a position of strength at a time when union power in general was waning. But union leaders recognized that attitude and economic circumstance could only sustain the union to a point. Concessions would have to be made.

The coming talks – and the PMA's aggressive attitude – caused great concern among importers and exporters, who began developing alternate plans and stockpiling inventory in advance of the old contract expiring. But when one union controls the entire West Coast and the two biggest container ports in the nation, the alternatives are limited.

The PMA began gathering data to establish a baseline of terminal productivity that would later be used to prove the union workers were deliberately slowing down the flow of cargo. Miniace was adamant. A slowdown was essentially a strike with pay, he said.

"I will not pay workers to strike," he declared.

When the contract expired on July 1, 2002, there was no agreement, but talks between the two sides continued. By September, union members began slowing down the pace of work along the waterfront. Miniace accused the union of being willing to jeopardize the national economy in order to get their way. The union, on the other hand, denied there was a slowdown, claiming the drop in productivity was due to a shortage of workers being deployed to the job.

On Friday, September 27, the members of the PMA shut down their West Coast terminals at 6 p.m. and locked out the ILWU. It was a rare show of strength for the employers – a signal that it was not only the union that was willing to play hardball. The terminals would remain closed until 8 a.m. on Sunday. The impact of the thirty-eight-hour lockout was immediate. Truck drivers were suddenly out of work, and ships that had been waiting for longshore workers were stuck at the dock. New arrivals would have to drop anchor and wait for the terminals to open once again.

But when the workers returned on Sunday morning, the PMA decided that the pace of work was still below what the PMA had benchmarked, and at 6 p.m. it locked out the union once more. This time the PMA vowed that the terminals would remain closed until the union was ready to sign a new contract.

The action prompted a national crisis. The local impact was felt first. Toyota had to send home forty workers at its processing terminal in the Port of Long Beach. The terminal processed several hundred vehicles a day, but the ship with the next load of 3,000 cars and trucks was among those stuck offshore. Huge auto carriers normally called at the terminal with new vehicles every two or three days. Many truck drivers, who lived from check-to-check, had to look for other jobs. Machinists who worked on the cranes and other equipment at the SSA Terminal on Pier J had to brave a gauntlet of ILWU picketers, who jeered at them and called them scabs for going through the picket line. The issue was complicated by the fact that the ILWU had been trying to gain jurisdiction over the machinists' jobs at West Coast ports.

Shippers were also up in arms. The nationwide economic impact from the port shutdown was being estimated at $1 billion a day. The cargo needed to stock store shelves for the holidays was being held hostage. Dole Food Co. of Westlake Village had 8.3 million perishable pounds of bananas, plantains, and yuccas locked in refrigerated containers behind closed terminal gates. If it were not possible to get access to the containers immediately, it would cost the company more than $1.7 million and raise the price of bananas at supermarkets across the country. Sunkist Growers said losses in citrus export sales were costing it $2.1 million a week. Mitsubishi Motors Corp. had to halt production at its car assembly plant in Normal, Illinois, because it couldn't get the necessary parts from Asia. The New United Motor Manufacturing Inc. plant in Fremont, California – a joint venture of Toyota and General Motors – managed to reopen after it chartered 747 jumbo jet freighters to deliver parts, including heavy transmissions, to the area.

"It's one thing if those two sides want to play brinkmanship," complained Robin Lanier of the West Coast Waterfront Coalition, which represented big retailers. "But it's another thing if they jump off the cliff, because they take us with them."

The manufacturers, retailers, and other trade-dependent businesses called for President George W. Bush to step in, invoke the Taft-Hartley Act, declare a national economic emergency, and force the ports to reopen and the workers to return. Under Taft-Hartley, the two sides would be ordered to return to the bargaining table during an eighty-day cooling off period. On October 8, the president ordered the lockout to end. The ports reopened the following day.

In the end, the two sides settled their differences and agreed in November 2002 to a tentative contract – this one for six years instead of the usual three-year contracts of the past. It was later approved by the rank-and-file longshore membership.

Miniace's get-tough policy may have put the union on notice that the PMA would no longer be the pushover to which the union had grown accustomed, but it had come at a very high price for the shipping lines, the terminal operators, and their customers.

Two years later, the PMA fired the get-tough leader who had called the union's bluff. Miniace filed suit against the PMA, seeking $1 million in severance pay, a bonus, retirement, health benefits, and punitive damages. The PMA countersued, charging that Miniace conspired with former PMA Chief Financial Officer Thomas McMahon to "flip" a PMA executive insurance policy to their own advantage without telling the PMA board. The exchange of allegations and charges spread out management's dirty laundry for the world to see. Miniace portrayed the PMA in court documents as a secretive and dysfunctional collection of rival companies.

> *PMA's member companies are either direct competitors or have entirely different economic interests. Members have to guard their own sensitive information from other members, guard PMA's sensitive information from the ILWU, and pursue their separate agendas and PMA's at the same time. These conflicting obligations led to two relevant practices at PMA: (i) the delegation of sensitive issues to smaller and smaller groups in order to avoid stalemate and maintain confidentiality; and (ii) not documenting sensitive information for fear that it would get in the wrong hands ... PMA is unlike any for profit corporation, with a bottom line shared vision to make money, or a non-profit whose backers have a shared vision or purpose.*

The PMA laid out its own allegations concerning its former president, painting a picture of Miniace as a runaway chief executive, making important, often self-serving deals without consulting his board, and treating himself to an extravagant lifestyle at PMA expense. The court dismissed Miniace's demand for severance pay and any payment for his emotional distress. Federal Judge Susan Illston ruled in 2006 that there was enough evidence of misconduct for Miniace to lose any claim for severance, and the emotional distress claimed by Miniace was the normal conflict between employer and employee. An attempt by the ILWU to join in the suit was rejected by the judge.

More important than Miniace's fall from grace was the issue of technology on the waterfront. That remains a long-term issue for both the union and the port. In the new technological age, change is happening on an almost-daily basis. At some point in the future, when ships are discharged automatically by giant robotic cranes, and cargo-handling equipment no longer needs drivers at the wheel – developments once beyond the scope of imagination, but now relatively close – what will be the role of the union? The early and oft-stated reason for having a port was the local jobs it generated. There is no doubt that having well-paid longshoremen as part of the community strengthens the local economy.

A port is more than just a business. It's a geographic and monumental fact that cannot be moved to an inland state and can only be replicated at other coastal sites at huge expense. But if its only purpose is as an artery for commerce – if the port becomes so efficient that it no longer employs thousands of workers – of what benefit is it to the city? Is there a danger that at some point Long Beach and the port could become just a checkpoint alongside the river of freight that pours through the area? These are the questions to be answered by the next generation, but there is historic precedent.

In the last half of the 19th century, towns throughout the West clamored for a rail connection. Having the train come through one's town ensured a link to the rest of the nation for people and freight. Now the rail lines in many of those towns are merely a nuisance. The train no longer stops, it just roars through town several times a day – a noisy and inconvenient intrusion into the lives of the residents whose predecessors once saw the train as part of the local economy. Times change. As machines take over the tasks of people, it's not just the union that has to look to its future, but the ports and the cities as well.

Clean Air Action Plan

The most ambitious effort undertaken in the new century, and perhaps ever in the history of the port, was the Clean Air Action Plan – a joint effort by the Long Beach and Los Angeles ports to dramatically reduce air pollution generated at the two ports. It marked a clear break from previous efforts to chip away at the problem, efforts that were quickly undone by the rapid growth of trade through the area.

A draft of the two ports' Clean Air Action Plan was unveiled by the ports in July 2006. Since the ports had no legal authority as regulatory agencies, it would have to use the terms negotiated into the leases with its tenants to implement the changes. Although those were typically long-term leases, they often had to be renegotiated for updating the terms of the agreement to reflect changing times. At those points, the ports would insist upon new environmental restrictions as part of the lease – restrictions that went far beyond both federal and state environmental regulations.

It was a bold move. Southern California, with its 18 million consumers in residence and rail connections to the rest of the nation, was a place the shipping lines could not afford to boycott. If the kinds of environmental practices included in the plan were to become a normal part of doing business worldwide, it would have to start in Southern California. A demand that ships turn off their onboard diesel engines and plug into a shore-side power source meant expensive modifications to ships as well as the terminals.

Long Beach Harbor Commission President James Hankla said the economy of Southern California would collapse without the ports of Long Beach and Los Angeles. Although the two ports often went their own ways, collaboration between them was not new, he said. The Alameda Corridor was an example of a successful joint effort that cleaned up the environment, as well as enabled faster freight connections.

The quest for clean air as outlined in the plan would come at a high price – almost $2 billion. The two ports and the South Coast Air Quality Management District, commonly called the AQMD, had committed to $200 million of that cost. The source for the other 90 percent was not yet identified, but the ports planned to lobby for an $800 million slice of a $1 billion air quality portion of a state transportation bond issue, assuming that voters approved the bonds. The $2 billion price tag did not include the cost to private industry to comply with the new regulations, or the indirect costs such as loss of revenues, or loss of business to other ports.

The Clean Air Action Plan included stringent requirements for ships, trains, trucks, and cargo-handling equipment.

Trucks and the trucking industry were a special challenge – so much so that the ports instituted a Clean Trucks Program as a subset of the Clean Air Action Plan. A digital survey done at port terminals, using optical character recognition software, found 41,000 individual trucks delivering and picking up containers at the ports, with 16,800 of those trucks coming to the port more than three and a half times a week. Trying to clean up that many trucks – most of them with individual owners – was an unprecedented challenge.

The Clean Trucks Program was aimed at restricting access to port terminals to newer model trucks with clean-burning engines. The program was phased in over time with the older, polluting trucks gradually being banned according to model year. Compliant trucks received radio-frequency ID tags that allowed them inside terminal gates. Non-compliant trucks that were used to pick up containers were assessed a fee charged to the cargo owner. The fees were collected by terminal operators and turned over to the ports to help finance replacement of older trucks.

The program also led to a dispute between the two ports. The Port of Los Angeles wanted to insert a requirement that any truck calling at the port would have to be driven by an employee – not an independent contractor. That would limit the number of individually owned trucks arriving at the port and the number of small trucking companies that did business there. Many of those smaller companies didn't actually own any trucks, but contracted for their labor needs with independent owner-operators.

Confusing the issue was an alliance between the environmental groups and the politically powerful International Brotherhood of Teamsters. The Teamsters also were closely aligned to Los Angeles Mayor Antonio Villaraigosa, a former union organizer who had received financial support from the union in the past.

If the drivers had to be employees, then the Teamsters would be free to organize them and would once again regain union dominance in port trucking. The drivers were regularly portrayed in Teamsters' and environmental statements at the time as an exploited underclass who worked long hours and barely made enough money to support their families. It was not an entirely inaccurate portrayal – many drivers did fall into that class. But there were others, perhaps a minority, who managed to make decent livings and enjoyed the freedom of working to their own schedules. As independent truckers, they were able to work the hours they wished, take time off when they wanted, and even pick up other trucking work during periods when port work was slow.

Long Beach had a different view of how to handle the question of owner-operator truck drivers. In February 2008, the Long Beach Harbor Commission released its own version of a trucking plan that would slash truck emissions, but allow trucking companies to use employee-drivers, owner-operators, or a combination of the two. Whatever kind of drivers they used, however, would have to abide by the environmental restrictions imposed by the port. Long Beach's position was that cleaning up truck pollution was an environmental issue; dictating a business model to trucking companies was a labor issue. The Port of Long Beach had committed to the environmental objective, but it refused to get drawn into the labor mandate being pushed by Los Angeles.

That, of course, presented a new problem. The same drivers serviced both ports. If the two ports had separate plans – if all the drivers servicing the Los Angeles ports had to be employees but the ones in Long Beach could be employees or not – would that result in a breakdown of the system? Long Beach obviously didn't think so, and there was little evidence to suggest that it would.

Much of what was happening at the time was being driven by a lawsuit brought by the American Trucking Associations – a nationwide trucking industry group – against both ports. The ATA's position was that while it wasn't against environmental restrictions, it was against a local jurisdiction dictating how an interstate business should operate. That was the purview of the federal government, the ATA argued. In October of 2009, Long Beach settled its dispute with the ATA and was dropped from the suit. Both the Teamsters and the environmentalists criticized the settlement, claiming that owner-operators would be financially unable to pay for or maintain their clean trucks. When that happened it would cause the entire program to unravel, they claimed.

The program, however, did not unravel. In the end it succeeded. The Port of Los Angeles mandate for employee-drivers was later rejected in federal court. The Supreme Court unanimously rejected such requirements as trucking companies having to put "How am I driving" placards on their trucks with a phone number where people could report safety or environmental concerns. The court also overturned a provision that would make companies subject to criminal sanctions for violations of the rules.

By 2012, truck emissions at the two harbors had been cut by 90 percent, according to the ports. That success did not come without costs that went beyond the price paid for clean trucks and cargo-moving equipment. A number of small companies were driven out of business, and a number of drivers also were forced out by the new rules – perhaps the unavoidable consequences of cleaning up the air.

Was it worth the incredible amount of money it took to accomplish, and was it the best use of money to clean up the air in Southern California? So far, at least, most people seem to agree that it was.

Worn Out and Obsolete
The Gerald Desmond Bridge was long overdue when it finally opened in 1968, connecting downtown Long Beach to Terminal Island. It replaced the old, dangerous, and often malfunctioning pontoon bridge that had been built as a temporary wartime measure in 1943, but was still carrying traffic back and forth across the Long Beach ship channel twenty-five years later. But the four-lane Gerald Desmond Bridge was never designed for the kind of traffic and constant pounding received from several thousand container-hauling big rigs crossing it daily.

By 2001, the Port of Long Beach was in the middle of spending $34 million on a five-year upgrade of the Gerald Desmond span. The bridge was being rehabilitated in anticipation of turning it over to Caltrans – the state Department of Transportation. But it was growing apparent that before the port spent too much money fixing up the bridge, it might think about tearing it down and building a new one.

Although it had already spent millions to do a seismic retrofit to the bridge and to widen it from four lanes to five – there were several reasons for the port board to hold off and look at its options. For one thing, repainting the bridge, the final phase of the do-over, was expected to cost another $50 million. The bridge had not been painted since it was built and before it could be repainted, all the toxic lead paint would have to be stripped off and taken away for disposal. For another thing, the bottom of the span was only 155 feet above the channel, already a tight squeeze for ships passing beneath, and bigger ships would soon be on their way. Building a new bridge also would allow the port to dredge out a wider channel. The large container ships with more than 100 feet of containers and bridge house above the waterline were tough to navigate beneath the bridge, especially when there was a crosswind blowing.

If all the port did was retrofit the bridge, it would in the end still have an old bridge near the end of its service life. An engineering assessment of the Gerald Desmond gave it a "bridge deficiency rating" of 53 out of 100, even with the seismic upgrade. When bridges dip below 50, they are usually seen as candidates for replacement.

Despite the seismic upgrade, the bridge continued to deteriorate, with chunks of concrete breaking loose from below the span and falling to the ground and

LOOKING TO THE FUTURE: *The replacement for the Gerald Desmond Bridge in a rendering looking south. The higher span will allow larger ships to pass under; the new bridge will accommodate more traffic and will also sport a bike and pedestrian path.*

TERMINAL OF TOMORROW: *The massive Middle Harbor development will combine two aging terminals into the greenest cargo terminal in the world. Construction of the first phase was to be completed in 2015.*

channel below. While many of the chucks were "not much larger than a baseball, a few have been the size of a football and substantially heavier," reported harbor engineers. Nets had been installed below the eastern side of the bridge in 2001 to stop concrete from falling on Fire Station No. 20. In 2004 the port expanded the netting to the other side of the bridge to protect property and people on that side of the channel. A concrete football falling from the bottom of the bridge would hit the ground at about sixty miles an hour – enough to do sizable damage to whomever or whatever it hit.

It took longer than expected to arrange the funding for the new bridge. The original plan called for the bridge to open in 2008, but the groundbreaking ceremony for the new bridge didn't actually come until January 2013. It didn't take long for builders to run into some unexpected history that resulted in substantial cost overruns for the project – which was already expected to cost $1.1 billion. Beneath the ground was a maze of old and active oil well pipes and utility lines, many of them abandoned from the early days of oil drilling. They all had to be cleared and capped before 180-foot-long steel and concrete piles could be driven into the soil to support the new structure. The extra cost for the project was estimated at about $200 million.

But the work went on. When it is finished, the new cable-stayed bridge will have a 205-foot clearance above the water, three lanes in each direction, bike and pedestrian access, and a great view of the waterfront. It will be the distinguishing landmark for Long Beach for decades to come.

Worn Out and Obsolete Part II

The other worn out and obsolete structure was the Port of Long Beach Harbor Administration Building, which opened with hoopla and bathing beauties in 1960. By the turn of the century, it was not only old and overcrowded, it was also seismically unsafe. It would cost nearly as much to fix as to replace, so designers were hired and plans laid for a new nine-story building to be erected across the street along with a port maintenance yard on seventeen acres. By 2008, the port board was ready to draw up the final plans and break ground on the new building. The price of the new structure, which would include the latest environmentally friendly features, would be about $220 million. The new port maintenance facility would be an additional $60 million.

In September 2010, Long Beach Mayor Bob Foster vetoed the expenditure for the building in the port budget, explaining that the port should secure office space somewhere else and use the savings to invest in its core business. The port in 2014 moved out of its old administration building to a temporary office site by the Long Beach Airport – eight miles from the port. Early in 2015, harbor commissioners and port executives agreed to join plans for a new Civic Center in downtown Long Beach. Expected to be complete around 2020, the Civic Center was planned to have space for Port headquarters, City Hall, and a new Main Library, as well as a hotel, condominiums, retail stores, and restaurants.

Charting Its Own Path

After the departure of Maersk-Sealand to Los Angeles, Long Beach embarked on a plan for mega-terminals that would be environmentally cleaner, more efficient, and create new jobs. That effort eventually focused on redeveloping the 105-acre Long Beach Container Terminal on Pier F and the 130-acre California United

Terminal on Pier D and E into one large terminal. The Middle Harbor Project would use landfill to expand the two container terminals into one 304-acre terminal.

California United Terminals, a subsidiary of Hyundai Marine, pulled up stakes in Long Beach and moved to Los Angeles in 2010 to sublease a ninety-eight acre portion of the APM Pacific Terminal on Pier 400. APM Pacific is a Maersk subsidiary. Following California United Terminals' departure, Long Beach signed a forty-year, $4.6 billion lease with Orient Overseas Container Line to operate the new facility through its Long Beach Container Terminal subsidiary.

By 2013, cost overruns due to unforeseen utility relocation issues and other construction problems were expected to increase the cost by as much as $85 million – which would push the final cost for the project to more than $1.3 billion.

Meanwhile, Long Beach and Los Angeles continued their sometimes cooperative, often contentious relationship into the new century. In 2013, the city of Long Beach filed a lawsuit to stop Los Angeles and the BNSF Railroad from developing a $500 million near-dock railyard dubbed the Southern California International Gateway. The negative effects of the railyard would be borne almost entirely by residents in West Long Beach, the suit contended. Los Angeles and the railroad, which had spent eight years preparing the plans and going through the environmental process to build the yard, denied that the concerns of Long Beach residents had been ignored.

The episode led to what has been a recurrent theme in the history of the Port of Long Beach – the call by people from Los Angeles for the two ports to merge into one. This time the proposal came from the Los Angeles 2020 Commission, a group set up at the city's behest by lawyer Mickey Kantor, the U.S. secretary of commerce during the Clinton administration. The 2020 Commission found that Los Angeles was a city in decline. One of the solutions it recommended was for the Port of Long Beach to merge with the Port of Los Angeles. Instead of two ports competing with each other, there would be one port that would focus on building the regional economy.

As has always been the case, Long Beach was not interested. Long Beach Mayor Bob Foster said he found the commerce secretary's idea "mysterious, condescending, and disrespectful." Nobody on the 2020 Commission had the courtesy to call the Port of Long Beach or the mayor before issuing the recommendation. Harbor Commission President Doug Drummond said he had requested the chance to talk about the issue, but was not given the opportunity to do so. He called the merger "an awful idea."

The upside to such a merger from the Long Beach perspective is hard to find. Long Beach had a history of squabbles between the port board and the City Council, but the port had retained its quasi-independent status and the city had profited from it. Remaining a department of the city or becoming part of a merged port authority for Long Beach would be the difference between living in a city with a port and living in a city beside a port. In the first case, the people of Long Beach have local control; in the second they would not.

A New Vision

By mid-2014, new leadership was in place at the Port of Long Beach. Joining Harbor Commissioners Doug Drummond and Rich Dines, both appointed in 2011, were former city Finance Director Lori Ann Farrell and Long Beach City

College Executive Vice President Lou Anne Bynum, resulting for the first time in the Long Beach Harbor Commission having a majority of women. When Harbor Commissioner Susan Anderson Wise stepped down at the end of her six-year term in July 2014, newly elected Mayor Robert Garcia appointed another woman, environmental attorney Tracy Egoscue, to take her place.

Former Port Executive Director Dick Steinke had retired in November 2011. His successor, Chris Lytle, left to take a job as Port of Oakland executive director in June 2013. Chief Harbor Engineer Al Moro filled in as interim executive director until the port hired former FedEx Canada President Jon Slangerup for the new top spot in July 2014.

A new age had dawned at the Port of Long Beach. The new port commissioners and their new executive director had definite ideas on how to make the port a relevant and valuable asset for the city and for its customers – both tenants and other supply chain partners.

The vision as Slangerup came on board was that the port would move further away from the traditional landlord port concept, in which the port leased out terminals, collected rents, and responded to the needs of its tenants. Under the new business model, the port would take a much stronger leadership role in managing the supply chain. The port would continue to lease out terminals to private operators, but it would establish itself as an honest broker, a neutral party that would act as a clearing house for information gathered from sources up and down the supply chain – data that would help the various partners in the supply chain process prepare for anticipated demand. Although a more efficient port would lead to higher worker productivity, jobs would continue to increase due to greater cargo volume, Slangerup predicted.

The new strategy called for reinventing the process of port development. For example, the port already had been moving toward an all-electric operation. The new vision was that the port would become an energy island – using solar and wind power supplemented by natural gas to generate the power needed to run the port and protect it in case the regional electric grid were to fail. Excess generated power would be used for emergency facilities in the city, such as police and fire operations and hospitals. Excess power generated by solar or wind power would be stockpiled and stored in batteries being recharged for use in the electric-powered cargo-moving equipment. Natural gas would be used not only for generating electricity when needed, but also as a fuel supply for new dual-fuel ships and as an export commodity.

The path ahead will not be an easy one – but it never has been.

Many of the challenges are old. The port comprises 3,000 acres of land, 4,500 acres of water, ten piers, eighty berths, and twenty-two shipping terminals. The water and much of the fill land is tidelands, granted to the city, but with certain conditions attached. Many make the case that the tidelands belong to the state, which has merely granted the city the right of administration, but it is not that simple. The ownership of the real estate is complex, and Long Beach has always been willing to fight for its ownership rights in that regard. The port was first developed and paid for by private investors. After the city took over the venture, the people of Long Beach voted to tax themselves to pay for maintaining and improving the port. Money from oil allowed the port to prosper, but even after the city lost much of that revenue, the port continued to be self-sufficient, profiting without money from local taxpayers. Taxpayers in the Pacific Northwest subsidize port operations with tax dollars. In Long Beach the port provides both money for tideland projects and support for local institutions, as well as jobs and local business opportunities.

The Port of Long Beach is a city asset because generations of Long Beach people have made it so. When the port strayed off course, as sometimes had happened over the years, the people who owned it, the citizens of Long Beach, joined together to set things right. It wasn't always pretty, but in the end Long Beach has always mitigated the negatives and enhanced the positives of being a Port Town.

In these rapidly changing times, the future remains uncertain, but if the past teaches us anything, it is that the world moves forward in spite of – or maybe even because of – people serving their own unique perspectives, making their judgments – and sometimes mistakes – and then correcting those mistakes, as they make their own history.

Bibliography

BOOKS

Aitchison, Peter. *The Noblest Work of God, The Memoirs of James Lough, Master Mariner, Eyemough, Berwickshire and John Craig, Shipbuilder, Toledo, Ohio*. Great Britain: Birlinn Ltd., 2005.

Alameda Corridor Transportation Authority. *The Alameda Corridor Story*. California. 2013.

Barra, Allen. *Inventing Wyatt Earp: His Life and Many Legends*. New York: Carroll & Graf, 1998.

Bell, Horace. *Reminiscences of a Ranger: Early Times in Southern California*. United States: University of Oklahoma Press, 1999.

Berner, Loretta. *A Step Back In Time*. Long Beach, Calif.: Historical Society of Long Beach, 1990.

Boone, Christopher G. "Zoning and Environmental Inequity in the Industrial East Side." In *Land of Sunshine: An Environmental History of Metropolitan Los Angeles*, edited by William Deverell and Greg Hise. Pittsburgh: University of Pittsburgh Press, 2005.

Bulmer-Thomas, Victor, John H. Coatsworth and Roberto Cortes Conde, eds. *Cambridge Economic History of Latin America Volume 1: The Colonial Era and the Short Nineteenth Century*. New York: Cambridge University Press, 2006.

Case, Walter H. *History of Long Beach and Vicinity, Vol. I*. Chicago: The S.J. Clarke Publishing Company, 1927.

---. *History of Long Beach and Vicinity, Vol. II*. Chicago: The S.J. Clarke Publishing Company, 1927.

Chapman, Charles Edward. *A History of California. The Spanish Period*. New York: The MacMillan Company, 1921.

---. *The Founding of Spanish California. The Northwestward Expansion of New Spain 1687-1783*. New York: The MacMillan Company, 1916.

Clay, Karen. Troesken, Werner. "Ranchos and the Politics of Land Claims." In *Land of Sunshine: An Environmental History of Metropolitan Los Angeles*, edited by William Deverell and Greg Hise. Pittsburgh: University of Pittsburgh Press, 2005.

Cook, Sherburne F. *The Conflict Between the California Indian and White Civilization*. Berkeley and Los Angeles: University of California Press, 1976.

Dakin, Susanna Bryant. *A Scotch Paisano in Old Los Angeles*. Berkeley, Calif.:

University of California Press, 1978.

Dawson, Michael. "Folio Three: Transitions in Southern California Landscape Photography, 1900-1940." In *Land of Sunshine: An Environmental History of Metropolitan Los Angeles*, edited by William Deverell and Greg Hise. Pittsburgh: University of Pittsburgh Press, 2005.

Deverell, William and Hise, Greg. *Land of Sunshine: An Environmental History of Metropolitan Los Angeles*, edited by William Deverell and Greg Hise. Pittsburgh: University of Pittsburgh Press, 2005.

Dana, Richard Henry Jr. *Two Years Before the Mast: A Personal Narrative of Life at Sea*. London: Adam and Charles Black, 1899.

Dollar, Robert. *Memoirs of Robert Dollar*. San Francisco: W.S. Van Cott & Co., 1921.

Dumke, Glenn S. *The Boom of the Eighties in Southern California*. San Marino, Calif.: The Henry E. Huntington Library and Art Gallery, 1991.

Erie, Steven P. *Globalizing L.A. Trade, Infrastructure, and Regional Development*. Stanford, Calif.: Stanford University Press, 2004.

Gottlieb, Robert. "Epilogue: The Present as History." In *Land of Sunshine: An Environmental History of Metropolitan Los Angeles*, edited by William Deverell and Greg Hise. Pittsburgh: University of Pittsburgh Press, 2005.

Grobaty, Tim. *Long Beach Chronicles: From Pioneers to the 1933 Earthquake*. Charleston S.C.: The History Press, 2012.

Guinn, J.M. *A History of California and an Extended History of its Southern Coast Counties, Also Containing Biographies of Well Known Citizens of Past and Present*. Los Angeles: Historic Record Company, 1907.

Gumprecht, Blake. "Who Killed the Los Angeles River?" In *Land of Sunshine: An Environmental History of Metropolitan Los Angeles*, edited by William Deverell and Greg Hise. Pittsburgh: University of Pittsburgh Press, 2005.

Harkness, Terry. "Folio Two: Lost Landscapes/Past Lives." In *Land of Sunshine: An Environmental History of Metropolitan Los Angeles*, edited by William Deverell and Greg Hise. Pittsburgh: University of Pittsburgh Press, 2005.

Hillburg, Bill. *Long Beach: The City and its People*. Carlsbad, Calif.: Heritage Media Corporation, 2000.

Igler, David. *The Great Ocean: Pacific Worlds from Captain Cook to the Gold Rush*. New York: Oxford University Press, 2013.

Irwin, Lew. *Deadly Times: The 1910 Bombing of the Los Angeles Times and America's Forgotten Decade of Terror*. Connecticut: Globe Pequot Press, 2013.

Jackson, Robert H. and Edward Castillo. *Indians, Franciscans, and Spanish Colonization: The Impact of the Mission System on California Indians*. New Mexico: University of New Mexico Press, 1996.

Johnson, Daniel. "Pollution and Public Policy at the Turn of the Twentieth Century." In *Land of Sunshine: An Environmental History of Metropolitan Los Angeles*, edited by William Deverell and Greg Hise. Pittsburgh: University of Pittsburgh Press, 2005.

Jurmain, Claudia, David Lavender and Larry L. Meyer. *Rancho Los Alamitos: Ever Changing, Always the Same*. Berkeley, Calif.: Heyday, 2011.

Kelsey, Harry. *Juan Rodriguez Cabrillo*. San Marino, Calif.: Huntington Library, 1998.

Kimeldorf, Howard. *Reds or Rackets? The Making of Radical and Conservative Unions on the Waterfront*. Berkeley, Calif.: University of California Press, 1992.

Krythe, Maymie. *Port Admiral: Phineas Banning 1830-1885*. San Francisco: California Historical Society, 1957.

Larrowe, Charles P. *Harry Bridges: The Rise and Fall of Radical Labor in the U.S.* Chicago: Lawrence Hill & Co. Publishers, Inc., 1972.

Lassiter, Unna and Jennifer Wolch. "Changing Attitudes Toward Animals Among Chicanas and Latinas in Los Angeles." In *Land of Sunshine: An Environmental History of Metropolitan Los Angeles*, edited by William Deverell and Greg Hise. Pittsburgh: University of Pittsburgh Press, 2005.

Latourette, Kenneth Scott. *The History of Early Relations between the United States and China, 1784-1844.* New Haven, Conn.: Yale University Press, 1917.

Levinson, Marc. *The Box: How the Shipping Container Made the World Smaller and the World Economy Bigger.* Princeton, N.J.: Princeton University Press, 2006.

Lewis, Oscar. *The Big Four: The Story of Huntington, Stanford, Hopkins, and Crocker, and of the Building of the Central Pacific.* New York:. Alfred A. Knopf, 1938.

Marquez, Ernest. *Port Los Angeles: A Phenomenon of the Railroad Era.* San Marino, Calif.: Golden West Books, 1975.

Marquez, Ernest and Veronique DeTurenne. *Port of Los Angeles.* Santa Monica, Calif.: Angel City Press, 2007.

Matthews, Glenna. *The Golden State in the Civil War.* New York: Cambridge University Press, 2012.

Maurer, Noel and Carlos Yu. *The Big Ditch, How America Took, Built, Ran, and Ultimately Gave Away the Panama Canal.* Princeton, N.J.: Princeton University Press, 2011.

Mauroni, Albert J. *Chemical and Biological Warfare: A Reference Handbook.* Santa Barbara, Calif.: ABC-CLIO Inc., 2007.

McCawley, William. *The First Angelinos: The Gabrielino Indians of Los Angeles.* Banning, Calif.: Malki Museum Press/Ballena Press, 1996.

McClung, William. "Folio One: Southern California, 1900." In *Land of Sunshine: An Environmental History of Metropolitan Los Angeles*, edited by William Deverell and Greg Hise. Pittsburgh: University of Pittsburgh Press, 2005.

McKinzie, Joe. *San Pedro Bay.* South Carolina: Arcadia Publishing, 2005.

McMahon, Joseph M. and Peter Sonne. *Hollister.* Mount Pleasant, S.C.: Arcadia Publishing, 2012.

McPhee, John. "Los Angeles Against the Mountains." In *Land of Sunshine: An Environmental History of Metropolitan Los Angeles*, edited by William Deverell and Greg Hise. Pittsburgh: University of Pittsburgh Press, 2005.

McPhee, John. *Uncommon Carriers.* New York: Farrar, Straus and Giroux, 2006.

McWilliams, Carey. *Southern California: An Island on the Land.* Utah: Gibbs Smith, 1946.

Meyer, Larry L. and Patricia L. Kalayjian. *Long Beach – Fortune's Harbor.* Tulsa, Okla.: Continental Heritage Press, 1983.

Mickelson, Joan. *Joseph W. Young Jr. and the City Beautiful: A Biography of the Founder of Hollywood, Florida.* Jefferson, N.C.: McFarland & Company, Inc., 2013.

---. *A Guide to Historic Hollywood, A Tour Through Place and Time.* Charleston, S.C.: The History Press, 2005.

Miller, Bruce W. *The Gabrielino.* Los Osos, Calif.: Sand River Press, 1991.

Morris, Charles. *The Story of Mexico.* Philadelphia: Universal Book and Bible House, 1914.

Myers, Paul A. *North to California: The Spanish Voyagers of Discovery 1533-1603.* United States: Llumina Press, 2004.

Myers, William A. *Iron Men and Copper Wires: A Centennial History of the Southern*

California Edison Company. Glendale, Calif.: Trans-Anglo Books, 1986.

Nelson, Bruce. *Workers on the Waterfront: Seamen, Longshoremen, and Unionism in the 1930s*. Chicago: University of Illinois Press, 1990.

Neushul, Peter. "Seaweed for War: California's World War I Kelp Industry." *Technology and Culture*. Vol. 30, No. 3. Maryland: The Johns Hopkins University Press, 1989.

Newmark, Harris. *Sixty Years in Southern California 1853-1913*. New York: The Knickerbocker Press, 1916.

Norton, Henry K. *The Story of California from the Earliest Days to the Present*. Chicago: A.C. McClurg & Co., 1913.

Orsi, Jared. "Flood Control Engineering in the Urban Ecosystem." In *Land of Sunshine: An Environmental History of Metropolitan Los Angeles*, edited by William Deverell and Greg Hise. Pittsburgh: University of Pittsburgh Press, 2005.

Port of Long Beach. *The Port of Long Beach Celebrating a Centennial*. La Quinta, Calif.: Desert Springs Publishing, 2011.

Price, Jennifer. "Thirteen Ways of Seeing Nature in L.A." In *Land of Sunshine: An Environmental History of Metropolitan Los Angeles*, edited by William Deverell and Greg Hise. Pittsburgh: University of Pittsburgh Press, 2005.

Queenan, Charles F. *Long Beach and Los Angeles A Tale of Two Ports*. Northridge, Calif.: Windsor Publications, Inc., 1986.

Raab, L. Mark. "Political Ecology of Prehistoric Los Angeles." In *Land of Sunshine: An Environmental History of Metropolitan Los Angeles*, edited by William Deverell and Greg Hise. Pittsburgh: University of Pittsburgh Press, 2005.

Rayner, Richard. *The Associates: Four Capitalists Who Created California*. New York: W.W. Norton & Company., 2008.

Richman, Irving Berdine. *California Under Spain and Mexico 1835-1847*. New York, Boston: Houghton Mifflin Company, 1911.

Robertson, Donald B. *Encyclopedia of Western Railroad History – Volume IV: California*. Idaho: The Caxton Printers, Ltd., 1998.

Robinson, John W. *Los Angeles in Civil War Days 1860-1865*. Norman, Okla.: University of Oklahoma Press, 2013.

---. *Southern California's First Railroad*. Palmdale, Calif.: Omni Publications, 1985.

Robinson, W.W. *Land in California*. Berkeley and Los Angeles: University of California Press, 1948.

Sabin, Paul. "Beaches vs. Oil in Greater Los Angeles." In *Land of Sunshine: An Environmental History of Metropolitan Los Angeles*, edited by William Deverell and Greg Hise. Pittsburgh: University of Pittsburgh Press, 2005.

Sackman, Douglas C. "A Garden of Worldly Delights." In *Land of Sunshine: An Environmental History of Metropolitan Los Angeles*, edited by William Deverell and Greg Hise. Pittsburgh: University of Pittsburgh Press, 2005.

Schiffman, Paula M. "The Los Angeles Prairie." In *Land of Sunshine: An Environmental History of Metropolitan Los Angeles*, edited by William Deverell and Greg Hise. Pittsburgh: University of Pittsburgh Press, 2005.

Shaler, William. "Journal of a Voyage Between China and the North-western Coast of America, Made in 1804." In Part I, Vol. III of *The American Register: or General Repository of History, Politics and Science*, edited by Charles Brockden Brown and Robert Walsh. Philadelphia: T & C Palmer, 1808.

Sharpsteen, Bill. *The Docks*. Berkeley and Los Angeles: University of California Press, 2011.

Sitton, Tom. "Private Sector Planning for the Environment." In *Land of Sunshine: An Environmental History of Metropolitan Los Angeles,* edited by William Deverell and Greg Hise. Pittsburgh: University of Pittsburgh Press, 2005.

---. *Grand Ventures: The Banning Family and the Shaping of Southern California.* San Marino, Calif.: Huntington Library, 2010.

Smith, Andrew F. *American Tuna: The Rise and Fall of an Improbable Food.* California: University of California Press, 2012.

Smith, Sarah Bixby. *Adobe Days.* Nebraska: University of Nebraska Press, 1987.

Starr, Kevin. *Embattled Dreams: California in War and Peace, 1940-1950.* New York: Oxford University Press, 2002.

Stimson, Grace Heilman. *Rise of the Labor Movement in Los Angeles.* California: University of California Press, 1955.

Strawther, Larry. *A Brief History of Los Alamitos and Rossmoor.* South Carolina: The History Press, 2012.

Townsend, Robert S., Christopher J. Carr, William M. Sloan, and Miles H. Imwalle. *California Tideland and Submerged Land Leasing for Conservation Purposes.* San Francisco: Morrison & Foerster LLP., 2009.

Tygiel, Jiles. *The Great Los Angeles Swindle: Oil, Stocks, And Scandal During the Roaring Twenties.* New York: Oxford University Press, 1994.

Vickery, Oliver. *Harbor Heritage.* United States: An Authors Book Company Publication, 1979.

Weir, Stan. *Singlejack Solidarity.* Minneapolis: University of Minnesota Press, 2004.

White, Michael D. *The Port of Long Beach.* Mount Pleasant, S.C.: Arcadia Publishing, 2009.

Willard, Charles Dwight. *The Free Harbor Contest at Los Angeles: An Account of the Long Fight Waged by the People of Southern California to Secure a Harbor Located at a Point Open to Competition.* California: Kingsley-Barnes & Neuner Company, Publishers, 1899.

Winslow, Calvin, ed. *Waterfront Workers: New Perspectives on Race and Class.* Urbana, Ill.: University of Illinois Press, 1998.

Wright, Doris Marion. *A Yankee in Mexican California: Abel Stearns, 1798-1848.* Santa Barbara, Calif.: Wallace Hebberd, 1977.

NEWSPAPERS

Newspaper	Years
The Cunningham Report	1996 – 2010
Daily Telegram	1904 – 1916
Independent, Press-Telegram	1938 – 1981
Long Beach Press	1887 – 1924
Los Angeles Times	1881 – Present
Los Angeles Herald Examiner	1903 – 1989
Los Angeles Star	1851 – 1879
The New York Times	1851 – Present
Press-Telegram	1981 – Present
Sacramento Union	1851 – 1994
San Francisco Call	1856 – 1895
Seattle Times	1891 – Present

About the Authors

George and Carmela Cunningham are husband and wife with a love of both history and books. Both were late bloomers.

George grew up in Florida. He worked as a surveyor for the state, was a construction inspector on a bridge-building project, painted buildings, flipped burgers, held a job as a draftsman, and worked in a variety of other blue-collar occupations. He served in Vietnam as a paratrooper in the 173rd Airborne Brigade, received a degree in journalism from the University of Florida, and worked for twenty-seven years as a writer and editor at newspapers in Florida and California.

Carmela grew up in Southern California in a strong Italian-American family, where macaroni was a daily dish and Sunday breakfast lasted until late in the afternoon. She worked selling ads at the Register newspaper, writing for a legal newspaper, and escorting press and producing internal publications at Rockwell's B1B division. She left the corporate world to study history and received her degree from UCLA in 1991. In 1995, she wrote *Information Access and Adaptive Technology*, which became the premier book for providing computer access and services to students with disabilities.

The Cunninghams have been together since 1978, but didn't marry until 1995. They were the founders and publishers of The Cunningham Report – a weekly newsletter on trade and transportation – which debuted in 1996 and closed fifteen years later. During that time, Carmela also worked as the chief operations officer for UCLA's Institution for Digital Research and Education.

George and Carmela live in Long Beach with their 14-pound Yorkie, Henry.

Index

Absaroka (freighter torpedoed in WWII), 291-292
Ada Hancock (coastal steamer in fatal accident), 82, 84, 94, 96
Aero Club of Southern California (Spruce Goose owner), 444
air quality, 395, 397, 415-416, 449, 494
    pollution, 308, 397, 399
    Port expansion dispute, 449
Air Transport Command's Ferry Division, 295
Alameda Boulevard/Street, 93, 310, 418, 460
    "Direct Road to Tokyo," 307
Alameda Corridor, 419, 432, 442, 460-464, 472, 473 (photo) 474-475, 484, 494
Alameda Corridor Transportation Authority (ACTA), 461-462, 472, 474
Alamitos Bay, 26, 115, 116, 141, 169, 191, 194, 197, 198, 199, 201, 209, 216, 334, 340
Alamitos Bay Marina, 114, 359
Alamitos Beach, 114, 118
Alamitos Land Co., 114
Alaska Packers' Association, 266
Albion Hall (union faction), 262-265
Alexander, David, 68-72, 91
    George Alexander (brother), 69
    and Phineas Banning, 68-69
Alexander Hotel, 229
    Scott Alexander (owner), 229
Alger, Russell A. (secretary of war), 130, 132, 134
Allen, E. Dan (Port chief harbor engineer), 456
Allied Engineers Inc. of Los Angeles, 295
Alta California, 27, 33-34, 35 (photo) 36, 38, 40-42, 45-48, 50, 51 (photo) 52, 54, 57-60
Alvarado (oil and lumber freighter), 205 (*see also* Long Beach Steamship Co.)
Amar, Eloi J. "Frenchy" (Port general manager), 278, 317 (photo), 318, 326, 339
American-Asiatic Oil Co., 208
American Colony, 47, 107
American Colony Railway, 108, 110, 113
American Federation of Labor (AFL), 183, 259, 262, 265-266, 269, 285, 310-312, 314, 368

AFL-CIO, 368
    Central Labor Council, 314
    Masters, Mates, and Pilots Union, 312
    Bud Satre, president, 314
American National Bank of Long Beach (*see* National Bank of Long Beach)
    merger with First National Bank of Long Beach (1909), 137
    (*see also* banking)
American Potash Co., 185-188
American Products Co., 187, 199-201
American Trader (oil spill of 1989), 440, 441
American Trucking Associations, 495
Anaheim, city of, 40, 92, 101, 103, 107, 114, 115, 441, 443, 468
    and Disneyland, 443-444, 451
    and DisneySea project (*see* Disney-DisneySea)
Anaheim Colony, 78
Anaheim Landing, 78, 92, 115
Anaheim Street (Long Beach), 172, 185, 284, 309, 432, 453
Anderson, Glenn M., (Long Beach congressman), 415, 460
Ardery, Maj. Edward D. (Army Corps of Engineers), 232-233, 236
Army Board of Engineers of Rivers and Harbors (*see* United States Army Board of Engineers of Rivers and Harbors)
Army Corps of Engineers (*see* United States Army Corps of Engineers)
Aquarium of the Pacific, 451-452, 455, 460, 478
automobile industry, 120, 220, 277, 328, 398
    and air pollution, 397
    imported cars, 365, 380, 398
    and roadway construction, 213
    (*see also* Ford Motor Co., General Motors, Toyota Motor Sales)
Bancroft, George (secretary of the Navy, Mexican War), 63
Bank of Long Beach, 137 (*see* National Bank of Long Beach)

banking, 137, 141, 162, 173, 242, 250, 256, 277

Bandini, Juan, 47
    Arcadia Bandini (daughter) *(see* Abel Stearns*)*

Banning family,
    Banning Co., The, 152
    Beatrice Banning (wife of General Patton, first cousin to Phineas Banning), 298-299
    Hancock Banning (son of Phineas and Rebecca Banning), 94, 133
    John Banning and William Lowber (grandfathers of Phineas Banning), 67
    Joseph B. Banning, Jr. (grandson of Phineas Banning), 266
    Mary Elizabeth Hollister (wife of Phineas Banning), 94, 96-98
    Phineas Banning, 67, 72-73, 77, 78, 79 (photo), 80-81, 83, 86-87, 89, 91, 94, 96-98, 102-105, 111-112, 115
    Rebecca Sanford (wife of Phineas Banning), 70, 81, 82-84, 94, 96, 152
    unions, position against, 153
    William Banning (son of Phineas and Rebecca Banning), 152

Barbour, Henry Parkhurst, 140-141, 143-144, 147
    Dana Burks Syndicate, 141, 143, 147

beauty pageants, 346

Beck, Dave (Teamsters Union), 285, 335-336

Bell, Charles W., (Pasadena congressman), 193

Belmont Heights, 168

Belmont Shore, 216

Berlin Wall, 343, 405
    impact on Long Beach defense industry, 440

Bethlehem Steel, Terminal Island, 284, 297, 306

Bixby family, 104, 107-108, 114
    and California Immigrant Union, 107
    Flint, Bixby & Co., 94, 97-98
    George H. Bixby (grandson of Jotham Bixby), 113, 161, 171, 177, 194, 200, 206-207
        (see also Western Steam Navigation Co.*)*
    J. Bixby & Co., 98, 105, 107-108, 114
    John W. Bixby (cousin of Jotham Bixby), 104, 114-115
    Jotham Bixby (younger brother to Lewellyn Bixby), 73, 97-98, 104, 107-108, 112, 136-137, 144, 169, 177
    and unions, 104, 107
    Lewellyn Bixby, 73-74, 94, 97, 104-105, 176, 225
    Llewellyn Bixby, Jr. (Long Beach harbor commissioner, grandson of Lewellyn Bixby), 365, 378, 401
    Marcellus Bixby (brother to Jotham Bixby), 73
    Margaret Hathaway (wife of Jotham Bixby), 104, 108
    Rancho Los Alamitos, as owners of, 114
    Rancho Los Cerritos (owned by J. Bixby & Co.), 107
    and William Willmore, 107

(see also American Colony *and* American Colony Association*)*

Bloody Thursday (strike of 1934) *(see* strikes and shutdowns*)*

"Blue Book" Union, 262-264

breakwaters, 90, 92, 97, 121, 124, 125, 127-128, 130-132, 132-135, 149, 155, 228, 232-234, 235 (photo), 236-237, 240-242, 246-248, 252-253, 272, 274, 279-281, 288, 290, 298, 323, 364, 365, 369, 375, 419, 441, 449, 454, 466 *(see also* San Pedro Bay, United States Army Board of Engineers, United States Army Corps of Engineers, United States Navy*)*

Bridges, Alfred Renton "Harry," 260, 261 (photo), 262, 263, 264, 265, 284, 286, 336, 351, 353
    on Franklin Roosevelt, 315
    and the International Longshoremen's and Warehousemen's Union (ILWU), 285, 308, 310, 313, 334, 335, 336, 351-354, 356, 370, 390, 401, 490, 504
    "Strike Committee," 265

bridges, Long Beach area
    Anaheim Street Bridge, 340
    Badger Avenue Bridge, 249, 254
    Broadway Bridge, 326
    Gerald Desmond Bridge, 142-143, 153, 362-363 (photo), 496 *(see also* Gerald Desmond*)*
    Gerald Desmond Bridge Replacement, 496-497 (rendering)
    Heim Bridge, Commodore Schuyler, 298, 307, 327, 361, 431, 455
    Henry Ford Bridge (rail), 361
    John H. Davies Bridge, 340
    Ninth Street Bridge, 339
    Ocean Boulevard Bridge, 334, 340
    pontoon bridge, 297, 307, 316, 326, 361, 363 (photo), 496
    Queensway Bridge, 380, 383, 398, 460
    Robert R. Shoemaker Bridge, 337 (photo), 339-340
    Salt Lake Railroad Bridge ("jack-knife"), 145 (photo), 153
    Second Street Bridge, 340
    Vincent Thomas Bridge, 399, 405-406, 485

Brown, Edmund Gerald "Pat" (Calif. attorney general, governor), 333, 364, 378-379, 385
    vs. city of Long Beach, 333-334

Brown, Paul (Port management), 434, 446-447

Brown, Willie (assemblyman), 378

Buffum, Charles A. (Long Beach mayor, businessman), 138, 166, 176, 219, 233, 256, 271
    Buffum's Department Stores, 256, 444
    Edwin E. Buffum (brother), 138, 160
    Otis Chandler (grandson), 379

Burks, Dana, 140-141, 143, 147, 160-161, 172, 177
    Dana Burks Syndicate, 177

Burlington Northern Santa Fe (BNSF) Railroad, 499 *(see also* Santa Fe Railroad*)*

Burroughs, Gary (Long Beach city auditor), 445

Bush, George W., 492

Bynum, Lou Anne (Long Beach harbor commissioner), 12, 500

Cabrillo, Juan Rodríguez, 26-27, 29-34, 210
    landing at San Pedro Bay (October 1542), 26

Cabrillo Marina, 446

Cage Submarine project, 202-205
    J.E. Meyer Co. (financial sponsors), 202
    John M. Cage and James C. Harvey, 202-203
    Los Angeles Submarine Boat Co. (operators), 202

California (State) Air Resources Board, 397, 399, 415
    Mary Nichols, (chairwoman), 415
    Tom Quinn, (chairman), 397

California Association of Port Authorities, 419

California Fish Co. (East San Pedro), 188

California Glass Insulator factory, 185
    merger with Bloom Jar Co., 185

California Gold Rush, 54, 64, 65, 73, 75, 134, 224, 389, 503

California Immigrant Union, 98, 104, 106-107
    effect on labor unions, 98-99, 101

California Indians (*see* Indians - California)

California Mexico Petroleum, 223, 224

California Railroad Commission, 129

California Shipbuilding Co., 187, 206, 207, 284, 287, 291
    SS Hattiesburg Victory, 306
    and United States Emergency Fleet Corporation, 207

California (State) Transportation Commission, 461

California Woolen Mills Manufacturing Co., 185

Californios, 45
    Battle of San Gabriel, 64
    Fort Hill, 63
    and Mexican War, 58-61, 63-64, 66
    surrender to U.S. forces, 64

Camp Drum, 81, 85, 89, 91
    Drum Barracks Project (Wilmington), 96

Camp Latham, 81-82

Campbell, James (engineer, railroad manager), 115, 116

Campbell, Adm. Robert L. (Navy Base commander), 330

Campbell, Thomas (agricultural advisor), 257

Campbell, Walter M. (attorney), 141

canneries, 185, 188-189, 293, 394
    South Coast Canning Co., 188
    Los Angeles Tuna Canning Co., 189

Cargo Theft Security Council, 422
    Cargo Criminal Apprehension Team (Cargo CATs), 422

Carrillo, Capt. José Antonio (Californio captain, Mexican War), 63

Carter, Jimmy, 372-373, 402, 407, 410

Caspian Sea, MV (Chinese cargo ship), 383

Central Labor Council (*see* American Federation of Labor)

Central Pacific Railroad, 98-99, 101

Cerritos Channel, 184, 210, 211, 216, 227, 228, 232, 233, 236, 240, 242, 244, 248, 280, 284, 290, 297, 307, 326-328, 340, 361, 410, 411, 431, 448, 453, 455, 487

Cerritos Slough, 71, 140, 142, 144, 146, 192

Chandler, Otis (grandson of Charles Buffum; Los Angeles Times publisher), 379

Chestnut Avenue (Long Beach), 108, 326

Chico, Col. Mariano (Alta California governor), 53, 102

China Ocean Shipping Co. (COSCO), 383, 409, 466, 468-472, 475, 485

China Shipping Co. (not to be confused with COSCO), 485-486

Chinese Exclusion Act, 106

Chiquita Brands International (*see* United Fruit Co.)

citrus industry (at Long Beach), 141, 338, 353, 382, 492

Civil War, 66, 77-78, 80-82, 86-87
    California as free state, 65
    California gold, importance of during war, 78
    Grand Union Demonstration, 80
    Los Angeles Union Guard, 77

Clark, Thomas (Long Beach mayor), 412

Clark, William A. (Montana senator; Salt Lake Railroad), 169

Clean Air Action Plan, 494

Clean Trucks Program, 489 (photo), 494-496

Cleveland, Grover, 113, 128
    and William Wallace Lowe, 112-113

Clinton, William J., 438, 470, 471, 499

Coast Labor Commissions Committee, 313

Coastwise Marine Disposal Co., 365
    and radioactive waste 365

Coffman, Richard M. (WWII head of San Pedro Bay shipping operations), 290

Cold War, 278, 304, 436, 440, 465

Colonial Chocolate Co., 228

Columbus Canada and the ILWU, 477

Columbia Steel Plant, 282

Communist Party (in the United States), 260
    longshoremen and stevedores, 262, 264, 265
    Southern California, 265-266

Congress of Industrial Organizations (CIO), 310-315, 334-335, 352
    Marine Engineers Beneficial Association, 312

Consolidated Steel Corp., 284, 296, 306
    C-1 freighters, 284
    C-2 freighters, 357

Consolidated Transportation Corridor Joint Powers Authority (CTCJPA), 461 (*see also* Alameda Corridor Transportation Authority)

Cordero, Mario (Long Beach harbor commissioner), 499

COSCO (*see* China Ocean Shipping Co.)

containerization, 341, 351, 356-358, 369-370, 387-390, 421-422, 424, 436, 490 (*see also* Matson Navigation Co., Malcom McLean, Sea-Land Service)

Craig family,
    Eleanor Craig (daughter of John F. Craig), 208
    James Craig, Jr. (Long Beach harbor commissioner, grandson of John F. Craig), 265, 401
    John Craig (father of John F. Craig), 157, 174, 502
    John F. Craig (son of John Craig), 157, 160, 163, 173-174, 175 (photo), 176, 192, 194, 198, 202, 204, 205, 207-208, 228, 253, 256, 338-339, 365, 375
    Ruth Craig (daughter of John F. Craig), 82
    (*see also* Western Steam Navigation Co.)

Craig Shipbuilding Co. (Long Beach Harbor), 159 (photo), 173-174, 192, 207, 210, 228, 230, 234, 253, 284, 296, 338-339, 375
    anti-union sentiment, 338-339
    later as Long Beach Shipbuilding Co., 207, 210, 228
    strike of June 1, 1910, 173-174

Craighill, Col. William P. (San Pedro-Santa Monica harbor study), 124-125

Crescent Wharf Co., (subsidiary of Salt Lake Railroad), 151-152

Crowe, Ida, 136

Curtis, Clinton James (Los Angeles Dock and Terminal Co.), 16, 141, 146, 160, 161-162, 165, 172, 177, 192, 338

Dana, Richard Henry (author), 49, 68

Daugherty Field, 295
    Reserve Navy aviation base, 295

Davis, John P. (Long Beach harbor commissioner), 349-350, 355

Dayman, Bromell P. (Long Beach mayor), 137, 140, 163
    (*see also* Townsend-Dayman Investment Co.)

deep-water harbor, 122, 124, 125, 127, 128, 129, 132, 170 (*see also* San Pedro Bay)

Depression (*see* Great Depression)

Descanso Street (Orange Avenue), 118

Desmond, Gerald (city councilman, city attorney), 333, 362 (*see also* Bridges - Gerald Desmond Bridge)

Desmond, Walter (attorney), 144, 199, 230
    and Long Beach Consolidated Oil Co., 230

Deukmejian, George (California governor), 419, 436

Diamond Match Co. (Los Angeles Harbor), 187
    (*see also* Pacific Kelp Manufacturer's Association)

Dillenbeck, Steve (Port executive director), 434, 446-447, 453-454, 463, 474-476

Dines, Rich (Long Beach harbor commissioner), 12, 500

Disney Co., 428-430, 441-448
    Disneyland, 428
    Disneyland Hotel, 428
    DisneySea Theme Park, 441, 443-444, 447-448
    and Industry Equity (Pacific) Ltd., 430
    Port Disney, 441-443

Dock and Terminal Co. (*see* Los Angeles Dock and Terminal Co.)

Dollar Steamship Co. and Terminal, 234, 246, 248-249, 256
    and Bent Brothers Construction Co., 246
    Robert Dollar, 234, 246,
    Southern Pacific-Dollar Line and Terminal (later known as), 234, 236, 246, 254, 268
    Stanley Dollar (son of Robert Dollar), 246, 256-257

Douglas Aircraft Co., 295, 306, 339, 368, 440, 444, 456
    Donald Douglas, 295

Downs, Frank H. (Long Beach mayor) 152, 165

Doyle, Clyde, (Long Beach congressman), 324

Drake, Col. Charles River (Long Beach developer), 138, 160

dredging, 122, 142, 146-147, 155, 160-163, 191-194, 197-201, 209, 227-228, 230, 236, 242, 279, 288, 396-397, 419-420, 453, 466
    deepening channels, 197, 419
    and ecology, 397, 453, 469
    Ford frontage, 244
    Long Beach Harbor, 194, 209
    Los Angeles Dredging Co., 210
    Los Angeles Harbor Channels, 233
    North American Dredging Co., 142
    Western Dredging and Marine Construction Co., 162-163, 200

droughts, 21, 26, 38, 86-87, 97,104-105, 251
    and Great Depression, 251
    Great Drought of 1862-64 (Southern California), 86, 97
    "Okies," 251
    and Rancho Los Alamitos (Jotham Bixby), 104-105
    smallpox outbreak, 86

drug(s), 259, 345
    smuggling (and containerization), 422, 470-471

Drum Barracks (*see* Camp Drum)

Drummond, Doug (Long Beach harbor commissioner), 7, 12, 445, 455, 499

Ebell Club, 158, 170

earthquakes, 75, 136, 257, 326, 438, 448, 458
    1933 Long Beach quake, 257, 273 (photo) 458

East San Pedro, 149-151, 154-155, 163, 166-167, 188

Egoscue, Tracy (Long Beach harbor commissioner), 12, 500

Eisenhower, Dwight D., 321 (photo), 322, 331-332, 343
    state ownership of coastal waters, 322

Eisner, Michael (Disney Co. president), 430, 441

Emory, Adm. William (Great White Fleet), 170

Eno, Rufus A. (Long Beach mayor), 148-149, 156-157

Evans, David (Los Angeles Dock and Terminal Co.), 141

Exchange Bank (Long Beach), 17

Exxon Long Beach (1989), 441

Farmers and Merchants Bank of Long Beach, 16, 105, 229

Farmers and Merchants Bank of Los Angeles, 105

Farrell, Lori Ann (Long Beach harbor commissioner), 12, 500

Federal Water Pollution Control Act (of 1965), 370

fires,
    at Channel 3, 298
    at Colonial Chocolate Co., 228
    at Echo Park Lake (Los Angeles), 220
    and fire protection, 148, 452, 461, 472, 500
    at Ford Motor plant, 328, 329 (photo)
    Gale Avenue, Four Corners Pipeline No. 8, 413-415
    at Golden State Refinery Co., 239
    at Golden State Woolen Mills, 228
    and gushers, 222-224, 238
    at the Long Beach Hotel (of 1888), 115
    at Long Beach Fisheries Co., 228
    at Lorned Manufacturing Plant, 187-188
    at Los Angeles Times, and bombs at 183
    at Municipal Pavilion, 156
    at National Kelp and Potash Co., 187
    of *Queen Elizabeth*, 382
    Shell Oil fires, 222-224
    Signal Hill fires, 238-239
    at "Stingaree Town" (squatters' town), 153-154, 167
    at Walter Fisher Well, 239

First National Bank of Long Beach (*see* National Bank of Long Beach)

Flint, Col. Edward A. (Los Angeles & San Pedro Railroad), 92

Flint family,
    Flint-Bixby partnership, 73-74, 94, 97-98, 104
    Flint, Bixby & Co., 94, 97-98
    Flint brothers, Thomas and Benjamin, 73-74, 97

flood control projects (*see* Los Angeles River)

floods (*see* water)

Ford Motor Co., 244, 245 (photo), 249, 254, 270, 274, 280, 290, 307, 324, 326-328, 329 (photo), 431, 448, 453, 455 (*see also* Bridges - Henry Ford Bridge, fires, subsidence)

Foreign Trade Zone, 400, 401,
    Foreign Trade Zone 50, 425, 427 (photo)

Fort Hill, 63

Fort Tejon, 70-71, 77, 80, 83, 86, 91

Foster, Bob (Long Beach mayor), 498-500

Free Harbor Fight (*see* San Pedro Bay)

freeway systems, 307-308, 350, 399, 409, 418-419, 431-433, 444, 460, 462, 475, 484-485
    Artesia (91) Freeway, 462
    Harbor (110) Freeway, 362
    Long Beach (710) Freeway, 339-340, 362, 396, 413, 416, 420, 424, 442-443, 462
    San Diego (405) Freeway, 416, 420
    Terminal Island (47/103) Freeway, 329 (photo), 410

freighters, 157, 202, 252, 290-291, 356, 492
    and Alaska Freighter's Association, 266
    and California Shipbuilding, 207
    and Consolidated Steel, 284
    and containerization modifications, 356
    jumbo jet freighters, 492
    and Long Beach Shipbuilding, 208, 230
    oil discharge into bay, 230
    and scrap steel, 278
    Western Steam Navigation Co., 230
    and World War II, 256

Friedland, Joel (Long Beach harbor commissioner), 434, 447, 459-460

Fries, Capt. Amos (Army Corps of Engineers), 144, 147, 155

Fronke, Robert (city auditor), 445

Gabrielinos (Indians), 21, 24, 31, 36-37, 504

Garcia, Dr. Robert (Long Beach mayor), 500

General Hubbard (first Southern Calif. steel ship), 171, 173, 175 (photo), 176
    (*see also* Craig Family, Craig Shipbuilding Co.)

General Motors, 350, 492

General Petroleum, 270, 330

Gerald Desmond Bridge (*see* bridges - Gerald Desmond Bridge)

Gunsul, Myrtelle L. (Long Beach city auditor), 225, 226, 242-243

Guyett, Bob (deputy fire chief), 413 (*see also* fires - Gale Avenue Fire)

GOP Railway, "Get Out and Push," 108 (*see also* Robert M. Widney)

Gray, James (Long Beach harbor commissioner), 434

Great Depression, 214, 249, 250-253, 258, 263-264, 271, 274, 275, 284, 303, 430

Great White Fleet (*see* United States Navy - Great White Fleet)

Halfhill, Alfred P., 188
    Halfhill Tuna Co., 228

Hancock, Capt. Winfield Scott (Civil War), 80, 82, 89
    Army Southern District for the Department of the Pacific, 80

Hancock Park, 89

Hankla, James (Long Beach city manager, harbor commissioner), 446, 451, 456, 474, 494

Hanjin Shipping Co., 448, 455-456, 472, 487
    move to Pier A, 487
    move to Pier C, 455

Hanna, E. John (Long Beach harbor commissioner),

401

Harding, Warren G., 214, 230
    and Charles H. Windham, 230
Harrington, William A. (Long Beach harbor commissioner), 346
Hatch, D.P. (San Pedro franchise holder), 158
Hatch, Ira (Long Beach mayor), 179 (photo), 190, 204
    Iola Hatch (wife), 190
Hatch, Philander Ellsworth (P.E.) (businessman), 16, 137, 162, 173, 194, 200, 206
    (*also see* National Bank of Long Beach)
Hauge, Oscar (Long Beach mayor), 254
Hauser, David (Long Beach harbor commissioner), 431, 434, 453, 463, 474
Hearrean, Roy (Long Beach harbor commissioner), 455, 459, 483
Hellman, Isaias W. (Farmers and Merchants Bank, Los Angeles), 105, 114, 350
Heim, Cdre. Schuyler F. (Navy Base commander), 298, 307 (*see also* bridges - Heim Bridge)
Heldmaier & Neu, 132-134, 143
Henry Ford Bridge (*see* bridges - Henry Ford Bridge)
Hercules H-4 flying boat (*see* Spruce Goose)
"Herman the German" crane, 337 (photo), 338, 428
Hewes, Charles E. (Long Beach city manager), 218-219, 224-227, 230
Hill, Leland (Port management), 434, 446, 447
Hiuka America Corp., 448
Hollister, Col. Joseph Hubbard, 74, 94, 96
Hollister, Mary Elizabeth Hollister (*see* Banning family)
Hollister, Col. William Welles, 74, 96
Holman, Lee (International Longshoremen's Association), 263-266
Hopkins, Mark, 98, 100, 102, 134
Hosmer, Craig (Long Beach congressman), 321 (photo)
Howser, Huell, 457, 467-470
Hughes, Howard, 315-316, 318, 382, 398, 400, 409, 428
    Hughes Aircraft Corporation, 316
    Hughes Glomar Explorer (drill ship), 398
    Hughes Summa Corporation, 282, 400
    (*see also* Spruce Goose)
Humble Oil supertanker terminal, 384
Hunter, Duncan (San Diego congressman), 456, 471-472
Huntington Beach, 40, 98, 440
Huntington Park, 461
Huntington, Collis, 73, 98, 99, 100, 101, 102, 103, 117, 122, 124-128, 130, 132, 134-135, 138, 165, 504
    Henry Huntington, nephew, 138
Huntington, Henry E., 138, 156, 350 (*see also* Pacific Electric Railroad)
Iaqua, SS (steam schooner, 1911), 15, 16, 177

imports, 249, 383, 389, 425
    automobiles (*see* automobile industry)
    banana, 383
    barley and copra, 348
    gypsum, 349,
    industrial zone, 425
    sake, 389
    salt, 349
Independent, Press-Telegram (*see* Press-Telegram)
Industrial Workers of the World (Wobblies, IWW), 183, 259, 262, 352
Indians, native American peoples
    California Indians, 22, 36, 503
    Gabrielino Indians, (*see* Gabrielinos)
    Shoshone people, 20, 23
Intermodal Container Transfer Facility (ICTF), 416, 418, 432, 461, 464-465, 484
International Brotherhood of Teamsters, 285, 335-336, 353, 370, 383, 407, 478, 495
    James "Jimmy" Hoffa, 353
International Immigrant Union. 98 (*see also* California Immigrant Union)
International Longshoremen's Association (ILA), 262, 263-269, 285, 310, 336, 353, 389
    strike of 1934 and Bloody Thursday (see unions - strikes)
International Longshore and Warehouse Union (ILWU - before 1997 International Longshoremen's and Warehousemen's Union), 261 (photo) 269, 285-286, 308-315, 334-336, 351-355, 370, 383, 390, 391 (photo), 392-393, 401, 406-408, 432, 464-465, 476-477, 487, 488, 490-493, 500
    Local 13, 312, 335, 354
    (*see also* Bridges, Alfred Renton "Harry")
International Transportation Service (ITS), 431-433, 443
Interstate Commerce Commission, 407
Iron Workers Union, 183
Jacobsen Pilot Service 339, 476
J.A. Jacobsen, 318
Japanese internment (*see* World War II)
Johnston, Gen. Albert Sidney (Civil War), 80
Johnston, Albert Sidney Jr., 82
Joint Labor Relations Committee, 354
Jones Act, 227, 434
"K" Line, 380, 431, 443 (*see also* International Transportation Service)
Kaiser Steel, 296
    Eagle Mountain Mine, 349
Kell, Ernie (Long Beach mayor), 432, 441, 445, 458-459
kelp, 186-188, 199-200, 397
Keystone Canyon, and Huntington Beach, 440, 441
Kinney, Abbot ("Doge of Venice"), 140, 161
Koppel Bulk Terminals, 347 (photo), 348,
Ku Klux Klan, 226
labor (*see* unions)

Lakewood, city of, 40, 169, 256, 411, 418

Langslet, Robert (Long Beach harbor commissioner), 459

Larkin, Thomas (U.S. consul, Mexican War), 59-60

Lewis, W.J. (International Longshoremen's Association), 266

Lisenby, William T. (Long Beach mayor), 202

Looff Amusement Device factory, 185

Long Beach & San Pedro Railway Co., 115-116

Long Beach Board of Harbor Commissioners, 6, 202, 253, 270, 354, 362, 428, 483, 495

Long Beach Chamber of Commerce, 14, 174, 219, 229, 253

Long Beach City Council, 113, 117, 144, 173-174, 200, 202, 209, 217-219, 225, 227, 229-234, 236-238, 244, 246, 249, 253, 270, 272, 288, 326, 332, 338, 362, 366, 376, 378, 383-386, 394, 399-400, 411-412, 418, 432-433, 437, 445, 449-450, 460-461, 463, 465, 470, 475-476, 482, 499-500

Long Beach, city of, 14, 75, 101, 112, 114, 119 (photo), 128, 136-138, 152, 156-157, 172-173, 184, 192, 193, 197-198, 200-201, 209, 211, 215-216, 224-227, 228-229, 231, 232-234, 236, 242, 252, 253, 254, 269-270, 274, 280, 286-288, 318-320, 331-334, 362-364, 367, 379, 393, 398, 413-414, 432, 436, 442, 452, 454, 461, 471, 498

    1933 earthquake (*see* earthquakes)

    and alcohol, 108, 113, 117-118, 163, 189-190, 211, 258 (*see also* Prohibition)

    annexation attempts by Los Angeles, 164-166, 168-169, 215-216

    city manager form of governance, 217-219

    Empire Day disaster (1913), 190

    incorporation (1888), disincorporation (1897), and reincorporation (1897), 113, 117-118

    naming of, 110, 112

    and Signal Hill, 238-239

    Terminal Island annexation fight with San Pedro, 147-151, 166-167

    (*see also* Willmore City)

Long Beach Consolidated Oil Co., 222-223, 230

Long Beach Container Terminal, 408-409, 498-499

Long Beach Development Co., 113-114, 116-117, 138, 340

Long Beach Heritage, 467-469

Long Beach Hotel, 110, 112, 113, 115

Long Beach Improvement Co., 14, 16-17, 177

Long Beach International Coal Terminal, 410-412

Long Beach Iron Works, 185

Long Beach Land and Navigation Co., 140, 144, 146

Long Beach Municipal Band, 14, 189-190, 256, 386, 424, 478

Long Beach Naval Hospital (*see* United States Navy)

Long Beach Naval Shipyard (*see* United States Navy)

Long Beach Naval Station (*see* United States Navy)

Long Beach Oil Development Co., 330

Long Beach, Port of (*see* Port of Long Beach)

Long Beach Press-Telegram (*see* Press-Telegram)

Long Beach Redevelopment Agency, 430, 451, 459, 460

Long Beach Shipbuilding Co. (*see* Craig Shipbuilding Co.)

Los Alamitos, city of, 40, 46, 295

Los Angeles & San Pedro Railroad Co., 91, 93, 103-104

Los Angeles Chamber of Commerce, 125, 137, 132, 144, 156, 199, 248, 311

    and Greater Harbor Committee, 241

Los Angeles City Council, 242, 288, 338, 394

    as Los Angeles Common Council, 78, 98

Los Angeles, city of, 8, 38, 16, 168-169, 193, 455

    consolidation with San Pedro and Wilmington, 164-168

    harbor bond, 232

    landfill dumps, dispute, 410

    and Port of Long Beach, 9

    and Port of Los Angeles, 8, 168

    property dispute with Navy, 295

    railroad system, 90

    and San Pedro, 165, 337-338, 358

Los Angeles County Board of Supervisors, 70, 84, 86, 90, 91, 96, 117, 187, 191, 196, 238-239, 396, 461

Los Angeles County Transportation Commission, 461

Los Angeles Dock and Terminal Co., 16-17, 141-144, 146-147, 152, 158, 160-162, 164, 166, 172, 173, 176-177, 189, 191-192, 197, 199, 200-202, 228-230, 232-234, 338-339, 350 (*see also* Clinton James Curtis)

Los Angeles Flood Control Channel (*see* Los Angeles River)

Los Angeles Harbor Commission, 199, 228, 339, 354, 358-360, 386, 394, 448, 463

    and World Trade Center (San Pedro) scandal, 384-387

Los Angeles Herald,

    on consolidation of San Pedro and Wilmington with Los Angeles, 165, 168

Los Angeles, Port of (*see* Port of Los Angeles)

Los Angeles River, 26, 39, 76, 85, 140-141, 191, 198-199, 214, 326

    and Arroyo Seco confluence, 39

    flood control projects, 140, 196-197, 199, 209, 214, 227-228, 232, 239, 241-242, 246, 252, 274, 279-280, 297-298, 326, 334, 340, 368-370, 375

    Los Angeles Flood Control Channel, 334, 368, 375

    Los Angeles Flood Control Association, 196

    as the San Gabriel River, 140-141

Los Angeles Shipbuilding and Boat Dry Dock Co., 284, 287, 291

Los Angeles Submarine and Boat Co., 202-203, 205

    W.L. Cleveland Co., 205

    (*also see* Cage Submarine Project)

Los Angeles Terminal Line (1891), 142

Los Angeles Terminal Railroad, 116, 122, 129, 133, 142

Los Angeles Times,
  on annexation of Long Beach by Los Angeles, 216
  bombing and deaths at Times building (1910), 183
  on City Auditor Myrtelle L. Gunsul office space dispute, 225
  on Collis Huntington's death, 135
  on conservation of oil, 222
  on consolidation of San Pedro and Wilmington, 165
  on Harry Bridges, 286, 309, 315, 353
  on industry in Long Beach, 201
  on Long Beach swimwear ordinance, 218
  on Phineas Banning, 111
  on Press-Telegram influence on Long Beach policy, 379
  on *Queen Mary* purchase, 376-379
  on Russell A. Alger (secretary of war), 130
  "totemites" and "dupes" (opinion of union members), 153
  "Trouble on the Waterfront" (special series, 1959), 353
  vs. unions, 153, 183, 265, 315, 353
  on World Trade Center (San Pedro) scandal (see Los Angeles Harbor Commission)
Los Angeles Transportation Co., 452
Los Angeles Tuna Canning Co., 189
Los Angeles Tuna Packing Co., 228
Lowenthal, Alan (Long Beach councilman), 445
Lundeberg, Harry (Sailors Union of the Pacific), 310-311, 314
Lytle, Chris (Port executive director), 500
Maersk Shipping Line of Denmark, 442, 443, 454
  Maersk Terminal, Pier J, 454
  A.P. Moller-Maersk Line, merger with Sea-Land Services, 486, 498-499
  Maersk-Sea-Land, and relocation to Port of Los Angeles, 487, 498-499
Mansell, John (Long Beach city manager), 331, 378
Marine Service Bureau (Long Beach and San Pedro company union), 262
Martin-Decker Corp., 275
Martin-Loomis Co., 274-275
Martin, W.R. "Frosty" (Long Beach harbor commissioner), 274-275, 339
Masters, Mates, and Pilots Union, 312
Matson Navigation Co., 263, 264, 354, 357, 369, 387-388, 456, 477
McDonnell Douglas, 295, 306, 339, 368, 440, 444, 456
McJunkin, James H. (Port executive director), 410, 412, 432, 433, 434, 446
McLean, Malcom, 340-341, 356-357, 359 (*see also* containerization, Sea-Land Service)
McLendon, Ben W. (Long Beach police chief), 224-226
Mechanization and Modernization Agreement (*see* unions)

Mendell, Col. George H. (Army Corps of Engineers), 121, 125, 133
  and survey from Point Dume to Capistrano, 122
Mendoza, Antonio de, 29-30
Metal Trades Union, 208
Metropolitan Transportation Commission, 474
Mexico, 27-29, 30, 33, 45-47, 50, 52-53, 56-59, 60-66, 68, 75, 80, 97, 144, 163, 183-184, 207, 222-224, 244, 249, 254, 292, 302, 310, 349, 392, 438, 478, 504, 505
Middle Harbor Project, 497 (photo), 498
mission(s), 34, 36-41, 46-48, 58, 503;
  and Fr. Junipero Serra, 34; 36-38, 42, 46, 47, 48, 50
  and Fr. Pedro Benito Gambón, 36
  Mission San Carlos Borromeo, 36
  Mission San Gabriel, 21, 36-37, 39-40, 48, 50, 54
  secularization of, 57
Missouri, USS, 302, 420
Mobil Oil Corp., 328, 364
Montgomery, Capt. John B. (Mexican War), 60
movie studios (and Long Beach), 189, 190
  Balboa Amusements Producing Co., 189
  Flying Irishman, The (movie), and Douglas Corrigan, 252
  Howard Hughes as movie producer, 316
Montana Land Co., 169
Mormon community in Southern California, 71-72, 74
Mormon Island, 149-150, 154, 155, 167
Motor Carrier Act of 1980, 407
Myler, Capt. J.J., 133
Nagumo, Adm. Chuichi (Pearl Harbor attack commander), 289
Naples (Long Beach), 114, 141, 169, 198, 216, 239, 340,
National Bank of Long Beach, 16-17, 173 (*see also* Hatch, P.E.)
National Labor Relations Board (NLRB), 312-314
National Recovery Administration (NRA), 263
National Steel and Shipbuilding Co., 471
New Jersey, USS, 421
Nichols, Mary (California Air Resources Board), 415
Nieto, Dominguez, 40
Nixon, Richard M., 304, 343, 372-373, 392, 393, 407, 438
North American Free Trade Agreement (NAFTA), 438
O'Neill, Beverly (Long Beach mayor), 468
Ocean Boulevard (Long Beach), 14, 112, 114, 158, 184, 232, 271, 274, 279, 298, 326, 327, 333, 334, 339, 340, 393, 410, 424, 425, 466, 487
  as Seaside Boulevard, 279, 288, 295, 317 (photo)
oil (drilling, refineries, terminals), 7, 8, 88-89, 185, 186, 220-221 (photo), 223-224, 238, 254, 272, 275, 320, 328, 330, 332, 370, 383, 395, 397, 416, 440-

441, 453, 498
- drilling rights, issue with Navy, 279, 288, 295
- dumping, 394
- freighters, oil (*see* freighters)
- and Great Depression, 254
- kerosene, 88-89
- oil islands (Long Beach), 362-364
- oil fires (*see* fires)
- pollution, water and air, 229, 385, 394-395, 397, 399, 410, 412-413, 416, 418, 431, 433, 441, 443, 459, 460, 475, 484-485, 494-495
- spills, 89, 220, 229, 231, 370, 394-397, 440-441
- whale oil, 88-89
- (*see also* subsidence)

on-dock rail (*see* rail and railroads)
Orient Overseas Container Line (OOCL), 380, 409, 499
Oregon and California Railroad, 137, 230
"Our Marina," 431
Pacific Coast Federation of Longshoremen (Local No. 3), 152
Pacific Coast Steel Co., 233-234, 236, 246, 340
Pacific Container Terminal(s), 409, 466, 472
Pacific Dock and Terminal Co., 339
Pacific Electric Railway (Red Cars), 138, 140, 156, 172, 184, 350-351
- as Pasadena and Los Angeles Electric System, 137

Pacific Far East Line, 398
Pacific Fleet (*see* United States Navy - Pacific Fleet)
Pacific Maritime Association (PMA), 335, 353-355, 406, 472, 476-477, 487-488, 490-493
- as Waterfront Employers Association, 335

Pacific Southwest Exposition, 245 (photo), 249, 254
Pacific States Electric Co., 185
Palos Verdes Peninsula, 39, 46, 85, 89, 125, 170, 186-187, 199, 288, 291
Pasadena and Los Angeles Electric System (*see* Pacific Electric Railway)
Pasadena Street Railroad, 137
Paternoster, Robert (Long Beach planning director), 419
Patton, Gen. George S., Jr., 298
Patton, Gen. George S., Sr. (Los Angeles County district attorney), 298
Pearl Harbor and Long Beach, 277, 281, 288-291, 293-295, 303, 323, 365, 421
Peek, William M. (commissioner of public safety), 217-218, 224-225
Peleliu, USS, 420
Perez, Carmen (Long Beach harbor commissioner), 459
Philippines, 33, 41, 249, 254, 304, 353, 402
Pierpoint Landing, 298, 326, 348, 383-384
Pike Amusement Center, 138, 189, 442
Pioneer Oil Co., 89
Point Dume, 125, 187

surveys, train proposals, 125, 127
kelp beds, 187
Point Fermin, 125
- and kelp beds, 186, 187
- defense zone (1940), 280
- lighthouse, 292

Pomeroy and Mills Real Estate, 110
pontoon bridge (*see* bridges - pontoon bridge)
Port Los Angeles (proposed Santa Monica Bay port), 126 (*see also* San Pedro Bay - Free Harbor Fight)
Port of Long Beach,
- as Long Beach Harbor Department, 242, 280, 400
- Pier A (old Navy Victory Pier, renamed Pier F in 1993), 241, 273 (photo), 339, 348, 409
- Pier A (after 1993, formerly North Harbor area), 455, 472, 487
- Pier B, (after 1993, formerly North Harbor Area), 254
- Pier C (renamed Pier E in 1993), 325
- Pier C (after 1993, formerly Seventh Street Peninsula), 254, 245 (photo), 400, 409, 455-456, 487
- Pier D, 252, 280, 297, 326, 409, 498
- Pier E ("Pier Echo," renamed as part of Pier T in 1993), 250, 280, 316, 339, 348, 376, 382, 398, 400, 409, 441
- Pier E (after 1993, formerly Piers B and C), 252, 326
- Pier F (after 1993 includes the former Pier A) 273 (photo), 326, 339, 380, 383, 409, 489 (photo), 498
- Pier G, 349, 380, 410-411, 431
- Pier J, 350, 365, 368, 379-380, 397, 400, 409, 431
- Pier S (former Union Pacific property), 487
- Pier T (former Navy Base and Shipyard), 316, 348, 409, 448, 457 (photo), 472, 487
- proposed merger of Long Beach, Los Angeles ports, 193, 194, 199, 210-211, 215-216, 228-229, 237, 240-242, 244-245, 246-248, 336, 338, 358-359, 385-387, 406, 418, 499
- Seventh Street Peninsula (renamed Pier C in 1993), 245 (photo), 409, 430, 455
- (*see also* Port of Los Angeles - rivalry with Port of Long Beach)

Port of Los Angeles,
- Pier 400, 466, 487, 499
- rivalry with Port of Long Beach, 199, 216, 232-236, 271-272, 278-279, 286-288, 318, 326, 339, 359-361, 370-371, 380, 390, 396-398, 406, 418, 431-432, 447, 448-449, 453-454, 456, 466-472, 483, 487, 495-496, 498-499

PortAdventure development (*see* Wrather Corp.)
Post, A. Alan (California legislative analyst), 379
Press-Telegram (before 1981 Independent, Press-Telegram), 243, 256, 274-275
- on City Attorney Irving Smith, 333
- influence on Long Beach policy, 379

as Long Beach Independent, 274-275
on Port attitudes and influences, 399
on *Queen Mary* purchase, 378-379

Prevratil, Joseph (Port executive director, businessman), 428, 430, 434, 445-446, 483

Prisk, William F. (Press-Telegram publisher), 200, 243, 256

Procter & Gamble, 245 (photo), 249, 254, 255 (photo), 274, 291, 324, 430, 448

Prohibition (21st Amendment), 120, 163, 211, 258-259

    repeal of, 258

    San Francisco, The, (line freighter), 258

"Queen City" (Long Beach), 367

Queen Mary (ocean liner), 367-368, 376, 378-380, 383-384, 398, 400, 405, 424-426, 428, 430, 434, 441-442, 444-446, 450, 452, 483

Queensway Bay, 368, 375, 383, 430, 441-442, 451

Queensway Bridge (opened 1970), 380

Quinn, Tom (California Air Resources Board), 397

Quinn, Walter J. (California auditor general's office), 379

Railroad Act, 99

rail and railroads, 66, 71, 73, 88, 90-94, 96, 98-106, 108, 110-111, 113, 115, 120, 122, 124, 127-128, 137-138, 140, 142-143, 147, 151-152, 153, 154, 163, 167-168, 172, 176, 194, 197, 220, 230-231, 234, 237, 249, 256, 274, 326, 328, 332, 353, 369, 416, 418, 432, 460-465, 472, 477, 484-485

    bridge (railroad), 153

    connection, east-west, 194

    mini-bridge service, 389-390

    near-dock rail yards, 399, 416 , 431, 432, 484, 499

    on-dock rail, 431-434, 454

        proposed Hanjin container terminal, 455

        and "K" Line's International Transportation Service (ITS), 432

        Maersk Terminal, 454-455

        Pier 300 (Port of Los Angeles), 449

        push-back, 432-434, 449

    Railroad Act, the, 99

    Union Pacific and Central Pacific link, 98-99, 101

    sound walls, 484-485

    (*see also* Alameda Corridor, individual railroad companies)

Rainbow Pier, 253, 254, 290

Rancho Cucamonga, 83

Rancho Dominguez, 446

Rancho Lomas de Santiago, 97

Rancho Las Bolsas, 46

Rancho Los Alamitos, 46, 54, 68, 86-87, 104-105, 114, 503

Rancho Los Cerritos, 46, 54, 65, 68, 97-98, 104, 107, 112, 114

Rancho Los Coyotes, 46

Rancho Los Nietos, 40, 46

Rancho Los Palos Verdes, 46, 89

Rancho San Joaquin, 97

Rancho San Justo, 74, 97

Rancho San Pasqual, 74, 89

Rancho San Pedro, 39-40, 45, 46, 50, 63, 71, 92

Rancho San Rafael, 39

Rancho Santa Fe, 338

Rancho Santa Gertrudes, 46

Rancho Santiago de Santa Ana, 97

ranchos, the movement: 39-40, 45, 46, 48, 10, 51 (map), 54, 57-58, 74-75, 84, 87, 104, 107, 502-503

Rattlesnake Island (*see* Terminal Island)

Reagan, James R., (Flood Control District chief), 197, 209

Reagan, Ronald W., 402-404, 420, 428

Red Cars (*see* Pacific Electric Railway)

Redevelopment Agency, Long Beach, 451, 459, 460

Redlands National Bank, 141

Richfield Oil Terminal (later Tesoro), 243, 254, 348, 349

Ridings, H.E. "Bud" (Long Beach harbor commissioner), 360, 378

Rivers and Harbors Act of 1912, 192

Rivers and Harbors Appropriation Act of 1899, 142-143

Roosevelt, Franklin Delano, 250, 258, 263, 265, 280-281, 289, 294-296, 302, 315-316

    criticized by Harry Bridges, 315

    Col. Elliott Roosevelt, 316

    death of (1945), 302

    and defense zone, 280; 281

    deployment of Pacific Fleet, 289

    end of Prohibition, 258

    Executive Order 9066 (*see also* World War II - Japanese population), 294

    National Industrial Recovery Act, 263; 265

    Roosevelt Base (Long Beach), 295, 296

Roosevelt, Theodore, 121, 170, 171, 182

    Great White Fleet (*see also* United States Navy)

RORO ships (roll-on/roll-off), 380, 381 (photo)

Sailors Union of the Pacific, 262-263, 310-311, 314, 335 (*also see* Bridges, Alfred Renton "Harry")

Salmarine Soap Co., 185

Salt Lake Railroad (see San Pedro, Los Angeles, and Salt Lake Railroad)

San Gabriel River, 194

San Pedro, 31, 39, 41, 49-50, 52, 54, 60, 61-63, 65, 67, 68, 69-72, 77, 79 (photo), 82, 84-85, 90, 92, 114-115, 116, 121-132 (photos), 134-135, 158, 169, 188, 205, 210, 227, 259, 267, 271, 272, 286-287, 288, 296, 336, 338, 358, 361-362, 405-406, 407, 424, 433, 448-449, 483

    consolidation with Los Angeles, 164-168

    Terminal Island annexation fight with Long Beach, 147-150

    World Trade Center (San Pedro) scandal (*see* Los Angeles Harbor Commission)

San Pedro, Los Angeles, and Salt Lake Railroad (the Salt Lake Railroad), 116-117, 142, 144, 145 (photo), 147-148, 151-154, 158, 163, 168-169, 172, 187

San Pedro Bay, 26, 30, 32, 40, 42, 45, 46, 49, 50, 51 (map), 67-68, 71, 72, 78, 79 (photo), 89-90, 92, 95 (map), 105, 112, 115, 116-117, 121, 123 (map), 124-125, 127, 131 (photo), 132-133, 144, 147, 170, 188, 190, 210, 211, 271-272, 298, 318

    as Bahia de los Humos y Fuegos (Bay of Smokes and Fires), 31, 33

    and Mexican War, 59-60

    vs. Santa Monica Bay as port site (Free Harbor Fight), 121-135

San Pedro Salt Works, 142, 144

San Sebastian Development Co. (*see* Los Angeles Harbor Commission)

Santa Barbara (steam schooner), 14, 16

Sanford, William (Douglass & Sanford), 67-71, 82-83, 94

Santa Fe Railroad, 110, 122, 140, 382, 418 (*see also* Burlington Northern Santa Fe Railroad)

Savannah, NS (nuclear-powered merchant ship), 366-367

Sea-Land Service, 357, 359, 361, 369, 380-381 (photo), 387-388, 458, 486-487 (*see also* containerization)

Sea Launch, 479 (photo)

Seaside Container Terminal, 399

Seaside Village, 112

Seaside Water Co., 138, 140, 144 (*see also* Long Beach Development Co.)

Seawise University, SS, 382

Seal Beach, 40, 46, 78, 92, 115, 239, 340

Shaler, Capt. William (first foreign trader at San Pedro), 41-43, 57

Shell Oil Co., 220-223

    Alamitos No. 1, Shell Oil Well, 220, 222

    Martin No. 1, Shell Oil Well, 223

shipbuilding, 228, 295, 482

    during WWI, 282

    decline of production, 482

    (*see also* Craig Shipbuilding Co.)

Signal Hill, 136, 141, 169, 220, 222-224, 230-231, 237-239, 257, 269, 274, 414

    Cherry Avenue, 224, 256, 295

    (*see also* oil)

Signal Hill Civil League, 136

Slangerup, Jon (Port executive director), 500

Sloat, Cdre. John D. (Mexican War), 59, 60, 62

South Coast Air Quality Management District (AQMD), 494

South Coast Canning Co., at Long Beach Harbor (1910), 188

South Coast Regional Coastal Commission, 395, 396, 398, 420, 469

Southern California Edison, 184, 210, 244-245 (photo), 280, 288, 323, 324, 326-327, 330-331, 345, 383, 395, 410, 453

Southern Pacific Railroad, 102-103, 108, 110-111, 113-117, 122, 124-129, 153, 155, 165, 172, 234, 236, 246, 249, 254, 256, 280, 350, 382, 416, 418, 432, 460, 463-465, 477

Spanish settlers, 37-38, 41

Spruce Goose, 315-316, 317 (photos) 318, 382, 398, 400, 409, 426, 428, 429 (photo), 430, 441-442, 444, 446, 483

Standard Oil, 136, 207, 223, 280

Standard Oil of California, 396

Standard Oil of Ohio (Sohio), 396-398, 409

Standard Shipbuilding Co., 296

Stanford, Leland, 98-100, 102, 134

State Lands Commission, 359, 367, 378-379, 385, 426, 451

Steamship Association of Southern California, 394, 433, 442, 451

Stearns, Abel, 46-50, 52-54, 55 (photo), 58, 61, 65, 68, 76, 85, 90, 104, 506

    Arcadia Bandini Stearns (wife), 53-54

steel, role of, 99, 106, 176, 233, 234, 246, 253, 295-296, 328, 332, 341, 356, 365, 431

    ban on scrap steel sales, 282

    burial in steel vault, 398

    and railroads, 106

    scrap steel, 274, 278, 351, 410, 448

    short supply, 296, 414

    steel workers, 308

    and vessels, 106, 284

Steinke, Dick (Port executive director) 476, 500

Stevens, Irwin M. (Long Beach harbor commissioner), 253

Stevenson, Adlai, 322

Stockton, Cdre. Robert F. (Mexican War), 60-63

strikes and shutdowns, 212, 259, 262

    of 1906, 152

    of 1934 and Bloody Thursday, 264-269

    of 1946, 309-312

    of 1948, 313-315

    of 1971, 390, 391 (photo), 392

    of 1972, 392-393

    1990 shutdown, 464

    lockout of 2002, 491-492

    pilot's union (Los Angeles), 476

    vs. Craig Shipbuilding, 173-174, 176, 208

    (*see also* unions)

SSA Marine (Stevedoring Services of America), 456, 464, 472, 492

subsidence, 9, 323-324, 326-328, 330-331, 334, 336, 339-340, 345-346, 362, 364, 371, 397, 430, 455

Talin, George (Long Beach harbor commissioner), 434, 446, 458-459

    Talin Tire Inc., 446, 459

Taft, William Howard, 178, 182, 223

    visit to Long Beach (1911), 178

Taft-Hartley Labor Act, 312-314, 392, 492

    invoked by President George W. Bush, 492

    invoked by President Richard Nixon, 392

Teague, Col. Gwynn A. (Army Corps of Engineers), 415

Tallichet, David (businessman, restaurateur), 349, 378

Teamsters Union (*see* International Brotherhood of Teamsters)

Temple, John, 48-49, 52, 54, 65, 68, 71-72, 75-76, 85, 87, 97-98

    August F. Hinchman (brother-in-law), 78

    and Abel Stearns, 52, 54, 58, 75-76

    and David W. Alexander, 65

    and George Rice (partners), 49

    John Temple (nephew), 98

    Rafaela Cota (wife), 54

    Temple Block, 97

terminal(s), 6, 8, 116, 228, 234, 236-237, 243, 246, 249, 254, 268, 270, 274, 280, 313, 326, 332, 348-349, 355, 360, 365, 369, 380, 382-384, 386, 388, 392, 395-399, 407, 409-412, 414, 426, 430-432, 441-443, 448-449, 452-456, 458-459, 464-472, 475-478, 485-488, 490-491, 494-495, 498-501

    (*see also* individual terminal operators)

Terminal Island, 116, 140-142, 144, 147-152, 154-155, 164-169, 228, 232, 236, 244, 246, 248, 254, 268, 270, 272, 279-280, 284, 288, 290-291, 295-298, 306-307, 316, 323-324, 326-327, 330, 339, 348, 351, 361-361, 382, 284, 395, 406, 410, 424, 426, 448-449, 454, 488, 496

    Brighton Beach resort, 147, 155

    and Japanese village, 293-294

    Navy Dry Docks (*see* United States Navy)

    as Rattlesnake Island, 72, 92, 97, 116, 121-122, 142, 147

    squatter community, 151-152, 153-155, 167-170

Texas and Pacific Railroad, 102-103

Thomas, Vincent (San Pedro assemblyman), 336, 358, 361, 362, 384, 405-406 (*see also* bridges - Vincent Thomas Bridge)

Thorley, Thomas (Port general manager), 347 (photo), 348, 380, 401

THUMS (Texaco, Humble, Union, Mobil, Shell), 364

Tichenor, Adelaide (former president of Ebell Club), 158

Tichenor, Henry Baldwin, 92, 93

    Banning Tichenor Partnership, 92

tidelands, 149, 151, 155-156, 279, 280, 320, 331, 332, 334, 338

Tidelands Grant (of 1911), 185, 201, 270, 318, 332, 346

Toko Kaiun Kaisha, Tokyo Steel Shipbuilding Co., 380

Total Terminals International (TTI), 472

Toyota Motor Sales, 365, 380, 409, 436, 455, 492

Townsend-Dayman Investment Co., 136-137, 140-141, 146

    (*also see* Townsend, Stephen)

    (*also see* Dayman, Bromell P.)

Townsend, Stephen (Long Beach mayor, developer), 17, 136-137, 138, 140-141, 146, 149, 163, 171, 219

and Dana Burks, 141, 171, 176

    (*see also* Long Beach Navigation Co., Townsend-Dayman Investment Co., Western Steam Navigation Co.)

trade, international, 7, 9, 45, 322, 358, 416, 419, 421, 424-425, 433, 460

Transocean Gateway Corporation, 369

Transportation Communications Union, 465

Trojan Transportation Co., 452

Truman, Harry S., 302, 303, 304, 309, 310, 311, 313, 314, 320, 322, 343

    Wage Stabilization Board, 311

tuna industry, 188, 189, 228, 229, 348, 383

Union Oil (refinery), 185, 210, 220, 222, 228-229, 240

Union Pacific Railroad, 6, 99, 101-102, 236, 280, 382, 411, 418

    Union "Pathetic," 477

Union Pacific oil field (Terminal Island), 288, 323, 326, 455

unions, 98, 102, 106-107, 152-153, 174, 182-183, 198, 202, 208, 212, 250, 259, 262-269, 284-286, 304, 308-315, 334-336, 351-356, 367-370, 390, 392, 401, 406-408, 420, 435, 464-465, 471, 476-478, 488, 490-491

    "A" men and "B" men, 353-354

    anti-union sentiments, 171, 265, 315, 339, 379 (*see also* Los Angeles Times)

    Mechanization and Modernization Agreement, 351, 353, 370, 390

    nuclear powered ships, opposition to, 367

    trucking, 407-408, 478

    walk-offs, 174

    Wilmington Bowl, 309, 311, 313

    (*see also* strikes and shutdowns, individual unions)

United Fruit Co. (Chiquita Brands International), 234

United States Army Board of Engineers for Rivers and Harbors, 193, 196-197, 233, 234, 247

United States Army Corps of Engineers, 194, 198, 232-233, 247, 396, 415, 419-420, 449

    river diversion (flood control), 199

United States Steel, 246

United States Navy, 15, 211, 244, 247-248, 170-171, 271-272, 273 (photos)

    and 1933 Long Beach earthquake, 257

    and Great Depression, 254

    Great White Fleet, 170-171

    Long Beach Naval Hospital, 288, 444, 456

    Long Beach Naval Shipyard (1948-1997), 296, 324, 330-331, 338, 339, 345, 377 (photo), 393, 401, 420, 456, 458, 466-469, 471, 482

    Long Beach Naval Station, 295, 324, 350, 365, 393, 420, 444, 456, 457 (photo), 458, 465-471

    Naval Dry Docks at Roosevelt Base (1943-45, later Terminal Island Naval Shipyard and Long Beach Naval Shipyard), 279, 296, 298, 306, 323, 324, 368

    Pacific Fleet, 60, 211, 253, 257, 271, 289

pollution (oil), 395
Roosevelt Base, 295-296
submarine contracts, 204-206
Terminal Island Naval Shipyard (1945-48, later Long Beach Naval Shipyard), 296
(see also San Pedro Bay - Free Harbor Fight)
U.S. Maritime Administration (MARAD), 366-367
U.S. Naval Dry Docks at Roosevelt Base (see United States Navy)
Van Camp Sea Food Co., 347 (photo), 348
Vickers, Charles L. (Port assistant and then general manager), 339, 353, 360, 362, 370, 380
Vietnam War,
    Duncan Hunter and Randy Cunningham (San Diego congressmen), 471
    and Port of Long Beach, 365, 467
Vincent Thomas Bridge (see bridges - Vincent Thomas Bridge)
Virgil Bogue, (Western Pacific tug), 163
Virginia Hotel (Long Beach), 14, 138, 160, 163, 170, 171, 178, 192, 194, 234, 243, 254
Wade, Edwin W. (Long Beach mayor), 349, 354, 359, 378
Wagner, Clarence (Long Beach mayor), 298
Walker, C.J. 16, 137, 140, 200, 229
    as president of Farmers and Merchants Bank, 16, 137
    Principal of Long Beach Land and Navigation Co., 146
    Walker Real Estate Co., 140
    Walker-Western, 223
Walker, Adm. John C., 129
    Walker Board, 129-130, 132
    (see also San Pedro Bay - Free Harbor Fight)
Walt Disney Co., (see Disney Co.)
Walter, Dr. Mike (Long Beach harbor commissioner), 499
water, 10, 14, 21, 26, 69, 71, 76, 85-86, 107
    Federal Water Pollution Control Act (of 1965), 370
    flood control channel (see Los Angeles River)
    floods, 9, 21, 23, 26, 73, 85-86, 191, 194, 196-199, 205, 209, 223, 227, 327-328
    Long Beach Land and Water Co., 110-113
    Los Angeles County Flood Control District (see Los Angeles River)
    oil spills (see oil)
    wastewater dumping, 370, 394
waterfront, the, 6-8, 14, 115, 262, 263
    and the Bixbys, 105
    at San Pedro, 70-72, 105, 115
    at Wilmington, 91
    and Southern Pacific, 116
    West Coast Waterfront Coalition, 492
Waterfront/Rail Truckers Union, 408
Western Boat Works (Cerritos Slough), 142, 185
Western Dredging and Marine Construction, 162-164; 172-173, 176-177, 191-192, 197, 199, 200-202, 228-230, 232-234, 350, 338
Western Pacific Railroad Co., 163
Western Pipeline and Steel Co., 296, 306
Western Steam Navigation Co., 171, 177, 192, 205, 230
    Bixby, George H.; Craig J.F.; Townsend, Stephen (principals), 171
    The Camino (with Craig Shipping Co.), 192, 205
    The General Hubbard (with Hammond Lumber Co.) 171, 173
    The Navajo (passenger ship, San Diego-Portland), 171, 192
Whealton, Louis N. (Long Beach mayor), 194, 200
White, Stephen M. (California senator), 127, 128-130, 131 (photo), 132
Widney, Dr. Joseph, 107
Widney, Judge Robert M. ("Get Out and Push Railroad"), 107-108, 110, 113
Wiley, Harry (Long Beach Municipal Band), 14, 189
Williams, Paul R., 295, 467
Williams, Reed M. (Long Beach harbor commissioner), 401
Willmore City (later Long Beach), 106-108, 110, 113, 136
Willmore, William Erwin (founder of Long Beach), 101-102, 106-108, 109 (drawing), 110-112, 117, 136
    American Colony, 107
    (see also Willmore City)
Wilmington, 164-169, 188-189, 199, 227, 232, 270, 286-287, 316, 336, 338, 358, 445, 448
    as New San Pedro 77, 81-82, 84-85
    Wilmington Bowl, 309, 311, 313
Wilmington Oil Field, 270-271, 232
Wilmington Transportation Co., 104, 241
Wilson, Adrian, 295
Wilson, Benjamin D., 68, 81, 90, 111, 298
    as partner of Phineas Banning, 91, 96, 97, 102
Wilson, Don Benito (Los Angeles mayor), 68-69
Wilson, Pete (San Diego mayor), 394
Wilson, Richard (Long Beach harbor commissioner), 412
Wilson, Woodrow, 182, 184, 204, 212, 230
Windham, Charles Henderson (Long Beach mayor, city manager, developer, "Father of the Port"), 16, 137-138, 139 (photo), 162, 192, 219, 228, 230
    Charles H. Windham (dredger), 163
    as Father of the Port of Long Beach (1902), 137
Wise, George E., 469
Wise, Susan Anderson (Long Beach harbor commissioner), 12, 500
World Campus Afloat Program (Chapman College and *The Queen Elizabeth*), 380
World Trade Center (Long Beach), 401, 422, 423 (photo), 424-425, 433, 450, 452, 455, 483-484
World Trade Center scandal (San Pedro), (see Los

Angeles Harbor Commission)

World War I, 207-208
    and shipbuilding (in Long Beach and Los Angeles), 282

World War II, 277, 293, 297, 315, 342, 357, 421, 430
    Arsenal of Democracy (Long Beach and Los Angeles), 294, 458
    and cargo ships, 356, 388
    economic stimulus, 250, 315
    and Japanese population, 293, 294, 421
    Pacific veterans, 306
    (*see also* "Herman the German," Pearl Harbor and Long Beach)

Wrather Corp., 426, 428, 430, 434, 441
    PortAdventure development, 428, 430, 441

Wrather, Bonita Granville, 428

Wrather, Jack, 426, 428

Yugoslav Hall (Dalmatian-American Hall), 362

Zaddart, Capt. F.B., 14, 16, 86

Zaferia District, 172

Zim-American Israeli Shipping Co., 476

Zumwalt, Adm. Elmo "Bud," 393

Made in the USA
San Bernardino, CA
22 June 2015